Knowledge Discovery Practices and Emerging Applications of Data Mining:

Trends and New Domains

A.V. Senthil Kumar
CMS College of Science and Commerce, India

A volume in the Advances in Data Mining
and Database Management (ADMDM)
Book Series

Information Science
REFERENCE
An Imprint of IGI Global

Managing Director:	Lindsay Johnston
Senior Editorial Director:	Heather Probst
Book Production Manager:	Sean Woznicki
Development Manager:	Joel Gamon
Development Editor:	Joel Gamon
Acquisitions Editor:	Lindsay Johnston
Typesetters:	Milan Vracarich, Natalie Pronio
Print Coordinator:	Jamie Snavely
Cover Design:	Lisa Tosheff

Published in the United States of America by
Information Science Reference (an imprint of IGI Global)
701 E. Chocolate Avenue
Hershey PA 17033
Tel: 717-533-8845
Fax: 717-533-8661
E-mail: cust@igi-global.com
Web site: http://www.igi-global.com

Library of Congress Cataloging-in-Publication Data

Knowledge discovery practices and emerging applications of data mining: trends and new domains / Av Senthil Kumar, editor.
     p. cm.
  Includes bibliographical references and index. Summary: This book introduces the reader to recent research activities in the field of data mining, covering association mining, classification, mobile marketing, opinion mining, microarray data mining, internet mining and applications of data mining on biological data, telecommunication and distributed databases. Provided by publisher.
  ISBN 978-1-60960-067-9 (hardcover) -- ISBN 978-1-60960-069-3 (ebook) 1. Data mining. 2. Knowledge acquisition (Expert systems) I. Senthil kumar, A., 1966-
  QA76.9.D343K 5645 2010
  006.3'12--dc22
                                        2010027734

This book is published in the IGI Global book series Advances in Data Mining and Database Management (ADMDM) (ISSN: 2327-1981; eISSN: 2327-199X).

British Cataloguing in Publication Data
A Cataloguing in Publication record for this book is available from the British Library.

All work contributed to this book is new, previously-unpublished material. The views expressed in this book are those of the authors, but not necessarily of the publisher.

Advances in Data Mining and Database Management (ADMDM) Book Series

David Taniar
Monash University, Australia

ISSN: 2327-1981
EISSN: 2327-199X

MISSION

With the large amounts of information available to businesses in today's digital world, there is a need for methods and research on managing and analyzing the information that is collected and stored. IT professionals, software engineers, and business administrators, along with many other researchers and academics, have made the fields of data mining and database management into ones of increasing importance as the digital world expands. The **Advances in Data Mining & Database Management (ADMDM) Book Series** aims to bring together research in both fields in order to become a resource for those involved in either field.

COVERAGE

- Cluster Analysis
- Customer Analytics
- Data Mining
- Data Quality
- Data Warehousing
- Database Security
- Database Testing
- Decision Support Systems
- Enterprise Systems
- Text Mining

IGI Global is currently accepting manuscripts for publication within this series. To submit a proposal for a volume in this series, please contact our Acquisition Editors at Acquisitions@igi-global.com or visit: http://www.igi-global.com/publish/.

Titles in this Series

For a list of additional titles in this series, please visit: www.igi-global.com

Data Mining in Dynamic Social Networks and Fuzzy Systems
Vishal Bhatnagar (Ambedkar Institute of Advanced Communication Technologies and Research, India)
Information Science Reference • copyright 2013 • 412pp • H/C (ISBN: 9781466642133) • US $195.00 (our price)

Ethical Data Mining Applications for Socio-Economic Development
Hakikur Rahman (University of Minho, Portugal) and Isabel Ramos (University of Minho, Portugal)
Information Science Reference • copyright 2013 • 359pp • H/C (ISBN: 9781466640788) • US $195.00 (our price)

Design, Performance, and Analysis of Innovative Information Retrieval
Zhongyu (Joan) Lu (University of Huddersfield, UK)
Information Science Reference • copyright 2013 • 508pp • H/C (ISBN: 9781466619753) • US $195.00 (our price)

XML Data Mining Models, Methods, and Applications
Andrea Tagarelli (University of Calabria, Italy)
Information Science Reference • copyright 2012 • 538pp • H/C (ISBN: 9781613503560) • US $195.00 (our price)

Graph Data Management Techniques and Applications
Sherif Sakr (University of New South Wales, Australia) and Eric Pardede (LaTrobe University, Australia)
Information Science Reference • copyright 2012 • 502pp • H/C (ISBN: 9781613500538) • US $195.00 (our price)

Advanced Database Query Systems Techniques, Applications and Technologies
Li Yan (Northeastern University, China) and Zongmin Ma (Northeastern University, China)
Information Science Reference • copyright 2011 • 410pp • H/C (ISBN: 9781609604752) • US $180.00 (our price)

Knowledge Discovery Practices and Emerging Applications of Data Mining Trends and New Domains
A.V. Senthil Kumar (CMS College of Science and Commerce, India)
Information Science Reference • copyright 2011 • 414pp • H/C (ISBN: 9781609600679) • US $180.00 (our price)

Data Mining in Public and Private Sectors Organizational and Government Applications
Antti Syvajarvi (University of Lapland, Finland) and Jari Stenvall (Tampere University, Finland)
Information Science Reference • copyright 2010 • 448pp • H/C (ISBN: 9781605669069) • US $180.00 (our price)

Text Mining Techniques for Healthcare Provider Quality Determination Methods for Rank Comparisons
Patricia Cerrito (University of Louisville, USA)
Medical Information Science Reference • copyright 2010 • 410pp • H/C (ISBN: 9781605667522) • US $245.00
(our price)

www.igi-global.com

701 E. Chocolate Ave., Hershey, PA 17033
Order online at www.igi-global.com or call 717-533-8845 x100
To place a standing order for titles released in this series, contact: cust@igi-global.com
Mon-Fri 8:00 am - 5:00 pm (est) or fax 24 hours a day 717-533-8661

Table of Contents

Section 1
Concepts, Tools and Techniques

Section 2
Research and Learning

Detailed Table of Contents

Section 1
Concepts, Tools and Techniques

Rahime Belen, Informatics Institute, METU, Turkey
Tuğba Taşkaya Temizel, Informatics Institute, METU, Turkey

This chapter presents the methods to detect disguised missing values by visual inspection and also describe the methods used to detect these values automatically. At the same time, the framework to detect disguised missing data is also proposed and a demonstration of the framework on spatial and categorical data sets is provided.

Giulia Bruno, Politecnico di Torino, Italy
Alessandro Fiori, Politecnico di Torino, Italy

Chapter 2 presents a review of four popular data mining techniques (i.e., Classification, Feature Selection, Clustering and Association Rule Mining) applied to microarray data. This chapter also describes the main characteristics of microarray data in order to understand the critical issues which are introduced by gene expression values analysis. Each technique is analyzed, examples of pertinent literature are reported and the prospects of data mining research on microarray data are provided in this chapter.

Chapter 3

This chapter proposes a technique that is developed to explore frequent temporal itemsets in the database. The basic idea of this technique is to first partition the database into sub-databases in light of either common starting time or common ending time. Then for each partition, the proposed technique is used progressively to accumulate the number of occurrences of each candidate 2-itemsets. A Directed graph is built using the support of these candidate 2-itemsets (combined from all the sub-databases) as a result of generating all candidate temporal k- itemsets in the database. This technique may help researchers to understand about generating frequent large temporal itemsets and to find temporal association rules among transactions within relational databases.

Chapter 4

This chapter highlights how one can be benefited by using Data Mining and Knowledge Discovery techniques in achieving an acceptable level of quality of service of telecommunication systems. It also discusses the application of data mining and knowledge discovery process in analyzing the QoS issues.

Chapter 5 focuses on using association rules and classification mining to select the persistently strong association rules. The process for finding persistent strong rules was executed against two data sets obtained from the American National Election Studies. Analysis of the first data set resulted in one persistent strong rule and one persistent rule, while analysis of the second data set resulted in 11 persistent strong rules and 10 persistent rules. This chapter suggests that these rules are the most robust, consistent, and noteworthy among the much larger potential rule sets.

Section 2
Research and Learning

Chapter 6

Ana Azevedo, CEISE/STI, ISCAP/IPP, Portugal

Manuel Filipe Santos, University of Minho, Portugal

This chapter introduces an architecture that can conduct to an effective usage of Data Mining (DM) in Business Intelligence (BI). This architecture includes a DM language that is iterative and interactive in nature. This chapter suggests that the effective usage of DM in BI can be achieved by making DM models accessible to business users, through the use of the presented DM language.

Chapter 7

Udai Shanker, Madan Mohan Malviya Engineering College, India

Abhay N. Singh, Madan Mohan Malviya Engineering College, India

Abhinav Anand, Madan Mohan Malviya Engineering College, India

Saurabh Agrawal, Madan Mohan Malviya Engineering College, India

This chapter proposes Shadow Sensitive SWIFT commit protocol for Distributed Real Time Database Systems (DRTDBS). Also the performance of Shadow Sensitive SWIFT is compared with shadow PROMPT, SWIFT and DSS-SWIFT commit protocols for both main memory resident and disk resident databases with and without communication delay. The chapter further points out that the proposed protocol improves the system performance up to 5% as transaction miss percentage.

Chapter 8

Giovanni Giuffrida, Universita' di Catania, Italy

Diego Reforgiato, University of Maryland, USA

Catarina Sismeiro, Imperial College London, England

Giuseppe Tribulato, Neodata Group s.r.l., Italy

This chapter focuses on the competition among mobile phone operators in developed countries in switching customers away from competitors with extremely discounted telephony rates. This fierce competitive environment is the result of a saturated market with small or inexistent growth and has caused operators to rely increasingly on Value-Added Services (VAS) for revenue growth. This chapter also describes novel methods now available to mobile phone operators to optimize targeting and improve profitability from VAS offers.

Chapter 9 discusses how to mine system execution traces, which are a collection of log messages describing events and states of a distributed system throughout its execution lifetime, generated by distributed systems so that the validation of QoS properties is not dependent on a SEM tool's capabilities. A real-life case study is used in this chapter to illustrate how data mining system execution traces can assist in discovering potential performance bottlenecks using system execution traces.

Chapter 10

This chapter highlights how each one profits from the other and illustrates their cooperation in existing systems developed in the medical domain. It also identifies different types of cooperation that combine elicitation and data mining for knowledge acquisition, use expert knowledge to enact the knowledge discovery, use discovered knowledge to validate expert knowledge, and use discovered knowledge to improve the usability of an expert system. The chapter also highlights authors experience in combining expert and discovered knowledge in the development of a system for processing medical isokinetics data.

Section 3
Case Studies

This chapter compares the performance of different Associative Classifiers (AC) like Classification Based on Association (CBA), Classification based on Multiple Association Rules (CMAR), Predictive Rule Mining (PRM), Classification based on Predictive Association Rules (CPAR) and Total From Partial Classification (TFPC) in terms of classification accuracy, efficiency, number of rules to be generated, quality of such rules, and the maximum number of attributes in rule-antecedents, with respect to MSC differentiation analysis. After the comparison between the five AC approaches, CMAR is suggested to be the most suitable approach for this study, and possibly also suitable to other similar studies such as the tissue engineering related data analysis.

Chapter 12 describes and differentiates World Wide Web (WWW), Semantic Web, Data Grid, and Knowledge Grid with the literature survey. The chapter also presents fuzzy XML technique to represent domain and meta knowledge into the knowledge repositories. To experiment the proposed generic architecture, an application of e-Learning is selected and a multiagent system mining knowledge grid is discussed with detailed methodology and role of agents in the system.

Chapter 13

This chapter focuses on the area of opinion mining and discuss the SentiWordNet lexicon of sentiment information for terms derived from WordNet. The results of the research in applying this lexicon to sentiment classification of film reviews along with a novel approach that leverages opinion lexicons to build a data set of features used as input to a supervised learning classifier are also presented. Furthermore, the results obtained through the research are in line with other experiments based on manually built opinion lexicons with further improvements obtained by using the novel approach, and are indicative that lexicons built using semi supervised methods such as SentiWordNet can be an important resource in sentiment classification tasks.

This chapter presents a pipeline for biological data integration and discovery of a priori unknown relationships between gene expressions and metabolite accumulations. In this pipeline, two standard clustering methods are compared against a novel neural network approach. The neural model provides a simple visualization interface for identification of coordinated patterns variations, independently of the number of produced clusters. This chapter also illustrates several quality measurements for the evaluation of the clustering results obtained on a case study involving transcriptomic and metabolomic profiles from tomato fruits. Moreover, a method is proposed for the evaluation of the biological significance of the clusters found.

Chapter 15

In Chapter 15, the author discusses about how the Internet forums attract dedicated users who build tight social communities. This chapter also highlights the abundance of Internet forums covering all aspects of human activities: politics, sports, entertainment, science, religion, leisure, hobbies, etc. This chapter eventually shows social role discovery as a important issue in discovery of valuable knowledge from Internet forums. This chapter also discusses the architecture of Internet forums, presents an overview of data volumes involved and outlines technical challenges of scraping Internet forum data.

Foreword

Recent developments of computer technology and the requirements of various applications have led to the increase in the volume and complexity of data. This makes manual analysis of such data very difficult. Data mining helps in automatic extraction of hidden predictive information from these data using other techniques like neural networks, decision trees, genetic algorithms and support vector machines. Some of the applications of data mining are predicting the trend of an industry based on the behaviors of customers, multifactor dimensionality reduction to detect the interaction of genes, condition monitoring of electrical equipments, surveillance, psychological and social network analysis.

Data mining tools also help in integrating all medical information from different systems, databases. Thus they provide physicians with certain information which are sometimes not provided by certain clinical decision support tools. Powerful information extraction tools have been developed to collect, retain and analyze the huge volume of data which is being transferred by people in the world. This can largely help a government in finding suspicious data linkages and patterns to control terrorist activities. Data mining tools provide engineers with the knowledge obtained from maintenance of products. This knowledge can be either obtained from the designers' own experiences or from the resources in their organization. This knowledge can help the engineers to design new products without the defects of old products. Data mining in Bioinformatics helps in finding motifs in sequences to predict folding patterns, to discover genetic mechanisms responsible for a disease, to decide the rules for multiple DNA or protein sequences etc. Biological Knowledge Discovery from Databases (BIOKDD) plays a significant role in analyzing the data and in solving emerging problems.

The objective of this book is to introduce the reader to recent research activities in the field of data mining. This book covers areas like association mining, classification, mobile marketing, opinion mining, microarray data mining, internet mining and applications of data mining on biological data, telecommunication and distributed databases. This book would be very helpful in understanding and implementation of data mining techniques in emerging domains.

This book will be very useful to researchers, engineers, scientists and individuals working in the field of data mining. This book would enable the readers to work on new research domains in data mining which would be useful for the society.

C. Swaminathan
Vice Chancellor
Bharathiar University, India

C. Swaminathan *known well for his institution-building abilities and keen interest in the field of higher education, was born to Thiru. A. Chinnappan and Thirumathi C. Ponnammal at Thingalur near Erode, Tamilnadu, India. Coming from a family of farmers, he had his schooling at Thingalur Government HSS. He then went on to do his B.A. at C. N. College, Erode and M.A. at Pachaiappa's College, Chennai. Continuing his studies, he obtained M.Phil. from the University of Madras after which he took up a faculty position as Lecturer in History at CBM College, Coimbatore in 1980. The researcher in him would make no allowance for any rest inspite of a demanding teaching career and he went on to get his Ph.D. in 2000.*

Preface

Data Mining and Knowledge Discovery in databases have been attracting a significant amount of research, industry, and media attention of late. Data Mining may be defined as the process of extracting trends or patterns from data and the technique. Data Mining involves the use of sophisticated data analysis tools to discover previously unknown, valid patterns and relationships in large datasets. These tools can include statistical models, mathematical algorithms, and machine learning methods. Consequently, data mining consists of more than collecting and managing data, it also includes analysis and prediction.

Knowledge Discovery (KD) may be characterized as the process that can be applied to the results of data mining, to make sense of them. A KD process includes data warehousing, target data selection, cleaning, preprocessing, transformation and reduction, data mining, model selection, evaluation and interpretation, and finally consolidation and use of the extracted knowledge. Specifically, data mining aims to develop algorithms for extracting new patterns from the facts recorded in a database. Hitherto, data mining tools adopted techniques from statistics, neural network modeling, and visualization to classify data and identify patterns. Ultimately, KD aims to enable an information system to transform information to knowledge through hypothesis testing and theory information. It sets new challenges for database technology: new concepts and methods are needed for basic operations, query languages, and query processing strategies.

Recent progress in scientific and engineering applications has accumulated huge volumes of high-dimensional data, stream data, and spatial and temporal data. There is an urgent need for a new generation of computational theories and tools to assist humans in extracting useful information (knowledge) from the rapidly growing volumes of digital data. These theories and tools are the subject of the emerging field of Knowledge Discovery in Databases (KDD) (Fayyad, Piatetsky-Shapiro, & Smyth, 1996).

Subsequently, the KDD process can be viewed as a multidisciplinary activity that encompasses techniques beyond the scope of any one particular discipline such as machine learning. KDD places a special emphasis on finding understandable, patterns that can be interpreted as useful or interesting knowledge. KDD also emphasizes scaling and robustness properties of modeling algorithms for large noisy data sets. Related AI research fields include machine discovery, which targets the discovery of empirical laws from observation and experimentation (Shrager & Langley, 1990), glossary of terms common to KDD and machine discovery (Kloesgen & Zytkow, 1996), and causal modeling for the inference of causal models from data (Spirtes, Glymour, & Scheines, 1993). Statistics in particular has much in common with KDD (Glymour, Madigan, Pregibon, & Smyth, 1996).

A number of advances in technology and business processes have contributed to a growing interest in data mining in both the public and private sectors. Some of these changes include the growth of computer networks, which can be used to connect databases; the development of enhanced search-related techniques such as neural networks and advanced algorithms; the spread of the client/server computing model, allowing users to access centralized data resources from the desktop; and an increased ability to combine data from disparate sources into a single searchable source (Makulowich, 1999).

In addition to these improved data management tools, the increased availability of information and the decreasing costs of storing it have also played a role. Over the past several years there has been a rapid increase in the volume of information collected and stored, with some observers suggesting that the quantity of the world's data approximately doubles every year. At the same time, the costs of data storage have decreased significantly from dollars per megabyte to pennies per megabyte. Similarly, computing power has continued to double every 18-24 months, while the relative cost of computing power has continued to decrease.

KDD is an attempt to address a problem that the digital information era made a fact of life for all of us: data overload and various KDD applications have been deployed in operational use on large-scale real-world problems in science and in business. In science, main KDD application areas includes, astronomy, biomedical engineering, telecommunications, geospatial data and climate data and the earth ecosystems. In business, main KDD application areas includes marketing, finance, fraud detection, manufacturing, telecommunication, and Internet agents. These are just a few of the numerous such systems that use KDD techniques to automatically produce useful information from large mass of raw data.

Along these approaches to enable practitioners in improving their researches and participate actively in solving practical problems related to various knowledge practices and emerging applications of data mining a complete reference will be an essential need. A book featuring all these aspects can fill an extremely demanding knowledge gap in the contemporary world.

Furthermore, in selecting potential KDD applications, which can be divided into practical and technical categories various criteria should be followed. The practical criteria for KDD projects are similar to those for other applications of advanced technology and include the potential impact of an application, the absence of simpler alternative solutions, and strong organizational support for using technology. For application dealing with personal data, one should also consider the privacy and legal issues (Piatetsky-Shapiro, 1995). The technical criteria include considerations such as the availability of sufficient data(cases).

This book seeks to provide the latest research and the best practices in the field of data mining. At the same-time it gives an in-depth look into the various emerging applications in data mining. Furthermore, this book provides an overview on the main issues of data mining (temporal association rule mining, classifiers, integration etc.,), various new concepts in data mining and the application of data mining in various fields.

WHERE THE BOOK STANDS

In the global context, advanced mining techniques in data mining are important, especially in the realm of emerging domains. Data mining techniques are the outcome of an extensive process of study, research and product development. In essence, this evolution began when entrepreneurs started arching business data in computers, efforts continued with improvements in easier data access, and more recently researches generated technologies that allow users to navigate through their data in real time. Well developed information and communication network infrastructure and knowledge building applications in emerging domains are important to promote information exchange among users, data analysts, system developers, and data mining researchers to facilitate the advances available from data mining research, application development, and technology transfer.

Advanced data mining techniques in emerging domains can yield substantial knowledge from even raw data that are primarily gathered for wider range of applications. The primary objective of the book is to develop various advanced data mining techniques and algorithms in emerging domains. Research in the field of data mining and knowledge discovery to evolve rapid and efficient ways of archiving and treating data has become a major field of study of mining in emerging domains.

Eventually, data mining is becoming a significant tool in science, engineering, industrial processes, healthcare, medicine, and other social services for making intelligent decision. However the datasets in these fields are predominantly large, complex, and often noisy. Therefore, extracting knowledge from data requires the use of sophisticated, high-performance and principled analysis techniques and algorithms, based on sound statistical foundations. These techniques in turn necessitate powerful visualization technologies; implementations that must be carefully tuned for performance; software systems that are usable by scientists, engineers, and physicians as well as researchers; and infrastructure that support them.

In this context, this book provides an overview on the main issues of data mining (temporal association rule mining, classifiers, integration etc.), various new concepts in data mining like disguised missing data, persistent strong rules, opinion mining, internet forums, and the application of data mining in the fields like telecommunication systems, biology, mobile marketing, microarrays and so forth.

ORGANIZATION OF CHAPTERS

This book includes fifteen chapters and they are divided into three sections: Concepts, Tools and Techniques; Research and Learning; and Case Studies. Section I has five chapters, and they illustrate the various tools and techniques for various emerging applications of data mining. Section II has five chapters, and they discuss policy and decision-making approaches of data mining for the development of business in terms of Intelligence and Marketing. The third section has five chapters and these chapters show various case studies on various trends and new domains of data mining applications.

In Chapter 1, the authors have explained the basic visual methods to detect some forms of disguises and the frameworks to identify them without requiring any domain expert. The chapter recognizes a data quality problem is that of disguised missing data which arises when an explicit code for missing data such as NA (Not Available) is not provided and a legitimate data value is used instead. Presence of these values may affect the outcome of data mining tasks severely such that association mining algorithms or clustering techniques may result in biased inaccurate association rules and invalid clusters respectively. Detection and elimination of these values are necessary but burdensome to be carried out manually. In this chapter, the methods to detect disguised missing values by visual inspection are explained first. Then, the authors describe the methods used to detect these values automatically. Finally, the framework to detect disguised missing data is proposed and a demonstration of the framework on spatial and categorical data sets is provided.

Chapter 2 provides a microarray technology tool analyze thousands of gene expression values with a single experiment. Authors state that due to the huge amount of data, most of recent studies are focused on the analysis and the extraction of useful and interesting information from microarray data. They also provide examples of applications which includes detecting genes highly correlated to diseases, selecting genes which show a similar behavior under specific conditions, building models to predict the disease outcome based on genetic profiles, and inferring regulatory networks This chapter presents a review of four popular data mining techniques (i.e., Classification, Feature Selection, Clustering and Association Rule Mining) applied to microarray data. It describes the main characteristics of microarray data in order to understand the critical issues which are introduced by gene expression values analysis. Each technique is analyzed and examples of pertinent literature are reported. Furthermore, it provides the prospects of data mining research on microarray data.

Chapter 3 proposes a technique that is developed to explore frequent temporal itemsets in the database. The basic idea of this technique is to first partition the database into sub-databases in light of either common starting time or common ending time. Then for each partition, the proposed technique is used progressively to accumulate the number of occurrences of each candidate 2-itemsets. A Directed graph is built using the support of these candidate 2-itemsets (combined from all the sub-databases) as a result of generating all candidate temporal k- itemsets in the database. Therefore, the technique used in this chapter may help researchers not only to understand about generating frequent large temporal itemsets but also helps in understanding of finding temporal association rules among transactions within relational databases.

Chapter 4 discusses and reports how one can be benefited by using Data Mining and Knowledge Discovery techniques in achieving an acceptable level of quality of service of telecommunication systems. The quality of service is defined as the metrics which is predicated by using the data mining techniques, decision tree, association rules and neural networks. It further states that digital telecommunication networks are highly complex systems and thus their planning, management and optimization are challenging tasks. The user expectations constitute the Quality of Service (QoS). It also states that to gain a competitive edge on other operators, the operating personnel have to measure the network in terms of QoS.

Chapter 5 demonstrates a process to identify especially powerful rules. More specifically, this chapter focuses on using association rules and classification mining to select the persistently strong association rules. Persistently strong association rules are association rules that are verifiable by classification mining the same data set. Further, the process for finding persistent strong rules was executed against two data sets obtained from the American National Election Studies. Analysis of the first data set resulted in one persistent strong rule and one persistent rule, while analysis of the second data set resulted in 11 persistent strong rules and 10 persistent rules. This chapter further suggests these rules are the most robust, consistent, and noteworthy among the much larger potential rule sets.

Chapter 6 discusses the relevance of Data Mining (DM) integration with Business Intelligence (BM), and its importance to business users. From the literature review, it was observed that the definition of an underlying structure for BI is missing, and therefore a framework is presented in this chapter. It was also observed that some efforts are being done that seek the establishment of standards in the DM field, both by academics and by people in the industry. Supported by those findings, this chapter introduces an architecture that can conduct to an effective usage of DM in BI. It also includes a DM language that is iterative and interactive in nature. This chapter suggests that the effective usage of DM in BI can be achieved by making DM models accessible to business users, through the use of the presented DM language.

Chapter 7 proposes Shadow Sensitive SWIFT commit protocol for Distributed Real Time Database Systems (DRTDBS), where only abort dependent cohort having deadline beyond a specific value (Tshadow_creation_time) can forks off a replica of itself called a shadow, whenever it borrows dirty value of a data item. It defines the new dependencies Commit-on-Termination external dependency between final commit operations of lender and shadow of its borrower and Begin-on-Abort internal dependency between shadow of borrower and borrower itself. The performance of Shadow Sensitive SWIFT is compared with shadow PROMPT, SWIFT and DSS-SWIFT commit protocols for both main memory resident and disk resident databases with and without communication delay. The chapter also shows that the proposed protocol improves the system performance up to 5% as transaction miss percentage.

In recent times, competition among mobile phone operators is now focused on switching customers away from competitors with extremely discounted telephony rates. In particular, this fierce competitive environment is the result of a saturated market with small or inexistent growth and has caused operators to rely increasingly on Value-Added Services (VAS) for revenue growth. Though mobile phone operators have thousands of different services available to offer to their customers, the contact opportunities to offer these services are limited. In this context, statistical methods and data mining tools can play an important role to optimize content delivery. In Chapter 8 the authors describe novel methods now available to mobile phone operators to optimize targeting and improve profitability from VAS offers.

Chapter 9 looks at various System Execution Modeling (SEM) tools which enable distributed system testers to validate Quality-of-Service (QoS) properties, such as end-to-end response time, throughput, and scalability, during early phases of the software lifecycle. Analytical capabilities of QoS properties, however, are traditionally bounded by a SEM tool's capabilities. This chapter discusses how to mine system execution traces, which are a collection of log messages describing events and states of a distributed system throughout its execution lifetime, generated by distributed systems so that the validation of QoS properties is not dependent on a SEM tool's capabilities. It also uses a real-life case study to illustrate how data mining system execution traces can assist in discovering potential performance bottlenecks using system execution traces.

Chapter 10 highlights how each one profits from the other and illustrates their cooperation in existing systems developed in the medical domain. Through a study, the authors have identified different types of cooperation that combine elicitation and data mining for knowledge acquisition, use expert knowledge to enact the knowledge discovery, use discovered knowledge to validate expert knowledge, and use discovered knowledge to improve the usability of an expert system. The chapter also describes the authors experience in combining expert and discovered knowledge in the development of a system for processing medical isokinetics data.

Chapter 11 focuses on discovering how Mesenchymal Stem Cells (MSCs) can be differentiated is an important topic in stem cell therapy and tissue engineering. In a general context, such differentiation analysis can be modeled as a classification problem in data mining. Specifically, this is concerned with the single-label multi-class classification task. The main aim of this chapter is to compare the performance of different associative classifiers, in terms of classification accuracy, efficiency, number of rules to be generated, quality of such rules, and the maximum number of attributes in rule-antecedents, with respect to MSC differentiation analysis.

Chapter 12 considers knowledge as a strategic weapon to get success in any business. Span of modern business applications have increased from a specific geographical area to the global world. The necessary resources of the business are available in distributed fashion using platform / technology like world wide web and grid of computational facilities. The prime intention of the grid architecture is to utilize scarce resources in objective to efficiently mine information from distributed resources. This chapter describes and differentiates World Wide Web (WWW), Semantic Web, Data Grid, and Knowledge Grid with the literature survey. Considering the limitations of the existing approaches, a generic multilayer architecture is designed and described with detailed methodology for each layer. The chapter also presents fuzzy XML technique to represent domain and meta knowledge into the knowledge repositories. To experiment the proposed generic architecture, an application of e-Learning is selected and a multiagent system mining knowledge grid is discussed with detailed methodology and role of agents in the system.

In Chapter 13, the authors have introduced the concept "Opinion Mining" which is an emerging field of research concerned with applying computational methods to the treatment of subjectivity in text, with a number of applications in fields such as recommendation systems, contextual advertising and business intelligence. In this chapter the authors survey the area of opinion mining and discuss the SentiWordNet lexicon of sentiment information for terms derived from WordNet. Furthermore, the results of their research in applying this lexicon to sentiment classification of film reviews along with a novel approach that leverages opinion lexicons to build a data set of features used as input to a supervised learning classifier are also presented.

It is observed that the volume of information derived from post genomic technologies is rapidly increasing. Due to the amount of involved data, novel computational methods are needed for the analysis and knowledge discovery into the massive data sets produced by these new technologies. Furthermore, data integration is also gaining attention for merging signals from different sources in order to discover unknown relations. Chapter 14 presents a pipeline for biological data integration and discovery of a priori unknown relationships between gene expressions and metabolite accumulations. In this pipeline, two standard clustering methods are compared against a novel neural network approach. The neural model provides a simple visualization interface for identification of coordinated patterns variations, independently of the number of produced clusters. Moreover, the chapter proposes a method for the evaluation of the biological significance of the clusters found.

Finally, in Chapter 15, the authors focus on Internet forum, a web application for publishing user-generated content under the form of a discussion. Messages posted to the Internet forum form threads of discussion and contain textual and multimedia contents. Moreover the chapter addresses an important feature of Internet forums is their social aspect. Internet forums attract dedicated users who build tight social communities. The chapter discusses the architecture of Internet forums, presents an overview of data volumes involved and outlines technical challenges of scraping Internet forum data. A broad summary of all research conducted on mining and exploring Internet forums for social role discovery is also presented in this chapter.

CONCLUSION

Recent progress in scientific and engineering applications has accumulated huge volumes of high-dimensional data, stream data, and spatial and temporal data. Highly scalable and sophisticated data mining tools for such applications represent are of the most active research frontiers in data mining. Emerging applications like stream data, moving object data, RFID data, data from sensor networks, multi-agent data , semantic web, web search, biomedical engineering, telecommunications, geospatial data , climate data and Earth's ecosystems etc. involve great management challenges that also represent new opportunities for data mining research.

In light of the tremendous amount of fast-growing and sophisticated types of data and comprehensive data analysis tasks, data mining technology may be only in its infancy, as the technology is still far from adequate for handling the large-scale and complex emerging application problems. Research is needed to develop highly automated, scalable, integrated reliable data mining systems and tools. Moreover, it is important to promote information exchange among users, data analysts, system developers, and data mining researchers to facilitate the advances available from data mining research, application development and technology transfer.

The book incorporate various advanced data mining techniques and algorithms in emerging domains. Implementation of advanced data mining techniques will be very helpful for scientists, engineers, and physicians as well as researchers, and infrastructures that support them. In addition to these, as researchers revealed data mining is the process of automatic discovery of patterns, transformations, associations and anomalies in massive databases, and is a highly interdisciplinary field representing the confluence of multiple disciplines, such as database systems, data warehousing, machine learning, statistics, algorithms, data visualization, and high-performance computing. Utilizing advanced data mining techniques in emerging domains like stream data mining, mining multi-agent data, mining semantic web, ubiquitous knowledge discovery etc. can improve data mining process.

REFERENCES

Fayyad, U., Piatetsky-Shapiro, G., & Smyth, P. (1996). From Data Mining to Knowledge Discovery in Databases. *American Association for Artificial Intelligence*, 37-54.

Glymour, C., Madigan, D., Pregibon, D., & Smyth, P. (1996). Statistics and Data Mining. *Communication of the ACM* (Special Issue on Data Mining).

Makulowich, J. (1999). *Government Data Mining Systems Defy Definition*. Washington Technology.

Piatetsky-Shapiro, G. (1995). Knowledge Discovery in Personal Data versus Privacy – A Mini-Symposium. *IEEE, 10*(5).

Shrager, J., & Langley,P. (Eds.) (1990). *Computational Models of Scientific Discovery and Theory Formation*. San Francisco, Calif.: Morgan Kaufmann.

Sprites,P., Glymour, C., & Scheines, R. (1993). *Causation, Prediction and Search*. New York: Springer-Verlag.

Acknowledgment

The editor would like to acknowledge the assistance from all individual in the entire process of manuscript preparation and raw process, without whose support the project could not have been satisfactorily completed. I am indebted to all the authors and reviewers who provided their relentless and generous supports. Thanks go to my close friends at CMS College of Science and Commerce for their whole hearted encouragements during the entire process.

Special thanks also go to the dedicated publishing team at IGI Global. Particularly to Kristin M. Klinger – Director of Editorial Content, Erika L. Carter – Acquisition Editor and Joel Gamon –Development Editor for their continuous suggestions, supports and feedbacks. Finally, I would like to thank my wife, daughter and all my family members for their love and support throughout this period.

A.V. Senthil Kumar, Editor
Director, Hindusthan College of Arts and Science
Bharathiar University, India
February, 2010

Section 1
Concepts, Tools and
Techniques

Chapter 1
A Framework to Detect Disguised Missing Data

Rahime Belen
Informatics Institute, METU, Turkey

Tuğba Taşkaya Temizel
Informatics Institute, METU, Turkey

ABSTRACT

Many manually populated very large databases suffer from data quality problems such as missing, inaccurate data and duplicate entries. A recently recognized data quality problem is that of disguised missing data which arises when an explicit code for missing data such as NA (Not Available) is not provided and a legitimate data value is used instead. Presence of these values may affect the outcome of data mining tasks severely such that association mining algorithms or clustering techniques may result in biased inaccurate association rules and invalid clusters respectively. Detection and elimination of these values are necessary but burdensome to be carried out manually. In this chapter, the methods to detect disguised missing values by visual inspection are explained first. Then, the authors describe the methods used to detect these values automatically. Finally, the framework to detect disguised missing data is proposed and a demonstration of the framework on spatial and categorical data sets is provided.

INTRODUCTION

Information management has become challenging with the ever-increasing data volumes. This data deluge has made the data miners and decision makers more enthusiastic than ever about discovering hidden and precious information by applying sophisticated data mining algorithms. However, once they realize that the data quality is poor, these databases often turn out to be data tombs that are rarely or no longer used.

Data quality ensures the completeness, timeliness, accuracy, validity and consistency of data. The systems having high-quality data are usually systems that implement and follow a data quality management plan in a timely fashion. Data quality problems arise when some systems lack of a plan or when for some, a plan is carried out during the design and implementation phases but neglected afterwards. Data quality also suffers in

DOI: 10.4018/978-1-60960-067-9.ch001

systems that change or evolve in time with a data quality management plan that does not take into consideration the new constraints (Hipp, Guntzer, & Grimmer,2001). As Geiger (2004) states, "The viability of the business decisions is contingent on good data and good data is contingent on effective approach to data quality management". Data quality is a multidimensional, complex and morphing concept (Dasu, 2003). In the last decade, it has become a popular issue in the areas of database statistics, workflow management, and knowledge engineering.

Poor data quality is pervasive. It makes it difficult to understand the data in relation to the nature of the phenomena in databases and make appropriate decisions concerning the customers. As a result, the customer satisfaction may be affected. Implementing data warehouses with poor data quality levels is, at best, very risky. Despite of all these risks, a proper data quality management plan can be a unique source of competitive advantage (Redman, 1997).

A well-known data quality problem is that of explicitly missing data that is indicated by using special codes such as "NaN" or "0" which arises when data is not provided or unknown. There are many algorithms to deal with this problem in the literature. On the other hand, missing values can appear as valid values that disguise themselves within the true values. Since they are not explicitly represented, disguise values have less chances of becoming detectable and may easily become a part of an analysis which may lead to biased and inaccurate results. Therefore, disguised missing data impair the data quality surreptitiously. For an example, consider a case where users are asked to select their "gender" in a form where the default selected value in the select box is "female". If the users do not want to reveal their gender information, they may skip the question. Consequently, the default value is recorded incorrectly for male users who have skipped the question. Another example is a website requiring registration in which users tend to leave the default values as they are

or select the first entries in the select box lists. Fields like date of birth or place of birth can be given as examples that are frequently left out and cause disguised missing values to emerge. In such datasets, many people are recorded as if they were born in 'Alabama' (first state in the list of U.S.) or on January 1 (the first value in the pop-up lists of month and day, respectively), which is formally valid but factually incorrect.

A well-known example of disguised missing data is that of Pima Indian diabetes dataset from UCI Machine Learning Example (Pima Indians Diabetes Data Set, 2009). Its metadata file indicates that there are no missing data values. However, Berault (2001) points out that five of seven attributes exhibit biological implausible *zero* values, suggesting that this metadata is incorrect and many analyses were conducted without taking into consideration these values in which some constitute 48% of the data set. When they inspected the data set, they realized that these values disrupted the mean and standard deviation of the distribution of variables, in some cases severely. For example while the mean of serum insulin concentration values was 79.8 mu U/ml on raw data, the mean increased to 155.55 after the removal of disguise values.

The disguise values bring about serious drawbacks in data analysis and mining tasks. For example a hypothesis test was conducted to measure whether there was any difference on diastolic blood pressures between diabetic and nondiabetic patients (Pearson, 2006). The tests showed significantly different results when performed on raw and cleansed data sets even though the discrepancy between the two sets only constituted 5% of them. So hypothesis results can be affected severely even with the existence of small amount of disguise values. Data mining results can also be affected negatively. For example, in k-means clustering algorithm, the disguise values can produce centroids that are shifted towards the disguise values thus form inaccurate clusters. In the presence of disguised missing data, some simple statistics such as standard deviation may shift to some anomalous values. Moreover, correlation analysis and regressions using disguised missing data may give misleading results. An association rule mining procedure may result in generating rules with high support and confidence, which will obscure real findings. At times, companies may suffer from decisions based on these obscure findings in terms of losses in profits or increasing costs.

So far the nature of disguised missing data and its effects were discussed. It is also important to identify the reasons of the emergence of disguised missing values. One of the reasons is the fact that some systems do not allow the users to skip the questions in the forms. Because during the system development phase it has been anticipated that all mandatory data fields are necessary for the application or they may become valuable in a data analysis in the future. However, the consequences of enforcing data entries as mandatory could be severe. Aforementioned examples of disguised missing values for the fields such as gender, date of birth and place of birth can be counted in this context. Users may not enter any information when the provided entries do not provide the information they ask for. For example, if the user is only allowed to select a city in U.S. as place of birth but the user was actually born outside U.S., they may tend to select first entry in the select list box.

Disguise values may appear even the system provides a comprehensive list of options for selection. For example, the users may have bad intentions; they may be neglectful; they may misinterpret the data fields or they deliberately disclose inaccurate information for security or personal reasons i.e. some people may not want to disclose their gender or age information. This is actually becoming a more and more common occurrence with data coming of the Internet and the emergence of CRM applications. Every company wants a database of loyal customers and desires to tailor marketing programs accordingly. However, they end up with a lot of incorrect data in their databases because the information they ask people for is more than people are willing to provide or is perceived to be an invasion of privacy. People may also obtain an advantage by deliberately entering inaccurate information. Such a case occurs very often in banks, manufacturers, and insurance companies when the company policy can encourage people to deliberate falsify information in order to gain a personal benefit (Olson, 2003).

Another reason for disguised missing values to emerge is the *lack of standard missing data representation*. This is due to the fact that the missing data representation code selected by the dataset creator is not conveyed clearly to other individuals or organizations in the analysis of the dataset (Pearson, 2006). Different software environments represent the missing data with different symbols (e.g. 0, -99, '.' or NaN) and even within a single data file, multiple codes are frequently seen for missing data. Pima Indian Diabetes Dataset (Pima Indians Diabetes Data Set, 2009) provides a good illustration for this problem (Hua & Pei, 2007). The data set includes many zero values that are biologically implausible but this value is essentially used to indicate a missing entry. However, since some researchers were not aware of it betimes, 70 experiments were conducted on the complete set including all these zero values. This oversight was reported as extremely serious since some of the missing data fractions reach 48.7% (Pearson, 2006). Multiple codes for missing data can also be seen when one wants to articulate different meaning with each code such as "Other", "Not apply", "Not known", "Not exist". Although each code's meaning is different from each other, they all indicate that none of the provided legitimate values are applicable and therefore can be treated as missing values.

Data importing and data cleansing tools used to find and correct errors in datasets cause data imperfections in the form of disguised missing data as a side effect (Maydanchik, 2007). The problems arise since these package tools are used without understanding the data in sufficient detail. Consequently, faulty specifications result in generating erroneous data from even perfect data and vice versa. These specifications can change the imperfect data into valid values that may be in fact potentially disguised missing data. For example all the missing values may be filled with a rough imputation technique which causes most of the missing values to be filled with the same value. In such a case, imputed data appears to be disguised missing and impair the data quality. As a result, companies may make their data dirtier contrary to their beliefs that they have made it cleaner.

In this chapter, disguised missing data which impairs the quality of data severely is focused particularly. Although other main aspects of data quality issues have already been discussed extensively in the literature, the problems regarding the disguised missing data have recently been recognized.

BACKGROUND

There is very limited previous study on cleansing disguised missing data. Pearson (2006) first coined the term disguised missing data, and suggested outlier mining and distribution anomaly detection methods to uncover disguised missing data. The first framework to automatically detect disguised missing data which requires no domain knowledge was proposed by Hua and Pei (2007). They proposed Embedded Unbiased Heuristic to detect disguised missing values. Both these methodologies are explained in detail in the following sections.

Pearson (2006) defined the disguised missing data formally as follows: Let's define a recorded matrix $\tilde{T} = [v_{ij}]_{mxn}$ that consists of data observations and a matrix $M = [m_{ij}]_{mxn}$ that corresponds to a missingness array, where $m_{ij} = 1$ if v_{ij} is missing and $m_{ij} = 0$ if v_{ij} is not missing. A special code such as "NaN" in the set of available metadata $\dot{X}$ defined

for $\tilde{T}$ is used to denote a missing value. Disguised missing data emerges when M cannot be constructed from $\tilde{T}$ by using data array $\tilde{T}$ and set of metadata $\dot{X}$. Pearson (2006) has stated that the disguise values can appear as outliers and inliers. There are few ways to discover them with the help of statistical methods.

Abnormal Values and Outliers

One can detect suspicious values in a given data set by examining the range of the valid data values. If a reliable metadata set is available, these values can be easily detected. However poor attention is paid to create and maintain accurate metadata repositories. Turkish Census Data Set for year 2000 (Statistics, 2000) is a good example in that matter. In this dataset there are tuples in which the attribute 'Age' is recorded as 999 which is practically impossible. This value is probably used instead of 'unknown' but since it is not mentioned in the data dictionary, it can be overlooked. A domain expert can easily eliminate these values before the analysis.

Another way to detect these values is to use data profiling tools. Like in census data set, data models and catalogues may become inaccurate over time. Data profiling generates valuable metadata in which basic statistics like value frequencies and distribution charts are utilized (Maydanchik, 2007). It enables the data quality experts to learn what the data looks like in terms of subject, attributes, relationships, dependencies and lifecycle of state-dependent objects. For example, *attribute profiling* produces basic aggregate statistics, frequency and distribution information about individual data attributes in order to give insight to the user about the meaning and attribute range. By using these techniques, disguised missing data that have abnormal values even when there is a lack in domain knowledge can be detected.

Outlier detection algorithms may also be used to uncover disguised missing data. This method works for Pima Indians diabetes dataset because zero values are biologically impossible values which fall far outside the ranges. Outlier detection algorithms will not work for many datasets because not all the disguised missing data values will necessarily be detected as outliers. Pearson (2006) states that another problem which needs attention is that outlier detection methods will return not only disguised missing data values but also additional outliers which requires examining the results further to find the disguised missing values.

Distribution Anomalies, Inliers

Disguised missing data values may also appear as inliers. While outliers are erroneous observations located farther away from the sample mean, inliers are erroneous observations located closer to the mean. Although outliers are well known and widely discussed problems in the literature, inliers are less well-known and in many cases disguised missing data values are observed as inliers.

In such a case, unusually high frequencies can help us to detect these values. Zero values in Triceps Skin Fold thickness (TSF) included in the Pima Indians diabetes demonstrates the problem. Approximately 30% of the tuples take zero value and they seem to be inliers rather than outliers. Similar problem is also observed for the city of İstanbul in Turkish Census Data Set (Statistics, 2000). In this dataset the attribute 'Place of birth' is specified by using the traffic license plate codes of the cities (1 for Adana, 2 for Adıyaman, …, 34 for Istanbul etc…). Approximately 4% of the data set takes zero value in this attribute. As it is not provided in the data catalogue, the authors conclude that it is highly possible to overlook these zero values without a domain expert.

(Pearson, 2006) suggests using Quantile-Quantile (Q-Q) plot to detect distribution anomalies of this type. Q-Q plot informally assesses the approximate normality of data sequence. In this plot, repeated value distributional anomalies are highlighted as given in Figure 1. Horizontal lower tail provides clear evidence of the distribution

Figure 1. Q-Q plot on the attribute of "Place of birth" on census data set

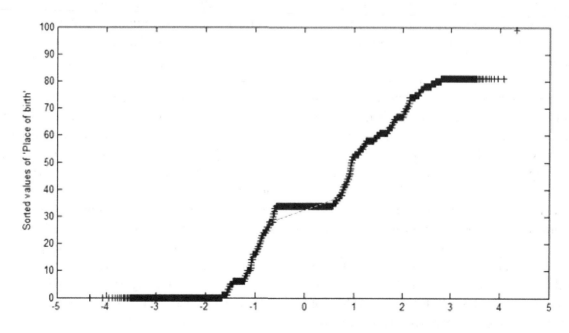

Figure 2. Normal Q-Q plots constructed from 200 randomly distributed data values between 1 and 10

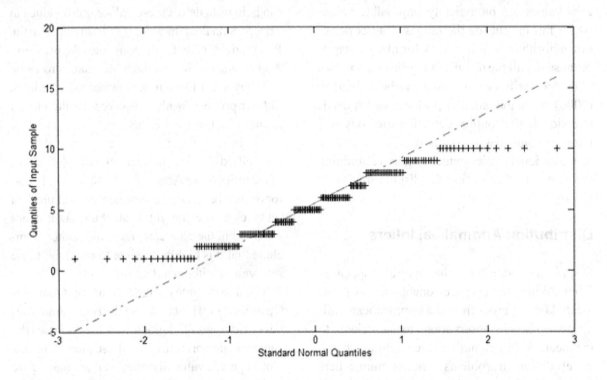

anomaly caused by repeated zero values in the dataset. Flatness in the middle corresponds to the value 34 which represents the city of Istanbul. This means that there is a large portion (44% of the sample set) of people living in their hometown. However, it cannot be sure whether this statistics is true. There is also a possibility that value 34 could be a disguise value which emerges due to bad input form design. For example, the design of the form may not be very user friendly so that users may misunderstood the fields and put a correct value in the wrong field i.e. they have misinterpreted the question as 'the city of residence' instead of 'place of birth'. Flatness at the value 81 also brings to mind a data distribution abnormality, but since its frequency is very low (0.2%), it can be ignored.

If every portion of the Q-Q plot is flat, then it shall be concluded that these flatness are not indicative of data anomaly for the variable. For example, for a randomly generated data set, sev-

eral flat portions will be got when their Q-Q plot is generated as shown in Figure 2 although the data set does not include any disguise value. Pearson (2006) describes such cases as the difficult ones but if the width of one of the flatness is relatively higher, it raises the question whether that value is over-represented for the variable.

Pearson (2006) gave an example to *inliers* disguised missing data values in 2002 AERS demographic dataset (Adverse Event Reporting System (AERS), 2009) and explained an anomaly caused by the value "January 1" of the field Event Date. He observed that January 1 is suspicious value in each year. These results were interpreted as "January 1" was commonly used as surrogate for "date unknown".

As a result, Pearson (2006) did not provide a monolithic framework which can handle all type of disguised missing data but he provided a substantial guidance which can be used to generate one. Consequently the first framework was published one year later by Hua and Pei (2007).

A FRAMEWORK TO DETECT DISGUISED MISSING DATA

Hua and Pei (2007) generated a framework based on the assumption that the projected database of a disguise value often contains a large unbiased sample of the whole dataset. This is to say that if a disguise value often appears randomly and frequently in a dataset, one can expect that each element in any subset containing disguise value has equal chance of being selected as in the whole dataset except the disguise value itself. In other words, this subset should represent the population in the whole dataset well. Based on this property, they utilized the Embedded Unbiased Sample (EUS) heuristic.

General Approach

This approach is based on the heuristic that only a small number of values are frequently used as disguise values (one or two in an attribute) in real world data.

The Embedded Unbiased Sample (EUS) Heuristic

According to the EUS heuristic, the recorded table $\tilde{T}$ is formed of the tuples with true values $\tilde{R}$ and tuples containing disguise values S. For example, if the disguise value in Age attribute is 0 and used frequently in the dataset, the recorded table $\tilde{T}_{age=0} = \tilde{R}_{age=0} + S_{age=0}$.

EUS is defined as follows (Hua & Pei, 2007):

If v is a frequently used disguise value on attribute A, then $T_{A=v}$ contains a large subset $S_v \subseteq \tilde{T}_{=v}$ such that S_v is an unbiased sample of $\tilde{T}$ except for attribute A where $\tilde{T}_{A=v} = \{ \tilde{t} \in \tilde{T} | \tilde{t}.A = v \}$.

Frequently used notations used in this chapter are shown in Table 1.

An example for a biased sample can be shown on a subset of a population satisfying certain criteria and/or constraints. For example, in a census data set, a subset of people who are under

Table 1. Frequently used notations in the text

Symbol	Explanation
T	The truth table
$\tilde{T}$	The recorded table
$\tilde{T}'$	A subset of $\tilde{T}$
$\tilde{t}$	A tuple in the recorded table
$\tilde{t}.A$	An entry in the recorded table
$\tilde{T}_v$	The projected database of value v
S_v	The disguised missing set of v
M_v	The maximal embedded unbiased sample of v
$\phi(\tilde{T}, \tilde{T}')$	The correlation-based sample quality score

18 years old will be unmarried as it is illegal to get married before this age in some countries. This subset will be biased and different than the rest of the data set that also comprise the people who are older than 18 and their marital status could be unmarried, married, widowed or divorced. Hence, this chosen subset is regarded as a biased sample of the whole set. On the other hand, disguised missing values are assumed to appear randomly in a data set. If they are in sufficient amount, they will be seen with every value of each attribute in the dataset. If these tuples comprising v as a subset $\tilde{T}$ is selected, it will contain both accurate tuples $\tilde{R}$ and contaminated tuples S_v. As a result, the aim is to find the subset S_v from $\tilde{T}$ which is unbiased sample of the whole set. In other words, S_v will be the unbiased sample of $\tilde{T}$ except for the attribute including disguise value. The larger the S, the more suspicious the v is for being a disguise value.

EUS Based Framework

If $\tilde{T}$ is recorded correctly without any disguise values, then $\tilde{T} = T$. The truth table shows how the data should be but this table is not available or known to the user. For each value v on attribute A, let T_v be the set of tuples carrying value v in the truth table. Then $T_v \subseteq \tilde{T}_v$ will be the result. This is to say that the projected table both includes the legitimate tuples and tuples injected with disguised missing values v if any. So, the disguised missing set S_v will be $(\tilde{T}_v - T_v)$ if v is used as the disguise on attribute A. According to the EUS heuristic, S_v is an unbiased sample of $\tilde{T}$. The larger the size of S_v, the more frequently v is used as the disguise value. Like the truth table, S_v is unknown to the user. It is difficult to find the exact S_v, but it can be approximated to S_v by using Maximal Embedded Unbiased Sample (MEUS). For each suspected disguise values v, $\tilde{T}_v$ can be obtained. The aim is to find M_v, the largest subset

of $\tilde{T}_v$ which will contain unbiased sample of the whole table. So, there is a need to measure the similarity of all attributes between the subset and the whole database except $A=v$. Similarity can be computed by using correlation (Hua & Pei, 2007). Another factor to be taken into account is the size of the unbiased sample subset. The large subsets increase v's likelihood of being selected as disguise value. After computing M_v for each v in the metadata set $\dot{X}$, MEUS values are sorted according to their values in descending order. The values with large and high quality MEUS should be reported as the suspicious frequent disguise values.

How to Measure Whether a Given Set is an Unbiased Sample of a Table Using Correlation Based Sample Quality Score (CBSQS)

CBSQS was proposed and employed by Hua and Pei (2007). According to this approach, if the values correlated in $\tilde{T}$ are also correlated in $\tilde{T}'$ and vice versa, then the possibility of $\tilde{T}$ and $\tilde{T}'$ having a similar distribution will be high. The correlation based sample quality score is defined as follows: Given table $\tilde{T}$, on attributes $A_1 \ldots A_m$ and subset $\tilde{T}' \subset \tilde{T}$, whether $\tilde{T}'$ is a good sample of $\tilde{T}$. If values which are correlated in $\tilde{T}$ are also correlated in $\tilde{T}'$ and vice versa, then it is likely that $\tilde{T}'$ and $\tilde{T}$ are of similar distribution.

The correlation between v_i and v_j is given by;

$$Corr(v_i, v_j) = \frac{P(v_i, v_j)}{P(v_i)P(v_j)} = \frac{P(v_i \mid v_j)}{P(v_j)} \qquad (1)$$

The CBSQS $\phi(\tilde{T}, \tilde{T}')$ is defined as follows:

$$\sum_{P_{\tilde{T}'}(v_i, v_j) > 0} \left(\frac{P_{\tilde{T}'}(v_i, v_j)}{1 + \mid Corr_{\tilde{T}}(v_i, v_j) - Corr_{\tilde{T}'}(v_i, v_j) \mid^a} \right)$$

$$(2)$$

The score returned from CBSQS is a non-negative number. The higher the score, more likely $\tilde{T}'$ is an unbiased sample of $\tilde{T}$. q is the order imitating Minkowski distance and was suggested as 1 in the experiments. If the subset is the unbiased sample of the whole set, the correlation difference in the denominator is expected to be zero or a very small number. Note that this task is carried out for every pair of v.

How to Compute a Maximal Embedded Unbiased Sample

Recall that to measure whether a value v is a frequent disguise value; they consider both quality of MEUS and relative size of M_v with respect to $\tilde{T}'_v$. So the disguise value score (DV-score) of a subset $U \subseteq \tilde{T}_v$ is defined as:

$$dv(v,U) = \frac{|U|}{|\tilde{T}_v|}\phi(\tilde{T}'_v, U) \qquad (3)$$

Based on this formula, frequent disguise value score is defined as;

$$dv(v) = \max_{U \subseteq \tilde{T}_V}\left\{dv(v,U)\right\} = \max_{U \subseteq \tilde{T}_V}\left\{\frac{|U|}{|\tilde{T}_v|}\phi(\tilde{T}_v, U)\right\} \qquad (4)$$

M_v is selected as the subset maximizing the DV-score. That is,

$$M_v = \arg\max_{U \subseteq \tilde{T}_V}\left\{\frac{|U|}{|\tilde{T}_v|}\phi(\tilde{T}_v, U)\right\} \qquad (5)$$

However, DV-score is not monotonic with respect to the set containment relation. That is to say that any subset of U may have a lower or higher DV-score than $dv(v,U)$. As a result, a greedy approach is used to deal with the problem. The algorithm starts with $\tilde{T}_v$ as the initial sample U. They remove each tuple from the table U tempo-rarily to compute DV-score for (U-$\{\tilde{t}\}$). They repeat this operation for every tuple in the U and then, the one with the largest (U-$\{\tilde{t}\}$) is chosen and removed from the table for good. This operation is repeated until DV-score cannot be improved any further.

PROBLEMS WITH THE CURRENT FRAMEWORK

In this section the cases in which EUS based framework fails are discussed.

The Characteristics of the Data Set

The framework better works with data sets in which *most of the projected databases are not unbiased samples* (Hua & Pei, 2007). For example, many people tend to submit tax returns on the deadline day. As a result, the projected database $\tilde{T}_{submission\ date=deadline}$ will include large unbiased samples of all tax returns although the attribute value is not disguised missing value. In addition, disguised missing values should not be randomly distributed in the domain of the attribute. Otherwise, it will be difficult to identify them.

Highly Dependent Attributes

Two attributes are called dependent when the value of the first attribute influences possible values of the second attribute (Maydanchik, 2007). If a projected database $\tilde{T}_v$ include such dependent attribute couple(s), Equation 2 may return a high score even if $\tilde{T}_v$ is not a good sample.

Recall that CBSQS in Equation 2 is based on joint probability and correlation difference. When the attributes are highly dependent, joint probability between their values will converge to 1. They will also be highly correlated both in $\tilde{T}_v$ and the whole dataset which will cause the denominator to converge to one. Therefore value couples of dependent attributes will provide considerable increment in Equation 2. Even though the value couples of other attributes return low results, total result may still be high and a biased sample can be detected as an unbiased sample.

Consider a dataset with the attributes A, B and C. Assume that A can take 3 different values; a_1, a_2 and a_3, B can take 3 values as b_1, b_2 and b_3 and finally C can take 2 values as c_1 and c_2. Let's assume that values of A are highly dependent with values of B under some circumstances. For example, when the attribute C takes the value c_1, A and B take the value a_1 and b_1 respectively. However, when the attribute C takes a value other than c_1, the rule breaks and B takes the value disregarding the value of A. In this dataset if disguised missing data for the attribute C is to be detected, a projected table for the value c_1 as given in Figure 3 shall be taken.

For this projected database $\tilde{T}_v = c_1$ the formula turns out to be;

$$\phi(\tilde{T}, \tilde{T}') = \frac{P_{\tilde{T}'}(A = a_1, B = b_1)}{1 + |\ Corr_{\tilde{T}}(a_1, b_1) - Corr_{\tilde{T}'}(a_1, b_1)\ |^2}$$

(6)

In a dataset where the ratio of tuples having the value c_1 is high, the nominator will be directly high. In the denominator, the difference between the correlation in the D and correlation

in the $\tilde{T}_v = c_1$ will be computed where the correlation function is defined as;

$$Corr(a_1, b_1) = \frac{P(a_1 \mid b_1)}{P(b_1)}$$

(7)

Then the correlation will be calculated as 1 for the $\tilde{T}_v = c_1$ and D because both the nominator and denominator is 1. So the equation turns out to be;

$$\phi(\tilde{T}, \tilde{T}') = \frac{P_{\tilde{T}}(A = a_1, B = b_1)}{1 + |1 - 1|^2} = P_{\tilde{T}'}(A = a_1, B = b_1)$$

(8)

So the result of

$$\phi(\tilde{T}, \tilde{T}')$$

will be high enough to select value c_1 as disguised missing value even though its projected table is not an unbiased sample of D.

Data miners should be aware of the fact that they can come across with such highly dependent attributes in many applications. For example in a legacy systems database, the redundant attributes that refer to the same attribute of a given entity are created on purpose. Such attributes are used for data quality assessment purposes, i.e. the value of an attribute must be compatible with the value of its redundant attribute. Other attribute dependen-

Figure 3. The projected database for $\tilde{T}_v = c_1$. $C = c_1$ only appears when $A = a_1$ and $B = b_1$

A	B	C
a_1	b_1	c_1
a_1	b_1	c_1
a_1	b_1	c_1
a_2	b_2	c_2
a_3	b_3	c_2

Main table D

$C = c_1$ ⟹

A	B
a_1	b_1
a_1	b_1
a_1	b_1

Projected database $\tilde{T}_v = c_1$

cies that also need attention are *derived attributes*, *partially dependent attributes*, *attributes with dependent optionality*, and *correlated attributes* (Maydanchik, 2007). Although they are used to derive data quality rules, they may bias the results while detecting disguise values using CBSQS.

Random Attributes

EUS heuristic will not work when disguise value for a random attribute is to be detected. However the heuristic still fails when computing a disguise value for a nonrandom attribute in a dataset that comprises random attributes. The deficiency is caused by the fact that the random attributes will probably have similar distribution in any sub sample $\tilde{T}_v$ and the whole dataset which causes them to return high scores in Equation 2. Although the attribute couples other than the random attributes do not have similar distributions in sub sample $\tilde{T}_v$ and the whole dataset, the score of random attribute couple(s) can still lead to a high CBSQS. For a detailed proof regarding the effect of highly dependent attributes (Belen, 2009).

Required Features

Since the approach is based on the correlation between attribute couples, importance to which attributes to cover is to be attached. Should all or some of the attributes within the dataset be used? If some of the attributes are utilized, how to decide which to be chosen? The inclusion of the irrelevant attributes will increase the computational requirements unnecessarily. In addition, they make the detection of the disguise values rather difficult; if not impossible. The problem with feature selection will be demonstrated in the Experimental Results section.

SOLUTIONS AND RECOMMENDATIONS

In order to eliminate the aforementioned deficiencies CBSQS have been revised. Recall that CBSQS returns a nonnegative number for an attribute couple with no upper limit. Consequently when the scores of attribute couples are added together, highly dependent or totally independent attribute couples may bias the result returning high scores than can dominate the summation. As a remedy, distribution hypothesis tests which are not sensitive to such cases can be of benefit to use.

The authors have decided on **Chi Square Two Sample Test** which checks whether two data samples come from the same distribution without specifying what that common distribution is (Heckert, 2006). The Chi-square Two Sample Test works on categorical data. If a data set contains discrete attributes besides categorical ones, then binning should be carried out on the discrete ones. The basic idea is to measure whether a projected database $\tilde{T}_v$ is an unbiased sample of the whole data set by using Chi Square Two Sample Test instead of correlation.

More formally, the chi-square two-sample test statistic can be defined as follows.

H$_0$: The two samples come from a common distribution.
H$_a$: The two samples do not come from a common distribution.
Test Statistic: For the chi-square two-sample tests, the data is divided into k bins and the test statistic is defined as:

$$x^2 = \sum_{i=1}^{k} \left(\frac{(K_1 R_i - K_2 S_i)^2}{R_i + S_i} \right) \tag{9}$$

where k is the number of categories (or bins), R_i is the observed frequency of bin i for the first sample, and S_i is the observed frequency of bin

Figure 4. The pseudo code used for data transformation and computing sample quality

---

Input: D data set, subset $U \subseteq \tilde{T}_v$, A_v attribute which is being analyzed for disguise missing value.

Output: Sample quality score sqs of the subset U and $\tilde{T}_v$ will be calculated on the transformed subset U' and $\tilde{T}_v''$

// C_D and C_U indicate the class label columns for the whole data set and the subset respectively.

```
1.  k = 1;
2.  sqs = 0;
3.  for i = 1 → n − 1
4.      for j = 1 → n
5.          if A_i ≠ A_v and A_j ≠ A_v
6.              Generate corresponding class label columns C_Dk and C_Lk for A_i and A_j in U and T̃_v respectively;
7.              Insert C_Lk and C_Dk to U' and T̃_v'' respectively;
8.              Measure the distribution similarity s between C_Dk and C_Lk using "Chi Square Two Sample Test"
9.              sqs = sqs + s;
10.             k = k + 1;
11.         end if
12.     end for
13. end for
14. RETURN sqs
```

---

i for the second. K_1 and K_2 are scaling constants that are used to adjust for unequal sample sizes. Specifically,

$$K_1 = \sqrt{\frac{\sum_{i=1}^{k} S_i}{\sum_{i=1}^{k} R_i}}$$

$$K_1 = \sqrt{\frac{\sum_{i=1}^{k} R_i}{\sum_{i=1}^{k} S_i}} \qquad (10)$$

The aim is to measure the distribution similarity between attribute couples of the dataset and the projected subset. In order to achieve this, the dataset is represented as a means of *value couples* they include. For example, new class labels for all the *value pairs* in attributes A_1 and A_2 that appear together have been generated. If A_1 and A_2 have p and k number of categories respectively, p x k new class labels have been generated, in

turn a new attribute column is created and finally put the new class labels that the value couples belong to. This data transformation is repeated for every attribute couple and for a dataset of n number of attributes a new dataset D' containing $\binom{n}{2}$ attributes is generated. See Figure 4.

In order to clarify the pseudo code, the example for highly dependent couples given in Figure 3 is revisited. For this dataset $\binom{3}{2} = 3$ attributes will be got. Before giving the transformed dataset, the value couples need to be classified as shown in Table 2.

By generating the class labels for each value couple the dataset can be transformed as seen in Figure 5.

In transformed dataset D', C_{D1} indicates the classes of value couples of attribute A and B, C_{D2} indicates the classes of value couples of attribute A and C and finally C_{D3} indicates the classes of

Table 2. Class labels for value couples

Value1	Value2	Class label
a_1	b_1	1
a_1	b_2	2
a_1	b_3	3
a_2	b_1	4
a_2	b_2	5
a_2	b_3	6
a_3	b_1	7
a_3	b_2	8
a_3	b_3	9
a_1	c_1	10
a_1	c_2	11
a_2	c_1	12
a_2	c_2	13
a_3	c_1	14
a_3	c_2	15
b_1	c_1	16
b_1	c_2	17
b_2	c_1	18
b_2	c_2	19
b_3	c_1	20
b_3	c_2	21

value couples of attribute B and C. Checking the labels for couples from Table 2, transformed dataset can be generated accordingly. As the class label columns are generated for the main dataset D, class label columns are generated for each subset $U \subseteq \tilde{T}_v$ and sample quality scores are calculated by using Chi Square two sample tests as shown in Figure 7.

The same MEUS calculations in Equations 3, 4 and 5 are used but the analyses are conducted on the transformed data set. CBSQS assumes a linear relationship between values. If an attribute has multiple dependency relationships, it may fail. For example, relations in XOR problem cannot be captured correctly by CBSQS as the result depends on both values of the two attributes. In order to find the relations that are dependent together on triple, quartet or more attributes, data transformations are provided. Chi-square two sample test can run on these labels despite the computational costs.

Transformations can be undertaken by the method given in Figure 4 which will be computed once for the whole dataset. These class labels

Figure 5. Transforming the dataset D

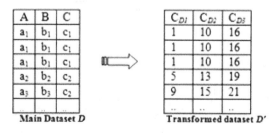

A	B	C
a_1	b_1	c_1
a_1	b_1	c_1
a_1	b_1	c_1
a_2	b_2	c_2
a_3	b_3	c_2
..		

Main Dataset D

C_{D1}	C_{D2}	C_{D3}
1	10	16
1	10	16
1	10	16
5	13	19
9	15	21
..	..	..

Transformed dataset D'

Figure 6. Projected database of value c_1

C_{D1}	C_{D2}	C_{D3}
1	10	16
1	10	16
1	10	16
5	13	19
9	15	21
..	..	..

Main table D

C_{U1}	C_{U2}
1	13
1	13
1	13

Projected database $\tilde{T}_v = c_1$

Figure 7. Main Framework

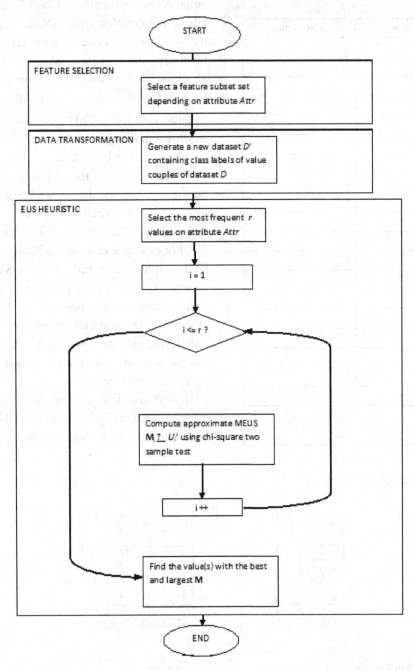

are then used to compare the distribution of the projected dataset with the whole data set. In order to demonstrate the improvements of the methodology, the problems mentioned in the "Problems with the Current Framework" section is revisited.

Highly Dependent Attributes

Recall that highly dependent attributes cause problems since CBSQS is based on the joint probability and correlation difference. Using Data

Transformation and Chi-Square Two Sample Test, this deficiency is inherently eliminated. Transforming the data also prevents the drawback of highly dependent attributes in CBSQS. Recall that the problem in CBSQS arises when the dependent attributes return relatively high scores and dominate the summation. As the correlation factor and the calculations that have been undertaken on the transformed data set are eliminated, the negative impact of highly dependent attributes will be eliminated from the calculations. If the class labels have similar distributions in the projected table with the main dataset, the result will be high accordingly. The example given in Figure 5 is again considered. Similar transformation can be seen in Figure 6.

In order to detect if $\tilde{T}_v = c_1$ is an unbiased sample, distribution similarity between columns C_{U1} and C_{D1} is calculated first via Chi-square two sample test. This will return a score between 0 and 1. Finally the similarity between columns C_{U2} and C_{D2} is calculated and added to the score. Since most of the values observed in C_{D1} and C_{D2} are not observed in C_{U1} and C_{U2} respectively, the scores in Equation 6 will be high and sample quality score will return low accordingly.

Random Attributes

Redundant attributes can be eliminated by using feature selection methods such as minimum-redundancy maximum-relevancy algorithm. The goal of the algorithm is to select a feature subset set that best characterizes the statistical property of a target classification variable, subject to the constraint that these features are mutually as dissimilar to each other as possible, but marginally as similar to the classification variable as possible (Peng, Long, & Ding, 2005). If the classification variable is selected as A_v the attribute comprising the candidate disguise value, the attributes that are dissimilar to A can be found out $_v$ and remove them from the calculations. As a consequence,

independent attributes which cause biased results will be eradicated. Selecting the feature subset also increases computational efficiency which has a significant effect while working with large datasets. Since value sets of attributes are dealt with, dimension reduction decreases the time required to run the method significantly. The overall process can be seen in Figure 7.

EXPERIMENTAL RESULTS

The performance of the proposed framework on three data sets with different characteristics has been evaluated.

Pima Indians Diabetes Data Set

This dataset include records about Pima Indian females who are at least 21 year old and tested either positive or negative for diabetes. There are 768 instances with 8 attributes which are used to determine the class of the patient whether s/he is diabet or not. This data set was also used by Hua and Pei (2007) in their analyses. The attributes of the data set and results can be found in Table 3.

On the attributes *diastolic blood pressure*, *triceps skin fold thickness*, *2-hour serum insulin*, and *body mass index*, there are 35, 227, 374, and 11 tuples that have value 0 respectively. All these methods find 0 (appear as outliers) as the most frequent disguise value for each of these attributes. These results are compatible with the domain knowledge since those attributes do not take values 0 for a person of reasonable condition. *Age* 21 is picked up as a frequent disguise values in both methods which is an inlier.

As seen in Table 3, the same results except for the attribute DIA is obtained. On the attribute "*diastolic blood pressure*", DIA, the method based on CBSQS detects 0 as the most frequent disguise value. The result agrees with the domain knowledge. But while analyzing $T_{v=0}$ the dependency effect is also observed. There are 35 tuples

Table 3. Comparison between CBSQS, Chi-Square Sample Test and the approach used in this chapter

ATTRIBUTE	Hua and Pei (2007)'s Approach based on CBSQS			Approach used in the chapter		
	Most Frequent Disguise Value	Number of Occurrences	Number of tuples in the approximate MEUS	Most Frequent Disguise Value	Number of Occurrences	Number of tuples in the approximate MEUS
Number of times pregnant (NPG)	0	111	110	0	111	110
Plasma glucose concentration at 2 hours (PGL)	91	9	9	91	9	9
Diastolic blood pressure (mm Hg) (DIA)	0	35	35	70	35	35
Triceps skin fold thickness (mm) (TSF)	0	227	227	0	227	226
2-Hour serum insulin (mu U/ml) (INS)	0	374	374	0	374	373
Body mass index (weight in kg/(height in m)^2) (BMI)	0	11	11	0	11	12
Diabetes pedigree function (DPF)	No	No	No	No	No	No
Age (years) (AGE)	21	63	57	21	63	62

having value 0 in DIA attribute and each of these tuples have value 0 in the attribute "*2 hour serum insulin*" and 33 of them have 0 in "*triceps skin fold thickness*". Such a dependency can bias the results and subsets in which many values couples are excluded may be detected as unbiased samples. Here, the result for DIA obtained via CBSQS is true but this algorithm may find a non-disguise value as disguise in a different set. For example consider the example given in Figure 3. The a_1, b_1 and c_1 values of three attributes *A*, *B* and *C* appear together but they cannot be observed with any other values. Hence they are highly dependent with each other. Such highly dependent relations can be monitored in real world applications i.e. a device may malfunction and produce specific output only under specific conditions. However, Hua and Pei (2007) commented on their results as although the frequency of the value 70 is greater than the frequency of the value 0, their method did not pick up just the most frequent one. For

a detailed proof regarding the effect of highly dependent attributes (Belen, 2009). On the other hand, the results based on chi-square test show that data transformation and method still need improvement.

Pima Indians Diabetes Data Set with Redundant Attributes

To demonstrate the effects caused by random attributes on the performance of CBSQS computations, Pima Indian Diabetes dataset is used.

Initially an attribute comprising uniformly distributed random values between 1 and 20 is created and included them in the data set. The algorithm was run on the new dataset. Then the process continued to add attributes with random values incrementally to observe the effects. Table 4 shows the detected disguise values for each dataset.

Recall that for the attributes TSF and INS, 0 is by far the most frequent value (29.6% and 48.7%

Table 4. The most frequent disguise values found by CBSQS algorithm in each run

Attribute	Original dataset	Dataset with 1 random attribute	Dataset with 2 random attributes	Dataset with 3 random attributes	Dataset with 4 random attributes	Dataset with 5 random attributes	Dataset with 6 random attributes
NPG	0	0	0	0	0	0	0
PGL	**91**	**106**	**111**	111	**102**	**105**	**108**
DIA	0	0	70	70	70	70	70
TSF	0	0	0	0	0	0	0
INS	0	0	0	0	0	0	0
BMI	0	0	0	0	0	0	0
DPF	NO	NO	NO	NO	NO	NO	NO
AGE	21	21	**22**	**21**	**22**	22	22

of the attributes TSF and INS have the value 0 respectively) and therefore they are still detected as the most frequent disguise values despite the random attribute(s). Zero value in the attribute DIA is an example for a disguise value that appears to be an outlier. In this attribute the value 70 can become the most frequent disguise value when more than 2 redundant attributes are added. Therefore data miners should give extra attention to the attributes that they would like to work with. In the framework used in the chapter, as the redundant attributes are eliminated before starting calculation, consistent results are obtained.

Highway Traffic Accidents Data Set

The highway traffic accidents data set includes the traffic accidents happened between 2006 and 2008 for all the cities in Turkey. The data set has got 22 attributes: *Date, Time, Town, Number of people died, Number of people injured, Latitude of accident, Longitude of accident* are some of these attributes. The data was entered by the traffic inspectorates around the country. When an accident takes place, the local officer should enter the details of the accident, i.e. time and date of the accident, town, city, the road name, road type, accident type, number of dead and wounded people, latitude and longitude of the accident, all

of which are mandatory. The system implements basic data quality checks. For example, the system lets officers to put the requested information only in specific formats and range such that users cannot specify an invalid date or road name.

In this experiment, cities of İzmir for 2008, Osmaniye for 2006, Istanbul for 2008 and Adana for 2008 have been analyzed as these were reported as the most problematic ones among all by the domain expert. They have 118, 262, 108, 1379 tuples respectively.

The disguise values were investigated on *X coordinate* and *Y coordinate* which hold latitude and longitude respectively of the point on the highway where the accident happened because the values of the coordinates were reported as unreliable by the experts. As a black spot is represented by two coordinates, both values together should be taken into consideration instead of analyzing individual attributes. So new point labels for each *X* and *Y* coordinate couples are generated. In fact this resulted in a huge number of points for a city. Recall that EUS heuristic depends on the assumption that the projected database of a disguise value often contains a large unbiased sample of the whole dataset. In such an attribute with numerous values, none of the projected database will probably contain a *large* unbiased sample. Consequently it will be impossible to find disguise values.

However, the data collection environment is also to be considered as it may give valuable information about the characteristics of the data set. In this environment, the coordinate information is obtained by the GPS devices. However, the domain expert stated the following reasons which may cause the incorrect specification of the coordinates:

a. GPS devices may malfunction due to a problem in the projection system and consequently inaccurate coordinate information may be obtained.
b. Longitude information may be entered in lieu of latitudes and vice versa. This situation arises especially when these coordinates are very close in a particular town.
c. Users may enter the coordinate information inaccurately in the database.
d. The coordinate information may be obtained before GPS devices get ready (GPS devices should receive information from at least three satellites before giving an accurate measure.)
e. The borders of a town or city may be changed or may have been defined incorrectly in the system's database.
f. Users may enter the same coordinates to the database systematically for any given points. The reasons may be numerous: users may not know the exact location; users may enter the same values to save time and it is easy; users may use dated reports to enter values. Such values are called as disguised missing values.

As a result, working on *areas* rather than the individual *points* is thought to be more valuable and effective which was also confirmed by the domain expert. So those areas that are frequently used as disguise values should be known. For this, 100 is used as binning range which gave the most reasonable results in the previous studies

with some cities in the rest of the data set. The minimum-redundancy maximum-relevancy algorithm returned the five most relevant attribute as: "Official Report Number", "Name of the Officer", "Road ID", "Town" and "Day of the Week" which were all approved by the domain expert.

Table 5 shows the results for four spatial datasets. The results of the framework used in this chapter were shown to the domain expert and all the results were verified. The domain expert stated that attributes *Road ID* and *Town* are correlated with the blackspot where the accident occured and added that these attribute values are expected to be the same for the coordinates that are marked as disguise values in the experiments.

The performance of the method used in this chapter is compared with respect to CBSQS. Hua and Pei (2007)'s method was able to find the disguise values in Osmaniye and İzmir correctly since these points ([36; 37] and [0;0]) were frequently used as disguises. For example in Osmaniye, 66 accidents out of 108 were recorded at the coordinate [36.00, 37.00] which is apparently suspicious. This value was recorded on 5 different highways and 4 towns. The algorithm used in this chapter as well as EUS heuristic returned this point as the most frequent disguised missing value. However, the other method failed to identify the coordinates correctly for Adana and Istanbul. Therefore, those algorithms were executed based on the areas (coordinate bins) that have been created as a part of the framework. CBSQS marked the area where the X coordinate ranges between 35,2265 to 35,2313 and Y coordinate ranges between 37,0001 to 37,0038 as the most frequent disguise value area. When the projected database of this area is analyzed, it was observed that the reason why the sample is detected as unbiased sample is the random attribute effect. Because all 22 attributes were used in their computations as opposed to the method in which only 5 relevant attributes were used. As a result, the irrelevant attributes such as *Number of people injured* or *Time* have affected their results nega-

Table 5. The most frequent disguise values found by the algorithm

Dataset	Detected disguise values	Number of tuples in the approximate MEUS	Problem observed by domain expert
Adana	35,7478-35,7509; 36,9881-36,5000	11	Accident points that are recorded very close to each other are said to be on different roads (although they should be stated on the same road); some of which do not fall into this area.
Istanbul	28,8204-28,8245; 41,0255-41,0337	31	Some accident points do not fall onto any roads. Accident points that are recorded very close to each other are said to be on different roads. The same points are sometimes marked as they are in different towns.
Osmaniye	36,000; 37,000	66	Not a point on any road in the region. The same point is recorded in 4 different towns.
Izmir	0;0	146	Outlier

tively. When the same five attributes were used for the other algorithm, an area where only two accidents happened returned as a result and still could not the ones that were supposed to be found.

Here, there are two challenges; how to decide binning ranges and how to decide optimum number of selected features. It is important to note that by creating these ranges, linearly bounded areas (squares or rectangles) were obtained. At that point it is very difficult to decide if this partitioning is reasonable. Depending on the number of accidents, larger or smaller areas may be needed. Deciding on the optimum number of features is another crucial issue. Therefore it is highly suggested to work with domain experts during these processes.

FUTURE RESEARCH DIRECTIONS

The importance of data quality has been realized in the recent years as a result of ever increasing database sizes. One particular challenge is that of disguised missing values that emerge mostly because of human error. Although the problem has been known for years, there are only few methods to handle this problem to some degree. As a result, there are several research challenges awaiting for the researchers to be solved. In current studies, it is assumed that there are only few disguise values frequently found in databases.

It is believed that disguise values emerge as a result of similar behaviors of users i.e. the first default entries in a select box usually give rise to disguise values. On the other hand, if several databases are integrated into a single database, several different disguise values may appear and it may be hard to detect them correctly. One can carry out disguised missing value detection algorithm for each database, correct all and then integrate them. Different disguise values may arise due to the different actions of different users. For example, in highway traffic accidents data set for city of Istanbul, since the population of the city is very high, the accidents are recorded by many different people from different regions in the city. Consequently, it is realized that different disguise values have come out which were in relation to the number of system users. So algorithms may become incapable to detect them. But once the dataset is partitioned into well-known geographical regions by taking into consideration the data enterer profiles, better results may be obtained.

To design the detection methods which works offline, data is collected first to derive some meaning out of the data set. Then, it is measured how "*good*" the quality of the data set is and prepare the dataset for further analyses by cleansing. But it cannot be ensured that the output data set is 100% accurate. It is always important to take timely precautions to make the database highly accurately populated. Developing methods working in real time that detect the occurrence of such values, by whom and when may help us improve the quality of databases. For example, if the details of people who tend to enter inaccurate values at certain times because of tiredness or other reasons are known, the enterprise or the organization may work on solutions to deal with the problem. If a person systematically enters wrong values, it may be because of unawareness of any standard metadata. If the data model is explained to the user in detail, the same problems from emerging again can be precluded. Another reason could be the fact that information is missing or inaccurate in the data catalogue. After interviewing with the user, data models or catalogues can be updated accordingly.

Disguised missing values may emerge in databases that are populated with automatic measures of sensors and measurement devices. If such devices malfunction or some specific external circumstances occur, they may record erroneous information including disguised missing values. It would have been interesting to scrutinize these databases and compare the performances and accuracy of the algorithms. Some deficiencies of the disguised missing value detection methods have been demonstrated. Improvements can still be made for more accurate calculation of dv-score and unbiased sample scores. The authors believe that factor analysis will be worthwhile to investigate in this respect for a future study. In particular, the analysis could be a remedy for the aforementioned problems about derived and dependent attribute values.

CONCLUSION

Detection of disguised missing data is mainly focused in this chapter. The authors have explained the basic visual methods to detect some forms of disguises and the frameworks to identify them without requiring any domain expert. Regardless of the method or framework chosen, elimination of redundant attributes may help to improve the results. The authors have also demonstrated that such attributes bias the calculation of dv-score. In particular, the approach proposed by Pearson (2006) and Hua and Pei (2007) in terms of its deficiencies and capabilities have been analyzed and an improvement based on Chi-Square Two Sample Test is proposed. The effects of redundant attributes on survey, medical and spatial datasets have been expressed.

In EUS based framework (Hua & Pei, 2007), the value whose projected database is the unbiased sample of whole dataset is identified as disguised missing value. In order to measure whether a set of tuples is an unbiased sample of a dataset, a method called *correlation-based sample quality score*, *CBSQS*, is used which is based on joint probability and correlation differences. Here it is assumed that if the values that are correlated in a dataset are also correlated in its subset, the subset can be considered as an unbiased sample of the dataset. But in reality many cases may emerge which do not meet the aforementioned expectations. When a subset includes highly dependent attributes, value couples of dependent attributes will result in considerable increment in the equation. Although the value couples of other attributes return low results, the total result may still be high and a biased sample can be detected as unbiased sample. Problems will also arise when dataset includes random attributes which have similar distributions in the main dataset and in any projected database. Therefore they will lead to a high score although the rest of the attribute couples do not have similar distributions in the main dataset and the subset.

In the light of the observed deficiencies, a new methodology to measure sample quality score based on *Chi-square Two Sample Test* have been generated which checks whether two data samples come from the same distribution without specifying what that common distribution is. In this methodology, the authors represent the dataset as a means of value couples they include. The data transformation reduces the negative impact of highly dependent attributes on the results and captures the multiple dependency relationships. After this process, the similarity of distributions in the main dataset and subsets using *Chi-square Two Sample Tests* is measured. The authors adhered to the MEUS calculations proposed by Hua and Pei (2007) in their proposed framework.

The importance of taking the nature of the dataset into account in order to detect disguised missing data accurately is highlighted. For example, disguised missing values may emerge differently in spatial data sets compared with the survey data sets. While in the survey data set only few disguises are used frequently, disguise values may be present within a specific area in the spatial sets. In the former case regarding survey data, users tend to select specific values from a select or list box. On the other hand in the latter case, users may select a coordinate (X and Y) by clicking on a map to register an event/occasion. Also it could be that measurement devices may malfunction or they are not calibrated. As it is possible to see minor changes between the latitudes and longitudes of the locations of the incidents on the same black spots that are recorded manually, it is advisable to seek disguise value ranges instead of a single value in a spatial data set. Therefore, before conducting the analysis the coordinates should be transformed into spatial regions.

Disguise values, when found, can be treated like explicitly missing values in some conditions. However, it is important to note that not all tuples comprising disguise values are actually missing values. Recalling the gender example given in the introduction section, while some people enter their gender information correctly, there will be some who have entered incorrectly. If other collected data provides sufficient information regarding the gender such as forename, it can be corrected to some degree. Otherwise it will be difficult to identify which data is given inaccurately that is to be marked in fact as missing. Also there are well-known techniques to impute missing data in the literature that can be used (Grzymala-Busse & Hu, 2001).

REFERENCES

Adverse Event Reporting System (AERS). Retrieved June 1, 2009, from U.S. Food and Drug Administration: http://www.fda.gov/cder/aers/default.htm

Belen, R. (2009). *Detecting disguised missing data.* Unpublished MSc thesis, Ankara Turkey: ODTU

Berault, J. (2001). Data mining diabetic databases: Are rough sets a useful addition? In *Proceedings of. 33rd Symposium on the Interface, Computing Science and Statistics, Fairfax.* Fairfax, VA. Costa Mesa (CA): The Interface Foundation of North America.

Dasu, T. J. T. (2003). *Exploratory Data Mining and Data Cleaning.* New York: Wiley-Interscience.

Geiger, J. (2004). Data Quality Management The Most Critical Initiative You Can Implement. In *Proceedings of the Twenty-Ninth Annual SAS® Users Group International Conference.* Montreal, Canada: SAS Institute Inc.

Grzymala-Busse, J. W., & Hu, M. (2001). A Comparison of several approaches to missing attribute values in Data Mining. *Lecture Notes in Computer Science*, 378–385. doi:10.1007/3-540-45554-X_46

Heckert, A. (2006). Chi Square Two Sample. *Tarihinde,* Retrieved June 11, 2009, from http://www.itl.nist.gov: http://www.itl.nist.gov/div898/software/dataplot/refman1/auxillar/ chi2samp.htm

Hipp, J., Güntzer, U., & Grimmer, U. (2001). *Data Quality Mining: Making a Virtue Neccessity.*

Hua, M., & Pei, J. (2007). Cleaning Disguised Missing Data: A Heuristic Approach. In *Proceedings of the 13th ACM SIGKDD International Conference on Knowledge Discovery and Data Mining* (pp. 950-958). California: IEEE.

Maydanchik, A. (2007). *Data Quality Assessment (Data Quality for Practitioners Series). Technics Publications*. LLC.

Olson, J. E. (2003). *Data Quality: The Accuracy Dimension*. San Francisco: Morgan Kaufmann.

Pearson, R. K. (2006). The Problem of Disguised Missing Data. *ACM SIGKDD Explorations Newsletter, 8*(1), 83–92. doi:10.1145/1147234.1147247

Peng, H., Long, F., & Ding, C. (2005). Feature selection based on mutual information: Criteria of max-dependency, max-relevance, and min-redundancy. *IEEE Transactions on Pattern Analysis and Machine Intelligence, 27* (8), 1226-1238. *Pima Indians Diabetes Data Set.* (2009). Retrieved June 21, 2009, from http://archive.ics.uci.edu/ml/datasets/Pima+Indians+Diabetes

Redman, T. C. (1997). *Data Quality for the Information Age*. Norwood, MA, USA: Artech House Publishers.

Statistics, N. I. (2000). *2000 National Census Data Set: The Social and Economic attributes of the population*. Ankara: National Institute of Statistics.

KEY TERMS AND DEFINITIONS

Chi-Square Two Sample Test: A test which is used to check whether two data samples come from the same distribution without specifying what that common distribution is.

Correlation Based Sample Quality Score: A score which is used to measure the similarity between the projected subset and the whole set based on the correlation method.

Data Quality: Refers to the degree of excellence exhibited with respect to the completeness, timeliness, accuracy, validity and consistency of data.

Disguised Missing Value: A value which is missing in the data set but a legitimate data value is used instead of using an explicit code for missing values.

Inlier: Erroneous observations located closer to the mean.

Maximal Embedded Unbiased Sample: A maximal subset of the projected database of the disguise value.

Missing Value: No data value is provided for a variable in an observation and can be explicitly indicated in a database by using different codes such as *NA* to imply *not available*.

Outlier: Observation that lies an abnormal distance from other values in a random sample from a population.

Chapter 2
Microarray Data Mining:
Issues and Prospects

Giulia Bruno
Politecnico di Torino, Italy

Alessandro Fiori
Politecnico di Torino, Italy

ABSTRACT

Microarray technology is a powerful tool to analyze thousands of gene expression values with a single experiment. Due to the huge amount of data, most of recent studies are focused on the analysis and the extraction of useful and interesting information from microarray data. Examples of applications include detecting genes highly correlated to diseases, selecting genes which show a similar behavior under specific conditions, building models to predict the disease outcome based on genetic profiles, and inferring regulatory networks. This chapter presents a review of four popular data mining techniques (i.e., Classification, Feature Selection, Clustering and Association Rule Mining) applied to microarray data. It describes the main characteristics of microarray data in order to understand the critical issues which are introduced by gene expression values analysis. Each technique is analyzed and examples of pertinent literature are reported. Finally, prospects of data mining research on microarray data are provided.

INTRODUCTION

With the developing of new technologies and revolutionary changes in biomedicine and bio-technologies, there was an explosive growth of biological data during the last few years. Genome wide expression analysis with DNA microarray technology has become a fundamental tool in genomic research. Since microarray technology was introduced, scientists started to develop informatics tools for the analysis and information extraction from this kind of data. Due to the characteristics of microarray data (i.e. high levels of noise, high cardinality of genes, small samples size) data mining approaches has become the suitable tools to perform any kind of analysis on these data. Many techniques can be applied to analyze microarray data, which can be grouped in four categories: Classification, Feature Selection, Clustering and Association Rule Mining.

DOI: 10.4018/978-1-60960-067-9.ch002

Classification is a procedure used to predict group membership for data instances. Given a training set of samples with a specific number of attributes (or features) and a class label (e.g., a phenotype characteristic), a model of classes is created. Then, the model is exploited to assign the appropriate class label to new data. Model quality is assessed by means of the classification accuracy measure, i.e., the number of correct label predictions over the total number of unlabeled data. The classification of microarray data can be useful to predict the outcome of some diseases or discover the genetic behavior of tumors.

Since genetic data are redundant and noisy, and some of them do not contain useful information for the problem, it is not suitable to apply the classification directly to the whole dataset. Feature Selection techniques are dimensional reduction methods usually applied before classification in order to reduce the number of considered features, by identifying and removing the redundant and useless ones. Moreover, feature selection algorithms applied to microarray data allow identifying genes which are highly correlated with the outcome of diseases. Another way to identify redundant genes is to group together sets of genes which show a similar behavior, and then select only a representative for the group. Furthermore, genes with similar expression pattern under various conditions or time course may imply co-regulations or relations in functional pathways, thus providing a way to understand functions of genes for which information has not been previously available.

Finally, relationships among genes or annotations and sample conditions can be detected also by exploiting the association rule mining techniques, which extract correlations among dataset attributes. This technique is also used to analyze time-series microarray data to discover gene regulatory networks.

In this review, application of data mining techniques on microarray data is focused, with the aim of making researchers aware of the benefits of such techniques when analyzing microarray data. The chapter is organized as follows. The first two sections provide a description of microarray data, to highlight the issues concerned with their analysis, and a brief discussion about the data cleaning approaches that can be exploited to prepare data before data mining. The following four sections provide a survey of classification, feature selection, clustering and association rule mining techniques based on their aims and characteristics. Finally, the last two sections describe new trends and provide some prospects of data mining application to microarray data.

DATA MINING TECHNIQUES FOR MICROARRAY

Microarray Datasets

A microarray dataset E can be represented in the form of a gene expression matrix, in which each row represents a gene and each column represents a sample. For each sample, the expression level of all the genes under consideration is measured. Element e_{ij} in E is the measurement of the expression level of gene i for sample j, where $i=1,...,N$, $j=1, ..., M$ and usually $N >> M$. Each sample is also characterized by a class label, representing the clinical situation of the patient or the biological condition of the tissue. The domain of class labels is characterized by C different values and label l_j of sample j takes a single value in this domain.

The format of a microarray dataset conforms to the normal data format of machine learning and data mining, where a gene can be regarded as a feature or attribute and a sample as an instance or a data point. However, the main characteristics of this data type are the high number of genes (usually tens of thousands) and the low number of samples (less then one hundred). This peculiarity causes specific challenges in analyzing microarray data (e.g., complex data interactions, high level of noisy, lack of biological absolute knowledge) which have to be addressed by data mining methods (Piatetsky-Shapiro & Tamayo, 2003).

In recent years an abundance of microarray datasets have become public available due to the increase of publication in bioinformatics domain. A large collection of public microarray data is stored by the ArrayExpress archive (http://www.ebi.ac.uk/microarray-as/ae/). The datasets, stored in MIAME and MINSEQE format, are all preprocessed, but also the raw data (for a subset of the collection) can be downloaded. One of the best features of this archive is the possibility to browse the entire collection or perform queries on experiment properties, submitter, species, etc. In the case of queries, the system retrieves summaries of experiments and complete data. Other datasets can be also downloaded from the author or tool websites (Chang & Lin, 2001; Statnikov, Aliferis, Tsamardinos, Hardin, & Levy, 2005).

Data Cleaning

The term data cleaning refers to the task of detecting and correcting or removing corrupted or inaccurate records from a dataset, before applying to it a data mining algorithm. Microarray data cleaning includes the following issues.

Normalization

Normalization is needed to adjust the individual hybridization intensities to balance them appropriately so that meaningful biological comparisons can be made. It ensures that differences in intensities are due to differential expression and not some printing, hybridization or scanning artifacts. Several normalization methods have been proposed in literature (Stekel, 2003) and some software packages have been developed for the analysis of microarray data. One of the most popular and general purpose software packages for microarray data is Bioconductor (http://www.bioconductor.org/). Other softwares are distributed by the companies that produce the microarray

technology, like Affymetrix and Agilent (Zahurak et al., 2007).

Missing Value Estimation

Missing values in microarray data arise due to technical failures, low signal-to-noise ratio and measurement errors. For example, dust present on the chip, irregularities in the spot production and inhomogeneous hybridization all lead to missing values. It has been estimated that typically 1% of the data are missing affecting up to 95% of the genes (Hyunsoo, Golub, & Park, 2005). To limit the effects of missing values several works addressed the problem of missing value estimation (Troyanaskaya et al., 2001), and the most used approach is the k-nearest neighbors algorithm.

Outlier Detection

The problem of outliers defined as "anomalous data points" often arises in large datasets. The aim of outlier detection methods is to detect and remove or substitute outliers. A broad survey of methods that have been found useful in the detection and treatment of outliers on microarray data analysis is presented in Pearson et al. (2003). Usually outliers are detected by computing the mean and the standard deviation of values. The values outside the range $\mu \pm \sigma$ are considered outliers. Other techniques have been proposed by replacing the mean and the standard deviation values, for example by using 3σ instead of σ. An alternative specifically used in the microarray data analysis community is the Hampel identifier (Davies & Gather, 1993), which replaces the mean with the median and the standard deviation with the median absolute deviation.

After data have been cleaned through the previously discussed methods, the appropriate data mining technique can be applied.

Classification

An important problem in microarray experiments is the classification of biological samples using gene expression data, especially in the context of cancer research. Conventional diagnostic methods are based on subjective evaluation of the morphological appearance of the tissue sample, which requires a visible phenotype and a trained pathologist to interpret the view. In some cases the class is easily identified by cell morphology or cell-type distribution, but in many cases apparently similar pathologies can lead to very different clinical outcomes. Examples of diagnostic classes include cancer versus non-cancer, different subtypes of tumor, and prediction of responses to various drugs or cancer prognosis. The prediction of the diagnostic category of a tissue sample from its expression array phenotype given the availability of similar data from tissues in identified categories is known as classification (Yeung & Bumgarner, 2003). Firstly in Golub (1999), the feasibility of cancer classification based solely on gene expression monitoring is demonstrated.

Classification Challenges

A critical issue in classifying microarray data is the limited number of samples that are available, thus it is difficult to asses the statistical significance of results. Moreover, the high number of genes could introduce noise affecting the classification model. Different algorithms were studied and proposed to define classification models for microarray data. The algorithms often used are reported below. Next, the methods which deal better with the characteristics of microarray data are discussed. However, the comparison of results is another critical issue, because of the amount of different exploited experimental designs. In fact, the classification accuracy of an algorithm strongly depends on the exploited experimental design.

Classification Algorithms

The most used classification algorithms exploited in the microarray analysis belong to four categories: Decision Tree, Bayesian Classifiers and Naïve Bayesian, Artificial Neural Networks and Support Vector Machines.

Decision Tree

Decision trees are derived by using the simple divide-and-conquer algorithm. In these tree structures, leaves represent classes and branches represent conjunctions of features that lead to those classes. At each node of the tree, the attribute that most effectively splits samples into different classes is chosen. To predict the class label of an input, a path to a leaf from the root is found depending on the value of the predicate at each node that is visited. The most common algorithms of the decision trees are ID3 (Quinlan, 1986) and C4.5 (Quinlan, 1993). An evolution of decision tree exploited for microarray data analysis is the random forest (Breiman, 2001), which uses an ensemble of classification trees. Dìaz-Uriarte and Alvarez de Andres (2006) showed the good performance of random forest for noisy and multi-class microarray data.

Bayesian Classifiers and Naïve Bayesian

From a Bayesian viewpoint, a classification problem can be written as the problem of finding the class with maximum probability given a set of observed attribute values. Such probability is seen as the posterior probability of the class given the data, and is usually computed using the Bayes theorem. Estimating this probability distribution from a training dataset is a difficult problem, because it may require a very large dataset to significantly explore all the possible combinations. Conversely, Naïve Bayesian is a simple probabilistic classifier based on Bayesian theorem with the (naïve) independence assumption. Based on that rule, using the joint probabilities of sample observations and classes, the algorithm attempts to estimate the conditional probabilities of classes given an observation. Despite its simplicity, the Naïve Bayes classifier is known to be a robust method, which shows on average good performance in terms of classification accuracy, also when the independence assumption does not hold (Michalski & Kaufman, 2001).

Artificial Neural Networks (ANN)

An Artificial Neural Network is a mathematical model based on biological neural networks. It consists of an interconnected group of artificial neurons and processes information using a connectionist approach to computation. Neurons are organized into layers. The input layer consists simply of the original data, while the output layer nodes represent the classes. Then, there may be several hidden layers. A key feature of neural networks is an iterative learning process in which data samples are presented to the network one at a time, and the weights are adjusted in order to predict the correct class label. Advantages of neural networks include their high tolerance to noisy data, as well as their ability to classify patterns on which they have not been trained. In Linder et al. (2007) a review of advantages and disadvantages of neural networks in the context of microarray analysis is presented.

Support Vector Machines (SVM)

Support Vector Machines are a relatively new type of learning algorithm, originally introduced by Vapnik (1998). Intuitively, SVM aims at searching for the hyper plane that best separates the classes of data. SVMs have demonstrated the ability not only to correctly separate entities into appropriate classes, but also to identify instances whose established classification is not supported by data. Although SVMs are relatively insensitive to the

distribution of training examples in each class, they may still get stuck when the class distribution is too skewed.

Sometimes, a combination of the presented methods may outperform the single technique. For example, a method which combines both the Neural Network Classifier and Bayesian methods is proposed in Zheng et al. (2005). In order to consider the correlations among genes, they build a neural network where the weights are determined by a Bayesian method. Yu et al. (2008) proposed a Bayesian approach combined with SVM to determine the separating hyper plane of an SVM, once its maximal margin is determined in the traditional way.

Comparison for Classification Methods

Some works tried to compare classifier performances on microarray dataset. However, since a huge benchmark of microarray datasets is missing in literature, a comparison of results presented in different works is very difficult. Particularly, the main problem is the choice of the experimental design used to compute the classification accuracy. In fact, different types of experimental design (i.e., leave-one-out, k-fold cross-validation, bootstrap and resubstitution) exist and are exploited in different works. In Ling and Hasan (2006) the four classification techniques previously described were compared on three microarray datasets and the accuracy is computed by applying a 10-fold cross-validation technique. The best performance is reached by SVM and ANN. For all datasets, the decision tree presents the worst performance. A similar result is presented in Pirooznia et al. (2008). The robustness of SVMs is also remarked in Li et al. (2004) where the SVM outperforms all the other methods in the most of analyzed microarray datasets. On the other hand, the decision tree shows always the worst performance (Wang et al., 2005).

According to the experimental results presented in these studies, the best method for classifying microarray datasets seems to be the SVM, because it is the most powerful method to deal with the main characteristics of microarray data (i.e., few samples and high number of features). In fact, SVM reaches the best accuracy on almost every dataset. Therefore, the SVM represents the state-of-art for classification task on microarray. By regarding the experimental design, Braga-Neto and Dougherty (2004) conclude that the k-fold cross validation seems to be the best estimator of classification performance compared to the other methods, because bootstrap has a high computational cost and resubstitution tends to be biased.

Feature Selection

Since the number of genes is usually significantly greater than the number of samples, and only a subset of the genes is relevant in distinguishing different classes, a feature selection is usually applied before classification. In this way, the performance of classifiers generally improves, because of the reduction in data dimensionality, the speed up of the learning process and the increasing in model interpretability (Yeung & Bumgarner, 2003). Furthermore, when analyzing microarray datasets, feature selection helps in providing a deeper understanding of the molecular basis of diseases. In fact, by selecting only the most relevant genes, the biologists are allowed to investigate only a subset of genes which are strongly correlated with the considered classes (i.e., different diseases, different tumor types, and different relapse times).

Feature selection techniques can be divided in two high level groups: supervised methods, which takes into account the sample class information, and unsupervised methods, which analyzes only the data distribution without using sample class labels. Among the first type, a further categorization can be done among filter, wrapper and embedded methods. In the following, first the common challenges of feature selection methods are described. Then, an overview of recent works in each category is presented, and finally a comparison of their main characteristics is provided.

Feature Selection Challenges

The first challenge in the feature selection applications for microarray is that a ground truth of biological knowledge about the genes which are responsible for the outcoming diseases is missing. Thus, the validation of results is an open problem. Some ontologies, such as UMLS and GO, try to model the biological processes and the correlations among genes/proteins and the diseases. However, methods that integrate this heterogeneous knowledge are very few (Qi & Tang, 2007; Papachristoudis, Diplaris, & Mitkas, 2009). Furthermore, some of the feature selection methods evaluate each gene in isolation, thus ignoring gene correlations. This problem is known as univariate approach, in contrast with the multivariate approach that considers the effects of groups of genes working together.

Finally, the evaluation of feature selection methods is highly dependent on classification task. Usually the experimental sections which are addressed to show the goodness of a method use the classification accuracy as measure of performance. A challenge in this direction should be the identification of a benchmark and a ground truth of biological processes to separate the gene list accuracy from the accuracy provided by a classifier.

Unsupervised Feature Selection Methods

The unsupervised techniques do not require the class information on samples and can be applied when the information in biological datasets is incomplete. Since more effective supervised feature selection methods have been developed, there are only few unsupervised methods proposed in recent works. The simplest unsupervised evaluation of the features is the variance. Higher the variance is, higher the gene relevance, because its expression varies among different conditions. On the contrary, if a gene expression does not vary very much, it can be considered irrelevant for the analysis. Although the data variance criteria finds features that are useful for representing data, it is not suited for selecting ones that must be useful for discriminating between samples in different classes. Thus, variance is generally used in addition to other methods (Ding, 2003).

Varshavsky et al. (2006) used the SVD decomposition to compute the SVD-entropy as a feature selection method. They propose several selection strategies such as Simple Ranking (SR), Forward Selection (FS) and Backward Elimination (BE). However, the SVD-entropy is very expensive in term of computational cost in the case of large number of features as in microarray datasets. Another unsupervised feature selection approach is the Laplacian score (He, Cai, & Niyogi, 2006). It is based on the observation that two data points are probably related to the same topic if they are close to each other. The assumption is that in many learning problem the local structure of the data space is more important than the global structure. The score computes how a feature respects the structure of a nearest neighbor graph of the dataset. An improvement of the Laplacian score is the LLDA-RFE (Niijima & Okuno, 2007). While the Laplacian score is a univariate approach, the LLDA-RFE is multivariate allowing in this way to select features that contribute to the discrimination with other features. Also this approach has problems of complexity due to the computation of SVD and eigen vectors.

Other methods of unsupervised feature selection are based on clustering algorithms in order to identify groups of similar genes and perform further analyses on these subsets. For example, Mitra et al. (2002) presented a method based on measuring similarity between features in order to remove redundancy. The method partitions the dataset into distinct clusters using a new measure, called maximum compression index, and then selects a representative feature for each cluster.

Supervised Feature Selection Methods

While the unsupervised methods analyze only the intrinsic characteristics of data (e.g., variance), the supervised techniques perform analyses considering the data distribution according to the sample classes. Among supervised feature selection methods, a further categorization can be done among filter methods, which assess the relevance of features by looking only at the data characteristics, wrapper methods, which use the model hypotheses to select the feature subset, and embedded methods, which search the optimal subset while the classifier model is built.

Filter Methods

Filter methods aim at evaluating the differential expressions of genes and rank them according to their ability to distinguish among classes. A gene is differentially expressed if it shows a certain distribution of expression levels under one condition and a significantly different distribution under the other conditions. In literature many techniques have been proposed to address the problem of detecting differentially expressed genes and define new ranking procedures (Loo et al., 2007). Classic statistical approaches for detecting differences between two groups include t-test, Wilcoxon test, and Mann-Whitney test. For multiclass problems the statistical tests ANOVA, Kruskal-Wallis test, and Friedman test are exploited. These methods have the virtue of being easily and very efficiently computed. The disadvantage is that some of these methods require assumptions on the data distribution. For example, the t-test requires that expression levels are normally distributed and homogeneous within groups and may also require equal variances between them. These assumptions may be inappropriate for subsets of genes.

Other filter methods (e.g., information gain, gini index, max minority, sum minority, sum of variance, towing rule) are implemented in the RankGene software (Su, Murali, Pavlovic, Schaffer, & Kasif, 2003). These measures are widely used in literature for gene expression analysis. They attempt to quantify the best class predictability that can be obtained by dividing the full range of expression values of gene in two disjoint intervals (e.g. up-regulated, down-regulated). Each measure belonging to this category quantifies the error in prediction in a different manner.

A deficiency of ranking genes by assessing a score to each one (i.e., the univariate approach) is that the features could be correlated among themselves. For example, if two genes are top ranked but they are also highly correlated (i.e., they distinguish the same samples), their combination does not form a better feature. This raises the issue of redundancy within the feature set. The advantages of reducing the redundancy are that with the same number of features the subset is more representative of the targeted phenotypes and the same accuracy is reached by a smaller subset of features than larger conventional feature sets. Ding and Peng (2005) proposed a method to expand the space covered by the feature set by requiring the features to be maximally dissimilar to each other (e.g., by maximizing their mutual Euclidean distance or minimizing their pair wise correlations).

Wrapper Methods

Feature Selection using wrapper methods offers an alternative way to perform a multivariate gene subset selection, incorporating the classifier's bias into the search and thus offering an opportunity to construct more accurate classifiers. Since the features to analyze are generally tens of thousands, wrapper techniques can not be applied alone and require a further step to avoid the exhaustive search among all the possible solutions. In fact, the number of feature subsets grows exponentially with the number of features, making enumerative search infeasible. Wrapper methods typically require extensive computation to search the best features and depend on the learning algorithm used (Juliusdottir et al., 2005). Furthermore, they do not always achieve better classification performance (Lai, Reinders, & Wessels, 2005), depending on the quality of the heuristics applied to the huge subset space. For these reasons, usually filter methods are preferred.

Some works combine a filter and a wrapper approach to gain the advantages of both. For example, Ni and Liu (2004) proposed a hybrid gene selection method. The first step is a filter technique in which each gene is evaluated according to a proximity degree metric. In the second step a wrapper procedure is performed using a genetic algorithm to choose the optimized gene subsets from the top-ranked genes. In this way, a subset of top-ranked genes are pre-selected and then a classification algorithm is applied on these genes to further select only a subset of them. Another interesting hybrid filter-wrapper approach is introduced in Ruiz et al. (2006), crossing a univariate pre-ordered gene ranking with an incrementally augmenting wrapper method.

Embedded Methods

The embedded approaches have the advantage of including the interaction with the classification model, while at the same time being far less computationally intensive than wrapper methods. For example, the random forest can be used to compute the relevance of a single gene in classification task (Jiang et al., 2004; Dìaz-Uriate & Alvarez de Andres, 2006). Guyon et al. (2002) proposed the SVM-RFE feature selection based on SVM. The approach iteratively trains the classifier optimizing the weights of the features, and then compute the ranking criterion for all features. Finally, the features with smallest ranking criterion are eliminated from the model. The weights given by the linear classifiers show the relevance of a feature in a multivariate way allowing the removing of irrelevant features represented by low weights. Draminski et al. (2008) proposed a feature selection algorithm based on Monte Carlo approach and tree classifier performance. The method considers a particular feature to be important, or informative, if it is likely to take part in the process of classifying samples into classes more often than not. The embedded methods, as wrapper approaches, have a high level of complexity due to the high number of features in microarrays.

Comparison for Feature Selection Methods

As for the classification task, a benchmark of microarray data for comparing feature selection techniques is missing. Some works try to find out which method is the best for a particular dataset or presents a robust behavior on different datasets. Jeffery et al. (2006) compared eleven feature selection methods on six datasets. The gene lists produced by analyzed methods are very dissimilar and produce different discrimination performance. The authors noticed that the t-statistic methods performed relatively poorly. Since microarray data could present high levels of noise together with low samples sizes, computing a t-statistic can be problematic, because the variance estimation can be skewed by the genes which have a low variance. Thus, genes with a low variance present a large t-statistic but they could be falsely predicted to be differentially expressed. An interesting result is presented in Lai et al. (2006). The authors illustrated that it is not always true that multivariate approach perform better than univariate ones, because the correlation structures, if present, are difficult to extract due to the small number of samples, and that consequently, overly-complex gene selection algorithms that attempt to extract these structures are prone to overtraining.

The comparison presented in Li et al. (2004) analyzes in more details the behavior of feature selection methods respect to the classifier em-

ployed for model construction. They compare eight feature selection algorithms implemented in Rank-Gene (Su et al., 2003) software on 9 microarray datasets changing the number of selected features in a range from 1 to 250. The conclusion is that the accuracy of classification is highly dependent on the choice of the classification method. This choice becomes more important than the choice of feature selection method when the number of selected genes is higher than 150 since little variation on accuracy are detected. Moreover, a clear winner seems not to exist. In fact, each method shows different performance behavior on different datasets. In some cases, when a high number of genes are selected, the majority of genes are shared by all the gene lists.

According to the results presented in Li et al. (2004) and Wang et al. (2005), the best classifier on which a feature selection method should be tested is the decision tree. In fact, the decision tree algorithm shows in most of analyzed microarray data the worst performance. Thus, a good feature algorithm with a low number of features may improve dramatically the performance of a decision tree that is not so robust to the noise present in gene expression data.

Feature Extraction

Another way to improve classification accuracy instead of selecting relevant genes is to combine them to obtain new artificial features, usually called meta-genes. Meta-genes combine the characteristics of many genes, thus few of them could reach a high classification accuracy. The most popular method belonging to this category is the Principal Component Analysis (PCA). PCA is a technique that transforms the original attribute space in a new space in which the attributes are uncorrelated and ranked based on the amount of variation in the original data that they account for. The PCA is an unsupervised approach, therefore it does not use the available class membership information for the samples. For this reason on microarray datasets the performance achieved by a classifiers applied on the new feature space are worst than supervised methods (Jeffery, Higgins, & Culhane, 2006).

The Fischer's Linear Discriminant Analysis (FLDA) is another popular feature extraction technique (Duda, Hart, & Stork, 2001). When compared with PCA, FLDA is a supervised algorithm, which maximizes the ratio between the inter-class and the intra-class variances. The FLDA is more accurate in multiclass problems with respect to the PCA, since there is no reason to assume that the principal components obtained by the PCA must be useful to discriminate between data in different classes. The FLDA was applied with good results on microarray data by Dudoit et al. (2002). However, in some cases the accuracy of FLDA decreases due to the small training set and a fairly large number of genes that bias the estimation of covariance matrices. Hanczar et al. (2003) proposed a reduction algorithm to identify classes of similarity among genes and create representative genes for each class by means of a linear combination of genes with a high degree of similarity. Then SVM classifier is applied to evaluate its accuracy. The aim of this kind of analysis is to reach the highest possible accuracy, instead of selecting the most relevant genes, because producing a correct prediction of a relapse or a patient response to specific treatments is more important.

The main critical issue of feature extraction methods is the meaning of meta-genes. Since they are a combination of genes, they are not useful for diagnostic test or biomarker development. Thus, this kind of techniques can be exploited only to improve classification accuracy without a real biological meaning, while feature selection methods can be used also to identify real genes responsible of disease outcome.

Clustering

The goal of clustering in microarray technology is to group genes or experiments into clusters according to similarity measures (Datta & Datta, 2006). For instance, genes that share a similar expression pattern under various conditions may imply co-regulations or relations in functional pathways. Thus, clustering could provide a way to understand the functioning of genes for which information has not been available in previous processes (Jiang, Tang, & Zhang, 2004). Furthermore, clustering can be used as a pre-processing step before a feature selection or a classification algorithm, to restrict the analysis to a specific category or to avoid redundancy by considering only a representative gene for each cluster. Many conventional clustering algorithms have been applied or adapted to gene expression data (Fu & Medico, 2007; Jiang et al., 2003; Thalamuthu et al., 2006) and new algorithms, which specifically address gene expression data, have recently been proposed (Gu & Liu, 2008). The main challenges of clustering methods are described first. Then, an overview of recent works which apply the clustering to microarray data is presented, and finally a comparison of their main characteristics is provided below.

Clustering Challenges

The main challenges regarding the application of clustering to microarray data are (i) the definition of the appropriate distance between objects, (ii) the choice of the clustering algorithm, and (iii) the evaluation of final results. Especially evaluating the results of clustering is a non-trivial task. Each article justifies a specific evaluation criterion, and in literature many criteria exist, such as measures which evaluate the obtained clusters without knowing the real class of objects (i.e., homogeneity and separation), measures which evaluate the agreement between the obtained clusters and the ground truth, and measures which involve the comparison with biological databases (i.e., GO) to measure the biological homogeneity of clusters. In addition, some works also highlight the problem of giving a user friendly representation of clustering results. Another evaluation criterion could be the clustering computational complexity, even if an evaluation of the complexity and efficiency of a method is very difficult to perform without resorting to extensive benchmark.

Clustering Algorithms

The similarity between objects is defined by computing the distance between them. Gene expression values are continuous attributes, for which several distance measures (Euclidean, Manhattan, Chebyshev, etc.) may be computed, according to the specific problem. However, such distance functions are not always adequate in capturing correlations among objects because the overall gene expression profile may be more interesting than the individual magnitude of each feature (Wang, Wang, Yang, & Yu, 2002). Other widely used schemes for determining the similarity between genes use the Pearson or Spearman correlation coefficients, which measure the similarity between the shapes of two expression patterns. However, they are not robust with respect to outliers. The cosine correlation has proven to be more robust to outliers because it computes the cosine of the angle between the expression gene value vectors. Other kinds of similarity measures include pattern based (which considers simple linear transformation relationships) and tendency based (which considers synchronous rise and fall of expression levels in a subset of conditions).

Once the distance measure has been defined, the clustering algorithms are divided based on the approach used to form the clusters. A detailed description of clustering algorithms applied to microarray has been provided by Shamir and Sharan (2001). Mainly, they can be grouped in two categories, partitioning and hierarchical algorithms.

Partitioning Algorithms

This family of clustering algorithms works similarly to k-means (MacQueen, 1967). K-means is one of the simplest and fastest clustering algorithms. It takes the number of clusters (k) to be calculated as an input and randomly divides points into k clusters. Then it iteratively calculates the centroid for each cluster and moves each point to the closest cluster. This procedure is repeated until no further points are moved to different clusters. Despite its simplicity, k-means has some major drawbacks, such as the sensibility to outliers, the fact that the number of clusters has to be known in advance and that the final results may change in successive runs because the initial clusters are chosen randomly.

Several new clustering algorithms have been proposed to overcome the drawbacks of k-means. For example, the genetic weighted k-means algorithm (Wu, 2008) is a hybridization of a genetic algorithm and a weighted k-means algorithm. Each individual is encoded by a partitioning table which uniquely determines a clustering, and genetic operators are employed. Authors show that it performs better than the k-means in terms of the cluster quality and the clustering sensitivity to initial partitions.

Dembélé and Kastner (2003) described the application of the fuzzy c-means to microarray data, to overcome the problem that a gene can be associated to more than one cluster. The fuzzy c-means links each gene to all clusters via a real-valued vector of indexes. The values of the components of this vector lies between 0 and 1. For a given gene, an index close to 1 indicates a strong association to the cluster. Inversely, indexes close to 0 indicate the absence of a strong association to the corresponding cluster. The vector of indexes thus defines the membership of a gene with respect to the various clusters. However, there is a problem of parameter estimation in this approach.

Au et al. (2005) proposed the Attribute Cluster Algorithm (ACA), which adopts the idea of the k-means to cluster genes by replacing the distance measure with the interdependence redundancy measure between attributes and the concept of mean with the concept of mode (i.e., the attribute with the highest multiple interdependence redundancy in a group).

Hierarchical Algorithms

Hierarchical clustering typically uses a progressive combination (or division) of elements that are most similar (or different). The result is plotted as a dendrogram that represents the clusters and relations between the clusters. Genes or experiments are grouped together to form clusters and clusters are grouped together by an inter-cluster distance to make a higher level cluster. Hierarchical clustering algorithms can be further divided into agglomerative approaches and divisive approaches based on how the hierarchical dendrogram is formed. Agglomerative algorithms (bottom-up approach) initially regard each data object as an individual cluster, and at each step, merge the closest pair of clusters until all the groups are merged into one. Divisive algorithms (top-down approach) start with one cluster containing all the data objects, and at each step splits a cluster until only singleton clusters of individual objects remain. For example, Eisen et al. (1998) applied an agglomerative algorithm called UPGMA (Unweighted Pair Group Method with Arithmetic mean) and adopted a method to graphically represent the clustered data set, while (Alon et al., 1999) split the genes through a divisive approach, called the deterministic-annealing algorithm.

A variation of the hierarchical clustering algorithm is proposed in Jiang et al. (2003). The authors have applied a Density-based Hierarchical Clustering method (DHC) on two datasets for which the true partition is known. DHC is developed based on the notions of density and attraction of data objects. The basic idea is to consider a cluster as a high-dimensional dense area, where data objects are attracted with each other. At the core part of the dense area, objects are crowded closely with each other, and thus have high density. Objects at the peripheral area of the cluster are relatively sparsely distributed, and are attracted to the core part of the dense area. Once the density and attraction of data objects are defined, DHC organizes the cluster structure of the data set in two-level hierarchical structures, one attraction tree and one density tree. However, to compute the density of data objects, DHC calculates the distance between each pair of data objects in the data set, which makes DHC not efficient. Furthermore, two global parameters are used in DHC to control the splitting process of dense areas. Therefore, DHC does not escape from the typical difficulty to determine the appropriate value of parameters.

Comparison for Clustering Methods

Richards et al. (2008) provided a useful comparison of several recent clustering algorithms by concluding that k-means is still one of the best clustering method because it is fast, does not require parallelisation, and produces clusters with slightly high levels of GO enrichment. Despite this consideration, the hierarchical clustering algorithms are the most used in biological studies. The main advantage of hierarchical clustering is that it not only groups together genes with similar expression pattern but also provides a natural way to graphically represent the data set (Jiang et al., 2004). The graphic representation allows users to obtain an initial impression of the distribution of data. However, the conventional agglomerative approach suffers from a lack of robustness because a small perturbation of the data set may greatly change the structure of the hierarchical dendrogram. Another drawback of the hierarchical approach is its high computational complexity.

In general, microarray data are clustered based on the continuous expression values of genes. However, when additional information is available (e.g., biological knowledge or clinical information), it may be beneficial to exploit it to improve cluster quality (Huang & Pan, 2006). Clinical information can be used to build models for the prediction of tumor progression. For example Wang et al. (2007) used epigenetic data to determine tumor progression in cancer, and Bushel et al. (2007) presented a method to incorporate phenotypic data about the samples.

Au et al. (2005) presented a particular validation technique for clustering. They selected a subset of top genes from each obtained cluster to make up a gene pool, and then they run classification experiments on the selected genes to see whether or not the results are backed by the ground truth and which method performs the best. Thus, they exploit class information on samples to validate the results of gene clustering. The good accuracy reached by selecting few genes from the clusters reveals that the good diagnostic information existing in a small set of genes can be effectively selected by the algorithm. It is an interesting new way of clustering validation, by integrating clustering and feature selection.

Biclustering

Due to the high complexity of microarray data, during the last few years scientists focused their attention on biclustering algorithms. The notion of biclustering was first introduced in Hartigan (1972) to describe simultaneous grouping of both row and column subsets in a data matrix. It tries to overcome some limitations of traditional clustering methods. For example, a limitation of traditional clustering is that gene or an experimental condition can be assigned to only one cluster. Furthermore, all genes and conditions have to be assigned to clusters. However, biologically a gene or a sample could participate in multiple biological pathways, and a cellular process is generally active only under a subset of genes or experimental conditions. A biclustering scheme that produces gene and sample clusters simultaneously can model the situation where a gene (or a sample) is involved

in several biological functions. Furthermore, a biclustering model can avoid those noise genes that are not active in any experimental condition.

Biclustering of microarray data was first introduced in Cheng and Church (2000). They defined a residual score to search for sub matrices as biclusters. This is a heuristic method and can not model the cases where two biclusters overlap with each other. Segal et al. (2003) proposed a modified version of one-way clustering using a Bayesian model in which genes can belong to multiple clusters or none of the clusters. But it can not simultaneously cluster conditions/samples. Bergmann et al. (2003) introduced the Iterative Signature Algorithm (ISA), which searches bicluster modules iteratively based on two predetermined thresholds. ISA can identify multiple biclusters, but is highly sensitive to the threshold values and tends to select a strong bicluster many times. Gu and Liu (2008) proposed a biclustering algorithm based on Bayesian model. The statistical inference of the data distribution is performed by a Gibbs sampling procedure. This algorithm has been applied to the yeast expression data, observing that majority of founded biclusters are supported by significant biological evidences, such as enrichments of gene functions and transcription factor binding sites in the corresponding promoter sequences.

Association Rule Mining

Another typical data mining task exploited to analyze gene expression data is the Association Rule Mining, which is used to find correlations in large dataset. In fact, a challenging problem in bioinformatics is to discover relationships and interactions among genes. Association rules have been widely used in the market basket analysis to represent sets of items that are likely to be purchased together (Agrawal & Srikant, 1994). This method detects sets of elements that frequently co-occur in a database and establish relationships between them of the form of $X \rightarrow Y$, which means that when X occurs it is likely that Y also occurs. X and Y are named itemsets, and are sets of pairs (attribute, value). The left hand side of the rule is named antecedent and the right hand side is named consequent. The significance of these associations is assessed by different quality measures, such as the support (the percentage of data that are covered by the rule, i.e., which contain both X and Y) and the confidence (the percentage of data which contain X over the data which contain both X and Y).

Association Rule Mining (ARM) technique has been recently proposed to the analysis of gene expression data in order to extract associations and relationships among subsets of genes (Creighton & Hanash, 2003). In this context, an expression profile can represent a single transaction, and each gene a single item. However, the association rule mining can not be directly applied to microarray data, because they are continuous values. Instead, there is the need to discretize the gene expression domain by defining appropriate value intervals. Binning the values helps to alleviate problems with noise, by focusing the analysis on the more general effects of genes. Usually gene expression data are binned into two levels, up-regulated (i.e. highly expressed) or down-regulated (i.e. inhibited) according to specific fixed thresholds. Sometimes there is also a third state (neither up nor down regulated) which is not considered in the analysis. In this case, both the degree of discretization and the computational cost are low. By using a higher degree the computational cost increases and the representation of the information is more accurate. Most of the works use fixed thresholds, i.e. at zero (Li et al., 2006), at the average gene expression value (Ponzoni, Azuaje, Augusto, & Glass, 2007), at other arbitrary values (Creighton & Hanash, 2003). Some works exploits k-means clustering (Bulashevska & Eils, 2005) to bin gene expression values or compare different discretization techniques (Baralis, Bruno, & Ficarra, 2008). However, there is no consolidating discretization method for microarray data.

In the following, the main challenges of association rule mining methods are described first. Then, an overview of recent works that apply the association rule to microarray data is presented. For each method, the strengths and the weaknesses with respect to the individuated challenges are provided finally.

Association Rule Mining Challenges

Association rule discovery can reveal biologically relevant associations between different genes or between experimental conditions and gene expressions. Furthermore, association rule mining can reveal temporal patterns of gene co-expression inferring participation in gene networks. It offers also the advantage that each gene can be annotated with several topics and all of them will be independently taken into account to discover latent relationships. One of the major limitations of association rule mining is the large amount of rules that are generated, which becomes a major problem in many applications. Rule estimation is another critical task. Basically rules are evaluated on support and confidence values, but these indexes may fail in capturing the real interestingness of rules. Another challenge is the biological validation of extracted rules, because many relationships among genes are still unknown, especially in the temporal context.

Association Rule Mining Algorithms

From the results of the ARM method, it is possible to discover interactions between correlated expressions of genes in microarray experiments as well as correlation between gene expressions or biological annotations and sample conditions.

In the context of correlations among genes, the kind of extracted rules is in the following form: {[+]g1, [+]g2} → {[+]g3}. It means that when gene 1 and 2 are over-expressed within a situation, then often gene 3 is over-expressed too. An association-rule miner identifies every rule that is frequent and interesting according to the user-defined thresholds of support and confidence. The reference algorithms for association rule mining are Apriori (Agrawal & Srikant, 1994) and FP-Growth (Han, Pei, & Yin, 2000). Usually new methods are compared with them to prove the efficiency. For example, Jiang and Gruenwald (2005) presented an algorithm (FIS-tree) to extract association rules from microarray data and report experimental results comparing the FIS-tree with Apriori and FP-Growth in terms of execution time. The FIS-tree mining algorithm performs better than the other two algorithms when the support threshold is low, or the database size in terms of the number of transactions is large, or the number of 2-item frequent itemsets is high. However, no biological validation of extracted rules is performed.

Carmona-Saez et al. (2006) proposed an algorithm to integrate gene expression profiles and gene annotations to extract rules in the form: {cell cycle} → {[+] condition 1, [+] condition 2, [-] condition 3}. It means that, in the dataset, a significant number of the genes annotated as "cell cycle" are over-expressed in condition 1, 2 and under-expressed in condition 3. The rules are extracted by means of the Apriori algorithm and then evaluated by means of the confidence and support values. Also a biological discussion is provided. However, two limitations are present in this work: (i) it uses the two-fold change cut-off method for discretizing expression measures in three intervals, without discussing such choise, and (ii) extracted rules are restricted to a single form, i.e., annotations in the left-hand-side and biological condition in the right-hand-side.

A tentative to overcome these problems is presented by Martinez et al. (2008), who presented the GenMiner algorithm. It allows different kinds of rules, such as genes → genes, genes → annotations, annotations → genes, and annotations → annotations. It exploits a Java implementation of the Close algorithm (Pasquier, Bastide, Taouil, & Lakhal, 1999) to extract the rules, because it limits the search space and the number of dataset scans to reduce execution times and memory space usage and it extracts only non-redundant rules to improve the results relevance.

Temporal Association Rule Mining Algorithms

The final goal of many analyses is to learn gene interaction networks, to describe and simulate how genes or groups of genes interact with each other, with activating or inhibiting mechanisms (Styczynski & Stephanopoulos, 2005). Thus, association rule mining has been exploited in the detection of gene regulatory networks. A gene regulatory network aims at representing relationships that govern the rates at which genes in the network are transcribed into mRNA. Genes can be viewed as nodes whose expression levels are controlled by other nodes (Ponzoni et al., 2007).

By considering single-time-point expression data, it is possible to discover sets of co-regulated genes, which show a similar behavior under different conditions. This analysis does not consider regulations which happen with a time delay. Since there can be a significant delay between the expression of a regulator gene and its effects (i.e. the activation or inhibition of another gene), not all the genes that induct the expression level of a gene are necessarily observed in a single microarray. Some methods only consider the static gene expression profiles, so they cannot be used to interpret the time-delayed gene regulations.

Recently, researchers have addressed time-series expression data. For example, Agrawal and Mitta (2005) identified temporal networks by using correlation among genes, considered as discrete signals. However, the correlation, defined as the degree of similarity between two signals, can not represent the causality relationships between them. Nam et al. (2009) proposed a method, referred to as Temporal Association Rule Mining (TARM), which can extract temporal dependencies among related genes. The authors tried different combinations of the algorithm parameters (i.e., discretization thresholds, minimum values of support and confidence) and select the best in term of precision and recall is selected. A biological validation of extracted rules is performed.

Association Rule Mining Comparison

The problem of the large amount of generated rules has been already pointed out in several studies, where some post-processing pruning methods have been proposed to reduce the number of generated rules. For example, (Creighton & Hanash, 2003) imposed constraints on the size of the rules, while (Tuzhilin & Adomavicius, 2002) proposed several post-processing operators for selecting and exploring interesting rules from the whole set. Other related works focuses on detecting high confident associations only (Li, Zhang, Dong, Ramamohanarao, & Sun, 1999), or avoiding redundancy (Carmona-Saez et al., 2006).

The problem of rule quality evaluation is another critical task. Basically rules are evaluated on support and confidence values, but these indexes may fail in capturing the real interestingness of rules. Support prunes items that occur very infrequently in the data set, although they might produce interesting and potentially valuable rules. Confidence is sensitive to the support of the consequent. Consequents with higher support automatically produce high confidence values even if exists no association between the items. Such false rules can be detected by determining whether the antecedent and the consequent are statistically independent. This inspired a number of measures for association rule interest, such as the lift, which calculates the ratio between the rule confidence and the support of the itemset in the rule consequent.

The third problem is the biological validation of extracted rules. Since there is not a benchmark in this context, the most used method to perform a rule validation is to manually extract the known gene interactions from biological databases, and then compare the extracted rules with the biological knowledge. Some measures such as precision or recall can be computed to measure the quality of the rules.

New Trends and Applications

Recently many studies were addressed to integrate microarray data with heterogeneous information. Since microarray experiments present few samples, the accuracy of the hypotheses extracted by means of data mining approaches could be low. Using different sources of information (e.g., ontologies, functional data, published literature), the biological conclusions achieve improvements in specificity. For example, multiple gene expression data sets and diverse genomic data can be integrated by computational methods to create an integrated picture of functional relationships between genes. These integrated data can then be used to predict biological functions or to aid in understanding of protein regulations and biological networks modeling (Hersh, 2008).

For feature selection approaches some works integrate Gene Ontology (GO) in the computation of most relevant genes. For example, Qi and Tang (2007) proposed a method that combines the discriminative power of each gene using a traditional filtering method with the discriminative values of GO terms. Moreover, redundancy is eliminated using the ontology annotations. The result shows an improvement of classification performance using fewer genes than the traditional filter methods.

The analysis of published literature on some specific topic could improve the results on DNA microarray data. With microarray experiments, hundreds of genes can be identified as relevant to the studied phenomenon by means of feature selection approaches. The interpretation of these gene lists is challenging as, for a single gene, there can be hundreds or even thousands of articles pertaining to the gene's function. Text-mining can alleviate this complication by revealing the associations between the genes that are apparent from literature (Krallinger, Valencia, & Hirschman, 2008). Unfortunately, current works are focused on keyword search and abstract evaluation that limit the extraction of biological results done in previous studies, and requires the researchers to further filter the results (Hoffmann & Valencia, 2005).

The interpretations of microarray results can be improved by using ontologies such as MESH or GO (Osborne, Zhu, Lin, & Kibbe, 2007). For example, GOEAST (Zheng & Wang, 2008) is a web-based user friendly tool, which applies appropriate statistical methods to identify significantly enriched GO terms among a given list of genes extracted by gene expression analysis.

Clustering is usually considered as an unsupervised learning approach because no *a priori* knowledge is assumed at the beginning of the process. However, in the case of gene expression data, some prior knowledge is often available (i.e., some genes are known to be functional related). Thus, integrating such knowledge can improve the clustering results. In recent years, some semi-supervised clustering methods have been proposed so that user-provided constraints or sample labels can be included in the analysis. For example, Tari et al. (2009) proposed a semi-supervised clustering method called GO fuzzy c-means, which enables the simultaneous use of biological knowledge and gene expression data. The method is based on the fuzzy c-means clustering algorithm and utilizes the Gene Ontology annotations as prior knowledge to guide the process of grouping functionally related genes. By following the approach of using prior biological knowledge for the fuzzy c-means algorithm, other clustering algorithms such as hierarchical and k-means can be adapted to use prior biological knowledge as well.

FUTURE RESEARCH DIRECTIONS

In microarray data analysis a critical issue is the definition of evaluation methods which allow the

researchers to compare the results with previous works. Some well-known datasets which are used widely are (Golub,1999; Alon et al.,1999; Pomeroy et al., 2002), but a benchmark defined by the community is still missing. Moreover, the experimental design is usually different between papers that treat the same topic. Different evaluators, like k-fold cross-validation or bootstrap approaches, are used producing different results difficult to compare. Finally, classification algorithms applied in other domains, such as Relevance Vector Machine (RVM), and adapted to face the small sample size, could improve the performance of classification models. In cluster analysis an unambiguous annotation of correlations between genes is not still defined. Different data source (e.g., KEGG) store information about pathways and correlations among genes, but the employment of them to validate the biological results is a critical issue due to different gene annotations and limited knowledge of some processes.

Another open problem is the biological validation of the results retrieved by data mining methods. Some works discussed in the previous section try to overcome this open issue integrating different data sources, but a well-define strategy to compare biological hypotheses with ground-truth knowledge is still missing. Finally, the authors believe that contribution of other data mining approaches could improve the results on gene expression data, giving a deeper understanding of the genetic aspect of biological processes.

CONCLUSION

Microarray data analysis provides a powerful approach to understand biological processes and gene interactions. Many tools and algorithms were proposed to address different biological problems. This chapter reviews the main contributions of classification, feature selection, clustering and association rule mining to microarray data analysis. Particularly, new techniques have been developed to address the specific microarray problems of large input dimensionality and the small samples size. These aspects caused the failure of some feature selection methods (e.g., statistical tests) and classifiers usually exploited in other data mining applications (such as decision tree), while the robustness of others (such as SVM) appears. In the association rule mining context a large number of rules are generated, thus requiring new methods for rule estimation and validation. For clustering, the difficult of creating meaningful clusters is increased by the large number of data. However, the integration of microarray data with other biological knowledge has been demonstrated to be the future trend for applications, trying to overcome the open problems of classical data mining methods.

REFERENCES

Agrawal, A., & Mitta, A. (2005). Identifying Temporal Gene Networks Using Signal processing Metrics on Time-Series Gene Expression Data. In *Proceedings of 3rd IEEE ICISIP Conference* (pp. 86-92).

Agrawal, R., & Srikant, R. (1994). Fast Algorithms for Mining Association Rules. In *Proceedings VLDB Conference*.

Alon, U., Barkai, N., Notterman, D., Gish, K., Ybarra, S., Mack, D., & Levine, A. (1999). Broad Patterns of Gene Expression Revealed by Clustering Analysis of Tumor and Normal Colon Tissues Probed by Oligonucleotide Array. In *Proceedings of National Academy Science* (pp. 6745-6750). USA.

Au, W., Chan, K., Wong, A., & Yang, W. (2005). Attribute Clustering for Grouping, Selection, and Classification of Gene Expression Data. *IEEE/ACM Transactions on Computational Biology and Bioinformatics*, *2*(2), 83–101. doi:10.1109/TCBB.2005.17

Baralis, E., Bruno, G., & Ficarra, E. (2008). Temporal Association Rules for Gene Regulatory Networks. In *IEEE International Conference on Intelligent Systems*.

Bergmann, S., Ihmels, J., & Barkai, N. (2003). Iterative Signature Algorithm for the Analysis of Large-Scale Gene Expression Data. *Physical Review*, *67*(3).

Braga-Neto, U., & Dougherty, E. (2004). Is Cross-validation valid for Small-Sample Microarray Classification? *Bioinformatics (Oxford, England)*, *20*(3), 374. doi:10.1093/bioinformatics/btg419

Breiman, L. (2001). Random Forests. *Machine Learning*, *45*(1), 5–32. doi:10.1023/A:1010933404324

Bulashevska, S., & Eils, R. (2005). Inferring Genetic Regulatory Logic from Expression Data. *Bioinformatics (Oxford, England)*, *21*(11), 2706–2713. doi:10.1093/bioinformatics/bti388

Bushel, P., Wolfinger, R., & Gibson, G. (2007). Simultaneous Clustering of Gene Expression Data with Clinical Chemistry and Pathological Evaluations Reveals Phenotypic Prototypes. *BMC Systems Biology*, *1*(1), 15. doi:10.1186/1752-0509-1-15

Carmona-Saez, P., Chagoyen, M., Rodriguez, A., Trelles, O., Carazo, J., & Pascual-Montano, A. (2006). Integrated Analysis of Gene Expression by Association Rules Discovery. *BMC Bioinformatics*, *7*(1), 54. doi:10.1186/1471-2105-7-54

Chang, C., & Lin, C. (2001). *LIBSVM: A Library for Support Vector Machines*. Retrieved from http://www.csie.ntu.edu.tw/~cjlin/libsvm.

Cheng, Y., & Church, G. (2000). Biclustering of Expression Data. In *Proceedings of Eighth International Conference Intelligent Systems for Molecular Biology* (pp.93-103).

Creighton, C., & Hanash, S. (2003). Mining Gene Expression Databases for Association Rules. *Bioinformatics (Oxford, England)*, *19*(1), 79–86. doi:10.1093/bioinformatics/19.1.79

Datta, S., & Datta, S. (2006). Evaluation of Clustering Algorithms for Gene Expression Data. *BMC Bioinformatics*, *7*(Suppl 4), S17. doi:10.1186/1471-2105-7-S4-S17

Davies, L., & Gather, U. (1993). The identification of Multiple Outliers. *Journal of the American Statistical Association*, *88*, 782–801. doi:10.2307/2290763

Dembélé, D., & Kastner, P. (2003). Fuzzy C-means method for Clustering Microarray Data. *Bioinformatics (Oxford, England)*, *19*(8), 973–980. doi:10.1093/bioinformatics/btg119

Dìaz-Uriarte, R., & Alvarez de Andres, S. (2006). Gene selection and classification of microarray data using random forest. *BMC Bioinformatics*, *7*(3), 1471–2105.

Ding, C. (2003). Unsupervised feature selection via Two-Way Ordering in Gene Expression Analysis. *Bioinformatics (Oxford, England)*, *19*(10), 1259–1266. doi:10.1093/bioinformatics/btg149

Ding, C., & Peng, H. (2005). Minimum Redundancy Feature selection from Microarray Gene Expression Data. *Journal of Bioinformatics and Computational Biology*, *3*(2), 185–206. doi:10.1142/S0219720005001004

Draminski, M., Rada-Iglesias, A., Enroth, S., Wadelius, C., Koronacki, J., & Komorowski, J. (2008). Monte Carlo feature selection for Supervised Classification. *Bioinformatics (Oxford, England)*, *24*(1), 110. doi:10.1093/bioinformatics/btm486

Duda, R., Hart, P., & Stork, D. (2001). Pattern Classification.

Dudoit, S., Fridlyand, J., & Speed, T. (2002). Comparison of Discrimination methods for the classification of Tumors using Gene Expression Data. *Journal of the American Statistical Association*, *97*(457), 77–88. doi:10.1198/016214502753479248

Eisen, M., Spellman, P., Brown, P., & Botstein, D. (1998). Cluster Analysis and Display of Genome-wide Expression Patterns. In *Proceedings of National Academy of Science* (pp. 14863-14868). *USA*.

Fu, L., & Medico, E. (2007). FLAME, A Novel Fuzzy Clustering method for the analysis of DNA Microarray Data. *BMC Bioinformatics*, *8*(1), 3. doi:10.1186/1471-2105-8-3

Golub, T. (1999). Molecular Classification of Cancer: Class Discovery and Class Prediction by Gene Expression Monitoring. *Science*, *286*(5439), 531–537. doi:10.1126/science.286.5439.531

Gu, J., & Liu, J. (2008). Bayesian Biclustering of Gene Expression Data. *BMC Genomics*, *9*(Suppl. 1), S4. doi:10.1186/1471-2164-9-S1-S4

Guyon, I., Weston, J., Barnhill, S., & Vapnik, V. (2002). Gene selection for Cancer Classification using Support Vector Machines. *Machine Learning*, *46*(1), 389–422. doi:10.1023/A:1012487302797

Han, J., Pei, J., & Yin, Y. (2000). Mining Frequent Patterns without Candidate Generation. In *Proceedings of ACM-SIGMOD International Conference Management of Data*.

Hanczar, B., Courtine, M., Benis, A., Hennegar, C., Clement, K., & Zucker, J. (2003). Improving Classification of Microarray Daya using Proptotype-based Feature Selection. *SIGKDD Explorations*, *5*(2), 23–30. doi:10.1145/980972.980977

Hartigan, J. (1972). Direct Clustering of a Data Matrix. *Journal of the American Statistical Association*, *67*(337), 123–129. doi:10.2307/2284710

He, X., Cai, D., & Niyogi, P. (2006). Laplacian Score for Feature Selection. *Advances in Neural Information Processing Systems, 18*, 507.

Hersh, W. (2008). *Information Retrieval: A Health and Biomedical Perspective*. Springer Verlag.

Hoffmann, R., & Valencia, A. (2005). Implementing the iHOP concept for navigation of Biomedical Literature. *Bioinformatics (Oxford, England), 21*(2). doi:10.1093/bioinformatics/bti1142

Huang, D., & Pan, W. (2006). Incorporating biological knowledge into distance-based clustering analysis of microarray gene expression data. *Bioinformatics (Oxford, England), 22*(10), 1259–1268. doi:10.1093/bioinformatics/btl065

Hyunsoo, K., Golub, G., & Park, H. (2005). Missing Value Estimation for DNA Microarray Gene Expression Data: Local Least Squares Imputation. *Bioinformatics (Oxford, England), 21*(2), 187–198.

Jeffery, I., Higgins, D., & Culhane, A. (2006). Comparison and Evaluation of methods for generating Differentially Expressed Gene Lists from Microarray. *BMC Bioinformatics, 7*(1), 359. doi:10.1186/1471-2105-7-359

Jiang, D., Pei, J., & Zhang, A. (2003). DHC: A Density-based Hierarchical Clustering method for Time Series Gene Expression Data. In *Proceedings of the IEEE Symposium on Bioinformatics and Bioengineering* (pp.393-400).

Jiang, D., Tang, C., & Zhang, A. (2004). Cluster Analysis for Gene Expression Data: A Survey. *IEEE Transactions on Knowledge and Data Engineering, 16*(11), 1370–1386. doi:10.1109/TKDE.2004.68

Jiang, H., Deng, Y., Chen, H., Tao, L., Sha, Q., & Chen, J. (2004). Joint Analysis of Two Microarray Gene-Expression Data Sets to Select Lung Adenocarcinoma Marker Genes. *BMC Bioinformatics, 5*(1), 81. doi:10.1186/1471-2105-5-81

Jiang, X., & Gruenwald, L. (2005). Microarray Gene Expression Data Association Rules Mining based on BSC-tree and FIS-tree. *Data & Knowledge Engineering, 53*.

Juliusdottir, T., Keedwell, E., Corne, D., & Narayanan, A. (2005). Two-Phase EA/k-NN for Feature selection and Classification in Cancer Microarray Datasets. In *Proceedings of IEEE Symposium on Computer Intelligence in Bioinformatics and Computing Biology* (pp.1-8).

Krallinger, M., Valencia, A., & Hirschman, L. (2008). Linking Genes to Literature: Text Mining, Information Extraction, and Retrieval Applications for Biology. *Genome Biology, 9*(2), S8. doi:10.1186/gb-2008-9-s2-s8

Lai, C., Reinders, M., Van't Veer, L., & Wessels, L. (2006). A Comparison of Univariate and Multivariate Gene Selection Techniques for Classification of Cancer Datasets. *BMC Bioinformatics, 7*(1), 235. doi:10.1186/1471-2105-7-235

Lai, C., Reinders, M., & Wessels, L. (2005). Multivariate Gene Selection: Does it help? In *Proceedings of the IEEE CSB Conference Workshops*.

Li, J., Zhang, X., Dong, G., Ramamohanarao, K., & Sun, Q. (1999). *Efficient Mining of High Confidence Association Rules without Support Thresholds* (pp. 406–411). PKDD.

Li, T., Zhang, C., & Ogihara, M. (2004). A Comparative Study of Feature Selection and Multiclass Classification methods for Tissue Classification based on Gene Expression. *Bioinformatics (Oxford, England), 20*(15), 2429–2437. doi:10.1093/bioinformatics/bth267

Li, X., Rao, S., Jiang, W., Li, C., Xiao, Y., & Guo, Z. (2006). Discovery of Time-delayed Gene Regulatory Networks based on Temporal Gene Expression Profiling. *BMC Bioinformatics, 7*(26).

Linder, R., Richards, T., & Wagner, M. (2007). Microarray Data classified by Artificial Neural Networks. *Methods in Molecular Biology-Clifton Then Totowa, 382*, 345.

Ling, N., & Hasan, Y. (2006). Classification on Microarray Data. In *Proceedings of the 2nd IMT-GT Regional Conference on Mathematics, Statistics and Applications*.

Loo, L., Roberts, S., & Hrebien, L. (2007). New Criteria for Selecting Differentially Expressed Genes. *IEEE Engineering in Medicine and Biology Magazine, 26*(2), 17–26. doi:10.1109/MEMB.2007.335589

MacQueen, J. B. (1967). Some Methods for Classification and Analysis of Multivariate Observations. In *Proceedings of 5-th Berkeley Symposium on Mathematical Statistics and Probability* (pp.281-297).

Martinez, R., Pasquier, N., & Pasquier, C. (2008). *GenMiner: Mining Informative Association Rules from Integrated Gene Expression Data and Annotations*. Bioinformatics.

Michalski, R., & Kaufman, K. (2001). Learning Patterns in Noisy Data: The AQ Approach. *Machine Learning and its Applications*, 22-38.

Mitra, P., Murthy, C., & Pal, S. (2002). Unsupervised Feature Selection Using Feature Similarity. *IEEE Transactions on Pattern Analysis and Machine Intelligence*, 301–312. doi:10.1109/34.990133

Nam, H., Lee, K., & Lee, D. (2009). Identification of Temporal Association Rules from Time-Series Microarray Data Sets. *BMC Bioinformatics*, 10.

Ni, B., & Liu, J. (2004). A Hybrid Filterwrapper Gene Selection Method for Microarray Classification. In *Proceedings of the Third International Conference on Machine Learning and Cyherneucs*.

Niijima, S., & Okuno, Y. (2007). Laplacian Linear Discriminant Analysis Approach to Unsupervised Feature selection. *IEEE/ACM Transactions on Computational Biology and Bioinformatics, 10*, 20.

Osborne, J., Zhu, L., Lin, S., & Kibbe, W. (2007). Interpreting Microarray results with Gene Ontology and MeSH. *Methods in Molecular Biology-Clifton then Totowa, 377*, 223.

Papachristoudis, G., Diplaris, S., & Mitkas, P. (2009). SoFoCles: Feature filtering for Microarray Classification based on Gene Ontology. *Journal of Biomedical Informatics*.

Pasquier, N., Bastide, Y., Taouil, R., & Lakhal, L. (1999). Efficient Mining of Association Rules using Closed Itemset Lattices. *Information Systems, 24*(1), 25–46. doi:10.1016/S0306-4379(99)00003-4

Pearson, R., Gonye, G., & Schwaber, J. (2003). *Outliers in Microarray Data Analysis*. Springer.

Piatetsky-Shapiro, G., & Tamayo, P. (2003). Microarray Data Mining: Facing the Challenges. *SIGKDD Exploration Newsletter, 5*(2), 1–5. doi:10.1145/980972.980974

Pirooznia, M., Yang, J., Yang, M., & Deng, Y. (2008). A Comparative Study of Different Machine Learning Methods on Microarray Gene Expression Data. *BMC Genomics, 9*(Suppl. 1), S13. doi:10.1186/1471-2164-9-S1-S13

Pomeroy, S., Tamayo, P., Gaasenbeek, M., Sturla, L., Angelo, M., & McLaughlin, M. (2002). Prediction of Central Nervous System Embryonal Tumour Outcome based on Gene Expression. *Nature, 415*(6870), 436–442. doi:10.1038/415436a

Ponzoni, I., Azuaje, F., Augusto, J., & Glass, D. (2007). Inferring Adaptive Regulation Thresholds and Association Rules from Gene Expression Data through Combinatorial Optimization Learning. *IEEE/ACM Transactions on Computational Biology and Bioinformatics, 4*(4), 624–634. doi:10.1109/tcbb.2007.1049

Qi, J., & Tang, J. (2007). Integrating Gene Ontology into Discriminative Powers of Genes for Feature Selection in Microarray Data. In *Proceedings of 2007 ACM Symposium on Applied Computing* (pp.434).

Quinlan, J. (1986). Induction of Decision Trees. *Machine Learning*, *1*, 81–106. doi:10.1007/BF00116251

Quinlan, J. (1993). *C4.5. Programs for Machine Learning*. San Francisco: Morgan Kaufmann Publishers.

Richards, A., Holmans, P., O'Donovan, M., Owen, M., & Jones, L. (2008). A Comparison of Four Clustering methods for Brain Expression Microarray Data. *BMC Bioinformatics*, *9*(1), 490. doi:10.1186/1471-2105-9-490

Ruiz, R., Riquelme, J., & Aguilar-Ruiz, J. (2006). Incremental Wrapper-based Gene Selection from Microarray Data for Cancer Classification. *Pattern Recognition*, *39*(12), 2383–2392. doi:10.1016/j.patcog.2005.11.001

Segal, E., Battle, A., & Koller, D. (2003). Decomposing Gene Expression into Cellular Processes. In *Proceedings of Pacific Symposium on Biocomputing* (pp.89-100).

Shamir, R., & Sharan, R. (2001). *Algorithmic Approaches to Clustering Gene Expression Data*. Current Topics in Computational Biology.

Statnikov, A., Aliferis, C., Tsamardinos, I., Hardin, D., & Levy, S. (2005). A Comprehensive Evaluation of Multicategory Classification methods for Microarray Gene Expression Cancer Diagnosis. *BMC Bioinformatics*, *21*(5), 631–643.

Stekel, D. (2003). *Microarray Bioinformatics*. Cambridge, UK: Cambridge University Press. doi:10.1017/CBO9780511615535

Styczynski, M., & Stephanopoulos, G. (2005). Overview of Computational Methods for the Inference of Gene Regulatory Networks. *Computers & Chemical Engineering*, *29*, 519–534. doi:10.1016/j.compchemeng.2004.08.029

Su, Y., Murali, T., Pavlovic, V., Schaffer, M., & Kasif, S. (2003). RankGene: Identification of Diagnostic Genes based on Expression Data. *Bioinformatics (Oxford, England)*, *19*(12), 1578. doi:10.1093/bioinformatics/btg179

Tari, L., Baral, C., & Kim, S. (2009). Fuzzy c-means Clustering with Prior Biological Knowledge. *Journal of Biomedical Informatics*, *42*(1), 74–81. doi:10.1016/j.jbi.2008.05.009

Thalamuthu, A., Mukhopadhyay, I., Zheng, X., & Tseng, G. (2006). Evaluation and Comparison of Gene Clustering methods in Microarray Analysis. *Bioinformatics (Oxford, England)*, *22*(19), 2405–2412. doi:10.1093/bioinformatics/btl406

Troyanskaya, O., Cantor, M., Sherlock, G., Brown, P., Hastie, T., & Tibshirani, R. (2001). Missing Value Estimation methods for DNA Microarrays. *Bioinformatics (Oxford, England)*, *17*(6), 520–525. doi:10.1093/bioinformatics/17.6.520

Tuzhilin, A., & Adomavicius, G. (2002). Handling very large numbers of Association Rules in the Analysis of Microarray Data. In *Proceedings of Eighth ACM SIGKDD International Conference on Data Mining and Knowledge Discovery* (pp.396-404).

Vapnik, V. (1998). *Statistical Learning Theory*. Wiley.

Varshavsky, R., Gottlieb, A., Linial, M., & Horn, D. (2006). Novel Unsupervised Feature Filtering of Biological Data. *Bioinformatics (Oxford, England)*, *22*(14). doi:10.1093/bioinformatics/btl214

Wang, H., Wang, W., Yang, J., & Yu, P. (2002). Clustering by Pattern Similarity in Large Data Sets. In *Proceedings ACM SIGMOD International Conference on Management of Data* (pp.394-405).

Wang, Y., Makedon, F., Ford, J., & Pearlman, J. (2005). HykGene: A Hybrid Approach for Selecting Marker Genes for Phenotype Classification using Microarray Gene Expression Data. *Bioinformatics (Oxford, England)*, 21(8), 1530–1537. doi:10.1093/bioinformatics/bti192

Wang, Z., Yan, P., Potter, D., Eng, C., Huang, T., & Lin, S. (2007). Heritable Clustering and Pathway Discovery in Breast Cancer Integrating Epigenetic and Phenotypic Data. *BMC Bioinformatics*, 8(1), 38. doi:10.1186/1471-2105-8-38

Wu, F. (2008). Genetic Weighted k-means Algorithm for Clustering Large-scale Gene Expression Data. *BMC Bioinformatics*, 9.

Yeung, K., & Bumgarner, R. (2003). Multiclass Classification of Microarray Data with Repeated Measurements: Application to Cancer. *Genome Biology*, 4.

Yu, J., Cheng, F., Xiong, H., Qu, W., & Chen, X. (2008). A Bayesian Approach to Support Vector Machines for the Binary Classification. *Neurocomputing*, 72(1-3), 177–185. doi:10.1016/j.neucom.2008.06.010

Zahurak, M., Parmigiani, G., Yu, W., Scharpf, R., Berman, D., & Schaeffer, E. (2007). Pre-processing Agilent Microarray Data. *BMC Bioinformatics*, 8(142), 1471–2105.

Zheng, G., George, E., & Narasimhan, G. (2005). *Neural Network Classifiers and Gene Selection methods for Microarray Data on Human Lung Adenocarcinoma*. Methods of Microarray Data Analysis IV.

Zheng, Q., & Wang, X. (2008). GOEAST: A Web-based Software Toolkit for Gene Ontology Enrichment Analysis. *Nucleic Acids Research*, 36, W358. doi:10.1093/nar/gkn276

ADDITIONAL READING

Furlanello, C., Serafini, M., Merler, S., & Jurman, G. (2003). Entropy-based Gene Ranking without Selection Bias for the Predictive Classification of Microarray Data. *BMC Bioinformatics*, 4(1), 54. doi:10.1186/1471-2105-4-54

Guyon, I., & Elisseeff, A. (2003). An Introduction to Variable and Feature Selection. *Journal of Machine Learning Research*, 3, 1157–1182. doi:10.1162/153244303322753616

Guyon, I., Gunn, S., Nikravesh, M., & Zadeh, L. (2006). *Feature Extraction: Foundations and Applications (Studies in Fuzziness and Soft Computing)*. Springer-Verlag.

Halkidi, M., Batistakis, Y., & Vazirgiannis, M. (2001). On Clustering Validation Techniques. *Journal of Intelligent Information Systems*, 17, 107–145. doi:10.1023/A:1012801612483

Kaski, S., Nikkila, J., Sinkkonen, J., & Lahti, L. (2005). *Associative Clustering for Exploring Dependencies between Functional Genomics Data Sets*. IEEE/ACM Transactions on Computational Biology and Bioinformatics.

Li, Y., Campbell, C., & Tipping, M. (2002). Bayesian Automatic Relevance Determination Algorithms for Classifying Gene Expression Data. *Bioinformatics (Oxford, England)*, 18(10), 1332–1339. doi:10.1093/bioinformatics/18.10.1332

Liu, B., Cui, Q., Jiang, T., & Ma, S. (2004). A Combinational Feature Selection and Ensemble Neural Network method for Classification of Gene Expression Data. *BMC Bioinformatics*, 5(1), 136. doi:10.1186/1471-2105-5-136

Liu, H., & Motoda, H. (2008). *Computational methods of Feature Selection*. Chapman and Hall/CRC.

Liu, H., & Yu, L. (2005). Toward Integrating Feature Selection Algorithms for Classification and Clustering. *IEEE Transactions on Knowledge and Data Engineering*, 491–502.

Liu, J., Wang, W., & Yang, J. (2004) Gene Ontology Friendly Biclustering of Expression Profiles. In *IEEE Computational Systems Bioinformatics Conference*.

Lockhart, D., Dong, H., Byrne, M., Follettie, M., Gallo, M., & Chee, M. (1996). Expression monitoring by Hybridization to High-density Oligonucleotide Arrays. *Nature Biotechnology*, *14*, 1675–1680. doi:10.1038/nbt1296-1675

Madeira, S. C., & Oliveira, A. L. (2004). *Biclustering Algorithms for Biological Data Analysis: A Survey*. IEEE/ACM Transactions on Computational Biology and Bioinformatics.

McLachlan, G., Do, K., & Ambroise, C. (2004). *Analyzing Microarray Gene Expression Data*. Wiley-IEEE.

Saeys, Y., Inza, I., & Larranaga, P. (2007). A Review of Feature Selection Techniques in Bioinformatics. *Bioinformatics (Oxford, England)*, *23*(19), 2507. doi:10.1093/bioinformatics/btm344

Shyamsundar, R., Kim, Y., Higgins, J., Montgomery, K., Jorden, M., & Sethuraman, A. (2005). A DNA Microarray Survey of Gene Expression in Normal Human Tissues. *Genome Biology*, *6*(3), R22. doi:10.1186/gb-2005-6-3-r22

Thompsona, R., Deoa, M., & Turner, D. (2007). Analysis of microRNA Expression by in situ Hybridization with RNA Oligonucleotide Probes. *Methods (San Diego, Calif.)*, *43*(2), 153–161. doi:10.1016/j.ymeth.2007.04.008

Tjaden, B., & Cohen, J. (2006). A Survey of Computational methods used in Microarray Data Interpretation. *Bioinformatics (Oxford, England)*, *6*, 21–39.

Turner, H. L., Bailey, T. C., Krzanowski, W. J., & Hemingway, C. A. (2005). *Biclustering models for Structured Microarray Data*. IEEE/ACM Transactions on Computational Biology and Bioinformatics.

Wang, J., Bø, T. H., Jonassen, I., Myklebost, O., & Hovig, E. (2003). Tumor Classification and Marker Gene Prediction by Feature Selection and Fuzzy c-means Clustering using Microarray Data. *BMC Bioinformatics*, *4*(1), 60. doi:10.1186/1471-2105-4-60

Wang, Y., Makedon, F., Ford, J., & Pearlman, J. (2005). HykGene: A Hybrid approach for selecting Marker Genes for Phenotype Classification using Microarray Gene Expression Data. *Bioinformatics (Oxford, England)*, *21*(8), 1530–1537. doi:10.1093/bioinformatics/bti192

Xu, R., & Donald Wunsch, I. I. (2005). Survey of clustering algorithms. *IEEE Transactions on Neural Networks*, *16*(3), 645. doi:10.1109/TNN.2005.845141

Yang, K., Cai, Z., Li, J., & Lin, G. (2006). A Stable Gene Selection in Microarray Data Analysis. *BMC Bioinformatics*, *7*(1), 228. doi:10.1186/1471-2105-7-228

Yeung, K., Bumgarner, R., & Raftery, A. (2005). Bayesian Model Averaging: Development of an Improved Multi-class, Gene selection and Classification tool for Microarray Data. *Bioinformatics (Oxford, England)*, *21*(10), 2394–2402. doi:10.1093/bioinformatics/bti319

Zhang, G. (2000). Neural Networks for Classification: A Survey. *IEEE Transactions on Systems, Man, and Cybernetics*, *30*(4), 451–563. doi:10.1109/5326.897072

KEY TERMS AND DEFINITIONS

Association Rule Mining: The data mining task of extracting rules with the aim of discover interesting relations between variables in large datasets.

Biclustering: A variation of simple clustering, which considers the simultaneous grouping of both row and column subsets in a data matrix.

Classification: The data mining task of building a classification model by analyzing a training data set with the aim of predict the value of a target variable.

Clustering: The data mining task of grouping together elements with similar characteristics.

Data Mining: A specific task in the KDD process, which includes classification, clustering, rule mining and feature selection.

Feature Selection: The data mining task of detecting the more relevant attributes of a dataset with respect to a specific target.

Knowledge Discovery in Data (KDD): The process of extract hidden information from data. It includes the tasks of data selection, preprocessing, transformation, mining, and evaluation.

Microarray: An ordered set of DNA fragments fixed to solid surfaces, used to monitor the gene expression value in thousands of genes simultaneously.

Chapter 3
Temporal Association Rule Mining in Large Databases

A.V. Senthil Kumar
Hindusthan College of Arts and Science, Bharathiar University, India

Adnan Alrabea
Al Balqa Applied University, Jordan

Pedamallu Chandra Sekhar
New England Biolabs Inc., USA

ABSTRACT

Over the last couple of years, data mining technology has been successfully employed to various business domains and scientific areas. One of the main unresolved problems that arise during the data mining process is treating data that contains temporal information. A thorough understanding of this concept requires that the data should be viewed as a sequence of events. Temporal sequences exist extensively in different areas that include economics, finance, communication, engineering, medicine, weather forecast and so on. This chapter proposes a technique that is developed to explore frequent temporal itemsets in the database. The basic idea of this technique is to first partition the database into sub-databases in light of either common starting time or common ending time. Then for each partition, the proposed technique is used progressively to accumulate the number of occurrences of each candidate 2-itemsets. A Directed graph is built using the support of these candidate 2-itemsets (combined from all the sub-databases) as a result of generating all candidate temporal k- itemsets in the database. The above technique may help researchers not only to understand about generating frequent large temporal itemsets but also helps in understanding of finding temporal association rules among transactions within relational databases.

INTRODUCTION

In recent years, data mining has attracted more attention in database communities because of its wide applicability. Similarly, the digital data acquisition and storage technology made great process

which has resulted in the growth of huge databases. One can find these huge databases in walks of life, from the mundane (includes supermarket transaction data, credit card usage records, telephone call details, government statistics, etc.) to more exotic (includes images of astronomical bodies, molecular databases, medical records, etc.). There were several advancements occurred in the area of

DOI: 10.4018/978-1-60960-067-9.ch003

generation, collection and storage of data. Some of main contributing factors in these advancements include computerization of businesses, scientific and government transactions, advances in data collection tools ranging from scanned text and image platforms to satellite remote sensing systems and cheap storage space. Furthermore, internet is playing a big role as a global information system that flooded us with a tremendous amount of data and information. These databases plays vital role in understanding the real-time systems and helps researchers as knowledge repositories to understand and design strategies for future. This explosion of growth in stored data has generated an urgent need for new and novel techniques and automated tools that can intelligently assist us in transforming the vast amounts of data into useful information and knowledge. The discipline that emerged to retrieve and analyze information from these databases is known as *data mining*. Data mining can be defined as a process of extracting patterns from data. It is becoming an increasingly important tool to transform these data into information. Data mining can also be defined as the analysis of observational data sets to find unsuspected relationships and to summarize the data in novel ways that are both understandable and useful to the data owner.

The goal of data mining is to discover hidden patterns, unexpected trends or other subtle relationships in the data using a combination of techniques from machine learning, statistics and database technologies. This new discipline today finds application in a wide and diverse range of business, scientific and engineering scenarios. For example, large databases of loan applications are available which record different kinds of personal and financial information about the applicants (along with their repayment histories). These databases can be mined for typical patterns leading to defaults which can help determine whether a future loan application must be accepted or rejected. Several terabytes of remote-sensing image data are gathered from satellites around the globe.

Data mining can help reveal potential locations of some (as yet undetected) natural resources or assist in building early warning systems for ecological disasters like oil slicks etc. Other situations where data mining can be of use include analysis of medical records of hospitals in a town to predict, for example, potential outbreaks of infectious diseases, analysis of customer transactions for market research application etc. Srivatsan Laxmanan and Sastry (2006) listed detailed review on wide variety of application areas for data mining in the recent years.

Data mining can be performed on data represented in quantitative, textual, or multimedia forms. It has a flexibility to use a variety of parameters to examine the data. Those parameters include association (patterns where one event is connected to another event, such as purchasing a pen and purchasing paper), sequence or path analysis (patterns where one event leads to another event, such as the birth of a child and purchasing diapers), classification (identification of new patterns, such as coincidences between duct tape purchases and plastic sheeting purchases), clustering (finding and visually documenting groups of previously unknown facts, such as geographic location and brand preferences), and forecasting (discovering patterns from which one can make reasonable predictions regarding future activities, such as the prediction that people who join an athletic club may take exercise classes). The relationships and summaries derived through a data mining exercise are often referred to as models or patterns. Examples include linear equations, rules, clusters, graphs, tree structures, and recurrent patterns in time series. The discovery of association relationship among a huge database has been known to be useful in selective marketing, decision analysis, and business management (Hipp, Guntzer, & Nakhaeizadeh, 2000).

An important research issue that extends from the mining of association rules is the discovery of temporal association patterns in temporal databases due to the wide variety of applications on various domains. In this chapter, a new technique is developed to explore frequent temporal itemsets in the database. The basic idea of this technique is to first partition the database into sub-databases in light of either common starting time or common ending time. Then for each partition, the proposed technique is used progressively to accumulate the number of occurrences of each candidate 2-itemsets. A Directed graph is built using the support of these candidate 2-itemsets (combined from all the sub-databases) as a result of generating all candidate temporal k- itemsets in the database.

BACKGROUND

In data mining, association rule learning is a popular and well researched method to identify collection of data attributes that are statistically related in the underlying data. The general idea of finding association rules originated in application involving "market-basket data". Each transaction or data are usually recorded in a database in which observation consists of an actual basket of items (such as grocery items), and the variables indicate whether or not a particular item was purchased. One can think of this type of data in terms of a data matrix of *n* rows (corresponding to baskets) and *p* columns (corresponding to grocery items). Such a matrix can be very large, with *n* in the number of millions and *p* in the tens of thousands, and is generally very sparse, since a typical basket contains only a few items. Association rules were invented as a way to find simple patterns in such data in a relatively efficient computational manner. The task in association rule discovery is to find all rules fulfilling given pre-specified frequency and accuracy criteria. This task might seem a little daunting, as there is no exponential number of potential frequent sets in the number of variables of the data, and that number tends to be quite large in, say, market basket applications. Fortunately, in real data sets it is the typical case that there will be relatively few frequent sets (for

example, most customers will buy only a small subset of the overall universe of products).

There are several algorithms proposed for generating association rules such as *a priori* algorithm, Eclat algorithm, FP-growth algorithm, and so on. The main drawback from the established association rule mining approach is that they ignore the time variable. However, almost all applications in real-time system are dynamic and vary over the time which leads to new data bases known as temporal database. A temporal database is a database with built-time aspects (http://en.wikipedia.org/wiki/Temporal_database). More specifically the temporal aspects usually include valid-time and transaction time. For time-variant temporal databases, there is a strong demand to develop an efficient and effective method to mine various temporal patterns. Temporal association rule mining is a technique that used to discover the valuable relationship among the items in the temporal database. Surveys on temporal databases and data mining techniques are available in the literature (Srivatsan Laxman & Sastry, 2006). The following section presents a detailed description on temporal data mining and its related tasks and motivated from Srivatsan Laxman and Sastry (2006).

TEMPORAL DATA MINING

Temporal Data Mining is a rapidly evolving area of research that is at the intersection of several disciplines that includes statistics, temporal pattern recognition, temporal databases, optimization, visualization, high-performance computing, and parallel computing. It is one of the fast-developing areas concerned with processing and analyzing high volume, high speed data. Temporal data mining can be defined as the activity of looking for interesting correlations or patterns in large sets of temporal data accumulated for other purposes. It has the capability of mining activity, inferring associations of contextual and temporal proximity, some of which may also indicate a cause-effect association. Temporal data mining looks very similar to classical time series analysis, but they differ in several points as listed below. The first difference is the size and nature of data sets and the manner in which the data is collected. Often temporal data mining methods have capability to analyze data sets that are prohibitively large for conventional time series modeling techniques to handle efficiently. The other main difference is in the kind of information that needs to be estimated or uncover from given dataset. The main scope of temporal data mining extends beyond the standard forecast or control applications of time series analysis. The ultimate goal of temporal data mining is to discover hidden relations between sequences and sub-sequences of events. By sequential data, it means data that is ordered with respect to some index.

The discovery of relations between sequences of events involves mainly three steps:

1. Representation and modeling of data sequence in a suitable form,
2. Definition of similarity measures between sequences, and
3. Application of models and representations to actual mining problems.

Roddick and Spiliopoulou (2001) investigated the confluence of data mining and temporal databases and present a survey and issues to be explored in temporal data mining. The three dimensions used in that paper are data type, mining operations and type of timing information. The approach used to solve the problem may be quite different and is depends on the nature of the event sequence. A sequence composed by a series of nominal symbols from a particular alphabet is usually called a *temporal sequence* and a sequence of continuous, real-valued elements, is known as a *time series*.

Temporal Data Mining Tasks

The temporal data mining tasks are grouped into five main tasks includes prediction, classification, clustering, search & retrieval and pattern discovery. Among these five tasks, the first four tasks are extensively investigated in traditional time series analysis and pattern recognition. However, there is very limited research has been made in pattern discovery and most of the algorithms for pattern discovery in large databases mainly discussed in data mining literature (Srivatsan Laxman & Sastry, 2006).

Prediction

The main goal of this task is to forecast the future value from the past sample (or available data set). Prediction is one of the five tasks in time series analysis and temporal data mining. The forecasting of future values can be achieved through building a predictive model from the known data set. Yule in 1927 developed the first such model to perform forecasting of future values from past data. There are several predictive models developed to date to perform the task of prediction which are listed as follows:

- The autoregressive family of models which can be used to predict a future value as a linear combination of earlier sample values and provided the time series is assumed to be stationary (Box, Jenkins, & Reinsel, 1994; Chatfield, 1996; Hastie, Tibshirani, & Friedman, 2001).
- Linear nonstationary models like ARIMA models have also been found useful in many economic and industrial applications where some suitable variant of the process (e. g. differences between successive terms) can be assumed to be stationary. Another popular work-around for nonstationarity is to assume that the time series is piece-wise (or locally) stationary. The

series is then broken down into smaller "frames" within each of which, the stationarity condition can be assumed to hold and then separate models are learnt for each frame.

- In addition to this standard ARMA family of models, there are many nonlinear models for time series prediction. For example, neural networks have been put to good use for nonlinear modeling of time series data (Sutton, 1988).

Classification

The main goal of this task is to automatically determine the analogous category for given input sequence which can be achieved from sequence classification. In sequence classification, it is assumed that each sequence presented to the system belongs to one of finite number of classes or categories (predefined). There are several applications for sequence classification in literature. Some of the applications are speech recognition (O'Shaughnessy, 2003; Gold & Morgan, 2000), gesture recognition (Darrell & Pentland, 1993 ; Yamato, Ohya, & Ishii, 1992 ; Starner & Pentland, 1995), handwritten word recognition, demarcating gene and non-gene regions in a genome sequence, on-line signature verification etc. Sequence classification is also used in pattern recognition applications, images are viewed as sequences. One of the popular applications is images of handwritten words (Kundu, He, & Bahl, 1988; Nag, Wong, & Fallside, 1986; Nalwa, 1997) which is used for signature identification, etc.

Over the years, sequence classification has been employed in both pattern-based as well as model based methods. In case of typical pattern-based method, prototype feature sequences are available for each class such as gesture for each word, etc. The classifier then searches over the space of all prototypes, for the one that is closest (or most similar) to the feature sequence of the new pattern. Typically, the prototypes and the given features vector sequences are of different lengths. Thus, in order to score each prototype sequence against the given pattern, sequence aligning methods like Dynamic Time Warping are needed. Another popular class of sequence recognition techniques is a model-based method that uses Hidden Markov Models (HMMs). Here, one HMM is learnt from training examples for each pattern class and a new pattern is classified by asking which of these HMMs is most likely to generate it. In recent years, many other model-based methods have been explored for sequence classification. For example, Markov models are now frequently used in biological sequence classification (Baldi, Chauvin, & Hunkapiller, 1994; Ewens & Grant, 2001). Machine learning techniques like neural networks have also been used for protein sequence classification (e.g see Wu, Berry, Shivakumar, & McLarty, 1995). Haelsteiner and Pfurtscheller (2000) use time-dependent neural network paradigms for EEG signal classification.

Clustering

Clustering of sequences or time series is concerned with grouping a collection of time series (or sequences) based on their similarity. Clustering is of particular interest in temporal data mining since it provides an attractive mechanism to automatically find some structure in large data sets that would be otherwise difficult to summarize (or visualize). There are many applications where a time series clustering activity is relevant. For example in web activity logs, clusters can indicate navigation patterns of different user groups. In financial data, it would be of interest to group stocks that exhibit similar trends in price movements. Another example could be clustering of biological sequences like proteins or nucleic acids so that sequences within a group have similar functional properties. There are a variety of methods for clustering sequences. At one end of the spectrum, it includes model-based sequence clustering methods (Smyth, 1997; Law & Kwok, 2000).

Learning mixture models, for example, constitute a big class of model-based clustering methods. In case of time series clustering, mixtures of, e. g., ARMA models (Xiong & Yeung, 2002) or Hidden Markov Models (Cadez, Heckerman, Meek, Smyth, & White, 2000; Alon, Sclaroff, Kollias, & Pavlovic, 2003) are in popular use. The other broad class in sequence clustering uses pattern alignment-based scoring (Corpet, 1988; Fadili, Ruan, Bloyet, & Mazoyer, 2000) or similarity measures (Schreiber & Schmitz, 1997 ; Kalpakis & Puttagunta, 2001) to compare sequences.

Search and Retrieval

Searching for sequences in large databases is another important task in temporal data mining. Sequence search and retrieval techniques play an important role in interactive explorations of large sequential databases. The problem is concerned with efficiently locating subsequences (often referred to as queries) in large archives of sequences (or sometimes in a single long sequence). Query-based searches have been extensively studied in language and automata theory. While the problem of efficiently locating exact matches of (some well-defined classes of) substrings is well solved, the situation is quite different when looking for *approximate* matches (Wu & Manber, 1992). In content-based retrieval, a query is presented to the system in the form of a sequence (Wu & Manber, 1992). Search and retrieval is a task meant to search a large database of sequential data and retrieve it sequences or subsequences *similar* to the given query sequence. For example, search and retrieval a track from music database (Ghias, Logan, Chamberlin, & Smith, 1995). In search and retrieval tasks there is a need to quantify the extent of similarity between any two (sub) sequences. Measure of similarity between two sequence elements of equal length can be defined by considering distances between corresponding elements of the two sequences. The individual elements of the sequences may be vectors of real numbers or symbolic data. Euclidean distance can be used similarity measure between two sequence elements if the sequence elements are feature vectors with real components. However, sometimes the Euclidean norm is unable to capture subjective similarities effectively.

There are several methods proposed in literature to define the similarity measure between two sequences based on application of area. For example, Time warping methods have been used for sequence classification and matching for many years (Kruskal, 1983; Juang & Rabiner, 1993; Gold & Morgan, 2000). Dynamic Time Warping (DTW) is a systematic and efficient method (based on dynamic programming) that identifies which correspondence among feature vectors of two sequences is best when scoring the similarity between them. In recent times, DTW and its variants are being used for motion time series matching (Chang, Chen, Men, Sundaram, & Zhong, 1998; Sclaroff, Kollios, Betke, & Rosales, 2001) in video sequence mining applications as well. DTW can in general, be used for sequence alignment even when the sequences consist of symbolic data. There are many situations in which such symbolic sequence matching problems find applications. Many problems in bioinformatics relate to the comparison of DNA or protein sequences, and time-warping-based alignment methods are well suited for such problems (Ewens & Grant, 2001; Cohen, 2004). Another approach that has been used in time series matching is to regard two sequences as similar if they have enough non-overlapping time-ordered pairs of subsequences that are similar. The idea was applied to find matches in a US mutual fund database (Agrawal, Lin, Sawhney, & Shim, 1995).

Pattern Discovery

Unlike in search and retrieval applications, in pattern discovery there is no specific query to search the database. Pattern discovery is unsupervised / supervised natured operation which is meant only for data mining methods. The main goal of pattern discovery is to discover all 'interesting' patterns in the data. There is no universal notion for defining a pattern. However, one concept that is found very useful in data mining is frequent patterns. A frequent pattern is one that occurs many times in the data. Most of the data mining literature is concerned with formulating useful pattern structures and developing efficient algorithms for discovering all patterns which occur frequently in the data. Methods for finding frequent patterns are considered important because they can be used for discovering useful rules. These rules can be used to infer some interesting regularities in the data. A *rule* consists of a pair of Boolean-valued propositions, namely, a left-hand side proposition (the antecedent) and a right-hand side proposition (the consequent). The rule also states that when the antecedent is true, then the consequent will be true as well. For several years, in machine learning and artificial learning rules have been popular representations of knowledge. Decision tree classifiers, for example, yield a set of classification rules to categorize data. One of the earliest attempts at discovering patterns (of sufficiently general interest) in sequential databases is a pattern discovery method for a large collection of protein sequences (Wang, Chirn, Marr, Shapiro, Shasha, & Zhang, 1994).

Temporal Association Rule Mining to Find Frequent Temporal Itemsets

In this subsection, a review is done on the temporal association rule mining techniques to find frequent temporal itemsets and their limitations. The discovery of relevant *association rules* is one of the most important methods used to perform data mining on transactional databases. Frequent itemset construction aims at generating all possible itemsets that satisfy the minimum support threshold condition. Various algorithms have been evolved over the years to tackle this problem and they differ in the number of scans required, data structures employed and the methodology used in the construction of frequent itemsets.

In general, in the first iteration the support of individual items has been identified and count number is generated for these items. Then, the items that have count greater than threshold value is filtered out i.e. the items which have minimum support value. In each following iterations, the set of itemsets found above the threshold value in the last iteration has been used as the base for generation of new potential itemsets, called *candidate* itemsets. A count has been made to find the actual support for these candidate itemsets during the pass over the dataset. The candidate itemsets which are actually large is identified at the end of the pass, which forms a base for the next iteration. The same process is repeated until no other new large itemsets are found. Apriori algorithm is one of the first few algorithms proposed for this process which is based on a candidate set generation logic (Agrawal & Srikant, 1994; Agrawal, Imielinski, & Swami, 1993).

Many variants of mining association rules are been studied to explore more mining capabilities, such as incremental updating (Ayad, El-Makky, & Taha, 2001), mining of generalized and multi-level rules (Srikant & Agrawal, 1995) and temporal association rule discovery (Chen & Petr, 2000; Ale & Rossi, 2000). The algorithms provide researchers with very important results and enabled a new direction of research which is integration of association mining and fast searching algorithms and their mining methods. However, these integrated and traditional mining algorithms are observed that they are not effectively applied to the transactional database where the exhibition periods of the items are different which is a common. For example, most of the customers order egg and coffee as breakfast sack in the morning hours between 7 to 11 AM. In this interval the items eggs and coffee items have higher support and confidence of 40% to occur together where as in another interval for the same items has.005% support and confidence value to occur together in other transaction (Yingjiu, Peng Ning, Sean Wang, & Sushil Jajodia, 2003).

The main difference between normal association rule mining and temporal associational rule mining is extra variable time, in temporal asocial rule mining it adds time constraint to the association rule. A transaction with time information can be described as: $\{TID, I_1, I_2, \ldots\ldots I_n, T_s, T_e\}$. TID is the ID for each transaction; n-itemsets means there are n items in the itemset; Ts and Te represent the start and the end of transaction respectively in terms of valid time. Valid time indicates the event occurring time and transaction time indicates the database time. In case of the transaction occurs at the moment, Ts may be equal to Te (for example, in sale records in the supermarket).

After going several real-time examples and thorough literature review, it is found that different association rules may be discovered while considering different time intervals associated to it. Many items are introduced or removed from the database which is termed as items lifespan (means that item is valid on specific time interval). Discovery such temporal intervals together with the association rules that hold during the time interval may leads to useful knowledge and the rules are known as temporal association rule. From the above discussion, temporal association rule can be defined as an association rule that holds during specific time intervals. The common equations used in temporal association rule are given as follows.

Frequency of a itemset over time period T

$$= \frac{\text{No. of transaction in which the itemset occus}}{\text{Total of transactions over that period}}$$

In the same way,

Confidence of an item with another item

$$= \frac{\text{Tranasction of both items over the period}}{\text{Transaction of first item of that period}}$$

Support value of A

$$= \frac{\text{Frequency of occurrenaces of A in specified time interval}}{\text{Total number of tuples in specified time interval}}$$

Confidence of A $(A \Rightarrow B[Ts, Te])$

$$= \frac{\text{Support count } (A \cup B) \text{ over interval}}{\text{Occurence of A interval}}$$

where, Ts indicates the valid start time and Te indicate valid time according to temporal data.

The basic steps are listed in discovery of temporal association rules are as follows: 1. Find all frequently occurring patterns in the sequence; 2. Eliminate which of them seem to be related to each other.

Apriori algorithm suffers a major limitation of repeated scan limitation in developing association rules. However, several algorithms have been proposed in literature to overcome this problem. Some of them are pattern growth based approach (FP-Growth), dynamic item counting, etc. FP-Growth (Han, Pei, & Yin, 2000) is one of the major improvements proposed to overcome the repeated scan limitation. It is a pattern growth based approach and requires only two overall scans of the original input for the frequent itemset construction process. A dynamic itemset counting is another algorithm proposed to overcome the repeated scan limitation and also reduces the number of scans by constructing frequent itemsets in a simultaneous fashion (Brin & Rajeev Motwani, 1997). The major limitation of these and related algorithms are lack in temporal aspects in them. These algorithms are efficient ones for transactional database mining but not for databases bound by temporal properties. Some research effort have been made in adapting the above defined methods to deal with temporal information which to leads to whole new approaches. Guimaraces (2000) proposed a method that uses common sub-sequences to derive association rules with predictive value, for instance, in the analysis of discretized, multi-dimensional time series.

The main problem of mining general temporal association rules is to discover all possible frequent general temporal association rules from the large database. This problem is divided into two steps: Generate all frequent maximal Temporal Itemsets (TI) and the corresponding maximal temporal Sub-Itemsets (SI) with their relative supports and derive all frequent general temporal association rules that satisfy min-confidence from these frequent TI. Deriving the frequent general temporal association rules is straight- forward once we obtained the frequent TI and SI with their supports. However, the major challenge of mining general temporal association rules is the exhibition periods of the items in the transaction database are allowed to be different from one to another.

Strong temporal association rule mining can be divided into 4 steps:

1.   Data pre-processing which includes data cleaning, data integration, data exchange and data reduction. In virtue of data pre-processing, we can get high quality data mining object. This is an important step of data mining.
2.   To find the frequent itemsets which have the support no less than minimum support value (min_s).
3.   To generate association rules with frequent itemsets which is different to generate association rules without time because it adds time information on frequent itemsets. So, the association rules are temporal ones.
4.   To generate rule sets and output.

Das et al. (1998) proposed a possible approach that extends the notion of a typical rule i.e. X _Y (which states if X occurs then Y occurs) to be a rule with a new meaning i.e. X _T Y (which states that if X occurs then Y will occur within time T). However, Juan et al. (2000) proposed the temporal aspect of association rule, in which transaction in the database are time stamped and user specified time intervals to divide the data into disjoint segments, like month, days and years. Ozden et al. (1998) proposed a frequent pattern approach for mining the time sensitive data using cyclic rules. A *cyclic rule* is the one that occurs at regular time intervals, for example at every first Monday of a month. In order to discover these rules, it is necessary to search for them in a restrict intervals of time, since they may occur repeatedly at specific time instants but on a little portion of the global time considered. A method to discover such rules is applying an algorithm similar to the *apriori*, and after having the set of traditional rules, detects the cycles behind the rules. A more efficient approach to discover cyclic rules consists on inverting the process: first discover the cyclic large *itemsets* and then generate the rules. A natural extension to this method consists in allowing the existence of different time units, such as days, weeks or months, and is achieved by defining calendar algebra to define and manipulate groups of time intervals and the rules discovered are designated as *calendric association rules* (Ramaswamy,Mahajan, & Silberschatz, 1998). Lu et al. (1998) proposed an approach to the discovery of relations in multivariate time sequences is based on the definition of N-dimensional transaction databases. Transactions in these databases are obtained by discretizing, if necessary, continuous attributes. Then, this type of databases can then be mined to obtain association rules. However, for mining such databases needs new definitions for association rules, support and confidence. The great difference is the notion of address, which locates each event in a multi-dimensional space and allows for expressing the confidence and support level in a new way. The authors have proposed a novel approach in the next section that would overcome the drawbacks of currently available approaches.

Table 1. Transaction Sub-database

T.No	Items
T1	a c d e f
T2	a b c e f
T3	b c e f
T4	b e

TECHNIQUE USED FOR FINDING FREQUENT TEMPORAL ITEMSETS

In data mining, association ship is a vital component which is used to analyze data transformation for making intelligent and efficient decisions. The results will no longer be accurate if we ignore the items which are infrequent in whole dataset but frequent in a particular time period. In literature, there is very limited attention had been made in considering infrequent items. To overcome that drawback, a new technique that aims at exploring frequent large temporal itemsets is proposed which could detect the temporal relationships or temporal associations between specific values of categorical variables in large data sets. In the proposed technique, a Directed Graph Approach has been developed to partitions the database into sub-databases in light of the exhibition period of each items. The partitions have been constructed in such a way that items in each partition (sub-database) will have either the common starting time or the common ending time. Then, for each partition, occurrences of all the candidate set of large 1-itemsets are counted which are then used to generate candidate 2-itemsets. These candidate 2-itemsets from all the sub-databases are combined and is used to form the Directed Graph which explores the possible candidate temporal k-itemsets in the database.

Directed Graph Approach

The construction of a directed graph begins by partitioning the database into sub-databases where the items are allowed to have different exhibition periods and the determination of their supports is made accordance with their exhibition periods. For each sub-database, all the transactions of the sub-database are scanned to count the support of the 1-itemsets. With the help of the candidate 1-itemset, candidate 2-itemsets are generated. For these candidate 2-itemsets brought from the previous partition, their numbers of occurrences will be cumulated from the previous partition to the correct one. The candidate 2-itemsets from all the sub-databases are combined together and by using these candidate 2-itemsets a directed graph is generated from which possible frequent temporal k-itemsets in the database can be identified. To illustrate this, a transaction sub-database, which is partitioned from the database in light of common starting time (exhibition period of each item), has been considered as shown in Table 1.

As a first step, all the transactions of the sub-database are scanned to count the support of the 1-itemsets to form the set of 1-itemsets i.e. $C_1 = \{\{a\}, \{b\}, \{c\}, \{d\}, \{e\}, \{f\}\}$. For this purpose, a hash table (C_1) is built on the fly, for the purpose of efficient counting. For each item in the database, it is checked with the item in the hash table. If the item is already present in the hash table, then the corresponding count of this item is incremented by one. If the item is not present in the hash table, then the new item is inserted into the hash table and the count is initialized as one. After occurrences of all the 1-subsets are counted, using candidate 1-itemsets all the 2-itemsets with their counts are generated as shown in Figure 1. The 2-itemsets with number of occurrences greater than the filtering threshold *(minimum support s)*, for example, whose value is 2, are been selected and viewed as candidate 2-itemsets and are transferred to the next sub-database for further processing. The method employs the same technique for generation of candidate 2-itemsets in the second database and counts their occurrences as well. Also for the candidate 2-itemsets transferred from the previous sub-database, their numbers of occurrences is cumulative occurrences of current

Figure 1. Generation of candidate 2-itemsets in sub-database

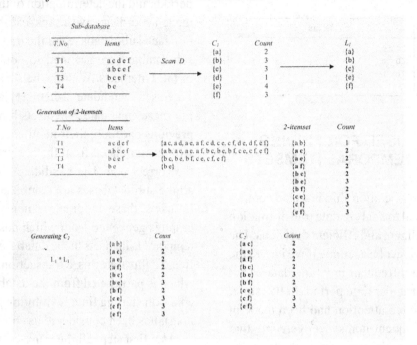

dataset to the pervious sub-database. The same process will be terminated when there are no partitions to be processed. In this approach, there is significant number of 2-itemsets has been filtered out in the early partitions which leads to final list of 2-itemsets that are very close to frequent 2-itemsets. Figure 2 illustrates the resultant list of candidate 2-itemsets after processing all partitions.

A directed graph has been constructed from possible candidate 2-itemsets to generate / discover the potential temporal *k-itemsets*. The constructed directed graphs will serve as a prevailing technique to depict associations. A directed graph is denoted as ($G = \{V, E\}$) where V is finite set of vertices elements and E is subset of edge elements i.e. $E \subseteq V \times V$. In the directed graph, an edge element is denoted as ordered pair $[u, v]$ where u and v are the vertices of the graph that are adjacent to each other. Moreover, edge can be defined as the *incident* from the vertex u and *incident* to the vertex v. The association graph can quickly turn into a tree display with as few as

dozen rules. Figure 3 illustrates the directed graphs constructed for the candidate 2-itemsets.

The nodes of the trees in Fig *3(i), 3(ii), 3(iii)* and *3(iv)* represents the respective pairs of the root nodes, i.e., candidate 2-itemsets, which are identified from the given database. The values of the edges represent the number of counts of each pair from the candidate 2-itemsets. The edges which as the *minimum support s,* for example, whose value is 5, are high lightened. After directed graphs for candidate 2-itemsets have been constructed, a directed graph is constructed for generating all candidate temporal *k-itemsets* by using the directed graphs generated using candidate 2-itemsets as shown in Figure 4.

The edges which have the minimum support 5 are high lightened and are used for the identification of the frequent temporal *k-itemsets*. Figure 4 itemsets {a b c e} and {a b c f} represents the possible frequent temporal *k-itemsets* and itemsets {a b}, {a d}, {a f}, {b c}, {b f}, {c e}, {c f} represents the possible frequent 2-itemsets for the given database.

Figure 2. List of candidate 2-itemsets in the database

2-itemsets	Count
{a b}	6
{a d}	10
{a e}	4
{a f}	7
{b c}	6
{b f}	6
{c e}	7
{c f}	8
{e f}	4

CONCLUSION

In the dynamic world, analysis and understanding of data is a very crucial component to design and develop efficient strategies or policies. Data mining technology has been successful in analyzing data set from various business domains and scientific areas. However, databases with temporal information are not well tackled by available data mining techniques that create space for novel approaches to analyze databases with temporal information. In this chapter, a new technique to explore frequent temporal itemsets in the database is proposed. The basic idea of this approach is to first partition the database into sub-databases based on either common starting time or common ending time. Then for each partition, the proposed technique has been used progressively to accumulate the number of occurrences of each candidate 2-itemsets. A Directed graph is built using the support of these candidate 2-itemsets (combined from all the sub-databases) as a result of generating all candidate temporal k- itemsets in the database. This technique may help researchers not only to understand about generating

Figure 3. Directed Graphs for the frequent 2-itemsets with minimum support

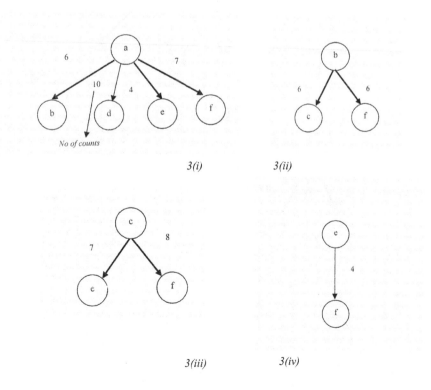

3(i)   3(ii)

3(iii)   3(iv)

frequent large temporal itemsets but also helps in discovering interesting temporal association relationships among large amounts of data which in turn helps in marketing, decision making and business management.

REFERENCES

Agrawal, R., Imielinski, T., & Swami, A. (1993). Mining Association Rules between Sets of Items in Large Databases. In *Proceedings of ACM SIG-MOD* (pp. 207-216).

Agrawal, R., Lin, K. I., Sawhney, H. S., & Shim, K. (1995). Fast similarity search in the presence of Noise, Scaling and Translation in Time Series Databases. In *Proceedings of 21ˢᵗ International Conference on Very Large Data Bases (VLDB 95)* (pp. 490-501).

Agrawal, R., & Srikant, R. (1994). *Fast Algorithms for Mining Association Rules* (pp. 487–499). VLDB.

Ale, J., & Rossi, G. (2000). An Approach to Discovering Temporal Association Rules. *Symposium on Applied Computing.*

Figure 4. Generation of candidate temporal k-itemsets

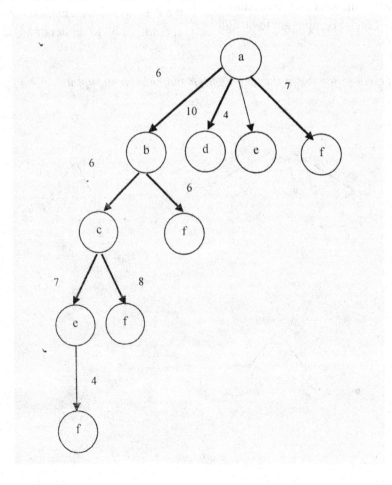

Alon, J., Sclaroff, S., Kollios, G., & Pavlovic, V. (2003). Discovering Clusters in Motion Time Series Data. In *Proceedings of 2003 IEEE Comput. Soc. Conf. on Computer Vision and Pattern Recognition* (pp. I.375–I.381).

Ayad, A. M., El-Makky, N. M., & Taha, Y. (2001). Incremental Mining of Constrained Association Rules. In *Proceedings of the First Conference on Data Mining.*

Baldi, P., Chauvin, Y., Hunkapiller, T., & McClure, M. (1994). Hidden Markov models of Biological Primary Sequence Information. In *Proceedings of National Academy Science* (pp. 1059-1063). USA 91.

Box, G. E. P., Jenkins, G. M., & Reinsel, G. C. (1994). *Time Series Analysis: Forecasting and Control.* Singapore: Pearson Education Inc.

Brin, S. J., & Rajeev Motwani, D. (1997). Dynamic Itemset Counting. In *Proceedings of ACM SIGMOD Conference* (pp. 255-264).

Cadez, I., Heckerman, D., Meek, C., Smyth, P., & White, S. (2000). *Model-based Clustering and Visualization of Navigation Patterns on a Website. Technical Report CA 92717-3425.* Irvine, CA: Dept. of Information and Computer Science, University of California.

Chang, S. F., Chen, W., Men, J., Sundaram, H., & Zhong, D. (1998). A Fully Automated Content based Video Search Engine supporting Spatiotemporal Queries. *IEEE Transactions on Circuits and Systems for Video Technology, 8*(5), 602–615. doi:10.1109/76.718507

Chatfield, C. (1996). *The Analysis of Time Series.* New York, NY: Chapman and Hall.

Chen, X., & Petr, I. (2000). Discovering Temporal Association Rules: Algorithms, Language and System. In *International Conference of Data Engineering.*

Cohen, J. (2004). Bioinformatics – An Introduction for Computer Scientists. *ACM Computing Surveys, 36*(2), 122–158. doi:10.1145/1031120.1031122

Corpet, F. (1988). Multiple Sequence Alignment with Hierarchical Clustering. *Nucleic Acids Research, 16*, 10881–10890. doi:10.1093/nar/16.22.10881

Darrell, T., & Pentland, A. (1993). Space-time Gestures. In *Proceedings of 1993 IEEE Comput. Soc. Conf. on Computer Vision and Pattern Recognition* (pp. 335–340).

Das, G., Mannila, H., & Smyth, P. (1998). *Rule Discovery from Time Series* (pp. 16–22). KDD.

Ewens, W. J., & Grant, G. R. (2001). *Statistical methods in Bioinformatics: An Introduction.* New York: Springer-Verlag.

Fadili, M. J., Ruan, S., Bloyet, D., & Mazoyer, B. (2000). A Multistep Unsupervised Fuzzy Clustering Analysis of fMRI Time Series. *Human Brain Mapping, 10*, 160–178. doi:10.1002/1097-0193(200008)10:4<160::AID-HBM20>3.0.CO;2-U

Ghias, A., Logan, J., Chamberlin, D., & Smith, B. C. (1995). Query by Humming – Musical Information Retrieval in an Audio Database. In *Proceedings of ACM Multimedia 95.* San Francisco, CA.

Gold, B., & Morgan, N. (2000). *Speech and Audio Signal Processing: Processing and Perception of Speech and Music.* New York: John Wiley & Sons.

Guimarães, G. (2000). *The Induction of Temporal Grammatical Rules from Multivariate Time Series* (pp. 127–140). ICGI.

Han, J., Pei, H., & Yin, Y. (2000). Mining Frequent Patterns without Candidate Generation. In *Proceedings of the Conference on the Management of Data (SIGMOD '00).* New York: ACM Press.

Haselsteiner, E., & Pfurtscheller, G. (2000). Using Time-dependent Neural Networks for EEG Classification. *IEEE Trans. Rahab. Eng, 8*, 457–463. doi:10.1109/86.895948

Hastie, T., Tibshirani, R., & Friedman, J. (2001). *The Elements of Statistical Learning: Data mining, Inference and Prediction.* New York: Springer-Verlag.

Hipp, J., Guntzer, U., & Nakhaeizadeh, G. (2000). Algorithms for Association Rule Mining – A General Survey and Comparison. *SIGKDD Explorations, 2*(1), 58–64. doi:10.1145/360402.360421

Juan, M. Ale., Gustavo, H., & Rossi, R. (2000). An Approach to Discovering Temporal Association Rules. In *ACM SIGDD.*

Juang, B. H., & Rabiner, L. (1993). *Fundamentals of Speech Recognition.* Englewood Cliffs, NJ: Prentice Hall.

Kalpakis, K., & Puttagunta, D. G. V. (2001). Distance measures for Effective Clustering of ARIMA Time Series. *IEEE International Conference on Data Mining.* San Jose, CA.

Kruskal, J. B. (1983). An Overview of Sequence Comparison: Time warps, String edits and Macromolecules. *SIAM Review, 21*, 201–237. doi:10.1137/1025045

Kundu, A., He, Y., & Bahl, P. (1988). Word Recognition and Word Hypothesis generation for Handwritten Script: A Hidden Markov Model based approach. In *Proceedings 1988 IEEE Comput. Soc. Conf. on Computer Vision and Pattern Recognition* (pp. 457–462).

Law, M. H., & Kwok, J. T. (2000). Rival penalized competitive learning for Model-based Sequence Clustering. In *Proc. IEEE Int. Conf. on Pattern Recognition.* Barcelona, Spain.

Lu, H., Han, J., & Feng, L. (1998). Stock Price Movement Prediction and N-Dimensional Inter-Transaction Association Rules. In *ACM SIGMOD Workshop on Research Issues in Data Mining and Knowledge Discovery* (pp.12.1-12.7).

Nag, R., Wong, K. H., & Fallside, F. (1986). Script recognition using Hidden Markov Models. In *Proceedings of 1986 IEEE Int. Conf. on Acoustics, Speech and Signal Processing* (pp. 2071–2074).

Nalwa, V. S. (1997). Automatic On-line Signature Verification. *Proceedings of the IEEE, 85*, 215–239. doi:10.1109/5.554220

O'Shaughnessy, D. (2003). *Speech Communications: Human and Machine.* Piscataway, NJ: IEEE Press.

Ozden, B., Ramaswamy, S., & Silberschatz, A. (1998). Cyclic Association Rules. In *Proceedings of 14th International Conference on Data Engineering (ICDE'98)* (pp.412-421). Orlando, Florida.

Ramaswamy, S., Mahajan, S., & Silberschatz, A. (1998). *On the Discovery of Interesting Patterns in Association Rules* (pp. 368–379). VLDB.

Roddick, J., & Spiliopoulou, M. (2001). A Survey of Temporal Knowledge Discovery Paradigms and Methods. *IEEE Transactions on Knowledge and Data Engineering, 13.*

Schreiber, T., & Schmitz, A. (1997). Classification of Time Series data with Nonlinear Similarity Measures. *Physical Review Letters, 79*, 1475–1478. doi:10.1103/PhysRevLett.79.1475

Sclaroff, S., Kollios, G., Betke, M., & Rosales, R. (2001). Motion Mining. In *Lecture notes in Computer Science; Proc. 2nd Intl. Workshop on Multimedia Databases and Image Communication.* Heidelberg: Springer-Verlag.

Smyth, P. (1997). Clustering Sequences with Hidden Markov Models. *Adv. Neural Inf. Process, 9*, 648–655.

Srikant, R., & Agrawal, R. (1995). Mining Generalized Association Rules. In *Proc. of the 21ˢᵗ International Conference on Very Large Databases* (pp.407-419).

Srivatsan Laxman, & Sastry, P.S. (2006). A Survey of Temporal Data Mining. *Sadhana, 31,* 173–198. doi:10.1007/BF02719780

Starner, T. E., & Pentland, A. (1995). Visual Recognition of American Sign Language. In *Proceedings of 1995 Int.Workshop on Face and Gesture Recognition.* Zurich.

Sutton, R. S. (1988). Learning to predict by method of Temporal Differences. *Machine Learning, 3*(1), 9–44. doi:10.1007/BF00115009

Wang, J. T.-L., Chirn, G.-W., Marr, T. G., Shapiro, B., Shasha, D., & Zhang, K. (1994). Combinatorial Pattern Discovery for Scientific Data: Some Preliminary Results. In *Proceedings of 1994 ACM SIGMOD International Conference on Management of Data* (pp. 115-125). Minneapolis, Minnesota.

Wu, C., Berry, M., Shivakumar, S., & McLarty, J. (1995). Neural Networks for Full-scale Protein Sequence Classification: Sequence Encoding with Singular Value Decomposition. *Machine Learning, Special issue on applications in Molecular Biology, 21*(1-2), 177-193.

Wu, S., & Manber, U. (1992). Fast Text searching allowing Errors. *Communications of the ACM, 35*(10), 83–91. doi:10.1145/135239.135244

Xiong, Y., & Yeung, D. Y. (2002). Mixtures of ARMA models for Model-based Time Series Clustering. In *2002 IEEE International Conference on Data Mining* (pp. 717-720). Maebashi City, Japan.

Yamato, J., Ohya, J., & Ishii, K. (1992). Recognizing Human action in Time-sequential Images using Hidden Markov Model. In *Proceedings of 1992 IEEE Comput. Soc. Conf. on Computer Vision and Pattern Recognition* (pp. 379-385). Champaign, IL.

Yingjiu Li. Peng Ning, X., Sean Wang., & Sushil Jajodia, R. (2003). Discovering Calendar-based Temporal Association Rules. *Data & Knowledge Engineering,* Vol. 4, Elesvier Publisher,193-214.

ADDITIONAL READING

Bastide, Y., Taouil, R., Pasquier, N., Stumme, G., & Lakhal, L. (2000). Mining Frequent Patterns with Counting Interface. *SIGKDD Explorations, 2*(2). doi:10.1145/380995.381017

Brockwell, P. J., & Davis, R. A. (1986). *Time Series: Theory and Methods*. Springer Series in Statistics.

Chen, M.-S., Han, J., & Yu, P. S. (1996). Data Mining: An Overview from Database Perspective. *IEEE Transactions on Knowledge and Data Engineering, 8*(6), 866–883. doi:10.1109/69.553155

Chudova, C., & Smyth, P. (2002). Pattern discovery in sequences under a Markovian assumption. In *Proceedings of Eighth ACM SIGMOD International Conference on Knowledge Discovery and Data Mining*. Edmonton, Canada.

Claudia, A., & Arlindo, O. Temporal Data Mining: An Overview. In *KDD Workshop on Temporal Data Mining* (pp. 1-13). San Francisco.

Dieterich, T. G., & Michalski, R. S. (1985). Discovering Patterns in Sequences of Events. *Artificial Intelligence, 25,* 187–232. doi:10.1016/0004-3702(85)90003-7

Frawely, W. J., Piatesky-Shapiro, F., & Matheus, C. J. (1991). *Knowledge Discovery in Databases: An Overview*. AAAI/MIT Press.

Garofalakis, M., Rastogi, R., & Shim, K. (2002). Mining Sequential patterns with regular expression constraints. *IEEE Transactions on Knowledge and Data Engineering, 14,* 530–552. doi:10.1109/TKDE.2002.1000341

Gusfield, D. (1997). *Algorithms on Strings, Trees and Subsequences.* New York: University of Cambridge Press. doi:10.1017/CBO9780511574931

Han, J., & Fu, Y. (1995). Discovery of Multiple-Level Association Rules from Large Databases. In *Proceedings of the 21st International Conference on Very Large Databases* (pp. 420-431).

Hoppner, F. (2001). *Learning Temporal Rules from State Sequences* (pp. 25–31). Seattle, USA: WLTSD.

Keogh, E. J., & Pazzani, M. (2000). Scaling up Dynamic Time Warping for Data Mining Applications. In *Proceedings of 6th ACM SIGKDD International Conference on Knowledge Discovery and Data Mining* (pp. 285-289). Boston, MA.

Kotsiantis, S., & Kanellopoulos, D. (2006). Association Rules Mining: A Recent Overview. *GESTS International Transactions on Computer Science and Engineering, 32*(1), 71–82.

Ma, S., & Hellerstein, J. L. (2001). Mining partially periodic event patterns with unknown periods. In *Proceedings of 17th International Conference on Data Engineering (ICDE '01)* (pp. 205-214).

Ng, R. T., Lakshmanan, L. V. S., Han, J., & Pang, A. (1998). Exploratory mining and pruning optimizations of constrained association rules. In *Proceedings of 1998 ACM SIGMOD International Conferences on Management of Data* (pp. 13-24). Seattle, Washington.

Perng, C.-S., Wang, H., Zhang, S. R., & Parker, D. (2000). Landmarks: A new model for similarity-based pattern querying in time series databases. In *16th International Conference on Data Engineering (ICDE00)* (pp.33). San Diego, CA.

Roberto, J. Bayardo, Jr., & Agrawal, R. (1999). Mining the Most Interesting Rules. In *Proceedings of the 5th ACM SIGMOD International Conference on Knowledge Discovery and Data Mining* (pp. 145-154). ACM Press.

Srikant, R., & Agrawal, R. (1996). Mining quantitative association rules in large relational tables. In *Proceedings of 1996 ACM SIGMOD Conference on Management of Data.*

Tesic, J., Newsam, S., & Manjunath, B. S. (2003). Mining Image Datasets using perceptual Association Rules. In *Proceedings of SIAM 6th International Workshop on Mining Scientific and Engineering Datasets in conjunction with 3rd SIAM International Conference on SDM* (pp. 71-77).

Wang, J., & Han, J. (2004). Efficient mining of Frequent Closed Sequences. In *20th International Conference on Data Engineering.* Boston, MA.

Wang, K., He, Y., & Han, J. (2000). Mining Frequent Itemsets Using Support Constraints. In *Proceedings of 2000 International Conference on Very Large Databases.*

Yan, X., Han, J., & Afshar, R. (2003). CloSpan: Mining closed sequential pattern in large datasets. In *Proceedings 2003 International SIAM Conference on Data Mining (SDM03).* San Fransisco, CA.

Yang, C., Fayyad, U., & Bradley, P. (2001). Efficient discovery of Error-tolerant Frequent Itemsets in high dimensions. In *Seventh ACM SIGKDD International Conference on Knowledge Discovery and Data Mining.*

Zaiane, O. R., Han, J., Li, Z., & Hou, J. (1998). Mining Multimedia Data. In *Proceedings of CASCON* (pp. 83-96).

Zaki, M. (1998). Efficient Enumeration of Frequent Sequences. In *Proceedings ACM 7th International Conference Information and Knowledge Management (CIKM).*

KEY TERMS AND DEFINITIONS

Association Rules: Used for discovering regularities between products in large scale transaction data recorded by Point-Of-Sale (POS) systems in supermarkets.

Data Mining: The process of extracting patterns from data.

Database: An integrated collection of logically-related records or files consolidated into a common pool that provides data for one or more multiple uses.

Directed Graph: It is a pair $G=(V,A)$ of a set V, whose elements are called vertices or nodes, a set A of ordered pairs of vertices, called arcs, directed edges, or arrows (and sometimes simply edges).

Frequent Itemset: A set of items that appears at least in a pre-specified number of transactions.

Temporal Data Mining: Data mining from temporal databases and/or discrete time series.

Time Series: It is a sequence of data points, measured typically at successive times spaced at uniform time intervals.

Chapter 4
Optimizing and Managing Digital Telecommunication Systems Using Data Mining and Knowledge Discovery Approaches

Adnan I. Al Rabea
Al Balqa Applied University, Jordan

Ibrahiem M. M. El Emary
King Abdulaziz University, Kingdom of Saudi Arabia

ABSTRACT

This chapter is interested in discussing and reporting how one can be benefited by using Data Mining and Knowledge Discovery techniques in achieving an acceptable level of quality of service of telecommunication systems. The quality of service is defined as the metrics which is predicated by using the data mining techniques, decision tree, association rules and neural networks. Digital telecommunication networks are highly complex systems and thus their planning, management and optimization are challenging tasks. The user expectations constitute the Quality of Service (QoS). To gain a competitive edge on other operators, the operating personnel have to measure the network in terms of QoS. In current times, there are three data mining methods applied to actual GSM network performance measurements, in which the methods were chosen to help the operating staff to find the essential information in network quality performance measurements. The results of Pekko (2004) show that the analyst can make good use of Rough Sets and Classification and Regression Trees (CART), because their information can be expressed in plain language rules that preserve the variable names of the original measurement. In addition, the CART and the Self-Organizing Map (SOM) provide effective visual means for interpreting the data set.

DOI: 10.4018/978-1-60960-067-9.ch004

INTRODUCTION

In response to human communication needs, telecommunications have developed into cellular radio networks, which enable subscribers to connect and communicate regardless of their location and even movement. The first generation networks were analogue, but the benefits of digital transmission, such as fewer transmission errors and more efficient use of radio frequencies, have paved the way for second-generation networks (2G) digital mobile telecommunication networks, whose most widely spread realizations are based on the Global System for Mobile communications standard (GSM World, 2003). The next generation, 3G networks are now being built, and the GSM successor is based on the Universal Mobile Telecommunications System (UMTS) standard. The UMTS network extends user connectivity on a global scale and provides more bandwidth for the user, enabling even multimedia transmissions. Digital mobile telecommunication networks are highly complex systems and thus their planning, management and optimization are not trivial tasks. The systems' complexity arises from elements such as switches, controllers, transceiver stations, to name just a few, which jointly form the radio interface of a network for mobile stations. The basic units of this complex network are base transceiver stations with antennas pointed to a radio coverage area, called the cell.

The subscribers, connected to the network via their mobile stations, expect network availability, connection throughput, and affordability. Moreover, the connection should not degrade or be lost abruptly as the user moves within the network area. These user expectations constitute Quality of Service (QoS), specified as "the collective effect of service performances, which determine the degree of satisfaction of a user of a service" (ITU-T E.800). To gain a competitive edge over other operators, the operating personnel have to measure the network in terms of QoS. By analyzing the information of their measurements, they can

manage and improve the quality of their services. With the information, they can also optimize the parameters and the configuration of the network.

However, because the operating staff is easily overwhelmed by hundreds of measurements, the measurements are aggregated into performance indicators, the most important of which are the Key Performance Indicators (KPI), which again can be divided into cost efficiency and QoS indicators (Lempiläinen & Manninen, 2001). Personnel expertise with the KPIs and the problems occurring in the cells of the network vary widely, but each personnel know the desirable KPI value range at least. Furthermore, the operators have their individual ways to judge if the KPIs in the cell indicate that the cell is performing as expected and if the cell is in its normal state. Their judgment may be based on simple rules such as "if any of the KPIs is unacceptable, then the state of a cell is unacceptable". The acceptance limits of the KPIs and the labeling rules are part of the a priori knowledge for analysis. When the operating personnel improve the QoS on the basis of their a priori knowledge, they face a lot of questions given below:

- What is the most common combination of KPI values when the state of a cell is unacceptable?
- Which KPIs is the most useful one for detecting problems?
- Which cells have the best QoS and how does KPI data manifest this?
- Whether all the KPIs relevant for analysis?

In finding the answers for QoS related questions, the personnel's main goal is to locate the problem areas in the network. Also, to support QoS improvement, one should know the best areas in the network. Should there be any; the configurations of well performing areas could be used to configure the problem areas of the network. Finally, even if most cells in the network perform as expected, it is useful to find cell groups that differ from each other and investigate if the groups could be optimized separately. The competence of the operating staff combined with the answers to the above questions should clarify the causes of the problems. Some complications may be solved by copying the parameter and configuration values learned from the best performing cells into the worst cells. Reliable knowledge of performance issues in the network gives the network operator a competitive edge over its rivals, as the knowledge helps solve the QoS related problems. Then how can the information about QoS performance are achieved? One potential answer is, it can be achieved through advanced approaches like data mining and knowledge discovery which are presented in the next section.

DATA MINING AND KNOWLEDGE DISCOVERY PROCESS

Data mining is the science and technology of exploring data in order to discover previously unknown patterns. Data Mining is a part of the overall process of Knowledge Discovery in Databases (KDD). The accessibility and abundance of information today makes data mining a matter of considerable importance and necessity. Most data mining techniques are based on inductive learning, where a model is constructed explicitly or implicitly by generalizing from a sufficient number of training examples. The underlying assumption of the inductive approach is that the trained model is applicable to future, unseen examples. Strictly speaking, any form of inference in which the conclusions are not deductively implied by the premises can be thought of as induction. Traditionally data collection is considered to be one of the most important stages in data analysis. An analyst (e.g., a statistician) used the available domain knowledge to select the variables to be collected. The number of variables selected was usually small and the collection of their values could be done manually (e.g., utilizing hand-

written records or oral interviews). In the case of computer-aided analysis, the analyst had to enter the collected data into a statistical computer package or an electronic spreadsheet. Due to the high cost of data collection, people learned to make decisions based on limited information.

However, since the information-age, the accumulation of data became easier and storing it inexpensive. It has been estimated that the amount of stored information doubles every twenty months. Unfortunately, as the amount of machine readable information increases, the ability to understand and make use of it does not keep pace with its growth. Data mining is a term coined to describe the process of shifting through large databases in search of interesting patterns and relationships. Practically, Data Mining provides tools by which large quantities of data can be automatically analyzed. Some of the researchers consider the term "Data Mining" as misleading and prefer the term "Knowledge Mining" as it provides a better analogy to gold mining (Klosgen & Zytkow, 1996). The Knowledge Discovery in Databases (KDD) process was defined my many, for instance Fayyad et al. (1996) define it as "the nontrivial process of identifying valid, novel, potentially useful, and ultimately understandable patterns in data". Frietman et al. (2001) considers the KDD process as an automatic exploratory data analysis of large databases. Hand et al. (2001) views it as a secondary data analysis of large databases. The term "Secondary" emphasizes the fact that the primary purpose of the database was not data analysis. Data Mining can be considered as a central step of the overall process of the Knowledge Discovery in Databases (KDD) process. Due to the centrality of data mining in the KDD process, there are some researchers and practitioners who use the term "data mining" as synonymous to the complete KDD process.

The purpose of a knowledge discovery process is to find new knowledge from an application domain (Klosgen & Zytkow, 1996). The process consists of many separate, consecutive tasks of

Figure 1. Knowledge Discovery process [Pekko, 2003]

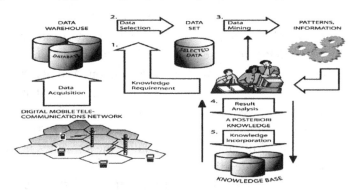

which data mining phase produces the patterns and information to be analyzed. Knowledge discovery deals with the data in a data warehouse or database. Several descriptions of a KDD and data mining processes have been published; solid representations are for example in publications (Fayyad, Piatetsky-Shapiro, & Smyth, 1996; Han & Kamber, 2001). For the purpose of knowledge discovery in the mobile telecommunications the authors suggest five main phases for KDD and further five within data mining,

- Knowledge requirement
- Data selection
- Data mining
  - a. Data reduction;
  - b. Data mining method selection;
  - c. Data preprocessing;
  - d. Data preparation;
  - e. Use of data mining methods
- Result analysis
- Knowledge incorporation

The suggested processes (Pekko, 2003) are depicted in Figure 1 and Figure 2 respectively.

The first step of knowledge discovery is to specify the knowledge requirement, that is, to define what it is that the analyst wants to find out from the application domain. To be able to specify the knowledge requirement the analyst has to have some a priori knowledge of the application domain. Generally speaking, knowledge

Figure 2. Data Mining process [Pekko, 2003]

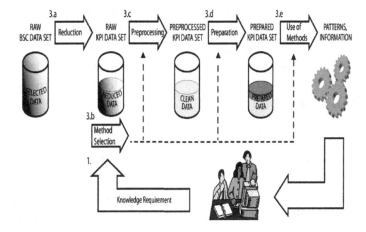

requirement is to find out problem related information from the data, more specifically, "what is the most common combination of KPIs when cell state is 'unacceptable'?, which KPIs indicate problems and what is the most common problem in the network?"

The second step is to select, possibly from several sources, the right data to support the knowledge requirement. Again, the skills and a priori knowledge of the analyst are needed. He should state what measurements, cells, and time periods are of interest. The necessary measurements are then fetched from a database, aggregated to KPIs and organized to a data table. For this study, the authors have given a KPI data set from a real operator. The data set consists of 53 measurements, covering three months period of 30 cells totaling in 3069 observations.

The third step, data mining - a process by itself – is now ready to start from the reduction of the selected data set. Result analysis and knowledge incorporation are considered steps of the KDD process.

Data Reduction

The raw data from a base controller database are commonly aggregated to KPIs according to pre-determined equations. The author of the equations can either be the manufacturer of the network management system or the network operating staff can make the KPIs by themselves. The authors have done aggregation to their data and reduced the amount of the data over seven times instead of the original 53 measurements. Sometimes data reduction is regarded as a part of preprocessing.

Data Mining Method Selection

The selection of an analysis method is dependent on the knowledge requirement and the preference of the analyst. An important requirement was the method's ability to retain the original KPI name in the results. It was also desired that results

should be in the same rule format as the a priori knowledge. Additionally, visual representations were needed to quickly address the analysis to the data structures. On this basis, Rough Sets, Classification And Regression Trees (CART) and Self-Organizing Map (SOM) were selected. Rough Sets and CART are capable of producing rules whereas both CART and SOM are used to visualize the structures in the data.

Data Preprocessing

The purpose of data preprocessing is to ensure that the analysis methods are able to extract the required information from the data. The most important phase of preprocessing is the feature extraction that is affected by the overall goals of the analysis, method selection and a priori knowledge. According to Kumpulainen et al. (2003), preprocessing is viewed as an iterative process. In feature extraction step, data integration, reduction, cleaning and transformation tasks can be recognized (Fayyad et al., 1996), but the tasks overlap somewhat. For the data set used, the integration was not needed as the data was acquired from a single source. The calculation of KPIs is a data reduction step, but at this point it is possible for the analyst to further reduce the amount of data by omitting some of KPIs. Data cleaning was done by omission of the measurements that had missing values. Visual inspection of the data was done to sort out the obvious outliers from the data. Several transforming operations were done, first of those was the attachment of the pre classification result to the data set as a new variable. Two other transformations, discretization and normalization were needed because rough sets are only usable for discrete data and SOM is usually trained with normalized values.

Data Preparation

Because rough sets are only usable for discrete data, the preprocessed data set had to be trans-

Figure 3. Discretization limits of the dropped calls KPI

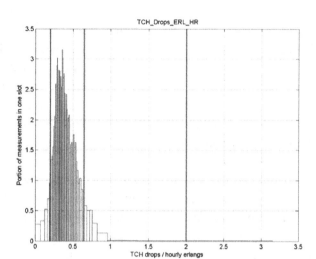

formed accordingly. This is called discretization and it is used to transfer all the continuous values of the selected data set to just few, discrete values. The limits for semantic values ("unacceptable", "bad", "normal", "and good") were given by an expert and they were further modified by visual inspection of the distributions. An example is given in Figure 3, where dropped calls are given discrete limits of 0, 20, 0, 65 and 2, 0 to discretize the variable to the respective "good", "normal", "bad" and "unacceptable" zones. SOM algorithm is based on the measurement of Euclidian distances between the measurements. Different scales of variables can greatly distort the results if the variables are supposed to have equal importance (Vesanto, Himberg, Alhoniemi, & Parhankangas, 2000). As this was the case for the data used, it was decided to give equal importance to all the KPIs and each KPI was scaled to the range of [0 … 1, 0].

Use of Data Mining Methods

Figure 4 depicts Simple Classification Tree of four levels. After the preprocessing and preparation, the data is ready for processing with the selected methods.

Figure 4. Simple Classification Tree of four levels

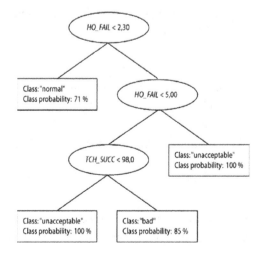

USING THE KNOWLEDGE DISCOVERY PROCESS FOR DETECTING AN ERROR IN ESS SWITCH: CASE STUDY

The KDD process employed in the case study of this chapter is very similar to the process used in many other projects. The steps in this process are given below.

Understanding the Data Mining Problem

The first step in the process involves gaining an understanding of the application domain and the goals of the KDD task. In this case, such an understanding had been acquired through previous work on the ANSWER expert system. The goal is influenced by a previous effort that attempted to use data mining techniques to predict catastrophic failures of 4ESS switches (Weiss, Eddy, & Weiss, 1998). A catastrophic failure is one in which the functioning of the entire 4ESS switch is compromised. The previous effort was seriously hampered by the rarity of catastrophic failures; only 50 such failures had been recorded and were available for study. Because of this experience, and to get the results be more widely applicable, the more general goal of predicting individual component failures was focused on. The data mining task, as described previously, is not well defined since neither the term "prediction" nor "pattern" was defined. To be meaningful, a prediction must apply to a specific time period. A prediction of a component failure is said to be correct if and only if the prediction occurs more than warning time and less than monitoring time before the actual failure. For example, given a warning time of one minute and a monitoring time of eight hours, a prediction must occur between one minute and eight hours prior to the actual failure for the failure to be considered successfully predicted. The warning time parameter ensures that there is sufficient time to respond to a failure prediction prior to the actual failure and the monitoring time parameter allows the user to control the specificity of the prediction. A prediction is "issued" if one of a pre-specified set of patterns (i.e., patterns identified by the data mining process) occurs in the stream of alarms coming from the 4ESS switch.

Patterns are described using a pattern language. Key features of this language were identified based on knowledge of the telecommunication domain. First, because alarms can be generated as a result of unrelated problems, the pattern language must provide a way of specifying a pattern so that the presence of an alarm does not prevent a pattern from matching. Secondly, because a fault may manifest itself in slightly different ways at different times; perhaps due to different activity occurring outside of the faulty component, there must be a way of specifying a pattern without fixing the order of all alarms within the pattern. Finally, because time is such an important factor, and because the behavior of the system will change in response to a fault, it must be possible to associate a time period with each pattern. Given these three requirements, it should be possible to specify the pattern "3 types-alarms and 2 type-B alarms occur, in any order, within a 5 minute period" (Weiss et al., 1998).

Selecting a Target Dataset

The target dataset was formed by collecting two weeks worth of alarms from the database at one of the two technical control centers. The resulting dataset contained 148,886 alarms, where each alarm contained approximately 20 variables. Based on knowledge of the domain and what variables are most important for diagnosis, five variables were selected to describe each alarm. These variables were:

- The time of generating the alarm;
- A unique identifier for the device associated with the alarm;
- The type of device;
- The diagnostic code associated with the alarm; and
- The severity of the alarm.

Thus, an alarm is represented by the tuple <time, device-id, device-type, diag-code, sever-

ity>. There are several dozen types of devices in a 4ESS switch, hundreds of diagnostics codes, and three severity levels (warning, minor, and major). Because the 4ESS switch recognizes component failures and automatically generates alarms for such failures, no additional effort was required in order to record these failures in the alarm stream. Preprocessing and Transforming the Data Components can fail for a variety of reasons. Because there is no need to distinguish between different types of failures, the various failure alarms were replaced with a common failure alarm. Also, because routine maintenance testing will cause failed components to generate additional failure alarms, a simple software program was applied to the target dataset to prune the "redundant" failure alarms. The resulting dataset yielded 1045 failure alarms corresponding to 1045 distinct component failures. The data mining task is then to predict these failure alarms (Weiss et al., 1998).

Applying Data Mining

The next major step in the KDD process involves selecting the data mining task and the algorithm to be applied. For this case study, the data mining task is clearly a prediction task. Because each alarm record represents an event—an observation that occurs at a specific instant of time; as an event prediction task was referred. A temporal data mining algorithm is required because the dataset contains events, not examples, and because predicting component failures will require the identification of temporal relationships in the data. Other important considerations in selecting a data mining method include the fact that the component failures are rare and known to be difficult to predict. Given these characteristics, the data mining algorithm may need to find patterns that occur very infrequently in the data and have relatively low predictive accuracy—perhaps well below 50%. Most data mining methods are not well suited to problems with these characteristics. The genetic-based data mining algorithm can be

developed to solve this data mining task (Weiss et al., 1998).

Interpretation of Results

The data mining algorithm produces a set of patterns for predicting component failures (i.e., each pattern x can be viewed as a rule of the form "x $\Rightarrow$ device failure"). Recall and precision values are computed for each pattern. For this domain, a pattern's recall is the percentage of the total component failures that it predicts and its precision is the percentage of times a prediction is correct. Note that if these patterns/rules are viewed as association rules, then recall corresponds to support and precision to confidence. To help select the most appropriate subset of the generated patterns, data mining software orders the patterns from most to least precise and then uses this ordering to generate a precision/recall curve. This curve is generated by viewing the most precise pattern as a solution, the two most precise patterns as another solution, etc., and then plotting the precision and recall for each solution. For this domain, as for most domains in the real world, these costs are not precisely known. In this case, these values may be estimated. Alternatively, several solutions can be given to a domain expert, who could then choose the most attractive solution based on the precision and recall values (Weiss et al., 1998).

The KDD process is an iterative process and it is common to use results as feedback into earlier stages in the KDD process. In this case study, the warning and monitoring times are parameters to the data mining software, and preliminary results were used as feedback to modify these parameter values. The values selected for evaluation were partly based on the "sensitivity" of the results to these parameters. For example, if a small increase in the monitoring time significantly improved the ability to predict a failure correctly, then additional points in this neighborhood can be explored. This exploration provides an insight into the nature of the prediction problem. For example, decreasing the warning time enables much better predictions to be made. This indicates that there is some useful information for predicting failures that occurs shortly before the actual failure. The final step involves consolidating the discovered knowledge. This was accomplished by documenting and distributing the key results. Most importantly, these results were then to be incorporated into the ANSWER expert system in the form of rules (Weiss et al., 1998).

APPLICATION OF DATA MINING AND KNOWLEDGE DISCOVERY PROCESS IN ANALYZING THE QOS ISSUES

Information needed to analyze QoS issues exists in KPI data, but sometimes it is not easy to recognize. The techniques of Knowledge Discovery in Databases (KDD) and Data Mining help us to find useful information in the data. In early 1990's, Data Mining and KDD have been much discussed in research topics. However, since the terminology still varies and the definitions overlap, the present research must find its own definitions. In this work, data mining is defined as a partially automated KDD subprocess, whose purpose is the nontrivial extraction of implicit and potentially useful patterns of information from large data sets. When Data Mining and KDD are taken into consideration, the former is to be seen as a subprocess of the latter. The KDD process starts with a knowledge requirement and ends, after the information produced by data mining has been interpreted, with knowledge that fulfills the requirement. However, data mining deals with a given set of data and produces patterns of information from it. KDD is the framework that sets up a need for information, whereas data mining is the tool that provides it. To date, a fully automatic KDD process has not yet been realized, because systems producing large amounts of data are also very complex. Problems in a complex system are

not solved by using merely the information in the measured data. A human analyst is a must for successful analysis, because he can provide a priori knowledge not present in the data yet needed for KDD. Human participation is needed to select the right data for KDD, to provide additional information for the data mining methods, and to judge the usefulness of the information patterns. KDD does not begin with specifications as to how data should be collected or measured but with the data already stored in the database. This does not mean that the knowledge gained could not be used to improve measurement and data recording.

After defining the knowledge requirement, the data set that supposes to contain relevant information should be selected. The selected data set must be preprocessed before actual data mining methods can be applied to it. The methods then automatically extract "valid, novel, useful and understandable" (Fayyad et al., 1996) patterns of information from the preprocessed data. Validity, novelty, usefulness, and intelligibility define the interestingness of the pattern (Han & Kamber, 2001). Human judgment is then needed to decide whether the extracted information is interesting. And if the patterns are deemed interesting, the interpreting person gains new knowledge by comparing the results with his a priori knowledge. Because of the rather loose definition of data mining, several methods can be used to extract and summarize information from the data. Choosing a method is largely up to the analyst applying KDD. The methods should suit the knowledge requirement task, but choosing a suitable data mining software package may be difficult because the knowledge requirement is task-specific. If suitable methods are not available, the analyst has to program the methods into a computer or even re-specify the knowledge requirement.

The most important criterion considered in the process of selecting data mining methods is their suitability as tools for the operating staff of a digital mobile telecommunications network to alleviate the task of interpreting QoS-related information from measured data. Three methods were chosen that fulfilled the criterion: rough sets, classification trees, and self-organizing map type neural networks. Classification trees and neural networks are commonly used in data mining software packages. Rough Sets (Pawlak, 1982) can be used to find out features in the data that can be expressed in the form of rules. Rough sets sort out those variables that contain relevant information for analysis. However, before they can be used, a priori knowledge has to be added into the selected data set. Classification And Regression Trees (CART), a common analytic method developed by Breiman et al. (1984), produce results similar to rough sets. Classification trees give features as rules similar to rough sets and only relevant variables are taken into account. In addition, classification trees provide a visual tree-shaped structure that can help the analyst understand the features in the data.

The Self-Organizing Map (SOM) (Kohonen, 1995) works best as a visualization tool for data, as it shows the structure of a data set usually as a two-dimensional map. Data points are placed on to the map, and the differences between measurements are visualized in color. The structure can be further simplified by clustering the map into just a few groups. These three methods provide three views of the features of a data set; the final choice and usefulness of a method depend on the analyst's knowledge requirement and preference.

Data mining, KDD, and related applications in telecommunication networks have been reported (Chen, Dayal, & Hsu, 2000; Garofalakis & Rastogi 2001; Klementtinen, 1999). Challenges to the operational management of telecommunications networks are discussed in Terplan (2001), where four main tasks are listed for operational management:

- Resolving service problems,
- Managing service quality,
- Maintaining and restoring a network,
- Collecting and managing data.

The most important task for the management personnel is to guarantee the level of quality service the customer requires, and for that they have to master the above tasks. Terplan (2001) suggests a choice of appropriate tools for the task, tools that should be useful for monitoring components, collecting data, and correlating information from many sources to help solve problems. It also points out that a large amount of data poses problems, and that advanced, automated methods are needed to help the personnel analyze the problems. More specifically, methods such as expert systems, neural networks, knowledge conservation, case-based reasoning, and data mining (Terplan, 2001) but it omits more detailed discussion of the subject.

The basis for handling massive data sets is laid by Suutarinen (1994), which presents a solution for managing a GSM base station system and shows that aggregating raw network measurements into fewer performance measurements helps manage the network tasks. Aggregation helps change the focus of analysis and simplify it because of less data. Also Ni (2001) has approached the QoS management of GSM network, but from the viewpoint of dynamic channel allocation, not from data mining. Mattison (1997) brings up some general ideas about data mining for telecommunications and describes the business value of data warehousing and data mining technology. Its focus is not on the scientific or technological aspects of data mining but rather on general concepts and their clarification and some examples of the use of commercial programs in data warehousing and data mining in telecommunications. Also Sasisekharan et al. (1996) have a rather general approach to data mining in telecommunications. They describe a data mining process that starts from extraction of features from the data and ends in finding classification rules. They do not focus much on the problem domain as on describing the properties of the rule sets discovered. In their analysis, they use a commercial program called SCOUT (Sasisekharan, Hsu, & Simen, 1993). Chen et al. (2000) have studied data mining and on-line analytical processing for customer profiling. Železný et al. (2000) have studied rule discovery for the autoimmunization of switchboard operations. Garofalakis and Rastogi (2001) discuss storage, exploration, and analysis of data sets in network management and present methods for compression of data and fault management. Weiss et al. (1998) describe the use of data mining to predict failures of telecommunication equipment. Ezawa and Norton (1995) applied the knowledge discovery approach and Bayesian network to fraud detection in telecommunications, whereas (Sterrit, Adamson, Shapcott, & Curran, 2000a, 2000b) applied Bayesian network to fault management. Klementtinen (1999) studied data mining by analyzing alarms generated in a mobile network and presented a KDD process that make use of two rule-based analyses to discover recurrent alarm patterns in the data.

Quality Performance Measurements

First generation analogue mobile networks, such as the Nordic Mobile Telephone (NMT) standard, have become obsolete in favor of the second generation (2G) digital mobile networks. The most widely spread 2G networks are based on the Global System for Mobile communications (GSM) standard. GSM World (2003) predicts that the number of GSM subscribers will exceed one billion in late 2003 or early 2004. Second generation networks have been operational and constantly developed since the early 1990's. The

GSM standard has been updated to the GSM Phase 2+ standard with added features and services. The additions extend the lifetime of the GSM standard at least till the end of 2010. The third generation (3G) digital networks such as the Universal Mobile Telecommunications System (UMTS) were developed at the outset of the third millennium to provide more data bandwidth for subscribers. Moreover, it is forecasted that by 2006 the GSM family, including UMTS, will have close to 85% of the world market (Nokia 2003). The popularity of the communications services available via 2G and 3G networks proves clearly that the technology has met with consumers' expectations. Public Land Mobile Network (PLMN) consists of several systems and their subcomponents. The PLMN has to provide communication services for the subscriber reliably and promptly. A skilled network operator and an appropriate network management system are required to respond to user expectations, for an important part of the operation is to monitor and analyze the quality of service provided for the user.

Telecommunications Management Network Tasks

The Telecommunications Management Network (TMN) model shown in Figure 5, is a collection of standards to provide a framework for managing the business of a telecommunications service provider. The model consists of four layers – business, service, network, and element management – which

Figure 5. A detailed network management operations map forms the content of the network management layer in the TMN model

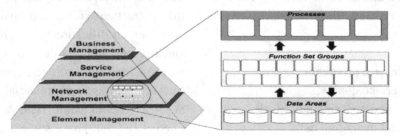

communicate information to one another. The purpose of the information transfer is to manage the telecommunications network. The model's top layers need information from the layers below to support decisions, and the bottom layers are the ones to provide it.

Operational processes in each layer are documented in the Telecommunications Operations Map (TOM) (Laiho, 2002;TMF 910). Network management operations reside in the network management layer. The TMN model lists five processes in network management, which are network

- Development & planning;
- Provisioning;
- Inventory management;
- Maintenance & restoration; and
- Data management

Terplan (2001) and Tisal (2001) recognize and discuss network data operations and their management. Quality analysis is an important part of data management with one of its main goals being to "provide sufficient and relevant information to verify compliance/ non-compliance to Service Level Agreements and QoS levels" (TMF 910). The methods and the results in Pekko (2004) are discussed from the viewpoint of the operations personnel who are responsible for managing network data operations (Figure 6) in the network management layer. The functions and data areas of the process are shown in Figure 6 as a detailed operations map of the network management layer. The areas corresponding to network data management are highlighted. An alternative view of network data management is given in Figure 7 in terms of its inputs and outputs.

Quality Performance Measurements

Suutarinen (1994) laid the foundation for quality performance measurements by developing a solution for managing the performance of a GSM base station system. He suggested a task oriented approach to network management and listed four management categories:

- Implementation of a new network, which means that if problems occur, the functionality of the network must be verified from base station sub-system observations,
- Monitoring, that is, daily evaluation of services and the necessary control tasks,
- Tuning, which requires verifying adequate service levels, identifying problems, optimization, and analysis of the network?
- Planning, aiming for the optimal configuration of the network is a perpetual process.

Figure 6. Processes function set groups, and data areas of a detailed network management operations map

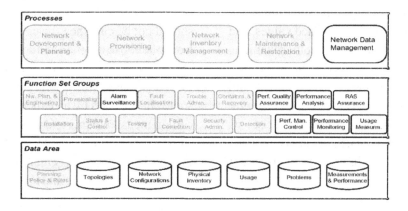

Figure 7. Network data management process

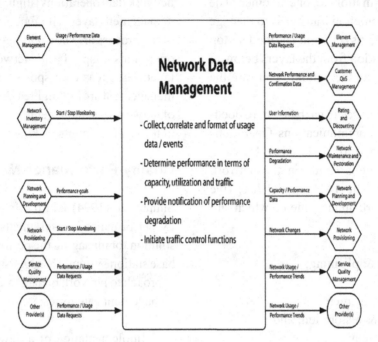

Each task category must have defined goals and information criteria, and means must be developed to get the information from the network management system. For monitoring and tuning, the measurement data from the BSS is thus very important. Suutarinen (1994) shows that instead of using raw measurements from the BSS, attributes constructed of the measurements are easier to understand and thus preferable in managing the network. Measurements from a PLMN contain information about the state of the network. And though the state of the network has not been defined universally, it can be judged roughly. For example, the state of the network is normal, when measurements fall within predefined values, and no alarms occur in the network. Another example, albeit undesirable, of a network state is the situation in which one or several measurements fall outside the predetermined limits and trigger alarms. However, should a problem arise, its causes should be investigated, and once they are known, the same or similar problems are easier to avoid in the future.

The network should be optimized and if some cells in the PLMN perform better than others, the reason should also be investigated. It may be that if the parameters set for well-performing cell are copied to normal or poorly-performing cells, the performance of the latter will improve. Furthermore, excess and shortage of capacity in a cell should be avoided. The states of the network must be recognized before problems and their causes can be sorted out. Past experience (a posteriori) and a priori knowledge can be used to help in recognition: calls in the network should get through with a predetermined probability, only a certain number of dropped calls are acceptable, the connection should not be cut when the calls are handed over from one cell to another, and so forth. This a priori knowledge can also be considered a requirement for acceptable network performance. Furthermore, some simple rules by an expert can be applied to certain measurements and used as boundaries of a normal operating state. Alternatively, a method to classify the data purely mathematically, though even here the operator must provide information about the quality of the state of found classes, at least a division into normal and problem states.

Selection of a Data Set

Data selection must support the knowledge discovery tasks. To support the discovery tasks, four main issues must be specified in measurement selection:

- Sampling rate,
- Time period,
- Geographical area,
- Variable selection.

Raw measurements are mostly event-based counters stored in BSC databases. KPIs are calculated from the raw counters, based on either the network operator's or the network management software provider's preferences. Depending on the KPIs required for the analysis, a database is queried and the relevant counters are fetched from the BSC databases. Based on the KPI equations, the KPIs are formed and stored in a separate KPI database. The KPIs were divided into two main groups, capacity- and quality-related KPIs. The capacity-related KPIs were to provide information on how efficiently the radio network was used, and the quality-related KPIs on how the radio interface affected the QoS. KPIs were available only as 24h measurements, which meant that it was not feasible to select a large number of cells over a short period of time, say a week, because only few measurements per cell were then available. Thus the data set was chosen to cover a period of 138 consecutive days to ensure that it represented long-term changes in intrinsic QoS. The data set contains measurements from 33 cells spanning a geographical area of closely located cells. However, neither the cells' exact geographical position nor their adjacency information was available. The fact that the cells were from the same general network area is yet enough to interpret the results.

Preprocessing

Preprocessing the selected data set was rather simple: observations containing missing values were removed from the set. If any KPI values were missing in a single observation, the whole data row was removed. If the cells were to be compared, a whole day had to be removed from the data. The removal of missing values left 93 days out of the original 138, a reduction of approximately 33%. However, the removal was necessary to ensure the validity of the results of any data mining method, as missing values would invalidate a method.

Limits Based on a Priori Knowledge

The analyst knows roughly the normal range of KPI values, and he knows also which end of the scale is desirable. For instance, his a priori knowledge of SDCCH access is that it is normal for KPI values to be close to 100. He also knows that if the value drops below 100, a problem ensues because the signaling channels should be available all the time. To ensure that his a priori knowledge is justified, the analyst can plot the KPIs' Probability Density Function (PDF) estimates, assuming that the data is acquired from a network that has been under normal operational control. PDF estimates are plotted so that variable data is divided into slots along the horizontal axis, which represents a KPI's value. Each slot has an equal number of data points, which means that the height of the slot is proportional to the density of data points over the range of one slot. When the analyst scrutinizes the plotted KPI PDF-distributions, he can justify and possibly refine the limits of a good, normal, bad and unacceptable KPI. Based on the limits and his a priori knowledge, the operator can then write out his rules to interpret the data as a labeling function.

Key Performance Indicators

A Key Performance Indicator (KPI) is considered an important performance measurement. In GSM network management, KPIs may be used for several purposes; thus selecting KPIs for analysis is a subjective matter (Laiho et al., 2002). However, KPIs can be divided roughly into cost efficiency- and quality-related KPIs (Lempiläinen & Manninen 2001). The QoS related KPIs in this thesis are based on the measurement of SDCCH and TCH logical channels and handovers. Intrinsic QoS analysis depends on quality-related KPI measurements available from the network elements. In the GSM network, the most important services are bearer and teleservices. The intrinsic QoS of a bearer service means that the network's radio coverage is available for the subscriber outdoors and indoors. However, the subscriber accepts that the network is unavailable in sparsely populated areas and when the signal is obstructed by the terrain. Likewise, the network signal can be blocked because of dense walls and when the subscriber moves underground. However, availability of the network is necessary for teleservices; therefore, KPI data contains information about those cells where the bearer service is degraded. Teleservices require a functional bearer service and a successful connection. Speech, SMS, fax, and data depend on the bearer service, and the subscriber's need for teleservices has to be filled in most cases. The subscriber is cognizant, however, of the fact that it is not always possible to use the services, especially in situations in which many people try to use the services contemporaneously within a small area. Should cell coverage be provided in extreme situations, investment in hardware would become financially unsound for the operator.

Five of the KPIs related to QoS refer to the use of the logical channels of the GSM network that require physical channels. The UM interface of the GSM network uses both Time Division Multiple Access (TDMA) and Frequency Division Multiple Access (FDMA) for receiving and transmitting information (Penttinen, 2001). TDMA means that each frequency channel is divided into eight repeated time slots. A separate time slot is a physical channel, and one physical channel can contain logical channels defined as Traffic CHannels (TCH) for call data and Control CHannels (CCH) for transmitting service data between the nodes of the network. In a time slot, the two types of logical channels can be combined (Penttinen 2001; Tisal 2001). Several TCH types are available for carrying traffic in a GSM network, and they can be divided into two groups: channels used for carrying speech and those for carrying data (GSM 05.02). As the performance measurements used in this thesis are indifferent to the types of traffic, it is adequate for the purpose here that the abbreviation TCH refers to any or all types of traffic channels. CCHs are used to signal or synchronize data and can be divided into four categories: Broadcast, Common, Dedicated and Cordless Telephony System (CTS) (GSM 05.02). Broadcast channels are used only in the downlink direction and are thus not very useful for performance measurements. A Common CCH (CCCH) is equally useless for the same reason; it transmits only in one direction. A CCH is used for CTS when a mobile station is used in a home environment and not connected to a PLMN.

The performance measurement data set in this work contains measurements only about a Stand-alone Dedicated Control CHannel (SDCCH). A SDCCH serves many communication purposes between the network and an MS. First of all, it is used when a call is initiated and information about the TCH and Slow Associated Control CHannel (SACCH) used for the call is transmitted. Secondly, Um interface protection signaling, used for encryption, is carried in the SDCCH. Furthermore, a SDCCH is also needed to deliver short messages, when an MS is not involved in a call (Penttinen, 2001). Finally, successful handovers are an important element of a mobile network. Handover means switching a connection from a physical channel to another. Handovers are divided into intra-cell and inter-cell handovers.

CONCULSION

In this chapter, data mining is presented as a tool to manage quality of service in digital telecommunications networks. Three data mining methods and a priori knowledge were applied to a real quality of service data set to interpret and summarize the information content of key performance indicators. These methods − Rough Sets, CART, and SOM. According to the results, Rough Sets are best suited for analyzing the QoS of single cells in a network, the CART for ruling out the most important KPIs and detecting potential outliers in the data, and the SOM for visualizing data features and checking a priori decision making. While the methods here are only a fraction − though an important one − of all the available data mining methods, the KDD framework in this chapter is solid and provides a systematic approach to dealing with information in data. Future challenges in knowledge discovery lie in the clear formulation of the discovery task, further automation of the knowledge discovery loop, and in reliable means to assess every step in KDD. To be more specific, suppose if it is possible to formulate a fair discovery task, then it should also find automatic, robust and reliable means to

- Use a priori knowledge,
- Acquire measurement data both sufficient for and relevant to the discovery task,
- Apply basic statistical analysis to verifying the quality of the data,
- Preprocess data,
- Select data mining method(s) suitable for the discovery task,
- Prepare the chosen data,
- Select parameters for the method(s),
- Assess the validity and usefulness of the information produced, and
- Store useful information as knowledge.

It should be able to automatically analyze the feasibility of the data for the discovery task by basic statistical analysis and exploration methods. Such automated analysis has already been considered in Vesanto (2002) and Wright (1998). Obvious faults in the data, such as missing values or clear outliers, should be fixed with less effort, for the validation of data is now laborious. It is hard to automate the selection of a data mining method, though attempts have been made (Spiliopoulou, Kalousis, Faulstich, & Theoharis, 1998). Automatic selection is hard because it depends on the discovery task, available data, and the analyst's preference. Currently, the decision on the applicable method is left largely to the analyst and the constrains set by the KDD system. A priori knowledge of both domain and method is needed when a data set is prepared. In this thesis, the preparation was manual, except that a decision variable was used. Automated preparation is now actively being researched (Pyle, 1999). Analyst expertise was called again when the methods' parameters were set for desired results. However, to decrease the threshold for data mining, a good KDD system should be able to suggest appropriate parameters for a given discovery task and data set.

Perhaps the most difficult task is to automate final steps, that is, to assess the validity and usefulness of information patterns, to interpret information to knowledge, and to decide how and in what form the knowledge is stored. However, it is questionable if in the near future automated and reliable means will be possible for interpreting information without human intervention. Penttinen and Ritala (2002) have considered issues of knowledge management from the technical angle. Over the past years, telecommunications have been rapidly becoming more and more important with no end in sight for their expansion. As people and life become increasingly dependent on telecommunications services, networks require increasingly detailed management and control. This chapter shows that data mining can be applied successfully to telecommunications.

In the future, such application is a must. Further research concentrates on the preprocessing; the aim is to ensure that the methods produce robust and understandable results. Also the role of the metadata and information required in the phases of the process is an interesting topic of further study. While the research concentrates on the methods presented in this paper, other methods such as fuzzy clustering could be useful for this type of data.

REFERENCES

Breiman, L., Friedman, J., Olshen, R., & Stone, C. (1984). *Classification and Regression Trees*. Boca Raton, FL: Chapman & Hall/CRC Press LLC.

Chen, Q., Dayal, U., & Hsu, M. (2000). OLAP-Based Data Mining for Business Intelligence Applications in Telecommunications and E-commerce. In Bhalla, S. (Ed.), *Proceedings of Databases in Networked Information Systems, International Workshop DNIS 2000* (pp. 1–19). Aizu, Japan. doi:10.1007/3-540-44431-9_1

Ezawa, K., & Norton, S. (1995). Knowledge Discovery in Telecommunication Services Data Using Bayesian Network Models. In U. Fayyad & R. Uthurusamy (Eds.), Proceedings of the First International Conference on Knowledge Discovery & Data Mining, Montreal (pp. 100-105). Canaak, AAAI Press, Menlo Park, CA.

Fayyad, U., Piatetsky-Shapiro, G., & Smyth, P. (1996). From Data Mining to Knowledge Discovery. An Overview. In Fayyad, U., Piatetsky-Shapiro, G., Smyth, P., & Uthurusamy, R. (Eds.), *Advances in Knowledge Discovery and Data Mining* (pp. 1–34). Cambridge, MA: The MIT Press.

Frietman, E., Hill, M., & Khoe, G. (2001). A Kohonen Neural Network Controlled All-Optical Router System. *International Journal of Computer Research, 10*(2), 251–267.

Garofalakis, M., & Rastogi, R. (2001). The NEMESIS. In *Proceedings of Data Mining and Knowledge Discovery DMKD 2001*. Santa Barbara, CA: Data Mining Meets Network Management.

Han, J., & Kamber, M. (2001). *Data Mining: Concepts and Techniques*. San Francisco: Morgan Kaufmann Publishers.

Hand, D., Mannila, H., & Smyth, P. (2001). *Principles of Data Mining*. Cambridge, MA: The MIT Press.

ITU-T E.800 (1994). Terms And Definitions Related to Quality of Service And Network Performance Including Dependability. ITU-T Recommendation E.800.

Klementtinen, M. (1999). A Knowledge Discovery Methodology for Telecommunication Network Alarm Databases. Thesis (PhD), University of Helsinki.

Klosgen, W., & Zytkow, J. (1996). Knowledge Discovery in Databases Terminology. In Fayyad, U., Piatetsky-Shapiro, G., Smyth, P., & Uthurusamy, R. (Eds.), *Advances in Knowledge Discovery and Data Mining* (pp. 573–592). Cambridge, MA: The MIT Press.

Kohonen, T. (1995). *Self-Organizing Maps*. Berlin: Springer-Verlag.

Kumpulainen, P., Hätönen, K., & Vehviläinen, P. (2003). Automatic Discretization in Preprocessing for Data Analysis in Mobile Network. In XVII IMEKO World Congress Metrology in the 3rd Millennium. Cavtat- Dubrovnik, Croatia.

Laiho, J. (2002). Radio Network Planning and Optimizations for WCDMA. Thesis (Doc. Tech.), Helsinki University of Technology.

Lempilainen, J., & Manninen, M. (2001). *Radio Interface System Planning for GSM/GPRS/UMTS*. Dordrecht, The Netherlands: Kluwer Academic Publishers.

Mattison, M. (1997). *Data Warehousing and Data Mining for Telecommunications*. Norwood, MA, USA: Artech House, Inc.

Ni, S. (2001). Network Capacity and Quality of Service Management in F/TDMA Cellular Systems. Thesis (Doc. Tech.), Helsinki University of Technology.

Nokia Inc. (2003). *A History of Third Generation Mobile 3G*. Nokia Inc.

Pawlak, Z. (1982). Rough Sets. *International Journal of Computer and Information Sciences*, *11*(5), 341–356. doi:10.1007/BF01001956

Pekko, V. (2004). Data Mining for Managing Intrinsic Quality of Service in Digital Mobile Telecommunications Networks. (Thesis) Ph.D, Tampere University of Technology Publications.

Penttinen, I., & Ritala, R. (2002). *2002* (pp. 154–158). Stockholm, Sweden: XML-Based Process Control. In Proceedings of Control Systems.

Penttinen, J. (2001). *GSM-tekniikka. Järjestelmän toiminta ja kehitys kohti UMTS-aikakautta*. Helsinki: WSOY. (In Finnish)

Pyle, D. (1999). *Data Preparation for Data Mining*. San Francisco: Morgan Kaufmann Publishers.

Sasisekharan, R., Hsu, Y., & Simen, D. (1993). SCOUT: An approach to Automating Diagnoses of Faults in Large Scale Networks. In Technical Program Conference Record, GLOBECOM '93, Global Telecommunications Conference (pp. 212-216).

Sasisekharan, R., Seshadri, V., & Weiss, S. (1996). Data Mining and Forecasting in Large-Scale Telecommunication Networks. *IEEE Expert*, *11*(1), 37–43. doi:10.1109/64.482956

Spiliopoulou, M., Kalousis, A., Faulstich, C., & Theoharis, T. (1998). NOEMON: An Intelligent assistant for Classifier Selection. In Wysotzki, F., Geibel, P., & Schädler, K. (Eds.), *Beiträge zum Treffen der GI-Fachgruppe 1.1.3 Maschinelles Lernen (FGML98)* (pp. 90–97). TU Berlin.

Sterrit, R., Adamson, K., Shapcott, M., & Curran, E. (2000b). Parallel Data Mining of Bayesian Networks from Telecommunications Network Data. In Proceedings of IPDPS 2000 Workshops. Cancun, Mexico.

Sterritt, R., Adamson, K., Shapcott, C., & Curran, E. (2000a). Data Mining Telecommunications Network Data for Fault Management and Development Testing. In Becken, N., & Brebbai, C. (Eds.), *Data Mining II* (pp. 299–308). Southampton: Wit Press.

Suutarinen, J. (1994). Performance Measurements of GSM Base Station System. Thesis (Lic. Tech.), Tampere University of Technology.

Terplan, K. (2001). *OSS Essentials: Support System Solutions for Service Providers*. Chichester, England: John Wiley & Sons, Ltd.

Tisal, J. (2001). *The GSM Network*. Chichester, England: John Wiley & Sons, Ltd.

TMF. (1999). *Network Management Detailed Operations Map. Evaluation Version 1.0*. Tele-Management Forum.

Vesanto, J. (2002). Data Exploration Based on the Self- Organizing Map. Thesis (Doc. Tech.), Helsinki University of Technology.

Vesanto, J., Himberg, J., Alhoniemi, E., & Parhankangas, J. (2000). *SOM Toolbox for Matlab 5*. Helsinki, Finland: Helsinki University of Technology.

Weiss, G. M., Eddy, J., & Weiss, S. (1998). Intelligent Telecommunication Technologies. In Jain, L. C., Johnson, R. D., Takefuji, Y., & Zadeh, L. A. (Eds.), *Knowledge-based Intelligent Techniques* (pp. 249–275). Boca Raton, Florida: CRC Press.

World, G. S. M. (2003). Website of the GSM Association [online]. Retrieved August 6, 2003, from: - http://www.gsmworld.com/index.shtml.

Wright, P. (1998). Knowledge Discovery Pre-Processing: Determining Record Usability. In Proceedings of the 36th Annual ACM Southeast Regional Conference (pp. 283-288). Marietta, GA, USA.

Zelezný, F., Mikšovský, P., Štepánková, O., & Zídek, J. (2000). KDD in Telecommunications. In DDMI 2000 Workshop (pp. 103-112). Porto: University of Porto.

KEY TERMS AND DEFINITIONS

Classification and Regression Trees (CART): Classification and regression trees are a set of techniques for classification and prediction.

Data Mining (DM): Data mining is a popular way of discovering new knowledge from large and complex data sets such as business transaction data, GIS data, environmental data, genomic data, text and web data, and so on.

Global System for Mobile communications (GSM): It is a globally accepted standard for digital cellular communication.

Key Performance Indicator (KPI): It is a visual cue that communicates the amount of progress made toward a goal.

Knowledge Discovery (KD): It is the process of constructing valid, new, interesting, and potentially useful knowledge from data.

Knowledge Discovery in Database (KDD): KDD consists of steps in discovering knowledge that lying in the database. Seven steps in KDD are: Goal Identification Create Target Data, Data Preprocessing, Data Transformation, Data Mining, Interpretation and Evaluation, Taking action.

Quality of Service (QoS): It is a set of technologies for managing network traffic in a cost effective manner to enhance user experiences for home and enterprise environments.

Self-Organizing Map (SOM): It is a clustering algorithm that is used to map a multi-dimensional dataset onto a (typically) two-dimensional surface.

Telecommunications Management Network (TMN): The Telecommunications Management Network (TMN) provides a framework for achieving interconnectivity and communication across heterogeneous operating systems and telecommunications networks. TMN was developed by the International Telecommunications Union.

Universal Mobile Telecommunications System (UMTS): It is the European standard for 3G mobile communication systems which provide an enhanced range of multimedia services.

Chapter 5
Finding Persistent Strong Rules:
Using Classification to Improve Association Mining

Anthony Scime
The College at Brockport, State University of New York, USA

Karthik Rajasethupathy
Cornell University, USA

Kulathur S. Rajasethupathy
The College at Brockport, State University of New York, USA

Gregg R. Murray
Texas Tech University, USA

ABSTRACT

Data mining is a collection of algorithms for finding interesting and unknown patterns or rules in data. However, different algorithms can result in different rules from the same data. The process presented here exploits these differences to find particularly robust, consistent, and noteworthy rules among much larger potential rule sets. More specifically, this research focuses on using association rules and classification mining to select the persistently strong association rules. Persistently strong association rules are association rules that are verifiable by classification mining the same data set. The process for finding persistent strong rules was executed against two data sets obtained from the American National Election Studies. Analysis of the first data set resulted in one persistent strong rule and one persistent rule, while analysis of the second data set resulted in 11 persistent strong rules and 10 persistent rules. The persistent strong rule discovery process suggests these rules are the most robust, consistent, and noteworthy among the much larger potential rule sets.

INTRODUCTION

In data mining, there are a number of methodologies used to analyze data. The choice of methodology is an important consideration, which is determined by the goal of the data mining and the type of data. Different methodologies can result in different rules from the same data. Association mining is used to find patterns of data that show

DOI: 10.4018/978-1-60960-067-9.ch005

conditions where sets of attribute-value pairs occur frequently in the data set. It is often used to determine the relationships among transaction data. Classification mining, on the other hand, is used to find models of data for categorizing instances (e.g., objects, events, or persons). It is typically used for predicting future events from historical data (Han & Kamber, 2001). Because association and classification methodologies or algorithms process data in very different ways, they yield different sets of rules. The process presented here exploits these differences to find particularly robust, consistent, and noteworthy rules among much larger potential rule sets. More specifically, this research focuses on using association rules and classification mining to select the persistently strong association rules, which are association rules that are verifiable by classification mining the same data set.

Decision tree classification algorithms construct models by looking at past performance of input attributes with respect to an outcome class. The model is constructed inductively from records with known values for the outcome class. The input attribute with the strongest association with the outcome class is selected from the training data set using a divide-and-conquer strategy that is driven by an evaluation criterion. The training data are divided based on the values of this attribute, thereby creating subsets of the data. Each subset is evaluated independently to select the attribute with the next strongest association to the outcome class along the subset's edge. The process of dividing the data and selecting the next attribute, which is the one with the next strongest association with the outcome class at that point, continues until a leaf node is constructed (Quinlan, 1993). The rules derived from the decision tree provides insight into how the outcome class's value is, in fact, dependent on the input attributes. A complete decision tree provides for all possible combinations of the input attributes and their allowable values reaching a single, allowable outcome class.

Classification decision trees have a root node. The attribute of this root node is the most predictive attribute of a record's class and is present in the premise of every rule produced by classification. The presence of the root node attribute in the premise of all the rules is a limitation of decision tree classification mining. There may be a domain theory where the root attribute is not relevant and/or another attribute is theoretically relevant and useful for predicting the value of the class attribute. Association mining may find rules in such instances. Further, the class attribute appears in the consequent of every classification rule. This class attribute is the goal of the data mining. It is the attribute that ultimately determines if a record supports a domain theory under consideration.

Association mining evaluates data for relationships among attributes in the data set (Agrawal, Imieliński, & Swami, 1993). The association rule mining algorithm Apriori finds itemsets within the data set at user-specified minimum support levels. An itemset is a collection of attribute-value pairs (items) that occurs in the data set. The support of an itemset is the percent of records that contain all the items in the itemset. The largest supported itemsets are converted into rules where each item implies and is implied by every other item in the itemset.

Given the limitations on decision tree classification rules, association mining may be applied to the classification attributes and data set to find other rules that address the domain. Unlike classification, association mining considers all the attribute combinations in the records. Also unlike classification, it does not have a goal of predicting the value of a specific attribute. As a result, association mining often produces a large number of rules (Bagui, Just, & Bagui, 2008), many of which may not be relevant. The strength of rules is an important consideration in association mining. Generally, a rule's strength is measured by its confidence level. Strong association mined rules are those that meet the minimum confidence level set by the domain expert (Han & Kamber, 2001).

The higher the confidence level the stronger the rule and the more likely the rule will be successfully applied to new data.

Measures of interestingness are either subjective or objective (Tan, Steinbach, & Kumar, 2006). Subjective interestingness is based on the domain expert's opinion of the rules found. A rule is subjectively interesting if it contradicts the expectations of an expert or is actionable in the domain (Silberschatz & Tuzhilin, 1996). Objectively measuring the interestingness of a rule is a major research area for both classification and association mining. In addition to being interesting, rules may be supportive (Scime, Murray, & Hunter, 2010). Knowledge in a domain is based on observations that are supported by substantial evidence from behavior in the domain and analysis of data from the domain. A data set representative of a domain should result in rules that support and confirm the domain's established knowledge, if the knowledge is correct, as well as be interesting when a rule contradicts the domain knowledge (National Academy of Sciences, 2008).

Although, different data mining methodologies yield different sets of rules, it is possible that different algorithms will generate rules that are similar in structure and supportive of one another. When this is the case, these independently identified yet common rules may be considered "persistent rules." Rules that are both persistent and strong can improve decision making by narrowing the focus to rules that are the most robust and consistent. In this research, the concept of persistent strong rules is explored. Further, the persistent-rule discovery process is demonstrated in the area of voting behavior, which is a complex process subject to a wide variety of factors. Given the high stakes often involved in elections, researchers, the media, candidates, and political parties devote considerable effort and resources in trying to understand the dynamics of voting and vote choice (Edsall, 2006). This research shows how strong persistent rules, found using both association and classification data mining algorithms, can be used to understand voters and their behavior.

This chapter is a continuation and extension of the work presented in Rajasethupathy et al. (2009), where the concept of persistent rules was first introduced and its utility for discovering robust, consistent, and noteworthy rules discussed. In particular, this chapter presents the algorithm for determining if a persistent rule is a persistent strong rule. The chapter begins with background on combining association and classification data mining to achieve results that are more meaningful than using the approaches individually. This is followed with a review of how rules are created by the Apriori association and the C4.5 classification algorithms. Included is how rules can be combined using rule reduction and supersession leading to the discovery of persistent rules and the determination of persistent strong rules. In the next section this methodology is applied to two independently derived data sets from the 1948-2004 American National Election Studies (ANES) Cumulative Data File. The first data set is used to identify individuals who are likely to vote, and the second is used to predict the political party for which a voter is likely to cast a ballot in a presidential election. These examples are followed by a short discussion on the future of data mining using multiple techniques. The chapter ends with a concluding section that summarizes persistent strong rule discovery in general and as applied to the two data sets.

BACKGROUND

The choice of association or classification mining is determined by the purpose of the data mining and the data type. Association mining is used to find connections between data attributes that may have real world significance, yet are not obvious to a real world observer. This analysis is often referred to as a market basket analysis because it can be used to find the likelihood that shopping items will be bought together. An association rule's consequent may have multiple attributes. Furthermore, one rule's consequent may be another rule's precedent. Classification mining builds a decision tree model with the goal of determining the likely value of a specific attribute based on the values of the other attributes. The consequent of all the classification rules of a model have the same attribute with its different values. Nevertheless, similar results have been obtained by mining the same data set using both methodologies. For example, Bagui (2006) mined crime data using association and classification techniques, as a result both indicates that in all regions of the United States, when the population is low, the crime rate is low.

Researchers have attempted to identify interesting rules by creating processes in which one applies other methodologies to data prior to the application of a data mining algorithm. For example, CMAR (Classification based on Multiple class-Association Rules) uses the frequent patterns and association relationships between records and attributes to do classification (Li, Han, & Pei, 2001). Jaroszewicz and Simovici (2004) employ user background knowledge to determine the interestingness of sets of attributes using a Bayesian Network prior to association mining. In their research, the interestingness of a set of attributes is indicated by the absolute difference between the support for the attribute's itemset in the Bayesian Network and as an association itemset.

A problem with association rules is that they must have high levels of support and confidence to be discovered by most association algorithms. Zhong et al. (2001) have gone beyond interesting association rules and found that peculiar rules are also to be interesting. These are rules that are derived from low support counts and attribute values that are very different from the other values for that attribute. Interesting association rules can also be identified through clustering (Zhao, Zhang, & Zhang, 2005). Rules are interesting when the attributes in the rule are very dissimilar. By clustering,

the distance or dissimilarity between attributes can be computed to judge the interestingness of the discovered rules. Geng and Hamilton (2006) have surveyed and classified interestingness measures for rules providing guidance on selecting the appropriate measurement instrument as a function of the application and data set.

Another problem with association mining is the very large number of rules typically found. Applying a rule template is a simple method to reduce the number of rules to those interesting to a particular question (Klemettinen, Mannilla, Ronkainen, Toivonen, & Verkamo, 1994). Zaki (2004) introduced the concept of closed frequent itemsets to drastically reduce the number of rules to present to the user. Rule reduction can also be accomplished by pruning association mining rules with rule covers (Toivonen et al., 1995). A rule cover is a subset of a rule set that matches all the records matched by the rule set. Rule covers produce useful short descriptions of large sets of rules. An interestingness measure can be used to reduce the number of association rules by 40-60% when the data are structured as a taxonomy. This is possible when the support and confidence of a rule are close to their expected values based on an ancestor rule, making the rule redundant (Srikant & Agrawal, 1995).

Data Dimensionality Reduction (DDR) can be used to simplify the data thus reducing the number of rules. Fu and Wang (2005) reduced data dimensionality using a separability-correlation measure to select subsets of attributes based on attribute importance with respect to a classification class attribute. Using a neural network classifier, the reduction in attributes lead to improved classification performance resulting in smaller rule sets with higher accuracies when compared with other methods. Expert knowledge has also been used to reduce data dimensionality while iteratively creating classification models (Murray, Riley, & Scime, 2007; Scime & Murray, 2007).

Classification mining has been improved by the prior application of association mining to data.

In this approach, the association mining creates itemsets that are selected based on achieving a given support threshold. The original data set then has an attribute added to it for each selected itemset, where the attribute values are true or false; true if the instance contains the itemset and false otherwise. The classification algorithm is then executed on this modified data set (Deshpande & Karypis, 2002; Padmanabhan & Tuzhilin, 2000) to find the interesting rules. Liu et al. (1998) used Apriori association mining limited to finding rules with a problem's class attribute in the rule consequent. These "classification association rules" are then used in a heuristic classifier to find interesting classification rules.

Combining association and classification is a multi-method approach to data mining. In Rajasethupathy et al. (2009), the concept of persistent rules to improve the usefulness of rules was first introduced, which is extended here to strong persistent rules. There are a large number of other approaches that apply multiple methods such as feature selection (Dy & Brodley, 2004), hybrid learning (Babu, Murty, & Agrawal, 2004; Vatsavai & Bhaduri, 2007; Wagstaff, Cardie, Bogers, & Schrodl, 2001; Wang, Zhang, & Huang, 2008), multi-strategy learning (Adomavicius & Tuzhilin, 2001; Dietterich, 2000; Li, Tang, Li, & Luo, 2009; Tozicka, Rovatsos, & Pechoucek, 2007; Webb & Zheng, 2004), model combination (Aslandogan, Mahajani, & Taylor, 2004; Lane & Brodley, 2003; Wang, Zhang, Xia, & Wang, 2008), multi-objective optimization (Chandra & Grabis, 2008), hybrid methods (Ramu & Ravi, 2008), and ensemble systems (Kumar & Ravi, 2008; Su, Khoshgoftaar, & Greiner, 2009).

ASSOCIATION PLUS CLASSIFICATION: PERSISTENT STRONG RULES

In data mining, data preparation is key to the analysis. A data set has attributes and instances. Attributes define the characteristics of the data set. Instances serve as examples and contain specific values of attributes. Attributes can be either nominal or numeric. Numeric attributes cannot be mined in association mining because they are continuous valued attributes. Therefore, they have to be converted into nominal or discrete valued attributes. During data preparation, numeric attributes are discretized (numeric to nominal) so that they can be mined using the association algorithm.

Association mining evaluates data for relationships among attributes in the data set (Witten & Frank, 2005). The association rule mining algorithm, Apriori, finds itemsets within the data set at user specified minimum support and confidence levels. The size of the itemsets is continually increased by the algorithm until no itemsets satisfy the minimum support level. The support of an itemset is the number of instances that contain all the attributes in the itemset. The largest supported itemsets are converted into rules where each item implies and is implied by every other item in the itemset.

For example, given an itemset of three items ($C1 = x$, $C2 = g$, $C3 = a$), twelve rules are generated:

```
IF (C1 = x AND C2 = g) THEN C3 = a    (1)
IF (C1 = x AND C3 = a) THEN C2 = g    (2)
IF (C2 = g AND C3 = a) THEN C1 = x    (3)
IF (C1 = x) THEN (C2 = g AND C3 = a)  (4)
IF (C2 = g) THEN (C1 = x AND C3 = a)  (5)
IF (C3 = a) THEN (C1 = x AND C2 = g)  (6)
IF (C1=x) THEN (C2=g)                 (7)
IF (C1=x) THEN (C3=a)                 (8)
IF (C2=g) THEN (C1=x)                 (9)
IF (C2=g) THEN (C3=a)                 (10)
IF (C3=a) THEN (C1=x)                 (11)
IF (C3=a) THEN (C2=g)                 (12)
```

Classification mining using the C4.5 algorithm, on the other hand, generates a decision tree. The goal of classification is to determine the likely value of a class variable (the outcome variable) given values for the other attributes of data. This is accomplished by the construction of a decision tree using data containing the outcome variable

Figure 1. Classification Decision Tree

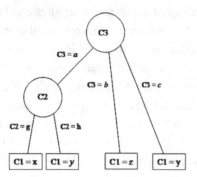

and its values. The decision tree consists of decision nodes and leaf nodes (beginning with a root decision node) that are connected by edges. Each decision node is an attribute of the data and the edges represent the attribute values. The leaf nodes represent the outcome variable; the expected classification results of each data instance. Using the three items from above with C1 as the outcome variable, Figure 1 represents a possible tree.

The branches of the decision tree can be converted into rules, whose consequent is the outcome variable with its legal values. The rules for the tree in Figure 1 are:

```
IF  C3 = a AND C2 = g THEN C1 = x      (13)
IF  C3 = a AND C2 = h THEN C1 = y      (14)
IF  C3 = b THEN C1 = z                 (15)
IF  C3 = c THEN C1 = y                 (16)
```

Rule Reduction and Supersession

The need to reduce the number of rules is common to classification and association techniques. This reduction may take place because the rule is not physically possible, the rule's confidence falls below the established threshold level, or the rule can be combined with other rules. In association mining, a minimum confidence level is set for the rules. Those rules whose confidence falls below that level are eliminated. In classification mining, a pruning process combines decision tree nodes to reduce the size of the tree while having a minimum effect on the classification result (Witten & Frank, 2005). It is possible that physically impossible or obviously coincidental rules remain after the algorithms reduce the number of rules. These rules should be identified by a domain expert and be eliminated, as well.

Furthermore, one rule may have all the properties of another rule in association mining. As a rule's premise takes on more conditions, the confidence of the rule generally increases. For example, given two rules, with the confidence levels given after the rule

```
IF A1 = r and A2 = s THEN A3 = t
(conf:.90)                          (17)
IF A1 = r THEN A3 = t (conf:.80)    (18)
```

Rule 18 has all the conditions of Rule 17. The additional condition in Rule 17 increases the confidence; however, if a confidence level of .80 is sufficient, then Rule 18 can supersede Rule 17 and Rule 17 is eliminated.

Persistent Strong Rule Discovery

Persistent rules are those that are obtained across independent data mining methods. That is, they are the subset of rules common to more than one method. If an association rule and a classification rule are similar, then the rule would be robust across methods and be considered persistent. Strong rules, on the other hand, are those found by association and classification algorithms that meet a domain expert's defined confidence level. Each algorithm has a mechanism for elimination of rules not meeting that confidence level. A persistent strong rule is not a new rule; it is an association rule that is both persistent by appearing in a classification decision tree and strong by exhibiting a similar confidence level in the classification rule. That is, the confidence levels fall within a tolerance defined by a domain expert.

Rules from association and classification can be compared when the rules contain the same attributes in the premise and the consequent. There are two ways an association rule can be matched to a classification rule. In the first case, the rule is a direct match. That is, the premise and the consequent of the classification rule match the association rule in attribute and value. A direct match exists in Rules 3 and 13, above, in which the premise is C2 = g AND C3 = a, and the consequent is C1 = x. In the second (and more common) case, the classification rules contain many conditions as the tree is traversed to construct the rule. That is, a condition exists for each node of the tree. As long as the entire association rule premise is present in a classification rule, the association rule can supersede the classification rule. When the classification rule drops conditions that are not present in the association rule, it becomes a rule-part.

However, there may be many identical rule-parts. The process of finding and evaluating the rule-parts that match an association rule involves the following steps:

1. Find association rules with the classification outcome variable as the consequent;
2. Find those classification rules that contain the same conditions as the association rule;
3. Create rule-parts by deleting the classification rule conditions that are not present in the corresponding association rule (Figure 2);
4. From the classification rule-parts add the number of total instances and
5. Add the number of correctly classified instances with the same consequent value;
6. If the consequent value rule-part does not match that of an association rule, then the entire rule results in an incorrect classification. The number of instances correctly classified by these rule-parts are subtracted from the number of correctly classified instances; and

7. Divide the correctly classified instances by the total classified instances to find the confidence level.

More formally, to determine a combined confidence level for classification rules (steps 4-7, above) the following is applied:

```
CCI = IC - IIC
ARC = CCI - ICAR
CF = ARC/IC
```

Where:

CCI: total number of Correctly Classified Instances
IC: total number of Instances Classified
IIC: total number of Instances Incorrectly Classified
ARC: total number of Instances Correctly Classified with respect to the Association Rule
ICAR: total number of Instances Incorrectly Classified with respect to the Association Rule
CF: ConFidence

Persistent strong rules are those that occur in association and classification rule sets with the same premise and consequent, and when the confidence levels of the independently found rules fall within a tolerance level, established by the

Figure 2. Rule-part Creation

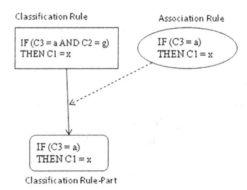

domain expert. When the confidence level is not within tolerance, the association rule continues to be persistent but not as strong.

The best possible rule is not one with the highest success rate. Sometimes the strongest rules may satisfy the instances in the training data set, but they may be both unreliable and unreasonable when applied to other data. However, when a rule is found independently through different data mining methods, the rule can be considered strong even when the confidence level may be less than that of a single rule. In other words, persistent rules across data mining methods are preferable to high-confidence rules found by only one data mining method. A rule found to be very strong (have a high confidence) by only one data mining method may be a result of the particular data set, whereas discovery of similar rules by independent data mining methods is not as likely to be caused by the data set. The persistent strong rule may have a lower confidence level; however, it is a more accurate confidence level and can reasonably assure researchers that it will maintain that confidence level when applied to other data sets.

The goal of the persistent strong rule discovery process is to find as many persistent strong rules as possible. A classification tree has one consequent whereas an association rule set can have many consequents. Therefore, because of the premise-consequent requirement, only some of the association rules can be compared to the classification rules. To accommodate more rule comparisons, classification is executed using each association rule consequent as the outcome variable. This insures the discovery of a greater number of persistent strong rules.

The persistent strong rules discovered by the above objective algorithm may or may not be interesting. Regardless of the rules' algorithmic origin–association, classification, persistent, or strong persistent–the interestingness must also be evaluated subjectively by a domain expert. A rule is subjectively interesting if it contradicts the expectations of the expert, suggests actions

to take in the domain (Geng & Hamilton, 2006; Silberschatz & Tuzhilin, 1996), or raises further questions about the domain. In addition to being interesting, rules are of value if they support existing knowledge in the domain (Scime, Murray, & Hunter, 2010). Rules that are strong persistent are those rules found by different data mining algorithms. These rules came from different analyses of the domain data and are supportive of each other. Other domain analyses, non-data mining analyses may come to the same conclusions as a persistent strong rules. In this case, which may be quite common, the persistent strong rule is providing more evidence that the situation outlined by the rule is in fact true in the domain. Persistent strong rules may be interesting or supportive in their domain.

MINING THE ANES DATA

The American National Election Studies (ANES, 2005) is an ongoing, long-term series of public opinion surveys intended to produce research-quality data for researchers who study the theoretical and empirical bases of American national election outcomes. The ANES collects data on items such as voter registration and choice, social and political values, social background and structure, partisanship, candidate and group evaluations, opinions about public policy, ideological support for the political system, mass media consumption, and egalitarianism. The ANES has conducted pre- and post-election interviews of a nationally representative sample of adults every presidential and midterm election year since 1948, except for the midterm election of 1950. The ANES data set is used primarily in the field of political science and contains a large number of records (47,438) and attributes (more than 900), which, for comparability, have been coded in a consistent manner from year to year. Because the data set is prepared for analysis, all the attribute values are coded numerically with predefined meanings. This study uses ANES data that had been previously selected and cleaned for data mining (Murray, Riley, & Scime, 2009; Scime & Murray, 2007). See the appendix for details on the pertinent survey items.

An important issue in political science is vote choice; that is, who votes for which candidate and why. For one project (Scime & Murray, 2007), the domain expert reduced the initial number of ANES attributes from more than 900 to the 238 attributes most meaningful for predicting presidential vote choice based on domain knowledge. Following the iterative expert data mining process using the C4.5 classification algorithm, the domain expert then further reduced the number of attributes to 13 attributes. These 13 specific survey questions effectively predict the party candidate for whom a voter will cast a ballot. The results suggest that such a survey will correctly predict vote choice 66% of the time. Previous studies using non-data mining techniques have shown only 51% accuracy.

Another important issue in political science and, in particular, for political pollsters is the likelihood of a citizen voting in an election. Again using the ANES, but selecting a different set of attributes and instances and using the CHAID classification algorithm, the domain expert identified two survey questions that together can be used to categorize citizens as voters or non-voters. These results met or surpassed the accuracy rates of previous non-data mining models using fewer input attributes. The two items correctly classify 78% of respondents over a three-decade period. Additionally, the findings indicate that demographic attributes are less salient than previously thought by political science researchers (Murray, Riley, & Scime, 2009).

The ANES attributes are of two types: Discrete and Continuous. Discrete-value attributes contain a single defined value such as party identification, which is indicated as Democrat, Republican, or other. Continuous-value attributes take on an infinite number of values such as the 0-100-scale "feeling thermometers," which measure affect toward a specified target, and subtractive scales,

which indicate the number of "likes" minus the number of "dislikes" mentioned about a target. It should be noted that in the previous studies the continuous-value attributes were left as continuous attributes.

As a result of the previous data mining methodology studies, the data sets had been cleaned and prepared for classification mining. To insure that discrete attributes were not misinterpreted as numeric values, an "a" or "A" was prepended to each value. Because association mining only uses discrete attributes, the continuous attributes were discretized. In this study, the WEKA (Waikato Environment for Knowledge Analysis) (Witten & Frank, 2005) software implementations of the association mining Apriori algorithm and the classification mining C4.5 algorithm were used. Shannon's entropy method was used to discretize the continuous attributes. When discretized, the values are presented as a range of numbers; the value closed by a parentheses is not included in that range of numbers. The value closed by a square bracket is included in the range of numbers. The values '–inf' and 'inf' represent negative and positive infinite, respectively.

Demonstrating Persistent Strong Rules: Identifying Likely Voters

The persistent-rule discovery process was applied to the data set used in the likely voter study (Murray, Riley, & Scime, 2009). The focus of this analysis is voter turnout – whether the respondent is expected to vote or not. This data set consists of three attributes and 3899 instances from the ANES. Association Apriori analysis resulted in three rules all of which have the intent to vote as the consequent. A three-fold C4.5 classification algorithm using intent to vote as the outcome variable generated a tree with three rules. In a three-fold process the data set is divided into three equal parts. Each part is independently used to assess the classification tree. The results of the assessments are averaged together to determine the tree's overall success rate and each individual rule's confidence.

The resulting rules were compared and evaluated, using a domain expert defined tolerance of 0.10. Persistent rules must have identical rule consequents generated independently by both data mining methodologies. Persistent strong rules must also have confidences within the tolerance.

The association rules are:

```
IF A_Voteval_V2 = A1 AND A_Prevvote = A1
THEN A_Intent = A1 (conf: 0.99)      (19)
IF A_Voteval_V2 = A1
THEN A_Intent = A1 (conf: 0.99)      (20)
IF A_Prevvote = A1
THEN A_Intent = A1 (conf: 0.96)      (21)
```

Rule 20 supersedes Rule 19, while retaining 99% confidence. Because intent to vote is the consequent for all the association rules, only one classification tree with intent to vote as the outcome variable is needed to find the persistent strong rules. The classification tree follows using A_Intent as the outcome variable:

```
A_Prevvote = A0
    A_Voteval_V2 = A0: A_Intent = A0 (IC
- 1042.85, IIC - 391.78)
    A_Voteval_V2 = A1: A_Intent = A1 (IC
- 378.15, IIC - 49.93)
    A_Prevvote = A1: A_Intent = A1 (IC -
3477, IIC - 144)
```

This tree can be converted into three rules:

```
IF A_Prevvote = A0 AND A_Voteval_V2 = A0
THEN A_Intent = A0 (conf: 0.62)      (22)
IF A_Prevvote = A0 AND A_Voteval_V2 = A1
THEN A_Intent = A1 (conf: 0.87)      (23)
IF A_Prevvote = A1
THEN A_Intent = A1 (conf: 0.96)      (24)
```

Rule 22 does not have as a consequent an association rule consequent; therefore, it does not support the persistence of any of the association rules. Rule 23 and Rule 24 have the same consequent as the association rules. Rule 23 has two rule-parts one of which matches Rule 20, allowing for supersession and a partial match. However, the confidence is outside the tolerance of 0.10, therefore Rule 20 is persistent, but not strong. Rule 24 is identical to Rule 21, and they both have 0.96 confidence. Hence, Rule 21 is a persistent strong association rule.

The single persistent strong rule found from the likely voter data set states that respondents to the survey who voted previously in a presidential election are likely to intend to vote in an upcoming Presidential election with a confidence of 96%. This rule may not be especially surprising. But, it strongly supports the fact that citizens interested in politics maintain that interest from election to election.

Demonstrating Persistent Strong Rules: Predicting Vote Choice

The persistent-rule discovery process was also applied to the data set used in the presidential vote choice studies (Murray & Scime, 2010; Scime & Murray, 2007). This data set consists of 14 attributes and 6677 instances from the ANES. The Apriori association algorithm was run on the data set, which generated 29 rules with a minimum 0.80 confidence and 0.15 support levels. All 29 rules concluded with the race attribute having the value "white." This suggested that the number of white voters in the data set was sufficiently large to skew the results. Further examination of the data set revealed that 83.5% of the voters were white. The domain expert concluded that race as an indicator of association is not useful. The race attribute was removed and the data set was rerun with the Apriori algorithm. This resulted in 33 rules with confidence levels between 0.60 and 0.85 and a support level of 0.15. Though the confidence levels had decreased, the rule consequents were varied and reasonable.

Next, the C4.5 classification algorithm using three folds was applied to the data set to which the Apriori association algorithm was applied (i.e., the data set that excluded the race attribute). A separate classification tree was constructed for each of the attributes appearing in an association rule consequent (depvarvotewho, awhoelect, affrep, aintelect, and affdem). The association and classification rules were compared and evaluated using a domain expert defined tolerance of 0.10.

As an example, the use of the outcome variable for the political party for which the voter reported voting (depvarvotewho) resulted in a classification tree with more complex rules than the rules obtained from association mining, and more complex than in the likely voter study. For example, one branch of the tree was

```
apid = a2
  affrepcand = '(-0.5-0.5]'
    demtherm = '(-inf-42.5]'
      aeduc = a1: depvarvotewho =
      NotVote
```

This branch of the tree translates into the rule:

```
IF Party identification (apid) = weak or
leaning Democratic (a2)
AND Affect towards Republican candidate
(affrepcand) = no affect,'(-0.5-0.5]'
AND Democratic thermometer (demtherm) =
not favorable '(-inf-42.5]'
AND Education of respondent (aeduc) = 8
grades or less (a1)
THEN Outcome variable, party voted for
(depvarvotewho) = Not Vote
```

With vote choice (depvarvotewho) as the subject of the classification mining, the association rules with vote choice as the consequent become candidates for identification as persistent rules. Ten of the 33 association rules met this requirement; two of these are superseded by another, leaving eight possibly persistent rules. For example, one of the eight association rules states:

```
IF Affect toward Republican candidate
(affrepcand) = extreme like, '(2.5-inf)'
THEN party voted for (depvarvotewho) =
Republican (conf: 0.75)
```

A review of the tree rules reveals that there are six classification rules whose premises and consequents match the premises and consequents of the association rules. The other rules are not considered further, because to be classified along a branch an instance must satisfy all the conditions (attribute-value pairs) of the branch. By supersession, the instances that satisfy the branch would also satisfy the association rule being evaluated. The six classification rules that incorporate the association rule each have the rule-part:

```
IF affrepcand = '(2.5-inf)' THEN REP
```

with a combined confidence of 0.78. Because this is within the tolerance (0.10) of the association rule's confidence (0.75), the rule is a persistent strong rule. The persistent strong rule discovery process was repeated on all eight association rules. Three of the persistent rules were found to be strong (persistent strong rules):

```
IF the affect toward the Republican can-
didate is positive
THEN the respondent votes for the Repub-
lican candidate.                    (25)
Association Confidence: 0.75
Classification Combined Confidence: 0.78
```

```
IF the affect toward the Democratic can-
didate is negative
THEN the respondent votes for the Repub-
lican candidate.                    (26)
Association Confidence: 0.65
Classification Combined Confidence: 0.64
```

IF the respondent identifies him or her-
self as a strong Democrat
THEN the respondent votes for the Demo-
cratic candidate.   (27)
Association Confidence: 0.63
Classification Combined Confidence: 0.68

The other five rules were found to be persistent, but not persistent strong. They are outside
the 0.10 tolerance between the confidence levels:

IF the feeling about Republican presiden-
tial candidate is positive
THEN the respondent votes for the Repub-
lican candidate.   (28)
Association Confidence: 0.65
Classification Combined Confidence: 0.34

IF the feeling about Democratic presiden-
tial candidate is positive
THEN the respondent votes for the Demo-
cratic candidate.   (29)
Association Confidence: 0.62
Classification Combined Confidence: 0.43

IF the feeling about Democratic presiden-
tial candidate is negative
THEN the respondent votes for the Repub-
lican candidate.   (30)
Association Confidence: 0.62
Classification Combined Confidence: 0.34

IF the affect toward the Republican Party
is mostly positive
THEN the respondent votes for the Repub-
lican candidate.   (31)
Association Confidence: 0.61
Classification Combined Confidence: 0.48

IF the affect toward the Democratic Party
is positive
THEN the respondent votes for the Democratic candidate.   (32)

Association Confidence: 0.61
Classification Combined Confidence: 0.80

The other four classification trees using awhoelect, affrep, aintelect, and affdem as outcome
variables result in an additional eight persistent
strong rules:

IF the feeling about Republican presiden-
tial candidate is positive
THEN the respondent thinks the Republican
will be elected.   (33)
Association Confidence: 0.81
Classification Combined Confidence: 0.79

IF the affect toward the Republican pres-
idential candidate is very positive
THEN the respondent thinks the Republican
will be elected.   (34)
Association Confidence: 0.80
Classification Combined Confidence: 0.87

IF the affect toward the Democratic pres-
idential candidate is negative
THEN the respondent thinks the Republican
will be elected.   (35)
Association Confidence: 0.73
Classification Combined Confidence: 0.70

IF the respondent voted Republican
THEN the respondent thinks the Republican
will be elected.   (36)
Association Confidence: 0.73
Classification Combined Confidence: 0.68

IF the affect toward the Republican pres-
idential candidate is positive
THEN the respondent thinks the Republican
will be elected.   (37)
Association Confidence: 0.68
Classification Combined Confidence: 0.77

```
IF the feeling about Republican vice
presidential candidate is positive
THEN the respondent thinks the Republican
will be elected.                    (38)
Association Confidence: 0.62
Classification Combined Confidence: 0.53
```

```
IF the affect toward the Republican pres-
idential candidate is negative
THEN the respondent thinks the Democratic
will be elected.                    (39)
Association Confidence: 0.62
Classification Combined Confidence: 0.55
```

```
IF the affect toward the Democratic Party
is neutral
THEN the affect toward the Republican
Party is neutral.                   (40)
Association Confidence: 0.70
Classification Combined Confidence: 0.68
```

Also, persistent but not persistent strong rules were found:

```
IF the respondent is a weak Republican or
leaning Republican
THEN the respondent thinks the Republican
will be elected.                    (41)
Association Confidence: 0.65
Classification Combined Confidence: 0.38
```

```
IF the respondent is a strong Democrat
THEN the respondent thinks the Democrat
will be elected.                    (42)
Association Confidence: 0.62
Classification Combined Confidence: 0.79
```

```
IF the respondent is interested in public
affairs most of the time
THEN the respondent is very much inter-
ested in campaigns.                 (43)
Association Confidence: 0.64
Classification Combined Confidence: 0.44
```

```
IF the affect toward the Republican Party
is neutral
THEN the affect toward the Democratic
Party is neutral.                   (44)
Association Confidence: 0.62
Classification Combined Confidence: 0.75
```

```
IF the affect toward the Republican pres-
idential candidate is neutral
THEN the affect toward the Republican
Party is neutral.                   (45)
Association Confidence: 0.61
Classification Combined Confidence: 0.45
```

In this example, then, there are 11 persistent strong association rules (25 - 27 and 33 - 40) and 10 persistent (not strong) association rules (28 - 32 and 41 - 45) among the original 33 rules.

The 11 persistent strong rules found from the vote choice data set collectively support political science's current understanding of the unparalleled strength of party identification as a predictor of political attitudes and behavior. Voters are loyal to their political party, and they assess the political environment through the lens of their partisanship.

FUTURE RESEARCH DIRECTIONS

Today, the use of the computer has become common for statistical analysis of data. Software packages are easy to use, inexpensive, and fast. But today's vast stores of data with immense data sets make comprehensive analysis all but impossible using conventional techniques. A solution is data mining. As data mining becomes an accepted methodology in the social sciences, domain experts will more routinely exploit the techniques as part of their normal analytical procedures.

Association mining discovers patterns in the data set. This technique comprehensively provides possible relationships between the data. The question is, which associations are viable. Currently, the domain expert decides the threshold level of confidence to select the strong rules. Classification mining can be used to find the strong association rules that are persistent. In the future, the domain expert will be able to conduct both association and classification simultaneously to determine the persistent strong rules from the data set. This combination of techniques will help the domain expert set the confidence threshold based on the data set itself. These rules can then be used with more confidence when making decisions within the domain.

Data mining is commonly conducted against transactional data, but data have gone beyond simple numeric and character flat file data. Today, data come in many forms: image, video, audio, streaming video, and combinations of data types. Data mining research is being conducted to find interesting patterns in data sets of all these data types. Beyond the different types of data, the data sources are also diverse. Data can be found in corporate and government data warehouses, transactional databases, the World Wide Web, and others. The data mining of the future will be multidimensional, accessing all these data sources and data types to find interesting, persistent strong rules.

Finding more interesting and supportive rules for a domain using multiple methods places constraints on the mining process. This is a form of constraint-based data mining. Constraint-based data mining use constraints to guide the process. Constraints that can be used can specify the data mining algorithm. Constraints can be placed on the type of knowledge that is to be found or the data to be mined. Dimension-level constraints research is needed to determine what level of a summary, or the reverse, detail is needed in the data before the algorithms are applied (Hsu, 2002).

Research in data mining will continue to find new methods to determine interestingness. Research is needed to determine what values of a particular attribute are considered to be especially interesting in the data and in the resulting rule set (Hsu, 2002). Currently there are 21 different

statistically based objective measures for determining interestingness (Tan, Steinbach, & Kumar, 2006). A leading area of research is to find new, increasingly effective measures. With regard to subjective measures of interestingness, research in domains that is both quantitative and qualitative can lead to new methods for determining interestingness. Further data mining research will find new methods to support existing knowledge and perhaps find new knowledge in domains where it has not yet been applied (Scime, Murray, & Hunter, 2010).

CONCLUSION

Data mining typically results in a set of rules that can be applied to future events or that can provide knowledge about interrelationships among data. This set of rules is most useful when it can be dependably applied to new data. Dependability is the strength of the rule. Generally, a rule's strength is measured by its confidence level. Association mining generates all possible rules by combining all the attributes and their values in the data set. The strong association rules are those that meet the minimum confidence level set by the domain expert (Han & Kamber, 2001). The higher the confidence level the stronger the rule and the more likely the rule will be successfully applied to new data. Classification mining generates a decision tree that has been pruned to a minimal set of rules. Each rule also has a confidence rating suggesting its ability to correctly classify future data.

This research demonstrates a process to identify especially powerful rules. These rules are strong because they have a confidence level at or exceeding the threshold set in association mining; they are persistent because they are also found by classification mining and hold a similar confidence level. These powerful rules, which are deemed "persistent strong rules," are those that are common to different algorithms and meet a pre-determined confidence level. Persistent rules are discovered by the independent application of association and classification mining to the same data set. Some of these rules have been identified as strong because they meet a minimum tolerance level established by a domain expert. While persistent rules may have a confidence level different from similar association rules and may not classify all future instances of data, persistent strong rules improve decision making by narrowing the focus to rules that are the most robust, consistent, and noteworthy.

In this case, the persistent strong rule discovery process is demonstrated in the area of voting behavior. In the likely voter data set, the process resulted in three association rules of which one persistent strong rule and one persistent rule were identified. In the vote choice data set, the process resulted in 33 association rules of which 11 persistent strong rules and 10 persistent rules were identified. The persistent strong rule discovery process suggests these rules are the most robust, consistent, and noteworthy of the much larger potential rule sets.

REFERENCES

Adomavicius, G., & Tuzhilin, A. (2001). Expert-driven Validation of Rule-based User Models in Personalization Applications. *Data Mining and Knowledge Discovery*, *5*(1-2), 33–58. doi:10.1023/A:1009839827683

Agrawal, R., Imieliński, T., & Swami, A. (1993). Mining Association Rules between Sets of Items in Large Databases. In *Proceedings of 1993 ACM SIGMOD International Conference on Management of Data* (pp. 207-216). Washington, D.C.

American National Election Studies (ANES). (2005). *Center for Political Studies*. Ann Arbor, MI: University of Michigan.

Aslandogan, Y. A., Mahajani, G. A., & Taylor, S. (2004). Evidence combination in Medical Data Mining. In *Proceedings of International Conference on Information Technology: Coding and Computing (ITCC'04), Vol. 2*, (pp.465-469). Las Vegas, NV.

Babu, T. R., Murty, M. N., & Agrawal, V. K. (2004). Hybrid Learning Scheme for Data Mining Applications. In *Fourth International Conference on Hybrid Intelligent Systems (HIS'04)* (pp. 266-271). Kitakyushu, Japan.

Bagui, S. (2006). An approach to Mining Crime Patterns. *International Journal of Data Warehousing and Mining*, *2*(1), 50–80.

Bagui, S., Just, J., & Bagui, S. C. (2008). Deriving Strong Association Mining Rules using a Dependency Criterion, the Lift Measure. *International Journal of Data Analysis Techniques and Strategies*, *1*(3), 297–312. doi:10.1504/IJDATS.2009.024297

Chandra, C., & Grabis, J. (2008). A Goal Model-driven Supply Chain Design. *International Journal of Data Analysis Techniques and Strategies*, *1*(3), 224–241. doi:10.1504/IJDATS.2009.024294

Deshpande, M., & Karypis, G. (2002). Using Conjunction of Attribute Values for Classification. In *Proceedings of the Eleventh International Conference on Information and Knowledge Management* (pp.356-364). McLean, VA.

Dietterich, T. G. (2000). Ensemble methods in Machine Learning. In *Proceedings of the First International Workshop on Multiple Classifier Systems* (pp.1-15). Cagliari, Italy.

Dy, J. G., & Brodley, C. E. (2004). Feature Selection for Unsupervised Learning. *Journal of Machine Learning Research*, *5*, 845–889.

Edsall, T. B. (2006). Democrats' Data Mining Stirs an Intraparty Battle. *The Washington Post*, March 8, A1.

Fu, X., & Wang, L. (2005). Data Dimensionality Reduction with application to improving Classification Performance and explaining Concepts of Data Sets. *International Journal of Business Intelligence and Data Mining, 1*(1), 65–87. doi:10.1504/IJBIDM.2005.007319

Geng, L., & Hamilton, H. J. (2006). Interestingness measures for Data Mining: A Survey. *ACM Computing Surveys, 38*(3), 9–14. doi:10.1145/1132960.1132963

Han, J., & Kamber, M. (2001). *Data Mining: Concepts and Techniques*. Boston, MA: Morgan Kaufman.

Hsu, J. (2002). Data Mining Trends and Developments: The Key Data Mining Technologies and Applications for the 21st Century. In *Proceedings of 19th Annual Conference for Information Systems Education (ISECON 2002)*, (Art 224b). San Antonio, TX.

Jaroszewicz, S., & Simovici, D. A. (2004). Interestingness of Frequent Itemsets using Bayesian Networks as Background Knowledge. In *Proceedings of 10th ACM SIGKDD International Conference on Knowledge Discovery and Data Mining* (pp.178-186). Seattle, WA.

Klemettinen, M., Mannila, H., Ronkainen, P., Toivonen, H., & Verkamo, A. I. (1994). Finding Interesting Rules from Large Sets of Discovered Association Rules. In *Proceedings of Third International Conference on Information and Knowledge Management (CIKM'94)* (pp. 401-408). Gaithersburg, Maryland, USA.

Kumar, D. A., & Ravi, V. (2008). Predicting Credit Card Customer Churn in Banks using Data Mining. *International Journal of Data Analysis Techniques and Strategies, 1*(1), 4–28. doi:10.1504/IJDATS.2008.020020

Lane, T., & Brodley, C. E. (2003). An Empirical Study of Two Approaches to Sequence Learning for Anomaly Detection. *Machine Learning, 51*(1), 73–107. doi:10.1023/A:1021830128811

Li, J., Tang, J., Li, Y., & Luo, Q. (2009). RiMOM: A Dynamic Multistrategy Ontology Alignment Framework. *IEEE Transactions on Knowledge and Data Engineering, 21*(8), 1218–1232. doi:10.1109/TKDE.2008.202

Li, W., Han, J., & Pei, J. (2001). CMAR: Accurate and Efficient Classification based on Multiple Class-Association Rules. In *Proceedings of 2001 IEEE International Conference on Data Mining* (pp. 369-376). San Jose, CA.

Liu, B., Hsu, W., & Ma, Y. (1998). Integrating Classification and Association Rule Mining. In *Proceedings of 4th International Conference on Knowledge Discovery and Data Mining* (pp. 27-31). New York, NY.

Murray, G. R., Riley, C., & Scime, A. (2007). *A New Age Solution for an Age-old problem: Mining Data for Likely Voters*. Paper presented at the 62nd Annual Conference of the American Association of Public Opinion Research, Anaheim, CA.

Murray, G. R., Riley, C., & Scime, A. (2009). Pre-election Polling: Identifying likely voters using Iterative Expert Data Mining. *Public Opinion Quarterly, 73*(1), 159–171. doi:10.1093/poq/nfp004

Murray, G. R., & Scime, A. (2010). Microtargeting and Electorate Segmentation: Data Mining the American National Election Studies. *Journal of Political Marketing, 9*(3), 143–166. doi:10.1080/15377857.2010.497732

National Academy of Sciences. (2008). *Science, Evolution, and Creationism*. Washington, D.C.: National Academies Press.

Padmanabhan, B., & Tuzhilin, A. (2000). Small is Beautiful: Discovering the minimal set of Unexpected Patterns. In *Proceedings of the Sixth ACM SIGKDD International Conference on Knowledge Discovery and Data Mining* (pp.54-63). Boston, MA.

Quinlan, J. R. (1993). *C4.5: Programs for Machine Learning*. San Francisco: Morgan Kaufmann.

Rajasethupathy, K., Scime, A., Rajasethupathy, K. S., & Murray, G. R. (2009). Finding "Persistent Rules": Combining Association and Classification Results. *Expert Systems with Applications*, 36(3P2), 6019-6024.

Ramu, K., & Ravi, V. (2008). Privacy preservation in Data Mining using Hybrid Perturbation methods: An application to Bankruptcy Prediction in Banks. *International Journal of Data Analysis Techniques and Strategies*, 1(4), 313–331. doi:10.1504/IJDATS.2009.027509

Scime, A., & Murray, G. R. (2007). Vote prediction by Iterative Domain Knowledge and Attribute Elimination. *International Journal of Business Intelligence and Data Mining*, 2(2), 160–176. doi:10.1504/IJBIDM.2007.013935

Scime, A., Murray, G. R., & Hunter, L. Y. (2010). Testing Terrorism Theory with Data Mining. *International Journal of Data Analysis Techniques and Strategies*, 2(2), 122–139. doi:10.1504/IJDATS.2010.032453

Silberschatz, A., & Tuzhilin, A. (1996). What makes Patterns interesting in Knowledge Discovery. *IEEE Transactions on Knowledge and Data Engineering*, 8(6), 970–974. doi:10.1109/69.553165

Srikant, R., & Agrawal, R. (1995). Mining generalized Association Rules. In *Proceedings of the 21st VLDB Conference* (pp. 407-419). Zurich, Switzerland.

Su, X., Khoshgoftaar, T. M., & Greiner, R. (2009). Making an Accurate Classifier Ensemble by Voting on Classifications from Imputed Learning Sets. *International Journal of Information and Decision Sciences*, 1(3), 301–322. doi:10.1504/IJIDS.2009.027657

Tan, P.-N., Steinbach, M., & Kumar, V. (2006). *Introduction to Data Mining*. Boston: Addison Wesley.

Toivonen, H., Klemettinen, M., Ronkainen, P., Hätönen, K., & Mannila, H. (1995). Pruning and Grouping of Discovered Association Rules. In *Proceedings of ECML-95 Workshop on Statistics, Machine Learning, and Discovery in Databases* (pp. 47-52). Heraklion, Crete, Greece.

Tozicka, J., Rovatsos, M., & Pechoucek, M. (2007). A Framework for Agent-based Distributed Machine Learning and Data Mining. In *Proceedings of the 6th International Joint Conference on Autonomous Agents and Multiagent Systems*, (Art 96). Honolulu, HI.

Vatsavai, R. R., & Bhaduri, B. (2007). A Hybrid Classification Scheme for Mining Multisource Geospatial Data. In *Proceedings of the Seventh IEEE International Conference on Data Mining Workshops (ICDMW 2007)* (pp. 673-678). Omaha, NE.

Wagstaff, K., Cardie, C., Rogers, S., & Schrödl, S. (2001). Constrained k-means Clustering with Background Knowledge. In *Proceedings of the Eighteenth International Conference on Machine Learning* (pp. 577-584). Williamstown, MA.

Wang, G., Zhang, C., & Huang, L. (2008). A Study of Classification Algorithm for Data Mining based on Hybrid Intelligent Systems. In *Ninth ACIS International Conference on Software Engineering, Artificial Intelligence, Networking, and Parallel/Distributed Computing* (pp. 371-375). Phuket Thailand.

Wang, Y., Zhang, Y., Xia, J., & Wang, Z. (2008). Segmenting the Mature Travel Market by Motivation. *International Journal of Data Analysis Techniques and Strategies*, 1(2), 193–209. doi:10.1504/IJDATS.2008.021118

Webb, G. I., & Zheng, Z. (2004). Multistrategy Ensemble Learning: Reducing Error by Combining Ensemble Learning Techniques. *IEEE Transactions on Knowledge and Data Engineering, 16*(8), 980–991. doi:10.1109/TKDE.2004.29

Witten, I. H., & Frank, E. (2005). *Data Mining: Practical Machine Learning Tools and Techniques* (2nd ed.). San Francisco: Morgan Kaufman.

Zaki, M. J. (2004). Mining Non-redundant Association Rules. *Data Mining and Knowledge Discovery, 9,* 223–248. doi:10.1023/B:DAMI.0000040429.96086.c7

Zhao, Y., Zhang, C., & Zhang, S. (2005). Discovering Interesting Association Rules by Clustering. *AI 2004: Advances in Artificial Intelligence, 3335,* 1055-1061. Heidelberg: Springer.

Zhong, N., Yao, Y. Y., Ohshima, M., & Ohsuga, S. (2001). Interestingness, Peculiarity, and Multi-database Mining. In *First IEEE International Conference on Data Mining (ICDM'01)* (pp.566-574). San Jose, California.

ADDITIONAL READING

Ankerst, M., Ester, M., & Kriegel, H. (2000). Towards an Effective Cooperation of the User and the Computer for Classification. In *Proceedings of the Sixth ACM SIGKDD International Conference on Knowledge Discovery and Data Mining* (pp. 179-188). Boston, MA.

Birrer, F. A. (2005). Data Mining to Combat Terrorism and the Roots of Privacy Concerns. *Ethics and Information Technology, 7*(4), 211–220. doi:10.1007/s10676-006-0010-6

Blos, M. F., Wee, H.-M., & Cardenas-Barron, L. E. (2009). The Threat of Outsourcing US Ports Operation to any Terrorist Country Supporter: A Case Study using Fault Tree Analysis. *International Journal of Information and Decision Sciences, 1*(4), 411–427. doi:10.1504/IJIDS.2009.027760

Cao, L., Zhao, Y., Zhang, H., Luo, D., Zhang, C., & Park, E. K. (2009). Flexible Frameworks for Actionable Knowledge Discovery. *IEEE Transactions on Knowledge and Data Engineering,* doi.ieeecomputersociety.org/10.1109/TKDE.2009.143.

Chen, H., Reid, E., Sinai, J., Silke, A., & Ganor, B. (2008). *Terrorism Informatics: Knowledge Management and Data Mining for Homeland Security*. New York: Springer.

Dalvi, N., & Domingos, P. Mausam, Sanghai, S. & Verma, D., (2004). Adversarial Classification. In *Proceedings of the Tenth ACM SIGKDD International Conference on Knowledge Discovery and Data Mining* (pp. 99-108). Seattle, WA.

Duda, R. O., Hart, P. E., & Stork, D. G. (2001). *Pattern Classification* (2nd ed.). New York: Wiley.

Giarratano, J. C., & Riley, G. D. (2004). *Expert Systems: Principles and Programming* (4th ed.). New York: Course Technology.

Hofmann, M., & Tierney, B. (2003). The involvement of Human Resources in Large Scale Data Mining Projects. In *Proceedings of the 1st International Symposium on Information and Communication Technologies* (pp. 103-109). Dublin, Ireland.

Jain, A. K., Duin, R. P. W., & Mao, J. (2000). Statistical Pattern Recognition: A Review. *IEEE Transactions on Pattern Analysis and Machine Intelligence, 22*(1), 4–37. doi:10.1109/34.824819

Kass, G. (1980). An Exploratory Technique for Investigating Large Quantities of Categorical Data. *Applied Statistics, 29*, 119–127. doi:10.2307/2986296

Kim, B., & Landgrebe, D. (1991). Hierarchical Decision Classifiers in High-Dimensional and Large Class Data. *IEEE Transactions on Geoscience and Remote Sensing, 29*(4), 518–528. doi:10.1109/36.135813

Lee, J. (2008). Exploring Global Terrorism Data: A Web-based Visualization of Temporal Data. *Crossroads, 15*(2), 7–14. doi:10.1145/1519390.1519393

Magidson, J. (1994). The CHAID Approach to Segmentation Modeling: Chi-squared Automatic Interaction Detection. In Bagozzi, R. P. (Ed.), *Advanced Methods of Marketing Research*. Cambridge, MA: Basil Blackwell.

Memon, N., Hicks, D. L., & Larsen, H. L. (2007). Harvesting Terrorists Information from Web. In *Proceedings of the 11ᵗʰ International Conference Information Visualization* (pp. 664-671). Washington, DC.

Memon, N., & Qureshi, A. R. (2005). Investigative data mining and its application in counterterrorism. In *Proceedings of the 5th WSEAS International Conference on Applied Informatics and Communications* (pp. 397-403). Malta.

Mingers, J. (1989). An Empirical Comparison of Pruning methods for Decision Tree Induction. *Machine Learning, 4*, 227–243. doi:10.1023/A:1022604100933

Murray, G. R., Hunter, L. Y., & Scime, A. (2009). Testing Terrorism using Iterative Expert Data Mining. In *Proceeding of the 2009 International Conference on Data Mining (DMIN 2009)* (pp. 565-570). Las Vegas, NV.

Murthy, S. K. (1998). Automatic construction of Decision Trees from Data: A Multi-disciplinary Survey. *Data Mining and Knowledge Discovery, 2*(4), 345–389. doi:10.1023/A:1009744630224

Quinlan, J. R. (1979). Discovering Rules by Induction from Large collection of Examples. In Michie, D. (Ed.), *Expert Systems in the Micro Electronic Age*. Edinburgh, Scotland: Edinburgh University Press.

Quinlan, J. R. (1987). Simplifying Decision Trees. *International Journal of Man-Machine Studies, 27*, 221–234. doi:10.1016/S0020-7373(87)80053-6

Scime, A., Murray, G. R., Huang, W., & Brownstein-Evans, C. (2008). Data Mining in the Social Sciences and Iterative Attribute Elimination. In Taniar, D. (Ed.), *Data Mining and Knowledge Discovery Technologies*. Hershey, PA: IGI Publishing.

Seno, M., & Karypis, G. (2001). LPMiner: An algorithm for finding Frequent Itemsets using Length-Decreasing Support Constraint. In *Proceedings of the 2001 IEEE International Conference on Data Mining* (pp. 505-512). San Jose, CA.

Turban, E., McLean, E., & Wetherbe, J. (2004). *Information Technology for Management* (3rd ed.). New York: Wiley.

Yi, X., & Zhang, Y. (2007). Privacy-Preserving Distributed Association Rule Mining via Semi-trusted Mixer. *Data & Knowledge Engineering, 63*(2), 550–567. doi:10.1016/j.datak.2007.04.001

KEY TERMS AND DEFINITIONS

Association Mining: A data mining method used to find patterns of data that show conditions where sets of attribute-value pairs occur frequently in the data set.

Association Rule: A rule found by association mining.

Classification Mining: A data mining method used to find models of data for categorizing instances; typically used for predicting future events from historical data.

Classification Rule: A rule found by classification mining.

Persistent Rule: A rule common to more than one data mining method.

Persistent Strong Rule: An association rule that is both persistent by appearing in a classification decision tree and strong by exhibiting a similar confidence level in the classification rule

Strong Rule: A rule found by association or classification mining that meets a domain expert's defined confidence level.

APPENDIX

ANES survey items in the likely voter data set:

Was respondent's vote validated? (A_Voteval_V2)

0.   No record of respondent voting.
1.   Yes.

"On the coming Presidential election, do you plan to vote?" (A_Intent) 0. No 1. Yes"Do you remember for sure whether or not you voted in that [previous] election?" (A_Prevvote)

0.   Respondent did not vote in previous election or has never voted
1.   Voted: Democratic/Republican/Other

ANES survey items in the vote choice data set:

Discrete-valued questions (attribute names)

What is the highest degree that you have earned? (aeduc)

1.   8 grades or less
2.   9–12 grades, no diploma/equivalency
3.   12 grades, diploma or equivalency
4.   12 grades, diploma or equivalency plus non-academic training
5.   Some college, no degree; junior/community college level degree (AA degree)
6.   BA level degrees
7.   Advanced degrees including LLB.

Some people do not pay much attention to political campaigns. How about you, would you say that you have been/were very much interested, somewhat interested, or not much interested in the political campaigns this year? (aintelect)

1.   Not much interested
2.   Somewhat interested
3.   Very much interested.

Some people seem to follow what is going on in government and public affairs most of the time, whether there is an election going on or not. Others are not that interested. Would you say you follow what is going on in government and public affairs most of the time, some of the time, only now and then, or hardly at all? (aintpubaff)

1.   Hardly at all
2.   Only now and then

3. Some of the time
4. Most of the time

How do you identify yourself in terms of political parties? (apid)

–3	Strong Republican
–2	Weak or leaning Republican
0	Independent
2	Weak or leaning Democrat
3	Strong Democrat

In addition to being American, what do you consider your main ethnic group or nationality group? (arace)

1. White
2. Black
3. Asian
4. Native American
5. Hispanic
6. Other

Who do you think will be elected President in November? (awhoelect)

1. Democratic candidate
2. Republican candidate
7. Other candidate

Continuous-valued questions

Feeling thermometer questions. A measure of feelings. Ratings between 50 and 100 degrees mean a favorably and warm feeling; ratings between 0 and 50 degrees mean the respondent does not feel favorably. The 50 degree mark is used if the respondent does not feel particularly warm or cold:

Feeling about Democratic Presidential Candidate. (demtherm)

Discretization ranges: (-inf - 42.5], (42.5 – 54.5], (54.5 – 62.5], (62.5 – 77.5], (77.5 – inf)

Feeling about Republican Presidential Candidate. (reptherm)

Discretization ranges: (-inf - 42.5], (42.5 – 53.5], (53.5 – 62.5], (62.5 – 79.5], (79.5 – inf)

Feeling about Republican Vice Presidential Candidate. (repvptherm)

Discretization ranges: (-inf - 32.5], (32.5 – 50.5], (50.5 – 81.5], (81.5 – inf)

Affect questions. The number of 'likes' mentioned by the respondent minus the number of 'dislikes' mentioned:

Affect toward the Democratic Party. (affdem)

Discretization ranges: (-inf - -1.5], (-1.5 - -0.5], (-0.5 - 0.5], (0.5 – 1.5], (1.5 – inf)

Affect toward Democratic presidential candidate. (affdemcand)

Discretization ranges: (-inf - -1.5], (-1.5 - -0.5], (-0.5 - 0.5], (0.5 – 2.5], (2.5 – inf)

Affect toward Republican Party. (affrep)

Discretization ranges: (-inf - -2.5], (-2.5 - -0.5], (-0.5 - 0.5], (0.5 – 2.5], (2.5 – inf)

Affect toward Republican presidential candidate. (affrepcand)Discretization ranges: (-inf - -2.5], (-2.5 - -0.5], (-0.5 - 0.5], (0.5 – 2.5], (2.5 – inf)

Section 2
Research and Learning

Chapter 6
A Perspective on Data Mining Integration with Business Intelligence

Ana Azevedo
CEISE/STI, ISCAP/IPP, Portugal

Manuel Filipe Santos
University of Minho, Portugal

ABSTRACT

Business Intelligence (BI) is an emergent area of the Decision Support Systems (DSS) discipline. Over the past years, the evolution in this area has been considerable. Similarly, in the last years, there has been a huge growth and consolidation of the Data Mining (DM) field. DM is being used with success in BI systems, but a truly DM integration with BI is lacking. The purpose of this chapter is to discuss the relevance of DM integration with BI, and its importance to business users. From the literature review, it was observed that the definition of an underlying structure for BI is missing, and therefore a framework is presented. It was also observed that some efforts are being done that seek the establishment of standards in the DM field, both by academics and by people in the industry. Supported by those findings, this chapter introduces an architecture that can conduct to an effective usage of DM in BI. This architecture includes a DM language that is iterative and interactive in nature. This chapter suggests that the effective usage of DM in BI can be achieved by making DM models accessible to business users, through the use of the presented DM language.

INTRODUCTION

Business Intelligence (BI) can be presented as an architecture, tool, technology or system that gathers and stores data, analyzes it using analytical tools, and delivers information and/or knowledge, facilitating reporting, querying, and, ultimately, allows organizations to improve decision making (Clark, Jones, & Armstrong, 2007; Kudyba & Hoptroff, 2001; Michalewicz, Schmidt, Michalewicz, & Chiriac, 2007; Moss & Shaku, 2003; Negash, 2004; Raisinghani, 2004; Thierauf, 2001; Turban, Sharda, Aroson, & King, 2008). To put it shortly, Business Intelligence can be defined as the process that transforms data into information and then into knowledge (Golfarelli, Rizzi, & Cella, 2004).

DOI: 10.4018/978-1-60960-067-9.ch006

Being rooted in the Decision Support Systems (DSS) discipline, BI has suffered a considerable evolution over the last years and is, nowadays, an area of DSS that attracts a great deal of interest from both the industry and researchers (Arnott & Pervan, 2008; Clark et al., 2007; Hannula & Pirttimäki, 2003; Hoffman, 2009; Negash, 2004; Richardson, Schlegel, Hostmann, & McMurchy, 2008; Richardson, Schlegel, & Hostmann, 2009).

Data Mining (DM) is being applied with success in BI and several examples of applications can be found (Linoff, 2008; Turban et al., 2008; Vercellis, 2009). Despite that, DM has not yet reached to non specialized users. The authors consider that the real issue is related with the fact that the Knowledge Discovery in Databases (KDD) process, as presented by Fayyad et al. (1996), is not fully integrated in BI. Consequently, its full potential could be not completely explored by decision makers using the systems. Currently, DM systems are functioning as separate isles, but the authors consider that only the full integration of the KDD process on BI can conduct to an effective usage of DM in BI.

The authors have point out three main reasons for DM to be not completely integrated with BI. Firstly, the models/patterns obtained from DM are complex and there is the need of an analysis from a DM specialist. This fact can lead to a non-effective adoption of DM in BI, being that DM is not really integrated on most of the implemented BI systems, nowadays. Secondly, the problem with DM is that there is not a user-friendly tool that can be used by decision makers to analyze DM models. Usually, BI systems have user-friendly analytical tools that help decision makers in order to obtain insights on the available data and allow them to take better decisions. Examples of such tools are On-Line Analytical Processing (OLAP) tools, which are widely used (Negash, 2004; Turban et al., 2008). Powerful analytical tools, such as DM, remain too complex and sophisticated for the average consumer. Finally, but extremely important, it has not been given sufficient empha-sis to the development of solutions that allow the specification of DM problems through business oriented languages, and that are also oriented for BI activities. With the expansion that has occurred in the application of DM solutions in BI, this is, currently, of increasing importance.

Most of the BI systems are built on top of relational databases. As a consequence, DM integration with relational databases is an important issue to consider when studying DM integration with BI. Codd´s relational model for database systems is long ago adopted in organizations. One of the reasons for the great success of relational databases is related with the existence of a standard language – SQL (Structured Query Language). SQL allows business users to obtain quick answers to ad-hoc questions, through queries on the data stored in databases. SQL is nowadays included in all the Relational Database Management Systems (RDBMS). SQL serves as the core above which are constructed the various Graphical User Interfaces (GUI's) and user friendly languages, such as Query By Example (QBE's), included in RDBMS. It is also necessary to define a standard language for data mining, which can operate likewise for data mining. Some efforts are being made in order to overcome this issue. Efforts involve the definition of standards for DM that arises both by academics and by people in the industry. It is the authors' belief that the effective integration of DM with BI systems must involve final business users' access to DM models. This access is crucial in order to business users to develop an understanding of the models, to help them in decision making. With this in mind, the authors present a high-level architecture that pretends to conduct to an effective usage of DM with BI. This architecture includes a DM language, named as Query Models By Example (QMBE), which is iterative and interactive in nature, thus allowing final business users to access and manipulate DM models.

Related Work

Research developed in Wang and Wang (2008) is aligned with the research considered in this chapter, in that they consider that business users have a crucial role in the development and analyses of DM models. However, they consider a different approach. A model that allows knowledge sharing among business insiders and DM specialists is presented. It is argued that this model can make DM more relevant to BI. The research presented in this chapter focus on making DM models to be directly manipulated by business users. It is considered that this can conduct to an understanding of DM models by business users, helping them on the decision making process and thus integrating DM with BI.

Han and Kamber (2006) states that the integration (coupling) of DM with database systems and/or data warehouses is crucial in the design of DM systems. They consider four possible integration schemes, which are, in increasing order of integration: no coupling, louse coupling, semi-tight coupling, and tight coupling. They present the concept of On-Line Analytical Mining (OLAM), which incorporates On-Line Analytical Processing with DM, as a way to achieve tight coupling. Nevertheless, the approach presented in this chapter is different in that DM models are stored in the database jointly with the data.

Several approaches have been proposed for the definition of data mining languages. In the literature there can be found some language specifications, namely, DMQL (Han, Fu, Wang, Koperski, & Zaiane, 1996), MINE RULE (Meo, Psaila, & Ceri, 1998), MSQL (Imielinski & Virmani, 1999), SPQL (Bonchi, Giannotti, Lucchesse, Orlando, Perego, & Trasarti, 2007), KDDML (Romei, Ruggieri, & Turini, 2006), XDM (Meo & Psaila, 2006), RDM (De Raedt, 2002), among others. These languages are generally part of a wider system, whose aim is, undoubtedly, to achieve the Knowledge and Data Discovery Management System (KDDMS) referred in Imielinski and Mannila (1996), that allows the high-level abstraction existent on the relational DBMS, and that integrates the complete KDD process. Despite the importance of the referred languages, they are not business oriented. To a greater extend, they are not oriented to the diverse BI activities. This issue is of increasing importance in organizations. The language introduced in this chapter differs from the above ones in such a way that it is oriented to business users and to BI activities.

Contributions and Chapter Layout

The main contribution of this chapter is to present the viability of developing DM languages that are oriented to BI activities as well as oriented to business users. In order to achieve these goals, a high-level architecture that intends to conduct to an effective usage of DM in BI is introduced. This architecture includes a new DM language that is iterative and interactive in nature, in order to allow business users to directly access and manipulate DM models. It also allows business users to answer ad-hoc questions through queries on the data and also on DM models.

This chapter also contributes to the design of a framework for BI, which helps to operationalize the state of the art in the field. An example for the framework for Business Intelligence is presented as it helps to understand some business questions that can be answered by a BI system. For the sake of doing a comparison, questions are presented that do not include DM usage, as well as questions including DM usage.

The remaining of the chapter is organized as follows. The authors initiate with an overview of the area of BI, presenting a framework for BI. They proceed with a clarification of some concepts related with the DM and KDD process. Next, the issue of DM integration with relational databases is presented. An architecture is introduced that intends to conduct to an effective usage of DM in BI. Finally, present future research directions and conclusion are discussed.

A FRAMEWORK FOR BUSINESS INTELLIGENCE

The roots for BI can be found in the field of DSS which "is the area of the Information Systems (IS) discipline that is focused on supporting and improving managerial decision-making" (Arnott & Pervan, 2008). DSS can also be presented as a computer-based solution that can be used to support complex decision making, and solving complex, semi-structured, or ill-structured problems (Nemati, Steiger, Iyer, & Herschel, 2002; Shim, Warkentin, Courtney, Power, Sharda, & Carlsson, 2002). The first reference to Business Intelligence was made by Lunh (1958). The term BI has replaced other terms such as Executive Information Systems and Management Information Systems (Negash, 2004; Turban et al., 2008). Nowadays it can be said that BI is an area of DSS that attracts a great deal of interest (Azevedo & Santos, 2009).

The Framework

BI refers to information systems aimed at integrating structured and unstructured data in order to convert it into useful information and knowledge, upon which business managers can make more informed and consequently better decisions. The main approaches presented in the literature are:

- The traditional approach to BI is concerned with, data aggregation, business analytics and data visualization (Kudyba & Hoptroff, 2001; Raisinghani, 2004; Turban et al., 2008). According to this approach, BI explores several technological tools, producing reports and forecasts, in order to improve the efficiency of the decision making. Such tools include Data Warehouse (DW), Extract-Transform and Load (ETL), OnLine Analytical Processing (OLAP), Data Mining (DM), Text Mining, Web Mining, Data Visualization, Geographic Information Systems (GIS), and Web Portals.

- On the next level there is a concern with the integration of business processes on BI (Eckerson, 2009; Golfarelli et al., 2004; Turban et al., 2008; Wormus, 2008; Zeller, 2007). According to this approach, "BI is a mechanism to bridge the gap between the business process management to the business strategy" (Zeller, 2008). In addition to all the tools in traditional BI, tools such as Business Performance Management (BPM), Business Activity Monitoring (BAM), Service-Oriented Architecture (SOA), Automatic Decision Systems (ADS), and dashboards, are included.

- Adaptive Business Intelligence is concerned with self-learning adaptive systems, that can recommend the best actions, and that can learn with previous decisions, in order to improve continuously (Michalewicz et al., 2007). Artificial Intelligence is incorporated on BI systems in this manner.

A schematic view of the framework for BI is depicted in Figure 1. The presented framework can be used as the basis for subsequent research, since it helps to operationalize the actual state of the art. Research could be developed along all the presented levels since there are open issues on all of them. Investigation areas on BI could include integration issues, analysis of usability, assessment, return on investment, and technological issues.

An Example of a Traditional Business Intelligence System

The research presented in this paper focus in traditional BI. Nevertheless, the system that is used considers the superficial usage of BPM tools, focusing mainly on dashboards. At the moment, a prototype of a traditional BI system is imple-

Figure 1. A framework for Business Intelligence

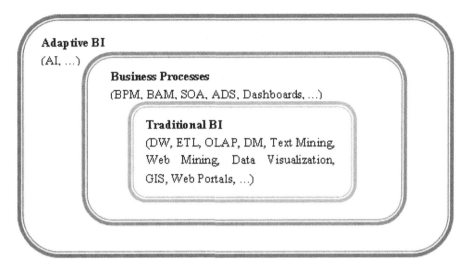

mented. Only some of the tools presented in the framework are implemented, namely, DW, ETL, OLAP, Data Visualization, Web portals, BPM, and Dashboards. In a near future, DM will be integrated in the system. The underlying relational database refers to a higher education institution. Almost all the business processes of the referred higher education institution are supported by an information system, build upon relational databases (Pereira, Azevedo, & Castilho, 2007). The direction board of the institution intends to expand the system with the inclusion of a BI system, which will come up from the presented prototype. The high-level architecture of the BI system currently implemented is presented in Figure 2.

At the moment, the system delivers information about students, but plans are being done in order to include teachers and employees. In Table 1, few examples of business questions that can be answered by the BI system are presented. All these questions can be converted into queries in any of the query languages offered by the RDBMS, for instance SQL. In addition, data visualization tools can help to understand some important aspects related with these questions. OLAP tools are also important as a way to obtain answers to the wide variety of ad-hoc questions posed to the

system by business users, considering different data dimensions.

DATA MINING AND KNOWLEDGE DISCOVERY IN DATABASES

The term Knowledge Discovery in Databases or KDD, for short, was coined in 1989 to refer to the broad process of finding knowledge in data, and to emphasize the "high-level" application of particular DM methods (Fayyad et al., 1996). Fayyad considers DM as one of the phases of the KDD process (Fayyad, 1996). The DM phase concerns, mainly, to the means by which the patterns are extracted and enumerated from data. As of the foundations of KDD and DM, several applications were developed in many diversified fields. The growth of the attention paid to the area emerged from the rising of big databases in an increasing and differentiate number of organizations. Nevertheless, there is the risk of wasting all the value and wealth of information contained on these databases, unless the adequate techniques are used to extract useful knowledge (Chen, Han, & Yu, 1996; Fayyad, 1996; Simoudis, 1996).

Figure 2. High-level architecture of the Business Intelligence System

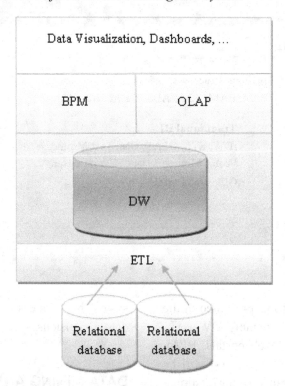

The application of DM techniques with success can be found in a wide and diversified range of applications. For instance, Salzberg (1999) apply DM techniques to gene discovery in DNA sequences. Wu et al. (2005) developed a framework that helps in the detection of depressive symptoms in psychiatry. Chiang et al. (2005) present a medical decision support system that can identify the patients who have polyps, while (Fung & Stoeckel, 2007) work helps on the identification of Alzheimer's disease. An intelligent decision support system is used to support intensive care medical activities (Gago & Santos, 2008; Gago, Fernandes, Pinto, & Santos, 2009; Santos, Pereira, & Silva, 2005). Silva et al.(2009) presents a study of the deforestation problem in Amazonia. Nlenanya (2009) applies a Geographical Information System (GIS) based on a knowledge discovery interface that can be used to stimulate sustainable development in sub-Saharan African region. Tadesse et al.(2009) work focus on monitoring and prediction of drought's impact on vegetation conditions. A system able

Table 1. Examples of business questions that can be answered by the Business Intelligence System

Question	Dimensions
Who are the best students?	
Who are the worst students?	By semester
How many students conclude the grades according to initial schedule?	By year
	By geographical origin
Which are the courses with higher retention taxes?	By studies field
How many students are there?	…
…	

to, after an oil spill, determine if an area is going to be contaminated or not is presented in Corchado et al. (2008). Santos et al. (2005) use DM techniques to do the automatic assessment of barrage water quality. A real-time decision support system for civil engineering structures is presented in Quintela et al. (2007). Lappas (2009) presents applications to societal benefit areas such as helpdesks and recommendation systems, digital libraries, e-learning, security and crime investigation, e-government services, and e-politics and e-democracy. There are DM applications even in sports. Bhandari et al.(1997) describe one application used by National Basketball Association (NBA) coaching staffs to discover interesting patterns in basketball game data.

There are several applications in the BI field. For instance, concerning the applications of DM to finance (John, Miller, & Kerber, 1996) refer to stock selection in order to obtain the best stock portfolio for investors. Other type of application, concerns the discovery of insurance risks (Apte, Grossman, Pednault, Rosen, Tipu, & White, 1999). DM techniques can also be used in credit card fraud detection (Chan, Fan, Prodromidis, & Stolfo, 1999). In Hu (2005), DM is used for analyzing retailing bank customer attrition. Santos et al. (2006) present a study of bankruptcy prediction based on data mining techniques. DM can be applied in the prediction of the ideal moment to replace aircraft components (Létourneau, Famimi, & Matwin, 1999). König and Gratz (2005) application is made in order to optimize manufacturing processes in the semiconductor industry. Most of the most popular applications of DM applications include market basket analysis and customer segmentation (Ghosh & Strehl, 2005; Simoudis, 1996). Hsu et al.(2004) propose a real data mining application for personalized shopping recommendation. Luck (2009) applies DM techniques on CRM data. Dzieciolowski and Kina (2008) examine how data mining can help identify best geographic areas for customer acquisition campaigns. A KDD approach was used to database marketing projects in Pinto

et al. (2006) and Santos et al. (2005). In Ezawa and Norton (1996) DM techniques are applied in order to predict uncollectible telecommunications accounts. Pan et al. (2007) aim at identifying customers who might switch to a competitor service provider. The problem of telephone calling fraud detection is presented in Cox et al.(1997). The problem of detecting cellular cloning fraud based on a database of call records is made in Fawcett and Provost (1997). Despite the importance of these applications, they work as separate isles, being that they are not truly integrated with BI systems.

Prediction and description were identified by Fayyad et al. (1996) as the two "high-level" primary goals of DM. To achieve these goals some tasks were used and its description can be found in the literature, namely, classification, prediction, clustering, association, and summarization. A significant number of methods/algorithms have been developed to accomplish each task, and different kinds of models/patterns can be obtained. There are different forms to evaluate models interestingness in each case. There is also the necessity of selecting between different models. There is a large variety of alternatives, including accuracy and error measures, and methods such as cross-validation, bootstrap, bagging and boosting, estimating confidence intervals, ROC curves.

The emergence of more complex types of data led to the development of new methods and models to cope with the new task of mining complex data like text mining (Prado & Ferneda, 2008), web mining (content, structure, and usage) (Markov & Larose, 2007), spatial data mining (Nlenanya, 2009), graph mining (Zhang, Hu, Xia, Zhou, & Achananuparp, 2008), mining time-series data (Liabotis, Theodoulidis, & Saraaee, 2006) etc.,

DM INTEGRATION WITH RELATIONAL DATABASES

Some efforts are being done that seek the establishment of standards in the DM area, both by academics, and by people in the industry field. The main goal is to integrate DM with relational databases, thus allowing an easiest application of DM to business systems, and making it more available to decision making.

Towards Standards for Data Mining

Examining the principal conferences and journals in the DM field, it can be concluded that the main issues for research are related with improving data preparation for data mining, developing better algorithms and methods for specific problems and applications, and measuring the utility of the obtained models. Nevertheless, the necessity to develop a theory for DM, similar to the one that was develop by Codd, with the Relational Model for database systems, arose (De Raedt, 2003; Imielinski & Mannila, 1996; Mannila, 2000). Over the past years, some efforts have been done in the development of standards for DM and KDD (Dzeroski, 2007; Mannila, 2000). These efforts arise both by academics and by people in the industry field. Being aware that they may be not completely covered here, the authors present the ones that they consider most important.

Industrial

Some of the efforts in the industrial field concern the definition of processes/methodologies that can guide the implementation of DM applications. For instance, SEMMA and CRISP-DM can be pointed out as such examples (Azevedo & Santos, 2008). It can be concluded that both can be considered as implementations of the KDD process, described above.

Over the past years several data mining suites have been developed (KDNuggets, 2009). These suites deliver user-friendly environments that allow users to apply data mining free and easy. Some of them have capabilities to integrate all the KDD process. Nevertheless, if these suites are used without the knowledge of a DM expert,

the obtained results may not be useful. This is due to the fact that the all KDD process must be considered, in spite of just applying DM algorithms without being aware of their characteristics. Also, these suites are oriented to DM specialists and not oriented to business users.

There are some efforts that intend to develop standards which allow model representation to be platform independent. One such example is the Knowledge Discovery Metamodel (KDM) (Object Management Group, 2008). Another example is Predictive Model Markup Language (PMML) (Data Mining Group, 2009). OLE DB for Data Mining can also be presented as an example (Tang & MacLennan, 2005). There is also a standard Java API for developing data mining applications and tools, named as Java Data Mining (JDM). These models seek mainly for portability among models obtained in different tools, and some of them are included in most of the BI tools in the market.

Academics

The academic efforts towards a theory for DM and KDD, above all, follow closely the theory developed by Codd for the Relational Model. According to Codd´s Relational Model, (Codd, 1970; Codd 1982), a database consists of a set of *relations*. Each *relation* is a set of *tuples*. Two formal languages were defined: the *Relational Algebra* and the *Relational Calculus*. One fundamental property of such languages is *closure*: the result of a query is a relation. A very popular language implemented nowadays in all the relational DBMS is SQL. Research towards a theory for DM and KDD, focus mainly on obtaining a theory, similar to Codd´s theory, giving DM and KDD a database perspective. Imielinski and Mannila (1996) compare *File Systems* to the actual *DM systems*, and refer the aim of developing Knowledge and Data Discovery Management Systems (KDDMS), similarly to the RDBMS.

One promising investigation line is that of *Inductive databases*, as presented by De Raedt

(2003) and Imielinski and Mannila (1996). According to the Inductive Database framework, data and models are stored on the same database and can be queried. Based on this framework, some theoretical research and prototypes have been developed, as well as some research about Data Mining Languages. These issues will be further explored in the next two sections. Catania et al. (2004) present a framework that keeps data and patterns separated. An algebra for DM, the K-algebra, is presented by Gerber and Fernandes (2004). A more theoretical approach is the 3W-model presented in Calders et al.(2006), which is an extension of the relational algebra. Nijssen and De Raedt (2007) presents IQL, an extension of the relational calculus.

Inductive Databases

"Inductive databases tightly integrate databases with data mining. The key ideas are that data and patterns (or models) are handled in the same way and that an inductive query language allows the user to query and manipulate the patterns (or models) of interest" (De Raedt, 2003). Inductive databases research goal is to replace the KDD process model by queries to an inductive database. Besides the traditional queries of the relational model, there is the necessity to consider inductive queries that will be used to generate and manipulate the models (Dzeroski, 2007). This can be provided in several distinct ways, and thus many different research lines can be found. For instance, Mielikäinen (2004) tries to clarify what distinguishes traditional databases from inductive databases, arguing that it is the ability of the second to rank or to grade queries. According to this line of investigation, queries consist of constraints and the aim is to develop a language of patterns and a set of constraints that patterns must satisfy.

An inductive database should provide the following features (Bonchi et al., 2007):

- Coupling with a database management system:
  - Capability for retrieving interesting data,
  - Data and patterns on the same DBMS;
- Expressiveness of the query language:
  - High-level vision of the pattern discovery system similarly to the high-level vision of the DBMS;
- Efficiency of the mining engine:
  - Capability for efficient query response time;
- Graphical user interface:
  - Capability for pattern visualization and existence of navigation tools.

The Inductive query language is a fundamental issue to consider in the research. Two different approaches can be found in the literature:

- Definition of special purpose languages;
- Using just standard SQL.

Definition of Special Purpose Languages

The definition of special purpose languages was the investigation line chosen by several researchers. One line of research, focus on the definition of extensions to SQL. There are also some languages based on XML. Logic-based languages can also be found.

SQL-Based

A Data Mining Query Language, DMQL, is presented in Han et al.(1996). DMQL has syntax similar to that of SQL. It allows the definition of the data to be mined, the kind of knowledge to be discovered, inclusion of background knowledge, and definition of thresholds. The kind of knowledge to be mined concerns different types of rules, for instance, association rules and classification rules.

Another approach is presented in Meo et al.(1998). The *MINERULE* operator, which is an extension of SQL and has got syntax similar to that of SQL, is presented. The operator mines for association rules, allowing the definition of groups to which mining is applied.

MSQL is presented in Imielinski and Virmani (1999). The language also has got syntax similar to that of SQL, and mines for rules. MSQL has got two main commands, namely, *GetRules* and *SelectRules*. *GetRules* generates rules from data and *SelectRules* queries a pre-existing database. The problem of providing little support to the pre-processing and pos-processing phases of the KDD process is common to all of these languages (Botta, Boulicaut, Masson, & Meo, 2004).

One language supporting pre- and post-processing phases is presented in Kramer et al. (2006), and is a component of SINBAD system. It consists of an extension of SQL, and several operators are defined. For instance, the operator *extend add as* is used to add the results of data mining operations as new attributes to a relation, and the operator *feature select* allows the selection of tuples in a relation by the definition of specific conditions. The authors sustain that the defined language can handle the pre-processing techniques discretization and feature selection, and the data mining techniques pattern discovery, clustering and classification, but there is no clear indication about the supported models.

SPQL (Simple Pattern Query Language) is presented in Bonchi et al. (2007). The language has got syntax similar to that of SQL, the mining being made with the clause TRANSACTION. The language mines for frequent patterns, and handles the pre-processing phase. The language serves as the base for a complete constraint based querying system, ConQuesSt, which is a human-guided, interactive and iterative system for pattern discovery.

Analyzing the presented languages, it can be concluded that all of them have limitations on the types of models they support, and that more research is needed in this area. Just to give a glance at the syntax of some of the presented data mining query languages, an example is given in Table 2 that allows a comparison between them. The language that is a component of the SINBAD system is not included because there is no sufficient information about the language syntax. SPQL is not included since this language does not allow for classification rules.

XML-Based

KDDML, which stands for KDD Markup Language, consists of a middleware language and system, as expressed by the authors in Romei et al.(2006). The language is entirely based in XML standards, including query syntax and data and model representations. Queries consist of XML documents and operations consist of XML tags. According to the presented examples, the kinds of models that are dealt by the system are trees, clusters and rules.

Another example of an XML-based system, named as XDM (XML for Data Mining), is presented in Meo and Psaila (2006). The basic idea consists on the definitions of two concepts: *Data Item*, which is a data/patterns container, and *Statement*, which is a description of an operator application. The aim of the system is the adoption of XML in the inductive database framework. The presented examples include association rules and clusters.

Logic-Based

De Raedt (2002) presents a constraint logic programming language, named as RDM, which stands for Relational Database Mining, developed to support DM. The language is embedded within Prolog. In this, examples are presented for association rules and experiments were made on graph structures.

Table 2. Comparison of SQL-Based languages syntax

	Schema: student(id,gender,age,nenroll,grant,grade) Classification Rules for grade in consequent Having grade<10; support>0.1; confidence>0.2
DMQL	use database school find classification rules as Classification Rules according to grade Related to gender, age, nenroll, grant From student Where student.grade<10 With support threshold > 0.1 With confidence threshold > 0.2
MineRule	MINE RULE ClassificationRules AS SELECT DISTINCT gender, age, nenroll, grant AS BODY, grade AS HEAD FROM student WHERE grade<10 EXTRACTING RULES WITH SUPPORT: 0.1, CONFIDENCE: 0.2
MSQL	GetRules (student) Into ClassificationRules Where consequent is {(grade<10)} and body in {(gender=*), (age=*), (nenroll=*), (grant=*)} and confidence > 0.2 and support > 0.1

Using Standard SQL

Using this approach, the inductive database can be queried using standard SQL. This approach has got advantages concerning extensibility and flexibility, over the approach of using special-purpose DM languages. One example, is the research presented in Boulicaut et al. (1999), where the principle is demonstrated for association rules. Sarawagi et al.(2000) use the same principle related to association rules and compare performances of several alternatives, by means of distinct SQL versions (SQL92 and SQL-OR). Using only basic SQL3 constructions and functions, Jamil (2004) shows that any object relational database can be mined for association rules. Rantzau (2004) investigates approaches based on SQL-92, and presents a new approach, named Quiver, that employs universal and existential quantifiers to find frequent itemsets. Calders et al.(2006) propose the extensions of RDBMS and introduces the notion of *virtual mining views*, which can be queried since they are traditional relational relations (views). Using association rules and frequent itemsets as an ex-

ample, they show that the user can query mining results by using only SQL. Trying to overcome the burden of the use of a limited type of models, Fromont et al.(2007) investigate how this approach can be used for models such as decision trees.

Knowledge and Data Discovery Management Systems (KDDMS)

The presented languages are part of bigger projects that intend to develop a complete system in order to incorporate the entire KDD process. The same goes to the projects using standard SQL. The common aim of all the presented projects and, in general, of research in the area of inductive databases is, undoubtedly, to achieve the KDDMS referred in Imielinski and Mannila (1996), that allows the high-level abstraction present on the RDBMS, and that integrates the complete KDD process.

The importance of KDDMS is similar to the importance of RDBMS. RDBMS released users from the technical details of file systems. This was achieved by means of logical independence between data and applications (Date, 2004;

Elmasri & Navathe, 2007). This allowed final business users to put ad-hoc questions directly to the systems, thus making systems truly available to them.

INTEGRATING DATA MINING WITH BUSINESS INTELLIGENCE

One of the main aspects of BI systems is that, its user-friendly tools makes systems truly available to the final business users. As presented above, powerful analytical tools, such as DM, remain too complex and sophisticated for the average consumer of BI systems. McKnight (2002) supports that bringing DM into the front line business personnel will increase their potential to attaining BI's high potential business value. Another fundamental issue that is pointed out as an important issue is the capability of DM tools to be interactive, visual, and understandable, to work directly on the data, and to be used by front line workers for intermediate and lasting business benefits. The authors consider that the framework of inductive databases, introduced in the previous section as a way to DM integration with relational databases, can also be a way to achieve the goal of a full integration of DM with BI, and leading to the end of, the already referred, BI isles.

Taking these issues into consideration, an architecture that allows an effective usage of DM with BI by business users in order to conduct to DM integration with BI, was envisaged. This architecture should:

- bring DM into the front line business users;
- be iterative, visual, and understandable by front line business users;
- work directly on data.

The authors consider that this can be achieved by means of a DM language that business users can understand and, consequently use it to manipulate and query DM models and data. Following these guidelines, in Figure 3 an architecture for integration of DM with BI is presented that intends to conduct to an effective usage of DM in BI. This architecture is an extension of the one that is presented in Figure 2. It includes two additional modules: DM module and a new language named as QMBE. As far as our knowledge, there is no similar architecture in the literature.

The DM module will feed the database with DM models. A new language, named as QMBE (Query Models By Example), will be developed to be similar to the QBE (Query By Example) languages presented in some relational DBMS (Date, 2004; Elmasri & Navathe, 2007). The user will be able to interact directly with the models, and be able to construct queries such as the ones presented in Table 3. All the questions can be converted into queries to the system, defined in the QMBE language.

The language has two important characteristics, which are interactivity, and iterativity. Just as in relational DBMS QBE languages, the user will be able to define different criteria, similar to the ones presented in Table 1 and Table 3, or other considered significant to business users. Considering that DM models are stored in the DW, thus stored in tables, they can be accessed and manipulated similarly to tables. The novelty of the QMBE language is that it is oriented to business users and to BI processes. This kind of approach allows business users too directly access and manipulate data and models. This will bring DM to the front line business users, alike the other BI tools, thus allowing DM integration with BI.

The presented architecture consists of a conceptual architecture, which will be implemented in a near future. It is also considered that the system's implementation is viable, since it is according to the inductive database framework. The authors argue that this system is according to the inductive database framework, since it provides the features, indicated in Bonchi et al. (2007), and that were already indicated above in this chapter, namely coupling with a database management system,

Figure 3. Architecture for integration of Data Mining with Business Intelligence

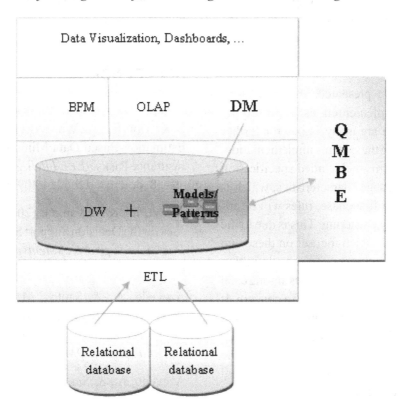

expressiveness of the query language, efficiency of the mining engine, and graphical user interface. In addition, the standards developed in the industry field will allow for the communication among the considered modules.

The system will support the complete KDD process, allowing many decisions to be made by the user in an interactive and iterative process. With this architecture the authors intend to demonstrate that the full integration of the KDD process with

BI can conduct to an effective usage of DM on BI, and consequently to DM integration with BI.

FUTURE RESEARCH DIRECTIONS

In a near future, the higher education institution intends to progress with the implementation of the developed prototype presented in Figure 2 in a real situation. The implementation on a real situ-

Table 3. Queries that can be posed to the extended Business Intelligence System

Queries on models	Queries on models and data
What are the characteristics of good students?	Select the actual students that can be good students.
What are the characteristics of bad students?	Select the actual students that can be bad students.
What are the characteristics of the students that do not conclude the grades according to initial schedule?	Select the actual students that can not conclude the grades according to initial schedule.
Are there different types of students in the school?	
…	…

ation will surely bring new and important inputs for improving the system. It is expected that the institution's decision makers will perceive all the value offered by the BI system and will demand for more features.

The architecture presented in Figure 3, is already being implemented as a prototype. Nevertheless, there are many issues for further research concerning the systems implementation. One of these concerns the detailed specification of the QMBE language characteristics, which is a critical issue. In a first phase, rules will be addressed followed by clustering. This is due to the application domain, which focuses on these two DM tasks. Another issue, concerns the definition of the communication of the modules among each others. Finally, user interface is also a concern. It is expected that when tests are finished the system will be integrated in a real situation, which is that of the referred higher education institution. The authors hope that the implementation on a real situation could help to support their claims, and to bring new useful insights.

CONCLUSION

The authors have presented the state of the art on BI and DM integration with relational databases and BI. They have also introduced an architecture that allows for DM integration with BI, including a new DM language: QMBE. The goal is to sustain that this is in fact possible. Even thought the architecture was presented in a rather informal way, the authors believe that it can be seen as a way that conducts to DM integration with BI, thus allowing an effective usage of DM in BI systems by business users. The interactive and iterative aspects of the system are crucial to achieve this goal. In summary, a new and comprehensive approach to DM integration with BI is presented. The main contribution of this chapter is to verify the viability of developing DM languages that

are oriented to BI activities as well as oriented to business users.

REFERENCES

Apte, C., Grossman, E., Pednault, E. P. D., Rosen, B. K., Tipu, F. A., & White, B. (1999). Probabilistic Estimation-Based Data Mining for Discovering Insurance Risks. *IEEE Intelligent Systems*, *14*(6), 49–58. doi:10.1109/5254.809568

Arnott, D., & Pervan, G. (2008). Eigth Key Issues for the Decision Support Systems Discipline. *Decision Support Systems*, *44*(3), 657–672. doi:10.1016/j.dss.2007.09.003

Azevedo, A., & Santos, M. F. (2008). KDD, SEMMA and CRISP-DM: A Parallel Overview. In. *Proceedings of the IADIS European Conference on Data Mining, DM2008*, 182–185.

Azevedo, A., & Santos, M. F. (2009). Business Intelligence: State of the Art, Trends, and Open Issues. In *Proceedings of the First International Conference on Knowledge Management and Information Sharing - KMIS 2009* (pp.296-300).

Bhandari, I., Colet, E., Parker, J., Pines, Z., Pratap, R., & Ramanujam, K. (1997). Advanced Scout: Data Mining and Knowledge Discovery in NBA Data. *Data Mining and Knowledge Discovery*, *1*(1), 121–125. doi:10.1023/A:1009782106822

Bonchi, F., Giannotti, F., Lucchesse, C., Orlando, S., Perego, R., & Trasarti, R. (2007). On Interactive Pattern Mining from Relational Databases. In S.Dzeroski & J. Struyf (Eds.), *Lecture Notes in Computer Science: Vol. 4747, Knowledge Discovery in Inductive Databases - 5th International Workshop - KDID 2006* (pp. 42-62). Berlin, Heidelberg: Springer-Verlag.

Botta, M., Boulicaut, J., Masson, C., & Meo, R. (2004). Query Languages Supporting Descriptive Rule Mining: A Ccomparative Study. In R. Meo, P.L. Lanzi & Mika Klemettinen (Eds.), *Lecture Notes on Artificial Intelligence: Vol. 2682, Database Support for Data Mining Applications - Discovering Knowledge with Inductive Queries* (pp. 24-51). Berlin, Heidelberg: Springer-Verlag.

Boulicaut, J., Klemettinen, M., & Mannila, H. (1999). Modeling KDD Processes within the Inductive Database Framework. In M. Mohania & A. M. Tjoa (Eds.), *Lecture Notes on Computer Science: Vol. 1676, Data Warehousing and knowledge Discovery - 1st International Conferense DaWak99* (pp. 193-202). Berlin, Heidelberg: Springer-Verlag.

Calders, T., Goethals, B., & Prado, A. (2006). Integrating Pattern Mining in Relational Databases. In J. Fürnkranz, T. Scheffer & M. Spiliopoulou (Eds.), *Lecture Notes on Artificial Intelligence: Vol. 4213, Knowledge Discovery in Databases - 10th European Conference on Principles and Practice of Knowledge Discovery in Databases - PKDD2006* (pp. 454-461). Berlin, Heidelberg: Springer-Verlag.

Calders, T., Lakshmanan, L. V. S., Ng, R. T., & Paredaens, J. (2006). Expressive Power of an Algebra for Data Mining. *ACM Transactions on Database Systems, 31*(4), 1169–1214. doi:10.1145/1189769.1189770

Catania, B., Maddalena, A., Mazza, M., Bertino, E., & Rizzi, S. (2004). A Framework for Data Mining Pattern Management. In J. Boulicaut, F. Esposito & F. Giannotti (Eds.), *Lecture Notes on Artificial Intelligence: Vol. 3202, Knowledge Discovery in Databases - 8th European Conference on Principles and Practice of Knowledge Discovery in Databases - PKDD2004* (pp. 87-98). Berlin, Heidelberg: Springer-Verlag.

Chan, P. K., Fan, W., Prodromidis, A. L., & Stolfo, S. J. (1999). Distributed Data Mining in Credit Card Fraud Detection. *IEEE Intelligent Systems, 14*(6), 67–74. doi:10.1109/5254.809570

Chen, M., Han, J., & Yu, P. S. (1996). Data Mining: An Overview from a Database Perspective. *IEEE Transactions on Knowledge and Data Engineering, 8*(6), 866–883. doi:10.1109/69.553155

Chiang, I., Shieh, M., & Hsu, J., Y. & Wong, J. (2005). Building a Medical Decision Support System for Colon Polyp Screening by Using Fuzzy Classification Trees. *Applied Intelligence, 22*(1), 61–75. doi:10.1023/B:APIN.0000047384.85823.f6

Clark, T. D., Jones, M. C., & Armstrong, C. P. (2007). The Dynamic Structure of Management Support Systems: Theory Development, Research, Focus, and Direction. *Management Information Systems Quarterly, 31*(3), 579–615.

Codd, E. F. (1970). A Relational Model of Data for Large Shared Data Banks. *Communications of the ACM, 13*(6), 377–387. doi:10.1145/362384.362685

Codd, E. F. (1982). Relational Database: A Practical Foundation for Productivity. *Communications of the ACM, 25*(2), 109–117. doi:10.1145/358396.358400

Corchado, J. M., Mata, A., Paz, F. D., & Pozo, D. D. (2008). A Case-Based Reaosoning System to Forecast the Presence of Oil Slicks. In. *Proceedings of the IADIS European Conference on Data Mining, 2008*, 3–10.

Cox, K. C., Eick, S. G., Wills, G. J., & Brachman, R. J. (1997). Visual Data Mining: Recognizing Telephone Calling Fraud. *Data Mining and Knowledge Discovery, 1*(2), 225–231. doi:10.1023/A:1009740009307

Data Mining Group. (2009). Predictive Model Markup Language (PMML). Retrieved August 1, 2009, from http://www.dmg.org/.

Date, C. J. (2004). *An Introduction to Database Systems*. Upper Sadle River, New Jersey: Pearson Education.

De Raedt, L. (2002). Data Mining as Constraint Logic Programming. In A.C.Kakas & F. Sadri (Eds.), *Lecture Notes on Artificial Intelligence: Vol. 2408, Computational Logic: Logic Programming and Beyond - Essays in Honour of Robert A. kowalski - Part II* (pp. 526-547). Berlin, Heidelberg: Springer-Verlag.

De Raedt, L. (2003). A Perspective on Inductive Databases. *SIGKDD Explorations, 4*(2), 69–77. doi:10.1145/772862.772871

Dzeroski, S. (2007). Towards a General Framework for Data Mining. In S. Dzeroski & J. Struyf (Eds.), *Lecture Notes in Computer Science: Vol. 4747, Knowledge Discovery in Inductive Databases - 5th International Workshop, KDID 2006* (pp. 259-300). Berlin, Heidelberg: Springer-Verlag.

Dzieciolowski, K., & Kina, D. (2008). Data Mining in Marketing Acquisition Campaigns. In. *Proceedings of the IADIS European Conference on Data Mining, 2008*, 173–175.

Eckerson, W. W. (2009). Research Q&A: Performance Management Strategies. *Business Intelligence Journal, 14*(1), 24–27.

Elmasri, R., & Navathe, S. B. (2007). *Fundamentals of Database Systems*. Upper Sadle River, New Jersey: Pearson Education.

Ezawa, K. J., & Norton, S. W. (1996). Constructing Bayesian Networks to Predict Uncollectible Telecommunications Accounts. *IEEE Expert, 11*(5), 45–51. doi:10.1109/64.539016

Fawcett, T., & Provost, F. (1997). Adaptive Fraud Detection. *Data Mining and Knowledge Discovery, 1*(3), 291–316. doi:10.1023/A:1009700419189

Fayyad, U. M. (1996). Data Mining and Knowledge Discovery: Making Sense Out of Data. *IEEE Expert, 11*(5), 20–25. doi:10.1109/64.539013

Fayyad, U. M., Piatetski-Shapiro, G., & Smyth, P. (1996). From Data Mining to Knowledge Discovery: An Overview. In Fayyad, U. M., Piatetski-Shapiro, G., Smyth, P., & Uthurusamy, R. (Eds.), *Advances in Knowledge Discovery and Data Mining* (pp. 1–34). Menlo Park, California: AAAI Press/The MIT Press.

Fromont, É., Blockeel, H., & Struyf, J. (2007). Integrating Decision Tree Learning into Inductive Databases. In S. Dzeroski & J. Struyf (Eds.), *Lecture Notes in Computer Science: Vol. 4747. Knowledge Discovery in Inductive Databases - 5th International Workshop, KDID 2006* (pp. 81-96). Berlin, Heidelberg: Springer-Verlag.

Fung, G., & Stoeckel, J. (2007). SVM feature selection for classification of SPECT images of Alzheimer's disease using spatial information. *Knowledge and Information Systems, 11*(2), 243–258. doi:10.1007/s10115-006-0043-5

Gago, P., Fernandes, C., Pinto, F., & Santos, M. F. (2009). INTCare: On-line Knowledge Discovery in the Intensive Care Unit. In. *Proceedings of INES, 2009*, 159–164.

Gago, P., & Santos, M. F. (2008). Towards an Intelligent Decision Support System for Intensive Care Units. In O. Okun & G. Valentini (Eds.), *Proceedings of the 18th European Conference on Artificial Intelligence: Vol. 1. Workshop on Supervised and Unsupervised Ensemble Methods and their Applications* (pp. 21-25). Patras, Greece.

Gerber, L., & Fernandes, A. A. A. (2004). An Abstract Algebra for Knowledge Discovery in Databases. In Benczúr, A., Demetrovics, J., & Gottlob, G. (Eds.), *Advances in Database and Information Systems* (pp. 83–98). Berlin, Heidelberg: Springer-Verlag.

Ghosh, J., & Strehl, A. (2005). Clustering and Visualization of Retail Market Baskets. In Pal, N. R., & Jain, L. (Eds.), *Advanced Techniques in Data Mining and Knowledge Discovery* (pp. 75–102). London, UK: Springer-Verlag. doi:10.1007/1-84628-183-0_3

Golfarelli, M., Rizzi, S., & Cella, I. (2004). What`s Next in Business Intelligence. In *DOLAP '04* (pp. 1–6). Beyond Data Warehousing.

Han, J., Fu, Y., Wang, W., Koperski, K., & Zaiane, O. (1996). DMQL: A Data Mining Query Language for Relational Databases. In *Proceedings of the SIGMOD '96 Workshop on Research Issues on Data Mining and Knowledge Discovery (DMKD '96)* (pp.27-34).

Han, J., & Kamber, M. (2006). *Data Mining: Concepts and Techniques*. San Francisco: Morgan Kaufman Publishers.

Hannula, M., & Pirttimäki, V. (2003). Business Intelligence Empirical Study on the Top 50 Finnish Companies. *Journal of American Academy of Business*, 2(2), 593–599.

Hoffman, T. (2009). 9 Hottest Skills for '09. *Computer World, January 1* (1), 26-27.

Hsu, C., Chung, H., & Huang, H. (2004). Mining Skewed and Sparse Transactions Data for Personalized Shopping Recommendation. *Machine Learning*, 57(1-2), 35–59. doi:10.1023/B:MACH.0000035471.28235.6d

Hu, X. (2005). A Data Mining Approach for Retailing Bank Customer Attrition Analysis. *Applied Intelligence*, 22(1), 47–60. doi:10.1023/B:APIN.0000047383.53680.b6

Imielinski, T., & Mannila, H. (1996). A Database Perspective on Knowledge Discovery. *Communications of the ACM*, 39(11), 58–64. doi:10.1145/240455.240472

Imielinski, T., & Virmani, A. (1999). MSQL: A Query Language for Database Mining. *Data Mining and Knowledge Discovery*, 3(4), 373–408. doi:10.1023/A:1009816913055

Jamil, H. M. (2004). Declarative Data Mining Using SQL3. In R. Meo, P. Lanzi & M. Klemettinen (Eds.), *Lecture Notes on Artificial Intelligence: Vol. 2682, Database Support for Data Mining Applications - Discovering Knowledge with Inductive Queries* (pp. 52-75). Berlin, Heidelberg: Springer-Verlag.

John, G. H., Miller, P., & Kerber, R. (1996). Stock Selection Using Rule Induction. *IEEE Expert*, 11(5), 52–58. doi:10.1109/64.539017

KDNuggets. (2009). Data Mining Software Suites. Retrieved August 5, 2009, from http://www.kdnuggets.com/software/suites.html.

König, A., & Gratz, A. (2005). Advanced Methods for the Analysis of Semiconductor Manufacturing Process Data. In Pal, N., & Jain, L. (Eds.), *Advanced Techniques in Data Mining and Knowledge Discovery* (pp. 27–74). London, UK: Springer-Verlag. doi:10.1007/1-84628-183-0_2

Kramer, S., Aufschild, V., Hapfelmeier, A., Jarasch, A., Kessler, K., Reckow, S., et al. (2006). Inductive Databases in the Relational Model: The Data as the Bridge. In F.Bonchi & J. Boulicault (Eds.), *Lecture Notes on Computer Science: Vol. 3933. Knowledge Discovery in Inductive Databases - 4th International Workshop - KDID2005* (pp. 124-138). Berlin, Heidelberg: Berlin-Verlag.

Kudyba, S., & Hoptroff, R. (2001). *Data Mining and Business Intelligence: A Guide to Productivity*. Hershey, PA: Idea Group Publishing.

Lappas, G. (2009). Machine Learning and Web Learning: Methods and Applications in Societal Benefit areas. In Rahman, H. (Ed.), *Data Mining Applications for Empowering Knowledge Societies* (pp. 76–95). Hershey, PA: IGI Publishing. doi:10.4018/978-1-59904-657-0.ch005

Létourneau, S., Famimi, F., & Matwin, S. (1999). Data Mining to Predict Aircraft Component Replacement. *IEEE Intelligent Systems, 14*(6), 59–65. doi:10.1109/5254.809569

Liabotis, I., Theodoulidis, B., & Saraaee, M. (2006). Improving Similarity Search in Time Series Using Wavelets. *International Journal of Data Warehousing and Mining, 2*(2), 55–81.

Linoff, G. S. (2008). Survival Data Mining Using Relational Databases. *Business Intelligence Journal, 13*(3), 20–30.

Luck, D. (2009). The Importance of Data Within Contemporary CRM. In Rahman, H. (Ed.), *Data Mining Applications for Empowering Knowledge Societies* (pp. 96–109). Hershey, PA: IGI Publishing. doi:10.4018/978-1-59904-657-0.ch006

Lunh, H. P. (1958). A Business Intelligence System. *IBM Journal of Research and Development, 2*(4), 314–319. doi:10.1147/rd.24.0314

Mannila, H. (2000). Theoretical Frameworks for Data Mining. *SIGKDD Explorations, 1*(2), 30–32. doi:10.1145/846183.846191

Markov, Z., & Larose, D. T. (2007). *Data mining the Web: Uncovering Patterns in Web content, Structure, and Usage.* Hoboken, New Jersey: Wiley-Interscience.

McKnight, W. (2002). Briging Data Mining to the Front Line, Part 1. *Information Management magazine, November* (2002), Retrieved July 16, 2009, from http://www.information-management.com/issues/200211001/5980-1.html.

Meo, R., & Psaila, G. (2006). An XML-Based Database for Knowledge Discovery. In T. Grust, H. Höpfner, A. Illarramendi, S. Jablonski, M. Mesiti, S. Müller, P. Patranjan, S. Kai-Uwe, M. Spiliopoulou & J. Wijsen (Eds.), *Lecture Notes in Computer Science: Vol. 4254. Current Trends in Database Technology - EDTB 2006 Workshops* (pp. 814-828). Berlin, Heidelberg: Springer-Verlag.

Meo, R., Psaila, G., & Ceri, S. (1998). An Extension to SQL for Mining Association Rules. *Data Mining and Knowledge Discovery, 2*(2), 195–224. doi:10.1023/A:1009774406717

Michalewicz, Z., Schmidt, M., Michalewicz, M., & Chiriac, C. (2007). *Adaptive Business Intelligence.* Berlin, Heidelberg: Springer-Verlag.

Mielikäinen, T. (2004). Inductive Databases as Ranking. In Y. Kambayashi, M. Mohania & W. Wöb (Eds.), *Lecture Notes on Computer Science: Vol. 3181, Data Warehousing and Knowledge Discovery - 6th International Conference DaWak2004* (pp. 149-158). Berlin, Heidelberg: Springer-Verlag.

Moss, L. T., & Shaku, A. (2003). *Business Intelligence Roadmap: The Complete Project Lifecycle for Decision-Support Applications.* Upper Saddle River, NJ: Pearson Education.

Negash, S. (2004). Business Intelligence. *Communications of the Association for Information Systems, 13*(1), 177–195.

Nemati, H. R., Steiger, D. M., Iyer, L. S., & Herschel, R. T. (2002). Knowledge Warehouse: An Architectural Integration of Knowledge Management, Decision Support, Artificial Intelligence and Data Warehousing. *Decision Support Systems, 33*(1), 143–161. doi:10.1016/S0167-9236(01)00141-5

Nijssen, S., & De Raedt, L. (2007). IQL: A Proposal for an Inductive Query Language. In S. Dzeroski & J. Struyf (Eds.), *Lecture Notes in Computer Science: Vol. 4747, Knowledge Discovery in Inductive Databases - 5th International Workshop, KDID 2006* (pp. 189-209). Berlin, Heidelberg: Springer-Verlag.

Nlenanya, I. (2009). Building an Environmental GIS Knowledge Infrastucture. In Rahman, H. (Ed.), *Data Mining Applications for Empowering Knowledge Societies* (pp. 262–279). Hershey, PA: IGI Publishing.

Object Management Group. (2008). Knowledge Discovery Model (KDM). Retrieved August 1, 2009, from http://kdmanalytics.com/kdm/index.php.

Pan, J., Yang, Q., Yang, Y., Li, L., Li, F. T., & Li, G. W. (2007). Cost-Sensitive-Data Preprocessing for Mining Customer Relationship Management Databases. *IEEE Intelligent Systems, 22*(1), 46–51. doi:10.1109/MIS.2007.7

Pereira, R. H., Azevedo, A., & Castilho, O. (2007). Secretaria On-Line From Iscap: A Case of Innovation. In *Proceedings of the IADIS International Conference WWW/Internet 2007* (pp.301-305).

Pinto, F., Gago, P., & Santos, M. F. (2006). Data Mining as a New Paradigm for Business Intelligence in Database Marketing Projects. In *Proceedings of the 8th International Conference on Enterprise Information Systems - ICEIS 2006* (pp.144-149).

Quintela, H., Santos, M. F., & Cortez, P. (2007). Real-Time Intelligent Decision Support System for Bridges Structures Behavior Prediction. In J. Neves, M.F. Santos & J.Machado (Eds.), *LNAI: Vol. 4874, Proceedings of the 13th Portuguese Conference on Aritficial Intelligence, EPIA 2007* (pp. 124-132). Berlin Heidelberg, Germany: Springer-Verlag.

Raisinghani, M. (2004). *Business Intelligence in the Digital Economy: Opportunities, Limitations and Risks*. Hershey, PA: Idea Group Publishing.

Rantzau, R. (2004). Frequent Itemset Discovery with SQL Using Universal Quantification. In R. Meo, P. Lanzi & M. Klemettinen (Eds.), *Lecture Notes on Artificial Intelligence: Vol. 2682. Database Support for Data Mining Applications - Discovering Knowledge with Inductive Queries* (pp. 194-213). Berlin, Heidelberg: Springer-Verlag.

Richardson, J., Schlegel, K., & Hostmann, B. (2009). *Magic Quadrant for Business Intelligence Platforms*. Core Research Note: G00163529, Gartner.

Richardson, J., Schlegel, K., Hostmann, B., & McMurchy, N. (2008). *Magic Quadrant for Business Intelligence Platforms, 2008*. Core Research Note: G00154227, Gartner.

Romei, A., Ruggieri, S., & Turini, F. (2006). KDDML: A Middleware Language and System for Knowledge Discovery in Databases. *Data & Knowledge Engineering, 57*(2), 179–220. doi:10.1016/j.datak.2005.04.007

Salzberg, S. L. (1999). Gene Discovery in DNA Sequences. *IEEE Intelligent Systems, 14*(6), 44–48. doi:10.1109/5254.809567

Santos, M., Pereira, J., & Silva, Á. (2005). A Cluster Framework for Data Mining Models: An application to intensive medicine. In *Proceedings of the 7th International Conference on Enterprise Information Systems - ICEIS 2005* (pp.163-168).

Santos, M. F., Cortez, P., Pereira, J., & Quintela, H. (2006). Corporate Bankruptcy Prediction Using Data Mining Techniques. In A. Zanasi, C.A. Brebbia & N.F.F. Ebecken (Eds.), *WIT Transactions on Information and Communication Tecchnologies: Vol. 37, Data Mining VII: Data, Text and Web Mining and their Business Applications* (pp. 349-357). Southampton, UK: WIT Press.

Santos, M. F., Cortez, P., Quintela, H., Neves, J., Vicente, H., & Arteiro, J. (2005). Ecological Mining - A Case Study on Dam Water Quality. In A. Zanasi, C.A. Brebbia & N.F.F. Ebecken (Eds.), *WIT Transactions on Information and Communication Tecchnologies: Vol. 35. Data Mining VI: Data mining, Text Mining and their Business Applications* (pp. 481-489). Southampton, UK: WIT Press.

Santos, M. F., Cortez, P., Quintela, H., & Pinto, F. (2005). A Clustering Approach for Knowledge Discovery in Database Marketing. In A.Zanasi, C.A. Brebbia & N.F.F. Ebecken (Eds.), *WIT Transactions on Information and Communication Tecchnologies: Vol. 35. Data Mining VI: Data, Text and Web Mining and their Business Applications* (pp. 367-376). Southampton, UK: WIT Press.

Sarawagi, S., Thomas, S., & Agrawal, R. (2000). Integrating Association Rule Mining with Relational Database Systems: Alternatives and Implications. *Data Mining and Knowledge Discovery, 4*(2-3), 89–125. doi:10.1023/A:1009887712954

Shim, J. P., Warkentin, M., Courtney, J. F., Power, D. J., Sharda, R., & Carlsson, C. (2002). Past, Present, and Future of Decision Support Technology. *Decision Support Systems, 32*(1), 111–126. doi:10.1016/S0167-9236(01)00139-7

Silva, M. S., Câmara, G., & Escada, M. I. (2009). Image Mining: Detecting Deforestation Patterns Through Satellites. In Rahman, H. (Ed.), *Data Mining Applications for Empowering Knowledge Societies* (pp. 55–75). Hershey, PA: IGI Publishing.

Simoudis, E. (1996). Reality Check for Data Mining. *IEEE Expert, 11*(5), 26–33. doi:10.1109/64.539014

Tadesse, T., Wardlow, B., & Hayes, M. J. (2009). The Application of Data Mining for Drought Monitoring and Prediction. In Rahman, H. (Ed.), *Data Mining Applications for Empowering Knowledge Societies* (pp. 280–291). Hershey, PA: IGI Publishing.

Tang, Z., & MacLennan, J. (2005). *Data Mining with SQL Server 2005*. Indianapolis, IN: Wiley Publishing.

Thierauf, R. J. (2001). *Effective Business Intelligence Systems*. West Port, CP: Quorum Books.

Turban, E., Sharda, R., Aroson, J. E., & King, D. (2008). *Business Intelligence: A Managerial Approach*. Upper Sadle River, New Jersey: Pearson Prentice Hall.

Vercellis, C. (2009). *Business Intelligence: Data Mining and Optimization for Decision Making*. West Sussex, United Kindgom: John Wiley & Sons.

Wang, H., & Wang, S. (2008). A Knowledge Management Approach to Data Mining Process for Business Intelligence. *Industrial Management & Data Systems, 108*(5), 622–634. doi:10.1108/02635570810876750

Wormus, T. (2008). Complex Event Processing: Analytics and Complex Event Processing: Adding Intelligence to the Event Chain. *Business Intelligence Journal, 13*(4), 53–58.

Wu, C., Yu, L., & Jang, F. (2005). Using Semantic Dependencies to Mine Depressive Symptoms from Consultation Records. *IEEE Intelligent Systems, 20*(6), 50–59. doi:10.1109/MIS.2005.115

Zeller, J. (2007). Business Intelligence: The Chicken or the Egg. Retrieved from http://www.information-management.com/bissues/20070601/2600340-1.html.

Zeller, J. (2008). Business Intelligence: The Road Trip. *Information Management Special Reports, December 2, 2008,* Retrieved from http://www.information-management.com/specialreports/2008112/100002266-1.html.

Zhang, X., Hu, X., Xia, J., Zhou, X., & Achananuparp, P. (2008). A Graph-Based Biomedical Literature Clustering Approach Utilizing Term's Global and Local Importance Information. *International Journal of Data Warehousing and Mining, 4*(4), 84–101.

KEY TERMS AND DEFINITIONS

Architecture: General structure and logical organization of a systems.

Business Intelligence: BI refers to information systems aimed at integrating structured and unstructured data in order to convert it into useful information and knowledge, upon which business managers can make more informed and consequently better decisions.

Business Users: Usually business users have low technical skills and use Information System to help him/her run his/her business.

Data Mining Language: A data mining language allows users to directly manipulate data and models at the same level.

Data Mining: One of the phases of the KDD process and concerns, mainly, to the means by which the patterns/models are extracted and enumerated from data.

Framework: A structure intended to serve as a support or guide.

Inductive Database: In an Inductive Database data and models are stored on the same database and can be queried.

Integration: The process by which a new element adapts to a system, thus allowing its inclusion.

Relational Model: According to Codd's Relational Model a database consists of a set of relations. Each relation is a set of tuples.

Standards: That obeys to settled parameters.

Chapter 7
Shadow Sensitive SWIFT:
A Commit Protocol for Advanced Data Warehouses

Udai Shanker
Madan Mohan Malviya Engineering College, India

Abhay N. Singh
Madan Mohan Malviya Engineering College, India

Abhinav Anand
Madan Mohan Malviya Engineering College, India

Saurabh Agrawal
Madan Mohan Malviya Engineering College,, India

ABSTRACT

This chapter proposes Shadow Sensitive SWIFT commit protocol for Distributed Real Time Database Systems (DRTDBS), where only abort dependent cohort having deadline beyond a specific value ($T_{shadow\_creation\_time}$) can forks off a replica of itself called a shadow, whenever it borrows dirty value of a data item. The new dependencies Commit-on-Termination external dependency between final commit operations of lender and shadow of its borrower and Begin-on-Abort internal dependency between shadow of borrower and borrower itself are defined. If there is serious problem in commitment of lender, execution of borrower is started with its shadow by sending YES-VOTE message piggy bagged with the new result to its coordinator after aborting it and abort dependency created between lender and borrower due to update-read conflict is reversed to commit dependency between shadow and lender with read-update conflict and commit operation governed by Commit-on-Termination dependency. The performance of Shadow Sensitive SWIFT is compared with shadow PROMPT, SWIFT and DSS-SWIFT commit protocols (Haritsa, Ramamritham, & Gupta, 2000; Shanker, Misra, & Sarje, 2006; Shanker, Misra, Sarje, & Shisondia, 2006) for both main memory resident and disk resident databases with and without communication delay. Simulation results show that the proposed protocol improves the system performance up to 5% as transaction miss percentage.

DOI: 10.4018/978-1-60960-067-9.ch007

INTRODUCTION

Database systems are currently being used as backbone to thousands of applications. Some of these have very high demands for high availability and fast real-time responses. Typically, these systems generate a very large transaction workload against the distributed real time database, and a large part of the workload consists of read, write and update transactions. Unavailability of real time or slow response in processing these transactions used by business applications could, however, be financially devastating and, in worst case, cause injuries or deaths. Examples include telecommunication systems, trading systems, online gaming, sensor networks etc. Typically, a sensor network consists of a number of sensors (both wired and wireless) which report on the status of some real-world conditions. The conditions include sound, motion, temperature, pressure & moisture, velocity etc. The sensors send their data to a central system that makes decisions based on both present and past inputs. To enable the networks to make better decisions, both the number of sensors and the frequency of updates should be increased. Thus, sensor networks must be able to tolerate an increasing load. For applications such as health care in a hospital, automatic car driving systems, space shuttle control, etc., data is needed in real-time and must be extremely reliable as any unavailability or extra delay could result in loss of human lives (Huang, 1991).

Recent years have seen increasing interest in providing support for warehouse-like systems that support fine-granularity insertions of new data and even occasional updates of incorrect or missing historical data; these modifications need to be supported concurrently with traditional updates. Such systems are useful for providing flexible load support in traditional warehouse settings for reducing the delay for real-time data visibility and for supporting other specialized domains such as Customer Relationship Management (CRM) and data mining where there is a large quantity of data that is frequently added to the database in addition to a substantial number of read-only analytical queries to generate reports and to mine relationships. These "updatable warehouses" have the same requirements of high availability and disaster recovery as traditional warehouses but also require some form of concurrency control, commit protocol and recovery to ensure transactional semantics.

Data mining is the art and science of extracting hidden patterns from the accumulated data for decision-making. It has emerged as a valuable decision support tool with the recognition that:

1. Data Mining and advanced statistical techniques provide insights into data that mere slicing and dicing does not.
2. The human mind's ability to handle complexity is limited.
3. The advances in computing have made the cost of storing and processing data very affordable.

The three essential requisites of good data mining initiatives are:

1. Domain expertise in the area of business
2. Extensive knowledge of data mining tools, advanced statistics and modeling expertise
3. A data mining vision that includes willingness to commit time and other resources.

Many applications listed above using DRT-DBS require distributed transaction executed at more than one site. Traditional log-based systems require sites force-write log records to disk at various stages of commit processing in order to ensure atomicity. A commit protocol ensures that either all the effects of the transaction persist or none of them persist despite the failure of site or communication link and loss of messages. The Commit processing should add as little overhead as possible to transaction processing. Therefore, the design of a better commit protocol is very important for DRTDBS.

BACKGROUND

The Two Phase Commit protocol (2PC) referred to as the Presumed Nothing 2PC protocol (PrN) is the most commonly used protocol in the study of DDBS (Attaluri, Gopi, & Salem, 2002; Gray & Reuter, 1993; Gray, 1978). It guarantees uniform commitment of the distributed transaction by maintaining logs and by exchanging explicit messages among the sites. In the absence of failures, the protocol is straightforward in that a commit decision is reached if all cohorts are ready to commit, otherwise an abort decision is taken. Assuming no failures, it works as follows.

1. The coordinator sends a VOTE-REQ (vote request) message to all cohorts.
2. When a cohort receives a VOTE-REQ, it responds by sending a YES (PREPARED) or NO VOTE (ABORTED) to the coordinator. If the cohort votes NO, it decides to abort and stops.
3. The coordinator collects the VOTE messages from all cohorts. If all of them are YES and the coordinator's VOTE is also YES, the coordinator decides to COMMIT and sends COMMIT messages to all cohorts. Otherwise, the coordinator decides to abort and sends ABORT messages to all cohorts that voted YES.
4. Each cohort that voted YES waits for a COMMIT or ABORT message from the coordinator. When it receives the message, it decides accordingly, sends an acknowledgement (ACK) message to the coordinator and stops.
5. Finally, the coordinator, after receiving the ACK messages from all cohorts, writes an end log record, and then forgets the transaction.

The 2PC satisfies the listed rules for atomic commit protocols as long as failures do not occur. However, if due to some reason the communication between cohorts and the coordinator is distracted, it is possible that the cohort is in uncertain state. It can neither abort nor commit since it does not know what the other cohorts and the coordinator have decided. The cohort is in a blocked state and may wait until the failure is corrected. Unfortunately, this blocking may continue for an indefinitely long period of time. To handle the failures, 2PC ensures that the sufficient information is force-written on the stable storage to reach a consistent global decision about the transaction. Hence, 2PC imposes a great deal of overhead on the transaction processing. There has been a lot of research to mitigate the overhead of the 2PC. A number of 2PC variants (Misikangas, 1997) have been proposed and can be classified into following four groups (Inseon & Yeom, 2002).

1. Presumed Abort/Presumed Commit Protocols
2. One Phase Commit Protocols
3. Group Commit Protocols
4. Pre Commit/Optimistic Commit Protocols

Presumed Commit (PC) and Presumed Abort (PA) (Mohan, Lindsay, & Obermarck, 1986) are based on 2PC. Soparkar et al. (1994) have proposed a protocol that allows individual site to unilaterally commit. An optimistic commit protocol and its variant is proposed in Gupta et al. (1996;1997). Enhancement has been made in PROMPT commit protocol (Haritsa, Ramamritham, & Gupta, 2000), which allows executing transactions to borrow data in a controlled manner only from the healthy transactions in their commit phase. However, it does not consider the type of dependencies between two transactions. The impact of buffer space and admission control is also not studied. In case of sequential transaction execution model, the borrower is blocked for sending the WORKDONE message and the next cohort can not be activated at other site for its execution. It will be held up till the lender completes. If its sibling is activated at another site anyway, the cohort at this new site will not get the result of previous site because previous cohort has been blocked for sending of WORKDONE message due to being borrower (Shanker, Misra, & Sarje, 2008).

The concept of Shadow was proposed by Bestavros (1992), Bestavros and Braoudakis (1995) and Bestavros et al. (1993). In this approach, a copy of original transaction known as Shadow is made of the original transaction. The original transaction continues to run uninterrupted, while the shadow transaction is restarted on a different processor and allowed to run concurrently. In other words, two versions of the same transaction are allowed to run in parallel, each one being at a different point of its execution. Obviously, only one of these two transactions will be allowed to commit; the other will be aborted. The concept of Shadow was first used for commit processing in shadow PROMPT which is a modification of PROMPT commit protocol. In shadow PROMPT, a cohort forks off a replica of the transaction, called a shadow, without considering the type of dependency and its fruitfulness, whenever it borrows a data page.

Lam et al. (1999) proposed Deadline-Driven Conflict Resolution (DDCR) protocol which integrates concurrency control and transaction commitment protocol for firm real time transactions. DDCR resolves different transaction conflicts by maintaining three copies of each modified data item (before, after & further) according to the dependency relationship between the lock requester and the lock holder. This not only creates additional workload on the systems but also has priority inversion problem. The serializability of the schedule is ensured by checking the before set and the after sets when a transaction wants to enter the decision phase. The protocol aims to reduce the impact of a committing transaction on the executing transaction which depends on it. The conflict resolution in DDCR is divided into two

parts (a) resolving conflicts at the conflict time; and (b) reversing the commit dependency when a transaction, which depends on a committing transaction, wants to enter in the decision phase and its deadline is approaching.

If data conflict occurs between the executing and committing transactions, system's performance will be affected. Pang and Lam (1998) proposed an enhancement in DDCR called the DDCR with Similarity (DDCR-S) to resolve the executing-committing conflicts in DRTDBS with mixed requirements of criticality and consistency in transactions. In DDCR-S, conflicts involving transactions with looser consistency requirement and the notion of similarity are adopted so that a higher degree of concurrency can be achieved and at the same time the consistency requirements of the transactions can still be met. The simulation results show that the use of DDCR-S can significantly improve the overall system performance as compared with the original DDCR approach.

Based on PROMPT and DDCR protocols, Qin and Liu (2003) proposed Double Space Commit (2SC) protocol. They analyzed and categorized all kind of dependencies that may occur due to data access conflicts between the transactions into two types commit dependency and abort dependency. The 2SC protocol allows a non-healthy transaction to lend its held data to the transactions in its commit dependency set. When the prepared transaction aborts, only the transactions in its abort dependency set are aborted and the transactions in its commit dependency set execute as normal. These two properties of the 2SC reduce the data inaccessibility and the priority inversion that is inherent in distributed real-time commit processing. 2SC protocol uses blind write model. Extensive simulation experiments have been performed to compare the performance of 2SC with that of other protocols such as PROMPT and DDCR. The simulation results show that 2SC has the best performance. Furthermore, it is easy to incorporate it in any current concurrency control protocol.

Ramamritham and Chrysanthis (1996) have given three common types of constraints for the execution history of concurrent transactions. Qin et al. (2003) extend the constraints and give a fourth type of constraint. Then the weak commit dependency and abort dependency between transactions, because of data access conflicts, are analyzed. Based on the analysis, an optimistic commit protocol, Two-Level Commit (2LC) is proposed, which is specially designed for the distributed real time domain. It allows transactions to optimistically access the locked data in a controlled manner, which reduces the data inaccessibility and priority inversion inherent and undesirable in DRTDBS. Furthermore, if the prepared transaction is aborted, the transactions in its weak commit dependency set will execute as normal according to 2LC. Extensive simulation experiments have been performed to compare the performance of 2LC with that of the base protocols PROMPT and DDCR. The simulation results show that 2LC is effective in reducing the number of missed transaction deadlines. Furthermore, it is easy to be incorporated with the existing concurrency control protocols.

The commit protocol proposed by Shanker et al. (2006) first analyzes all kind of dependencies that may arise due to data access conflicts among executing-committing transactions when a committing cohort is allowed to lend its data to an executing cohort. It then proposes a static two-phase locking and high priority based, write-update type, ideal for fast and timeliness commit protocol i.e. SWIFT. In SWIFT, the execution phase of a cohort is divided into two parts, locking phase and processing phase and then, in place of WORKDONE message, WORKSTARTED message is sent just before the start of processing phase of the cohort. Further, the borrower is allowed to send WORKSTARTED message, if it is only commit dependent on other cohorts instead of being blocked as opposed to other existing commit protocol. This reduces the time needed for commit processing and is free from cascaded aborts. To ensure non-violation of ACID properties, checking of completion of processing and the removal of dependency of cohort are required before sending the YES-VOTE message. Simulation results show that SWIFT improves the system performance in comparison to earlier protocol. The SWIFT commit protocol is beneficial only if the database is main memory resident.

The unnecessary creation of shadow by Shadow PROMPT is solved to some extent in Dependency Sensitive Shadow SWIFT (DSS-SWIFT) commit protocol (Shanker, Misra, Sarje, & Shisondia, 2006). In DSS-SWIFT protocol, the cohort forks off a replica of itself called a shadow, whenever it borrows dirty value of a data item, and if, the created dependency is abort type as compared to creating shadow in all cases of dependency in Shadow PROMPT. Also, the health factor of cohort is used for permitting to use dirty value of lender rather than health factor of transaction as whole. However, DSS-SWIFT still creates the non beneficial shadows in some cases.

DISTRIBUTED REAL-TIME DATABASE SYSTEM MODEL

The structure of the simulation model including the description of its various components such as system model, database model, network model, cohort execution model, locking mechanism and the model assumptions is given in Figure 1. The common model for DRTDBS is given below (Shanker, Misra, & Sarje, 2006; Shanker, Misra, Sarje, & Shisondia, 2006). At each site, two types of transactions are generated: global transactions and local transactions. Each global transaction consists of m cohorts, where m is less than or equal to the number of database sites N_{site}. The same model is used for local and global transactions. Each local transaction has a coordinator and a single cohort both executing at the same site. Each transaction consists of N_{oper} number

Figure 1. Distributed real-time database system model

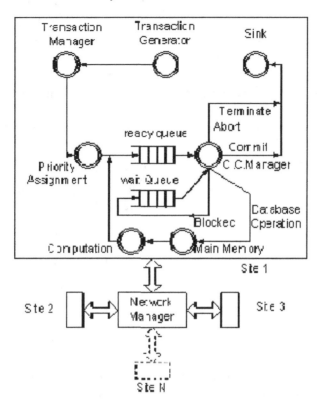

of database operations. Each operation requires locking of data items and then processing.

System Model

Each site consists of a transaction generator, a transaction manager, a concurrency controller, a CPU, a ready queue, a local database, a communication interface, a sink and a wait queue. The transaction generator is responsible for creating the transactions independent to the other sites using Poisson distribution with the given inter-arrival time. The transaction manager generates cohorts on remote site on behalf of the coordinator. Before a cohort performs any operation on a data item, it has to go through the concurrency controller to obtain a lock on that data item. If the request is denied, the cohort is placed in the wait queue. The waiting cohort is awakened when the requested lock is released and all other locks are available. After getting all locks, the cohort accesses the memory and performs computation on the data items. Finally, the cohort commits/aborts and releases all the locks that it is holding. The sink component of the model is responsible for gathering the statistics for the committed or terminated transactions.

Database Model

The database is designed by using a collection of data items that are uniformly distributed across all the sites. Transactions make requests for the data items and concurrency control is implemented at the data item level. No replication of data items at various sites is considered here.

Network Model

A communication network interconnects the sites. There is no global shared memory in the system. All sites communicate via messages exchange over the communication network. The network manager models the behavior of the communication network.

Cohort Execution Model

In this work, authors have considered the parallel execution of cohorts. The coordinator of the transaction spawns all cohorts together by sending messages to remote sites to activate them, lists all operations to be executed at that site and then cohorts may start execution at the same time in parallel. The assumption here is that a cohort does not have to read from its sibling and operations performed by one cohort during its execution are independent of the results of the operations performed by other cohorts at some other sites. In other words, the sibling cohorts do not require any information from each other to share.

Locking Mechanism

The main technique used to control concurrent execution of transactions is based on the concept of locking data items. A lock is a variable associated with a data item that describes the status of the item with respect to possible operations that can be applied to it. Generally there is one lock for each data item in the database. Locks are means for synchronizing the access of concurrent transactions to the database items. A transaction is said to follow the two phase locking protocol if all locking operations precede the first unlock operation in the transaction. There is a number of variations of the Two Phase Locking (2PL) such as Static Two Phase Locking (S2PL) and Dynamic Two Phase Locking (D2PL). The Static 2PL (S2PL) requires a transaction to lock all needed data items before the transaction begins execution, by predeclaring it's read-set and write-set. If any of the predeclared data item cannot be locked, the transaction does not lock any items; instead, it waits until all data items are available for locking.

Model Assumptions

It is assumed that the transactions are firm real time transactions. The model assumptions are listed below.

1. Processing of a transaction requires the use of CPU and data items located at local or remote site.
2. Arrival of the transactions at a site is independent of the arrivals at other sites and uses Poisson distribution.
3. Each transaction pre-declares its read-set (set of data items that the transaction will only read) and update-set (set of data items that the transaction will update).
4. The cohorts are executed in parallel.
5. A lending transaction cannot lend the same data item in read/update mode to more than one cohort to avoid cascaded abort.
6. A cohort already in the dependency set of another cohort cannot permit a third incoming cohort to perform read or update.
7. The communication delay considered is either 0ms or 100ms to study the impact of the network delay on the system.
8. A distributed real time transaction is said to commit, if the coordinator has reached to commit decision before the expiry of the deadline at its site. This definition applies irrespective of whether cohorts have also received and recorded the commit decision by the deadlines.
9. The database is in the main memory or in disk at all sites.

Shadow Sensitive SWIFT

In this sub section, the protocol which is combined with SWIFT is introduced. The conflict resolution in DDCR is solved by resolving the conflicts at the conflict time and reversing the commit dependency when a transaction, which depends on a committing transaction, wants to enter in its decision phase and its deadline is approaching. Here, in case of Write-Read conflict, the dependency can not be reversed if the lender has entered in decision phase. In the following sub section, we will discuss how the problem has been solved in Shadow Sensitive SWIFT with help of the concept of shadowing and deferred commitment of the transaction.

$T_{shadow\_creation\_time}$ Computation

The deadline of a transaction is controlled by the runtime estimate of a transaction and the parameter slack factor, which is the mean of an exponential distribution of slack time. Deadlines are allocated to arriving transactions using the method given below. The deadlines of transactions (both global and local) are calculated based on their expected execution times (Shanker, Misra, & Sarje, 2006; Lam, 1994). The deadline (D_i) of transaction (T_i) is defined as:

$$D_i = A_i + SF*R_i$$

where, A_i is the arrival time of transaction (T_i) at a site; SF is the slack factor; R_i is the minimum transaction response time. As cohorts are executing in parallel, the R_i can be calculated as:

$$R_i = R_p + R_c$$

where, R_p, the time for execution phase and R_c, the time for commitment phase are given as below. For global transaction

$$R_p = \max. ((2*T_{lock} + T_{process})*N_{oper\ local}, (2*T_{lock} + T_{process})*N_{oper\ remote})$$

$$R_c = N_{comm}*T_{com}$$

For local transaction

$$R_p = (2*T_{lock} + T_{process})*N_{oper\ local}$$

$$R_c = 0$$

where, T_{lock} is the time required to lock/unlock a data item; $T_{process}$ is the time to process a data item (assuming read operation takes same amount of time as write operation); N_{comm} is number of messages; T_{com} is communication delay i.e. the constant time estimated for a message going from one site to another; $N_{oper\ local}$ is the number of local operations; $N_{oper\ remote}$ is maximum number of remote operations taken over by all cohorts. If T_2 is abort dependent on T_1

$$T_{shadow\_creation\_time} = R_1 + R_2$$

where, R_1 = Deadline Time of T_1 and R_2 is minimum Time required for T_2 from sending YES-VOTE response to finally committing.

Types of Dependencies

Sharing of data items in conflicting mode creates dependencies among conflicting transactions and constraints their commit order. It is assumed that a cohort requests an update lock if it wants to update a data item x. The prepared cohorts, called as lenders, lend uncommitted data to concurrently executing transactions known as borrower. If a cohort fork off a replica of the transaction, it is called as shadow. The original incarnation of the transaction continues its execution, while the shadow is blocked after finishing its execution. If the lender finally commits, the borrower continues its on-going execution and the shadow is discarded; otherwise, borrower is aborted due to abort of lender and shadow is activated. Two new dependencies are defined apart from commit and abort dependencies. The modified definitions of dependencies used in this chapter are given below:

Commit Dependency (CD). If a transaction T_2 updates a data items read by another transaction T_1, a commit dependency is created from T_2 to T_1. Here, T_2 is called as commit dependent and is not allowed to commit until T_1 commits.

Abort Dependency (AD). If T_2 reads/updates an uncommitted data item updated by T_1, an abort dependency is created from T_2 to T_1. Here, T_2 is called as abort dependent. T_2 aborts, if T_1 aborts and T_2 is not allowed to commit before T_1.

Begin-on-Abort Dependency (BAD). This dependency is created between shadow and borrower who created it. Here, shadow of cohort will be activated, only if borrower aborts due to abort of its lender.

Commit-on-Termination Dependency (CTD). This dependency is created between final commit operations of lender and shadow of its borrower. The final commit operation by a lender is deferred and resumed only after termination (i.e. commit or aborts) of shadow.

Here, BAD is internal dependency while others are external dependencies (Xin, 2006). Each site maintains shadow set (DDDS) also, which is the set of shadows of those cohorts that are abort dependent on lender and deadline beyond $T_{shadow\_creation\_time}$.

DDDS (S_i): Shadow of those cohorts which are in abort dependency set of T_1

Hence, if T_2 is abort dependent on T_1 and fulfills the shadow creation criteria, then Shadow of T_2, S_2 is created and added in DDDS (T_1). Each transaction/cohort T_i, that lends its data while in prepared state to an executing transaction/cohort T_j, maintains three/four sets.

- Commit Dependency Set CDS (T_i): set of commit dependent borrower T_j, that has borrowed dirty data from lender T_i.
- Abort Dependency Set ADS (T_i): set of abort dependent borrower T_j that has borrowed dirty data from lender T_i.
- Begin-on-Abort Dependency Set BAD (T_j): set of shadow of borrower T_j who has created it. T_j has borrowed dirty data from lender T_i.
- Commit-on-Termination Dependency Set CTD (T_j): set of shadow of a borrower attached with its lender whose dependency has been reversed.

Type of Dependency in Different Cases of Data Conflicts

When data conflicts occur, there are three possible cases of conflicts.

Case 1: Read-Update Conflict

If T_2 requests update-lock while T_1 is holding a read-lock, a commit dependency is defined from T_2 to T_1. The transaction id of T_2 is added to the CDS (T_1). Then, T_2 acquires the update-lock.

Case 2: Update-Update Conflict

If both locks are update-locks and HF(T_1)≥MinHF, an abort dependency is defined from T_2 to T_1. The transaction id of T_2 is added to ADS (T_1). T_2 acquires the update-lock; otherwise, T_2 is blocked. In case of getting update-lock, the shadow of T_2 is only created and added to DDDS (S_i), if T_2 qualifies for shadow creation criteria. The transaction id of T_2 is added to BAD (T_2).

Case 3: Update-Read Conflict

If T_2 requests a read-lock while T_1 is holding an update-lock and HF (T_1)≥MinHF, an abort dependency is defined from T_2 to T_1. The transaction id of T_2 is added to ADS (T_1). T_2 acquires the read-lock. In case of getting read-lock, the shadow of T_2 is only created and added to DDDS (S_i), if T_2 qualifies for shadow creation criteria. The transaction id of T_2 is added to BAD (T_2).

The lock manager processes the data item accesses in conflicting mode as seen in Algorithm 1.

Mechanics of Interaction between Lender and Borrower Cohorts

If T_2 accesses a data item already locked by T_1, one of the following four scenarios may arise.

Scenario 1: T_1 Receives Decision before T_2 has Completed its Local Data Processing

- If the global decision is to commit,
  - ○ T_1 commits. All cohorts in ADS (T_1) & CDS (T_1) will execute as usual.
  - ○ T_2 completes its commit operation, if it has been deferred.
  - ○ Sets of ADS (T_1), BAD (T_2), DDDS (S_i) & CDS (T_1) will be deleted.

- If the global decision is to abort,
  - ○ T_1 aborts. Cohorts in the dependency set of T_1 will execute as follows:
  - ○ T_2 completes its commit operation, if it has been deferred.

Shadows of all cohorts Begin-on-Abort Dependent on T_2 in DDDS (S_i) will be activated and sends YES-VOTE to their coordinator, only if they can complete execution; otherwise, discarded;

Transactions in CDS (T_1) will execute normally.

Delete Set ADS (T_1), BAD (T_2), DDDS (S_i) and CDS (T_1).

Scenario 2: T_2 is about to Start Processing Phase after Getting all its Locks before T_1 Receives Global Decision

T_2 sends WORKSTARTED message to its coordinator.

Algorithm 1.

```
If (T2 CD T1)
{
        CDS (T1) =CDS (T1) {T2};
        T2 is granted Update lock;
}
else
{
        if ((T2 AD T1) AND (HF(T1) ≥ MinHF))
        {
                ADS (T1) =ADS (T1) {T2};
                T2 is granted the requested lock;
                If (deadline (T2)>Tshadow_creation_time)
                {
                        Add shadow of T2 in DDDS (Si);
                        BAD (T2) =BAD (T2) {T2's shadow};
                }
        }
        else if (T2 has read dirty value of T1 and received VOTE-REQ message from its coordinator)
        {
                CDS (shadow (T2)) =CDS (shadow (T2)){T1};
                CTD (T1) = CTD (T1) {T2};
Shadow of T2 is activated and granted the requested lock after aborting T2 and deleting T2 from ADS (T1);
        }
}
```

Scenario 3: T_2 Aborts before T_1 Receives Decision

In this situation, all works carried out by T_2 are undone and T_2 is removed from the dependency set of T_1.

Scenario 4: T_2 has Read Dirty Value of T_1 and Received Vote-Req Message From its Coordinator before T_1 Receives Commit Decision Message.

Abort T_2 and Delete T_2 from ADS (T_1).
  Activate execution of T_2 with its shadow.
  Add T_2 in CTD (T_1).
  Shadow sends YES-VOTE message piggy bagged with the new result to its coordinator.

Algorithm

On the basis of above discussions, the complete pseudo code of the protocol is given in Algorithm 2.

Main Contributions

1. Abort dependent cohort having deadline beyond a specific value ($T_{shadow\_creation\_time}$) can only forks off a replica of itself called a shadow.
2. Two new dependencies Begin-on-Abort and Commit-on-Termination are defined.
3. Reversing of abort dependency created between lender and borrower due to Update-Read conflict to commit dependency between shadow of borrower and lender. The final commit operations of lender and shadow is governed by Commit-on-Termination Dependency.
4. On activation of borrower transaction with help of shadow, it sends YES-VOTE message piggy bagged with the new result to its coordinator in case of abort of lender & borrower.

To maintain consistency of database, cohort sends the YES-VOTE in response to its coordinator's VOTE-REQ message only when its dependencies are removed & it has finished its processing, and, in case of reversal of dependency, final commit operation by a lender is deferred and resumed only after termination (i.e. commit or aborts) of shadow.

Performance Measures and Evaluation

The default values of different parameters for simulation experiments are given below in Table 1 and same as taken in Shanker (2006) and Lam (1994). The concurrency control scheme used is static two phase locking with higher priority (Lam, Hung, & Son, 1997). Miss Percentage (MP) is the primary performance measure used in the experiments and is defined as the percentage of input transactions that the system is unable to complete on or before their deadlines (Ulusoy, 1992). Since, there were no practical benchmark programs available in the market or with research communities (Lee, Lam, & Kao, 1999) to evaluate the performance of protocols and algorithms, an event driven based simulator was written in C language (Taina & Son, 1999). In the simulation used, a small database (200 data items per site) is used to create high data contention environment. For each set of experiment, the final results are calculated as an average of 10 independents runs. In each run, 100000 transactions are initiated.

Simulation Results

Simulation was done for both the main memory resident and the disk resident databases at communication delay of 0ms and 100ms. Shadow Sensitive SWIFT is compared with shadow PROMPT, SWIFT and DSS-SWIFT in this experiment. Figure 2, Figure 3, Figure 4, Figure 5 and Figure 6 show the Miss Percent behaviour under normal and heavy load conditions with/ without communication delay. In these graphs,

Algorithm 2.

```
if (T₁ receives global decision before, T₂ ends execution)
{if (T₁ is in Commit-on-Termination Dependency Set)
 Defer commit processing till termination of shadow.
 else
 {
 One: if (T₁'s global decision is to commit)
 {
 T₁ enters in the decision phase;
 T₂ completes its commit operation, if it has been deferred.
 Delete sets of ADS (T₁), BAD (T₂), DDDS (Sᵢ) and CDS (T₁);
 }
 else //T₁'s global decision is to abort
 {
 T₁ aborts;
 T₂ completes its commit operation, if it has been deferred.
 Transactions in CDS (T₁) will execute as usual.
 For all the abort dependent cohorts
 {
 if (shadow)
             {
                 IF (Shadow of cohort can complete its execution)
                   Execute Cohorts Shadow in DDDS (Sᵢ) and send YES-VOTE;
 else
 Discard shadow;
             }
 }
 Delete sets of ADS (T₁), BAD (T₂), DDDS (Sᵢ) and CDS (T₁);
 }
 }
 }
 else
 {
 if (T₂ aborted by higher transaction before T₁ receives decision OR T₂ expires its deadline)
 {
 Undo the computation of T₂;
 Abort T₂;
 Delete T₂ from CDS (T₁) & ADS (T₁);
 if (shadow)
 Delete T₂ from DDDS (Si);
 }
 else if (T₂ ends executing phase before T₁ receives global decision)
 T₂ sends WORKSTARTED message;

             else if (T₂ has read dirty value of T₁ and received VOTE-REQ message from its coordinator)
                 {
 Shadow of T₂ is activated and granted the requested lock after aborting T₂ and deleting T₂ from ADS (T₁);
 Shadow sends YES-VOTE message piggy bagged with the new result;
                 }
 }
```

the authors observe that there is a noticeable difference between the performances of the various commit protocols throughout loading range first.

Let us consider the case of update-read conflict. If there is serious problem in commitment of lender, the final commit decision can be delayed for an indefinite time. Meanwhile, it is possible that borrower has received VOTE-REQ message from its coordinator. Now, the execution of transaction can be started with borrower's shadow after aborting borrower itself and abort dependency created between lender and borrower due

Table 1. Default values for the model parameters

Parameters	Meaning	Default setting
N_{site}	Number of Site	4
AR	Transaction Arrival Rate	4 Transactions/ Second
T_{com}	Communication Delay	100 ms (Constant)
SF	Slack Factor	1-4 (Uniform Distribution)
N_{oper}	No. of Operations in a Transaction	3-20 (Uniform Distribution)
PageCPU	CPU Page Processing Time	5 ms
PageDisk	Disk Page Processing Time	20 ms
DBsize	Database Size	200 Data Objects/Site
P_{write}	Write Operation Probability	0.60

to update-read conflict is reversed to commit dependency between shadow and lender with read-update conflict. Now, the shadow sends YES-VOTE message piggy bagged with the new result (initial value of data item) to its coordinator. In this way, shadow and lender can proceed for their execution without any further much delay

and interferences. Only, the final commit operations of lender will be deferred till termination of shadow.

Again, let us take the case of update-update or update-read conflicts. If the lender and, in turn, its borrower have been aborted, the execution of borrower transaction can be started with its shadow

Figure 2. Miss% with (RC+DC) at Communication Delay= 0ms, Normal & Heavy Load. Main Memory Resident Database.

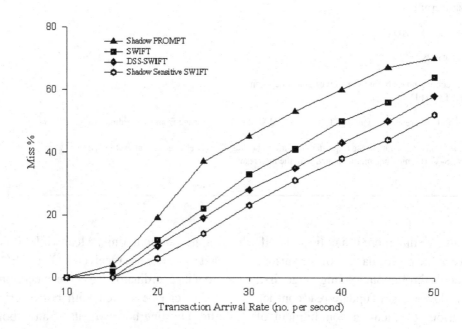

Figure 3. Miss% with (RC+DC) at Communication Delay= 100ms, Normal & Heavy Load. Main Memory Resident Database

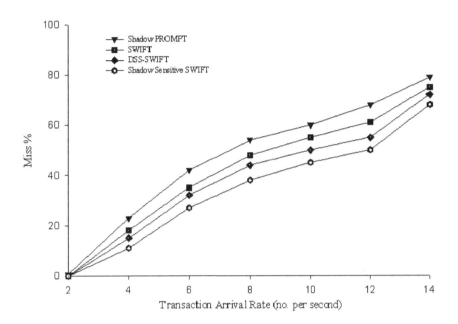

Figure 4. Miss% with (RC+DC) at Communication Delay= 0ms, Normal Load. Disk Resident Database

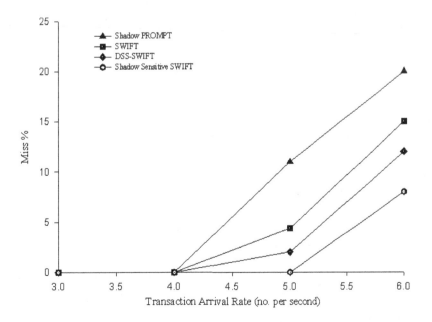

Figure 5. Miss% with (RC+DC) at Communication Delay= 0ms, Heavy Load. Disk Resident Database

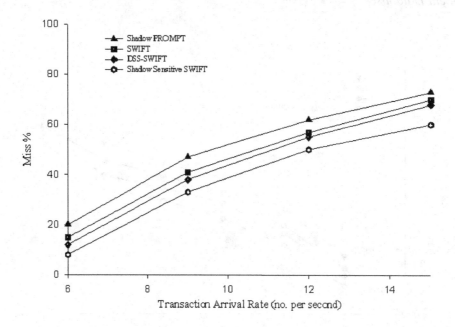

Figure 6. Miss% with (RC+DC) at Communication Delay=10 0ms, Normal & Heavy Load. Disk Resident Database

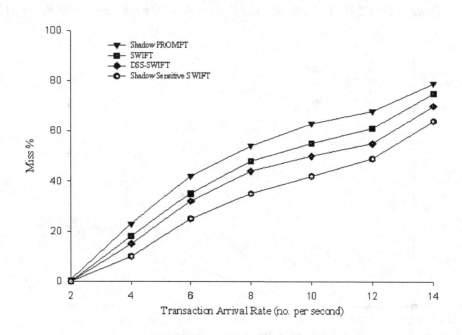

in case of any chance of completion. Here, the shadow sends YES-VOTE message piggy bagged with the new result (initial value of data item) to its coordinator because it has completed all the activities parallel with borrower's execution.

In both the above cases, the survival of transaction with borrower's shadow utilizes the concept of single phase commit protocol but sends YES-VOTE message as compared to WORKDONE Message. Due to this reason, it is free from disadvantage of single phase commit protocol of long duration data item locking. Here the work done by borrower is never wasted in most of the cases even if a wrong borrowing decision is made. Due to aforementioned reason, Shadow Sensitive SWIFT minimizes the number of messages needed for execution and commit of cohort, and is also free from long duration locking of data items. Hence, the Shadow Sensitive SWIFT commit protocol provides a performance that is significantly better than other commit protocols.

Disk Resident Database

FUTURE RESEARCH DIRECTIONS

Following are some suggestions to extend this work (Shanker, Misra, & Sarje, 2001; Shanker, 2006).

- Performance studies are based on the assumption that there is no replication. Hence, a study of relative performance of the topic discussed here deserves a further look under assumption of replicated data.
- The work can be extended for Mobile DRTDBS, pear-to-pear database systems, grid database systems etc. where memory space, power and communication bandwidth are bottleneck. There is a need to design various protocols for different purposes that may suit to the specific need of hand held devices.

- The integration and the performance evaluation of proposed commit protocol with 1PC and 3PC protocols.
- Although tremendous research efforts have been reported in the hard real time systems in dealing with hard real time constraints, very little work has been reported in hard real time database systems. So, the performance of Shadow Sensitive SWIFT can be evaluated for hard real time constrained transactions.
- Biomedical Informatics is quickly evolving into a research field that encompasses the use of all kinds of biomedical information, from genetic and proteomic data to image data associated with particular patients in clinical settings. Biomedical Informatics comprises the fields of Bioinformatics (e.g., genomics and proteomics) and Medical Informatics (e.g., medical image analysis), and deals with issues related to the access to information in medicine, the analysis of genomics data, security, interoperability and integration of data-intensive biomedical applications. Main issues in this field is provision of large computing power such that researchers have access to high performance distributed computational resources for computationally demanding data analysis, e.g., medical image processing and simulation of medical treatment or surgery and large storage capacity and distributed databases for efficient retrieval, annotation and archiving of biomedical data. What is missing today is full integration of methods and technologies to enhance all phases of biomedical informatics and health care, including research, diagnosis, prognosis, etc. and dissemination of such methods in the clinical practice, whenever they are developed, deployed and maintained. Hence it is another topic of research interest.

CONCLUSION

This chapter presents a new commit protocol Shadow Sensitive SWIFT with the help of Commit-on-Termination dependency between final commit operations of lender and shadow of its borrower, and Begin-on-Abort dependency between shadow of borrower and borrower itself. In case of delay in commitment of lender due to some serious problem, the execution of transaction is started via reversing the abort dependency with commit dependency in between borrower's shadow and lender with read-update conflict and final commit operation of lender is permitted to resume only after the termination of shadow. Also, the shadow has been allowed to send YES-VOTE message piggy bagged with the new result to its coordinator in case of abort of lender & borrower and activation of execution of transaction with help of borrower's shadow. In this way, the Shadow Sensitive SWIFT improves the system performance up to 5% by minimizing long duration locking of data items and reducing the number of messages needed for commit of cohort. It is very much beneficial in abort oriented system. It ensures the survival of transaction with shadowing approach.

REFERENCES

Attaluri, Gopi, K., & Salem, K. (2002). The Presumed-Either Two-Phase Commit Protocol. *IEEE Transactions on Knowledge and Data Engineering, 14(5)*, 1190-1196.

Bestavros, A. (1992). Speculative Concurrency Control. *Technical Report TR-16-92*. Boston University, Boston, MA.

Bestavros, A., & Braoudakis, S. (1995). Value Cognizant Speculative Concurrency Control. In *21st VLDB Conference*. Zurich, Switzerland.

Bestavros, A., Braoudakis, S., & Panagos, E. (1993). Performance Evaluation of Two-Shadow Speculative Concurrency Control. *Technical Report 1993-001*. Boston University, Boston, MA.

Gray, J. (1978). Notes on Database Operating Systems. Operating Systems: An Advanced Course. *Lecture Notes in Computer Science, Springer Verlag, 60*, 393–481.

Gray, J., & Reuter, A. (1993). *Transaction Processing: Concepts and Technique*. San Mateo, CA: Morgan Kaufman.

Gupta, R. Haritsa, J. R., & Ramamritham, K. (1997). More Optimism About Real-Time Distributed Commit Processing. *Technical Report TR-97-04*. Database System Lab, Supercomputer Education and Research Centre, I.I.Sc. Bangalore, India

Gupta, R., Haritsa, J. R., Ramamritham, K., & Seshadri, S. (1996). Commit Processing in Distributed Real Time Database Systems. *Real-time Systems Symposium*. Washington DC, San Francisco.

Haritsa, J. R., Ramamritham, K., & Gupta, R. (2000). The PROMPT Real Time Commit Protocol. *IEEE Transactions on Parallel and Distributed Systems, 11*(2), 160–181. doi:10.1109/71.841752

Huang, J. (1991). *Real Time Transaction Processing: Design, Implementation and Performance Evaluation*. Unpublished doctoral dissertation, University of Massachusetts, USA.

Inseon, L., & Yeom, H. Y. (2002). A Single Phase Distributed Commit Protocol for Main Memory Database Systems. In *16th International Parallel & Distributed Processing Symposium (IPDPS 2002)*. Ft. Lauderdale, Florida, USA.

Lam, K. Y. (1994). *Concurrency Control in Distributed Real-Time Database Systems*. Unpublished doctoral dissertation, City University of Hong Kong, Hong Kong.

Lam, K. Y., Hung, S. L., & Son, S. H. (1997). On Using Real-Time Static Locking Protocols for Distributed Real-Time Databases. *Real-Time Systems*, *13*, 141–166.doi:10.1023/A:1007981523223

Lam, K. Y., Pang, C., Son, S. H., & Cao, J. (1999). Resolving Executing-Committing Conflicts in Distributed Real - time Database Systems. *Journals of Computer*, *42*(8), 674–692. doi:10.1093/comjnl/42.8.674

Lee, Victor C. S., Lam, K. Y., & Kao, B. (1999). Priority Scheduling of Transactions in Distributed Real - Time Databases. *International Journal of Time-Critical Computing Systems*, *16*, 31–62.

Misikangas, P. (1997). *2PL and its Variants.* Seminar on Real - Time Systems. Department of Computer Science, University of Helsinki.

Mohan, C., Lindsay, B., & Obermarck, R. (1986). Transaction Management in the R* Distributed Database Management System. *ACM Transactions on Database Systems*, *11*(4). doi:10.1145/7239.7266doi:10.1145/7239.7266

Pang, C. L., & Lam, K. Y. (1998). On Using Similarity for Resolving Conflicts at Commit in Mixed Distributed Real-time Databases. In *5th International Conference on Real - Time Computing Systems and Applications*.

Qin, B., & Liu, Y. (2003). High Performance Distributed Real-time Commit Protocol. *Journal of Systems and Software, Elsevier Science Inc.*, *68*(2), 145–152.

Qin, B., Liu, Y., & Yang, J. C. (2003). A Commit Strategy for Distributed Real-Time Transaction. *Journal of Computer Science and Technology*, *18*(5), 626–631. doi:10.1007/BF02947122

Ramamritham, K., & Chrysanthis, P. K. (1996). A Taxonomy of Correctness Criteria in Database Applications. *Journal of the VLDB*, *5*, 85–97. doi:10.1007/s007780050017

Shanker, U. (2006). *Some Performance Issues in Distributed Real Time Database Systems.* Unpublished doctoral dissertation, Department of Electronics & Computer Engineering, Indian Institute of Technology Roorkee, India.

Shanker, U., Misra, M., & Sarje, Anil K. (2001). Hard Real-Time Distributed Database Systems: Future Directions. In *All India Seminar on Recent Trends in Computer Communication Networks* (pp. 172-177). Department of Electronics & Computer Engineering, Indian Institute of Technology Roorkee, India.

Shanker, U., Misra, M., & Sarje, Anil K. (2006). SWIFT- A New Real Time Commit Protocol. [Springer Verlag]. *International Journal of Distributed and Parallel Databases*, *20*(1), 29–56. doi:10.1007/s10619-006-8594-8

Shanker, U., & Misra, M. Sarje, Anil K., & Shisondia, R. (2006). Dependency Sensitive Shadow SWIFT. In *10th International Database Applications and Engineering Symposium* (pp. 373-376). Delhi, India.

Shanker, U., Misra, M., & Sarje, Anil K. (2008). Distributed Real Time Database Systems: Background and Literature Review. [Springer Verlag.]. *International Journal of Distributed and Parallel Databases*, *23*(2), 127–149. doi:10.1007/s10619-008-7024-5

Soparkar, N., Levy, E., Korth, H. F., & Silberschatz, A. (1994). Adaptive Commitment for Real - Time Distributed Transaction. In *3rd International Conference on Information and Knowledge Management* (pp.187-104). Gaithersburg, Maryland, United States.

Taina, J., & Son, S. H. (1999). Towards a General Real-Time Database Simulator Software Library. In *Proceedings of the Active and Real-Time Database Systems*.

Ulusoy, O. (1992). *Concurrency Control in Real-time Database Systems*. Unpublished doctoral dissertation, Department of Computer Science, University of Illinois, Urbana-Champaign, USA.

Xin, T. (2006). *A Framework for Processing Generalized Advanced Transactions*. Unpublished doctoral dissertation, Department of Computer Science, Colorado State University, USA.

ADDITIONAL READING

Agrawal, D., Abbadi, A. El., & Jeffers, R. (1992). Using Delayed Commitment in Locking Protocols for Real-Time Databases. In *ACM International Conference on Management of Data* (pp. 104-113). San Diego, California.

Agrawal, D., Abbadi, A. El., Jeffers, R., & Lin, L. (1995). Ordered Shared Locks for Real-time Databases. *International Journal on Very Large Data Bases, 4*(1), 87–126. doi:10.1007/BF01232473

Agrawal, S., & Abhay, N. Singh., Anand, A., & Shanker, U. (2010). SPEEDITY-A Real Time Commit Protocol. In *Proceedings of the International Conference on Futuristic Computer Applications*. IISc Bangalore, India, March 20-21.

Bestavros, A., Lin, K. J., & Son, S. H. (1997). *Real-Time Database Systems: Issues and Applications*. Kluwer Academic Publishers.

Boutros, S. Boutros, & Desai, B. C. (1996). A Two-Phase Commit Protocol and its Performance. In *7th IEEE International Workshop on Database and Expert Systems Applications* (pp. 100-105). Zurich, Switzerland.

Cooper, E. C. (1982). Analysis of Distributed Commit Protocols. In *Proceedings of the ACM International Conference on Management of Data (SIGMOD)* (pp. 175-183). Orlando, Florida.

Davidson, S. B., Lee, I., & Wolfe, V. (1991). Timed Atomic Commitment. *IEEE Transactions on Computers, 40*(5), 573–583. doi:10.1109/12.88481

Georgakopoulos, D. (1992). A Framework for Dynamic Specification of Extended Multidatabase Transactions and Interdatabase Dependencies. In *3rd Workshop on Heterogeneous Databases and Semantic Interoperability*.

Ghafoor, A., & Berra, P. B. (1989). An Efficient Communication Structure for Distributed Commit Protocols. *IEEE Journal on Selected Areas in Communications, 7*(3), 375–389. doi:10.1109/49.16870

Gray, J., & Lamport, L. (2004). Consensus on Transaction Commit. *MSR-TR-2003-96, 32*.

Gupta, R. (2000). *Commit Processing in Distributed On-Line and Real-time Transaction Processing Systems*. Unpublished Master of Science (Engineering) dissertation. Supercomputer Education and Research Centre, IISc Bangalore, India.

Gupta, R., & Haritsa, J. R. (1996). Commit Processing in Distributed Real-Time Database Systems. In *National Conference on Software for Real-Time Systems* (pp. 195-204). Cochin, India.

Haritsa, J. R., & Ramamritham, K. (2000). Real-Time Database Systems in the New Millennium. *Journal of Real Time Systems, 19*(3), 1–5.

Juhnyoung, L. (1994). *Concurrency Control Algorithms for Real - time Database Systems*. Unpublished doctoral dissertation, Department of Computer Science, University of Virginia, USA.

Kao, B., & Garcia-Monila, H. (1995). An Overview of Real-time Database Systems. *Advances in Real-time Systems*, 463-486.

Kim, Y. K. (1995). *Predictability and Consistency in Real Time Transaction Processing*. Unpublished doctoral dissertation, University of Virginia, USA.

Lindstrom, J. (2003). *Optimistic Concurrency Control Method for Distributed Real Time Database Systems*. Unpublished doctoral dissertation, Helsinki University, Finland.

Liu, M. L., Agrawal, D., & El Abbadi, A. (1994). The Performance of Two-Phase Commit Protocols in the Presence of Site Failures. In *24ᵗʰ International Symposium on Fault-Tolerant Computing* (pp. 234-243). Austin, Texas.

Mitrani, I. (1987). *Modeling of Computer and Communication Systems*. Cambridge, UK: Cambridge University Press.

Mittal, A., & Dandamudi, S. P. (2004). Dynamic versus Static Locking in Real-Time Parallel Database Systems. In *18ᵗʰ International Parallel and Distributed Processing Symposium*. Santa Fe, New Mexico.

Nagaraj, P. K. (1998). *Commit Processing in Distributed Secure and Real-time Transaction Processing Systems*. Unpublished M. E dissertation, Department of Computer Science, B.M.S. College of Engineering, Bangalore University, India.

Ramamritham, K. (1993). Real-time Databases. *Distributed and Parallel Databases. Special Issue: Research Topics in Distributed and Parallel Databases, 1*(2), 199–226. doi:10.1007/BF01264051

Ryu, I. K., & Thomasian, A. (1990). Analysis of Database Performance with Dynamic Locking. *Journal of the Association for Computing Machinery, 37*(3), 491–523.

Shanker, U., & Misra, M. (2006). Some Performance Issues in Distributed Real Time Database Systems. In VLDB PhD Workshop (2006). *The Convention and Exhibition Center (COEX)*. Seoul, Korea: Sarje, Anil K.

Soparkar, N., Levy, E., Korth, H. F., & Silberschatz, A. (1992). Adaptive Commitment for Real-time Distributed Transaction. *Technical Report TR-92-15*. Department of Computer Science, University of Texas, Austin.

Srinivas, R. (2002). *Network-Aided Concurrency Control in Distributed Databases*. Unpublished doctoral dissertation, University of Virginia, USA

Stankovic, J., Son, S. H., & Hansson, J. (1999). Misconception about Real-Time Database. *IEEE Computer, 32*(6), 29–36.

Tay, Y. C. (1995). Some performance issues for transactions with Firm Deadlines. In *Real-Time Systems Symposium* (pp. 322-331). Pisa, Italy.

Ulusoy, O., & Belford, G. (1993). Real-Time Transaction Scheduling in Database Systems. *Information Systems, 18*(8), 559–580. doi:10.1016/0306-4379(93)90024-U

Vrbsky, S. V., & Tomic, S. (1998). Satisfying Timing Constraints of Real Time Databases. *Journal of Systems and Software, 41*, 63–73. doi:10.1016/S0164-1212(97)10007-3

Wolfson, O. (1987). The Overhead of Locking (and Commit) Protocols in Distributed Databases. *ACM Transactions on Database Systems, 12*(3), 452–471. doi:10.1145/27629.28053

KEY TERMS AND DEFINITIONS

Cohort: The transaction manager generates cohorts on local or remote site on behalf of the coordinator to perform any operation on a data item.

Commit Protocols: Ensures that either all the effects of the transaction persist or none of them persist despite of the site or communication link failures and loss of messages.

Data Conflict: When more than one transaction try to use the same data item at the same time then we say that data conflict among them arises.

Deadline: It may be defined as the time allocated to a particular transaction by which it is expected to complete its execution.

Dependency: Sharing of data items in conflicting modes creates dependencies.

Distributed Real Time Database Systems: Collection of multiple, logically inter-related databases distributed over a computer network where transactions have explicit timing constraints, usually in the form of deadlines.

Firm Real Time Transaction: A Firm Real Time transaction loses its return value after its deadline expires.

Shadow: It is the copy of the transaction/cohort which runs in parallel with the transaction/cohort. However it may be noted that either the main transaction/cohort is committed or the shadow is committed but not both.

YES VOTE Message: This is the message sent by cohorts to the coordinator indicating that they are ready to commit.

Chapter 8
Mobile Marketing:
The Challenges of the New Direct Marketing Channel and the Need for Automatic Targeting and Optimization Tools

Giovanni Giuffrida
Universita' di Catania, Italy

Diego Reforgiato
University of Maryland, USA

Catarina Sismeiro
Imperial College London, England

Giuseppe Tribulato
Neodata Group s.r.l., Italy

ABSTRACT

In most developed countries competition among mobile phone operators is now focused on switching customers away from competitors with extremely discounted telephony rates. This fierce competitive environment is the result of a saturated market with small or inexistent growth and has caused operators to rely increasingly on Value-Added Services (VAS) for revenue growth. Though mobile phone operators have thousands of different services available to offer to their customers, the contact opportunities to offer these services are limited. In this context, statistical methods and data mining tools can play an important role to optimize content delivery. In this chapter the authors describe novel methods now available to mobile phone operators to optimize targeting and improve profitability from VAS offers.

INTRODUCTION

The mobile phone market is becoming increasingly saturated and competitive (Leppaniemi & Karjaluoto, 2007). In several European countries mobile phone penetration is now over 100% and first-time customers (new users that enter the market and expand the business) are practically inexistent (The Netsize Guide, 2009). In the US, similar competitive intensity has also become the norm after the introduction of wireless number

DOI: 10.4018/978-1-60960-067-9.ch002

portability by the Federal Communications Commission in November 2003. Facing saturated and stagnant markets, mobile service operators are now focused on attracting competitors' customers. Because one of the main factors influencing customers' operator choice is the availability of a more convenient telephony rate plan, (Eshghi, 2007), mobile operators are relying increasingly on price competition for customer acquisition while revenue expansion comes mostly from *Value-Added Services* (VAS). Examples of these services include the provision of sports information, news, and weather forecasts, download of ring-tones, games, music, short movies, and even TV shows, all for a fee. Occasionally some of these services are offered for free. In such cases the objective of the service is not generating revenue directly but doing so indirectly. For example, revenues can be generated indirectly through the charges related with the data transmission services or the browsing of additional web pages over the phone. In the case of free viral videos aimed at building brand awareness and word-of-mouth, firms usually wish to build or sustain future revenue streams and long-term goals which are even more difficult to assess (future revenues could be associated with product sales both via the mobile phone or offline, depending on the firm that launches the videos). In addition, services may be offered for free in order to improve users' experience, satisfaction, and loyalty. These products or services are produced by the mobile service provider itself or by external content providers, in which case revenue sharing contracts are established: mobile operators and content producers each take a percentage of the revenue generated, with the share of each depending on the type of content and on the power split between organizations.

Push Versus Pull Delivery Systems

In a Pull delivery system (one of the types of VAS delivery system), mobile phone users initiate on their own a search for a product or service they might be willing to buy (e.g., browse sites through the mobile phone to download videos, games, or a new ring-tone). Currently one of the most popular and successful Pull delivery system is the App Store, developed by Apple in conjunction with the iPhone launch. Anyone can now produce applications for the iPhone to be sold worldwide through the App Store once Apple approves the application. The App Store is a "moderated" type of services, that is, Apple has to make sure all material sold through its store is legal, does not violate operator restrictions (these differ from country to country), does not include offensive material, and so on. Apple is ultimately responsible for the applications sold at the store. These applications are also value-added services and the revenues obtained from their sale are split between Apple and the developer who designed and produced the application.

Notice that Apple does not send messages to iPhone users selling ("pushing") these applications, instead mobile users go to the App Store and search for the applications of their interest. These systems can be very successful and generate significant revenue. As a matter of fact, recently Apple announced (Kerris & Bowcock, 2009) that a total amount of more than 1.5 billion applications have been downloaded since its inception and more than 65,000 different applications are today available on its App Store.

Alternatively, in a Push delivery system (the other type of VAS delivery system), the mobile phone operator is the initiator of the communication with the user (i.e., actually it sends an offer to the user) to stimulate the purchase of a specific product/service, or to have the user respond to an offer. In such delivery systems periodically mobile phone operators send text (SMS) and/or multimedia (MMS) messages to mobile phone users that contain typically one or more commercial offers. These offers invite users to subscribe or acquire services and/or to download digital products (e.g., ring-tones, TV shows, video clips) that can be purchased directly from the mobile phone in a few clicks. Messages sent to mobile phones might also direct users to browse additional web pages or download data over the phone, which can also produce additional revenues depending on the type of service contract. Hence, in such Push systems mobile phone users are not the initiator of the communication and do not search for specific applications or products they might need or desire. Mobile phone operators are actively engaged in targeting users with specific offers (Wray & Richard, 2009), and users only need to respond to such offers. Figure 1 presents an example of an MMS commercial message sent to mobile phone users that offers a wallpaper image for download. Mobile users can simply click on the message to download the image and set it as wallpaper on their mobile phone. The cost of the service will be added to their monthly bill or deducted from their pre-paid account.

Push Delivery System

Push delivery system is focused mainly by the authors in this chapter. Their objective is to review and discuss how mobile operators can actively optimize the delivery and targeting of offers to their customer base. The goal of operators is to maximize revenues by delivering the offers with the highest profit potential. From the mobile operators point of view, it is noted that the Push delivery system is in general very cost

Figure 1. An example of a Multi Media Message (MMS) offer as shown on the mobile phone screen

effective. Whereas lower telephony rates that attract new telephony customers place a direct negative pressure on company revenues, and may even produce a (tolerated) loss. This type of Value-Added Services represent an additional revenue source and tend to be associated to significant profits when properly managed. The cost of operations is often dominated by the one-time investment on the message-delivery infrastructure and, subsequently, each message can be sent at zero (or close to zero) marginal cost. As a result, operators can easily reach millions of potential buyers at little cost making the profit potential of these advertising-related services very high.

Despite the great benefits mobile phone operators can extract from these Push value-added services, their effective management poses significant challenges: operators need to target users with a selection of messages from a massive catalogue of offers while facing limited testing capacity and heterogeneity in the content production process. Recently, and in response to these challenges, researchers have developed new tools and methods specific to this direct marketing channel that allow a more profitable use of value-added offers. These tools and methods take advantage of the detailed logs of customer interaction with the offered services kept by current infrastructures. These logs track all the messages and offers sent to a customer and the corresponding feedback (e.g., whether the customer opened a message, viewed a page, bought a video, or clicked on a link). The information contained in these logs can then be used by an automated targeting system to aid message selection and customer targeting.

The chapter reviews and analyzes the challenges faced by mobile operators in managing their VAS systems and discusses some of the methods available to improve profitability for the direct targeting activities of mobile phone operators engaged in the delivery of value-added services. Based on the vast experience in implementing optimization systems in this area, the authors describe many of the experiments they carried out.

Also the findings, which the authors believe, can aid mobile phone operators in the management and design of their offers is also explained. The remaining of this chapter is organized as follows. Next the challenges faced by this new direct marketing channel is described. Then the findings from previous research and from the authors own experiments regarding the management of these services is presented. The chapter concludes with discussing future areas of research in the mobile marketing domain.

CHALLENGES IN THE MANAGEMENT OF MOBILE VAS SYSTEMS

The management of mobile phone value-added services presents several significant challenges, which will be discussed in this section. In the following sections alternative methods that can be employed to deal with such challenges will be described.

Massive Number of Value-Added Service Offers and the Need for Fast-Learning Methods

Because VAS are now a significant revenue source, and central to profitability, mobile phone operators and external production companies have become increasingly creative and extremely fast in generating new services and offers. Virtually anyone with computer skills can create digital content to be offered to mobile users. As a result, production businesses have proliferated in the market and provide new offers to mobile phone operators on a daily basis. In addition, traditional media companies (music labels and TV networks) quickly transform their existing products into content to be delivered via mobile phones.

As a consequence of these market features, the number of alternatives that mobile operators have available to send to mobile phone users is now extremely large and growing quickly. It is not unusual in this context to have tens of thousands of possible products or services to advertise at any moment and, in most cases, the content catalogue grows by dozens of new items a day, a growth rate that is not likely to be reduced. This massive number of offers to be tested and studied poses some difficulties in terms of knowledge discovery. For example, previously the direct marketing industry had used human-intensive methods to classify, optimize, and test different offers and then target these to specific individuals. In the case of the thousands of multimedia messages available in current catalogues to be advertised to mobile users, it is simply too costly, thus prohibitive to rely on human experts for their content classification and testing. Instead, automatic systems that require minimum human intervention become essential.

Finally, because of the sheer size and growth rate of content catalogues and because of the limited life of many of the offers (e.g., many of the offers expire in a matter of few days; some expire on the same day of their release or even in a matter of few hours, as in the case of news videos), mobile operators face significant difficulties in the implementation of standard *pre-testing methods*. Traditionally, companies have relied on pre-testing to determine the best offers to be sent to specific target groups whenever facing a low cost of contact and a large target population (e.g., email marketing) (Nash, 2000). In such contexts, pre-testing is a simple and economical procedure that, in a nutshell, works as follows: alternative executions of a specific persuasive message are sent to different sub-samples from the target population; after a certain period of time, the responses from each execution are compared among themselves and the best ones are chosen for use with the rest of the population. Because of the massive number of offers that needs to be tested quickly (before they expire), this task becomes either not feasible or ineffective in the context of mobile marketing.

Limited Contact Opportunities per Customer and the Need for Targeting

Even though most mobile operators can contact millions of customers, the number of opportunities to contact *each* customer is quite small. In order to send commercial offers to mobile phones, many countries require the advertiser, content producers, or the telephony provider to obtain the receivers' permission in advance (though the requirements for opt-in or opt-out systems vary from country to country) (Barwise & Strong, 2002; Salo & Tahtinen, 2005). This factor significantly reduces the total available customer base for targeted offers.

In addition, mobile devices are highly personal instruments that users take with them almost everywhere at all times. Mobile operators have recognized that if messages are not accepted in advance, are not relevant to the receiver, arrive at an inconvenient time, or too frequent, the receiver can easily regard mobile offers as illegal, intrusive, and irritating (Wehmeyer, 2007; Ngai & Gunasekaran, 2007; Barnes & Scornavacca, 2008; Barwise & Strong, 2002). As a result, operators have now understood that offers sent to mobile phones should not be based on a mass communication paradigm. Instead, in order to avoid service cancellation or an operator switch, only a limited number of messages should be sent to individuals and these should be targeted and personalized to the receiver's needs. Confirming this belief, previous research has demonstrated that few well-targeted messages are more effective than many generic ones (Bauer, Neumann, & Reichardt, 2005).

As a result, today operators follow very strict business rules that limit the number of messages sent periodically to users. In many typical real-life applications operators have restricted to one per day the number of messages that could be sent to each user, though each company sets its own limits and often adjusts these to the country in which it is operating. Some operators are experiment-

ing new business models in which the telephony service is provided free of charge in exchange for advertising exposure (i.e., mobile users can make calls and send text messages if they are willing to be exposed to a certain number of daily ads). However, at the time this chapter is being written, reports from companies like Blyk in the UK and Mosh Mobile in the US that have adopted this business model are not extremely positive. Recently, Blyk has been acquired by Orange who reportedly plans to offer students a range of promotions, such as tickets and possibly free calls and texts, in return for receiving advertising on their mobile phones (Wray, 2009). Even when a message can contain more than one offer, the total number of offers per message varies typically from one to four due to the limited screen size of users' handsets. Hence, each person can only be exposed to no more than a very small fraction of all possible offers.

Because of these limitations and constraints, *message targeting*, which was once heralded as an advantage of mobile marketing, has now become a *requirement* in any VAS Push Management System together with systems that allow for the optimization of message design. However, with the reduced number of contact opportunities, these tasks (message targeting and design optimization) are also more challenging.

Structural Limitations and the Need to Cluster Users

A third challenge associated with the targeting and knowledge discovery in the context of mobile value-added services relates to structure limitations. Though each infrastructure might have different constraints, from the experience of the authors, current systems are typically restricted to sending no more than a few hundreds of *different* messages a day. Because each message can be sent to thousands of different individuals, message delivery systems can reach millions of customers a day as long as individuals are grouped in a meaningful way (e.g., in clusters based on previous response to offers) and all individuals in a cluster receives a common message.

These constraints might ease over time. However, full customization and personalization (one customized message sent to each individual) is not yet feasible in existing infrastructures and it is far from becoming feasible. As a result, methods to adequately cluster individuals and decide which message to send to each cluster are central for revenue optimization.

Content Categorization and the Need for Automatic Categorization Systems

A final challenge that mobile operators face in managing VAS relates to the different categorization of offers used by each content provider with whom the company contracts. Because each producer provides his own content, created independently, each producer has also developed their unique categorization schema and is not always willing to change it. For instance, a java game from producer A might be classified in a category called "Entertainment." A similar java game from producer B could instead be classified by that producer as "Online Games." Hence, the offers coming from multiple producers can be assigned to categories with very different names and with a very different breadth (e.g., "Entertainment" as a category will include many other types of offers, not only online games).

The differences in name and scope of vendor-specific categories pose another optimization challenge. Content categories could be powerful predictors of purchase for specific groups or individuals given their previous purchase history (similarly to applying collaborative filtering to categories and users). Despite this potential, given the way the category information is currently collected by mobile phone companies, this variable introduces mostly noise into the analysis. It is then necessary to develop approaches that can

overcome this problem to better learn message performance and decide on targeting and message optimization.

In sum, the challenges that any Push VAS optimization and management system needs to overcome are significant. However, the authors experience reveals that it is possible to design and implement systems that can deal with such challenges by relying on recent statistical and data-mining (Close, Pedrycz, Swiniarski, & Kurgan, 2007) techniques. The authors have also conducted several experiments whose results can help mobile operators in the development of such systems and the design of their offers. In the next section previous research in this area and the methods proposed to overcome the challenges discussed above is reviewed, and the results of some of the experiments is described.

CUSTOMER CLUSTERING

One of the challenges in managing Push VAS services is that current systems cannot send a customized offer to each mobile phone user. Instead, in order to reach millions of customers, current systems need to deliver a common message to groups of users. Clustering customers in a meaningful way is then essential to the management of such Push systems. The objective would be to group together customers with similar interests and then proceed to knowledge discovery, testing, and message targeting by taking into account and relying on these user clusters (Giuffrida, Sismeiro, & Tribulato, 2008).

Behavioral Clusters

User clustering can be achieved using efficient clustering algorithms that rely on non-supervised classifiers and on customer-centric data, which might include demographic information and the previous response to commercial offers (i.e., previous behavior). As noted, however that in many real-life mobile applications demographic information is often too noisy and sparse and, as in the case of mobile phone pre-paid accounts, might not be available all together.

Hence, from the experience, clustering and optimization systems that rely on demographic information are often unreliable, especially when compared with systems that rely on previous response and behavior. This result follows closely what researchers in marketing have found both in the online and bricks-and-mortar environments. Indeed, previous research has concluded that standard demographics information is rarely predictive of consumer decision making. Instead, past purchase and consumption behavior provides far better predictions of future purchases and consumption (Eshghi et al., 2007; Montgomery, 1999).

In the previous applications, the authors have relied successfully on user *behavior*, in the form of purchase histories, to cluster successfully mobile phone users. Purchase histories can be represented as a vector of dummy variables that specifies if an item has been bought, or not, by the user in the past; previous behavior can also be represented as a vector of integers reflecting how many times the user has bought from a specific offer category. Hence, it can be assumed that two customers are *similar* (and should be placed together in a cluster) if they buy similar content over time or, more precisely, if they shop in similar categories in a similar proportion. Different strategies exist to discover customer behavior patterns from such type of data (Sarwar, Karypis, Konstan, & Reidl, 2001) but any fast and efficient clustering algorithm with good scalability like the spherical k-means algorithm (Dhillon & Modha, 2001a; Dhillon, Fan, & Guan, 2001b; Zhong, 2005) can be used (this is a particular version of the historical k-means (Mac Queen, 1967) and is based on dot-product metrics that nicely fit with the mobile marketing domain as discussed in Giuffrida et al. (2008)).

Delta Clustering

The set of mobile phone customers that needs to be clustered is not static or stable: new customers join the service, others discontinue the service, and still others make purchases; all on a daily basis. Naturally that this will require that any system based on customer clustering takes into account these dynamics. In the limit, customers might need to be re-clustered on a daily basis, which might be a costly operation depending on the algorithm used, the number of customers, and the number of categories or items in the purchase history. Based on the authors experience, changes in the customer based are very low probability events. Because customer histories and customer status change very slowly, it is possible to overlook the evolution in the customer base over short periods and perform delta clustering without any significant loss in precision (Giuffrida et al., 2008). It can be re-assigned, each day if necessary, those users with new purchasing activity in the previous day; it can be started from the status of the latest cluster execution and use the centroids found in the latest run as a starting point (after the new purchase data is collected).

Cluster centroids, and a truly full clustering run, are conducted only over larger periods of time (e.g., every two weeks). This allows the considerable reduction of the execution time needed to analyze the data. The new clustering schema will include the recent users' activities, and depending on the purchasing of a specific content, a user might switch to a different cluster that in this new run shows a greater affinity with her new purchase history. Keeping clusters stable (or almost) for longer periods of time also provides additional benefits: not only does it reduce computation time, it also reduces the likelihood of sending multiple exposures of the same message to a significant number of users. Indeed, when customers with different past viewing histories are re-grouped together, it becomes more difficult to satisfy the no-multiple-show condition. Also, frequently changing customers might lead the system to discard a good offer too frequently, just because a significant part of the cluster has seen it before.

Hence, in the applications used in this chapter, the authors typically make a trade-off between how often to perform a complete re-clustering and how long to maintain the population within each cluster (relatively) stable. This is however an empirical question that can be investigated with some experimentation (e.g., It is able to define an adequate frequency for re-clustering after few trials only).

Managing Non-Clickers

One of the problems with clustering mobile phone users based on their previous behavior is that, at any point in time, there is always a significant portion of mobile users that never buy anything, that is, never click on the offers (called *non-clickers*). For example, in one of the previous applications only about 35% of the population had purchased something in the past (called *clickers*), whereas the remaining 65% had never purchased anything (*non-clickers*). As a result, only use the activity of a minority of the mobile users to perform the clustering could be used. For the majority of the users (*non-clickers)* historical information is not provided.

To try to get usable information from *non-clickers*, previous researchers have proposed simple heuristics that have performed well in real-life applications. For example, in Giuffrida et al. (2008) the authors send *good* offers to *non-clickers*, that is, non-clickers are targeted with offers that tend to perform well overall, among the entire clicker population (regardless of the clustering schema). In addition, and to avoid pushing only few offers, the authors split the non-clickers group into smaller sets (in their case each subset had about fifty thousand users). Then, the authors target each set of non-clickers following the empirical purchasing likelihood computed from the clicker population. By doing this the authors

also reduce the risk of picking one bad offer and sending it to a large number of customers. Note also that each new customer, upon arrival, needs to be first inserted into a non-clicker set. The customer will then be assigned to clicker groups (through full clustering or delta clustering) as soon as he/she makes a purchase. The results reported in Giuffrida et al. (2008) show this method works extremely well.

Number of Clusters

The task of choosing the right number of clusters k is always a challenging one (Sugar & James, 2003). This depends on many factors such as customer base size and number of categories. In general, a large number of clusters produces a more precise targeting. However, a large number of clusters requires a longer clustering execution time and data preparation time, larger storage space, and a longer message delivery process. Notice that sending messages to many clusters is time consuming, as the delivery engine has to pause for few seconds (or even minutes) between two consecutive deliveries (for technical reasons). In addition, for marketing reasons, most mobile operators require that all customers receive messages within a well-defined time frame. Hence, any optimization and targeting system needs to make sure that the number of cluster is small enough not to extend for too long the delivery phase.

The final choice on the number of clusters depends upon the available storage, computation power, and the gains that adding further clusters might provide in terms of predictive accuracy. In the previous applications authors have weighed all these factors and monitored the clustering performance as a function of the number of clusters to make a decision of how many clusters to use. For example, the spherical k-means clustering algorithm has an objective function one wants to minimize. The authors graph the value of this function for different numbers of clusters and then decide on how many clusters to use. Fig-

Figure 2. Clustering quality as a function of the number of clusters

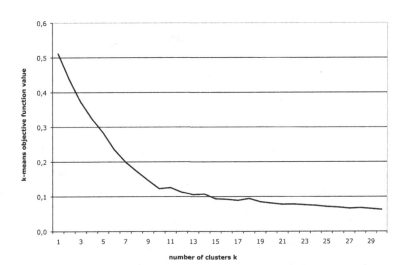

ure 2 shows the value of this k-means objective function for the clustering of a real database of mobile-phone users periodically targeted with commercial messages. The commercial messages could be classified in one of 12 mutually exclusive categories (these categories were obtained using a text-mining method similar to the one which is described in the subsequent section). The categories considered are: ring-tones, vocal ring-tones, wallpapers, videos, songs, news, games, calendars, services, promotions, sports, and multimedia. (User-specific 12-dimentional vector of purchase frequencies is used to cluster individuals.)

As it can be seen from Figure 2, using about 20 to 30 clusters provides very good results: performance improvements beyond the 11-cluster solution are minimal, and improvements beyond a 20 cluster solution are practically inexistent. In an application like this, unless there were technical problems of relevance (e.g., storage and delivery time) one would select about 20 clusters to be used in a real system.

Visualizing and Interpreting Clusters

To get a better understanding of the clusters obtained, it is possible to use several visualization tools. Figure 3 provides an example of a graphical representation of the outcome of the user clustering with 20 clusters.

In Figure 3, the first line represents the clusters. Each column, coded with two shades of green for easy differentiation, represents a cluster and the width of the column represents its size. There are 20 columns, one for each cluster, and clusters are listed from the smallest to the largest. The remaining lines represent the product categories and in the intersection of a cluster and a category the authors have coded the affinity between the two. Hence, given a row r and a column c, the element $[r,c]$ represents the affinity of cluster c to category r, and the darker the stronger this affinity (affinity is coded in different shades of grey, from almost white to almost black). For example, the darker elements of the matrix indicate a very strong affinity, meaning that all the users of that cluster have bought from the corresponding category. Very light grey indicates a weak affinity—

Figure 3. Affinity matrix representation

customers of that cluster were not interested in that category.

Wider clusters are strongly associated to one category and, as a result, are well defined in terms of possible targeting strategies. Clusters depicted in columns 15, 17 and 20 are good examples: users in these clusters bought products in only one category. Smaller clusters present strong affinity with at least one category, though often with more than one. Only the clusters depicted in second and sixth columns have less defined targeting strategies: their users bought products in almost every category.

To get a better understanding of how customers cluster together as a result of their purchasing history, user clusters have been depicted using Self-Organizing Maps (SOM), (De Hoon, 2002) which depict the customers' vectors from an N-dimensional space into two dimensions (the representation is such that if two items are close to each other in the N-dimensional space they will be close also in the two-dimensional space). Figure 4 represents the user density in a 2D space with respect to all the categories. The color scale shows the maximum density area in dark red and the minimum in dark blue (each image is normalized with respect to the size of the corresponding category).

This type of graph provides further rich information on the 20 clusters. For example, the three categories in the first column have dense areas (dark red groups of users) that are wide and not well defined, surrounded by low density areas group of people (shown in cyan). All the others categories have smaller dense areas, well defined,

and surrounded by dark blue areas. Categories such as ring-tones and games have some overlaps (the big cluster of users in the Games category is in the same area as the dense cluster of users associated with ring-tones) meaning that a subset of their customers are interested in both types of products. In contrast, sports and news have little overlap, with few common customers. This initial analysis provides the first insights into how user respond to the offers and how to possibly target them. There are however other tools that can significantly help in this task.

Figure 4. User concentration over categories

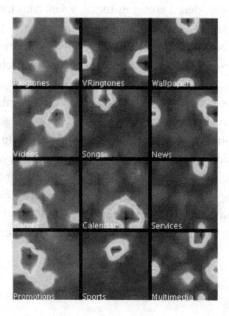

LEARNING ON NEW OFFERS

Though mobile user clustering resolves some of the challenges, it does not provide an answer to many others. One of the challenges that clustering does not resolve relates with the need to acquire knowledge on a very large (and growing) content catalogue. Every day dozens of new offers are added to the catalogue of mobile operators. To optimize targeting decisions, mobile operators need to learn how likely users are to respond to each offer and who (or which cluster) is likely to respond. Such learning needs to be performed while dealing with the challenges which are described previously and using the often limited information available to mobile operators. The mobile operator might know, for example, the offer's category, as defined by the content provider, the content (e.g., image and text), and the price of the product or service being featured. For all *new* offers mobile operators do *not* know how they have performed (as they have never been tested), though operators might know how mobile users have purchased in the past (if exposed to an offer) and the performance of offers previously delivered. In some cases mobile operators might know also the demographic information of mobile users, though such information might be too unreliable and, as in the case of pre-paid accounts, it might not even exist.

In addition, the learning phase in these optimized Push delivery systems should be as automatic as possible, requiring minimal human intervention and ideally, they should run unsupervised. Fortunately, recent research has proposed several automatic methods to improve the learning on new offers that can rely on the limited information set available to mobile operators. Next the authors reviews some of these methods and explain how they can be implemented in real systems.

Using Heterogeneous Category Information in Performance Prediction

Category information can be highly valuable to infer the purchasing likelihood of certain groups of mobile users in the absence of actual purchase histories specific to each new offer (mobile operators do not know how each new offer will perform before testing it or sending to the entire user population but they might know how offers of the same "type" have performed in the past). If mobile users have purchased in the past from specific categories (e.g., ring-tones or games), it is likely that they will keep on buying in those categories (Fennel, Allenby, Yang, & Edwards, 2003; Montgomery, 1999) for analyses in which previous behavior is a very good predictor of future behavior). Category information also allows researchers to learn on "types" of offers instead of learning on specific offers by applying sophisticated statistical or data-mining models on categories instead of individual offers. Also, when learning on categories of offers (instead of specific offers) it is possible to use the acquired knowledge on other new offers of the same type and researchers can capitalize on having more information available by pooling together offers of the same type. When learning on specific offers the knowledge is lost once the offer expires.

Despite the potential information contained in offer categories, there are two challenges when using these in predicting offer performance. First, with the categorizations different vendors provide, mobile phone operators get diversed. In addition, the library of offers is extremely large (as compared to the learning occasions) and expands at a significant pace, making it difficult to use a human-based labeling to create a common labeling for all offers. To solve these problems previous research has proposed the use of a common and finer categorization of all offers that is generated by an automatic system (Giuffrida et al., 2008). To obtain this categorization the authors in Giuffrida et al. (2008) propose to merge all categories from the original data into a single uniform schema using pattern matching and text-mining techniques applied to the offer's text and to the offer's original (and unstandardized) category label. Rules mapping the original offer's text and category to a new and common category labeling are then generated (Domingos & Pazzani, 1977; Freund & Schapire, 1997; Cover & Hart, 1967; Lui, Li, Lee, & Yu, 2004; McCallum & Nigam, 1999).

For example, rules can be had that assign the category 'songs' of provider A and the offer's text 'watch the video clip' of provider B to the category 'music' of the new labeling schema. The proposed approach avoids the manual creation of a labeled dataset, greatly reduces human intervention, and is particularly effective in mobile marketing applications in which the content category usually emerges from the text displayed in the offer (note that mobile users can only rely on the offer's text and/or on image to understand the type of content that is available for sale). Previous research has indeed demonstrated the usefulness of a categorization obtained using these text-mining techniques in a mobile marketing context. Indeed, the Click-Through-Rate (CTR) predictions based on new constructed categories were clearly superior to those using the original fragmented categorizations (Giuffrida et al., 2008).

Heterogeneity within Categories: Predicting an Offer's Performance before Testing

Though categories are useful in predicting mobile offer performance, it is very likely that different products or offers in the same category will show substantial differences in terms of purchasing probability (i.e., in terms of CTR). In addition, because the typical Push VAS application reviewed here are characterized by big and fast-growing catalogues with limited life-span, it is also not clear how best to select the offers that to be tested *first*, as the system might not have enough capacity to

learn on all new items and one might need to prioritize. It is likely that if the offers to be subjected to learning and testing is selected randomly, it will not be able to learn fast enough on all items and, most importantly, it will not be able to learn fast enough on the most promising items.

Based on the authors experience, it is found that, it is possible to devise heuristics to handle some of these challenges effectively. For example, one simple heuristic that seems to perform well is to rank categories based on overall performance and then learn first on those items belonging to the most attractive categories. Another heuristic would be to learn first on the *most recent* new offers and to mix content categories in each learning cluster to expose each learning cluster to a variety of topics (this tends to reduce fatigue and reduces the significant drop in performance typically observed in learning samples).

These are of course heuristics that, based on authors experience, have been extremely helpful. However, these heuristics do not rely on any grounded statistical or data-mining method and still require significant testing and fine-tuning to provide adequate performance. There are also other methods that can be applied to better learn the performance of different offers that rely on more sophisticated statistical and data-mining methods and can still be performed with minimal human intervention. One method proposed by Battiato et al. (2009a) and Battiato et al. (2009b) is to use the offer's price, text, and image to predict its performance. In that work the authors demonstrate how image- and text-mining techniques can be used to automatically characterize each offer. The result of this proposed automatic processing is a set of variables that describe both the visual and verbal content of each offer. In the example used in Figure 1, the authors propose the use of dummy variables to describe the text "Do you like this Puppy? Get it as a wallpaper for your phone." These dummy variables are set to 1 if a given word is included in the text and 0 otherwise. The authors remove very common words (e.g., 'a', 'for', 'this', 'your' will discriminate little across different offers) and very uncommon words that were unlikely to appear in other offers. The authors also allow for stemming, though no semantic analysis of the text (with the objective of understanding its meaning) is performed.

The variables that characterize the visual features are derived from Textons, a concept originally developed by Julesz (1981). In this case, the 'sleepy doggy' image of Figure 1 (together with all the images in the content catalogue) would be processed using a filter bank (Winn, Criminsi, & Minka, 2005) that includes low- and high-pass filters. The filtered values for each pixel of all images are then clustered and a vocabulary of "visual words" (or Textons) is created. Each image could then be characterized as a histogram of these visual words (i.e., one would "describe" each image in the catalogue, and any new image arriving at the catalogue, by determining how frequently a specific Texton was present in the image). Determining how many "visual words" (Textons) to make the visual vocabulary requires also some additional testing and, again, significant fine-tuning might be required.

After obtaining the visual and text-related variables that characterize each offer, the authors use these as predictors in regression models in which the dependent variable is the click-through-rate (CTR) or purchase likelihood (some of the regression models used include locally weighted regression, regression trees, simple regression, and also a cascade of regression models). These models are estimated using previously tested offers (offers previously sent to users and whose performance has been observed), and are then used to predict the performance for offers not yet tested. In their work, the authors demonstrate that price, image, and text all provide valuable information to predict an offer's performance and optimize VAS revenues. Textons—texture-based holistic cues (Renninger & Malik, 2004)—were found to be extremely powerful when compared to color-based cues. The offer's text shows also

significant predictive power especially when compared to the relative small effect of price, perhaps because text in this application served as a proxy for the offer's category (the authors in their work do not account for the offer's category, which they have explained previously can be very powerful predictors).

The authors in Battiato et al. (2009a) and Battiato et al. (2009b) further demonstrate that a system that pre-tests *only* the most promising offers as predicted by their models performs significantly better than a system that randomly selects which offers to test, whenever the learning constraints, which are described previously, are present and significant. Hence, when a new message arrives at the catalogue it is possible to improve performance, and deal with the challenges that are presented in this chapter, by first predicting the offer's likely performance (based on its features) and then test first the most promising offers. Whenever information on an offer's category is also available, it is possible to incorporate these also in the predictive model using discrete (dummy) variables. As an alternative, it is also possible to perform the same analysis category by category. Real-life systems relying at least in part in similar predictive models tend to perform significantly better than those relying on heuristics or simple rules. The believe that further developments of these basic ideas could still provide additional improvements.

Optimizing and Building Learning Samples

Traditional pre-testing, widely used in direct marketing applications like the one of mobile VAS, relies typically on a sample of the general population—also called learning sample or learning cluster—on which new offers are tested (untested offers are sent to this sample and performance monitored; results are then used to select which offers to send to the entire population).

As described previously, traditional pre-testing is not feasible in the context of mobile Push VAS because of the large and fast growing catalogue and the limited testing possibilities (this is despite the small cost of contact). Learning samples are however still used. For example, in the work of (Battiato et al., 2009a; Battiato et al., 2009b) though the offer's text, image, and price are used to predict the performance of new offers and decide which ones to subject to further testing (only the most promising offers will be subject to further testing), testing using a learning sample is still required. Also in the work of Giuffrida et al. (2008), learning samples are at the center of their approach.

Interestingly, from authors own field tests and previous research has demonstrated that learning samples should not be static. One of the problems individuals in learning clusters face is that they are more likely to receive (on average) an offer of "lower quality" (in the sense that it is an offer that does not meet the individuals' needs and tastes). As a result, annoyance and disappointment with

the offers accumulate over time and the result is a reduced attention given to commercial messages.

To demonstrate this, the authors have conducted a test using mobile commercial messages and the result is presented in the Figure 5. During four consecutive weeks they have monitored the performance of the messages sent to a learning sample (*learning cluster*) to the performance of those sent to the optimized sample (*revenue cluster*). Individuals in the learning cluster are sent random (new) messages without any type of optimization or attempt to match individuals' interests to offers. In the optimized or revenue cluster individuals receive messages that seem appropriate to their tastes and interests given their previous purchase behavior. Each cluster includes few thousand mobile users and these are kept fixed over time (individuals are not rotated).

As it can be seen from the Figure 5, a typical revenue cluster has a better CTR than a learning cluster, though it varies depending on the availability of quality content (i.e., the actual performance depends on the quality of the offers available). In contrast, a systematic decrease of CTR

Figure 5. Fixed learning cluster versus optimized cluster

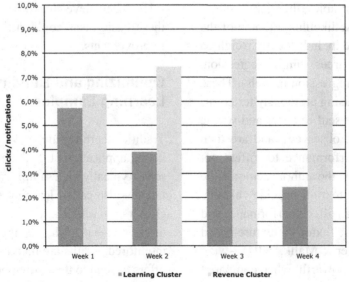

week after week in the learning cluster can be observed. This result indicates that customers might lose interest in the service if exposed to uninteresting content over a long period (i.e., if exposed to content that is not targeted to their specific interests). Indeed, the likelihood of receiving a bad offer is very high in a learning cluster as the offers are not filtered based on any previous learning. In fact, it is found that for learning clusters the number of weak offers is higher than the number of good ones, given the total number of active offers in any moment.

One way to prevent this type of problems is to rotate the individuals in the learning samples. Hence, learning clusters should be built periodically with new randomly assigned users to ensure that each mobile user is not exposed to testing (non-optimized) content for too long. That is also what is done in some of the state of the art optimization systems (Giuffrida et al., 2008). Basically, learning clusters can be formed by temporarily *borrowing* users from optimized clusters.

In order to monitor when such a rotation might be required the authors suggest to look at customer inactivity rate (i.e., the percentage of people that decide to stop downloading messages in the period under study), and at the rate of customer churn (i.e., the percentage of people that unsubscribe the service in the period under study). Both inactivity and churn are significantly higher in learning samples than among users who are sent targeted content. For example, during the four weeks of the test whose results are shown in Figure 5, about 3.8% of the customers unsubscribe the service for the learning cluster, against 1.6% for the revenue cluster. In addition, the learning clusters show an inactivity rate of 6.2% on average, versus 3.5% for the optimized clusters. Of course to determine what is the optimal moment to rotate clusters (i.e., what is the difference in churn and inactivity that should trigger a change) will require extensive monitoring and fine tuning, and further research should be performed in this area.

After significant field tests, the authors have opted to randomly assign new users to learning clusters every day, which is the minimum possible time period they can act on (due to the timing of message delivery and arrival of new information from the mobile operator systems). Finally, it is also noted that rotating users provides additional benefits. For example, by moving customers from an optimized cluster to a learning cluster, customers' interests may be learned more accurately. In fact, in the learning clusters people are exposed to a greater variety of offers. Because customers' interests can change over time (e.g., shopping for a new car when having a baby, or looking for a mortgage when marrying), by keeping a customer in optimized clusters for a long time can cause the system to expose him/her to a very limited number of offers and prevent the discovery of his/her new interests.

TARGETING USERS AND OFFER DESIGN

Once the system has learned on all the offers available for sending, it is necessary to target users optimally and to carefully design the offers to be sent. It is essential to fine-tune the targeting system in order to fully benefit from the learning phase. How messages are sent and how the content is included in each message seems to impact significantly final performance.

Due to the lack of research in this area, the authors have conducted several experiments to determine how message design and delivery might influence the CTR of each offer (and hence its profitability). Next the authors present some of these experiments and provide a summary of their conclusion, which they believe that might aid other researchers when implementing similar systems. In all the experiments random samples of about 11 to 12 thousand mobile-phone users have been used. The content being tested in these experiments was new content (i.e., it had never been sent to users), and no information regarding its effectiveness was available. In addition, the alternative offers were equally priced, allowing them to ignore the costing factor and any price effects.

Multiple Sending

Previous research seems to suggest that the number of exposures to a commercial message (e.g., a banner in the online) can have an influence on consumer response. For example in Chatterjee et al. (2003) the authors find that repeated banner exposures can increase the CTR rate. They have conducted a series of experiments to determine the relationship between offer exposure and clicks in commercial mobile offers. The goal is to understand how the CTR of a single offer changes with the number of exposures. To do so, repeated exposures of the same content is sent (e.g., content A) to a random sample of users over a period of 10 days. In the example below, results for a test in which the content was sent every three days can been seen. During the remaining days users were exposed to other offers (for a total of seven different offers, which was labeled *A, B, C, D, E, F,* and *G*). Only one offer (offer A) was sent

multiple times during these testing days and each message contained only one offer.

Figure 6 presents the results of one of these experiments. In this example the final pattern of exposure was **A** – B – C – **A** – D – E – **A** – F – G – **A**. The figure then shows the CTR of each one of the offers sent during the ten consecutive days from 19/07/09 till 28/07/09.

The results clearly show a significant decrease in CTR of a given content as the number of exposures increases which contradicts the results found in the online world (Chatterjee, Patrali, Hoffman, Donna, Novak, & Thomas, 2003). For example, in the example above, after the first exposure, the CTR of the second exposure is about 42% lower than the CTR of the first exposure; the CTR of the third exposure is also significantly lower and about 60% lower than the CTR of first exposure. This is indicative that unlike other contexts multiple exposures do not lead to an increase in the CTR. Instead, over time, if users have not clicked on a specific offer, by exposing users to those offers again, does not increase their likelihood of response.

In designing the targeting system it is believed that multiple exposures should be tested carefully and, in most cases, avoided. Notice that many other offers had a CTR significantly higher than

Figure 6. Click-Through-Rate of seven offers sent over ten consecutive days

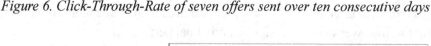

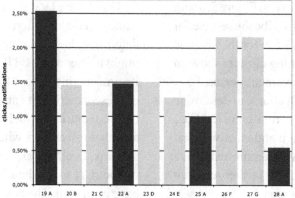

the third exposure of offer A. This would mean that it is possible to maximize profits by avoiding multiple exposures and instead send a new offer to the user population (of course an extremely good offer with very high CTR might still fair better in a second or third exposure than other relatively low performance offers, but in general, such situations will be rare). Perhaps the nature of the short commercial messages and the need for low levels of cognition and attention to fully understand the content in the domain would explain the result. However, the authors believe this is a result that deserves further research because it seems to distinguish it from other domains (Chatterjee et al., 2003). Though similar patterns across many experiments have been observed, it would be important to understand under what conditions and for what type of content does multiple exposure increase (or not) purchase likelihood.

Offer Position in a Message

Previous research suggests that content order has a significant impact on CTR (Ansari & Mela, 2003). In a second set of experiments how changing the offer's position in a message influences the final CTR in the mobile phone environment can be studied. In these experiments authors drew three groups of random customers (G_1, G_2 and G_3) and randomly selected three offers (content A, B and C). Then the same *three* offers in a *single* message is sent to each group, in which the order has been changed so that the contents would appear on the users' handsets.

Each mobile-phone user is sent one message but inside the message users are shown more than one offer, sequentially, as in a short slide-show (this type of effects are possible when sending commercial offers using MMS messaging; only those users with phones able to read these type of messages can be effectively sent the offers). Below experiments on the time between slides when showing multiple offers within a single message is discussed in more detail. The contents will be sent in the following order: (A, B, C) to group G_1, (C, A, B) to group G_2, and (B, C, A) to group G_3.

The average CTR for each position and across the different offers is computed and the results of one of these experiments is shown in Figure 7.

Figure 7 clearly shows that content sent in the first position is two times more likely to be effective than content sent in the second and third positions (the difference between the second and third position is not statistically significant at 5% significance level). This result follows closely what is found in the online world with banners and sponsored search ads in Google and Yahoo!: the ads on the top of the page or on the top of a search list have a much higher CTR and conversion rate (Ghose & Yang, 2009).

Figure 7. Average Click-Through-Rate at different positions

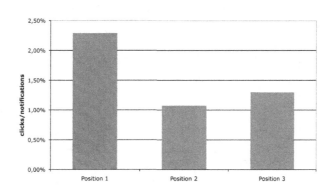

Another important issue, regarding message optimization, would be to determine how to position the alternative offers in the message: it can be known that the first offer will have a boost in CTR just because of its position (all else constant). However, which offer should be positioned first as each offer can have significantly different intrinsic levels of attractiveness (as measured by CTR)? For example, in this experiment, the contents based on user response is ranked. On average (and irrespective of position) users click on content A more often; content C is the second best, followed by content B, which is the offer with the lowest CTR.

It is possible that the CTR of each offer might interact with its position in the message. If such interaction occurs, any message optimization will need to take into account not only overall CTR, but also the best position in a message given the expected CTR.

Figure 8 provides a clear answer on whether CTR and content position in a message do interact. For example, content A, which is the best among all three offers, performs the best when positioned first in the message. The difference in performance is so substantial that makes the combination with offer A positioned first in the message the best performing message. Indeed, for this experiment the best combination is (A, B, C), that is the message with the best content in the best performing position (first in the message), the second best content (content C) in the second best position (third in the message), and the weakest content (content B) in the worst position (second in the message).

These results reveal that any system aimed at optimizing offer performance needs not only to consider the number of exposures but also the position in a message whenever a single message can contain more than one offer. Carefully modeling the interaction effects between position and quality of an offer is essential for the optimization of content delivery.

Time Between Slides

Another factor that might influence user response is the time in-between the visualization of sequential offers. In general, each message sent can be composed by a *sequence* of *slides* if sent under the MMS format and each slide will correspond to a specific offer. When setting up an MMS, it is possible to define a duration parameter for each slide. Given this parameter, most handsets automatically change slides after the defined duration.

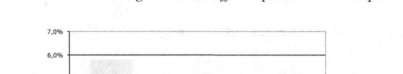

Figure 8. Changes in CTR while combining contents in different positions in the sequence

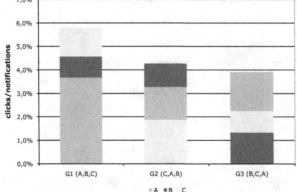

Changing this duration parameter might also have an impact on performance.

In a new set of experiments the authors wanted to measure exactly how this duration parameter impacted the CTR. To do so, three offers are sent (*A, B,* and *C* in this order) to four groups of random customers (G_1, G_2, G_3, and G_4). The only difference of the messages sent to each group is the time in-between slides. The time was set to five, eight, 11, and 14 seconds respectively for each group. The maximum CTR is observed when setting the duration to eight seconds. Hence, it seems that if too little time in-between slides (e.g. 5 seconds), customers do not have enough time to see each offer properly, and cannot process their content. The results also suggest that each user might have a maximum time allocated to process the entire message (a limited attention span). As a result, after a certain threshold, giving more time to process each content benefits the earlier offers but will hinder the ones shown later in the message because it limits the probability that the final offers will be seen or processed. In fact, the results show that if too much time is allowed in-between slides, an increase in the CTR of the first content is seen and significantly CTR of all remaining offers is reduced. However, in the experiments, this increase did not compensate the decrease in CTR of the final offers.

Again, these results clearly show that fine-tuning message-specific design factors can provide added improvements in performance. Each provider should carefully monitor and test their own offers and design variables. However, the gains that can be achieved from simpler experimentation are substantial. In the authors experience, beyond clustering users and predicting the CTR irrespective of message design, carefully tuning design variables like the time in-between slides and the position of the offers in a message provided significant profit increases for the mobile operator.

FUTURE RESEARCH DIRECTIONS

There are many areas still open and requiring further research. For example, though several results regarding message design are presented (e.g., the experiments on offer position and time in-between slides), there are many other design issues that need further research. What text to include in the offer and what type of image and dynamic content should be included? Structuring a system that does not only optimizes message targeting but also optimizes message design, possibly automatically, would represent a significant step forward.

Other future research avenues could also focus on the improvement of the targeting algorithm. So far most of the system relies on the observation of user's previous purchase behavior. Perhaps other behavioral indicators could also be added to better predict offer performance. For example, users can interact with the offers without actually buying (e.g., users can download the message and even open it without clicking and without buying). It is possible this additional behavioral information can provide better predictive accuracy.

In addition, the authors have not yet explored whether the sequential purchase information could contain further information to help predict future behavior. So far they have only considered the purchase frequency within each category to cluster individuals, but it is possible that purchase sequences might also be informative. Another interesting future research is to understand the best time of the day (and day of the week) to send a promotional message to each user. At this time the authors did not include any temporal consideration in the algorithm. MMS messages are currently sent at the same time to all customers. It is possible, however, the time of the day influences the purchasing probability and that not all individuals are equally responsive at the same time of the day.

In a similar manner, location-based information could be embedded (if available) into the recommendation engine. This would open up interesting research avenues as people may be treated differently depending upon their current geographical location at the moment the SMS/MMS is sent. In sum, there are still many avenues open for investigation and the authors hope this chapter will stimulate further research in this area.

CONCLUSION

By putting together the basic building blocks the authors have just reviewed user clustering, performance learning, and message design and targeting in this chapter and a state-of-the-art message optimization and delivery system for mobile-phone operators is structured. Every day, the system would need to perform the following steps:

1. *Data gathering and cleaning*: the database is updated with new data.
2. *User clustering*: customer base is clustered based on all available data.
3. *Computation of cluster- and offer-specific statistics*: summary statistics are computed for
   - Cluster affinity towards categories,
   - Generic category potential,
   - Contents seen by each cluster,
   - Content potential.
4. *Campaign scheduling*: the decision algorithm will select the content to be sent to each cluster and creates the related campaign. In a similar way, the system schedules content recently added to the catalogue, for the *learning clusters*.
5. *Sending*: campaign schedules and related customer groups are communicated to the delivery platform; the schedule specifies for each customer group the set of offers to send on that day.

The authors have implemented similar systems that have run successfully in a real business environment. The customer base comprises over two million customers and results show a considerable improvement when compared to a non-optimized solution. They were not allowed to set up a control panel, which would have been ideal for testing their system. Instead, they tested the overall system measuring performance before and after its implementation with full optimization (during the first months only learning data is collected which is used to cluster customers then and learn on new offers).

To demonstrate the gains an optimized system can provide the authors carried an initial test over a ten-week period, five weeks before the activation of their system and five weeks after. They did not consider holidays in order to make sure the two five-week periods were consistent. They computed the revenue per notification obtained before and after the use of the optimization system. Results show a significant increase in revenue using the optimization system. The revenue per notification is 0.07 during the first five weeks and 0.16 once the optimization system is used. This represents an improvement of 141% in performance. Even one year after the introduction of such optimization system, management perception was that of a substantial improvement in overall business performance with a substantial increase in revenue.

From these results it is clear that implementing a message optimization and delivery system based on state-of-the-art statistical and data mining methods can provide a significant increase in revenues and profits. Though review methods was not exhaustive, with this chapter the authors have provided a clear roadmap to aid anyone wishing to design an optimization system for the delivery of commercial offers to mobile phones. They have discussed several of the practical issues facing mobile operators and alternatives methods to solve such issues.

REFERENCES

Ansari, Asim., & Mela, Carl F. (2003). E-customization. *JMR, Journal of Marketing Research, 40*, 131–145. doi:10.1509/jmkr.40.2.131.19224

Barnes, S. J., & Scornavacca, E. (2008). The Strategic value of Enterprise Mobility: Case study insights. *Information-Knowledge-Systems Management, 7*(1-2), 227–241.

Barwise, P., & Strong, C. (2002). Permission-based Mobile Advertising. *Journal of Interactive Marketing, 16*(1), 14–24. doi:10.1002/dir.10000

Battiato, S., Farinella, G.M., Giuffrida, G., Sismeiro, C., & Tribulato, G. (2009a). Exploiting Visual and Text Features for Direct Marketing Learning in Time and Space Constrained Domains. *Pattern Analysis and Applications Multimedia Tools and Applications Journal - Special Issue on Metadata Mining for Image Understanding, 42*(1), 5-30.

Battiato, S., Farinella, G. M., Giuffrida, G., Sismeiro, C., & Tribulato, G. (2009b). Using Visual and Text Features for Direct Marketing on Multimedia Messaging Services Domain. *Multimedia Tools and Applications, 42*(1), 5–30. doi:10.1007/s11042-008-0250-z

Bauer, H. H., Neumann, M., & Reichardt, T. (2005). Driving Consumer Acceptance of Mobile Marketing - A Theoretical Framework and Empirical Study. In *Proceedings of the 4th International Marketing Trends Congress, ESCP-EAP Annual Conference* (pp. 181-192). Paris.

Chatterjee, Patrali, & Hoffman, Donna, L., Novak, & Thomas, P. (2003). Modeling the Clickstream: Implications for Web-Based Advertising Efforts. *Marketing Science, 22*(4), 520–541. doi:10.1287/mksc.22.4.520.24906

Close, K. J., Pedrycz, W., Swiniarski, R. W., & Kurgan, L. A. (2007). *Data Mining: A Knowledge Discovery Approach*. Springer.

Cover, T., & Hart, P. (1967). Nearest Neighbor Pattern Classification. *IEEE Transactions on Information Theory, 13*(1), 21–27. doi:10.1109/TIT.1967.1053964

De Hoon, M. (2002). Cluster 3.0 for Windows, Mac OS X, Linux, Unix. Retrieved August 18, 2009, from http://bonsai.ims.u-tokyo.ac.jp/~mdehoon/software/cluster/

Dhillon, I. S., Fan, J., & Guan, Y. (2001b). Efficient Clustering of Very Large Document Collections. *Data Mining for Scientific and Engineering Applications*, 357–381.

Dhillon, I. S., & Modha, D. S. (2001a). Concept Decompositions for Large Sparse Text Data using Clustering. *Machine Learning, 42*(1),143–175. Also appears as *IBM Research Report RJ 10147*, 1999.

Domingos, P., & Pazzani, M. (1997). On the Optimality of the Simple Bayesian Classifier under Zero-One Loss. *Machine Learning, 29*, 103–130. doi:10.1023/A:1007413511361

Eshghi, A., Haughton, D., & Topi, H. (2007). Determinants of Customer Loyalty in the Wireless Telecommunications Industry. *Telecommunications Policy, 31*, 93–106. doi:10.1016/j.telpol.2006.12.005

Fennell, G., Allenby, G. M., Yang, S., & Edwards, Y. (2003). The Effectiveness of Demographic and Psychographic Variables for Explaining Brand and Product Category Use. *Quantitative Marketing and Economics, 1*(2), 223–244. doi:10.1023/A:1024686630821

Freund, Y., & Schapire, R. E. (1997). A Decision-Theoretic Generalization of On-line Learning and an application to Boosting. *Journal of Computer and System Sciences, 55*, 1–34. doi:10.1006/jcss.1997.1504

Ghose, A., & Yang, S. (2009). (forthcoming). An Empirical Analysis of Search Engine Advertising: Sponsored Search in Electronic Markets. *Management Science*. doi:10.1287/mnsc.1090.1054

Giuffrida, G., Sismeiro, C., & Tribulato, G. (2008). Automatic Content Targeting on Mobile Phones. In *Proceedings of the 11th International Conference on Extending Database Technology: Advances in Database Technology* (pp. 630-639). Nantes, France. *EDBT '08*, Vol. 261. New York: ACM.

Julesz, B. (1981). Textons, the elements of Texture Perception, and their Interactions. *Nature, 290*, 91–97. doi:10.1038/290091a0

Kerris, N., & Bowcock, J. (2009). *Apple's App Store Downloads Top 1.5 Billion in First Year*. Retrieved August 18, 2009, from http://www.apple.com/pr/library/2009/07/14apps.html

Leppaniemi, M., & Karjaluoto, H. (2007). Mobile Marketing: From Marketing Strategy to Mobile Marketing Campaign Implementation. In *Proceedings of the 6th Annual Global Mobility Roundtable Conference*. Los Angeles.

Lui, B., Li, X., Lee, W. S., & Yu, P. S. (2004). Text Classification by Labeling Words. In *Proceedings of the 19th National Conference on Artificial Intelligence*. San Josè, California.

Mac Queen, J. B. (1967). Some methods for the Classification and analysis of Multivariate Observations. In *Proceedings of the Fifth Berkeley Symposium on Mathematical Statistics and Probability* (pp. 281–297).

McCallum, A., & Nigam, K. (1999). Text Classification by Bootstrapping with Keywords, EM and Shrinkage. In *ACL99* (pp. 52–58). Workshop for Unsupervised Learning in Natural Language Processing.

Montgomery, A. L. (1999). *Using Clickstream to predict WWW usage*. Retrived August 19, 2009, from http://www.andrew.cmu.edu/user/alm3/papers/predicting%20www%20usage.pdf

Nash, E. (2000). *Direct Marketing: Strategy, Planning, Execution*. New York: McGraw-Hill Education.

Ngai, E. W. T., & Gunasekaran, A. (2007). A Review for Mobile Commerce Research and Applications. *Decision Support Systems, 43*, 3–15. doi:10.1016/j.dss.2005.05.003

Renninger, L. W., & Malik, J. (2004). When is Scene Recognition just Texture Recognition? *Vision Research, 44*, 2301–2311.

Salo, J., & Tahtinen, J. (2005). Retailer use of Permission-based Mobile Advertising. In I. Clarke & Flaherty Theresa (Eds.), *Advances in Electronic Marketing, Idea Group Inc* (pp. 140-156).

Sarwar, B., Karypis, G., Konstan, J., & Reidl, J. (2001). Item-based collaborative filtering recommendation algorithms. In *Proceedings of the 10th International Conference on World Wide Web* (pp. 285-295). Hong Kong.

Sugar, C. A., & James, G. M. (2003). Finding the Number of Clusters in a Dataset. *Journal of the American Statistical Association, 98*(463), 750–763. doi:10.1198/016214503000000666

The Netsize Guide. (2009). *Mobile Society & Me: When Worlds Combine*. Retrieved from. [available at http://www.netsize.com/]

Wehmeyer, K. (2007). Mobile Ad Intrusiveness – The effects of Message type and Situation. In *Proceedings of the 20th Bled eConference eMergence*. Bled, Slovenia.

Winn, J., Criminisi, A., & Minka, T. (2005). Object categorization by Learned Universal Visual Dictionary. In *Proceedings of the Tenth IEEE International Conference on Computer Vision* (pp. 1800-1807). Washington, DC, USA.

Wray, R. (2009). *Orange to offer free gifts to students who agree to receive Ads on Mobiles*. Retrieved August 19, 2009, from http://www.guardian.co.uk/business/2009/jul/22/orange-free-gifts-advertising-blyk

Zhong, S. (2005). Efficient Online Spherical k-means Clustering. *Neural Networks, IJCNN'05, 5*, 3180-3185.

KEY TERMS AND DEFINITIONS

Clustering: Assignment of a set of observations into subsets so that observations in the same cluster are similar in some sense.

Data Mining: Process of extracting patterns from data. As more data is gathered it is becoming an important tool to transform these data into information.

Marketing Communications: Messages and related media used to communicate with a market.

MMS: Multimedia Message Service is a standard way to send messages that include multimedia content to and from mobile phones.

Mobile Marketing: Set of practices that enables organizations to communicate and engage with their audience in an interactive and relevant manner through any mobile device or network.

Mobile Phone: Electronic device used for mobile telecommunications over a cellular network of specialized base stations known as cell sites.

Targeting: Selection of a particular market segment toward which all marketing effort is directed. Market targeting enables the characteristics of the chosen segment to be taken into account when formulating a product or service and its advertising.

Chapter 9
Data Mining System Execution Traces to Validate Distributed System Quality-of-Service Properties

James H. Hill
Indiana University-Purdue University Indianapolis, USA

ABSTRACT

System Execution Modeling (SEM) tools enable distributed system testers to validate Quality-of-Service (QoS) properties, such as end-to-end response time, throughput, and scalability, during early phases of the software lifecycle. Analytical capabilities of QoS properties, however, are traditionally bounded by a SEM tool's capabilities. This chapter discusses how to mine system execution traces, which are a collection of log messages describing events and states of a distributed system throughout its execution lifetime, generated by distributed systems so that the validation of QoS properties is not dependent on a SEM tool's capabilities. The author uses a real-life case study to illustrate how data mining system execution traces can assist in discovering potential performance bottlenecks using system execution traces.

INTRODUCTION

Enterprise distributed systems, such as mission avionic systems, traffic management systems, and shipboard computing environments, are transitioning to next-generation middleware, such as service-oriented middleware (Pezzini & Natis, 2007) and component-based software engineering (Heineman & Councill, 2001). Although next-generation middleware is improving enterprise distributed system functional properties (i.e.,

its operational scenarios), Quality-of-Service (QoS) properties (e.g., end-to-end response time, throughput, and scalability) are not validated until late in the software lifecycle, i.e., during system integration time. This is due in part to the *serialized-phasing development* problem (Rittel & Webber, 1973).

As illustrated in Figure 1, in serialized-phasing development, the infrastructure and application-level system entities, such as components that encapsulate common services, are developed during different phases of the software lifecycle. Software design decisions that affect QoS properties,

DOI: 10.4018/978-1-60960-067-9.ch009

Figure 1. Overview of serialized-phased development in distributed systems

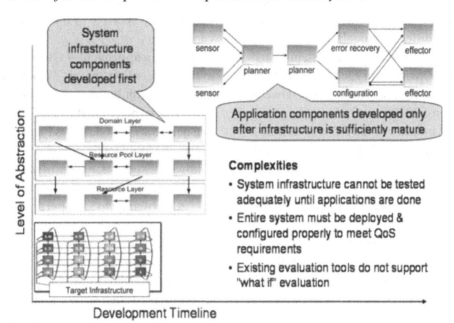

however, are typically not discovered until final stages of development, e.g., at system integration time, which is too late in the software lifecycle to resolve performance bottlenecks in an efficient and cost effective manner (Mann, 1996; Snow & Keil, 2001; Woodside, Franks, & Petriu, 2007).

System Execution Modeling (SEM) tools (Smith & Williams, 2001), which are a form of model-driven engineering (Schmidt, 2006), assist distributed system developers in overcoming the serialized-phasing development problem shown in Figure 1. SEM tools use domain-specific modeling languages (Ledeczi, Maroti, Karsai, & Nordstrom,1999) to capture both platform-independent attributes (such as structural and behavioral concerns of the system) and platform-specific attributes (such as the target architecture of the system) as high-level models. Model interpreters then transform constructed models into source code for the target architecture. This enables distributed system testers to validate QoS properties continuously throughout the software lifecycle while the "real" system is still under development. Likewise, as development of the real

system is complete, distributed system testers can incrementally replace *faux* portions of the system with its real counterpart to produce more realistic QoS validation results.

Although SEM tools enable distributed system developers and testers to validate distributed system QoS properties during early phases of the software lifecycle, QoS validation capabilities are typically bounded to a SEM tool's analytical capabilities. In order to validate QoS properties unknown to a SEM tool, distributed system testers have the following options:

- **Use handcrafted solutions:** This option typically occurs outside of the SEM. Moreover, this option is traditionally not applicable across different application domains because it is an *ad hoc* solution, e.g., handcrafting a solution to validate event response-time based on priority in a proprietary system;
- **Leverage model transformations to convert models to a different SEM tool:** This option implies the source and target

SEM tool supports the same modeling features and semantics. If the target SEM tools has different modeling features and semantics, then distributed system testers have discrepancies in QoS validation results (Denton, Jones, Srinivasan, Owens, & Buskens, 2008); or

• **Wait for updates to the SEM tool:** This is the best option for distributed system testers because it ensures consistency of QoS validation results when compared to the previous two options. In many cases, however, this option may not occur in a timely manner so that distributed system testers can leverage the updates in their QoS validation exercises. Distributed system testers therefore have to revert to either of the first two options until such updates are available, which can result in the problems previously discussed.

Consequently, relying solely on built-in validation capabilities of SEM tools can hinder distributed system testers to thoroughly validate enterprise distributed system QoS properties continuously throughout the software lifecycle. Distributed system testers therefore need improved

techniques that will enhance QoS analytical capabilities irrespective of the SEM tools existing capabilities.

Solution approach → QoS validation using system execution traces. To address problems associated with limited analytical capabilities of a SEM tool when validating QoS properties, there is a need for methodologies that extend conventional SEM tool methodologies and simplify the following exercises, as illustrated in Figure 2.

1. **Capturing QoS property metrics** without the SEM tool having *a priori* knowledge of what metrics (or data) is required to analyze different QoS properties. This step can be accomplished using system execution traces (Chang & Ren, 2007), which are a collection of log messages generated during the execution lifetime of a distributed system in its target environment. The log messages in the system execution trace are lightweight and flexible enough to adapt the many different QoS metrics that formulate throughout the software lifecycle and across different application domains;

2. **Identifying QoS property metrics** without requiring *a priori* knowledge of what data

Figure 2. Overview of using dataflow models to mine system execution traces and validate QoS properties

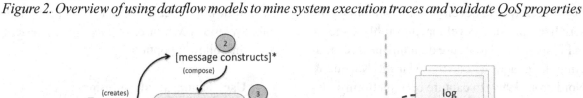

(or metrics) is being collected (i.e., the ability to learn at run-time). This step can be accomplished using *log formats*, which are expressions that identity the static and variable portions of log messages of interest within system execution traces generated in Step 1. The log formats are then used to mine system execution traces and extract metrics of interest for QoS validation; and

3. **Evaluating QoS properties** without *a priori* knowledge of how to analyze extracted QoS metrics. This step can be accomplished using dataflow models (Downs, Clare, & Coe, 1988) that enable distributed system testers auto-reconstruct end-to-end system execution traces for QoS validation. Distributed system testers then specify a domain-specific (i.e., user-defined) equation for validating QoS properties using metrics data minded in Step 2.

Using dataflow models to mine system execution traces enable distributed system testers to validate QoS properties independent of the SEM tool of choice. Likewise, as enterprise distributed systems continue increasing in size (e.g., number of lines of source code, and number of hardware/software resources) and complexity (e.g., envisioned operational scenarios), dataflow models can adapt without modification. This is because dataflow models operate at a higher level of abstraction than system composition (i.e., how components communicate with each other) and system complexity (i.e., the operational nature of the system in its target environment). Likewise, domain-specific analytics associated with dataflow models need not change.

This chapter illustrates the following concepts for using dataflow models to mine system execution traces and validate enterprise distributed system QoS properties:

- How to use high-level constructs to specify QoS metrics that are to be extracted from system execution traces;
- How to represent high-level constructs as dataflow models to ensure correct auto-reconstruction of end-to-end system execution traces; and
- How to use dataflow models to mine system execution traces and validate enterprise distributed system QoS properties using domain-specific analytical equations.

Distributed system testers therefore can focus more on using SEM tools to discover QoS bottlenecks specific to their application domain, and are ensured they will be able to perform such activities irrespective of a SEM tool's analytical capabilities.

BACKGROUND

Before beginning the discussion on using dataflow models to mine system execution traces and validate QoS properties, first let us understand existing techniques used to validate enterprise distributed system QoS properties. This section therefore summarizes current uses of system execution traces, data mining, and dataflow modeling, and conventional techniques for validating distributed systems QoS properties.

System Execution Traces

System execution traces can capture both metrics and the state of a system. Keeping this in mind, Chang and Ren (2007) has investigated techniques for automating the functional validation of test using execution traces. Likewise, Moe and Carr (2001) discuss techniques for understanding and detecting functional anomalies in distributed systems by reconstructing and analyzing (or data mining) system execution traces. Irrespective of how system execution traces are used, their key advantage to validating functional concerns is platform, architecture, and language independence. Therefore this helps to increase the quality of the overall solution (Boehm, Brown, & Lipow, 1976) so that it is applicable across different application domains.

Data Mining

Data mining system execution traces to locate faults is a well-studied research topic. For example, Denmat et al. (2005) reinterpreted Jones et al. (2002) problem to visualizing faulty statements (i.e., statements that could be potential sources of a bug) in execution traces as a data mining problem. In doing so, Denmat et al. (2005) were able to uncover limitations in Jones et al. solution approach and address some of the limitations. Likewise, Lo et al. (2007) contribute to the domain of *specification mining* (Ammons, Bodik, & Larus, 2002 ; Lo & Khoo, 2006), which is the process of inferring specifications from execution traces. In their work, Lo et al. (2007) developed several data mining algorithms that can reconstruct scenarios from execution traces for visualization as UML2 Sequence Diagrams. Finally, Lo et al. (2008) developed algorithms for data mining execution traces to discover temporal rules about program execution, which can help understand system behavior and improve program verification.

Although data mining system execution traces has been heavily researched (e.g., locating faults and understanding program behavior), existing research focuses primarily on functional properties of the system. Data mining system execution traces to validate QoS properties, such as end-to-end response time, throughput, and scalability, has not been studied in much detail – especially in the context of distributed systems. This chapter therefore provides contributions on enabling data mining of system execution traces for distributed systems and validation of QoS properties.

Distributed System Analysis

Mania et al. (2002) discusses a technique for developing performance models and analyzing component-based distributed system using execution traces. The contents of traces are generated by system events. When analyzing the systems performance, however, Mania et al. (2002) rely on synchronized clocks to reconstruct system behavior. Although this technique suffices in tightly coupled environments, if clocks on different hosts drift (as may be the case in ultra-large-scale systems), then the reconstructed behavior and analysis may be incorrect. Similarly, Mos and Murphy (2001) presents a technique for monitoring Java-based components in a distributed system using proxies, which relies on timestamps in the events and implies a global unique identifier to reconstruct method invocation traces for system analysis.

Parsons et al. (2006) presents a technique for performing end-to-end event tracing in component-based distributed systems. Their technique injects a global unique identifier at the beginning of the event's trace (e.g., when a new user enters the system). This unique identifier is then propagated through the system and used to associate data for analytical purposes (i.e., to preserve data integrity). In large- or ultra-large-scale enterprise distributed systems, however, it can be hard to ensure unique identifiers are propagated throughout components created by third parties.

Dataflow Modeling

Dataflow models, also known as dataflow diagrams, have been used extensively in software design and specification (Downs, Clare, & Coe, 1988; Jilani, Nadeem, Kim, & Cho, 2008), digital signal processing (Lee & Parks, 2002), and business processing modeling (Russell, van der Aalst, ter Hofstede, & Wohed, 2006). For example, Vazquez (1994) invested techniques for automatically deriving dataflow models from formal specifications of software systems. Likewise, Russell et al. (2006) investigates the feasibility of using UML activity diagrams within business processing process, which include dataflow modeling. In all cases, dataflow modeling was utilized because it provides a means for representing system functionality without being bounded to the systems overall composition. This is because the dataflow models, in theory, remain constant unless the system's specification changes.

To date, little research has investigated the use of dataflow models to mine system execution traces and validate QoS properties. Because system execution traces are dense and rich sources of information, they are good candidates for data mining to validate QoS properties. The main challenge, however, is extracting information from the system execution traces while (1) preserving data integrity and (2) analyzing extracted data (or metrics) at without *a priori* knowledge its structure and complexity.

As discussed later in this chapter, dataflow modeling is one part of the solution to data mining system execution traces to validate distributed system QoS properties. The dataflow models are used to capture how data is transmitted throughout a distributed system. This information is then used to reconstruct end-to-end system execution traces and preserve data integrity (i.e., ensuring metrics are correlated with their correct chain of events) so the user-defined evaluation function analyzes the metrics correctly.

MOTIVATIONAL CASE STUDY: THE QED PROJECT

The Global Information Grid (GIG) middleware (National Security Agency, 2009) is an enterprise distributed system from the class of Ultra-Large-Scale (ULS) systems (Software Engineering Institute, 2006). The GIG is designed to ensure that different applications can collaborate effectively and deliver appropriate information to users in a

timely, dependable, and secure manner. Due to the scale and complexity of the GIG, however, conventional implementations do not provide adequate end-to-end QoS assurance to applications that must respond rapidly to priority shifts and unfolding situations.

The QoS-Enabled Dissemination (QED) project (Loyall, Carvalho, Schmidt, Gillen, Martignoni, & Bunch, 2009) is a multi-organization collaboration designed to improve GIG middleware so it can meet QoS requirements of users and distributed applications and systems. QED's aim therefore is to provide reliable and real-time communication middleware that is resilient to the dynamically changing conditions of GIG environments. Figure 3 shows QED in the context of the GIG. At the heart of the QED middleware is a Java information broker based on the Java Messaging Service and JBoss that enables tailoring and prioritizing of information based on mission needs and importance, and responds rapidly to priority shifts and unfolding situations. Moreover, QED leverages technologies such as Mockets (Tortonesi, Stefanelli, Suri, Arguedas, & Breedy, 2006) and differentiated service queues (El-Gendy, Bose, & Shin, 2003) to provide QoS assurance to GIG applications.

The QED project is in the early phases of its software lifecycle and its development is slated to run for several more years. Since the QED middleware is infrastructure software, applications that use it cannot be developed until the middleware itself is sufficiently mature. It is therefore hard for QED developers to ensure their software architecture and implementations are actually improving the QoS of applications that will ultimately run on the GIG middleware. The QED project thus faces the serialized-phasing development problem as explained in the introduction section.

To overcome the serialized-phasing problem, QED developers are using SEM tools to automatically execute performance regression tests against the QED and evaluate QoS attributes

Figure 3. Overview of QED in the context of the GIG middleware

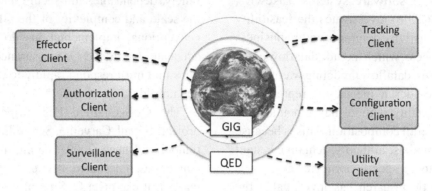

continuously throughout its development. In particular, QED is using the Component Workload Emulator (CoWorkEr) Utilization Test Suite (CUTS) (Hill, Slaby, Baker, & Schmidt, 2006), which is a platform-independent SEM tool for enterprise distributed systems. Distributed system developers and testers use CUTS by modeling the behavior and workload of their enterprise distributed system and generating a test system for their target architecture. Distributed system testers then execute the test system on the target architecture and validate QoS attributes. This process is repeated continuously throughout the software lifecycle to increase confidence levels in QoS assurance.

Previous research showed how integrating CUTS-like SEM tools with continuous integration environments provided a flexible solution for executing and managing distributed system tests continuously throughout the software lifecycle (Hill, Schmidt, Slaby, & Porter, 2008). This work also showed how system execution traces capture metrics of interest for validating QoS properties. Applying results from prior work to the initial prototype of the QED middleware, however, revealed the following limitations of adapting CUTS to the QED project:

- **Limitation 1: Inability to mine metrics of interest unknown *a priori* to SEM tools.** Data mining is the process of discov-

ering relevant information in a data source, such as a system execution trace, that can be used for analysis (e.g., validating QoS properties). In the initial version of CUTS, data mining was limited to metrics that CUTS knew *a priori*, i.e., at compilation time. It was therefore hard to identify, locate, and extract data for metrics of interest, especially if QoS evaluation functions needed data that CUTS did not know *a priori*, such as metrics extracted from a real component that replaces an emulate component and CUTS is not aware of its implementation.

QED testers therefore need a technique to identify metrics of interest that can be extracted from large amounts of system data. Moreover, the extraction technique should allow testers to identify key metrics at a high-level of abstraction and be flexible enough to handle data variation for effective application to enterprise distributed systems. This technique can be realized using log formats, which are high-level abstractions that capture variable and static portions of log messages in system execution traces. The variable portion of each log format is also used to mine and extract metrics of interest from system execution traces, which can later be used in user-defined equations that analyze QoS properties.

- **Limitation 2: Inability to analyze and aggregate extracted data unknown *a priori* to SEM tools.** Data analysis and aggregation is the process of evaluating extracted data based on user-defined equations, and combining multiple results (if applicable) into a single result. This process is necessary since evaluating QoS properties traditionally yields a scalar result, such as evaluating that the response-time of an event is 30.4 msec. In the initial version of CUTS, data analysis and aggregation was limited to functions that CUTS knew *a priori*, which made it hard to analyze data using user-defined functions.

QED testers needed a flexible technique for analyzing metrics using user-defined functions. Moreover, the technique should preserve data integrity (i.e., ensuring data is associated with its correct execution trace), especially as the system increases in both complexity and size. This technique can be realized using dataflow models and analyzing the dataflow using relational database theory techniques (Atzeni & Antonellis, 1993).

- **Limitation 3: Inability to manage complexity of dataflow model specification.** As enterprise distributed systems increase in size and complexity, challenges associated with Limitations 1 and 2 described above will also increase in complexity. For example, as distributed system implementations mature more components are often added and the amount of data generated for QoS attribute evaluation will increase. Likewise, the specification of a QoS attribute evaluation equations will also increase because there is more data to manage and filter.

QED testers need a flexible and lightweight technique that will ensure complexities associated with limitations 1 and 2 are addressed properly as the QED implementation matures and increases in size and complexity. Moreover, the technique should enforce constraints of the overall process, but be intuitive to use by QED testers. This technique can be accomplished using domain-specific modeling languages (Sztipanovits & Karsai, 1997; Gray, Tolvanen, Kelly, Gokhale, Neema, & Sprinkle, 2007), which are abstractions that capture the semantics and constraints of a target domain while providing intuitive graphical representations that shield end-users, such as the QED testers, from its complexities.

Due to the limitations described above, it was hard for QED testers to use the initial version of CUTS and validate QoS properties without being dependent on its analytical capabilities. Moreover, this problem extends beyond the QED project and applies to other projects need to validate QoS properties irrespective of a SEM tool's analytical capabilities. The following section discusses how system testers can data mine system execution traces generated by a distributed system to validate QoS properties and address the limitations previously described.

DATA MINING SYSTEM EXECUTION TRACES USING DATA FLOW MODELS

This section describes in detail the technique of using dataflow models to mine system execution traces and validate of distributed system QoS properties independent of the SEM tool's analytical capabilities. This section also describes how the technique is realized in an open-source tool called UNITE, which has been integrated into the CUTS SEM tool. Finally, this section concludes by illustrating how UNITE is applied to the QED project case study.

Specifying QoS Metrics to Mine from System Execution Traces

System execution traces, which are a collection of log messages generated throughout the lifetime of a system executing in its target environment, are essential in understanding the behavior of a system, whether or not the system is distributed (Joukov, Wong, & Zadok, 2005 ; Chang & Ren, 2007). Such artifacts typically contain key data that can be used to analyze the system online and/or offline. For example, Listing 1 shows a simple system execution trace produced by a distributed system that requires password authentication before clients can use its resources.

Listing 1. Example of system execution trace produced by a distributed system.

1.   activating LoginComponent
2.   *(more log messages)*
3.   LoginComponent received request 6 at 1234945638
4.   validating username and password for request 6
5.   username and password is valid
6.   granting access at 1234945652 to request 6
7.   *(more log messages)*
8.   deactivating the LoginComponent

As illustrated in Listing 1, each line in the system execution trace represents an effect in the system. Moreover, each line in Listing 1 captures the state of the system when the log message was produced. For example, line 3 states when LoginComponent received a login request and line 6 captures when LoginComponent granted access to the client.

Although a system execution trace contains key data for analyzing the system that produced it, a system execution trace is traditionally generated in a verbose format that can be understood by humans. This implies that information data captured in a system execution trace can be discarded. Each log message that appears in a system execution trace is also constructed from a well-defined format—called a *log format. Log formats* are high-level constructs that capture both constant and variable portions of individual, yet similar, log messages in a system execution trace. The information captured in the variable portion of a log format represents metrics that is data mined from the system execution trace and is usable in domain-specific analytical equations. This format remains constant throughout the execution lifetime of system, and only certain values (or variables) in each log format, e.g., time or event count, change over time. The challenge therefore is specifying what metrics should be data mined from the system execution trace so that the extracted data is useable in user-defined analytical equations.

Specifying log formats in UNITE. In UNITE, log formats are specified using high-level constructs composed of human readable text and placeholders identified by brackets { }. Table 1 shows the different placeholder types supported by UNITE). The brackets are used to tag variables (or metrics) that are to be data mined from a system execution trace generated by a distributed system. Each placeholder (or bracket) also represents variable change in a log message (such as those presented in Listing 1) over the course of the system's lifetime. This enables UNITE to address Limitation 1 introduced at the latter part of the case study.

UNITE caches the variables and converts the high-level construct into a regular expression, such as a PERL compatible regular expression (www.pcre.org). The regular expression is used during the data mining process to identify log messages that have candidate data for variables in log format.

Listing 2. Example of log formats for identifying metrics of interest

LF1: {STRING owner} received request {INT reqid} at {INT recv}

Table 1. Log format variable types supported by UNITE

Type	Description
INT	Integer data type
STRING	String data type (with no spaces)
FLOAT	Floating-point data type

LF2: granting access at {INT reply} to request {INT reqid}

PERL Compatible Regular Expression:

LF1: (?<owner>\\S+) received request (?<reqid>-?\\d+) at (?<reqid>-?\\d+)

LF2: granting access at (?<reply>-?\\d+) to request (?<reqid>-?\\d+)

Listing 2 highlights high-level constructs for two log message entries from Listing 1 and the corresponding PERL compatible regular expression. The First Log Format (LF1) is used to mine log messages related to receiving client login requests (line 3 in Listing 1). The second log format (LF2) is used to mine log messages related to granting access to a client's login request (line 6 in Listing 1). Overall, there are 5 variables in Listing 2. Only two variables, however, capture metrics of interest: recv in LF1 and reply in LF2. The remaining three variables (i.e., owner, LF1. reqid, and LF2.reqid) are used to determine causality and preserve data integrity.

Preserving Data Integrity during the Data Mining Process

In the log formats that are used for identifying log messages in system execution traces that contain data (or metrics) of interest, each log format contains a set of tags, which are representative of variables that are used to mine metrics for each log format. In the simplest case, a single log format can be used to validate QoS properties. For example, if a distributed system tester wants to know how many events a component received per second, i.e.,

the arrival rate of events, then the component could cache the necessary data internally and generate a single log message reflecting this metric when the system is shutdown.

Although this approach is feasible, i.e., caching data and generating a single log message, it is not practical in a distributed system because individual data points needed to validate a QoS property can be generated by different components. Moreover, data points can be generated by components deployed on different hosts. What is needed therefore is the capability of generating independent log messages and specifying how to associate independent log messages with each other to preserve data integrity. This capability can be realized using a dataflow model. In the context of data mining system execution traces, a dataflow model is defined as:

- A set of log formats that have variables identifying what data to mine from system execution traces; and
- A set of causal relations that specify the order of occurrence for each log format such that $CR_{i,j}$ means $LF_i \rightarrow LF_j$, or LF_i occurs before LF_j.

To understand how dataflow models can be used in this situation in a better way, it is necessary to understand the role of log formats first. As discussed in the previous section, system execution traces capture (ordered) events and the state of a distributed system throughout its execution lifetime. The individual log messages in a system execution trace also can be identified using log formats. Since the log formats are directly related to log messages in a system execution trace, the order of a log format will be the same as the order of occurrence for log messages in a system execution trace. If a dataflow model consists of nodes (i.e., individual data points) and relations (i.e., how data is transmitted between individual nodes), then log formats represent the individual nodes in the dataflow model. More specifically, log format variables represent the individual nodes in a dataflow model since they capture critical pieces of information in system execution traces need to construct it.

After defining the nodes in a dataflow model, the next step is to define the relations between nodes (i.e., the log formats). As a result, this paves the way for defining the causality in the dataflow model. Causal relations are traditionally based on time (Singhal & Shivaratri, 1994), such as determining that e_1 is causally related to e_2 because $t_1 < t_2$ when using a global clock to timestamp events. This notion of time, however, does not exist in dataflow models used to mine system execution traces. This is because log format variables are used to determine causality since the value of a variable is guaranteed to not change between two causally related log formats, and removes all ambiguity when determining causality of events in dense system execution traces.

Using log format variables to define causality between nodes in the dataflow model also has other several advantages over using time, such as: it alleviates dependencies on (1) using a globally unique identifier (e.g., a unique id generated at the beginning of a system execution trace and propagated throughout the system or a global clock) and (2) requiring knowledge of system composition to associate metrics across multiple log messages and to preserve data integrity.

Instead, the only requirement of the dataflow model is that two unique log formats can be associated with each other via their variables, and each log format is in at least one causal relation. This requirement, however, can result in circular relations between log formats. Circular relations therefore are not permitted because it requires human intervention to determine where the relation chain between log formats begins and ends.

Specifying dataflow models in UNITE. In UNITE, distributed system testers specify dataflow models by selecting what log formats are used to mine system execution traces. If more than one log format is needed, then they must specify

a causal relation between each log format. When specifying casual relations, distributed system testers select variables from the corresponding log format that represent the cause and effect.

For example, if a QED developer wants to calculate duration of the login operation, then they create a dataflow model using LF1 and LF2 from Listing 2. Next, a causal relation is defined between LF1 and LF2 as:

Listing 3. Example of a causal relation in a dataflow model

LF1.reqid = LF2.reqid

As Listing 3 illustrates, LF1 and LF2 are causally related to each other based on the value of reqid in either log format. Now that it is possible to define a dataflow model in terms of log formats and their causal relations, a discussion of how to evaluate dataflow models using user-defined evaluation functions based on metrics data mined from system execution traces is given in the next section.

Evaluating Dataflow Models Using User-Defined Equations

The previous sections discussed how log formats are (1) used to identify log messages that contains data of interest, and (2) used to construct dataflow models to mine system execution traces. The main purpose of the dataflow model is to preserve data integrity, which is essential to ensure all data points are associated with the execution trace (or event) that generated it. The final step in the process is therefore to evaluate the dataflow model using a user-defined equation, which represents validating a QoS property that is unknown to a SEM tool. For example, if a distributed system developer wanted to calculate the authentication time based on the system execution trace presented in Listing 1, they would define the following equation:

Figure 4. Four types of causal relations that can occur in a distributed system

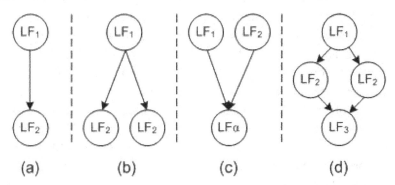

Listing 4. Example of a user-defined equation for evaluating authentication time

LF2.reply − LF1.recv

Before discussing how to evaluate a user-defined equation, such as the one presented in Listing 4, using a dataflow model and metrics data mined from system execution traces, it is necessary to first understand the different types of causal relations that can occur in a distributed system.

There are four types of causal relations that can occur in a distributed system and can affect the algorithm used to evaluate a dataflow model. As shown in Figure 4, the first type is (a) one-to-one relation, which is the most trivial type to resolve between multiple log formats. The second type is (b) one-to-many relation and is a result of a multicast event. The third type is (c) many-to-one, which occurs when many different components send an event type to a single component. The final type is (d) a combination of previous types (a)–(c), and is the most complex relation to resolve between multiple log formats.

If it is assumed that each entry in a message log contains its origin, e.g., hostname, then it is possible to use a dynamic programming algorithm and relational database theory (Atzeni & Antonellis, 1993) to reconstruct the data table that contains all the variables from a dataflow model. As shown

in Algorithm 1, first a directed graph where log formats are nodes and the casual relations are edges is constructed. Next, the directed graph is topologically sorted so the evaluation knows the order to process each log format. This step is also necessary because when causal relation types (b) – (d) are present in the dataflow model specification, processing the log formats in reverse order of occurrence reduces algorithm complexity for constructing the dataset. Moreover, it ensures the algorithm has rows in the dataset to accommodate the data from log formats that occur prior to the current log format.

Algorithm 1. General algorithm for evaluating dataflow models

```
1  procedure EVALUATE (dataflow, logmsgs) {
2    let dataflow' = topological_sort(dataflow);
3    let dataset = variables_table(dataflow);
4    let sorted = sort_host_then_time(logmsgs);
5
6    foreach (LF_i in dataflow') {
7      let K = C_i from CR_{i,j}
8
9      foreach (logmsg in sorted) {
10       if (logmsg matches LF_i) {
11         let V = values_of_variables(logmsg);
12
13         if (K is not empty set){
14           UPDATE dataset WITH V USING K;
15         }
16         else {
17           INSERT V INTO dataset;
18         }
19       }
20     }
21   }
22 }
```

After topologically sorting the log formats, a dataset, which is a table that has a column for each log format variable in the dataflow model, is constructed. This dataset is constructed by first sorting the log messages by origin and time to ensure correct message sequence for each origin. More importantly, this enables presentation of the data trend over the lifetime of the system before aggregating the results.

Finally, each log format is matched against each log messages (or all the log messages for each log format is selected for processing). If there is a match, then the value of each variable in the log message is extracted, and the dataset is updated based on the following rules:

- **Rule for appending data.** If there is no cause variable set for the current log format, then the values from the log message are appended to the end of the data set.
- **Rule for inserting data.** If there is a variable set for the cause log format, then all the rows in the dataset where the cause's values equal the effect's values are updated (see Listing 3 for an example).

Finally, all incomplete rows are purged from the dataset and it is evaluated using the user-defined evaluation function (see Listing 4).

Managing duplicate data entries. For long running systems, it is not uncommon to see variations of the same log message within the complete set of log messages. Moreover, log formats are defined to identify variable portions of a message. The evaluation process is therefore expected to encounter similar log messages multiple times.

When constructing the data set in Algorithm 1, different variations of the same log format creates multiple rows in the final data set. QoS properties, however, are a single scalar value, and not multiple values. The following techniques are therefore used to address this concern:

- **Aggregation.** A function used to convert a dataset to a single value. Examples of an aggregation functions are, but not limited to: AVERAGE, MIN, MAX, and SUM.
- **Grouping.** Given an aggregation function, grouping is used to identify datasets that should be treated independent of each other. For example, in the case of causal relation (d) in Figure 4, the values in the dataset for each sender (i.e., LF2) could be considered a group and analyzed independently.

Evaluating dataflow models in UNITE. UNITE implements Algorithm 1 using the SQLite relational database (www.sqlite.org). To construct the variable table, the data values for the first log format are first inserted directly into the table since it has no causal relations. For the remaining log formats, the causal relation(s) is transformed into a SQL UPDATE query, which allows UNITE to update only rows in the table where the relation equals values of interest in the current log message. Listing 5 shows an example SQL UPDATE query for inserting new data into the existing dataset based on causality relations between two log formats: LF1 and LF2.

Listing 5. SQL query for inserting new data into an existing dataset

```
UPDATE dataset SET LF1_recv = ?recv AND
LF1_reqid = ?reqid
WHERE LF2_reqid = ?reqid;
```

Table 2 shows the variable table (or dataset) constructed by UNITE for the example dataflow model. After the variable data table is constructed, the evaluation function and groupings for the dataflow model are used to create the final SQL query that evaluates it, thereby addressing Limitation 2 introduced at the latter part of the case study.

Listing 6 shows the example evaluation function as an SQL query, which is used to evaluate

Table 2. A sample dataset for evaluating dataflow model in UNITE

LF1.reqid	LF1.recv	LF2.reqid	LF2.reply
6	1234945638	6	1234945652
7	1234945690	7	1234945705
8	1234945730	8	1234945750

the dataset in Table 2. The final result of this example would be 16.33 msec. Likewise, if the AVERAGE aggregation function is removed, then distributed system testers can view the data trend for average login time, which can help discover potential performance bottlenecks.

Listing 6. SQL query for calculating average login time

SELECT AVG(LF2.reply − LF1.recv) AS result
FROM dataset;

Managing the Complexity of Dataflow Models

UNITE uses dataflow models to validate distributed system QoS properties. Although dataflow models enable UNITE to validate QoS properties independent of a SEM tool's capabilities, as dataflow models increase in size (i.e., number of log formats and relations between log formats) it becomes harder for distributed system developers to manage their complexity. This challenge arises since dataflow models are similar to finite state machines (i.e., the log formats are the states and the relations are the transitions between states), which incur state-space explosion problems (Harel, 1987).

To ensure efficient and effective application of dataflow models towards validating enterprise distributed system QoS attributes, UNITE leverages a model-driven engineering technique called domain-specific modeling languages (Sztipanovits & Karsai, 1997; Gray et al., 2007). Domain-specific

modeling languages capture both the abstractions and semantics of a target domain while providing intuitive abstractions for modeling and addressing concerns within the target domain. In the context of dataflow models, domain-specific modeling languages provide graphical representations that reduce the following complexities:

- **Visualizing dataflow.** To construct a dataflow model, it is essential to understand dataflow throughout the system, as shown in Figure 4. An invalid understanding of dataflow can result in an invalid specification of a dataflow model. By using domain-specific modeling languages, distributed system testers can construct dataflow models as graphs, which help visualize dataflow and ensure valid construction of such models, especially as they increase in size and complexity.

- **Enforcing valid relations.** The relations in a dataflow model enable evaluation of QoS attribute independent of system composition. Invalid specification of a relation, however, can result in invalid evaluation of a dataflow model. For example, distributed system developers and tests may relate a variable between two different log formats that are of a different type (e.g., one is of type INT and the other is of type STRING), but have the same variable name (e.g., id). By using domain-specific modeling languages, it is possible to enforce constraints that will ensure such relations are not possible in constructed models.

UNITE implements several Domain-specific modeling languages using an MDE tool called the Graphical Modeling Environment (GME) (Ledeczi, Bakay, Maroti, Volgyesi, Nordstrom, & Sprinkle, 2001). GME allows system and software engineers, such as distributed system developers and testers, to author Domain-specific modeling languages for a target domain, such as dataflow

Figure 5. Example dataflow model in UNITE's domain-specific modeling language

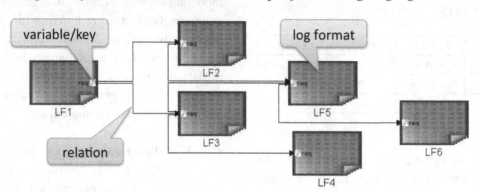

modeling. End-users then construct models using the specified domain-specific modeling language and use model interpreters to generate concrete artifacts from constructed models, such as a configuration file that specifies how UNITE should evaluate a dataflow graph.

Figure 5 shows an example dataflow model for UNITE in GME. Each rectangular object in this figure (i.e., LF1 and LF2) represents a log format in the dataflow model that contains variables for extracting metrics of interest from system execution traces. The lines between two log formats represent a relation between variables in either log format. When distributed system testers create a relation between two different variables, the domain-specific modeling language validates the connection (i.e., ensures the variable types are equal). Likewise, distributed system testers can execute the GME constraint checker to validate systemic constraints, such as validating that the dataflow model is acyclic.

After constructing a dataflow model using UNITE's domain-specific modeling language, distributed system testers use model interpreters to auto-generate configuration files that dictate how to mine system execution traces. The configuration file is a dense XML-based file that would be tedious and error-prone to create manually. UNITE's domain-specific modeling language graphic representation and constraint checking therefore reduces complexity in managing dataflow models, thereby addressing Limitation 3 introduced at the latter part of the QED case study.

EXPERIMENTAL RESULTS

As mentioned in motivational case study, the QED project is in the early phases of it software lifecycle. Although it is expected to continue for several years, QED developers do not want to wait until system integration time to validate the performance of their middleware infrastructure relative to stated QoS requirements. QED testers therefore are using CUTS and UNITE to perform early integration testing. All tests were run in a representative testbed at ISISlab (www.isislab. vanderbilt.edu), which is powered by Emulab software (Ricci, Alfred, & Lepreau, 2003). Each host in the experiment was an IBM Blade Type L20, dual-CPU, 2.8-GHz processor, with 1 GB RAM configured with the Fedora Core 6 operating system.

To test the QED middleware, QED developers first constructed several scenarios using CUTS' modeling languages (Hill & Gokhale, 2007). Each scenario was designed so that all components communicate with each other using a single server in the GIG (similar to Figure 3). The first scenario was designed to test different thresholds of the underlying GIG middleware to discover potential areas that could be improved by the QED middleware. The second scenario was more complex and emulated a multi-stage workflow that tests the underlying middleware's ability to ensure application-level QoS properties, such as reliability and end-to-end response time when handling applications with different priorities and privileges.

The QED multi-stage workflow has six types of components, as shown in Figure 6. Each directed line that connects a component represents a communication event (or stage) that must pass through the GIG (and QED) middleware before being delivered to the component on the opposite end. Moreover, each directed line conceptually represents where QED will be applied to ensure QoS between communicating components. The projection from the middle component represents the behavior of that specific component. Each component in the multi-stage workflow has a behavior model/workload (based on Timed I/O Automata) (Kaynar, Lynch, Segala, & Vaandrager, 2006) that dictates its actions during a test. Moreover, each behavior model contains actions for logging key data needed to validate QoS properties using dataflow models, similar to Listing 1 in the previous section. Listing 7 lists an example message from the multi-stage workflow scenario.

Listing 7. Example log messages from the multi-stage workflow scenario

- ○ MainAssembly.SurveillanceClient: Event 0: Published a SurveillanceMio at 1219789376684
- ○ MainAssembly.SurveillanceClient: Event 1: Time to publish a SurveillanceMio at 1219789376685

This log message contains information about the event, such as event id and timestamp. Each component also generates log messages about the events it receives and its state (such as event count). In addition, each component sends enough information to create a causal relation between

itself and the receiver, so there is no need for a global unique identifier to preserve data integrity when data mining the system execution trace. QED developers next used UNITE to construct log formats (as discussed in the previous section) for identifying log messages during a test run that contain metrics of interest. These log formats were also used to define dataflow models that validate QED's QoS properties. In particular, QED developers were interested in validating and understanding the following QoS properties using dataflow models in UNITE:

- **Multiple publishers.** At any point in time, the GIG will have many components publishing and receiving events simultaneously. QED developers therefore need to evaluate the response time of events under such operating conditions. Moreover, QED needs to ensure QoS when the infrastructure servers must manage many events. In order to improve the QoS of the GIG middleware, however, QED developers must first understand the current capabilities of the GIG middleware without QED in place. These results provide a baseline for evaluating the extent to which the QED middleware capabilities improve application-level QoS.

- **Time spent in server.** One way to ensure high QoS for events is to reduce the time an event spends in a server. Since a third-party vender provides the GIG middleware, QED developers cannot ensure it will generate log messages that can be used to calculate how it takes the server to process an event. Instead, QED developers must rely on messages generated from distributed application components whenever it publishes/sends an event.

For an event that propagates through the system, QED developers use Equation 1 to calculate how much time the event spends in the server

Figure 6. CUTS model of the multi-stage workflow test scenario

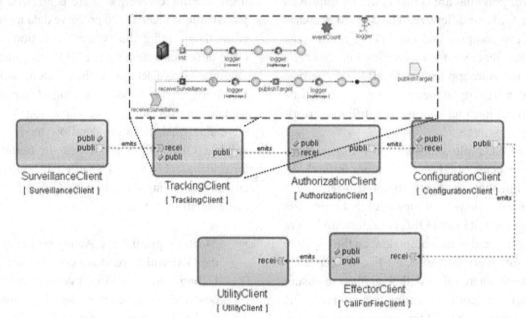

assuming event transmission is instantaneous, i.e., negligible.

$$(end_e - start_e) - \sum_c S_{c_e}. \qquad (1)$$

This equation also shows how QED developers calculate the time spent in the server by taking the response time of the event e, and subtracting the sum of the service time of the event in each component S_{c_e}.

Analyzing Multiple Publisher Results. Table 3 presents the results for tests that evaluate average end-to-end response time for an event when each publisher publishes at 75 Hz. As expected, the response time for each importance value was similar. When this scenario was tested using UNITE, the test results presented in Table 3 were calculated from two different log formats—either log format generated by a publisher and the subscriber.

UNITE also allows QED developer and testers to view the data trend for the dataflow models QoS validation of this scenario to get a more detailed understanding of performance. Figure 7 shows how the response time of the event increases over the lifetime of the experiment. It is known beforehand that this configuration for the test produced too much workload. UNITE's data trend and visualization capabilities, however, helped make it clear the extent to which the GIG middleware was being over utilized.

Analyzing maximum sustainable publish rate results. QED developers used the multi-stage workflow to describe a complex scenario tests the limits of the GIG middleware without forcing it into incremental queuing of events. Figure 8 graphs the data trend for the test, which is calculated by specifying Equation 1 as the evaluation for the dataflow model, and was produced by UNITE after analyzing (i.e., data mining metrics form) system execution traces. The test also consisted of several different log formats and causal relations, which were of types (a) and (b), as illustrated in Figure 4.

Figure 8 shows the sustainable publish rate of the multi-stage workflow in ISISlab. This figure shows how the Java just-in-time compiler and

Table 3. Average end-to-end Response Time (RT) for multiple publishers sending events at 75 Hz

Publisher Name	Importance	Average E2E Response Time (msec)
Client A	30	103931.14
Client B	15	103885.47
Client C	10	103938.33

other Java features cause the QED middleware to temporarily increase the individual message end-to-end response. By the end of the test, the time an event spends in the server reduces to normal operating conditions.

The multi-stage workflow results provided two insights to QED developers. First, their theory of maximum publish rate in ISISlab was confirmed. Second, Figure 8 helped developers speculate on what features of the GIG middleware might cause performance bottlenecks, how QED could address such problems, and what new test are need to illustrate QED's improvements to the GIG middleware. By providing QED testers with comprehensive testing and analysis features using dataflow models to mine system execution traces via UNITE helped guide the development team to the next phase of testing and integration of feature sets.

FUTURE RESEARCH DIRECTIONS

Based on the results and experience developing and applying UNITE to a representative distributed system, the following is a list of future research directions:

- **Investigating techniques to optimize data mining and evaluation time:** As the system execution traces increase in size, the evaluation time of the dataflow model increases. Future work therefore should investigate techniques for optimizing evaluation of dataflow models so evaluation time is not dependent on the size of the system execution traces.

- **Investigating techniques for enabling multiple viewpoints (or aspects):** Creating system execution traces can be an

Figure 7. Data trend graph of average end-to-end response time for multiple publishers sending events at 75 Hz

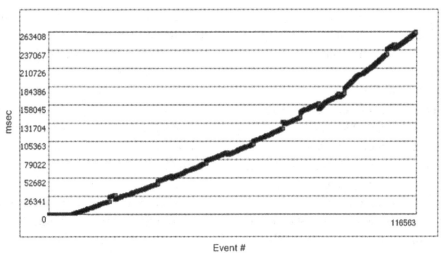

Figure 8. Data trend of the system placed in near optimal publish rate

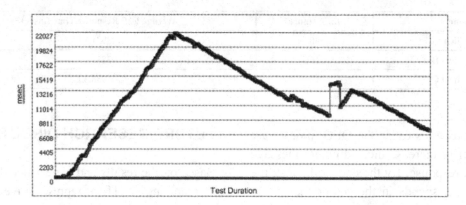

expensive process because it requires executing the system in its target environment. Currently, a single dataflow graph is used to mine a system execution trace and used to validate a single QoS property. QoS, however, is a multi-dimensional property. Future research therefore should investigate techniques for enabling multiple viewpoints using a single dataflow model and system execution trace.

- **Investigating techniques to use dataflow models to mine validate the distributed system state using system execution traces:** System execution traces not only capture metrics, but it also captures the state of the system. Future research therefore should investigate techniques for validating system state while the system is both online (i.e., in real-time) and offline (i.e., after the system is shutdown) using system execution traces.

- **Investigating techniques to mine system execution traces and auto-construct dataflow models:** Although UNITE's domain-specific modeling language was designed to reduce complexities associated with defining and managing dataflow models, it is tedious and error-prone to ensure their specification will extract the correct metrics. This is because there is discon-

nect between the log messages used to generate execution traces and log formats that extract metrics from log messages in a system execution trace. Future research therefore should investigate techniques for auto-generating dataflow models from system execution traces to ease the specification process.

CONCLUSION

This chapter describes and evaluates a technique of using dataflow models to mine system execution traces and validate QoS properties. The chapter also describes how the dataflow and data mining techniques has been realized in a tool called UNITE. UNITE enables distributed system testers to validate QoS properties irrespective of SEM tool of choice. Moreover, UNITE can be used to validate QoS properties irrespective of the SEM tool's existing analytical capabilities.

Based on the results and experience developing and applying UNITE to a representative enterprise distributed system, the following lessons were learned:

- **Dataflow modeling increases the level of abstraction for validating QoS properties.** Instead of requiring knowledge of system composition and implementation, dataflow models provided a platform-, architecture-, and technology-independent technique for validating QoS properties.

- **Domain-specific modeling languages help manage the complexity of data-flow models.** This is because the domain-specific modeling languages provide QED testers with visual abstractions that were clear representations of the target domain. It therefore made it easier for them to compose such models, and ensure they were valid before using them to mine system execution traces.

REFERENCES

Ammons, G., Bodik, R., & Larus, J. R. (2002). Mining Specifications. *ACM SIGPLAN Notices, 37*(1), 4–16. doi:10.1145/565816.503275

Atzeni, P., & Antonellis, V. D. (1993). *Relational Database Theory.* Redwood, CA, USA: Benjamin-Cummings Publishing Co.

Boehm, B. W., Brown, J. R., & Lipow, M. (1976). Quantitative Evaluation of Software Quality. In *The 2nd International Conference on Software Engineering* (pp. 592-605). San Francisco, CA: IEEE Computer Society Press.

Chang, F., & Ren, J. (2007). Validating System Properties Exhibited in Execution Traces. In *IEEE/ACM International Conference on Automated Software Engineering* (pp. 517-520). Atlanta, GA: ACM.

Denmat, T., Ducasse, M., & Ridoux, O. (2005). Data Mining and Cross-checking of Execution Traces: A Re-interpretation of Jones, Harrold and Stasko Test Information Visualization. In *20th IEEE/ACM International Conference on Automated Software Engineering* (pp. 396–399). Long Beach, CA: ACM/IEEE.

Denton, T., Jones, E., Srinivasan, S., Owens, K., & Buskens, R. W. (2008). NAOMI – An Experimental Platform for Multi-modeling. In *ACM/IEEE 11th International Conference on Model Driven Engineering Languages & Systems.* Toulouse, France.

Downs, E., Clare, P., & Coe, I. (1988). *Structured Systems Analysis and Design Method: Application and Context.* Hertfordshire, UK: Prentice Hall International (UK) Ltd.

El-Gendy, M. A., Bose, A., & Shin, K. (2003). Evolution of the Internet QoS and Support for Soft Real-time Applications. In *Proceedings of the IEEE* (pp. 1086-1104), 91 (7).

Gray, J., Tolvanen, J. P., Kelly, S., Gokhale, A., Neema, S., & Sprinkle, J. (2007). Domain-Specific Modeling. In P. Fishwick, *CRC Handbook on Dynamic System Modeling* (pp. 7.1-7.20). CRC Press.

Harel, D. (1987). Statecharts: A Visual Formalism for Complex Systems. *Science of Computer Programming, 8*(3), 231–274. doi:10.1016/0167-6423(87)90035-9

Heineman, G. T., & Council, W. T. (2001). *Component-based Software Engineering: Putting the Pieces Together.* Boston, MA: Addison-Wesley Longman Publishing Co., Inc.

Hill, J. H., & Gokhale, A. (2007). Model-driven Engineering for Early QoS Validation of Component-based Software Systems. *Journal of Software, 2*(3), 9–18. doi:10.4304/jsw.2.3.9-18

Hill, J. H., Schmidt, D. C., Slaby, J., & Porter, A. (2008). CiCUTS: Combining System Execution Modeling Tools with Continuous Integration Environments. In *15th Annual IEEE International Conference and Workshops on the Engineering of Computer Based Systems* (pp. 66-75). Belfast, Northern Ireland: IEEE Computer Society.

Hill, J. H., Slaby, J. M., Baker, S., & Schmidt, D. (2006). Applying System Execution Modeling Tools to Evaluate Enterprise Distributed Real-time and Embedded System QoS. In *12th International Conference on Embedded and Real-Time Computing Systems and Applications* (pp. 350-362). Sydney, Australia: IEEE Computer Society.

Jilani, A. A., Nadeem, A., Kim, T.-h., & Cho, E.-s. (2008). Formal Representations of the Data Flow Diagram: A Survey. *Advanced Software Engineering and Its Applications*, 153-158.

Jones, J. A., Harrold, M. J., & Stasko, J. (2002). Visualization of Test Information to Assist Fault Localization. In *24th International Conference on Software Engineering* (pp. 467 – 477). Orlando, FL: ACM.

Joukov, N., Wong, T., & Zadok, E. (2005). Accurate and Efficient Replaying of File System Traces. In *4th Conference on USENIX Conference on File and Storage Technologies* (p. 25). San Francisco, CA: USENIX Association.

Kaynar, D. K., Lynch, N., Segala, R., & Vaandrager, F. (2006). *The Theory of Timed I/O Automata*. San Rafael, CA, USA: Morgan and Claypool Publishers.

Ledeczi, A., Bakay, A., Maroti, M., Volgyesi, P., Nordstrom, G., & Sprinkle, J. (2001). Composing Domain-Specific Design Environments. *IEEE Computer, 34*(11), 44–51.

Ledeczi, A., Maroti, M., Karsai, G., & Nordstrom, G. (1999). Metaprogrammable Toolkit for Model-Integrated Computing. In *IEEE International Conference on the Engineering of Computer-Based Systems Conference*. Nashville, TN: IEEE Computer Society.

Lee, E. A., & Parks, T. M. (2002). *Dataflow Process Networks*. Norwell, MA, USA: Kluwer Academic Publishers.

Lo, D., & Khoo, S. (2006). SMArTIC: Towards Building an Accurate, Robust and Scalable Specification Miner. In *14th ACM SIGSOFT International Symposium on Foundations of Software Engineering* (pp. 265 – 275). Portland, OR: ACM.

Lo, D., Khoo, S., & Liu, C. (2008). Mining Past-time Temporal Rules from Execution Traces. In *International Workshop on Dynamic Analysis* (pp. 50 – 56). Seattle, WA: ACM.

Lo, D., Maoz, S., & Khoo, S. (2007). Mining Modal Scenario-based Specifications from Execution Traces of Reactive Systems. In *22nd IEEE/ACM International Conference on Automated Software Engineering* (pp. 465 – 468). Atlanta, GA: IEEE/ACM.

Loyall, J., Carvalho, M., Schmidt, D., Gillen, M., Martignoni, A. III, & Bunch, L. (2009). *QoS Enabled Dissemination of Managed Information Objects in a Publish-Subscribe-Query Information Broker*. Orlando, FL: Defense Transformation and Net-Centric Systems.

Mania, D., Murphy, J., & McManis, J. (2002). *Developing Performance Models from Nonintrusive Monitoring Traces*. IT & T.

Mann, J. (1996). *The Role of Project Escalation in Explaining Runaway Information Systems Development Projects: A Field Study*. Atlanta, GA: Georgia State University.

Moe, J., & Carr, D. A. (2001). Understanding Distributed Systems via Execution Trace Data. In *9th International Workshop on Program Comprehension* (pp. 60). Toronto, Canada: IEEE Computer Society.

Mos, A. M., & Murphy, J. (2001). Performance Monitoring of Java Component-Oriented Distributed Applications. In *9th International Conference on Software, Telecommunications and Computer Networks* (pp. 9-12). Dubrovnik, Croatia.

National Security Agency. (2009, June 28). *Global Information Grid*. Retrieved August 5, 2009, from http://www.nsa.gov/ia/programs/ global_industry_grid/ index. shtml

Parsons, T., Mos, A., & Murphy, J. (2006). J2EE Systems. In *IEE Proceedings-Software*. Non-Intrusive End-to-End Runtime Path Tracing for.

Pezzini, M., & Natis, Y. V. (2007). *Trends in Platform Middleware: Disruption Is in Sight*. Retrieved June 10, 2008, from www.gartner.com/ DisplayDocument?doc_cd=152076

Ricci, R., Alfred, C., & Lepreau, J. (2003). A Solver for the Network Testbed Mapping Problem. *SIGCOMM Computer Communications Review*, *33*(2), 30–44.

Rittel, H., & Webber, M. (1973). Dilemmas in a General Theory of Planning. *Policy Sciences*, *4*(2), 155–169. doi:10.1007/BF01405730

Russell, N., van der Aalst, W. M., ter Hofstede, A. H., & Wohed, P. (2006). On the Suitability of UML 2.0 Activity Diagrams for Business Process Modelling. In *3rd Asia-Pacific Conference on Conceptual Modelling* (pp. 95 – 104). Hobart, Australia: Australian Computer Society, Inc.

Schmidt, D. C. (2006). Model-Driven Engineering. *IEEE Computer, 39* (2).

Singhal, M., & Shivaratri, N. G. (1994). *Advanced Concepts in Operating Systems*. New York, NY, USA: McGraw-Hill, Inc.

Smith, C., & Williams, L. (2001). *Performance Solutions: A Practical Guide to Creating Responsive, Scalable Software*. Boston: Addison-Wesley Professional.

Snow, A., & Keil, M. (2001). The Challenges of Accurate Project Status Reporting. In *34th Annual Hawaii International Conference on System Sciences*. Maui, Hawaii: ACM.

Software Engineering Institute. (2006). *Ultra-Large-Scale Systems: Software Challenge of the Future. Carnegie Mellon University*. Pittsburgh, PA: Carnegie Mellon.

Sztipanovits, J., & Karsai, G. (1997). Model-Integrated Computing. *IEEE Computer*, *30*(4), 110–112.

Tortonesi, M., Stefanelli, C., Suri, N., Arguedas, M., & Breedy, M. (2006). Mockets: A Novel Message-Oriented Communications Middleware for the Wireless Internet. In *International Conference on Wireless Information Networks and Systems*. Setubal, Portugal.

Vazquez, F. (1994). Identification of Complete Dataflow Diagrams. *SIGSOFT Software Engineering Notes*, *19*(3), 36–40. doi:10.1145/182824.182832

Woodside, M., Franks, G., & Petriu, D. C. (2007). *The Future of Software Performance Engineering* (pp. 171–187). Minneapolis, MN: The Future of Software Engineering.

ADDITIONAL READING

Cascaval, C., Duesterwald, E., Sweeney, P. F., & Wisniewski, R. W. (2006). Performance and Environment Monitoring for Continuous Program Optimization. *IBM Journal of Research and Development*, *50*(2/3), 239–248. doi:10.1147/rd.502.0239

Chatterjee, A. (2007). Service-Component Architectures: A Programming Model for SOA. *Dr. Dobb's Journal*, *400*, 40–45.

Chilimbi, T. M., & Hauswirth, M. (2004). Low-overhead Memory Leak Detection using Adaptive Statistical Profiling. In *Proceedings of the 11th international Conference on Architectural Support for Programming Languages and Operating Systems*. Boston, MA.

Haran, M., Karr, A., Orso, A., Portor, A., & Sanil, A. (2005). Applying classification techniques to remotely-collected program execution data. In *Proceedings of the 10th European Software Engineering Conference held jointly with 13th ACM SIGSOFT International Symposium on Foundations of Software Engineering*. Lisbon, Portugal.

Hauswirth, M., Sweeney, P., Diwan, A., & Hind, M. (2004). Vertical Profiling: Understanding the Behavior of Object-Oriented Applications. *ACM SIGPLAN Notices, 39*(10), 251–269. doi:10.1145/1035292.1028998

Huselius, J., & Andersson, J. (2005). Model synthesis for Real-Time Systems. In *Proceedings of the Ninth European Conference on Software Maintenance and Reengineering*, Manchester, UK.

Kounev, S. (2006). Performance Modeling and Evaluation of Distributed Component-based Systems using queuing Petri nets. *IEEE Transactions on Software Engineering, 32*(7), 486–502. doi:10.1109/TSE.2006.69

Kounev, S., & Buchmann, A. (2003). Performance modeling and evaluation of Large-Scale J2EE Applications. In *Proceedings of the 29th International Conference of the Computer Measurement Group (CMG) on Resource Management and Performance Evaluation of Enterprise Computing Systems*. Dallas, TX.

Laugelier, G., Sahraoui, H., & Poulin, P. (2005). Visualization-based Analysis of Quality for Large-Scale Software Systems. In *Proceedings of the 20th IEEE/ACM International Conference on Automated Software Engineering*. Long Beach, CA.

Ledeczi, A., Nordstrom, G., Karsai, G., Volgyesi, P., & Maroti, M. (2001). On Metamodel Composition. In *Proceedings of the 2001 IEEE International Conference on Control Applications*. Mexico City, Mexico.

Li, Z., Sun, W., Jiang, Z. B., & Zhang, X. (2005). BPEL4WS Unit Testing: Framework and Implementation. In *Proceedings of the IEEE International Conference on Web Services*. Orlando, FL.

Memon, A., Porter, A., Nagarajan, A., Schmidt, D., & Natarajan, B. (2004). Skoll: Distributed Quality Assurance. In *Proceedings of the 26th IEEE/ACM International Conference on Software Engineering*. Edinburgh, Scotland.

Metz, E., Lencevicius, R., & Gonzalez, T. (2005). Performance data collection using a Hybrid Approach. In *Proceedings of the 10th European Software Engineering Conference held jointly with 13th ACM SIGSOFT International Symposium on Foundations of Software Engineering*. Lisbon, Portugal.

Mos, A., & Murphy, J. (2004). COMPAS: Adaptive Performance Monitoring of Component-Based Systems. In *Proceedings of 2nd ICSE Workshop on Remote Analysis and Measurement of Software Systems*. Beijing, China.

Odom, J., Hollingsworth, J. K., DeRose, L., Ekanadham, K., & Sbaraglia, S. (2005). Using Dynamic Tracing Sampling to measure Long Running Programs. In *Proceedings of the 2005 ACM/IEEE Conference on Supercomputing*. Seattle, WA.

Parsons, T., & Murphy, J. (in press). Detecting Performance Antipatterns in Component-based Enterprise Systems. *Journal of Object Technology*.

Saff, D., & Ernst, M. D. (2004). An experimental evaluation of continuous testing during development. In *Proceedings of the 2004 ACM SIGSOFT International Symposium on Software Testing and Analysis*. Boston, MA.

Schroeder, P. J., Kim, E., Arshem, J., & Bolaki, P. (2003). Combining Behavior and Data Modeling in Automated Test Case Generation. In *Proceedings of the 3rd International Conference on Quality Software*. Dallas, TX.

Srinivas, K., & Srinivasan, H. (2005). Summarizing application performance from a Components Perspective. In *Proceedings of the 10th European Software Engineering Conference held jointly with 13th ACM SIGSOFT International Symposium on Foundations of Software Engineering* Lisbon, Portugal.

Stewart, C., & Shen, K. (2005). Performance modeling and System Management for multi-component Online Services. In *Proceedings of the 2nd USENIX Symposium on Networked Systems Design and Implementation*. Boston, MA.

Wu, W., Spezialetti, M., & Gupta, R. (1996). Designing a Non-intrusive Monitoring Tool for developing Complex Distributed Applications. In *Proceedings of the 2nd IEEE International Conference on Engineering of Complex Computer Systems*. Washington, D.C.

KEY TERMS AND DEFINITIONS

Causal Relations: Relations that define how data in a dataflow model relates across different (application) contexts.

Dataflow Modeling: The process of identifying and modeling how data moves around an information system, such as an enterprise distributed system.

Domain-Specific Modeling Language: A modeling language that captures the abstractions and semantics (typically in the form of constraints) of a given domain and provides intuitive visual notations that enable end-users to easily construct valid models that realize concepts for the target domain.

Enterprise Distributed Systems: Systems characterized to be large at-scale, consists of many software components deployed on many hardware resources, and communicate via network to accomplish different operational scenarios.

Log Formats: High-level constructs that capture both constant and variable portions of individual, yet similar, log messages in a system execution trace.

Quality-of-Service (QoS) Validation: The process of evaluating quality-of-service (QoS) properties, such as end-to-end response time, throughput, and scalability, of a system on the target architecture.

System Execution Modeling: The process of using domain-specific modeling languages to model the behavior and workload of a system and use constructed models to validate different system properties, such as QoS properties.

System Execution Trace: A collection (or sequence) of text-based messages that capture the behavior and state of an application, such as an enterprise distributed system, throughout its execution lifetime.

Chapter 10
Cooperation between Expert Knowledge and Data Mining Discovered Knowledge

Fernando Alonso
Universidad Politécnica de Madrid, Spain

Loïc Martínez
Universidad Politécnica de Madrid, Spain

Aurora Pérez
Universidad Politécnica de Madrid, Spain

Juan Pedro Valente
Universidad Politécnica de Madrid, Spain

ABSTRACT

Although expert elicited knowledge and data mining discovered knowledge appear to be completely opposite and competing solutions to the same problems, they are actually complementary concepts. Besides, together they maximize their individual qualities. This chapter highlights how each one profits from the other and illustrates their cooperation in existing systems developed in the medical domain. The authors have identified different types of cooperation that combine elicitation and data mining for knowledge acquisition, use expert knowledge to enact the knowledge discovery, use discovered knowledge to validate expert knowledge, and use discovered knowledge to improve the usability of an expert system. The chapter also describes their experience in combining expert and discovered knowledge in the development of a system for processing medical isokinetics data.

INTRODUCTION

Expert knowledge and data mining discovered knowledge are two powerful instruments for producing knowledge-based systems. Together,

DOI: 10.4018/978-1-60960-067-9.ch010

expert knowledge and data mining discovered knowledge, maximize their individual qualities. Looking at the discipline of medicine, medical expert systems are a challenging field, now requiring cooperation between both types of knowledge.

From the late 1970s to the early 1990s medical expert systems to aid diagnosis were developed on the basis of rules or models entered and validated by the expert, and data input by the physician after examining the patient and the patient's medical record (Davis, Buchanan, & Shortliffe, 1977; Shortliffe et al., 1981). The system automatically suggested a diagnosis and helped the physician to make the final decision. These systems were useful because they automatically processed complex decision trees that provided a differential diagnosis. They were not, however, without weaknesses. For example, most of the time experts simplified the knowledge model entered in the system, as they were unable to express all their knowledge as rules.

More recently, automatic knowledge acquisition, discovery and maintenance have attracted a lot of interest. The manual definition of the model by the expert has been overtaken by the automatic discovery of models and reference patterns based on Data Mining (DM) techniques, i.e. automatic medical knowledge elicitation (discovery) from the comprehensive and contextual interpretation of patient data.

The fact is that these two approaches, knowledge discovery and knowledge elicitation from experts, complement rather than oppose each other. Applied together, they can output more realistic and efficient models and patterns: DM techniques can be used to support the tasks involved in Expert System (ES) or Knowledge-Based System (KBS) development, and expert knowledge can be used to improve the knowledge discovery process. The aim of this chapter is to highlight a series of relevant examples of the cooperation between expert knowledge and discovered knowledge and describe the characteristics and possibilities of this cooperation in the medical field. The authors also include an overview of current trends in this field of research. Finally the chapter describes their experience in this field, presenting a long-term project that integrates expert knowledge and DM-discovered knowledge to process isokinetics data.

BACKGROUND

The joint application of knowledge discovered through DM and heuristic knowledge elicited beforehand from the expert has the goal of optimizing and maximizing the performance of the resulting KBS.

To illustrate this cooperation, cases where knowledge is acquired through both expert knowledge acquisition and data mining and where expert knowledge is applied to improve knowledge discovery is presented. Cases where DM techniques are used to aid ES development with respect to aspects like ES validation, improving system usability and efficiency or validating the local application of generic knowledge is also highlighted. This section finalizes with a summary of related work and with an enumeration of major current trends in the field of combining ES and DM.

Knowledge Acquisition: Combining Elicitation and Data Mining

Acquisition of the knowledge to develop a KBS through elicitation from an expert and knowledge discovery is an applicable case of mutual cooperation taking place in the medical field. A rule-based expert system for diagnosing pulmonary tuberculosis, called TUBERDIAG, described by Phuong et al. (1999), presents this type of cooperation. Tuberculosis is still a frequent and very dangerous disease in developing countries. Pulmonary Tuberculosis (PT) is the most frequent form because it spreads easily. Even though it is relatively easy to treat, there are many PT patients because it is often difficult to diagnose. For this reason, the TUBERDIAG system was developed. This system can act like a high-ranking medical consultant specialized in PT diagnosis.

The system's most important components are: knowledge acquisition subsystem, knowledge base, reasoning engine, and explanation subsystem.The knowledge acquisition subsystem uses two sources of rules:

1. **Rules from Experts:** Most rules are formed by doctors. To form these rules, all the symptoms seen in the patient are listed (there are about 30 such symptoms), and these symptoms are classified by the frequency of their occurrence in PT patients. Then, all possible combinations of the most frequent symptoms are formed, and doctors are consulted to estimate the extent to which this combination of symptoms confirms or excludes PT.

2. **Statistical Approach:** For each combination of symptoms, the database of diagnosed patients is searched to find all the patients who had these symptoms, and, rather than asking an expert, the likelihood of the patient having PT is estimated. This approach is efficient and fast. The database stores both the diagnostic results of the expert system's and the doctors' diagnoses; the differences between these diagnoses help to correct the rules.

The medical knowledge base contains rules provided by the knowledge acquisition subsystem. These rules (rules from experts and rules automatically acquired applying the statistical approach) are previously debugged by a committee of leading doctors specialized in PT. If the committee notices a wrong diagnosis when applying the rules, it suggests a way to correct the rules. The medical knowledge base now contains more than 1000 rules.

The inference system follows the doctor's four-step diagnostic process:

1. Analyze the patient's symptoms to find the likelihood of PT; if this likelihood exceeds a certain threshold, go to next step.

2. Examine the patient's sputum for the presence of Koch's bacillus. If there are two or more positive sputum tests, treat as PT, else go to next step.

3. Take an X-ray of the lungs. Use the results of the X-ray and the patient's symptoms to compute the possibility of PT. If this new likelihood exceeds a threshold, start PT treatment else go to next step.

4. At this step, the system suggests a test treatment. This test treatment is directed against PT or against some other probable disease.

The system accepts fuzzy descriptions of the patient's symptoms, and the reasoning engine uses fuzzy logic and approximate reasoning to model the uncertainty of symptoms. The explanation subsystem shows its final conclusion, all sets of patient symptoms that were used in reasoning, and the rules that matched each set. As a result, the users can see the intermediate diagnostic conclusions from all four steps of the diagnostic process, and the way the rules affect the final conclusion.

Using Expert Knowledge in Knowledge Discovery

Another case of cooperation between expert knowledge and discovered knowledge occurs when you want to discover knowledge using DM techniques, and you need expert knowledge to enact the discovery process. This expert knowledge can be built into the actual knowledge discovery method, as shown in Tsumoto (1999), describing a rule induction system based on rough sets. This system, called PRIMEROSE-REX5, conforms to a diagnostic model based on expert reasoning (Matsumura, Matsunaga, Maeda, Tsumoto, Matsumura, & Kimura, 1988). This model establishes three kinds of reasoning processes: exclusive reasoning, inclusive reasoning and reasoning about complications.

Exclusive reasoning excludes a candidate disease when a patient does not have the symptom that is necessary to diagnose the disease. Inclusive reasoning suspects a disease in the

Table 1. Experimental Results (Headache)

Method	CHR-A	DR-A	COR-A
PR-REX5	95.0%	88.3%	96.2%
Experts	98.0%	95.0%	97.4%

output of the exclusive process when a patient has disease-specific symptoms. And reasoning about complications checks whether the inputs can be explained by the final diagnostic candidates. If not (and if these inputs are important for diagnosis of a specific disease), then complications should be considered and checked. Each reasoning type is rule based. There are, therefore, three rule types: characterization rules (for exclusive reasoning), discrimination rules (for inclusive reasoning) and complication rules.

PRIMEROSE-REX5 consists of two procedures that analyze all the attribute-value pairs from the database: one is an exhaustive search procedure to induce characterization and complication rules, and the other is a procedure to induce discrimination rules. Expert knowledge is applied in both procedures to define what thresholds the attribute-value pairs have to pass to be included in the rule. This knowledge is input by medical experts. PRIMEROSE-REX5 was evaluated on a medical dataset for the differential diagnosis of headache with 1477 samples (split into 738 for training and 739 for testing) and 34 attributes. Rules performed equally well as a medical expert, as shown in Table 1, where CHR-A is the characterization rule accuracy (how many training samples that do not belong to a class are excluded correctly from the candidates), DR-A is the discrimination rule accuracy (equivalent to

the averaged classification accuracy) and COR-A is the complication rule accuracy (how many symptoms that cannot be explained by diagnostic conclusions are detected by complication rules).

The knowledge discovered by PRIMEROSE-REX5 was used to develop the RH expert system (Rule-based system for Headache), which makes a differential diagnosis of headache.

RH was evaluated in an outpatient clinic on 186 patients. This evaluation showed that it performed almost as well as a medical expert (Table 2).

ES Validation and Enhancement of Rule Certainty Factors

A common case of cooperation between discovered knowledge and expert knowledge is when discovered knowledge is used to validate an ES developed with elicited knowledge. An example of this type of cooperation is described by Cooke et al. (2000), where DM techniques, applied to a patient database containing images and text, are used to validate the system and the confidence (certainty factors) in the heuristic rules of the PERFEX ES.

PERFEX is a rule-based expert system for the automatic interpretation of cardiac SPECT (Single Photon Emission Computed Tomography) data. This system infers the extent and severity of CAD (Coronary Artery Disease) from perfusion distributions, and outputs a patient report summarizing the condition of the three main arteries (LAD, LCX and RCA) and other key information. The overall goal is to assist in the diagnosis of CAD. The expert system presents the resulting diagnostic recommendations in both visual and textual forms in an interactive framework, thereby

Table 2. Evaluation of RH

Method	Classification Accuracy	Detection of Complications
RH	91.4% (170/186)	77.8% (21/27)
Experts	93.5% (174/186)	92.6% (25/27)

Table 3. Seven heuristic rules from PERFEX, with support (Sup), confidence (Conf) and certainty factors derived from data mining (DM CF), and the original certainty factors derived from the domain experts (PERFEX CF)

Rule	Sup	Conf	DM CF	PERFEX CF
If AnteroLateral then LAD	19%	66%	0.31	0.70
If AnteroSeptal then LAD	17%	72%	0.44	0.80
If SeptoAnterior then LAD	15%	79%	0.58	0.80
If Septonferior then LAD	15%	81%	0.62	0.70
If InferoSeptal then LAD	22%	69%	0.38	0.40
If LateroAnterior then LAD	25%	60%	0.20	0.40
If Apical then LAD	28%	70%	0.39	0.70

enhancing overall utility. A relational database combining textual and image information was generated from 655 patients who had undergone both stress/rest myocardial perfusion SPECT and coronary angiography. The patient population (449 men and 206 women) comprised 480 CAD patients and 175 healthy volunteers.

The PERFEX system contains 253 heuristic rules. These rules correlate the presence and location of perfusion defects on SPECT studies with coronary angiography (catheterization) demonstrated CAD and with expert visual interpretation. Each rule within the ES was originally assigned a Certainty Factor (CF) based on the experience of several domain experts (experts in the field of nuclear cardiology). When run against 655 patients, with these assigned certainty factors, PERFEX demonstrates a significantly lower sensitivity and higher specificity than the visual interpretation for identifying the presence and location of CAD versus catheterization.

Data mining was concentrated on heuristic rules involving myocardial perfusion defects and the LAD (Left Anterior Descending artery) vascular territory. The data mining resulted in 181 association rules, of which seven involved LAD stenosis, and were part of the 253 heuristic rules within the PERFEX ES. These 7 rules are shown in Table 3 along with their original CFs from PERFEX (derived from the domain experts)

and the CF discovered through data mining. These two values are clearly significantly different.

In view of the results shown in Table 3, the certainty of these seven heuristic rules in PERFEX was changed to the newly calculated CFs and run against the same 655 patients. When compared to the previous results, there were no statistical differences found in detecting or localizing CAD. DM validated the confidence of the heuristic rules and improved their certainty factors.

Improving System Usability and Efficiency

Frequently, KBS users have to answer a great many questions formulated by the system to gather information about the problem. In consultation systems, like these, the application of DM techniques to the stored results of previous system executions can optimize future question/answer sequences by reducing the number of questions. In the following, an example of this type of cooperation between discovered knowledge and expert knowledge is shown.

The problem of patient eligibility for clinical trials is an important issue for adequately evaluating new treatments in a timely manner. But accruing patients for clinical trials is a tedious and time-consuming task for clinicians that need them to have extensive knowledge of the specific criteria for all available clinical trials. To solve this problem, different systems have been developed for accrual to clinical trials (Fink, Kokku, Niki-forou, Hall, Goldgof, & Krischer, 2004; Seroussi, Bouaud, & Antoine, 2001). However, to get a system fielded in the clinic, it must be extremely easy and quick to use. A busy clinical practitioner will not be willing to answer redundant questions and hence will not use a system that asks them. So, it is of paramount importance to reduce the number of questions that clinicians are required to answer. This is what the research presented by Bethel et al. (2006) aims to do. It is based on the idea that a physician will immediately know the answers to some questions based on answers to others, that is, there is a clear implication that always holds.

The developed system is a web-based expert system to match eligible breast cancer patients with open clinical trials, or categorize the reasons if the patient was eligible and not put onto the trial. Through interviews with clinicians, implications were discovered that reduced the number of required questions/answers to determine eligibility. After gathering and recording data on past breast cancer patients, the questions asked by the expert system together with their answers were extracted and mined through the Apriori algorithm that generated implication rules such as (biopsy = yes) → (surgery = yes).

Initially the DM process was applied to a database of 135 patients and 1812 association rules were found. By sifting rules and discussing the interesting ones with some medical experts, it was determined that only 4 were to be considered newly discovered rules and added back into the expert system. However, they still did not find all the existing clinician-generated implication rules. Then a second DM process was run focusing just upon the two protocols for which there were 4 clinician-generated implication rules and using the most recent 100 patients' data.

In the experiment on the first protocol, with 100 patients, three of the four current system im-plications were found (in 831 discovered rules). There were 10 new rules of interest that required further research and only one of them was found valid by the clinical experts.

In the experiment on the second protocol, with 85 patients, 487 rules including one of the current system implications were discovered. There were 13 new rules of interest that would require further investigation to establish medical validity; three of the rules were verified as valid.

The result of this research is that the system recovered all the implication rules that were obtained from experts, as well as eight previously unknown implication or association rules from the knowledge base. These eight new rules were verified as correct by a clinical expert and added to the Clinical Trial Assignment Expert System to improve clinical ease of use, system efficiency, and accuracy.

Validating the Local Application of Generic Knowledge

When the knowledge base is built with generic global knowledge and ES behavior on a specific local problem is unknown (i.e. it is unknown whether it will correctly and completely account for all the cases that can occur in that local situation), discovered knowledge can be used to verify whether the elicited rules are representative enough for the local data and if the local data have any new correlation that the knowledge base does not contain.

This cooperation between discovered knowledge and expert knowledge was applied by Lama et al. (2006) to treat nosocomial infection. A hospital-acquired or nosocomial infection is a disease that develops around 48-72 hours after the patient is admitted to hospital. These infections are caused by bacteria with a very high resistance to antibiotics, and so they are much more dangerous than any infection acquired by the patient outside of the hospital. This is a very important problem arising in hospitals (it is third on the list of most costly and deadly infectious diseases in the USA).

The MERCURIO system was designed to support medical practitioners in the complex task of controlling nosocomial infections. MERCURIO combines expert knowledge and discovered knowledge. The system identifies critical situations for a single patient (e.g., unexpected antibiotic resistance of a bacterium) or for hospital units (e.g., contagion events), and warns the microbiologist. It also provides reports about the number of nosocomial infections in the various areas of the hospital. One of the system modules is a real-time validation and monitoring ES, called ESMIS. Given a newly isolated bacterium and the related antibiogram, ESMIS validates the culture results, reports the most suitable list of antibiotics for therapy, issues alarms regarding the newly isolated bacterium, issues alarms regarding the patient's clinical situation, and identifies potential epidemic events inside the hospital.

ESMIS' knowledge base was built from both the NCCLS (National Committee for Clinical Laboratory Standards) guidelines (NCCLS, 2005) and the expert's suggestions. These guidelines are quite general, since they were built considering data regarding many laboratories around the world. However, it is not clear that they can completely and correctly interpret the infections developed inside a particular hospital environment. For this reason, it was necessary to verify if the rules obtained from the NCCLS document are representative of the local hospital infections, and if there are other correlations in the local hospital infection data that are either not considered in the NCCLS document or unknown to the expert microbiologists.

To address these problems, data mining was applied to local hospital infection data to generate association rules that show the susceptibility or resistance of a bacterium to different antibiotics. The discovered association rules were transformed into alarm rules that were confirmed by experts and then used for data validation in ESMIS. Several

thousand rules were discovered, whereas there were only a few tens of interesting rules. There is a filtering program that helps to focus on certain rules. It can eliminate uninteresting rules on the basis of the microbiologist's interests rather than on support and confidence. This is very important since the interesting rules may represent rare events and thus have low support and confidence.

Summary of Related Work

In summary, the cooperation between expert knowledge and discovered knowledge can improve a medical system in different ways under diverse circumstances:

1. When medical experts exist and there is a database of already diagnosed patients, knowledge elicited from experts can be combined with knowledge discovered through DM to build the system.
2. When the system uses knowledge discovered using DM techniques, expert knowledge can be used to enact the discovery process and increase the system's reliability.
3. When the system uses heuristic rules with associated certainty factors and there is a database of correctly solved cases, DM techniques can be applied to validate the system and even improve these certainty factors.
4. When a system based on expert knowledge results in a long and costly consultation process for the end-user and there are data from previous system uses, then DM techniques can be applied to discover ways of improving the system usability and efficiency.
5. When the system uses general expert knowledge whose behavior is unknown under localized and real-world situations, DM techniques can be used to validate and improve the local behavior.

Current Trends

Some research indicating current trends in the cooperation between expert knowledge and data mining discovered knowledge in different fields of application follows.

- Chazard et al. (2009) presents the PSIP (Patient Safety through Intelligent Procedures in medication) project framework that uses data mining (e.g., decision trees) to electronically identify situations leading to risk of Adverse Drug Events (ADEs). They used 10,500 hospitalization records from Denmark and France. They automatically generated 500 rules from these records. These rules are currently being validated by experts. A decision support system to prevent ADEs is then to be developed. The article examines a decision tree and the rules in the field of vitamin K antagonists.

- To conquer the bottleneck problems existing in traditional rule-based reasoning disease diagnosis systems, such as low reasoning efficiency and lack of flexibility, etc., (Xu & Li, 2009) researched integrated Case-Based Reasoning (CBR) and Rule-Based Reasoning (RBR) technology and put forward a Litchi Disease Diagnosis Expert System (LDDES) with an integrated reasoning method. The method uses data mining and expert knowledge elicitation technology to set up a knowledge base and case library. It adopts rules to instruct CBR retrieval and matching, and uses association rules and the decision tree algorithms to calculate case similarity. The experiment shows that the method can increase system flexibility and reasoning ability, and improve the accuracy of litchi disease diagnosis.

- Brisson and Collard (2008) presents the KEOPS data mining methodology centered on domain knowledge integration. KEOPS is a CRISP-DM compliant methodology that integrates a knowledge base and ontology. They focus first on the preprocessing steps of business understanding and data understanding in order to build an Ontology-Driven Information System (ODIS). Then they show how the knowledge base is used for the post-processing step of model interpretation. They also explain the role of the ontology and define a part-way interestingness measure that integrates both objective and subjective criteria in order to evaluate model relevance according to expert knowledge.

- Safety on board airborne platforms relies heavily on their repair. This includes fixing and testing to reduce down time. Maintenance practices using these components are achieved using general- and special-purpose testing equipment within the existing Maintenance Management System (MMS). Haider et al. (2009) describe the work performed to improve the reliability and maintainability of avionics systems using an Intelligent Decision Support System (IDSS). To understand the shortcomings of the existing system, they research ongoing practices and methodologies. The paper reports the significant improvements made by integrating autonomous information sources as knowledge into an IDSS. Improvements are made by automating the existing data collection procedures to create an expert system using intelligent agents. Data mining techniques and intelligent agents operating on behalf of experts are employed to create an expert system. Using feedback, the IDSS generates forecasts, alerts and warnings before system availability is compromised. A knowledge base of all aspects of the logistics cycle is created as the system ages. This should help to make informed decisions about the platform, the Unit Under Testing (UUT) or even the unit's support environment.

- The prevention of customer churn through customer retention is a core issue of Customer Relationship Management (CRM). By minimizing customer churn a company can maximize its profit. Li et al. (2009) propose a novel churn model to deal with customer retention problems. To do this, it uses not only churn probability to classify customers, but also the achieved pattern and rules to make policies. To build the model, they integrate, with the help of fuzzy set theory and alpha-cuts, expert knowledge and data mining techniques. The proposed model provides a new route to guide further research into customer retention.

- Sun et al. (2009) gives the general definition of the concepts of extension knowledge, extension data mining and extension data mining theorem in a high dimensional space, and also builds the IDSS comprising rough sets, an expert system and a neural network, developing the relevant computer software. The results of diagnosis tests for the common diseases of myocardial infarction, angina pectoris and hypertension compared with tests run by physicians shows that the sensitivity, specificity and accuracy of diagnosis by IDSS are all greater than for physicians. Operating as a support system, IDSS can improve the accuracy rate of physicians' diagnosis, evidently leading to a lower mortality and disability rate and a higher survival rate. This has strong practical values and further social benefits.

COOPERATION BETWEEN EXPERT KNOWLEDGE AND DISCOVERED KNOWLEDGE: AUTHORS EXPERIENCE IN THE FIELD OF ISOKINETICS

An experiment was conducted with this cooperation as part of the I4 project (Intelligent Interpretation of Isokinetics Information) (1996-2007). I4 is a medical diagnosis system that uses underlying knowledge in the isokinetics domain, gathered by combining the expertise of a physician specialized in isokinetics techniques and DM techniques applied to a set of existing data. I4 is a significant example of cooperation between expert knowledge and discovered knowledge to solve new problems and improve solutions.

What is I4?

Muscle function assessment is a key goal of medical and sports scientists for evaluating the effects of training, for diagnosing muscular dysfunctions and for assessing the effectiveness of rehabilitation programs (Gleeson & Mercer, 1996). An isokinetics machine is a muscular evaluation device that consists of a physical support (Figure 1a) on which patients perform exercises using any of their joints (knee, elbow, ankle, etc.) within different ranges of movement and at a constant speed.

The graphic representation of these exercises (strength applied over time) looks like a sinusoidal curve, containing a lot of small peaks and other irregularities (Figure 1b). The mechanical component of existing isokinetics systems generally meets the demands of muscle strength assessment. When the project kicked off, however, the performance of the software built into these systems did not make the grade as far as isokinetics test interpretation is concerned. This meant that the massive data flow supplied by these systems could not be fully exploited.

The I4 project was developed in conjunction with the National Center of Sports Research and

Figure 1. a) Diagram of Isokinetics machine use. b) Exercises with inertia peaks and their elimination

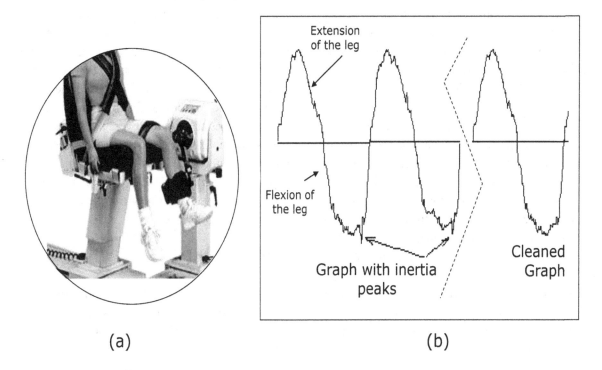

(a) (b)

Sciences (CNICD), with the key aim of performing a more comprehensive analysis of the data output by the isokinetics machine and offering users more support for decision making. The system was designed to operate on knee exercises. [1,2]

I4 Phase 1: ES Development

At the early stage, the plan was to build a user interface that would do a preliminary analysis of the data (data validity, curve morphology, simple comparative analysis). With the help of an expert in the subject with several years' experience running isokinetics tests on top-competition sportspeople and other patients, an ES was designed. The system's first task is to remove some irregularities in the curves caused by the inertia of the isokinetics machine. Several functions were created to fulfill this mission. These functions later turned out to be an ideal formalism for solving other questions.

Functions

These functions were created to address some of the pre-processing steps, involving data cleaning, noise reduction and other similar tasks. They also proved useful for providing medical users with relevant information. Functions were created after interacting iteratively with the expert, by gathering her knowledge about these tasks. This can be viewed as the first example of synergy between Expert Knowledge and DM in this research. The functions eliminate irregularities for which the patient is not responsible and assess the morphology of each isokinetics curve. Firstly, the strength curves are preprocessed to eliminate inertia peaks, that is, peaks produced by machine inertia rather than by the patient's actual strength.

Then, I4 functions detect exercise extensions and flexions that are invalid because the patient employed much less effort than in others, and movements that can be considered atypical as their morphology is unlike the others. The process for detecting these anomalies is used in part to detect the extensions and flexions that are most representative of the exercise, that is, the extensions and flexions that provide for a better patient muscle assessment. The analysis of the actual strength curves involves assessing different characteristics of the extension/flexion curve morphology. These characteristics are what the specialist is interested in and are inputs for patient assessment. The aspects evaluated are uniformity, regularity, maximum peak time, troughs, and curve shape.

The functions were unsatisfactory for this purpose. They represent procedural knowledge (especially calculations) very well, but they are not so good for representing fine-grain knowledge, like heuristic assertions "If there are many invalid exercises, repeat the tests". Therefore, the authors decided to add declarative knowledge represented by means of rules.

Rules

The rule-based expert system outputs concludes on three aspects of isokinetics analysis:

1. Protocol validation, determining that the protocol has been correctly applied. This is very important since the expertise used for the later parts of the analysis is very sensitive to the way in which the tests are performed.
2. Numerical analysis of data, in particular numerical features (maximum peak, total effort, gradients of the curve, etc.) for each leg and a comparison between both legs.
3. Morphological analysis of data, of each leg and its comparison in order to determine any kind of dysfunctions.

Figure 2 shows the user interface for rule-based analysis after selecting morphological analysis. There are icons for conclusions regarding each leg, its flexion and extension. The bottom window

shows an overall analysis for the right leg, indicating problems with the right flexors and extensors.

An additional goal of this system was to enable visually impaired physicians to use an isokinetics machine. The system included text-to-speech output to enable interaction and used the expert knowledge to provide a global interpretation of the strength curves. However, the system was based on the knowledge of just one expert, and there were no other known experts in the field capable of confirming these ideas. Additionally, a great many tests had been run and stored, but had not been processed.

I4 Phase 2: KDD

In view of this situation, it was decided to exploit the knowledge stored in all those exercises and design a KDD system to extend and validate the earlier ES built with the help of the expert. The work focused on detecting patterns in isokinetics curves and generating characteristic models of certain population groups.

Data Cleaning and Preprocessing

The aim of data cleaning is to raise data quality to a level suitable for the selected analyses. Data quality is a multifaceted issue posing one of the biggest challenges to data mining. Data quality refers to data accuracy and completeness. Data quality can also be affected by the structure and consistency of the data being analyzed. The presence of duplicate records, the lack of data standards, the timeliness of updates, and human error have a substantial impact on the effectiveness of the more complex data mining techniques, which are sensitive to possible subtle differences in the data.

To improve data quality, data cleaning deals with issues of removing duplicate records, normalizing the values used to represent information in the database, eliminating or accounting for missing data, identifying anomalous data (e.g.,

Figure 2. Window showing results from the rule subsystem

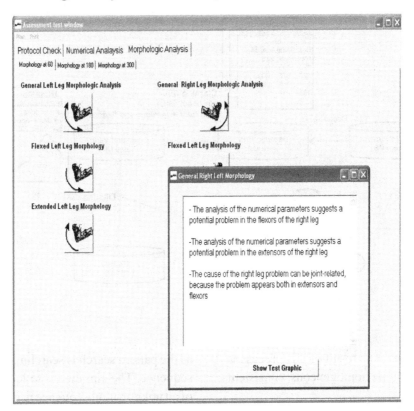

out-of-range values), standardizing data formats and so on. Exactly what data cleaning is to be performed depends on the purpose to which the data is to be put.

Other data preparation tasks include converting data types, if necessary, deriving new fields, field selection (identifying relevant data items for the business problem and removing unnecessary data fields), sampling or focusing. There are no established methodologies or practices for using data preprocessing techniques, as data preprocessing is heavily domain dependent. Yet good data preprocessing is essential for successfully analyzing real data (Seifert, 2006; Pyle, 1999). Data preparation was an extremely pressing question in I4 due to the poor quality of the stored data: incomplete or poorly run tests, missing data in some tests, etc. The ES built (especially the functions) was used to solve this problem and clean the data, as many

of the analyses run by the ES were specifically concerned with test completeness and quality.

Figure 3 summarizes the tasks that have to be carried out before the available data set could be used. The first task was decoding, as the input came from a commercial application (the isokinetics system) that had its own internal data format.

Then two data cleaning tasks were performed using expert knowledge:

1.   Removal of incorrect tests, in which the isokinetics test protocol had not been correctly applied.
2.   Elimination of incorrect extensions and flexions, due mainly to the patient not concentrating enough during the exercise.

The last task was to filter the exercises to remove noise introduced by the machine itself, using

Figure 3. Data preprocessing tasks

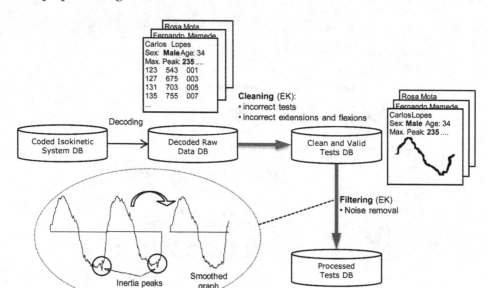

the above functions. The result of this process is a DB in which tests are homogeneous, consistent and noise free.

Pattern Detection

One relevant application of DM algorithms is to detect representative parts of the curve in order to characterize the series. In isokinetics the presence of this sort of patterns could be representative of some kind of injury, and the correct identification of the deviation could be an aid for detecting the injury in time. By identifying patterns, criteria can be established to classify the exercises (and the patients).

An algorithm was developed that detects similar patterns in exercises. Then this algorithm was used to detect any patterns that appear in exercises done by patients with injuries and do not appear in exercises completed by healthy individuals. This is not, strictly speaking, a partial comparison problem (Faloutsos, Ranganatha, & Manolopoulos, 1994), on which a lot of research was conducted in the early 21st century (Kahveci & Singh, 2001),

as the pattern search is searching for an unknown sequence. The aim then is to locate the presence of an unknown subsequence in a set of sequences: the problem involves finding subsequences that are frequently repeated in a set of times series, about which there is, however, no background knowledge. There are several examples of pattern searching in symbolic series. Han et al. (1998) try to find subsequences that are periodically repeated within a symbolic sequence. This work was the starting point for many other approaches to this problem. Geurts (2001) tried to classify a series of objects on the basis of time series variables. For this purpose, he defined a set of tests to give the measure of the presence of a pattern in a series, and these tests are the decision nodes of a future classification tree. The landmarks-based technique (Perng, Wang, Zhang, & Parker, 2000) is a method for characterizing and comparing time series based on the identification of landmarks, that is, the singular points of the curve (e.g. maximums, minimums and turning points).

Since time series are composed of continuous numerical values in the method proposed by the authors, it differs significantly from most of the above works. This makes it impossible to use symbolic pattern search methods, as a similarity measure needs to be introduced to detect when two subsequences are similar enough to be considered part of the same pattern. Only subsequences that are repeated in enough data series can be considered patterns, but there is no previous information about pattern shape, presence of characteristic points, size, etc. Blind search, that is, search without background knowledge, is an obstacle to be overcome by the method proposed later and also marks a departure from earlier work.

The proposed method reuses some existing ideas from Han (1998) periodic searching algorithm, the Apriori property to prune the search tree, etc. But major changes had to be made in order to consider variable-length patterns and pattern similarity. The method inputs are a collection of time series of variable length (S), the minimum confidence to consider that a pattern appears in a relevant number of series (min-conf) and the maximum distance between patterns to be considered similar (max-dist). The result is a set of patterns that appear in S with a confidence greater or equal to min-conf.

The method used in Alonso et al. (2003) is useful for finding significant patterns that are likely to characterize a set of non-uniform time series, even though important characteristics of these patterns, like length or position within the time series, are unknown. A real example is shown below. A set of eight exercises completed by injured female patients (knee cartilage disease) have been taken. This is a realistic number, because it is difficult to find more patients with the same sort of injury for evaluation in a given environment (in this case, Spanish top-competition athletes). The graphs of the exercises used are shown in Figure 4.

The aim of this test case was to detect patterns symptomatic of knee cartilage disease. The similar pattern-searching algorithm was able to identify patterns depending on the parameters used. For example, if min-conf is 0.8 and max-dist is 50, the algorithm finds a number of patterns, the most promising of which is shown in Figure 5a. This pattern corresponds to the lower part of the curves, as shown in Figure 5b. Then the authors tried to match this pattern against a set of healthy patients' exercises, and this pattern did not show up. After a positive expert evaluation, it was able to use this pattern as a symptom of knee cartilage disease.

Figure 4. Eight Isokinetics exercises performed by injured patients (knee cartilage disease)

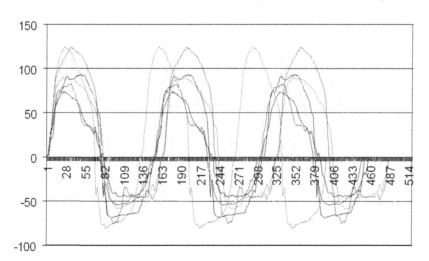

Creating Reference Models for Population Groups

One common task involved in assessing isokinetics exercises is to compare a patient's test against a reference model created beforehand. These models represent the average profile of a group of patients sharing common characteristics. All the exercises done by individuals with the desired characteristics (weight, height, sport, sex, etc.) are selected to create a reference model for a particular population. Normally, there is a majority subgroup of similar exercises, which represent the standard profile that the user is looking for, and a disperse set of groups of one or two exercises. The former is used to create a reference model unifying all the exercises' common characteristics.

This has found to be a difficult manual process since it was designed by an expert in isokinetics. Hence the authors tried to implement a semi-automatic mechanism. To do this, an automatic clustering process is enacted and the clusters are then shown for the expert to decide which set or sets of exercises the model should be based on. The next step is preliminary pre-processing. This step removes extensions and flexions that are correct but are not representative of the patient. The final step is to normalize the selected exercises and calculate the model taking the average of all exercises.

An isokinetics exercise for a patient, or a set of isokinetics exercises, will be able to compare with the models stored in the database. Thus, it will be able to determine what group the patients belong or should belong to and identify what sport they should go in for, what their weaknesses are with a view to improvement or how they are likely to progress in the future. The problem of comparing exercises is simplified using the discrete Fourier transform to transfer the exercises from the time domain to the frequency domain, resulting in a very efficient process. This is an important point as there are many exercises for comparison in the database.

The project at this stage produced two quite similar applications (Alonso et al., 2005). One, called Isokinetics Expert System (ISOCIN), was designed for use by visually impaired physicians. The other application, called Isokinetics Expert System for Sport (ISODEPOR), is being used at the National High Performance Center to evaluate the muscle strength of Spanish top-competition athletes.

These applications proved to be a very useful tool for isokinetics system users to compare patients, create models and classify patients and find patterns likely to characterize patients. Members of the center's staff claimed that this system improved the work of physicians in the field of isokinetics and listed the system's prominent features as follows:

Figure 5. Pattern possibly characteristic of cartilage disease

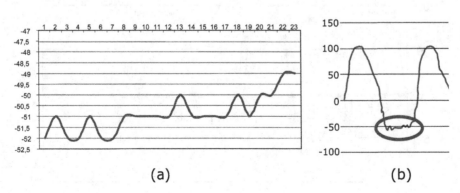

(a)　　　　　　　　　　　　　　　(b)

1. Physicians who are not isokinetics specialists can use the system to test interpretation, patterns and models.
2. The complex parameters that are used for interpreting the tests can be inferred more correctly and completely.
3. Population modeling increases the power of isokinetics systems, and is very useful for detecting both coincidences with and slight deviations from group norms. It is now planned to use the models for the early evaluation of the capabilities of young athletes.
4. I4 has provided friendly access for medical practitioners to the isokinetics parameters and an improved graphical presentation of the results of isokinetics tests.

Additionally, this system is extremely valuable as an instrument for disseminating isokinetics technology and encouraging non-expert medical practitioners to enter this field.

I4 Phase 3: Symbolic Analysis

From routine system use it has been found that, although the results of I4 are correct, the expert and the I4 system did not work exactly in the same way. The isokinetics machine produced numerical time series that are used to classify patients and produce models and patterns, whereas the expert analyzed the morphological characteristics of the isokinetics curves symbolically. As a result, medical specialists did not find the system conclusions, expressed in numerical terms, to be satisfactory and found it difficult to justify the findings.

To improve system usability, it was decided to redefine the process and, like the expert, work with symbolic data, that is, transform the numerical time series into symbolic series so that they can be interpreted in the same way as an expert does. The expert knowledge in this transformation of data into symbolic series is used to capture the key concepts from the viewpoint of series analysis.

To do this, the research focused on the design of an isokinetics symbols alphabet and a symbols extraction method that translates numerical time series into symbolic temporal series first. Next, a symbolic distance measure was designed. By using this, symbolic sequences can be automatically compared to detect similarities, classify patients, etc.

Isokinetics Symbols Alphabet

A vocabulary, called Isokinetics Symbols Alphabet (ISA) has been defined. These symbols were identified by analyzing together with the expert and the key aspects of each isokinetics curve (Alonso, Martinez, Perez, Santamaria, & Valente, 2006).The following symbols (shown in Figure 6) capture the meaningful information contained in the curves:

1. Ascent: the patient gradually increases applied strength.
2. Descent: the patient gradually decreases applied strength.
3. Peak: a spike in any part of the sequence.
4. Trough: a valley in any part of the sequence.
5. Curvature: the upper section of a region.
6. Transition: the changeover from extension to flexion or vice versa.

The symbols are labeled with the region to which they belong (extension or flexion).

The next step is to define types for each symbol. These types are shown in Table 4 and were elicited directly from the expert as the expert analyzed a set of supplied sequences.

Symbols Extraction Method

A Symbols Extraction Method (SEM) was designed to transform the isokinetics curves into symbolic sequences represented according to ISA. First, a numerical sequence is prepared and put

Figure 6. Symbols of an Isokinetics curve

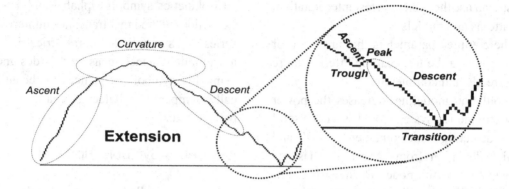

through the Domain-Independent Module (DIM), which outputs a set of domain-independent features, that is, peaks and troughs. These are used as input for the Domain-Dependent Module (DDM). The DDM outputs all the domain-dependent data of the sequence. The DDM is divided into three sub-modules:

1. Output of domain-dependent features selecting the relevant peaks and troughs and identifying ascents, descents and curvatures.
2. Filtering stage, which will, for instance, merge two similar consecutive symbols.
3. Assign types to symbols. This process is based on a set of rules that were built after a knowledge acquisition process with the expert, and actually constitute a mini-expert system within the expert system.

Comparing Symbolic Series: Isokinetics Symbolic Distance

None of the edited distances from the state of the art that was examined exactly fits the problem, because the symbols used in the isokinetics domain also have an associated type that needs to be taken into account to calculate the distances. This led the authors to propose a variation on the Needleman-Wunch distance (Needleman & Wunsch, 1970). The suggested distance – Isokinetics Symbolic Distance (ISD) – allocates a variable cost to the insert, substitute and delete operations. This cost depends on the symbol and symbol type to be inserted or deleted. The ISD between two series, S1, and S2, is defined as the cumulative cost of the operations (delete, insert and substitute) required to transform S1 into S2.

For qualitative and quantitative reasons, not all the operations or all the symbols can be allocated

Table 4. Isokinetics Symbols Alphabet (ISA)

Region	Symbol	Type		
EXT FLEX	Ascent	Sharp	Gentle	
	Descent	Sharp	Gentle	
	Trough	Big	Small	
	Peak	Big	Small	
	Curvature	Sharp	Flat	Irregular
	Transition	-		

an identical gapcost in the isokinetics field. For example, curvatures are symbols that are part of any extension or flexion, whereas peaks and troughs are circumstantial symbols, usually induced by minor patient injuries and, therefore, may or may not appear. Therefore, each symbol has to be allocated a different weight, and a distinction has to be made depending on the symbol type.

With the help of an isokinetics expert, both the cost of substituting one symbol type by another and the cost of inserting or deleting a particular symbol type have been defined. The insert and delete costs were unified to assure that the comparison of two series is symmetric. For the substitute cost, a graph structure, where the principal cost of substituting two symbols is determined mainly by the symbol was opted. The symbol type serves to refine that cost.

Having obtained the distances between each extension and flexion of the two sequences for comparison, these values go through a normalization process to assure that all the distances are defined in the interval [0, 1]. Then their arithmetic mean is calculated. This process outputs the ISD between the two compared sequences.

As one of the goals of the system is for the user to compare models and exercises on the basis of their symbolic features, the interface can also receive two input curves, translate them into symbolic curves and compare these curves. The user interface provides the user with three views of the isokinetics exercise: the original numerical series, the symbolic series edited by the ISA language (which is similar to how the expert works) and the symbolic series displayed graphically as a curve.

Summary: Cooperation between Expert Knowledge and Discovered Knowledge in the I4 System

In the I4 system there are several examples of cooperation between expert knowledge and DM -discovered knowledge. The tasks where this synergy was stronger are:

1. Expert knowledge was employed to build expert functions that were used to remove incorrect tests, to eliminate incorrect extensions and flexions and to remove noise for the data preparation task before applying DM.
2. Expert knowledge was used to select and validate the patterns discovered by the numerical DM system.
3. Expert knowledge was used to guide the early DM process, in particular for reference model generation (semi-automatic selection of the population to be used).
4. Finally, expert knowledge was used systematically in the third phase of I4, the symbolic analysis. The main idea of this phase was to bring the DM process closer to the expert by using the concepts that the expert was accustomed to working with and provide more intuitive conclusions for a medical user. Expert knowledge was used to generate the vocabulary, output the symbolic data from the numerical data and define the weights used in the symbolic distance, among other tasks.

FUTURE RESEARCH DIRECTIONS

The missing link to complete authors experience in the field of isokinetics is a method for creating symbolic reference models. With this, all the functionalities of the numerical operating mode would have their symbolic equivalent. This could pave the way for comparative studies of the two. This process would require cooperation between DM and expert knowledge, as reference models would be generated using a DM process on symbolic data driven by expert knowledge. All this would be a key milestone in this research.

Authors were analyzing several alternatives for refining the symbolic reference model generation method. Their first idea is to use brute force to try to generate the symbolic series that minimizes the distance to the set of time series that the reference model is to identify. Another idea on which they were working is to generalize the symbolic distance from two to *n* series, generating, in the process, the symbolic time series pattern that best matches the *n* series. In both cases, they found that there is a combinatorial explosion. In thier view, this rules out both methods.

Finally, the potentially better option of using Genetic Programming techniques (GP) for this purpose was examined. The aim then is to find, by evolving successive generations, the individual that best represents the set. To do this, there are two important factors that should be defined. The first is to use Grammar-Guided Programming (GGP) to improve the process. GGP requires a Context-Free Grammar (CFG) that guarantees the validity of the new individuals generated by crossovers and mutations in the evolutionary process. Second, a fitness function to direct the process towards the ultimate objective have to be choosed, in this case, the construction of a reference model. To do this, the best fitness function would provide the measure of the distance of the new individual to the population of which the individual is a member. This distance should be minimized to find the model candidates.

The generation of valid symbolic reference models will be vital for the cooperation between expert knowledge and DM discovered knowledge, as it will provide experts with models defined in their own language. This way, experts will be able gain new knowledge more easily than using numerical models.

CONCLUSION

Mutual cooperation between expert knowledge and DM discovered knowledge in the development of an ES or a KBS helps to create better systems and optimizes the performance of the resulting system. In actual fact, some systems could not even be built if it were not for the positive effects of such cooperation.

This cooperation, which takes place in many walks of life, is especially relevant in the medical field because medical databases tend to be very large and the medical domain is extremely complex. The authors have analyzed many papers describing such cooperation and presented a representative selection of the different forms that this cooperation can take. The analysis of all these cases and authors experience in the I4 project has revealed that cooperation between expert knowledge and discovered knowledge helps to build superior and better validated systems containing more, higher quality knowledge.

REFERENCES

Alonso, F., Caraça-Valente, J. P., Martínez, L., & Montes, C. (2003). Discovering Similar Patterns for Characterising Time Series in a Medical Domain. *Knowledge and Information Systems: An International Journal*, 5(2), 183–200. doi:10.1007/s10115-003-0098-5

Alonso, F., Caraça-Valente, J. P., Martínez, L., & Montes, C. (2005). Discovering Patterns and Reference Models in the Medical Domain of Isokinetics. In Kantardzic, M., & Zurada, J. (Eds.), *Next Generation of Data-Mining Applications* (pp. 393–414). New York: Wiley-IEEE Press.

Alonso, F., Martínez, L., Pérez, A., Santamaría, A., & Valente, J. P. (2006). Symbol Extraction Method and Symbolic Distance for Analyzing Medical Time Series. In *Proceedings of International Symposium on Biological and Medical Data Analysis.* [Berlin: Springer.]. *Lecture Notes in Computer Science*, 4345, 311–322. doi:10.1007/11946465_28

Bethel, C. L., Hall, L. O., & Goldgof, D. (2006). Mining for Implications in Medical Data. In Y.Y. Tang, S.P. Wang, G. Lorette, D.S. Yeung & H. Yan (Eds.), *Proceedings of the 18th International Conference on Pattern Recognition* (pp. 1212-1215). Los Alamitos, CA: IEEE Computer Society.

Brisson, L., & Collard, M. (2008). How to Semantically Enhance a Data Mining Process? In J. Filipe & J. Cordeiro (Eds.), *10th International Conference, ICEIS 2008, Revised Papers. Lecture Notes in Business Information Processing,* 19 (pp. 103-116). Berlin/Heidelberg: Springer.

Chazard, E., Preda, C., Merlin, B., Ficheur, G., & Beuscart, R. (2009). Data-Mining-based Detection of Adverse Drug Events. In H. -P Adlassnig, B. Blobel, J. Mantas & I. Masic (Eds.), *Medical Informatics in a United and Healthy Europe, Proceedings of MIE 2009. Studies in Health Technology and Informatics,* 150 (pp. 552-556). Amsterdam: IOS Press.

Cooke, C. D., Santana, C. A., Morris, T. I., DeBraal, L., Ordonez, C., & Omiecinski, E. (2000). Validating Expert System Rule Confidences Using data Mining of Myocardial Perfusion SPECT Databases. *IEEE Computers in Cardiology, 27,* 785–788.

Davis, R., Buchanan, B., & Shortliffe, E. H. (1977). Production Rules as a representation for a Knowledge-based Consultation Program. *Artificial Intelligence, 8*(1), 15–45. doi:10.1016/0004-3702(77)90003-0

Faloutsos, C., Ranganatha, M., & Manolopoulos, Y. (1994). Fast subsequence matching in Time Series Databases. In *Proceedings of the 3rd International Conference on Knowledge Discovery and Data Mining* (pp. 24-30). Menlo Park, CA: AAAI Press.

Fink, E., Kokku, P. K., Nikiforou, S., Hall, L. O., Goldgof, D. B., & Krischer, J. P. (2004). Selection of Patients for Clinical Trials: An Interactive Web-Based System. *Artificial Intelligence in Medicine, 31*(3), 241–254.

Geurts, P. (2001). Pattern Extraction for Time Series Classification. In *Principles of Data Mining and Knowledge Discovery, 5th European Conference, PKDD 2001. Lecture Notes in Computer Science,* 2168 (pp. 115-127). Berlin/Heidelberg: Springer. doi: 10.1007/3-540-44794-6.

Gleeson, N. P., & Mercer, T. H. (1996). The utility of Isokinetics Dynamometry in the Assessment of Human Muscle Function. *Sports Medicine (Auckland, N.Z.), 21*(1), 18–34. doi:10.2165/00007256-199621010-00003

Haider, K., Tweedale, J., & Jain, L. (2009). An Intelligent Decision Support System Using Expert Systems in a MAS. In Nakamatsu, K., Phillips-Wren, G., Jain, L. C., & Howlett, R. J. (Eds.), *New Advances in Intelligent Decision Technologies. Studies in Computational Intelligence, 199* (pp. 213–222). Berlin, Heidelberg: Springer. doi:10.1007/978-3-642-00909-9_21

Han, J., Dong, G., & Yin, Y. (1998). Efficient Mining of Partial Periodic Patterns in Time Series Database. In *Proceedings of the 4th International Conference on Knowledge Discovery and Data Mining* (pp. 214-218). Menlo Park, CA: AAAI Press.

Kahveci, T., & Singh, A. (2001). Variable Length Queries for Time Series Data. In *Proceedings of the 17th International Conference of Data Engineering* (pp 273-282). Heidelberg, Germany. doi: 10.1109/ICDE.2001.914838

Lama, E., Mello, P., Nanetti, A., Riguzzi, F., Storari, S., & Valastro, G. (2006). Artificial Intelligence Techniques for Monitoring Dangerous Infections. *IEEE Transactions on Information Technology in Biomedicine, 10*(1), 143–155. doi:10.1109/TITB.2005.855537

Li, Y., Xu, X., & Songram, P. (2009). A Novel Model for Customer Retention. In H. Wang, Y.Shen, T. Huang & Z. Zeng (Eds.), *Sixth International Symposium on Neural Networks (ISNN 2009). Advances in Intelligent and Soft Computing,* 56 (pp. 739-747). Berlin/Heidelberg: Springer. doi: 10.1007/978-3-642-01216-7.

Matsumura, Y., Matsunaga, T., Maeda, Y., Tsumoto, S., Matsumura, H., & Kimura, M. (1988). Consultation System for Diagnoses of Headache and Facial Pain: RHINOS. *Medical Informatics, 11,* 145–157. doi:10.3109/14639238609001367

NCCLS. (2005). *National Committee for Clinical Laboratory Standards (NCCLS)*. Retrieved 2005, from http://www.nccls.org.

Needleman, S. B., & Wunsch, C. D. (1970). A General method applicable to the search for Similarities in the Amino Acid Sequences of Two Proteins. *Journal of Molecular Biology, 48*, 443–453. doi:10.1016/0022-2836(70)90057-4

Perng, C., Wang, H., Zhang, S. R., & Parker, D. S. (2000). Landmarks: A New Model for Similarity-Based Pattern Querying in Time Series Databases *ACDE*, 33-44.

Phuong, N. H., Hung, D. H., Co, N. V., Duong, B. D., Thinh, P. T., Hoa, N. P., & Linh, N. N. (1999). TUBERDIAG: An Expert system for Pulmonary Tuberculosis Diagnosis. *International Journal of Uncertainty. Fuzziness and Knowledge Based Systems, 7*(4), 371–382. doi:10.1142/S0218488599000325

Pyle, D. (1999). *Data Preparation for Data Mining. The Morgan Kaufmann Series in Data Management Systems*. San Francisco: Morgan Kaufmann.

Seifert, J. W. (2006). Data Mining: An Overview. In Pegarkov, D. D. (Ed.), *National Security Issues* (pp. 201–217). Haupauge, NY: Nova Science Publishers.

Seroussi, B., Bouaud, J., & Antoine, E. C. (2001). ONCODOC: A Successful Experiment of Computer-supported Guideline Development and Implementation in the treatment of Breast Cancer. *Artificial Intelligence in Medicine, 22*(1), 43–64. doi:10.1016/S0933-3657(00)00099-3

Shortliffe, E. H., Scott, A. C., Bischoff, M. B., Campbell, A. B., van Melle, W., & Jacobs, C. D. (1981). ONCOCIN: An Expert System for Oncology Protocol Management. In *Proceedings of the Seventh International Joint Conference on Artificial Intelligence* (pp. 876-881). Vancouver, Canada: IJAI.

Sun, B., Li, Y., & Zhang, L. (2009). The Intelligent System of Cardiovascular Disease Diagnosis Based on Extension Data Mining. In Y. Shi, S. Wang, Y. Peng, J. Li & Y. Zeng (Eds.), *Cutting-Edge Research Topics on Multiple Criteria Decision Making, Proceedings of 20th International Conference on Multiple Criteria Decision Making. Communications in Computer and Information Science*, 35 (pp. 133-140). Berlin/Heidelberg: Springer. doi: 10.1007/978-3-642-02298-2.

Tsumoto, S. (1999). Discovery of Rules for Medical Expert Systems-Rough Set Approach. In *Proceedings of the Third International Conference on Computational Intelligence and Multimedia Applications* (pp. 212-216). Los Alamitos, CA: IEEE Computer Society.

Xu, B., & Liu, L. Q. (2008). Research of Litchi Diseases Diagnosis Expert System Based on RBR and CBR. In D. Li & C. Zhao (Eds.), *The Second IFIP International Conference on Computer and Computing Technologies in Agriculture (CCTA2008). IFIP Advances in Information and Communication Technology*, 293 (pp. 681-688). Boston: Springer.

ADDITIONAL READING

Adomavicius, G., & Tuzhilin, A. (2001). Expert-Driven Validation of Rule-Based User Model in Personalization Applications. *Data Mining and Knowledge Discovery, 5*, 33–58. doi:10.1023/A:1009839827683

Bernstein, A., Provost, F., & Hill, S. (2005). Toward Intelligent Assistance for a Data Mining Process: An Ontology-Based Approach for Cost-Sensitive Classification. *IEEE Transactions on Knowledge and Data Mining, 17*(4), 503–518. doi:10.1109/TKDE.2005.67

Ceruti, M. G. (2000). The Relationship between Artificial Intelligence and Data Mining: Application to Future Military Information Systems. In, *2000 IEEE International Conference on System, Man and Cybernetics* (pp. 1875).

Chin, H. H., & Jafari, A. A. (2001). Using Procedure Reasoning System for Knowledge Discovery in Data Mining. In, *Proceedings of the 33rd Southeastern Symposium on System Theory* (pp. 331-336).

Holmes, G., & Cunningham, S. J. (1993). Using Data Mining to Support the Construction and Maintenance of Expert Systems. In *Proceedings of Artificial Neural Networks and Expert Systems* (pp. 156-159). Dunedin, New Zealand.

Hong, T., & Han, I. (2002). Knowledge-based Data Mining of News Information on the Internet using Cognitive Maps and Neural Networks. *Expert Systems with Applications, 23*, 1–8. doi:10.1016/S0957-4174(02)00022-2

Hu, J., & Liu, Y. (2006). Designing and Realization of Intelligent Data mining System Based on Expert Knowledge. In K.H. Chai, C.C. Hang & M. Xie (Eds.), *IEEE International Conference on Management of Innovation and Technology* (pp. 380- 383). Singapore: IEEE Press.

Jing, W., & Song, J. D. (2001). Using Expert System and KDD in Optimization of Mobile Network. In Zhong, Y. X., Cui, S., & Wang, Y. (Eds.), International *Conferences on Info-Tech & Info-Net* (pp. 240–245). Beijing: IEEE Press.

Keedwell, E., Bessler, F., Narayanan, A., & Savic, D. (2000). From Data Mining to Rule Refining. A new tool for Post Data Mining Rule Optimisation. In *Proceedings of 12th IEEE International Conference on Tools with Artificial Intelligence (ICTAI)* (pp. 00-82). IEEE Computer Society.

Klemettinen, M., Mannila, H., & Toivonen, H. (1997). A Data Mining Methodology and Its Application to Semi-Automatic Knowledge Acquisition. In *Proceedings of the 8th International Workshop on Database and Expert Systems Applications* (pp. 670). Washington, DC: IEEE Computer Society Press.

Kohara, K., Ishikawa, T., Fukuhara, Y., & Nakamura, Y. (1997). Stock price prediction using Prior Knowledge and Neural Networks. *Intelligent Systems in Account. Financial Management, 6*, 11–22.

Kovalerchuck, B., Vityaev, E., & Ruiz, J. F. (2000). Consistent Knowledge Discovery in Medical Diagnosis. *IEEE Engineering in Medicine and Biology, 19*(4), 26–37. doi:10.1109/51.853479

Mejía-Lavalle, M., & Rodríguez-Ortiz, G. (1998). Obtaining Expert System Rules using Data Mining Tools from a Power Generation Database. *Expert Systems with Applications, 14*, 37–42. doi:10.1016/S0957-4174(97)00073-0

Mitchell, F., Sleeman, D. H., & Milne, R. (1995). How to do Knowledge Acquisition without completely Annoying your Expert. In *IEE Colloquium on Knowledge Discovery in Databases*. London.

Phuong, N. H., Phong, L. L., Santiprabhob, P., & De Baets, B. (2001). Approach to Generating Rules for Expert Systems Using Rough Set Theory. In M.H. Smith, W.A. Gruver & L.O. Hall (Eds.), *Proceedings of the Joint 9th IFSA World Congress and 20th NAFIPS International Conference* (pp.877-882). IEEE Computer Society Press. Dorian, Pyle. (1999). *Data Preparation for Data Mining*. The Morgan Kaufmann Series in Data Management Systems. Publisher: Elsevier Science & Technology Books.

Rennolls, K. (2005). An Intelligent Framework (O-SS-E) for Data Mining, Knowledge Discovery and Business Intelligence. In *Proceedings of the 16th International Workshop on Database and Expert Systems Applications (DEXA'05). Lecture Notes in Computer Science 3588*. Berlin: Springer.

Sleeman, D., & Mitchell, F. (1996). Towards Painless Knowledge Acquisition. In *Proceedings of the 9th European Knowledge Acquisition Workshop on Advances in Knowledge Acquisition. Lecture Notes in Computer Science* (pp.262-277). London, UK: Springer-Verlag.

Tao, L., & Li, Y. L. (2004). A Synthetic Intelligent System for Web Information Mining. In *Proceedings of the Third International Conference on Machine Learning and Cybernetics* (pp.1357-1360). Shangai: IEEE Computer Society.

Tsipouras, M. G., Exarchos, T. P., & Fotiadis, D. I. (2006). A Comparison of Methodologies for Fuzzy Expert System Creation - Application to Arrhythmic Beat Classification. In *Proceedings of the 28th Annual International Conference of the IEEE Engineering in Medicine and Biology Society* (pp.2316-2319). Washington, DC: IEEE

Tsipouras, M. G., Exarchos, T. P., & Fotiadis, D. I. (2007). Integration of Global and Local Knowledge for Fuzzy Expert System Creation - Application to Arrhythmic Beat Classification. In *Proceedings of the 29th Annual International Conference of the IEEE Engineering in Medicine and Biology Society* (pp.3840-3843). Piscataway, NJ: IEEE Engineering in Medicine and Biology Society.

Tsumoto, S., & Tanaka, H. (1996). Automated Discovery of Medical Expert System Rules from Clinical Databases based on Rough Sets. In *Proceedings of the 2nd International Conference on Knowledge Discovery and Data Mining (KDD'96,)* (pp. 63-69). Menlo Park, CA: The AAAI Press.

Turksen, I. B. (1998) Fuzzy Data Mining and Expert System Development. In *Proceedings 1998 IEEE International Conference on Systems, Man, and Cybernetics* (pp. 2057- 2062). Washington, DC: IEEE.

Vityaev, E., & Kovalerchuk, B. (2005). Relational Methodology for Data Mining and Knowledge Discovery. In *Proceedings of the 16th International Workshop on Database and Expert Systems Applications (DEXA'05). Lecture Notes in Computer Science 3588*. Berlin: Springer.

Wang, D. (2006). Data Mining for Building Rule-based Fault Diagnosis Systems. In *Proceedings of the 25th Chinese Control Conference* (pp. 2206-2211). Beijing: Beijing University of Aeronautics and Astronautics Press.

Weiss, S. M., Buckley, S. J., Kapoor, S., & Damgaard, S. (2003). Knowledge-Based Data Mining. In *Proceedings of the Ninth ACM SIGKDD International Conference on Knowledge Discovery and Data Mining (pp 456-461)*. New York: ACM.

Yen, S. J., & Chen, A. L. P. (1997). An Efficient Data Mining Technique for Discovering Interesting Association Rules. In *Proceedings of the 8th International Workshop on Database and Expert Systems Applications (DEXA '97)* (pp. 664). Berlin: Springer.

Zhang, J., & Figueiredo, R. J. (2006). Application Classification through Monitoring and Learning of Resource Consumption Patterns. In *Proceedings of the 20th International Parallel and Distributed Processing Symposium* (pp. 10). IEEE.

Zhang, S., & Wang, Y. (2004). An Extension of SEMEST: The Online Software Engineering Measurement Tool. *In Proceedings of the 2004 Canadian conference on Electrical and Computer Engineering (CCECE 2004 – CCGEI 2004)* (pp.1519-1522). IEEE CS Press.

KEY TERMS AND DEFINITIONS

Data Mining Discovered Knowledge: The extracted patterns, trends, associations, etc., output by the data mining phase of the knowledge discovery process are referred to as data mining discovered knowledge.

Expert Knowledge: Expert knowledge is a combination of a theoretical understanding of the problem and a collection of heuristic problem-solving rules that experience has shown to be effective in the domain. Expert systems are constructed by obtaining this knowledge from a human expert and coding it into a form that a computer may apply to similar problems.

Expert System: An expert system is a knowledge-based system whose core knowledge is composed primarily of expert knowledge elicited from one or more human experts in the domain. It is then a software system that aims to solve problems by emulating expert problem-solving procedures.

Genetic Programming: A systematic method for getting computers to automatically solve a problem starting from a high-level statement of what needs to be done. Genetic programming is a domain-independent method that genetically breeds a population of computer programs to solve a problem. Specifically, genetic programming iteratively transforms a population of computer programs into a new generation of programs by applying analogs of naturally occurring genetic operations.

Isokinetics System: System used to perform isokinetic exercises and measure the strength applied. An isokinetic exercise is the exertion of a joint across a kinetic field at a constant speed throughout.

Knowledge Discovery in Databases (KDD): Nontrivial extraction of implicit, previously unknown, and potentially useful information from data.

Knowledge-Based System (KBS): A knowledge-based system is a system based on artificial intelligence methods and techniques whose performance depends more on the explicit presence of a body of knowledge than on complex computational procedures. It core components are the knowledge base and the inference mechanisms.

Times Series, Numerical or Symbolic: A time series is a chronological sequence of observations on a particular variable. Usually the observations are taken at regular intervals, but the sampling could be irregular. Numerical time series are time series where the variable takes numerical values, whereas symbolic time series are time series where the observed variable has symbolic values.

ENDNOTES

[1]   The research and findings described in this chapter were completed in close cooperation with the Higher Sports Council, and particularly Dr. Africa Lopez Illescas, whom we would like to thank especially for the support and expertise she lent in the field of isokinetics.

[2]   The research described was part of the "VIIP: Sistema para el Analisis e Interpretacion de datos Isocineticos y Posturograficos" project, funded by the Spanish Ministry of Education and Science as part of the 2004-2007 National R&D&I Plan through the project DEP2005-00232-C03.

Section 3
Case Studies

Chapter 11
A Comparative Study of Associative Classifiers in Mesenchymal Stem Cell Differentiation Analysis

Weiqi Wang
University of Oxford, UK

Yanbo J. Wang
China Minsheng Banking Corporation Ltd., China

Qin Xin
Simula Research Laboratory, Norway

René Bañares-Alcántara
University of Oxford, UK

Frans Coenen
University of Liverpool, UK

Zhanfeng Cui
University of Oxford, UK

ABSTRACT

Discovering how Mesenchymal Stem Cells (MSCs) can be differentiated is an important topic in stem cell therapy and tissue engineering. In a general context, such differentiation analysis can be modeled as a classification problem in data mining. Specifically, this is concerned with the single-label multi-class classification task. Previous studies on this topic suggests the Associative Classification (AC) rather than other alternative (Classification) techniques, and presented classification results based on the CMAR (Classification based on Multiple Association Rules) associative classifier. Other AC algorithms include: CBA (Classification Based on Associations), PRM (Predictive Rule Mining), CPAR (Classification based

DOI: 10.4018/978-1-60960-067-9.ch011

on Predictive Association Rules) and TFPC (Total From Partial Classification). The main aim of this chapter is to compare the performance of different associative classifiers, in terms of classification accuracy, efficiency, number of rules to be generated, quality of such rules, and the maximum number of attributes in rule-antecedents, with respect to MSC differentiation analysis.

INTRODUCTION

Mesenchymal Stem Cells (MSCs) have been claimed to be an integral part of tissue engineering due to their pluripotent differentiation potential both *in vivo* and *in vitro* (Beeres, Atsma, van der Laarse, Pijnappels, van Tuyn, & Fibbe, 2005; Derubeis & Cancedda, 2004; Zhang, Li, Jiang, Wu, & Liu, 2004), and have become one of the most significant research topics in the past few decades. MSCs are able to differentiate along the osteogenic, chondrogenic, adipogenic, myogenic, tendonogenic, and neurogenic lineages under appropriate stimuli (Pittenger, Mackay, Beck, Jaiswal, Douglas, & Mosca, 1999; Roelen & Dijke, 2003; Tuan, Boland, & Tuli, 2003), generating bone, cartilage, fat, muscle, tendon, and neuron cells respectively (Figure 1). Other discoveries on plasticity and immunologic properties of MSCs have further increased the interest in their clinical applications (Krampera, Glennie, Dyson, Scott, Laylor, & Simpson, 2003; Muller, Kordowich, Holzwarth, Spano, Isenee, & Staiber, 2006). The significance of MSCs in clinical therapy has trig-

gered an urgent need for a better understanding and, if possible, computational prediction of MSCs differentiation (Griffith & Swartz, 2006).

In order to obtain a better understanding of MSCs, a significant number of studies have been conducted (Battula, Bareiss, Treml, Conrad, Albert, & Hojak, 2007; Hanada, Dennis, & Caplan, 1997; Lennon, Haynesworth, Young, Dennis, & Caplan, 1995; Magaki, Kurisu, & Okazaki, 2005; Meuleman, Tondreau, Delforge, Dejeneffe, Massy, & Libertalis, 2006; Muller et al., 2006), providing an enormous amount of experimental data for computational prediction. However, those studies and experiments were not interrelated with each other, i.e. different experiments focused on different combinations of factors affecting MSC differentiation, including species of cell donors, *in vitro* vs. *in vivo* environments where the experiments were executed, cell culture media, growth factors and supplements to the culture media, culture dimension (monolayer vs. 3D culture), cell attaching substrate (for monolayer culture) vs. scaffold (for 3D culture), and cell behaviors, especially the differentiation fates of

Figure 1. Differentiation fates of MSCs

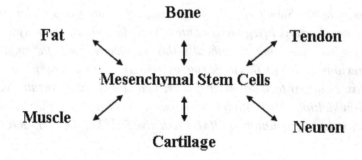

MSCs in terms of the different lineages to which the cells committed (Hanada et al., 1997; Haynesworth, Baber, & Caplan, 1996; Kuznetsov, Friedenstein, & Robey, 1997; Lennon et al., 1995; Muller et al., 2006). The scattered experimental data hence resulted in a large amount of noise in the database and a discrete data structure, which cannot take advantage of traditional mathematical modeling methods. As a consequence, it is extremely difficult to construct intracellular pathway models for MSC metabolism, especially for their differentiation process (Bianco, Riminucci, Gronthos, & Robey, 2001).

On the other hand, useful information and meaningful prediction for MSC differentiation can be derived based on knowledge discovery via data mining techniques. The nature of data mining is to discover useful, but hidden, information (knowledge) in data. Previous studies under this heading (Wang, Wang, Banares-Alcantara, Coenen, & Cu, in press; Wang, Wang, Banares-Alcantara, Cui, & Coenen, 2009) model the analysis of MSC differentiation as a classification problem (in data mining) — the task of assigning predefined categories (differentiation fates) to "unseen" (MSC) instances. Broadly speaking, classification can be separated into two divisions: *single-label* that assigns exactly one predefined category to each "unseen" instance; and *multi-label* that assigns one or more predefined category to each "unseen" instance. With regard to *single-label* classification, three distinct approaches can be identified: *one-class* which learns from positive data samples only, and either assigns the predefined category to a "unseen" instance or ignores the assignation of the instance; *two-class* (or *binary*) which learns from both positive and negative data samples, and assigns either a predefined category or the complement of this category to each "unseen" instance; and *multi-class* which simultaneously deals with all given categories comprising all data samples, and assigns the most appropriate category to each "unseen" instance. The study presented

in this chapter is concerned with the *single-label multi-class* classification task.

Mechanisms on which classification algorithms have been based include: decision trees, naive Bayes, k-NN (k-Nearest Neighbor), SVM (Support Vector Machine), genetic algorithm, neural networks, inductive learners (such as *FOIL* (First Order Inductive Learner) and RIPPER (Repeated Incremental Pruning to Produce Error Reduction)), association rules, etc. Among these mechanisms, classification based on association rules, i.e. Associative Classification (AC) or Classification Association Rule Mining (CARM), was suggested to address the MSC differentiation analysis problem (Wang et al., in press; Wang et al., 2009). It seems that AC (or CARM) offers a number of advantages over other classification approaches (Coenen, Leng, & Zhang, 2005; Shidara, Nakamura, & Kudo, 2007; Thabtah, Cowling, & Peng, 2005).

Coenen and Leng (2007) indicate:

- *"Training of the classifier is generally much faster using CARM (AC) techniques than other classification generation techniques such as decision tree (induction) and SVM (support vector machine) approaches"* (particularly when handling with the *multi-class* problem).
- *"Training sets with high dimensionality can be handled very effectively"*.
- *"The resulting classifier is expressed as a set of rules which are easily understandable and simple to apply to unseen data (an advantage also shared by some other techniques, e.g. decision tree classifiers)"*.
- In addition Liu et al. (1998) suggest that *"Experimental results show that the classifier built this way (AC) is, in general, more accurate than that produced by the state-of-the-art classification system"*.

Since the first introduction of AC (Ali, Manganaris, & Srikant,, 1997), a number of major (AC) algorithms have emerged, these include: CBA (Classification Based on Associations), CMAR (Classification based on Multiple Association Rules), PRM (Predictive Rule Mining), CPAR (Classification based on Predictive Association Rules), and TFPC (Total From Partial Classification). Broadly speaking, these AC algorithms can be categorized into two groups, described as follows, according to the way that the Classification Association Rules (CARs) are generated.

- **Two Stage Algorithms,** were a set of CARs are produced first (as "stage 1"), which are then pruned and placed into a classifier (as "stage 2"). Typical algorithms of this approach include CBA (Liu et al., 1998) and CMAR (Li et al., 2001).
- **Integrated Algorithms,** were the classifier is produced in a single processing step. Algorithms of this kind include PRM and CPAR (Yin & Han, 2003), and TFPC (Coenen & Leng, 2004, 2007; Coenen et al., 2005).

Previous studies in data mining (or knowledge discovery) based MSC differentiation analysis report a satisfactory performance using the CMAR associative classifier, with regard to an online MSC database (Wang, Wang, Banares-Alcantara, Coenen, & Cui, in press; Wang, Wang, Banares-Alcantara, Cui, & Coenen, 2009). In this chapter, the analysis of MSC differentiation by addressing a series of AC approaches is developed, and aim to find the most appropriate associative classifier for this MSC differentiation study, by comparing the performance of different (AC) approaches in several aspects, i.e. classification accuracy, efficiency, number of rules to be generated, quality of such rules, and maximum number of attributes in rule-antecedents.

Chapter Organization

The rest of this chapter is organized as follows. The following section describes some related data mining aspects, as the background knowledge of this chapter, in classification, Association Rule Mining (Cody, Boctor, Filley, Hazen, Scott, & Sharma, 2000), and Associative Classification (AC). In the third section, five existing AC approaches (i.e. CBA, CMAR, PRM, CPAR and TFPC) are described in detail. The construction of a domain-specific (MSC) database, as the data preparation of the study, is introduced in the fourth section. Experiments are presented in the fifth section that compares the performance of existing AC approaches in MSC differentiation study. The sixth section gives a discussion of the study, and further points out some future research directions there. Finally the chapter ends with the conclusion.

BACKGROUND

The focus of this chapter is to compare five existing AC approaches in the application of data analysis on MSC differentiation. AC in fact lies at the overlap between classification and ARM, which solves the traditional classification problem based on ARM techniques with regard to rule generation and presentation. As mentioned above, AC has been selected as a suitable technique for MSC differentiation analysis. In this section, the authors concentrate scientifically and technically on the depiction of (*single-label multi-class*) classification, ARM and AC.

Classification

Classification is a traditional school in the field of data mining, as well as in machine learning. It is a typical form of *"data analysis that can be used to extract models describing important data classes"* (Han & Kamber, 2006). Specifically, classification aims to assign predefined data categories/classes to "unseen" data instances, based on the study of a given set of training data examples — data instances associating with data category labels. Early studies of (data) classification can be dated back to the early 1960s, see for instance (Maron, 1961) with regard to such textual data. The process of classification consists of two steps: (1) *"a classifier is built describing a predetermined set of data classes or concepts"* — *"this is the learning step (or training phase), where a classification algorithm builds the classifier by analyzing or 'learning from' the training set"* (Han & Kamber, 2006); and (2) the classifier model is used for classifying "unseen" data samples into predefined classes as given in the training set — this is the classification step (or test phase). In step (2), the measure of accuracy has been widely used to evaluate the performance of classification, especially as presented in this chapter when dealing with the *single-label multi-class* classification task. Agrawal, Gadbole, Punjani and Roy (2007) confirm that *"in a classification problem, the classification system is trained on the training data and effectiveness is measured by accuracy on test data"*, which is the fraction of correctly predicted instance-class mappings.

Broadly speaking, mechanisms on which classification algorithms have been based can be separated into two "families": *direct classification* — classification without rule generation; and *rule based classification* — classification with rule generation (and presentation). The "family" of *direct classification* focuses on directly classifying "unseen" data instances into predefined categories, but has no concern for presenting to the end user why and how the classification predictions have been made. Since this group of mechanisms only aims to show that machines can learn and make correct classification decisions, such (Classification) approaches were proposed under the machine learning heading. In *direct classification*, typical mechanisms include: naive Bayes (Lowd & Domingos, 2005), SVM (Boser, Guyon, &

Vapnik, 1992), genetic algorithm (Freitas, 2002; Yang, Widyantoro, Ioerger, & Yen, 2001), neural networks (Han & Kamber, 2006), etc.

The "family" of *rule based classification* mines and generates human readable Classification Rules (CRs) from a given class-database D_C, with the objective of building a classifier to categorize "unseen" data records. Such mechanisms in this "family" were proposed under the data mining heading. Generally, D_C is described by a relational database table that includes a class attribute — whose values are a set of predefined class labels $C = \{c_1, c_2, ..., c_{|C|-1}, c_{|C|}\}$. The *two-step* process of *rule based classification* can be described formally as (1) CRs are generated from a set of training data instances $D_R \subset D_C$; and (2) "unseen" instances in a test dataset $D_E \subset D_C$ are assigned into predefined class groups. A D_C is established as $D_R \cup D_E$, where $D_R \cap D_E = \varnothing$. Both D_R and D_E share the same database attributes except the class attribute. By convention the last attribute in each D_R record usually indicates the predefined class of this record, noted as the class attribute, while the class attribute is missing in D_E. Typical mechanisms in *rule based classification* include: Decision Trees (Quinlan, 1993), *k*-NN (James, 1985), *FOIL* (Quinlan & Cameron-Jones, 1993), RIPPER (Cohen, 1995), Association Rules (Liu, et al., 1998; Wang, Xin, & Coenen, 2008), etc.

Association Rule Mining

Association Rule Mining (Cody et al. 2000), first introduced by Agrawal et al. (1993), aims to extract a set of Association Rules (ARs) from a given transactional database D_T. Association Rule describes an implicative co-occurring relationship between two sets of *binary*-valued (i.e. ABSENCE or APPEARANCE, 0 or 1) transactional database attributes (items), expressed in the form of an "antecedent $\Rightarrow$ consequent" rule. As indicated by Cornelis et al. (2006), the concept of mining ARs can be dated back to work in the 1960's (Hajek, Havel, & Chytil, 1966).

In a more general form, ARM can be defined as follows. Let $I = \{a_1, a_2, ..., a_{n-1}, a_n\}$ be a set of items, and $\mathcal{F} = \{T_1, T_2, ..., T_{m-1}, T_m\}$ be a set of transactions (data records), a transactional database D_T is described by $\mathcal{F}$, where each $T_j \in \mathcal{F}$ comprises a set of items $I' \subseteq I$. In ARM, two threshold values are usually used to determine the significance of an AR:

- **Support**: A set of items S is called an itemset. The *support* of S is the proportion of transactions T in $\mathcal{F}$ for which $S \subseteq T$. If the *support* of S exceeds a user-supplied *support* threshold σ, S is defined as a *frequent itemset*.
- **Confidence**:*Confidence* represents how "strongly" an itemset X implies another itemset Y, where $X, Y \subseteq I$ and $X \cap Y = \varnothing$. A *confidence* threshold α, supplied by a user, is used to distinguish high confidence ARs from low confidence ARs.

An AR $X \Rightarrow Y$ is said to be *valid* when the *support* for the co-occurrence of X and Y exceeds σ, and the *confidence* of the AR exceeds α. The computation of *support* is:

$$support(X \cup Y) = count(X \cup Y) / |\mathcal{F}|,$$

where $count(X \cup Y)$ is the number of transactions containing the set $X \cup Y$ in $\mathcal{F}$, and $|\mathcal{F}|$ is the *size* function (*cardinality*) of the set $\mathcal{F}$. The computation of *confidence* is:

$$confidence(X \Rightarrow Y) = support(X \cup Y) / support(X).$$

Informally, "$X \Rightarrow Y$" can be interpreted as: if X is found in a transaction, it is likely that Y also will be found.

In general, ARM involves a search for all *valid* rules. The most computationally difficult part of this is the identification of *frequent itemsets*. Since its introduction in 1994, the *apriori* algorithm de-

veloped by Agrawal and Srikant (1994) has been the basis of many subsequent ARM algorithms. In Agrawal and Srikant (1994) it was observed that ARs can be straightforwardly generated from a set of *frequent itemsets*. Thus, efficiently and effectively mining *frequent itemsets* from data is the key to ARM. The *apriori* algorithm iteratively identifies *frequent itemsets* in data by employing the "closure property" of itemsets in the generation of candidate itemsets, where a candidate (possibly frequent) itemset is confirmed as frequent only when all its subsets are identified as frequent in the previous pass. The "closure property" of itemsets can be described as follows: if an itemset is frequent then all its subsets will also be frequent; conversely if an itemset is infrequent then all its supersets will also be infrequent.

With regards to the history of ARM investigation, many algorithms have been introduced that mine ARs from identified *frequent itemsets*. These algorithms can be further grouped into different "families", such as Pure-*apriori* like, Semi-*apriori* like, Set Enumeration Tree like, etc.

- **Pure-*apriori* like** were *frequent itemsets* are generated based on the generate-prune level by level iteration that was first promulgated in the *apriori* algorithm. In this "family" archetypal algorithms include: *apriori*, *apriori*-Tid and *apriori*-Hybrid (Agrawal & Srikant, 1994), Partition (Savasere, Omiecinski, & Navethe, 1995), Sampling (Toivonen, 1996), DIC (Brin, Motwani, Ullman, & Tsur, 1997), CARMA (Hidber, 1999), etc.
- **Semi-*apriori* like** were *frequent itemsets* are generated by enumerating candidate itemsets but do not apply the *apriori* generate-prune iterative approach founded in (1) the join procedure, and (2) the prune procedure that employs the "closure property" of itemsets. In this "family" typical algorithms include: AIS (Agrawal et al., 1993), SETM (Houtsma & Swami, 1995),

OCD (Mannila, Toivonen, & Verkamo, 1994), etc.

- **Set Enumeration Tree like** were *frequent itemsets* are generated through constructing a *set enumeration tree* structure (Rymon, 1992) from D_T, which avoids the need to enumerate a large number of candidate itemsets. In this "family" a number of approaches can be further divided into two main streams: *apriori-TFP*[1] based (Coenen, Goulbourne, & Leng, 2001; Coenen & Leng, 2002; Coenen, Leng, & Ahmed, 2004; Coenen, Leng, & Goulbourne, 2004), and *FP-tree* based (El-Hajj & Zaiane, 2003; Han, Pei, & Yin, 2000; Liu, Pan, Wang, & Han, 2002).

Associative Classification

An overlap between ARM and *rule based classification* is AC (Associative Classification) or CARM (Classification Association Rule Mining), which strategically solves the traditional classification problem by applying ARM techniques. The idea of AC, first introduced in (Ali, Manganaris, & Srikant, 1997), aims to extract a set of Classification Association Rules (CARs) from a class-transactional database D_{C-T}. Let D_T be a transactional database, and $C = \{c_1, c_2, ..., c_{|C|-1}, c_{|C|}\}$ be a set of predefined class labels, D_{C-T} is described by $D_T \times C$. D_{C-T} can also be defined as a special class-database D_C, where all database attributes and the class attribute are valued in a *binary* manner — "*Boolean attributes can be considered a special case of categorical attributes*" (Srikant & Agrawal, 1996). A CAR is a special AR that describes an implicative co-occurring relationship between a set of *binary*-valued data attributes and a predefined class, expressed in the form of an "$X \Rightarrow c_i$" rule, where X is an itemset found in D_T (as "$D_{C-T} - C$") and c_i is a predefined class in C.

AC offers the following advantages with respect to the classification techniques mentioned above (Antonie & Zaiane, 2002; Yoon & Lee, 2005):

- The approach is efficient during both the training and categorization phases, especially when handling a large volume of data.
- The classifier built in this approach can be read, understood and modified by humans.

Furthermore, AC is relatively insensitive to noise data. AC builds a classifier by extracting a set of CARs from a given set of training instances. Possible CARs are determined by a large enough *support* and a large enough *confidence*. Usually, rules derived from noise in the data will fail to reach these thresholds and will be discarded.

In comparison, classification approaches other than AC, i.e. naive Bayes, SVM, genetic algorithm, neural networks, etc. do not present the classification in a human readable fashion, so that users do not see why the (Classification) predictions have been made by computers. While rules generated by decision tree classifier, RIPPER classifier, etc. can be read and understood by humans, however (Yin & Han, 2003) report that in many cases AC offers higher classification accuracy than other *rule based classification* approaches.

For these reasons it was decided to use an AC approach to address the prediction of mammalian MSC differentiation. One of the existing AC frameworks is the CMAR (Classification based on Multiple Association Rules) algorithm (Li et al., 2001). CMAR generates CARs (from a given set of training instances) through an *FP–tree* (Han, Pei, & Yin, 2000) based approach. Experimental results using this algorithm show that it could achieve high classification accuracy for a range of data sets (Li et al., 2001). Other alternative AC techniques are CBA, PRM, CPAR, TFPC, etc.

FIVE ASSOCIATIVE CLASSIFICATION APPROACHES

Classification Based on Associations

The Classification Based on Associations (CBA) algorithm (Liu et al., 1998) exemplifies the "two stage" approach (as opposite to the "integrated" approach), and was one of the first to make use of a general ARM algorithm for "stage 1". CBA uses a version of the well-known *apriori* algorithm (Agrawal & Srikant, 1994), using user-supplied *support* and *confidence* thresholds, to generate CARs which are then prioritized as follows (e.g. given two rules r_A and r_B):

- r_A has priority over r_B if the *confidence* value of r_A is greater than the *confidence* value of r_B.
- r_A has priority over r_B if the *confidence* values of r_A and r_B are equal, but the *support* value of r_A is greater than the *support* value of r_B.
- r_A has priority over r_B if the *confidence* values of r_A and r_B are equal, the *support* values of r_A and r_B are equal, but the rule-antecedent *size* (the number of items) of r_A is less than the rule-antecedent *size* of r_B.

In "stage 2", the ordered set of CARs is then pruned as follows:

- For each data record d in the training set, find the first CAR (the one with the highest precedence) that correctly classifies the record (the *cor-CAR*), and the first CAR that wrongly classifies the record (the *wro-CAR*).
- For each data record where the *cor-CAR* has higher precedence than the *wro-CAR*, such CARs are included in the classifier.
- For all data records where the *cor-CAR* does not have higher precedence than the *wro-CAR*, alternative CARs with lower precedence must be considered and added to the classifier.

CARs are added to the classifier according to their precedence. On completion the lower precedence CARs are examined and a default rule selected to replace these low precedence CARs. CBA illustrates the general performance drawback of "two stage" algorithms — the cost of the pruning stage is a product of the size of the data set and the number of candidate CARs, both of which may in some cases be large. It is clear, also, that the choice of *support* and *confidence* thresholds will strongly influence the operation of CBA. The ordering strategy, noted as *Confidence-Support-Antecedent* (CSA), seems to work well on some data sets.

Classification Based on Multiple Association Rules

The Classification based on Multiple Association Rules (CMAR) algorithm (Li et al., 2001) has a similar general structure to CBA, and uses the same rule prioritization approach as that employed in CBA. CMAR differs in the method used in "stage 1" to generate candidate CARs, which makes use of the *FP-tree* data structure coupled with the *FP-growth* algorithm (Han et al., 2000); this makes it more computationally efficient than CBA. Like CBA, CMAR tends to generate a large number of candidate CARs. The set of CARs is pruned by removing all rules with a χ squared value below a user-defined threshold and all rules where a more general rule with higher precedence exists. Finally, a database coverage procedure is used to produce the final set of CARs. This stage is similar to that of CBA, but whereas CBA finds only one CAR to cover each case, CMAR uses a coverage threshold parameter to generate a large number of CARs. When classifying an "unseen" data record, CMAR groups CARs that satisfy the record according to their class and determines the combined effect of the CARs in each group using a Weighted χ Squared (WCS) measure.

Predictive Rule Mining

Predictive Rule Mining (PRM) (Yin & Han, 2003), as an extension of the *FOIL* algorithm (Quinlan & Cameron-Jones, 1993), is a time-efficient algorithm based on the *greedy* paradigm in which rules to distinguish positive examples from negative ones are iteratively learnt. PRM repeatedly searches for the current "best" rule and decreases the weights of the positive examples when those positive examples are correctly covered by this selected "best" rule until all the positive examples in the (training) data set are covered. Note that (in comparison) the positive examples will be removed if such examples are covered by any selected "best" rule during each iteration of the rule selection in traditional *FOIL*. By performing such an approach, PRM can produce more rules than *FOIL* and each positive example is usually covered more than once. Consequently, it leads higher classification accuracy than *FOIL*. Similarly as the methodologies used in *FOIL*, a crucial function *gain* (*p*) is used to measure the information gained from adding the literal *p* to the current rule *r* during selection of literals, e.g. the number of bits saved in representing all the positive examples by adding *p* to *r*. In order to achieve a better efficiency than *FOIL*, PRM employs the standard approach (Gehrke, Ramakrishnan, & Ganti, 1998) based on a new data structure called *PNArray* to retail the computational burden on evaluation of every literal during searching stages for the one with the highest gain in *FOIL*. For *multi-class* (Classification) problems, PRM follows the standard framework from *FOIL*: for each class, its examples are used as positive examples and those of other classes as negative ones, and the rules for all classes are merged together to form the classifier (rule set).

Classification Based on Predictive Association Rules

Classification based on Predictive Association Rules (CPAR) (Yin & Han, 2003) inherits the basic idea of traditional *FOIL* in rule generation and integrates the features of associative classification of PRM. When selecting literals during the rule building process, PRM selects only one "best" literal in each iteration and ignores all the others. In fact, there are usually many rules with similar accuracy based on the remaining dataset in each iteration. The "best" rule among them in the remaining dataset may not be the "best" rule in the whole (training) dataset. This strategy may therefore lead to PRM missing some very important rules. Instead of ignoring all literals except the "best" one, CPAR keeps all close-to-the-best literals in each iteration during the rule building process. By performing such an approach, CPAR can select more than one literal at the same time and build several rules simultaneously. In comparison with PRM, CPAR has the following advantages: (1) CPAR generates a much smaller set with high-quality predictive rules directly from the given dataset; (2) to avoid producing redundant rules, CPAR generates each rule by taking into account the set of "already-generated" rules; and (3) when predicting the class label for a given example, CPAR uses the *best k rules* on which this example satisfies.

Total From Partial Classification

Several of the above AC methods apply coverage analysis to prune data instances/cases and reduce the number of rules generated in the training phase. It can be demonstrated that coverage analysis, especially when applied to a large D_{C-T} comprising many items and multiple transactions, includes a significant computational overhead. This is the motivation behind development of an algorithm that directly builds an acceptably accurate classifier without coverage analysis. The Total From

Partial Classification (TFPC) algorithm, proposed by Coenen et al. (2005), is directed at this aim. Coenen and Leng (2007) argue that the principal advantage offered by TFPC is that "*it is extremely efficient (because it dispenses with the need for coverage analysis)*".

TFPC is derived from the *apriori-TFP* ARM approach (Coenen, 2004; Coenen & Leng, 2004). It employs the same (*set enumeration tree*) structures and (mining) procedures as used in *apriori-TFP* to the task of identifying CARs in D_{C-T}. For this purpose, predefined class labels in D_{C-T} are considered as items, and set at the end of the item list (ordered in a descending manner based on the item frequency).

In its rule generation process, TFPC adopts the heuristic: "*if we can identify a rule X $\Rightarrow$ c which meets the required support and confidence thresholds, then it is not necessary to look for other rules whose antecedent is a superset of X and whose consequent is c*" (Coenen et al., 2005). The advantages of employing this heuristic can be listed as follows.

- It "*reduces the number of candidate rules to be considered*" thus "*significantly improving the speed of the rule-generation algorithm*" (Coenen & Leng, 2007).
- It reduces the number of final CARs to be generated, so that "*this 'on-the-fly' pruning replaces the expensive pruning step that other algorithms perform by coverage analysis*" (Coenen & Leng, 2007).
- It reduces the risk of *over-fitting* — i.e. the risk of producing a set of CARs that perform well on the training dataset but do not generalize well to the test dataset.

The classifier built by TFPC is finally represented as a list of CARs in a CSA rule ordering fashion. When classifying "unseen" cases TFPC typically uses the *best first rule* approach.

DATA PREPARATION

Parameter Selection from the Online MSC Database

In order to integrate mammalian MSC differentiation data, an online database[2] containing over 500 parameters that are believed to influence the MSC differentiation has been built in the previous studies (Wang et al., 2009). All the data in this online database have been published in the literature and marked with their respect references.

The current size of this database is 501 records, covering four types of MSC differentiation fates as predefined classes, which are osteogenesis, chondrogenesis, adipogenesis and proliferation without differentiation. The total number of parameters in this database is up to 500, including those which are believed to be most significant, such as donor species, *in vitro* vs. *in vivo* culture, culture medium, supplements and growth factors, culture dimension (monolayer vs. 3D culture), substrate (for monolayer culture) vs. scaffold (for 3D culture), those which are believed to be potentially important, such as age of donor, cell passage number, cell seeding density, incubation duration, those which usually act as supplementary comments, such as donor gender, MSC harvest place, and those representing cell behaviors as experimental results, including MSC differentiation fates, population doubling time, expression of cell markers, gene profiles, expansion fold of cell number, etc.

Among all the parameters in the database, those which are believed to be the most essential ones were abstracted and considered in this study. Table 1 shows all the parameters used for prediction in the current stage of this study. Consequently, the number of parameters in the abstracted database was reduced from 500 to 105.

Table 1. The abstracted database

Parameter groups	Significance/Description
Donor species	MSCs from different species of mammal in the same culture condition may lead to different results. The current database covers five different donor species.
Culture medium	The most essential of environment conditions where MSCs grow, proliferate and differentiate. A different culture medium has different effect on cells. The current database covers 16 types of culture media.
Supplements and growth factors	Chemicals that maintain MSC differentiation potential or influence their differentiation fates. The functions and effects of growth factors on MSCs vary from one to another, leading to different experimental results. The current database covers 64 types of supplements.
Culture dimension (2D vs. 3D) MSC differentiation sometimes differs significantly from monolayer to 3D culture, even under the same culture medium and supplements. This is one parameter with two possible values. Substrate (for 2D) /scaffold (for 3D)	Influences cell viability. A chemically modified substrate can even change MSCs' differentiation fate. The current database covers 10 types of substrates and 5 types of scaffolds.
Differentiation fate	To what lineage MSCs are committed to after differentiation. It is the most significant result after cell culture. Used to define the classes in the database; the objective of this study is to predict it. The current database covers four types of differentiation fates, as four classes.

Data Normalization and Cleaning

After parameter selection, the database was discretised and normalized using the LUCS-KDD Discretised Normalized (DN) software[3], so that data was made available in *binary* form and suitable for use by AC applications. In this study, the discretisation and normalization processes result in a data file with its number of attributes increased to 183.

This discretised and normalized data file contains noisy data, generally caused by the absence of culture condition parameters such as culture media, supplements & growth factors[4], etc. For example, if the insulin growth factor is absent in a record, this record will have an attribute representing "absence of insulin" after the discretisation and normalization process. This kind of attributes does not provide any useful information while increasing the complexity of the data file. Thus, all the attributes with a value of "absence" were

eliminated, with the resulting data file referred as the preliminary data file.

Data Pre-Processing

The preliminary data file was not directly used as input data file to the five AC approaches because it contains some overlapping attributes. For example, some records in the preliminary data file contain an attribute for the presence of "ITS-plus", because in some experiments "ITS-plus" is used as supplement to the culture medium ("ITS-plus" is a combination of 6.25 g/ml of bovine insulin, 6.25 g/ml of transferrin, 6.25 g/ml of selenous acid, 5.33 g/ml of linoleic acid, and 1.25 mg/ml of bovine serum albumin39). In this case, the attribute for "ITS-plus" overlaps with the attribute for "insulin", and hence should be converted into one attribute for "insulin" plus four more attributes for the other four chemicals indicated above. On the other hand, some attributes in the data file are not useful. For example, it is known that the pres-

Table 2. Pruning of the attributes in the preliminary data file during data pre-processing

Attributes before pre-processing	Attributes after pre-processing	Ref.
antibiotic-antimycotic, penicillin, streptomycin, gentamicin	none	n/a
L-glutamine, glutamine	glutamine	n/a
platelet lysate	PDGF-αα, PDGF-ββ, TGF-β, VEGF, EGF	(Celotti, Colciago, Negri-Cesi, Pravettoni, Zaninetti, & Sacchi., 2006; O'Connell, Impeduglia, Hessler, Wang, Carroll, & Dardik, 2008)
ITS-plus/ITS+permixTX, ITS+1	insulin, transferrin, selenous acid, LA-BSA	(Johnstone, Hering, Caplan, Goldberg, & Yoo, 1998; Mackay, Beck, Murphy, Barry, Chichester, & Pittenger, 1998)
SITE (from sigma)	selenous acid, insulin, transferrin, ethanolamine	(Liu, Wu, & Hwang, 2007)
ascorbic acid, scorbate-2-phosphate/ascorbic acid-2-phosphate	"ascorbic acid (-2-phosphate)"	n/a
IBMX, 8-MM-IBMX	"IBMX or 8-MM-IBMX"	n/a
TGF-β1, TGF-β3	TGF-β	n/a

ence of the supplement "antibiotic-antimycotic" is to prevent contamination and has no influence on MSC differentiation. Attributes concerned with this type of supplements should hence be eliminated from the preliminary data file. As a result of pruning the attributes according to Table 2, the preliminary data file became the input data file to the five AC approaches, with 95 attributes in total. This step is referred as data pre-processing, after which the five AC approaches were applied to segments of the input data file with a Ten-fold Cross Validation (TCV) accuracy setting (90% training set, 10% test set) (Schaffer, 1993), with the results shown in the next section.

EXPERIMENTS

In this work, comparison of five different AC approaches on the performance in MSC data analysis has been focused. The five AC approaches for comparison are CBA, CMAR, PRM, CPAR and TFPC. Experiments were run on a 2.00 GHz Intel(R) Core(TM) 2 CPU with 2.00 GB of RAM running under Windows Command Processor. The TCV evaluation undertaken used a *confidence* threshold value (α) of 50% and a *support* threshold

value (σ) of 1% for CBA, CMAR and TFPC with the intension to avoid *over-fitting* (Coenen & Leng, 2004; Coenen et al., 2005; Li et al., 2001; Wang, Xin, & Coenen, 2007), while for PRM and CPAR there is no such notion of *support* and *confidence*.

Performance Comparison

After the five AC approaches were applied to the input data file with TCV, each of them showed different performance, in terms of (1) classification accuracy in each TCV fold and the average accuracy, (2) number of CARs generated in each TCV fold and the average number of CARs generated, (3) maximum number of attributes in CAR antecedents, and (4) generation time after which the classification was accomplished.

The average accuracy, average number of CARs and generation time for each AC approach are shown in Table 3. Among all, CBA gave the highest average accuracy of 94.8%, while the lowest accuracy of 67.6% was obtained from CPAR. In terms of average number of CARs, CMAR showed a preeminent result of 290.7, while no other AC approach gave a number higher than 81.5. The sort ascending order of generation time for the five AC approaches is PRM, CPAR, CBA,

Table 3. Performance of the five AC approaches

	CBA	CMAR	PRM	CPAR	TFPC
Average accuracy (%)	94.8	90.42	69.0	67.6	90.6
Average num of CRs	58.8	290.7	34.6	38.0	81.5
Max. num of attributes in antecedents	4	6	4	4	3
Generation time (seconds)	2.58	57.61	0.33	0.55	2.73

TFPC and CMAR; however, CMAR has the largest maximum number of attributes in antecedents of 6, remarkably more than the other AC approaches.

Rule Comparison

For every independent AC approach, a number of rules were generated in each TCV fold, based on which AC makes classification prediction and evaluates the accuracy. These rules are important to this study because they may contain useful and valuable information (or knowledge) on stem cell differentiation. For the fairness of the comparison, the authors simply chose to compare the rules in the respect fold No.10 of each tested AC approach. Three most interesting rules in each AC approach were selected manually and listed in a descending order with the respect interpretation. The reader is reminded that for the rules from CBA, CMAR and TFPC, their *confidence* values were shown in square brackets, while the rules from PRM and CPAR do not have *confidence* values due to their algorithms. The evaluation to the rules in terms of their significance was elucidated in the next section, based on *a priori* knowledge.

- In CBA, the following rules were believed to be most interesting:
  1. **Rule # CBA20:** {FBS + ascorbic acid + dexamethasone + TCP} $\Rightarrow$ {osteo} [100.0%], which can be interpreted as: in the presence of FBS (Fetal Bovine Serum), ascorbic acid and dexamethasone, MSCs will undergo osteogenesis on the substrate of TCP (Tissue Culture Plastic).

  2. **Rule # CBA40:** {transferrin + dexamethasone + TGF-β + TCP} $\Rightarrow$ {chondro} [94.73%], interpreted as: with the help of transferrin, dexamethasone, TGF-β in the culture medium, MSCs is most likely to differentiate into cartilage on TCP substrate.

  3. **Rule # CBA13:** {β-glycerophosphate + BMP-2} $\Rightarrow$ {osteo} [100.0%], meaning that the combination of β-glycerophosphate and BMP-2 always stimuli MSCs to become bone cells.

- In CMAR, the selected rules are listed as follows:
  1. **Rule # CMAR89:** {FBS + ascorbic acid + dexamethasone + β-glycerophosphate + 2D + TCP} $\Rightarrow$ {osteo} [100.0%], meaning that MSC cultured on plastic substrate in monolayer culture will be induced into osteogenesis if supplemented with FBS, dexamethasone, β-glycerophosphate and ascorbic acid.

  2. **Rule # CMAR154:** {human + ascorbic acid + insulin + TGF-β} $\Rightarrow$ {chondro} [96.42%], meaning that human MSC is most likely to undergo chondrogenic differentiation under the stimuli of the combined treatment with insulin and TGF-β together with ascorbic acid (or ascorbic acid-2-phosphate).

  3. **Rule # CMAR127:** {human + FBS + dexamethasone + insulin + 2D + TPC} $\Rightarrow$ {adipo} [100%], suggesting that the culture conditions above is supportive for human MSC adipogenesis.

- In PRM, the selected rules are:
  1. **Rule # PRM1:** {DMEM + dexamethasone + β-glycerophosphate} ⇒ {osteo}, meaning that in the presence of the culture medium and supplements as above, MSCs will undergo osteogenesis.
  2. **Rule # PRM14:** {human + DMEM-HG + FBS + TCP} ⇒ {prolife}, meaning that DMEM-HG and FBS only helps human MSCs proliferate, without inducing them to any type of differentiation.
  3. **Rule # PRM9:** {TGF-β + proline} ⇒ {chondro}, meaning that TGF-β and proline may together promote chondrogenesis.
- In CPAR, the rules were exactly the same as those in PRM, except that the following three rules were found not to exist in PRM:
  1. **Rule # CPAR27:** {UltroserG serum substitute} ⇒ {prolife}, suggesting that the UltroserG serum substitute does not induce MSC differentiation.
  2. **Rule # CPAR33:** {DMEM-F12} ⇒ {osteo}, suggesting that DMEM-F12 may be biased on osteogenesis rather than other types of differentiation.
  3. **Rule # CPAR38:** {dexamethasone} ⇒ {chondro}, suggesting that in the current database, dexamethasone appears more frequently in chondrogenesis than other differentiation types.
- In TFPC, the selected rules are:
  1. **Rule # TFPC66:** {FBS + dexamethasone + insulin} ⇒ {adipo} [54.54%], meaning that in many cases the combination of FBS, dexamethasone and insulin can differentiate MSCs into fat cells, but not always.
  2. **Rule # TFPC46:** {DMEM-HG + ascorbic acid} ⇒ {chondro} [69.44%], meaning that ascorbic acid in the culture medium of DMEM-HG can promote chondrogenesis.
  3. **Rule#TFPC1:** {proline} ⇒ {chondro} [100.0%], suggest that proline may play a role in chondrogenesis.

As listed above, all the AC approaches can abstract classification rules containing information on MSC differentiation. However, the quality of these rules, in terms of the extent to which they correlate with a priori knowledge and how well the rules were integrated, has to be evaluated manually, as elucidated in the next section.

FUTURE RESEARCH DIRECTIONS

Five AC approaches have been used in this study with the aim of comparing their performance on prediction of MSC differentiation by classification, and abstraction of hidden rules from currently available experimental data.

Results from all the five AC approaches have been derived in terms of both computational performance (i.e. classification accuracy, number of CARs generated, maximum number of attributes in CAR antecedents, and time efficiency) and CARs abstracted from MSC data. From Table 3 it can be seen that all the classifiers gave accuracy higher than 90% except PRM and CPAR. However, CMAR showed a preeminent result of 290.7 on average number of CARs, with the largest maximum number of attributes in CAR antecedents of 6, remarkably higher than the other classifiers. Despite that the generation time of CMAR is the longest, the best AC approaches suggested in this study relies on the balance of the four types of performance and the quality of the mined CARs.

For CBA, all the three selected rules are consistent with observations in lab; however, the Rule # CBA20 is obviously not as good as Rule # CMAR89, because the former one is a subset of the latter one. In fact, due to the limited size of the CBA rules, CMAR excelled CBA in the similar cases for some other rules as well (data not shown). For PRM and CPAR, these two algorithms gave exactly the same rules, except for Rules # CPAR27, 33 and 38. After being analyzed, none of these three rules showed valuable information. For example, dexamethasone was known to participate also in osteogenesis and adipogenesis, whereas Rule # CPAR38 claims it to be only beneficial to chondrogenesis. Thus, CPAR is close to PRM on rule quality.

Among all the five classifiers, TFPC gave the most limited average length of rules, with the maximum number of attributes in antecedents of three. This results in the problem that few of the TFPC rules were well integrated, although their *confidence* values were relative high. In fact, over half of the TFPC rules have only one attribute in their respect antecedent, which makes it extremely difficult to provide useful biological information. In contrast to TFPC, CMAR generates CARs in a most integrated manner. For example, Rule # CMAR89 gives a more integrated abstraction for osteogenesis than Rule # CBA20. Rule # CMAR154 is believed to be better organized than Rule # TFPC46, as the former one contains more information. In many more cases, CMAR also exceeded the other four AC approaches on the quality of rules.

From the analysis above, an overview of rule quality for each AC approach can be derived, which is that CMAR performs best in generating rules with integrated information. Although PRM and CPAR cost much less generation time, CBA provides the highest accuracy and TFPC has a good balance in time efficiency, accuracy and number of CARs, CMAR is suggested as the most suitable classifier to this study due to its excelling rule quality and satisfactory accuracy. However, CMAR has the same problem with the other classifiers, which is that a number of rules do not make scientific sense. For example,

for Rule # CMAR204: {goat + 2D} ⇒ {osteo} [88.88%], it is obvious that only "Goat MSC" and "monolayer culture" are not enough to induce osteogenesis. Similarly, for Rule # CMAR274: {FBS + 3D} ⇒ {osteo} [72.41%], according to authors knowledge, FBS is not specifically for promoting osteogenesis but for maintaining cell survival without promoting effect towards any differentiation, independently of the fact that the culture is monolayer or 3D. In fact, all the five tested AC approaches have some rules without scientific sense. As a result, all the rules have to be reviewed by human beings for the rule quality. The generation of non-scientific rules is due to the size of the database and the sample properties of the data. Based on this reason, a conclusion can be made that if the MSC database is expanded in the future, the non-scientific rules could be pruned and more rules with scientific sense could be identified.

CONCLUSION

In this study, MSC data from an online database were processed and analyzed by five different AC approaches in order to compare their performance with respect to several aspects. Due to the capacity of AC, which is to harmonize the vast amount of experimental data and produce simple but useful rules, it is recommended as a suitable tool for this study. After the comparison between the five AC approaches, CMAR is suggested to be the most suitable approach for this study, and possibly also suitable to other similar studies such as the tissue engineering related data analysis. Due to the limited experimental data input at this stage, most of the identified rules are known by stem cell researchers. However, it will be possible to mine completely original rules if the size and contents of the MSC database are expanded in the future.

ACKNOWLEDGMENT

The authors would like to thank Professor Jian Lu from the School of Physics & Astronomy at the University of Manchester, and the following colleagues from the Department of Engineering Science at the University of Oxford for their valuable suggestions to this study: Paul Raju, Nuala Trainor, Dr. Cathy Ye, Dr. Xia Xu, Dr. Shengda Zhou, Dr. Renchen Liu, Professor James Triffitt, Clarence Yapp, Yang Liu and Zhiqiang Zhao.

The authors would also like to thank Professor Paul Leng from the Department of Computer Science at the University of Liverpool, Dr. Jiongyu Li and Fan Li from the Information Management Center in the China Minsheng Banking Corp. Ltd., and Zhijie Jia from the Beijing Friendship Hotel for their support with respect to the work described here.

REFERENCES

Agrawal, R., Imielinski, T., & Swami, A. (1993). Mining Association Rule between Sets of Items in Large Databases. In *Proceedings of the 1993 ACM SIGMOD International Conference on Management of Data* (pp. 207-216). Washington D.C.: ACM Press.

Agrawal, R., & Srikant, R. (1994). Fast Algorithm for Mining Association Rules. In *Proceedings of the 20th International Conference on Very Large Data Bases (VLDB-94)* (pp. 487-499). Santiago de Chile, Chile: Morgan Kaufmann Publishers.

Agrawal, S., Godbole, S., Punjani, D., & Roy, S. (2007). How much noise is too much: A study in Automatic Text Classification. In *Proceedings of the 7th IEEE International Conference on Data Mining (ICDM-07)* (pp. 3-12). Omaha, NE, USA: IEEE Computer Society.

Ali, K., Manganaris, S., & Srikant, R. (1997). Partial Classification using Association Rules. In *Proceedings of the 3rd International Conference on Knowledge Discovery and Data Mining* (pp. 115-118). Newport Beach, CA, USA: AAAI Press.

Antonie, M. L., & Zaiane, O. R. (2002). Text Document Categorization by Term Association. In *Proceedings of the 2002 IEEE International Conference on Data Mining* (pp. 19-26). Maebashi City, Japan: IEEE Computer Society.

Battula, V. L., Bareiss, P. M., Treml, S., Conrad, S., Albert, I., & Hojak, S. (2007). Human Placenta and Bone Marrow derived MSC cultured in Serum-free, b-FGF-containing medium express cell surface frizzled-9 and SSEA-4 and give rise to multilineage differentiation. *Differentiation*, *75*(4), 279–291. doi:10.1111/j.1432-0436.2006.00139.x

Beeres, S. L., Atsma, D. E., van der Laarse, A., Pijnappels, D. A., van Tuyn, J., & Fibbe, W. E. (2005). Human Adult Bone Marrow Mesenchymal Stem Cells repair experimental conduction block in rat Cardiomyocyte Cultures. *Journal of the American College of Cardiology*, *46*(10), 1943–1952. doi:10.1016/j.jacc.2005.07.055

Bianco, P., Riminucci, M., Gronthos, S., & Robey, P. G. (2001). Bone Marrow Stromal Stem Cells: Nature, Biology, and Potential applications. *Stem Cells (Dayton, Ohio)*, *19*(3), 180–192. doi:10.1634/stemcells.19-3-180

Boser, B. E., Guyon, I. M., & Vapnik, V. N. (1992). A Training Algorithm for Optimal Margin Classifiers. In *Proceedings of the 5th ACM Annual Workshop on Computational Learning Theory* (pp. 144-152). Pittsburgh, PA, USA: ACM Press.

Brin, S., Motwani, R., Ullman, J. D., & Tsur, S. (1997). Dynamic Itemset counting and Implication Rules for Market Basket Data. In *Proceedings of the 1997 ACM SIGMOD International Conference on Management of Data* (pp. 255-264). Tucson, Arizona, USA: ACM Press.

Celotti, F., Colciago, A., Negri-Cesi, P., Pravettoni, A., Zaninetti, R., & Sacchi, M. C. (2006). Effect of Platelet-rich plasma on Migration and Proliferation of SaOS-2 Osteoblasts: Role of Platelet-derived Growth Factor and Transforming Growth Factor-beta. *Wound Repair and Regeneration, 14*(2), 195–202. doi:10.1111/j.1743-6109.2006.00110.x

Cody, G. D., Boctor, N. Z., Filley, T. R., Hazen, R. M., Scott, J. H., & Sharma, A. (2000). Primordial Carbonylated Iron-Sulfur compounds and the synthesis of Pyruvate. *Science, 289*(5483), 1337–1340. doi:10.1126/science.289.5483.1337

Coenen, F. (2004). The LUCS-KDD Apriori-T Association Rule Mining Algorithm. *Department of Computer Science, The University of Liverpool, UK.* Retrieved from http://www.cxc.liv.ac.uk/~frans/KDD/Software/Apriori_T/aprioriT.html.

Coenen, F., Goulbourne, G., & Leng, P. (2001). Computing Association Rules using partial totals. In *Proceedings of the 5th European Conference on Principles and Practice of Knowledge Discovery in Databases* (pp. 54-66). Freiburg, Germany: Springer-Verlag.

Coenen, F., & Leng, P. (2002). Finding Association rules with some very Frequent Attributes. In *Proceedings of the 6th European Conference on Principles and Practice of Knowledge Discovery in Databases* (pp. 99-111). Helsinki, Finland: Springer-Verlag.

Coenen, F., & Leng, P. (2004). An Evaluation of Approaches to Classification Rule Selection. In *Proceedings of the 4th IEEE International Conference on Data Mining* (pp. 359-362). Brighton, UK: IEEE Computer Society.

Coenen, F., & Leng, P. (2007). The Effect of Threshold Values on Association Rule based Classification Accuracy. *Journal of Data and Knowledge Engineering, 60*(2), 345–360. doi:10.1016/j.datak.2006.02.005

Coenen, F., Leng, P., & Ahmed, S. (2004). Data Structures for Association Rule Mining: T-trees and P-trees. *IEEE Transactions on Data and Knowledge Engineering, 16*(6), 774–778. doi:10.1109/TKDE.2004.8

Coenen, F., Leng, P., & Zhang, L. (2005). Threshold Tuning for improved Classification Association Rule Mining. In *Proceedings of the 9th Pacific-Asia Conference on Knowledge Discovery and Data Mining* (pp. 216-225). Hanoi, Vietnam: Springer-Verlag.

Coenen, F. P., Leng, P., & Goulbourne, G. (2004). Tree Structures for Mining Association Rules. *Journal of Data Mining and Knowledge Discovery, 8*(1), 25–51. doi:10.1023/B:DAMI.0000005257.93780.3b

Cohen, W. W. (1995). Fast Effective Rule Induction. In *Proceedings of the 12th International Conference on Machine Learning* (pp. 115-123). Tahoe City, CA, USA: Morgan Kaufmann Publishers.

Cornelis, C., Yan, P., Zhang, X., & Chen, G. (2006). Mining Positive and Negative Association Rules from Large Databases. *Proceedings of the 2006 IEEE International Conference on Cybernetics and Intelligent Systems* (pp. 613-618). Bangkok, Thailand: IEEE Computer Society.

Derubeis, A. R., & Cancedda, R. (2004). Bone Marrow Stromal Cells (BMSCs) in Bone Engineering: Limitations and Recent Advances. *Annals of Biomedical Engineering, 32*(1), 160–165. doi:10.1023/B:ABME.0000007800.89194.95

El-Hajj, M., & Zaiane, O. R. (2003). Inverted Matrix: Efficient Discovery of Frequent Items in Large Datasets in the context of Interactive Mining. In *Proceedings of the 9th ACM SIGKDD International Conference on Knowledge Discovery and Data Mining* (pp. 109-118). Washington, DC: ACM Press.

Freitas, A. A. (2002). *Data Mining and Knowledge Discovery with Evolutionary Algorithm.* Germany: Springer-Verlag Berlin Heidelberg.

Gehrke, J., Ramakrishnan, R., & Ganti, V. (1998). RainForest: A Framework for Fast Decision Tree Construction of Large Datasets. In *Proceedings of International Conference on Very Large Data Bases* (pp. 416-427). New York, USA.

Griffith, L. G., & Swartz, M. A. (2006). Capturing complex 3D Tissue physiology in vitro. *Nature Reviews. Molecular Cell Biology, 7*(3), 211–224. doi:10.1038/nrm1858

Hajek, P., Havel, I., & Chytil, M. (1966). The GUHA Method of Automatic Hypotheses Determination. *Computing, 1*, 293–308. doi:10.1007/BF02345483

Han, J., & Kamber, M. (2006). *Data mining: Concepts and Techniques* (2nd ed.). San Francisco: Morgan Kaufmann Publishers.

Han, J., Pei, J., & Yin, Y. (2000). Mining Frequent Patterns without Candidate Generation. In *Proceedings of the 2000 ACM SIGMOD International Conference on Management of Data* (pp. 1-12). ACM Press, Dallas, TX, USA.

Hanada, K., Dennis, J. E., & Caplan, A. I. (1997). Stimulatory effects of basic Fibroblast Growth Factor and Bone Morphogenetic Protein-2 on Osteogenic differentiation of Rat Bone Marrow-derived Mesenchymal Stem Cells. *Journal of Bone and Mineral Research, 12*(10), 1606–1614. doi:10.1359/jbmr.1997.12.10.1606

Haynesworth, S. E., Baber, M. A., & Caplan, A. I. (1996). Cytokine expression by Human Marrow-derived Mesenchymal Progenitor Cells in vitro: Effects of Dexamethasone and IL-1 Alpha. *Journal of Cellular Physiology, 166*(3), 585–592. doi:10.1002/(SICI)1097-4652(199603)166:3<585::AID-JCP13>3.0.CO;2-6

Hidber, C. (1999). Online Association Rule Mining. In *Proceedings of the 1999 ACM SIGMOD International Conference on Management of Data* (pp. 145-156). Philadelphia, Pennsylvania, USA: ACM Press.

Houtsma, M., & Swami, A. (1995). Set-oriented Mining of Association Rules in Relational Databases. In *Proceedings of the 11th International Conference on Data Engineering* (pp. 25-33). Taipei, Taiwan: IEEE Computer Society.

James, M. (1985). *Classification Algorithm.* New York: Wiley-Interscience.

Johnstone, B., Hering, T. M., Caplan, A. I., Goldberg, V. M., & Yoo, J. U. (1998). In vitro Chondrogenesis of Bone Marrow-derived Mesenchymal Progenitor Cells. *Experimental Cell Research, 238*(1), 265–272. doi:10.1006/excr.1997.3858

Krampera, M., Glennie, S., Dyson, J., Scott, D., Laylor, R., & Simpson, E. (2003). Bone Marrow Mesenchymal Stem Cells inhibit the response of naive and memory antigen-specific T cells to their Cognate Peptide. *Blood, 101*(9), 3722–3729. doi:10.1182/blood-2002-07-2104

Kuznetsov, S. A., Friedenstein, A. J., & Robey, P. G. (1997). Factors required for Bone Marrow Stromal Fibroblast Colony Formation in vitro. *British Journal of Haematology, 97*(3), 561–570. doi:10.1046/j.1365-2141.1997.902904.x

Lennon, D. P., Haynesworth, S. E., Young, R. G., Dennis, J. E., & Caplan, A. I. (1995). A Chemically defined medium supports in vitro proliferation and maintains the osteochondral potential of Rat Marrow-derived Mesenchymal Stem Cells. *Experimental Cell Research, 219*(1), 211–222. doi:10.1006/excr.1995.1221

Li, W., Han, J., & Pei, J. (2001). CMAR: Accurate and Efficient Classification based on Multiple Class-Association Rules. In *Proceedings of the 2001 IEEE International Conference on Data Mining* (pp. 369-376). San Jose, CA: IEEE Computer Society.

Liu, B., Hsu, W., & Ma, Y. (1998). Integrating Classification and Association Rule Mining. In *Proceedings of the 4th International Conference on Knowledge Discovery and Data Mining* (pp. 80-86). New York City: AAAI Press.

Liu, C. H., Wu, M. L., & Hwang, S. M. (2007). Optimization of Serum free medium for Cord Blood Mesenchymal Stem Cells. *Biochemical Engineering Journal, 33*(1), 1–9. doi:10.1016/j.bej.2006.08.005

Liu, J., Pan, Y., Wang, K., & Han, J. (2002). Mining Frequent Item Sets by Opportunistic Projection. In *Proceedings of the 8th ACM SIGKDD International Conference on Knowledge Discovery and Data Mining* (pp. 229-238). Edmonton, Alberta, Canada: ACM Press.

Lowd, D., & Domingos, P. (2005). Naive Bayes Models for Probability Estimation. In *Proceedings of the 22nd International Conference on Machine Learning* (pp. 529-536). Bonn, Germany: ACM Press.

Mackay, A. M., Beck, S. C., Murphy, J. M., Barry, F. P., Chichester, C. O., & Pittenger, M. F. (1998). Chondrogenic differentiation of Cultured Human Mesenchymal Stem Cells from Marrow. *Tissue Engineering, 4*(4), 415–428. doi:10.1089/ten.1998.4.415

Magaki, T., Kurisu, K., & Okazaki, T. (2005). Generation of Bone Marrow-derived Neural Cells in Serum-free Monolayer Culture. *Neuroscience Letters, 384*(3), 282–287. doi:10.1016/j.neulet.2005.05.025

Mannila, H., Toivonen, H., & Verkamo, A. I. (1994). Efficient Algorithms for Discovering Association Rules. In *Proceedings of the 1994 AAAI Workshop on Knowledge Discovery in Databases* (pp. 181-192). Seattle, Washington, USA: AAAI Press.

Maron, M. E. (1961). Automatic Indexing: An Experimental Inquiry. [JACM]. *Journal of the ACM, 8*(3), 404–417. doi:10.1145/321075.321084

Meuleman, N., Tondreau, T., Delforge, A., Dejeneffe, M., Massy, M., & Libertalis, M. (2006). Human Marrow Mesenchymal Stem Cell Culture: Serum-free Medium allows better expansion than Classical Apha-MEM medium. *European Journal of Haematology, 76*(4), 309–316. doi:10.1111/j.1600-0609.2005.00611.x

Muller, I., Kordowich, S., Holzwarth, C., Spano, C., Isensee, G., & Staiber, A. (2006). Animal Serum-free culture conditions for Isolation and Expansion of Multipotent Mesenchymal Stromal Cells from Human BM. *Cytotherapy, 8*(5), 437–444. doi:10.1080/14653240600920782

O'Connell, S. M., Impeduglia, T., Hessler, K., Wang, X. J., Carroll, R. J., & Dardik, H. (2008). Autologous Platelet-rich Fibrin Matrix as Cell Therapy in the Healing of Chronic Lower-extremity Ulcers. *Wound Repair and Regeneration, 16*(6), 749–756. doi:10.1111/j.1524-475X.2008.00426.x

Pittenger, M. F., Mackay, A. M., Beck, S. C., Jaiswal, R. K., Douglas, R., & Mosca, J. D. (1999). Multilineage potential of Adult Human Mesenchymal Stem Cells. *Science, 284*(5411), 143–147. doi:10.1126/science.284.5411.143

Quinlan, J. R. (1993). *C4.5: Programs for Machine Learning*. San Mateo, CA, USA: Morgan Kaufmann Publishers.

Quinlan, J. R., & Cameron-Jones, R. M. (1993). FOIL: A Midterm Report. In *Proceedings of the 1993 European Conference on Machine Learning (ECML-93)* (pp. 3-20). Vienna, Austria: Springer-Verlag.

Roelen, B. A., & Dijke, P. (2003). Controlling Mesenchymal Stem Cell differentiation by TGFBeta Family Members. *Journal of Orthopaedic Science, 8*(5), 740–748. doi:10.1007/s00776-003-0702-2

Rymon, R. (1992). Search through Systematic Set Enumeration. In *Proceedings of the 3rd International Conference on Principles of Knowledge Representation and Reasoning* (pp. 539-550). Cambridge, MA, USA: Morgan Kaufmann Publishers.

Savasere, A., Omiecinski, E., & Navathe, S. (1995). An Efficient Algorithm for Mining Association Rules in Large Databases. In *Proceedings of the 21st International Conference on Very Large Data Bases* (pp. 432-444). Zurich, Switzerland: Morgan Kaufmann Publishers.

Schaffer, C. (1993). Selecting a Classification Method by Cross-Validation. *Machine Learning, 13*(1), 135–143. doi:10.1007/BF00993106

Shidara, Y., Nakamura, A., & Kudo, M. (2007). CCIC: Consistent Common Itemsets Classifier. In *Proceedings of the 5th International Conference on Machine Learning and Data Mining (MLDM-07)* (pp. 490-498). Leipzig, Germany: Springer-Verlag.

Srikant, R., & Agrawal, R. (1996). Mining Quantitative Association Rules in Large Relational Tables. In *Proceedings of the 1996 ACM SIGMOD International Conference on Management of Data* (pp. 1-12). Montreal, Quebec, Canada: ACM Press.

Thabtah, F., Cowling, P., & Peng, Y. (2005). The Impact of Rule Ranking on the Quality of Associative Classifiers. In *Proceedings of AI-2005, the Twenty-fifth SGAI International Conference on Innovative Techniques and Applications of Artificial Intelligence (AI-05) - Research and Development in Intelligent Systems XXII* (pp. 277-287). Cambridge, UK: Springer-Verlag.

Toivonen, H. (1996). Sampling Large Databases for Association Rules. In *Proceedings of the 22nd International Conference on Very Large Data Bases* (pp. 134-145). Mumbai (Bombay), India: Morgan Kaufmann Publishers.

Tuan, R. S., Boland, G., & Tuli, R. (2003). Adult Mesenchymal Stem Cells and Cell-based Tissue Engineering. *Arthritis Research & Therapy, 5*(1), 32–45. doi:10.1186/ar614

Wang, W., Wang, Y. J., Bañares-Alcántara, R., Coenen, F., & Cui, Z. (in press). Analysis of Mesenchymal Stem Cell differentiation in vitro using Classification Association Rule Mining. *Journal of Bioinformatics and Computational Biology.*

Wang, W., Wang, Y. J., Bañares-Alcántara, R., Cui, Z., & Coenen, F. (2009). Application of Classification Association Rule Mining for Mammalian Mesenchymal Stem Cell differentiation. In *Proceedings of the 9th Industrial Conference on Data Mining (ICDM-09) — Advances in Data Mining Applications and Theoretical Aspects* (pp. 51-61). Leipzig, Germany: Springer-Verlag Berlin Heidelberg.

Wang, Y. J., Xin, Q., & Coenen, F. (2007). A Novel Rule Ordering Approach in Classification Association Rule Mining. In *Proceedings of the 5th International Conference on Machine Learning and Data Mining* (pp. 339-348). Leipzig, Germany: Springer-Verlag.

Wang, Y. J., Xin, Q., & Coenen, F. (2008). Hybrid rule ordering in Classification Association Rule Mining. *Transactions on Machine Learning and Data Mining, 1*(1), 1–15.

Yang, L., Widyantoro, D. H., Ioerger, T., & Yen, J. (2001). An entropy-based adaptive Genetic Algorithm for learning Classification Rules. In *Proceedings of the 2001 Congress on Evolutionary Computation (CEC-01)* (pp. 790-796). Seoul, South Korea: IEEE Computer Society.

Yin, X., & Han, J. (2003). CPAR: Classification based on predictive Association Rules. In *Proceedings of the 3rd SIAM International Conference on Data Mining (SDM-03)* (pp. 331-335). San Francisco, CA, USA: SIAM.

Yoon, Y., & Lee, G. G. (2005). Practical Application of Associative Classifier for Document Classification. In *Proceedings of the Second Asia Information Retrieval Symposium* (pp. 467-478). Jeju Island, Korea: Springer-Verlag.

Zhang, Y., Li, C., Jiang, X., Zhang, S., Wu, Y., & Liu, B. (2004). Human placenta-derived Mesenchymal Progenitor Cells support culture expansion of long-term culture-initiating cells from Cord blood CD34+ cells. *Experimental Hematology, 32*(7), 657–664. doi:10.1016/j.exphem.2004.04.001

KEY TERMS AND DEFINITIONS

Association Rule (AR): A typical knowledge model in data mining, which describes an implicative co-occurring relationship between two non-overlapping sets of binary-valued transactional database attributes.

Association Rule Mining (ARM): A research field in data mining, which aims to extract association rules from a given transactional database.

Associative Classification (AC): An overlap between classification and association rule mining that solves the traditional classification problem by applying association rule mining techniques.

Cell differentiation: The process by which a less specialized cell becomes a more specialized cell type. For example, a multipotent MSC becomes an osteoblast (specialized in bone generation).

Classification Association Rule (CAR): A special association rule that describes an implicative co-occurring relationship between a set of binary-valued transactional database attributes and one or more predefined data categories.

Classification Rule (CR): A typical knowledge model in data mining, which describes an implicative relationship between data attributes and predefined data categories.

Classification: A research field in data mining, which aims to assign predefined data categories to "unseen" data instances, based on the study of a given set of training data examples associating with category labels.

Confidence: The support of an association rule in relation to the support of its antecedent.

Mesenchymal Stem Cells (MSCs): Multipotent stem cells that can differentiate into a variety of cell types. Cell types that MSCs have been shown to differentiate into include osteoblasts, chondrocytes, myocytes, adipocytes, endotheliums, etc.

Support: The overall frequency in a given transactional database where an association rule applies.

ENDNOTES

[1] The *apriori-TFP* and its related softwares may be obtained from http://www.csc.liv.ac.uk/~frans/KDD/Software

[2] The online MSC database can be visited from http://www.oxford-tissue-engineering.org/forum/plugin.php?identifier=publish&module=publish

[3] LUCS-KDD DN software may be obtained from http://www.csc.liv.ac.uk/~frans/KDD/Software/LUCS-KDD-DN/lucs-kdd_DN.html

[4] For related information, please find from http://www.oxford-tissue-engineering.org/forum/table3.doc

Chapter 12
Multiagent Knowledge-Based System Accessing Distributed Resources on Knowledge Grid

Priti Srinivas Sajja
Sardar Patel University, India

ABSTRACT

Knowledge is considered as a strategic weapon to get success in any business. Span of modern business applications have increased from a specific geographical area to the global world. The necessary resources of the business are available in distributed fashion using platform / technology like world wide web and grid of computational facilities. The prime intention of the grid architecture is to utilize scarce resources in objective to efficiently mine information from distributed resources. With simple data grid and semantic web technologies, it is difficult to offer higher level knowledge-based services on grid environment. Hence, development of a framework that helps mining and utilizing the required information from large, unstructured, and distributed resources in intelligent fashion becomes necessary. This chapter describes and differentiates World Wide Web (WWW), Semantic Web, Data Grid, and Knowledge Grid with the literature survey. Considering the limitations of the existing approaches, a generic multilayer architecture is designed and described with detailed methodology for each layer. The chapter also presents fuzzy XML technique to represent domain and meta knowledge into the knowledge repositories. To experiment the proposed generic architecture, an application of e-Learning is selected and a multiagent system mining knowledge grid is discussed with detailed methodology and role of agents in the system. The chapter concludes with advantages and application areas.

INTRODUCTION

The rapid development of Information and Communication Technology has strongly influenced the way in which people carry out their business. Success in any business depends on how better the scarce resources, information, and knowledge have been utilized for competitive advantages. To get such competitive advantages, demand of timely and reliable information is increasing

DOI: 10.4018/978-1-60960-067-9.ch012

exponentially. This leads to the concepts of data and knowledge grid. Resource on such grid can intelligently assist people to accomplish complex tasks and solve problems.

Grid applications often involve large amount of data and/or computing, and are not easily handled by today's Internet and Web infrastructures. Grid evolution had started since early 1990. The first generation grids, also called Computational Grids allowed interconnecting large supercomputing centers. Second-generation grids are characterized by their capability to link more than just few regional or nation-wide supercomputing centers, and by the adoption of standards (such as HTTP, LDAP, PKI, etc.) that enable the deployment of global-scale computing infrastructure (Cannataro & Talia, 2003). The motivation for third generation or next-generation grids is to simplify and structure the systematic building of grid applications through the composition and reuse of software components and the development on knowledge-based services and tools. Open Grid Services Architecture, Semantic Grid, and Knowledge Grids are the most promising approaches towards next-generation grids.

The prime intention of the latest generation of grid architecture is to utilize scarce resources in objective to efficiently mine information from distributed resources. This leads to an intelligent framework which helps mining and utilizing the required information. For this purpose, a knowledge-based system accessing distributed databases through a knowledge grid is designed and will be elaborated in the proposed chapter. The proposed architecture is a generic multi-tier architecture having Higher K-grid Layer, Core K-grid Layer and Data Grid Layer. To experiment the proposed design, academic domain has been selected and multiple activities in the domain were identified. As these activities were required to be loosely coupled and can be used independently, they have been conceived as autonomous agents.

The example multiagent system for the academic domain works on the top of the proposed architecture.

Besides presenting a multiagent application mining knowledge grid with detailed design and results, this chapter also elaborates other candidate applications and presents concluding remarks.

The chapter is organized as follows. First section describes and differentiates World Wide Web (WWW), Semantic Web, Data Grid, and Knowledge Grid. General structure of the data grid is also defined in this section. The parameters like computing efficiency, semantic ability, and capacity to hold knowledge is also compared in these technologies with interactive diagram.

In second section, concept of knowledge grid is elaborated with its characteristics, principles, and parameters affecting the power and role of knowledge grid. To meet described parameters and principles, a generic architecture of a knowledge grid is presented. The proposed structure encompasses three different layers namely Higher K-grid Layer, Core K-grid Layer and Data Grid Layer. This section also describes knowledge representation using fuzzy XML (with example membership functions in XML and DTD model) and for storing knowledge into the metadata repository and knowledge base. Third section presents typical applications and work done so far by elaborating different projects and applications developed in the area.

Fourth section presents a multiagent system application mining knowledge grid. The application is designed as to work on top of the proposed generic architecture of knowledge grid. This section briefly introduces agents and multiagent system fundamentals with characteristics and architecture. This section also describes the role of the multiagent knowledge grid in the area of e-Learning. The chapter concludes with advantages and application areas.

WWW, SEMANTIC WEB, DATA GRID AND KNOWLEDGE GRID

The World Wide Web (WWW) is a well-known example of a large scale distributed hypermedia system on the internet platform. The WWW is based on the *HTTP* for data transfer, *HTML* markup for content display on top of the Internet infrastructure that uses different protocols and content description schemes. According to Stork (2002), WWW can reach its full potential by addressing two issues (i) being the *"semantic" access and use* problem (i.e. access to and use of content and services, based on semantically sound resource description); (ii) being the *universality* of *physical access* via high-bandwidth local loops and broadband wireless channels.

Semantic Web is considered as an extension of the current Web in which information is given well defined meaning by associating metadata. Such metadata helps in better enabling computers and people to work in cooperation (Berners-Lee, Hendler, & Lassila, 2001). Basic objective of a semantic web is "Making content machine-understandable". The semantic web aims to allow Web entities (software agents, users, and programs) to interoperate, dynamically discovering and using resources, extracting knowledge, and solving complex problems. According to Cannataro and Talia (2004), a layered model of the Semantic Web comprises:

- A set of Web resources with a unique, global identity, described by metadata in a common and shared formalism with rules for inferring new metadata and knowledge through ontologies.
- A set of basic services such as reasoning and querying over metadata, ontologies, and semantic search engines. These services represent a great improvement over current Internet services, such as the Domain Name System (DNS) and key-based search.

- A set of high-level applications developed by using basic services.

Data grids are *large scale distributed computing systems* providing mechanisms for the controlled sharing of computing resources. Any grid needs generic 'middleware' components that enable efficient access to specific applications by using a configuration of heterogeneous resources, such as processors, storage, and network connections. In other words, grids are middleware services on distributed environment providing storage and access platforms to multiple autonomous applications within the environment. The grid provides a common infrastructure for creating global properties that span separate heterogeneous and independent resources (Moore, 2001; Foster & Kesselman, 1999). The common infrastructure is used to support a single sign-on authentication environment, uniform job submission mechanisms, uniform naming conventions for grid resources, and uniform scheduling systems. Therefore, grids serve as interoperability mechanisms for turning remote and heterogeneous resources into a globally accessible system.

Data grids support mainly data storage, data retrieval, and data discovery processes through the data management infrastructure and services on the top of the grid. Large number of data and information repository with homogeneous ontologies can be handled through such adapted grid. Through querying the repositories, discovery is done. The SDSC Storage Resource Broker (SRB) implemented on client-server platform as middleware and Metadata CATalog (MCAT) combines a data handling system with a collection to automate data discovery and retrieval (Baru, Moore, Rajasekar, & Wan, 1998). Current large-scale data grid projects include Biomedical Informatics Research Network (BIRN), Southern California Earthquake Center (SCEC), and Real-time Observatories, Applications, and Data management Network (ROADNet), all of which make use of the SDSC Storage Resource Broker

Figure 1. Data Grid Architecture

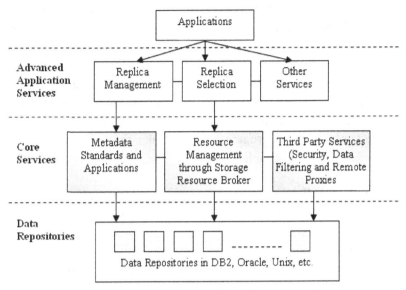

as the underlying data grid technology. These applications require widely distributed access to data by many people in multiple places. The data grid creates virtual collaborative environments that support distributed scientific and engineering research in coordination. In-Memory Data Grid is also referred to as IMDG. The typical data grid components are shown in Figure 1.

Both the web and grid are being operated on the Internet. The WWW primarily emphasize on content management and e-commerce support. The main functions of web are information provision, communication, and transactions for public businesses. The grid emphasizes on discovery of knowledge in scientific way. The major functions of grid are high performance computing and sharing of computing resources in controlled fashion. The grid application encompasses computationally hard and data intensive problems in science and engineering. However, as stated, both web and grid exists on the Internet platform and can be benefited by each other.

Further, Cannataro and Talia (2004) elaborates that the Semantic Grid seeks to incorporate the Semantic Web approach into the ongoing Grid.

Using semantics and ontologies in grids can offer high-level support for managing grid resources. It also helps in designing complex applications that will benefit from the use of semantics.

The discovery process through a data grid requires knowledge to correctly interpret the meaning and usability of the collected items within the repositories. It needs to understand logical/semantic, temporal, spatial, and functional relationship between the large amounts of data items stored within the grid. The typical data grids are basically collection-based infrastructure and hence, do not provide efficient mechanism to deal with such relationships. This results in comparatively poor data discovery. Above this, size of the repository makes the services of grid access slow and inefficient. If a knowledge component is added along with data items, the meaning associated with the data items help the smooth and effective execution of services. According to Zhuge (2004b) the existing web and Internet technologies do face problems like acquisition, representation, organization, processing semantic, and maintenance; which can be better solved by employing knowledge grid. This leads to development of knowledge grid where individual components possess knowledge and the services are also knowledge-based. This is a step ahead than a data grid and a semantic web where relationships between the data/information items are to be considered.

According to Foster and Kesselman (1999), the first generation of grid is considered as data grid or computational grid. Such grids connect large supercomputing centers and aggregate computational power which is not available in the individual sites.

Second-generation grids can link more than just a few regional or nationwide supercomputing centres. These grids use standards such as HTTP, LDAP (Lightweight Directory Access Protocol), and PKI (Public-Key Infrastructure) that enable the deployment of a global-scale computing infrastructure, link remote resources and allow collaboration between virtual organizations (Cannataro & Talia, 2004). Primary representatives of second-generation grids include systems such as Globus (www.globus.org), UNICORE (UNIform Interface to COmputing REsources), and Legion.

Foster et al. (2001) delineated a milestone between second and third generation grids when they defined the grid as a "flexible, secure, and coordinated resource sharing among dynamic collections of individuals, institutions, and resources—what we refer to as virtual organizations." The motivation for third generation grids was to simplify and structure the systematic building of grid applications, reusability, and the development of knowledge-based services and tools. Open grid service architecture is an example of the same.

Figure 2 shows the comparison of the data grid, semantic web, and knowledge grid.

Grid Computing environments must be constructed upon the following foundations (Joshy & Craig, 2004):

• Coordinated resources: Grid system is not advisable to build on coordinated resources. Instead of building grid systems with a centralized control, the necessary infra-structure for coordination among the resources may be provided. This infrastructure should be based on respective policies and service-level agreements.

• Open standard protocols and frameworks: Use of open standards provides interoperability and integration facilities. These standards must be applied for functionalities like resource discovery, resource access, and resource coordination.

The grid protocols are categorized in two broad classes (Casanova, 2005) namely:

i. Information protocols that obtain information about the structure and state of a resource like configuration, current load, and usage policy; and

ii. Management protocols that help in accessing shared resources define and apply resource requirements, determine operations to be performed on the resources, manage relationships among resources, and ensure the requested protocol operations are consistent with the policy under which the resource is to be shared etc. in a controlled fashion.

KNOWLEDGE GRID

Knowledge Grid is an intelligent interconnection environment that enables people or virtual roles to effectively capture, publish, share, and manage explicit knowledge resources as well as provide on-demand knowledge services to support people or services to carry out innovation, cooperative teamwork, problem-solving, and decision making (Zhuge, 2004a). A knowledge grid must support the following principles (Cannataro & Talia, 2003):

i. Data heterogeneity and large data sets handling;

ii. Algorithm integration and independence;

Figure 2. Data Grid, Semantic Web and Knowledge Grid

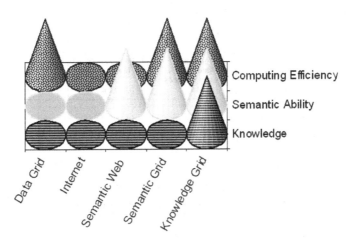

iii. Compatibility with grid infrastructure and grid awareness;

iv. Openness;

v. Scalability, and

vi. Security and data privacy.

Moreover, the architecture should support the following five parameters (Zhuge, 2004b):

i. **Space:** The capacity to hold a great variety of both individual and shared knowledge resources.

ii. **Time:** The direction of evolution.

iii. **Structure:** The construction of the environment and resources in the environment.

iv. **Relation:** Relationships among parameters and among resources.

v. **Measurement:** Evaluation of status and prospects of resources, processes, and their relationships.

According to Liu (2003), the knowledge grid and web with intelligence need to incorporate and standardize at least the following ten fundamental capabilities like:

i. Self-organization;

ii. Growth/Reproduction;

iii. Specialization/Association through self-organization and reproduction;

iv. Autocatalysis/Coordination;

v. Problem Solving support through tool like Markup Languages;

vi. Semantics;

vii. Meta knowledge;

viii. Personalization;

ix. Personalization and coordination; and

x. Planning.

Some of the principles and characteristics can not be effectively met without adding the higher level knowledge-based services. This leads to the development of a knowledge grid, which is a step towards next generation grid. One of the major creditability of any generic architecture is the ease of use and accessibility from given point to the knowledge stored in distributed resources. The architecture should manage the resources as well as users' profile in meaningful way.

The generic architecture and access mechanism in it is normally independent of the domain knowledge and users' information; hence the architecture is needed to be modular and clustered for ease of management and ease of development. Clustered knowledge and related services provide suitable on-demand knowledge services with underlying reasoning and explanation. Additionally, it should

Figure 3. Knowledge Grid Architecture

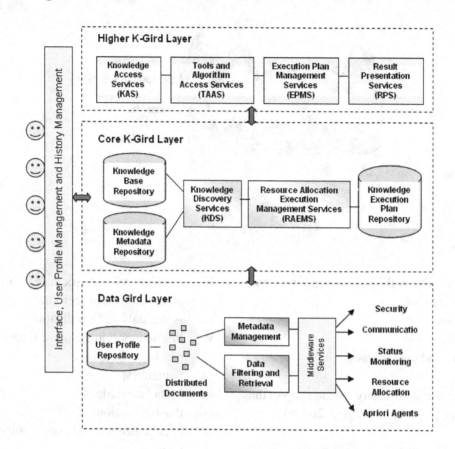

support the management of metadata. There should be ease of adding new knowledge from any point, and at the same time it is necessary to fuse the new knowledge with the existing knowledge. This makes the knowledge management service complete and keep the resources up-to-date and dynamically evolved.

Generic Architecture of Knowledge Grid

To meet the objectives and requirement discussed earlier, the following generic architecture of knowledge grid (denoted in Figure 3) is proposed.

The architecture is organized in a three loosely coupled layers namely Higher K-grid Layer, Core K-grid Layer, and Data Grid Layer. An in-

terface facility is also designed for friendly interface and ease of use.

Higher K-Grid Layer

This layer provides higher level knowledge grid service like knowledge access service and algorithms, execution plan management, and result presentation services. The Knowledge Access Services (KAS) are responsible for the semantic search, selection, extraction, transformation, and knowledge delivery through the core Knowledge Discovery Services (KDS). On the basis of user requirements and constraints, the KAS automates the searching and finding of resources to be analyzed based on KDS of the next layer, which is the core K-grid layer.

Tools and Algorithms Access Services (TAAS) are responsible for search, selection, and downloading of mining tools and algorithms. It takes the metadata regarding the availability of such algorithms and tools, reference etc. from the Knowledge Metadata Repository (KMR) of the K-grids layer, which is managed by the Knowledge Discovery Services (KDS) of the K-grid Layer. The interface may hold the tools, algorithms and intermediate results within the workspace it holds. Simultaneously, the history within the interface facility undergoes suitable update.

Execution Plan Management Services (EPMS) generate graphically designed execution plan which describes the interaction and flows between resources, extraction tools, DM tools, visualization tools, and store results in the Knowledge Base Repository (KBR). User will have options to choose a suitable plan from available multipurpose execution plans stored in Knowledge Execution Plan Repository (KEPR) .

Results Presentation Services (RPS) specifies how to generate present and visualize the output to the user of the system. For this, RPS takes help of the User Profile Repository (UPR) of the data grid layer. The output is stored in a suitable ontology, which afterwards is converted to another ontology/presentation scheme to provide better visualization to the user.

Core K-Grid Layer

The Core K-grid Layer has to support the definition, composition, and execution of a knowledge component over the grid. This actually serves as a knowledge repository layer having support to three different repositories namely: (i) Knowledge Base Repository (KBR), (ii) Knowledge Metadata Repository (KMR), and (iii) Knowledge Execution Plan Repository (KEPR). In other words, this layer manages all knowledge components, related metadata and their execution plan. For this, it requires services like Knowledge Discovery

Service (KDS) and Resource Allocation Execution Management Services (RAEMS).

The Knowledge Discovery Service (KDS) is responsible for discovering required knowledge component through metadata. For this, KDS manages Knowledge Metadata Repository (KMR). Some of the examples for metadata are algorithms, tools with reference, execution plans, etc. The markup languages can be used to effectively represent data. One may use fuzzy XML proposed by Sajja (2007; 2009). The XML stands for eXtensible Markup Language used to represent logic and content in web-based system through user defined tags. The XML can be further modified by defining application specific linguistic tags and supporting inference mechanism.

The function of any representation scheme is to capture the essential features of a problem domain and make the information available to a problem solving procedure. Starting from abstraction and procedural rules to multi-layer architectures, many effective knowledge representations have been developed (Sajja & Chourasia, 2005). For highly unstructured environment like Internet, there is a need of a specific tool, which manages *"Knowledge Network"* (Lee & Fischetti, 1999). For knowledge grid, a flexible and effective representation is one of the prime requirements for user acceptance. XML can be used for better representation of meta-knowledge, domain-knowledge, and other heuristic including the general problem solving strategies and models. As stated above, XML allows precise and exact data. However, to show correct status and usability of data, the precision and exactness of the data is practically less applicable. To overcome this limitation, inclusion of linguistic modifier is necessary. The notion of linguistic parameter is supported efficiently by fuzzy logic.

Fuzzy logic was formulated by Zadeh (1965) as multi-valued logic between 0 and 1. Fuzzy logic is widely applicable especially in the system controls that are very complex, uncertain, and cannot be modeled precisely even under various assumptions and approximations. Human style of decision processing includes vague and linguistic parameters like amount, price, age, etc. Values of such linguistic variables are not crisp, but fuzzy like 'low…medium…high… poor…moderate… rich', etc. Embedding fuzzy logic into XML framework offers opportunity for approximate reasoning and allows qualitative knowledge about a problem to implement into the system by using fuzzy rules. This makes system more user friendly, readable, easy to maintain, and effectively reduces the complexity by reducing number of rules. To exhibit intelligent behavior, fuzzy XML rule is represented in the format as follows:

```
<rule>
        <antecedent> .......</ante-
cedent>
        <consequent>
<generally>      ....... <modifi-
er>….</modifier>    ….. </generally>
<specifically>     ....... <modi-
fier>….</modifier>       ….</specifi-
cally>
        </consequent>
</rule>
```

The power of fuzzy logic comes from linguistic variable. As shown in the above format, a linguistic modifier (De Soto, Capdevila, & Fernández, 2003) is attached with XML rule to deal with the vagueness associated with the situation. The structure of the linguistic modifier along with a membership function is as follows:

For example, the variable temperature ($S(x)$, μ_x) is used here to construct a modifier *very* for label *low*:

```
<term label="low">
<modifier ="very">
<operator speed: type="Speed">
<w>15</w>
</operator>
```

```
</modifier>
</term>
```

The general structure of a fuzzy XML code which includes such modifiers and other user defined tags is give as follows:

```
<?xml version = "1.0"?>
//……..
// Formal models & general problem
solving strategies can be stored in
format of a block.
<model name= "…">
<block>
        <rule>.....</rule>
</block>
</model>         ….where name is the
encoded name of the model
//rules …..
<rule>
        <antecedent> .......</ante-
cedent>
        <consequent>
<generally>       .......<modifi-
er>….</modifier>  …. </generally>
<specifically> .......    <modifi-
er>….</modifier> …. </specifically>
        </consequent>
</rule>
…….
```

To obtain crisp values of the vague linguistic variables used, there is a need of defuzzification process. The formula for defuzzification along with its operators can also be placed in the above structure.

Figure 4 describes Document Type Definition (DTD) structure for the above model.

Data Grid Layer

This layer manages the users' profile, provides data filtering facility along with related data man-

Figure 4. Document Type Definition: Model

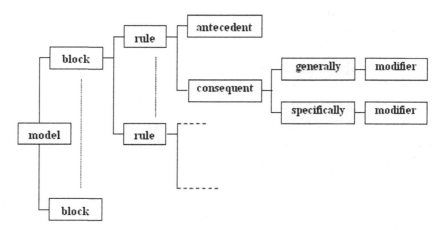

agement activities, and middleware services that enable physical access of the grid. The middleware services include security management, communication, resource allocation, and other agents. It may contain other typical component resources such as - broker agent, book-keeping facility, and replica catalog. It manages static data, dynamic data, and provides querying facility.

The replica catalog holds copies of the instances, or replicas, within specified storage systems. Sometimes it is not advisable to permanently modify the existing source of information. For example, a user-asserted correspondence and/ or temporary results are to be hold temporarily. In this case, replica of existing documents can be created and modified. A replica may be created to the new storage location to realize better performance, accessibility or availability from a particular location. A replica might be deleted when it is no longer useful for efficient management of storage location on the grid. Sometimes, the replica catalog also holds the reference to remote resource/documents. According to various performance criteria like speed, cost, and security a replica is selected from the replica catalog.

Typical replica management services include the functionality of replica management such as replica creation, deletion, and cataloging. For the effective management of these functionalities,

a dedicated replica manager module is needed. The temporary replica developed is to be used for limited period of time and hence, it is advisable to put the replica at client side. This leads to customized repository of replica on client side. It is possible to store some replica at a centrally available server, which is accessible by group of professionals of an institute instead of generating multiple similar copies of replicas. Another approach is to store replica on the gird itself. Where replicas or not available on individual client machine, replicas are to be selected through process of replica selection. The common criteria used to select replica is time taken to access it i.e. access speed (Allcock, Chervenak, Foster, Kesselman, Salisbury, & Tuecke, 2001).

Intelligent replica selection requires information about the capabilities and performance characteristics of a storage system (Allcock et al., 2001). Such problem is classified as information discovery problem and can be solved by leveraging machinery provided by the Globus Metacomputing Directory Service (GMDS) (Fitzgerald, Foster, Kesselman, vonLaszewski, Smith, & Tuecke, 1997), an information collection, publication, and access service for Grid resources. The approach of intelligent replica selection is described in the paper of Vazhkudai et al.(2001).

There is an Optimization module to minimize the content access times based on user profile, application nature, and history of utilization. The other middleware services and third party agents are security, resource allocation, agents to manage session, data retrieval, etc. The security functionality checks the user validity, authenticate users for different rights such as accessing, modifying, replica generation, etc. from the resources. Simultaneously, session agents/threads manage session generic checks, timings to expire/restart session and rollback mechanisms. The metadata repository provides the size of the file and other resource information like access rights, access methods and logical subsets of file instances.

Interface

The interface facility shown in the architecture manages interaction between users and system. This interface facilitates manages following typical activities such as:

- user profile creation for a new user by asking various questions regarding users basic information, users work place information and purpose to access the grid;
- user profile deletion for a profile which is no longer needed;
- change/removal of users information like contact details and change of purpose to a user profile;
- accessing user profile for information reading;
- etc.

A sample profile file containing user profile information is given below:

```
< profile class="user_profile">
<user_name = "myname"/>
<user_age = "myage" />
<user_jobtype = "myjobtype" />
<user_mail = "mymail" />
```

```
<user_purpose = "mypurpose"
/>
    . . .
. . .
</profile>
```

It also helps in managing history and temporary results. The stored user profile helps in predicting their requirements earlier and presents the content in more effective form. This layer provides workspace to hold temporary data and path of execution that can be further used to explain and justify the action taken by the system.

TYPICAL APPLICATIONS AND WORK DONE SO FAR

The Knowledge Grid Project in Italy (Cannataro & Talia, 2003) aims to provide an environment for designing, deploying, and executing distributed data mining applications on the Grid. However, it consists of only two hierarchical levels, namely the Core K-grid Layer (to manage metadata) and the High level K-grid Layer (to provide various services). VEGA is a prototype developed with a GUI for accessing the Knowledge Grid.

In UK, there are several projects related to Knowledge Grid. The Discovery Net Project (Sairafi, Emmanouil, Giannadakis, Guo, Kalaitzopolous, Osmond, Rowe, Syed, & Wendel, 2003) is architecture to support knowledge discovery and data mining processes in a Grid-enabled distributed computing environment with three major modules, namely, Resource Discovery Server, Knowledge Server, and Meta-information Server. An XML-based language called Discovery Process Markup Language (DPML) was proposed for modeling processes. Users can compose processes via a graphical user interface and in the area of bioinformatics context.

The myGrid Project in UK (Wroe, Stevens, Goble, Roberts, & Greenwood, 2003) encompasses distributed knowledge services in grid for problem solving using Semantic Web technology for matchmaking bioinformatics related requests and services/data. The proposed architecture consists of several key components namely Ontology server, FaCT reasoner, Matcher, and Ranker to make the matchmaking possible.

The Knowledge Grid Project (VEGA-KG) in China (Zhuge, 2004b; 2004c) introduces the concept of Knowledge Space which tries to specify a knowledge resource based on its location (e.g. URL), knowledge level (e.g. concept, axiom, rule, or method) and knowledge category (e.g. knowledge or information). It treats the Knowledge Grid somewhat as a distributed knowledge base and proposes a SQL-like language called KGQL for accessing knowledge resources and developing Knowledge Grid related applications. Knowledge Base Grid (KB-Grid) (Wu, Chen, & Xu, 2003) is also a Knowledge Grid project in China, which suggests a paradigm for organizing, discovering, utilizing, and managing web knowledge base resources; and has been applied to support knowledge services of Traditional Chinese Medicine.

Grid technologies are evolving towards an open grid architecture, called the *Open Grid Services Architecture* (*OGSA*), in which a grid provides an extensible set of services that virtual organizations can aggregate in various ways (Talia, 2002). OGSA defines uniform exposed-service semantics, the so-called Grid service, based on concepts, and technologies from both the Grid computing and Web services communities.

Fard et al. (2008) describe a novel discovery approach to sample a multi-expert disease diagnosis system using grid technology, soft computing, and game theory. The typical knowledge grid architecture is defined on top of Globus, a widely used toolkit to deploy geographically distributed grids. The knowledge grid services are organized in two hierarchic levels: the *Core K-grid Layer* and the *Higher K-grid Layer*. The proposed generic layer encompasses three layers for precise objectives.

MULTIAGENT SYSTEM APPLICATION MINING KNOWLEDGE GRID

The architecture defined in the previous section is the generic multi tier architecture enabling functions of the knowledge grid. On the top of the knowledge grid architecture any application can work which utilizes the functionalities of the knowledge grid. As the e-Learning application is selected for the academic environment, which is a large and complex system involving different independent tasks being executed in parallel fashion; a multiagent framework is chosen. The following subsection introduces necessary fundamentals and architecture of the proposed system on the generic knowledge grid architecture.

Introduction to Agents

An agent refers to a component of software and/or hardware that is capable of acting in a certain way to accomplish tasks on behalf of its user. Agents can be formally defined as follows:

An agent is a computational entity that -

- Acts on behalf of other entities in an autonomous fashion;
- Performs its actions with some level of proactivity and/or reactive ness; and
- Exhibits properties like learning, cooperation, and mobility to a certain extent.

The agents are autonomous, cooperative, and able to learn. By nature agents may be proactive or reactive. Table 1 describes major characteristics of agents. These characteristic and components of a typical agent described in Figure 5.

Modern business systems are becoming more complex day by day with increasing expectations from computing world. The systems the author need to analyze span different application areas (such as interdependencies of physical and economical infrastructures) and required to work with

Table 1. Characteristics of Agents (Akerkar & Sajja, 2009)

Characteristic	Description
Autonomy	Capability to work autonomously without human intervention. For this purpose, they are supposed to possess necessary skills and are enriched with required resources.
Cooperation	In order to complete their tasks, agents must interact with users, the environment, and other agents.
Learning	Agents should be able to learn from the entities with which they interact to complete their tasks.
Reactivity	Agents perceive their environment and respond in a timely fashion to changes enforced by the environment.

larger scope. This leads to the need for agents that can be asked to carry out their intended tasks independently and in parallel fashion. The intended application can be divided into multiple subtasks. These tasks can be independently entertained by one or more agents to achieve advantages of parallel processing. After completing the job, the agents may interact with each other in a cooperative fashion for resources or feedback. This saves time and offers a multidisciplinary solution, which would not have been possible with a stand-alone system.

The main advantages of agent technologies are as follows:

- They can be used to solve large and complex problems.
- They allow for the interconnection and interoperation of multiple existing legacy systems.
- They provide solutions to problems where information resources, expertise, and the problem itself are widely distributed.

Figure 5. Components of a Typical Agent

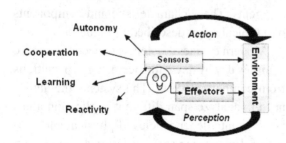

- They enhance modularity, speed, reliability, flexibility, and reusability in problem solving.

Agents are further categorized according to their nature of working and design. Some example categories are collaborative agents, interface agents, mobile agents, information agents, and query and interface agents. These categories are briefly described in Table 2. Agents having combine characteristics and/or design of two or more agents are identified as hybrid agents.

Multiagent System and Agents Communication

A multiagent system is comprised of several agents working together towards a goal or completion of a task. It is a loosely coupled network of problem-solving entity that work together to find answers to problems that are beyond the capacity of any individual problem-solving entity. Since agents of a multiagent system are loosely coupled functions of the application, they need to interact for resources and results.

An agent communication language consists of three parts:

- An inner language, known as the Knowledge Interchange Format (KIF);
- An outer language, known as Knowledge Query and Manipulation Language (KQML); and
- Common vocabularies (i.e. ontologies).

Table 2. Categories of Agents

Category of Agent	Characteristics of the Agent Type
Collaborative Agents	This type of agents work in co-operation with other entities/ agents of the environment in order to perform the specified tasks. These agents are quite useful when the problem domain is large; as the collaborative agents interconnect different standalone legacy components to define the problem and acquire resources and expertise from distributed areas.
Interface Agents	Interface agents are used to provide a user-friendly environment/ interface to work with a highly technical application. They work as personal assistants, helping users to interact with the system.
Mobile Agents	An agent's mobility refers to its ability to move around an electronic network/ distributed environment. For this purpose, such agents encompass techniques to interact with a wide area network, such as the World Wide Web (WWW). The typical tasks they can perform are searching information and executing tasks on behalf of their owners and interacting with the remote systems.
Information Agents	Information agents help by searching for and managing information on users' behalf. Such agents are enriched with dedicated techniques for information searching, ranking, extracting, and filtering according to need.
Hybrid agents	Hybrid agents combine two or more agent categories according to need of the application.

If a problem domain is particularly complex, large, or unpredictable, the only way it can reasonably be addressed is to develop a number of functionally specific and (nearly) modular components (agents) that are specialized at solving a particular problem aspect. This decomposition allows each agent to use the most appropriate paradigm for solving its particular problem (Capuano, Marsella, & Salerno, 2000). Besides providing necessary framework to multiple agents, a Multi Agent System (MAS) does the following:

- Provides an environment for the agents;
- Sets the relationships between the entities; and
- Provides a platform for a set of operations that can be performed by the agents.

MAS can manifest self-organization and complex behaviors, even when the individual strategies of all their agents are simple (Bobek & Perko, 2006). The dynamics of a multiagent system are defined by its agents. Multiagent systems can be classified into two categories - homogeneous and heterogeneous. When the agents within the system follow a similar topology, it is called a homogeneous multiagent system; otherwise, it is called a heterogeneous multiagent system.

Multiagent systems are successful due to several causes. Some of the major reasons are as follows:

- They are able to solve large problems, especially those where classical systems are not successful.
- They allow different systems to work together in an interconnected fashion.
- They provide efficient solutions where information is distributed among different places.
- They allow software reusability; therefore, there is more flexibility in adopting different agent capabilities to solve problems.

Table 3 presents characteristics of multiagent system:

Multiagent System for e-Learning

e-Learning is a step towards a learning economy (Bachman, 2000), emphasizing online delivery of information and hence, an accelerated learning process in a cost-effective way through IT

Table 3. Characteristics of a Multiagent System

Characteristic	Description
Reliability	A multiagent system is able to dynamically co-ordinate with the agents incorporated in it. In case, an agent fails, other functionalities would not be disturbed. The multiagent system's framework help in efficient recovery of component failures with controlled redundancy of the agents.
Extensibility	A multiagent system can incorporate a few agents on need. That is, number and capabilities of agents working on a problem can be altered easily from a structured framework without disturbing other agents.
Quality	Multiple objects working for a common goal increase the computational efficiency, which results in a significant increase of quality. Ability to isolate an agent leads to easy repairing and testing.
Reusability	The agents of a multiagent system can be reused in many similar applications.
Ease of development and maintainability	All the agents of a multiagent system can be developed in parallel and independently with "divide and conquer" approach. Such a structured system is easy to maintain and develop.

(Gotschall, 2000; Sajja, 2008; Shreiber & Berge, 1998). According to Drucker (2000), e-Learning is just-in-time education integrated with high-velocity value chains. It is the delivery of individualized, comprehensive, dynamic learning content in real time, aiding the development of communities of knowledge, linking learners and practitioners with experts. The major components of an e-Learning system are subject experts, media developers, instructors, editors, designers, and technical experts (Kanendran, Johnny, & Durga, 2004). All these components collectively contribute to three different aspects of e-Learning namely: content, service, and technology; which are denoted in Figure 6. To improve the overall quality of an e-Learning solution, these three basic aspects need to be strengthened. Improving the quality of each aspect individually increases the quality of the integrated-solution framework, thereby satisfying users at various levels.

According to Unwin (2003), the prime objectives of any e-Learning technique are (i) to ensure that access to high-quality information is integrated into course provisions; (ii) to equip e-learners with the skills to exploit the available information; (iii) to provide appropriate assistance to e-learners in information searching and utilization; and (iv) to address issues related to communications and cost.

A complete e-Learning system offers the following advantages:

- Presentation of required information in efficient and customized way on demand;
- Content is timely, accurate, and reliable;
- Ability to upgrade instantly and quickly;
- Documentation of knowledge for future use;
- Scalable and collaborative applications; and
- Cost-effective solutions by saving infrastructural cost and time.

Figure 6. Aspects of e-Learning Technology

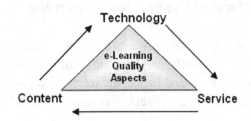

Many e-Learning platforms and systems have been developed and commercialized. Most of the traditional computer-aided software developed so far are typical full-fledged systems based on specific databases, providing only static presentation of information. The system developed for adult literacy in regional language, "Parichay" (Sajja 2006), calculates a learner's level of capability using domain heuristics and presents material according to the learner's need and capability. However, this solution is a single personal computer-based system and offers limited scope. Due to this limitation, learners cannot take advantage of building communities and groups for discussion.

e-Learning systems developed so far focused mainly on the content delivery for a specific domain (Pankratius & Vossen, 2003; Kuan-Ching, Chuan-Ko, Yin-Te, & Hsiao-His,2006; Foster et al.,2001). They are based on client-server, peer-to-peer, and web services architecture, with a major drawback being their limitations in scalability, availability, and distribution of computing power as well as storage capabilities. Instead of providing just an online repository of the content, an e-Learning system is supposed to offer customized advice and step-by-step assistance to help learners in friendly way. Moreover, standard e-Learning solutions are not integrated with functions like student monitoring, courseware management, mail and chatting, reporting, evaluation of quizzes and assignments, etc.

The e-Learning system should possess following major characteristics:

- Ability to hold and access the domain knowledge efficiently in a secured fashion;
- Ability to reuse the lower level knowledge component;
- Ability to identify learner's level and presentation of content in friendly way; and
- To retrieve, use, and learn new knowledge from the stored content repository and meta-knowledge.

For successful inclusion of the above listed requirements, it becomes trivial to add 'knowledge' component within the content and/or to provide knowledgeable services and techniques to access the content. This leads to the utilization of knowledge-grid platform for the e-Learning application.

Since e-Learning encompasses multiple independent tasks, there is a need for various independent lower-level components called agents. Vortals (vertical portals) and intelligent agents are the two most promising technologies in which e-Learning could be practically accomplished (Hill, 2003; Dan, Florin, & Mihai, 2003). Giotopoulos et al. (2007) has described a genetic algorithm-based e-Learning approach through various assessment agents and resource retrieval agents.

The proposed architecture utilizes agent technology on knowledge grid for e-Learning and offers dual advantages of agent-based system and knowledge grid. The architecture is shown in Figure 7.

The proposed system encompasses different agents for activities like user management, courseware management; tutorials; quizzes, drills, and practice assignments; performance evaluations; information retrieval and semantic search; and communication (mail and chat) facilities. All of these agents work in collaboration with the higher knowledge grid layer. Table 4 shows a brief summary of the agents used along with their objectives.

The data layer of the proposed architecture provides uniform resources and basic facilities to the system. The data grid layer works in conjunction with documentation and manages local, communication, and user management agents. This layer can be considered as the fabric of the grid architecture proposed here, which provides uniform interface to all the resources on the grid. On each client, this layer starts applications of resources provision, manages the sessions and history and presumes the user profile. Users are given grid login services with different access levels. At present four user levels have been designed namely: (i) administrator, (ii) instructor, (iii) students, and (iv) guest.

The administrator can create users and assign suitable rights to the user information along with access rights. User can be further provided a specific key to access the resources by the ad-

Figure 7. Multiagent System on Top of the Knowledge Grid

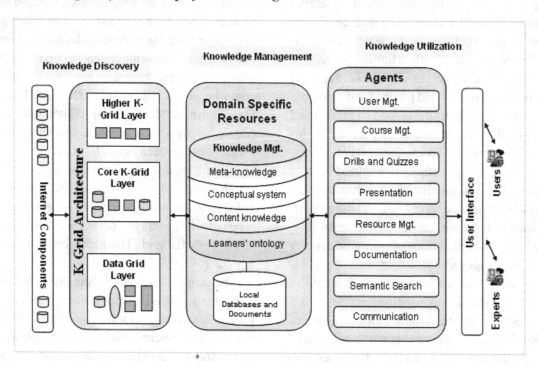

Table 4. Agents and their objectives

Agent	Objective the Agent
User management	- Manages operation like creation of users and assign rights (by administrator). - Managing profile of users and providing functionalities like edit, search, and delete information. - Automatic update to history of the content used.
Course management	- Manages creation of courses and subjects to be taught (by instructor). - Managing prerequisites and other constraints of the course, edit subject content, and set relation to the content and question bank.
Drills and quizzes	- Manages question bank by creating questions, providing solutions and marks for the correct answers.
Presentation	- Manages presentation of questions in random order, calculates speed correctness ratio and marks, and determines sequence of presentation according to user's learning level identified.
Resource management	- Manages resources of hardware and authenticates sessions.
Documentation	- Takes regular backup management. - Provide documentation of information stored in a structured way.
Semantic search	- Searches and presents necessary information like course content, administrative reports, results and students performance in a structured way.
Communication	- Provides facility to communicate with instructors and administrator and get information according to access rights. - Publishes the results and necessary announcements on networked platform.

ministrator. At this time, additional information about user is collected and stored in the user's profile. The user profile information is helpful to determine access to the facilities and presentation style and sequence of the content. For example, only instructors are allowed to edit question bank and course material of a given subject. Visitors and parents are not allowed to access the drills and quizzes, however, they can see announcements, published results, infrastructural facilities of the institute, etc.

After successful connection to the grid resources, requests of users for different facilities can be entertained. The core grid layer mainly supports knowledge repository for domain knowledge and meta knowledge. It utilizes XML to store the content as discussed earlier.

CONCLUSION

The described knowledge grid architecture provide higher level services for problem solving, searching resources, and designing knowledge discovery processes in a structured manner. The grid will be proved as an effective infrastructure for managing very large data sources and providing high-level mechanisms for extracting valuable knowledge from them in near future.

Grid computing is the most promising framework for future implementations of high performance data intensive distributed applications. Although today the grid is mainly used for scientific applications, in near future it will be used for industrial and commercial applications (Cannataro & Talia, 2003). In future, the knowledge grid will be used as a platform for implementing and deploying geographically distributed knowledge discovery (Kargupta & Chan, 1999) and knowledge management platforms and applications. Some ongoing efforts in this direction have recently been initiated. Examples of systems such as the Discovery Net (Ghanem, Guo, Rowe, & Wendel, 2002), the AdAM system (Hinke &

Novotny, 2000), and the knowledge grid discussed here show the feasibility of the approach and can represent the first generation of knowledge-based pervasive grids.

According to Liu (2003), the next paradigm shift in web intelligence and knowledge grid will be towards the notion of wisdom and the new web intelligence and knowledge grid technologies to be developed will be precisely determined by *human needs in a post-industrial era;* namely:

- information empowerment;
- knowledge sharing;
- virtual social clustering;
- service enrichment; and
- practical wisdom development.

To meet the strong demands for participation and the growing interests in WI, the Web Intelligence Consortium (WIC) was formed in spring 2002. The objective, promotion programs and publication related details can be seen at http://wi-consortium.org/. Such many consortium activities can be planned.

Other research challenges include developing automatic ontology creation, wisdom-based web/grid, testing techniques, and standards for the knowledge grid. One may think about the platform-independent virtual grid in future that evolves harmoniously with the applications. The semantics and versatile resources are fundamental elements for such grid environment specially when such application awareness and other social factors are concerned. This is a step towards 'wisdom web'. Other key issues which need further research and elaboration can be (i) normalization of the semantic space on grid; (ii) clustering, co-ordination, and self organization of grid resources/layers; (iii) evolution according to need; and (iv) an intelligent browser to display better and interpret the machine-understandable semantics.

The knowledge grid helps in increasing productivity by reducing total cost of ownership; and any type, any where, any time services are provided by/for all. As stated earlier, it is an infrastructure that implements dynamic virtual organizations.

REFERENCES

Akerkar, R. A., & Sajja, P. S. (2009). *Knowledge-based Systems*. Sudbury, MA: Jones & Bartlett Publishers.

Allcock, W., Chervenak, A., Foster, I., Kesselman, C., Salisbury, C., & Tuecke, S. (2001). The Data Grid: Towards an Architecture for the Distributed Management and Analysis of Large Scientific Datasets. *Journal of Network and Computer Applications, 23*, 187–200.

Bachman, K. (2000). *Corporate e-Learning: Exploring a new frontier*. W.R. Hambrecht and Co.

Baru, C., Moore, R., Rajasekar, A., & Wan, M. (1998). The SDSC storage resource broker. In *Proceedings of CASCON'98 Conference*, Toronto, Canada.

Berners-Lee, T., Hendler, J., & Lassila, O. (2001). The Semantic Web. *Scientific American, 279*(5), 34–43. doi:10.1038/scientificamerican0501-34

Bobek, S., & Perko, I. (2006). Intelligent Agent-Based Business Intelligence. *Current Developments in Technology-Assisted Education*, FORMATEX, 1047-1051.

Cannataro, M., & Talia, D. (2003). Knowledge grid: An architecture for distributed knowledge discovery. *Communications of the ACM, 46*(1), 89–93. doi:10.1145/602421.602425

Cannataro, M., & Talia, D. (2004). Semantics and Knowledge Grids: Building the Next-Generation Grid. *IEEE Intelligent Systems, 19*(1), 56–63. doi:10.1109/MIS.2004.1265886

Capuano, N., Marsella, M., & Salerno, S. (2000). ABITS: An Agent-based Intelligent Tutoring System for Distance Learning. In *Proceedings of ITS 2000*, Montreal, Canada. Retrieved from http://www.capuano.biz/Papers/ITS_2000.pdf

Casanova, M. A. (2005). *Grid Computing – Introduction*. Retrieved from http://www.inf.puc-rio.br/~casanova/INF2328-Topicos-WebBD/modulo6-Topicos/modulo6a-grid.PDF

Dan, G., Florin, L., & Mihai, H. (2003). e-Learning distributed framework using intelligent agents. *New Trends in Computer Science and Engineering*, Anniversary Volume, Technical University Gh. Asachi, Polirom Press, Iaşi, 159-163.

De Soto, A. R., Capdevila, C. A., & Fernández, E. C. (2003). Fuzzy Systems and Neural Networks XML Schemas for Soft Computing. *Mathware & Soft Computing, 10*(2-3), 43–56.

Drucker, P. (2000). Need to know: Integrating e-Learning with high-velocity value chains. *A Delphi Group White Paper*. Retrieved from http://www.delphigroup.com/research/ whitepaper_request_download.htm

Fard, A. M., Kamyar, H., & Naghibzadeh, M. (2008). Multi-expert Disease Diagnosis System over Symptom Data Grids on the Internet. *World Applied Science Journal, 3*(2), 244–253.

Fitzgerald, S., Foster, I., Kesselman, C., vonLaszewski, G., Smith, W., & Tuecke, S. (1997). A Directory Service for Configuring High-performance Distributed Computations. In *Proceedings of 7th IEEE Symposium on High Performance Distributed Computing* (pp.365-375).

Foster, I., & Kesselman, C. (1999). *The Grid: Blueprint for a new computing infrastructure*. San Francisco: Morgan Kaufmann.

Foster, I., Kesselman, C., & Tuecke, S. (2001). The Anatomy of the Grid: Enabling Scalable Virtual Organizations. *The International Journal of Supercomputer Applications, 15*(3), 6–13.

Ghanem, M., Guo, Y., Rowe, A., & Wendel, P. (2002). Grid-based Knowledge Discovery Services for High Throughput Informatics. In *Proceedings of 11ᵗʰ IEEE International Symposium on High Performance Distributed Computing* (pp. 416). Washington, DC: IEEE CS Press.

Giotopoulos, K., Alexakos, C., Beligiannis, G., & Likothanassis, S. (2007). Integrating Computational Intelligence Techniques and Assessment Agents in e-Learning Environments. *International Journal of Computational Intelligence*, *3*(4), 328–337.

Gotschall, M. (2000). e-Learning strategies for Executive Education and Corporate Training. *Fortune*, *141*(10), S5–S59.

Hill, L. (2003). *Implementing a Practical e-Learning System*. Retrieved from http://agora.lakeheadu.ca/pre2004/december2002/elearning.html

Hinke, T., & Novotny, J. (2000). Data Mining on NASA's Information Power Grid. In *Proceedings of 9ᵗʰ IEEE International Symposium on High Performance Distributed Computing* (pp.292-293). IEEE CS Press.

Joshy, J., & Craig, F. (2004). *Introduction to Grid Computing*. Upper Saddle River, NJ: Prentice Hall.

Kanendran, T. A., Johnny, S., & Durga, B. V. (2004). Technical report: Issues and strategies of e-Learning. *Sunway College Journal*, *1*, 99–107.

Kargupta, H., & Chan, P. (1999). *Advances in Distributed and Parallel Knowledge Discovery*. AAAI Press.

Kuan-Ching, L., Chuan-Ko, T., Yin-Te, T., & Hsiao-His, W. (2006). Towards design of e-Learning platform in Grid Environments. In *Proceedings of the 2006 International Conference on Grid Computing & Applications*. Las Vegas, Nevada.

Lee, T. B., & Fischetti, M. (1999). *Weaving the Web*. Harper, San Francisco.

Liu, J. (2003). Web Intelligence (WI): What makes Wisdom Web? In *Proceedings of the 18ᵗʰ International Joint Conference on Artificial Intelligence (IJCAI-03)* (pp.1596-1601). Acapulco, Mexico.

Moore, R. (2001). Knowledge-based Grids. In *Proceedings of the Eighteenth IEEE Symposium on Mass Storage Systems and Technologies* (pp. 29). San Diego, California

Pankratius, V., & Vossen, G. (2003). Towards e-Learning Grids: Using Grid Computing in Electronic. Learning. In *Proceedings of IEEE Workshop on Knowledge Grid and Learning Grid Intelligence* (pp.4-15). Halifax, Canada.

Sairafi, S. A., Emmanouil, F. S., Giannadakis, M., Guo, Y., Kalaitzopolous, D., & Osmond, M. (2003). The design of Discovery Net: Towards Open Grid services for Knowledge Discovery. *International Journal of High Performance Computing Applications*, *17*(3).

Sajja, P. S. (2006). Parichay: An Agent for Adult Literacy. *Prajna*, *14*, 17–24.

Sajja, P. S. (2007). Knowledge representation using Fuzzy XML Rules for Knowledge-based Adviser. *International Journal of Computer. Mathematical Sciences and Applications*, *1*(2-4), 323–330.

Sajja, P. S. (2008). Enhancing Quality in e-Learning by Knowledge-based IT support. *International Journal of Education and Development Using Information and Communication Technology*, *4*(1).

Sajja, P. S. (2009). Multi-tier Knowledge-based System accessing Learning Object Repository using fuzzy XML. In Yang, H., & Yuen, S. (Eds.), *Handbook of Research on Practices and Outcomes in e-Learning: Issues and Trends*. Hershey, PA: IGI Global Book Publishing.

Sajja, P. S., & Chourasia, N. N. (2005). Knowledge Representation Using XML in a Multi-Layer Knowledge-Based Adviser for Small-Scale and Cottage Industries. In *Proceedings of 2nd National Seminar on Data and Knowledge Engineering*, India.

Shreiber, D. A., & Berge, Z. L. (1998). *Distance training: How innovative organizations are using technology to maximize learning and business objectives*. San Francisco: Jossey-Bass.

Stork, H. (2002). Webs, Grids and Knowledge Spaces - Programmes, Projects and Prospects. *Journal of Universal Computer Science*, 8(9), 848–868.

Talia, D. (2002). The Open Grid Services Architecture: Where the Grid Meets the Web. *IEEE Internet Computing*, 6(6), 67–71. doi:10.1109/MIC.2002.1067739

Unwin, D. (2003). Information support for e-Learning: principles and practice. *UK eUniversities Worldwide Summer.*

Vazhkudai, S., Tuecke, S., & Foster, I. (2001). Replica Selection in the Global Data Grid. In *Proceedings of the 1st International Symposium on Cluster Computing and the Grid. Brisbane*, Australia.

Wroe, C., Stevens, R., Goble, C., Roberts, A., & Greenwood, M. (2003). A Suite of DAML+OIL Ontologies to describe Bioinformatics Web Services and Data. *International Journal of Co-operative Information Systems*, 12(2), 197–224. doi:10.1142/S0218843003000711

Wu, Z., Chen, H., & Xu, J. (2003). Knowledge Base Grid: A Generic Grid Architecture for Semantic Web. *Journal of Computer and Technology*, 18(4), 462–473. doi:10.1007/BF02948920

Zadeh, L. A. (1965). Fuzzy Sets. *Journal of Information and Control*, 8, 338–353. doi:10.1016/S0019-9958(65)90241-X

Zhuge, H. (2004a). Semantics, Resource and Grid. *Future Generation Computer Systems*, 20(1), 1–5. doi:10.1016/S0167-739X(03)00159-6

Zhuge, H. (2004b). *The Knowledge Grid*. China: Chinese Academy of Sciences.

Zhuge, H. (2004c). China's e-Science Knowledge Grid Environment. *IEEE Intelligent Systems*, 19(1), 13–17. doi:10.1109/MIS.2004.1265879

KEY TERMS AND DEFINITIONS

Agent: An Agent is a computational entity that acts on behalf of other entities in an autonomous fashion; and exhibits properties like learning, cooperation, and mobility to a certain extent.

Data Grid: Data Grids are *large scale distributed computing systems* providing mechanisms for the controlled sharing of computing resources. Data grids support mainly data storage, data retrieval, and data discovery processes through the data management infrastructure and services on the top of the grid.

e-Learning: e-Learning is a step towards a learning economy, emphasizing online delivery of information and hence, an accelerated learning process in a cost-effective way through IT.

Knowledge Grid: Knowledge Grid is an intelligent interconnection environment that enables people or virtual roles to effectively capture, publish, share, and manage explicit knowledge resources as well as provides on-demand knowledge services to support people or services to carry out innovation, cooperative teamwork, problem-solving, and decision making.

Multiagent Systems: A Multiagent System is comprised of several agents working together towards a goal or completion of a task. It is a loosely coupled network of problem-solving entities that work together to find answers to problems that are beyond the capacity of any individual problem-solving entity.

Semantic Grid: Semantic Grid seeks to incorporate the Semantic Web approach into the ongoing Grid. Using semantics and ontologies in grids can offer high-level support for managing grid resources and for designing complex applications that will benefit from the use of semantics.

Semantic Web: The Semantic Web is considered as an extension of the current Web in which information is given well defined meaning by associating metadata.

Chapter 13
Opinion Mining with SentiWordNet

Bruno Ohana
Dublin Institute of Technology, Ireland

Brendan Tierney
Dublin Institute of Technology, Ireland

ABSTRACT

Opinion Mining is an emerging field of research concerned with applying computational methods to the treatment of subjectivity in text, with a number of applications in fields such as recommendation systems, contextual advertising and business intelligence. In this chapter the authors survey the area of opinion mining and discuss the SentiWordNet lexicon of sentiment information for terms derived from WordNet. Furthermore, the results of their research in applying this lexicon to sentiment classification of film reviews along with a novel approach that leverages opinion lexicons to build a data set of features used as input to a supervised learning classifier are also presented. The results obtained are in line with other experiments based on manually built opinion lexicons with further improvements obtained by using the novel approach, and are indicative that lexicons built using semi supervised methods such as SentiWordNet can be an important resource in sentiment classification tasks. Considerations on future improvements are also presented based on a detailed analysis of classification results.

INTRODUCTION

Opinion information concerns people's expressed beliefs and judgments on a certain topic, and can be an important component used in making more accurate decisions in a number of scenarios. Companies for instance, have a keen interest in finding out what are customers saying about

their products and service offerings. Consumers on the other hand would benefit from accessing other people's opinions and reviews on products they wish to purchase, as recommendations from other users tend to play a part on influencing such decisions. Knowledge of other people's opinions is also important on other realms such as political activism, where for instance it could be of interest to discover the general sentiment towards a new piece of legislation or towards political parties and

DOI: 10.4018/978-1-60960-067-9.ch013

public figures; or in the detection of subjective bias on environments where there should be none, such as in monitoring news coverage.

In recent years, the internet has enabled access to opinions in the form of written text from a variety of sources and in a much larger scale: it is now easier for people to express their opinions on virtually any subject by means of specialized product review websites, discussion forums and blogs. This is in fact a growing trend, as pointed out in research performed by Horrigan (2008) over 30% of internet users have at one time posted a comment or review online about a product or service they've purchased suggesting an ever growing availability of opinion related information on the web. The same research states that, as on 2007, 81% of internet users in the United States have used the internet to perform research on a product they intended to purchase. Further evidence of the importance of opinions in guiding consumer decisions can be seen in a study on the online travel industry from (Akehurst, 2009) highlighting the perceived high credibility of information found in user generated content, and on the study relating transaction feedback posted by users and consumer behavior on online auction services (Dellarocas, 2003).

The internet is quickly becoming a vast repository of publicly available user generated content dedicated to expressing opinions on any topic of interest. However, there are challenges in extracting useful information from large volumes of data. In Horrigan (2008), 58% of internet users reported that researching product information online was either confusing, difficult to find, or have found the volume of information available to be overwhelming. Suggesting information overload issues may be present in online opinion repositories where these resources become too big to be analyzed in a timely fashion, and are poorly utilized as a result (Farhoomand & Drudy, 2002). Automated methods for efficiently extracting opinion knowledge from these resources appear an attractive proposition for both individuals who

would be able to make informed decisions and to companies who could quickly gauge opinions on their products and services, adding this knowledge to their product development processes. These goals are in essence closely related to those of the discipline of knowledge discovery proposed in Fayyad et al. (1996), which concerns computational methods aiming at finding "valid, novel, potentially useful and ultimately understandable patterns from data". In addition, opinions are generally expressed in textual form, making it a rich ground for the application of text mining techniques and natural language processing. Thus the motivating need to analyze large volumes of opinion information, coupled with advances in natural language processing and knowledge discovery methods gave rise to research in the emerging field of *Opinion Mining*.

This chapter introduces the reader to the research field of opinion mining by presenting a review of research literature, an outline of the potential applications of this technology and the intellectual challenges involved in extracting useful knowledge from opinions in text. Particular emphasis is given to the topics of predictive opinion mining and the application of sentiment lexicons to such tasks. The authors also present the results of their research with the SentiWordNet lexicon (Esuli & Sebastiani, 2006) applied to the task of sentiment classification of film reviews. This research presents a unique approach that uses opinion lexicons to build a set of features that can be used to train a classifier, which achieved improved classification results in the experiment. The results obtained are discussed together with findings and opportunities for future development.

OPINION MINING

The starting point for mining opinions in text is the abstraction that a document can be considered as a collection of objective and subjective statements, where objective statements refer to factual information contained in the text, while subjective statements relate to the expression of opinions, sentiment, evaluations and speculations (Wiebe, 1990), the latter being naturally the aspect that interests opinion mining research the most. Devising automated methods for extracting, exploring and analyzing opinion information from text is thus the scope of opinion mining research. The examples given below illustrate how such methods can be used in practical knowledge discovery applications.

Search Engines

One of the most direct applications of opinion mining is searching for opinions in document repositories. Finding out subjective statements related to a topic and their positive or negative orientation can extend the role of traditional search engines into recommendation engines by retrieving results on a given topic containing only positive or negative sentiment, for example in searching for products that have received good reviews on a particular area. Case studies of search technology incorporating opinion information are found in Grefenstette et al. (2004) where a query system uses both topic and sentiment information to retrieve results in a given subject; and in the review browser that retrieves product attributes and their relevant opinions (Dave, Lawrence, & Pennock, 2003). On the other hand, information retrieval systems that aim at providing factual information on a given topic can detect and discard opinion information to increase the relevance of results (Wiebe, Bruce, Martin, Wilson, & Bell, 2004), or can assist in alerting for the existence of opinionated bias where there should be none, such as in news reports (Mullen & Malouf, 2006).

Inappropriate Content

In a collaborative environment such as an online forum, opinion mining could be applied to automatically detect subjective statements contain-

ing overly heated or inappropriate remarks, also called *flaming* behavior (Kaufer, 2000). Similar techniques could assist more efficient online advertisement strategies by avoiding advertisement placements next to content that is topically related to the advertisement campaign, but carries unfavorable opinions towards a certain product or brand (Jin, Li, Mah, & Tong, 2007). Another closely related area is that of monitoring the activity of extremism in online forums (Abbasi, Chen, & Salem, 2008).

Customer Relationship Management

Systems that manage customer interactions can become more responsive by using sentiment detection as a tool to automatically predict the level of satisfaction of client feedback. An example for this is the automatic classification of customer feedback replies by email containing positive or negative sentiment (Konig & Brill, 2006), which could then be used for automatically routing of messages into the appropriate teams for corrective actions when necessary.

Business Intelligence

Opinion mining can add the subjective components of text as a new dimension in exploring and discovering new knowledge from textual data. This may take the form of aggregated sentiment bias information from user feedback which can be used to drive marketing campaigns or improve products. A case study involving a system designed to perform the analysis of opinions from product feedback posted by users is seen in Glance et al. (2005). In the financial area, opinions may have an effect on the market's perception on a given investment product, and assessing their effects has received considerable research attention. In Devitt and Ahmad (2007) a model for detection of sentiment on financial news sources is presented. The constant flow of incoming financial news from news sources is analyzed and sentiment information is extracted by inspecting words in the neighborhood of key financial terms, and presented in a stream of opinion strength over time (Ahmad, Cheng, & Almas, 2006). Sentiment in news items has shown a correlation to stock price movement as seen in the results from a classification experiment in Koppel and Shtrimberg (2004). The authors also suggests that this can be used to derive more robust data sets for opinion mining research, since price movement can be considered a reliable label for document sentiment.

The Scope of Opinion Mining Research

The survey presented in Pang and Lee (2008) maps the activities of the emerging field of opinion mining broadly into classification and extraction tasks. Classification entails research aiming at detecting in first instance if a given piece of text can be categorized as subjective or objective. If subjective, to be able to correctly predict the text's sentiment orientation or *polarity*; the extraction aspect of opinion mining shares the concerns of information retrieval in text, and attempts to identify within a text document what are the key attributes of an opinion, such as the opinion holder or to what entity or topic it refers to. Another formulation which is employed in this chapter appears in Esuli and Sebastiani (2006), where the primary objectives of opinion mining are categorized into:

- Determining the degree in which a given text is objective or subjective, or *subjectivity detection.*
- If a text is indeed subjective, determining whether it expresses a positive or negative bias, or *sentiment classification.*
- Determining the strength of the polarity of a given subjective text.

Other categorizations may fall into the realm of the analysis of subjective content in text, such as

mining author points of view on political discourse aiming at identifying party or political orientation (Mullen & Malouf, 2006). Indeed a formulation of opinion proposed in Kim and Hovy (2004) does take this into account. It is worth noting another field of research that shares some of the concerns of opinion mining: that of *affective computing*, aiming at the development of computational approaches for detecting human emotions such as anger, fear and humor (Strapparava & Valitutti, 2004). Affective computing has applications in human computer interaction, but is closely linked to the problem of detecting subjective text, since both relate to the expression of human emotions. More details in research literature in the field of predictive opinion mining: subjectivity detection and sentiment classification is inspected in the following sections. Whereas opinion extraction methods have also received considerable research attention, predictive tasks are more closely linked to our current research, and a thorough survey of opinion extraction research would be beyond the scope of this chapter.

Subjectivity Detection

In order to detect subjectivity in text, a computational model requires a formalization of what is understood by the concept. In Wiebe et al. (2004) the subjectivity of a sentence is defined based upon previous work in linguistics and literary theory, where *subjective elements* from a document are sought: these are the linguistic expressions that characterize private states of mind. A subjective element expresses the opinions, thoughts and speculations of a *source*, that is the document author or an entity mentioned in the text. It also has a *target*, or the object to which the opinion is directed to. Finally, opinions express a particular sentiment that broadly speaking can be gauged in terms of positive or favorable to negative or unfavorable. An abstraction of subjectivity encompassing the above elements is also seen in Kim and Hovy (2004), where an opinion is defined as a quadruple of the form [Topic, Holder, Claim, Sentiment] in which a *Holder* believes a *Claim* on a given *Topic*, with a given *Sentiment* associated with it. Subjectivity detection is generally concerned with finding clues that help in determining to what degree a piece of text is subjective, and locating the subjective elements in text when they exist.

Sentiment Classification

Following from subjectivity detection, the next important predictive task is determining what, if any, is the sentiment *orientation* of the opinions contained within a document. It is assumed in general that the document being inspected is subjective in nature, such as a product review, and that the document's opinion refers to a single entity (Pang & Lee, 2008). With this characterization, opinion orientation in a document can be classified as belonging to opposing positive or negative polarities, or ranked according to a spectrum of possible opinions as is the case with film reviews with feedback ranging from zero to five stars (Pang & Lee, 2005) or the assignment of a numeric satisfaction score to travel destinations seen in Baccianella et al. (2009).

The Challenges of Subjective Language

Subjective language may appear under a variety of guises, reflecting the diversity which human feelings can be conveyed in natural language. This diversity often translates to ambiguity and unclear distinctions between facts and opinions, and it appears that establishing the limits of subjective text and its orientation as positive, negative or neutral is not a trivial task, even for humans. Evidence of this can be seen in the often high levels of disagreement between human annotators when faced with the task of identifying text as subjective or objective, or opinions as positive or negative (Pang, Lee, & Vaithyanathan, 2002;

Andreevskaya & Bergler, 2006; Yu & Hatzivassiloglou, 2003; Wiebe et al., 2004).

Not only can expressions be conveyed in explicit statements, but also implicitly in discourse by means of irony, sarcasm and metaphors. This is noted in the categorization proposed in Nigam and Hurst (2004), where one of the components of subjective text relates to implicit versus explicit aspect, indicating how directly is opinion being conveyed. In a typically explicit statement such as *"It is an enjoyable read, full of insightful comments and written with style."*, the terms used in the sentence usually carry significant opinion information. In other cases, more elaborate expressions such as *"does the job"*, or *"worth a try"* may be used. On the other end of the scale, opinion is implicitly stated by the use of more sophisticated linguistic resources like metaphors seen in: *"The director lays visual and sound effects on thick, like ketchup, eventually drowning the movie."*; and sarcastic expressions such as the example: *"A trailer for a movie written by a team of bodybuilders and greeting card authors"*. Modality is also highlighted in this categorization as a source of opinion information, whereby conditions are attached to a certain sentiment, such as *"if only it would play all file formats"*. Lastly, attribution is also an aspect of opinion, specifying who might like or dislike a certain product, with possible implications to overall opinions depending on the context they are in. The example *"Only hard core fans of action movies will enjoy watching it."* could implicitly mean very few people actually will enjoy it, if the author is writing to a wide audience.

Opinionated text will often contain quite a high amount of factual content, as a more detailed description of the subject tends to appear in support of the author's point of view. This will pose challenges to correctly detecting subjectivity, but it is worth highlighting however that a clear distinction between what is fact and what is opinion at sentence level is not always possible and opinion information may be lost at the expense of filtering factual content. In the example: *"other impressive set pieces follow... and an extended sequence at a construction site, in which a hilarious pursuit through a maze of blue doors culminates in some exciting fights...",* author opinion comes together with plot description, and potentially useful opinion information can still be extracted from it. Moreover, as noted by Nigam and Hurst (2004), opinionated documents tend to refer to more than one entity, even when the main topic of the document is a specific product, it is likely to contain comparisons to other products and mention other people's opinions.

Finally, opinions are common on user generated content such as blog posts and social networks which are frequently written using informal language. A practical but crucial issue present on most sources of opinion is that informality is followed by issues such as incorrect spelling, inconsistent grammar usage, unusual jargons and colloquialisms that add to the complexity of analyzing this type of text. As an example, it was observed in Yang et al. (2007) that unusual spellings such as "greeeat" and non standard terms such as "supergood" can often be seen in the expression of sentiment in user generated content.

The above observations suggest different types of information can be extracted from texts which are relevant to the detection of opinions in text. These aspects have been explored in computational models proposed in the literature, which are surveyed in the next section.

Opinion Mining Techniques

Opinion mining shares common interests with other research fields, and thus is able to leverage advances from different areas such as natural language processing, text mining and machine learning, resulting in a wealth of approaches combining different techniques from those fields. In this section opinion mining techniques with particular emphasis on opinion lexicons is surveyed.

Exploring Annotated Corpora

Corpus approaches try to infer general relationships in a written language from a subset of documents with manually annotated opinion information. By applying computational method these relationships can be explored to derive generic approaches for the detection of subjectivity and sentiment classification. In Wiebe et al. (2004) a corpus of annotated subjective sentences based on newspaper articles is used to a subjectivity detection algorithm that applied linguistic rules based on proximity to other subjective terms. Further analysis of the document corpus also revealed how infrequent terms play a key role in detecting subjectivity – a factor also observed on the literature on Dave et al. (2003) and Yang et al. (2007). A corpus based learning approach is also seen in the work of Turney and Littman (2003) for inferring the orientation of a term based on its statistical relationship to a core set of terms extracted from the corpus.

Supervised Learning

Certain opinion mining tasks can be treated as a binary classification problem where a document is assigned to positive or negative, subjective or objective classes, and as such can be subject to supervised learning techniques commonly employed in text classification. With the increasing availability of data sets that can be used as sources of information for opinion mining, one natural approach is to apply data driven supervised learning methods by taking the traditional *bag-of-words* text mining representation of documents (Salton, Wong, & Yang, 1975). An application of these techniques to subjectivity detection is seen in Pang and Lee (2004), where a classifier is trained to predict objective or subjective sentences based on a training set of extracted documents from the internet. The subjective data set is comprised of 5000 text extracts from film reviews, whereas the objective set is built from 5000 extracts from film plot summaries. A similar approach is presented in Yu & Hatzivassiloglou (2003) where a Naïve Bayes classifier is trained to detect subjective documents and based on a data set of news sources known a priori to carry objective (news and business sections) and subjective (editorials and letters to the editor) content, with good results. The method is extended to sentence-level opinion detection by including parts of speech, sentence similarity measures and counting the presence of semantically oriented terms from a subset of manually labeled seed words. Results from Wiebe et al. (1999) also show positive results on Naïve Bayes classifiers trained a data set of subjective and objective documents, using features derived from part of speech, punctuation and syntax elements.

In sentiment classification, Pang et al. (2002) presents a series of experiments evaluating various classes of word vectors used to train supervised learning algorithms for classifying film reviews into positive or negative. The experiment achieves best results when using term unigrams rather than larger n-gram features, even though bigrams could capture sentiment encoded in the form of 2-term expressions such as "really good" or "much preferred". The poorer classification results could be attributed to the resultant increase in the model dimensionality causing a necessary increase in the volume of training data required to achieve good classification performance. Indeed, work from Cui et al. (2006) reports good results for word vectors with higher order n-grams where a significantly larger training data set comprised of over 320.000 product reviews was used. Another similar experiment based on word vectors and product reviews as the data set reports good results for tri-grams is seen in Dave et al. (2003).

Word vectors techniques applied to sentiment classification generate good classification performance results, but these results stay well below those obtained for topic-based document classification using the same techniques. Empirical performance metrics for text categorization surveyed in Sebastiani (2002) show how high

precision, high recall topic based classification can be achieved, based on results using well known experiment data sets. This observation, coupled with further analysis of opinion bearing documents suggests that sentiment information exists not only in document terms and needs to be captured by other means. For instance, one point highlighted in Pang et al. (2002) and often commented in the literature is the issue of *thwarted expectations*, as seen on the extract below:

This film should be brilliant. It sounds like a great plot, the actors are first grade... However, it can't hold up

In the above case a sentence contains a high number of positive statements, building up the expectation of a positive review, but the overall sentiment of the review is still negative, suggesting other factors such as the organization of terms within a sentence come into play when conveying opinions.

Term Disambiguation and Parts of Speech

Issues stemming from ambiguity in word meaning also arise on opinion mining tasks. In Wiebe and Mihalcea (2006), subjectivity detection is improved by adding a subjective feature to detect terms in need of disambiguation. This need has also been highlighted in Turney and Littman (2003) where corpus analysis may provide further clues for disambiguation of a term in relation to subjectivity and orientation. Classifying terms from a textual document into its grammatical roles, or parts of speech within a sentence has also been explored in opinion mining. A motivating factor is that detecting parts of speech can be considered a form of word disambiguation for the cases where word senses are associated with its grammatical use, such as noun or verb (Wiebe et al., 1999). Another factor is the finding that adjectives are considered good indicators of opinion information and have been seen to provide good correlation to sentiment orientation. In Pang et al. (2002), a study reports good results using only adjective words as features to perform sentiment classification using a machine learning method, however with poorer results than using words from the entire document as features. Parts of speech can also be applied as a pre-processing step for deriving features for opinion mining: In Yu and Hatzivassiloglou (2003) it is used as part of a feature set for performing sentiment classification on a data set of newswire articles, with similar approaches attempted in Pang et al. (2002), Salvetti et al. (2004) and Gamon (2004) on various data sets. In Turney (2002) a method that detects and scores patterns in part of speech is applied to derive features for sentiment classification, with a similar idea applied to opinion extraction for product features seen in Yi et al. (2003).

Writing Style and Document Structure

The subjective aspects of a document also have presented relationships to document structure and writing style, as in the example of thwarted expectations previously discussed in this section. One consideration is *term position* within the document is that it can be argued that the location of a specific opinion bearing term within a document can have greater or lesser influence in overall sentiment classification. If for instance this term is placed towards the end of the document, it may have a stronger correlation with the author's opinion as the end of the document is generally where concluding remarks are present. This aspect has been explored in the experiments presented in Pang et al. (2002), where it was seen to influence overall classification, even though in a small scale. Other attempts to model discourse structure can be seen in Devitt and Ahmad (2007) where a graph-based representation of text relationships is proposed based on linguistic models of lexical cohesion and other metrics extracted from the document, and in the annotation scheme using frames proposed in Somasundaran et al. (2008).

Detecting the existence of expressions that can increase, decrease or invert sentiment orientation of text is of importance to the accuracy of opinion mining techniques, as seen in the example:

There is just nothing original or intriguing about this film. It lacks real involvement with the audience.

In this case, overtly positive terms present in the sentence have their sentiment inverted by the negating terms "nothing" and "lacks". Predicting the correct sentiment conveyed by the text will require methods for detecting such cases. In Pang et al. (2002) negation detection is modeled as word vector features by adding a modifier prefix to negated terms, such as converting "great" into "NOT_great". Other modifiers such as "very", "just" or "extremely" were employed in conjunction with negation detection in a sentiment classification method exploring positive and negative term counting on Kennedy and Inkpen (2006). Several approaches have been studied for the detection of negation in the context of extracting information from medical records (Chapman, Bridewell, Hanbury, Cooper, & Buchanan, 2001; Huang & Lowe, 2007; Mutalik, Deshpande, & Nadkardi, 2001) of which, the *NegEx* algorithm (Chapman et al., 2001) is discussed in more details in this chapter.

Humoristic features like sarcasm and irony also do play a part in expressing author sentiment by indirectly evoking author's judgment on a given topic. These can be relatively more complex to identify, usually not depending on term sentiment alone but relying on word play, contrasts and domain knowledge. Other affective expressions like anger, joy and fear can also be closely related to author sentiment and therefore opinion (Strapparava, Valitutti, & Stock, 2006). Supervised approaches to humor detection have been investigated in Mihalcea and Strapparava

(2005) for a limited aspect of written humor, but with some success when experimented on a test data set.

Finally, it is to be expected that opinionated documents will also contain objective sections. On product reviews this may amount to sections describing the product features, as opposed to expressing an opinion on them. On film reviews the author may choose to present details of the plot, or the background of a certain actor to further support an argument. It can be speculated that the objective sections of an opinionated document in general will carry less opinion information than the subjective ones, and may cause a decrease in performance on overall document classification by providing little clues to overall opinion at the expense of a large volume of noise added to the model. A case where an actor dialogue is inserted by the author into a film review containing terms in opposition to authors opinion can be considered as an example. Similar issues have been observed in Pang et al. (2002), Kennedy et al. (2006) and Nigam et al. (2004). In Pang and Lee (2004) a subjectivity detection pre-processing step is used to filter out objective sentences before training a machine learning classifier for sentiment classification and obtained considerable improvements over a baseline classifier based solely on word vectors.

Opinion Lexicons

Intuitively, terms can be thought as a unit of opinion information within a document. The presence of words such as "good", "wonderful", or "disgusting" could be considered good indicators of whether the sentiment of a sentence or document is positive or negative. Lexicons of opinion bearing terms could provide readily available information for assisting the detection of sentiment, or making predictions on sentiment orientation. In addition, opinion lexicons can be applied in predictive tasks without a requirement for training data. For this reason these methods are often referred to as unsupervised learning approaches to opinion mining (Pang & Lee, 2008).

There are several opinion lexicons derived from the study of semantic orientation of words, and the motivation for opinion mining tasks. The most straightforward way to obtain a lexicon is by manually labeling terms as positive or negative with the assistance of human annotators. Manually built lexicons have been proposed in the literature, the General Enquirer being a popular one often used as a gold standard on research Stone et al. (1966), with similar resources used in Pang et al. (2002) and Wilson et al. (2005). Manually creating lexicons however is a time consuming effort and can also be subject to annotator bias. To mitigate these issues, *lexical induction* approaches have been proposed in the literature for generating opinion lexicons by expanding entries from a core of seed words known a priori to carry opinion information. The proposed approaches for induction involves exploring semantic term relationships or evaluating similarities in document corpora. In Hatzivassiloglou and McKeown (1997) it was demonstrated that it is possible to infer the orientation of adjectives from a set of core terms by examining co-occurrence patterns from a document corpus with a high degree of accuracy, thus offering a method for expanding an opinion lexicon beyond a manually labeled set of terms. In Turney and Littman (2003) a list of seed words is extended based on a proximity measure to other common terms extracted from a corpus based on querying an internet search engine for documents where terms co-occur.

Another popular approach is to derive opinion information from the WordNet database (Miller, Beckwith, Fellbaum, Gross, & Miller, 1990), typically by examining term relationships to a subset of core terms assumed to carry positive and negative opinion. This has been explored in Kamps et al. (2004) by evaluating synonym information from WordNet using the words "good" and "bad" as seed. Another semi supervised method of lexical induction leveraging graph patterns in WordNet is presented in Rao and Ravichandran (2009). A similar example of WordNet-based lexicon has been proposed for affective computing tasks (Strapparava et al., 2004).

Lexicons of opinion bearing terms applied to sentiment classification can be seen in manually assembled lists (Yi, Nasukawa, Bunescu, & Niblack, 2003; Pang et al., 2002). In Kennedy et al. (2006) a set of terms is derived from various manually built sources and applied to sentiment classification, with a similar approach used in Yang et al.(2007). Lexical induction based on proximity measures in document corpus applied to subjectivity detection can be seen in Turney and Littman (2003). Approaches that derive lexicons from WordNet are applied to subjectivity detection in Yu et al. (2003) and in sentiment classification experiments (Dave et al., 2003; Kim & Hovy, 2004; Salvetti et al., 2004).

WordNet Glosses

As noted in Rao and Ravichandran (2009), term relationships in the WordNet database form a highly disconnected graph, and thus expansion of opinion information from a core of seed words by examining semantic relationships such as synonyms and antonyms is bound to be restricted only to a subset of terms. To overcome this problem, information contained in term *glosses* – explanatory text accompanying each term – can be explored to infer term orientation, based on the assumption that a given term and the terms contained in its gloss are likely to indicate the same polarity. Further strengthening this point, Andreevskaia et al. (2006) presents a method for expansion of opinion terms based on WordNet glosses, and highlight that glosses text have a potentially low level of noise since they "are designed to match as close as possible the components of meaning of the word, have relatively standard style, grammar and syntactic structure". The approach is also seen in Esuli and Sebastiani (2005), where extending WordNet by exploring gloss information yields

positive accuracy improvements over a gold standard in comparison to some of the methods discussed in this section. This same approach is at the core of the *SentiWordNet* database (Esuli & Sebastiani, 2006).

SentiWordNet

SentiWordNet is a sentiment lexicon derived from WordNet by leveraging term relationships and term glosses. It is built via a semi supervised approach, which can easily be replicated to other WordNet-like lexicons, and also can easily be updated as future WordNet versions become available. Building on the strengths of WordNet's semantic relationships, SentiWordNet derives opinion scores for terms with a given meaning – or *synset* - using a semi-supervised method where only a very small portion of terms - the *paradigmatic* terms - are manually labeled, with the remaining database derived using an automated method. The process is summarized below:

1. Manually label a set of paradigmatic positive and negative WordNet terms known a priori to carry sentiment information.
2. Iteratively expand each label by adding terms from WordNet that are connected to already labeled terms by a relationship considered to reliably preserve term orientation. These are: "direct antonym", "attribute", "hyponymy" (pertains-to and derive-from), "also-see" and "similarity". Add terms in the "antonym" relationship to the opposing class.
3. Repeat steps 2 and 3 for a fixed number of iterations K.
4. For each labeled term from the previous steps, produce a word vector representation of its term glosses, and use it to train a committee of classifiers based on different algorithms on prediction of positive or negative sentiment for a given term. These classifiers are then used to determine the positive or negative

score of the remainder of WordNet terms yet unlabeled.

Steps 1-3 perform the expansion of the lexicon by inspecting WordNet's term relationships. Once this approach is exhausted, the glosses of the positive and negative terms found so far are used as training data for a text classification exercise on step 4. A committee of classifiers based on different algorithms is used to minimize algorithm bias.

Combining Approaches

Taking the view that different opinion mining methods capture different aspects of sentiment related information from a document, this survey of techniques is concluded by noting the contribution in the literature to research that combines different methods into a single predictive model. In Abbasi et al. (2008) a feature set using word vectors and writing style metrics is combined to produce a classifier with improved results over a baseline. In Yang et al. (2007) several lexicons of opinion term information, along with a database of low frequency terms are used to produce an overall document score to detect sentiment orientation of blog posts. In Mullen and Collier (2004) a combination of proximity metrics and term relationships extracted from a lexicon is used for classification of political opinions. Not only better feature sets can be generated from various sources, but the predictions of machine learning classifiers trained on distinct types of features can be combined. This can be done to address

induction bias from a specific classifier algorithm, and also to make better decisions from a pool of classification techniques, each leveraging different aspects of text. Applications of this idea to sentiment classification can be seen in Kennedy and Inkpen (2006), where a combination of the predictions from a classifier using word vectors and scores from counting terms from an opinion lexicon generate improved results over a baseline, with a similar approach reported in Yu and Hatzivassiloglou (2003).

SENTIMENT CLASSIFICATION WITH SENTIWORDNET

In the previous section lexicon-based approaches to opinion mining and results from experiments on both subjectivity detection and sentiment classification that use this type of resource have been discussed. The use of resources built by lexicon induction methods such as SentiWordNet could be of advantage on various instances. SentiWordNet could be applied to replace or extend manually built sentiment lexicons. In addition the building process used by SentiWordNet could be ported to languages other than English where resources similar to WordNet exist. Finally, by leveraging information in glosses SentiWordNet provides a more extensive coverage of sentiment terms in comparison to manually crafted lists. To illustrate the extent of term coverage obtained by SentiWordNet, Table 1 presents the number of terms marked with opinion information in the

Table 1. Coverage of Opinion Lexicons

Lexicon	Opinion Terms
General Enquirer[*] (Stone et al., 1966)	4216
Subjectivity Clues (Wilson et al., 2005)	7650 (out of 8221 terms)
Grefenstette et al. (2004)	2258
SentiWordNet (Esuli et al., 2006)	28431 (out of total 86994 WordNet terms)

(*) Latest version obtained from http://www.wjh.harvard.edu/~inquirer

database in comparison to some of the opinion lexicons seen in the literature.

Thus, validating automated methods that build lexicons such as SentiWordNet is an interesting research question, since such resources can be useful in improving the scalability of lexicon based opinion mining techniques. In this research, the authors wish to assess the use of SentiWord-Net as a tool for document-level sentiment classification.

Research Design

The research applies SentiWordNet to the classification of reviews using two distinct methods. To evaluate how the lexicon would compare with previous research using the same data set, the first experiment comprised the counting of positive and negative terms found in a document and determining sentiment orientation based on which class received the highest score. This approach is similar to the methods presented in Pang et al. (2002) and Kennedy and Inkpen (2006). Secondly, an alternative approach to term counting is proposed where a data set of features based on the calculation of SentiWordNet scores for different aspects of the document is built and used to train a machine learning sentiment classifier.

On both experiments, the "polarity" data set of film reviews presented in Pang and Lee (2004) will be used as the source of subjective documents. In this data set, the text for 1000 positive and 1000 negative film reviews was extracted from user feedback posted on the Internet Movie Database (http://www.imdb.com).

Each set of terms sharing the same meaning in SentiWordNet (*synsets*) is associated with two numerical scores ranging from 0 to 1, indicating the term's positive and negative orientation. The scores reflect the agreement amongst the classifier committee on the positive or negative label for a term, thus one distinct aspect of SentiWordNet is that it is possible for a term to have non-zero values for both positive and negative scores, according to the formula:

Pos. Score(term) + Neg. Score(term) + Objective Score(term) = 1   (1)

Where *Objective Score* is inferred from the positive and negative scores, and reflects Senti-WordNet's confidence in the term not carrying opinion information. The higher the score, the stronger the certainty of a term polarity assigned by the classifier committee. Terms in Senti-WordNet follow the categorization into parts of speech derived from WordNet, and therefore to correctly apply scores to terms, a part of speech tagger program was applied to the polarity data set. The *Stanford Part of Speech Tagger* described in Toutanova and Manning (2000) is used in the experiment.

Natural Language and Style Considerations

In the second part of the experiment, authors investigate how to derive features from Senti-WordNet taking into account metrics that can be extracted from the document by counting scores. One aspect evaluated by this experiment was the influence of applying weights to scores as a function of their position in the document. This would intuitively translate to the existence of areas within a document that tend to carry more opinion content, such as the end of the document where closing remarks reflecting the overall view of the author are likely to appear. Several adjusting schemes were attempted and the chosen method implements a linearly increasing weight adjustment to scores, as given by the formula below.

$$score_{adj} = score \frac{t_1}{T} C \qquad (2)$$

Table 2. Metrics derived from SentiWordNet

Metric Category	Features
Overall Scores	Sum of positive and negative scores found in SentiWordNet, for each part of speech. • Adjectives, adverbs and verbs were considered for the experiment. • A scoring function was applied to score calculation based on term position within the document.
Scores *Strength* per part of speech.	Ratio of overall score per total terms found, for each part of speech.
Ratios per part of speech.	Positive to negative ratio per part of speech.
Scores per document segment.	Ratios for the above metrics for each of N partitions of a document. • Each document was segmented into 10 partitions with equal number of terms.
Negation	Percentage of negated terms in document.

Where $score_{adj}$ reflects the adjusted score for a original term *score* extracted from SentiWordNet, with C being a constant numeric value, and t_i the position of the given term t relative to the total of terms T in the document.

Negation detection also plays an important element of the research. The authors have implemented a version of the *NegEx* algorithm (Chapman et al., 2001), which scans sentences based on a database of pre defined negation expressions. The algorithm maintains three distinct lists, depending on the scope of the negation: expressions that modify preceding terms, subsequent terms and pseudo-negation expressions with no effect on term polarity.

SentiWordNet Features

SentiWordNet scores were then applied to terms found according to part of speech, with additional document level metrics calculated. For each document, the total sum of positive and negative scores for each part of speech was computed. An indication of opinion strength is derived by dividing the total score for each part of speech by the number of occurrences. Intuitively this would measure whether authors use words that carry stronger opinion content to express their views. In addition the document was partitioned into a fixed number of segments with equal number of

terms, and scores calculated for each segment. By experimentation, using a total of 10 segments was found to be best suited to the size of documents in this data set. The final data set was generated from the source documents by extracting the above information with SentiWordNet. A total of 95 distinct features were generated, which are summarized in Table 2.

The above set of features was used to train a supervised learning algorithm to classify reviews in positive or negative, using algorithm implementations available in the *RapidMiner* (Mierswa, Wurst, Klinkenberg, Scholz, & Euler, 2006) data mining package.

Results

This section presents the research results for the two proposed approaches to sentiment classification of film reviews using SentiWordNet.

Term Counting

SentiWordNet scores were calculated as positive and negative terms which are found on each document, and used to determine sentiment orientation by assigning the document to the class with the highest score. This method yielded an overall accuracy of **65.85%**, with results detailed in Table 3.

Table 3. SentiWordNet results for Term Counting

Class	Positive	Negative
Predicted Positive	576	259
Predicted Negative	424	741
Total	1000	1000
Class Recall	57.6%	74.1%
Class Precision	68.98%	63.76%

Table 4. Accuracy results using features from SentiWordNet

Experiment	Accuracy Results
SentiWordNet Features using Support Vector Machine.	67.40%
- Including Linear Weight Scoring Function.	68.00%
- Including Negation Detection and Linear Weight Scoring.	68.50%
- Including Negation Detection, Linear Scoring, Feature Selection.	**69.35%**

SentiWordNet Features

The results for the sentiment classification experiment were measured according to classification accuracy. Initially, the features generated by SentiWordNet were used to train three different classifiers. Using 3-fold cross-validation, the best results were obtained by Support Vector Machines (67.4%), followed by Naïve Bayes (63.02%) and Nearest Neighbor (60.2%) algorithms. The initial results obtained with Support Vector Machine classifier were then improved by adding negation detection, the scoring weight function and a feature selection refinement step. Table 4 presents results for each stage of the experiment, with best accuracy results of 69.35%.

Feature selection was performed by progressively removing features that have the weakest correlation to the positive or negative label being trained according to a score based on feature information gain in relation to the predicted label. The final data set included 92 of the 95 features originally generated.

Findings

Table 5 illustrates how SentiWordNet was compared with other published results in the area using based on similar approaches that use opinion lexicons:

Term counting using SentiWordNet remains close to other results using manually built lexicons.

Table 5. Accuracy Comparisons

Method	Accuracy Results
SentiWordNet Term Counting (in this research)	**65.85%**
SentiWordNet Scores used as Features (in this research).	**69.35%**
Positive/Negative Word Lists (Pang et al., 2002).	69.00%
Term counting from General Enquirer Dictionary + Linguistic Features (Kennedy & Inkpen, 2006).	67.80%

In Pang et al. (2002) the results are based on term counting from a manually built word list for the domain of film reviews, whereas results from Kennedy and Inkpen (2006) follow the same principle, but leverage a combined lexicon and take into account *intensifier* and *diminishing* terms such as "very" and "seldom". The second method using SentiWordNet features and a supervised learning algorithm yielded improvements over the basic term counting approach. In addition, results seen in Table 4 indicate improvements can be achieved by applying linguistic methods such as negation detection, and by taking position of a term within the document into account during term scoring. Feature selection also played an important part in obtaining better results by re-moving uncorrelated features from the training process. These improvements helped the quality of final accuracy results when used in conjunction. Amongst the least correlated features are metrics on the number of negated terms for a document, suggesting the use of negating expressions in the narrative of a review is equally likely to appear on both positive and negative instances.

Misclassifications

Evaluating misclassified entries based on this method indicated certain patterns in writing style where term sentiment alone may be insufficient to correctly detect opinion orientation of a docu-ment. The concluding remarks of a film review presented on the below extract show that on bad reviews authors may choose to highlight good but relatively less important aspects of a film in order to provide a more balanced point of view:

... it looks great, it has a few notable performances and I suppose it's pretty well directed in a purely technical way.

Likewise, to obtain the same effect certain positive reviews displayed a somewhat restrained praise:

the only downfall of the opening sequence is the editing style used… it's choppy, slow motion which is unsettling and distracting.

The phenomenon of *thwarted expectations* discussed in Pang et al. (2002) can also affect the performance of this method. On those cases, sentences building up expectation would employ the number of terms with positive orientation whereas the conveyed sentiment is negative, thus affecting conclusions made by a classifier using data based on term polarity. In addition, the use of colloquial language and expressions where no opinion information exists; disambiguation of WordNet terms with more than one meaning; inaccuracies in the assignment of part of speech tags and the correct detection of named entities such as actor and film names were identified as contributing factors to misclassifications. Finally, the use of glosses as a source of information for detecting positive or negative opinion in terms may generate certain inaccuracies as shown in the example used in Table 6.

In this case both synsets contain generally positive SentiWordNet scores; however consider this term's use on the extract: *"the action in Ar-mageddon is so over the top, nonstop, and too ludicrous for words"*. It can be argued that the second synset term should contain a negative orientation, given its association with synonym terms such as "farcical" and "idiotic". However SentiWordNet assigned positive scores to this term, on the basis the text from the synset gloss is more likely to be associated with a positive oriented term than a negative one. Recalling that scores are expanded by applying a classification algorithm based on terms extracted from synset glosses, therefore terms such as "exuberance" and "clown" and the somewhat ambiguous "laugh-able" could be influencing the construction method in assigning incorrect scores. The depen-dence of SentiWordNet scores on term glosses could be a limiting factor in the accuracy of term

Table 6. Glosses in SentiWordNet

Term	Gloss	SentiWordNet Score (Pos, Neg)
Ludicrous	(adj) farcical, ludicrous, ridiculous (broadly or extravagantly humorous; resembling farce) "the wild farcical exuberance of a clown"; "ludicrous green hair"	(0.5, 0.125)
Ludicrous	(adj) absurd, cockeyed, derisory, idiotic, laughable, ludicrous, nonsensical, preposterous, ridiculous (incongruous; inviting ridicule) "the absurd excuse that the dog ate his homework"; "that's a cockeyed idea"; "ask a nonsensical question and get a nonsensical answer"; "a contribution so small as to be laughable"; "it is ludicrous to call a cottage a mansion"; "a preposterous attempt to turn back the pages of history"; "her conceited assumption of universal interest in her rather dull children was ridiculous"	(0.625, 0)

scores, and the overall classification accuracy of this method.

FUTURE RESEARCH DIRECTIONS

Findings from this research highlight certain limitations of employing lexicons on predictive opinion mining: opinion is not always conveyed directly, and often is subject to noise from other non relevant aspects present in the document. Further research on exploring linguistic methods that accurately detect such cases can assist on improving accuracy results. In addition, exploring the detection of patterns on text such as in the thwarted expectation example may help improving results of lexicon based approaches. It is also possible that expanding opinion lexicons beyond single terms and into more elaborate expressions may assist in detecting more instances where sentiment is being conveyed. Several opinion lexicons and lexicon generation approaches were surveyed in this research, and a comparison of the performance of these lexicons on opinion mining tasks could help in better understanding their strengths and weaknesses, and how they can be used together. This could be particularly beneficial in overcoming some of the limitations seen in SentiWordNet's reliance on glosses. Lexicon based methods can also be applied as a component of sentiment classification approaches that combine more than one source of information, as seen in Kennedy et al. (2006) and Mullen and Collier (2004) and further

developments in these methods could be obtained from the development of improved lexicons.

Progressing from the current research, another important line of enquiry concerns cross-domain sentiment classification, where techniques are designed to work in a domain-independent fashion and thus can be applied to a wider range of documents, possibly on cases where little or no training data is available. Techniques that apply opinion lexicons such as our method may be suitable since in principle they do not depend on domain information, but rely on a priori set of terms known to carry opinion bias. The research also shows that considerable improvements were achieved over the baseline by applying refinements such as feature selection and outlier removal to machine learning classification algorithm. Other encouraging results were reported in Abbasi et al. (2008) and indeed, a more comprehensive study of feature selection, feature generation, outlier analysis, and classification parameter tuning could improve results even further and provide a better understanding of the effect of these refinements to predictive opinion mining problems.

CONCLUSION

Opinion mining is an emerging field posing exciting research challenges. Its importance to knowledge discovery is clear as opinion adds a new dimension to the information that can be extracted from textual data, and has the potential of improving an organization's ability to create new knowledge and users to make better informed decisions. The variety of ways in which opinions can be conveyed in natural language makes the methods for detection and classification of opinions a difficult problem for human annotators and computers alike. This same richness means developments in both natural language processing and in data driven machine learning methods will have important roles to play as this technology evolves.

In this chapter the authors have presented the research field of opinion mining, surveying its potential applications and state of the art research with particular attention to research related to predictive opinion mining tasks. The survey also highlights the role of opinion lexicons and how they have been applied in previous research, and presented lexicons built by semi automated induction methods, such as the SentiWordNet lexical resource.

The research assessed the use of the SentiWordNet opinion lexicon in the task of sentiment classification of film reviews. Results obtained by simple word counting were similar to other results employing manual lexicons, indicating SentiWordNet performs well when compared with manual resources on this task. Using SentiWordNet as a source of features for a supervised learning scheme has shown improved results over pure term counting suggesting lexicons could be a good source for feature generation into predictive models. The relatively low dimensionality of a data set used in this approach - less than 100 features compared to several thousand typically seen on word vector approaches - could lead to more attractive models for real world applications with time critical constraints. Finally, the results of the study indicates how linguistic pre-processing plays an important role in lexicon based approaches, and also revealed opportunities where further refinements in this area may yield gains in classification accuracies.

REFERENCES

Abbasi, A., Chen, H., & Salem, A. (2008). Sentiment Analysis in Multiple Languages: Feature Selection for Opinion Classification in Web Forums. *ACM Transactions on Information Systems, 26*(3), 1–34. doi:10.1145/1361684.1361685

Ahmad, K., Cheng, D., & Almas, Y. (2006). Multilingual Sentiment Analysis of Financial News Streams. In *Proceedings of the 1st International Conference on Grid in Finance*. Palermo.

Akehurst, G. (2009). User generated content: The use of Blogs for Tourism Organizations and Tourism Consumers. *Service Business, 3*(1), 51–61. doi:10.1007/s11628-008-0054-2

Andreevskaya, A., & Bergler, S. (2006). Mining WordNet for Fuzzy Sentiment: Sentiment Tag Extraction from WordNet Glosses. In *Proceedings of EACL*.

Baccianella, S., Esuli, A., & Sebastiani, F. (2009). Multi-facet Rating of Product Reviews. In *Proceedings of the 31th European Conference on IR Research on Advances in Information Retrieval*. Toulouse, France.

Chapman, W., Bridewell, W., Hanbury, P., Cooper, G., & Buchanan, B. (2001). Evaluation of Negation Phrases in Narrative Clinical Report, In *Proceedings of 2001 AMIA Symposium*. (pp 105-109).

Cui, H., Mittal, V., & Datar, M. (2006). Comparative Experiments on Sentiment Classification for Online Product Reviews. In *Proceedings of the National Conference on Artificial Intelligence* (pp. 1265-1270). AAAI Press.

Dave, K., Lawrence, S., & Pennock, D. (2003). Mining the Peanut Gallery: Opinion Extraction and Semantic Classification in Product Reviews. In *Proceedings of the 12th International Conference on the World Wide Web - ACM WWW2003*. Budapest, Hungary.

Dellarocas, C. (2003). The Digitization of Word of Mouth: Promise and Challenges of Online Feedback Mechanisms. *Management Science.* Institute for Operations Research and Management Sciences, 1407-1424.

Devitt, A., & Ahmad, K. (2007). Sentiment Polarity Identification in Financial News: A Cohesion Based Approach. In *Proceedings of the 45th Annual Meeting of the Association of Computational Linguistics* (pp. 984–991).Prague, Czech Republic.

Esuli, A., & Sebastiani, F. (2005). Determining the Semantic Orientation of terms through Gloss Classification. In *Proceedings of the 14th ACM International Conference on Information and Knowledge Management* (pp. 617-624). Bremen, Germany.

Esuli, A., & Sebastiani, F. (2006). SentiWordNet: A Publicly Available Lexical Resource for Opinion Mining. In *Proceedings of the International Conference on Language Resources and Evaluation (LREC).* Genoa.

Farhoomand, A., & Drudy, D. H. (2002). Managerial Information Overload. *Communications of the ACM, 45*(10), 127–131. doi:10.1145/570907.570909

Fayyad, U., Piatetsky-Shapiro, G., & Smyth, P. (1996, November). The KDD Process for Extracting useful Knowledge from Volumes of Data. *Communications of the ACM, 11*(39), 27–34. doi:10.1145/240455.240464

Gamon, M. (2004). Sentiment Classification on Customer Feedback Data: Noisy Data, Large Feature Vectors, and the Role of Linguistic Analysis. In *Proceedings of the 20th International Conference on Computational Linguistics* (pp. 841). Geneva, Switzerland.

Glance, N., Hurst, M., Nigam, K., Siegler, M., Stockton, R., & Tomokiyo, T. (2005). Deriving Marketing Intelligence from Online Discussion. In *Proceedings of the 11th ACM SIGKDD International Conference on Knowledge Discovery in Data Mining* (pp. 419 – 428).

Grefenstette, G., Qu, Y., Shanahan, J., & Evans, D. (2004). Coupling Niche Browsers and Affect Analysis for an Opinion Mining Application. In. *Proceedings of the RIAO, 2004*, 186–194.

Hatzivassiloglou, V., & McKeown, K. (1997). Predicting the Semantic Orientation of Adjectives. In *Proceedings of the 35th Annual Meeting of the Association of Computational Linguistics (ACL'97)* (pp. 174-181). Madrid, Spain.

Horrigan, J. (2008). Online Shopping. *Pew Internet and American Life Project – Research Report.*

Huang, Y., & Lowe, H. (2007). A Novel Hybrid Approach to Automated Negation Detection in Clinical Radiology Reports. *Journal of the American Medical Informatics Association,* 14(3), May/June 2007.

Jin, X., Li, Y., Mah, T., & Tong, J. (2007). Sensitive Webpage Classification for Content Advertising. In *Proceedings of the 1st International Workshop on Data Mining and Audience Intelligence for Advertising* (pp. 28-33).

Kamps, J., Marx, M., Mokken, R. J., & De Rijke, M. (2004). Using WordNet to measure Semantic Orientation of Adjectives. In *Proceedings of the 4th International Conference on Language Resources and Evaluation (LREC 2004)* (pp. 1115-1118).

Kaufer, D. (2000) Flaming: A White Paper. *Carnegie Mellon Dept. of English.*

Kennedy, A., & Inkpen, D. (2006). Sentiment Classification of Movie Reviews Using Contextual Valence Shifters. *Computational Intelligence, 22,* 110–125. doi:10.1111/j.1467-8640.2006.00277.x

Kim, S., & Hovy, E. (2004). Determining the Sentiment of Opinions. In *Proceedings of Conference on Computational Linguistics (COLING-04)* (pp.1367-1373). Geneva, Switzerland.

König, A. C., & Brill, E. (2006). Reducing the Human Overhead in Text Categorization. In *Proceedings of the 12th ACM SIGKDD International Conference on Knowledge Discovery and Data Mining - KDD '06* (pp. 598-603). Philadelphia, PA, USA.

Koppel, M., & Shtrimberg, I. (2004). Good news or bad news? Let the market decide. *AAAI Spring Symposium on Exploring Attitude and Affect in Text*, 86-88. Springer.

Mierswa, I., Wurst, M., Klinkenberg, R., Scholz, M., & Euler, T. (2006). YALE: Rapid Prototyping for Complex Data Mining Tasks. In *Proceedings of the 12th ACM SIGKDD International Conference on Knowledge Discovery and Data Mining (KDD-06)*.

Mihalcea, R., & Strapparava, C. (2005). Making Computers Laugh: Investigations in Automatic Humour Recognition. In *Joint Conference on Human Language Technology/Empirical Methods in Natural Language Processing (HLT/EMNLP)*.

Miller, G. A., Beckwith, R., Fellbaum, C., Gross, D., & Miller, K. J. (1990). Introduction to Wordnet: An On-line Lexical Database. *International Journal of Lexicography, 3*(4), 235–244. doi:10.1093/ijl/3.4.235

Mullen, T., & Collier, N. (2004). Sentiment Analysis using Support Vector Machines with diverse Information Sources. In *Proceedings of EMNLP*.

Mullen, T., & Malouf, R. (2006). A Preliminary Investigation into Sentiment Analysis of Informal Political Discourse. In *Proceedings of the AAAI Symposium on Computational Approaches to Analyzing Weblogs* (pp.159-162).

Mutalik, P., Deshpande, A., & Nadkardi, P. (2001). Use of General-Purpose Negation Detection to Augment Concept Indexing of Medical Documents. *Journal of the American Medical Informatics Association, 8*(6).

Nigam, K., & Hurst, M. (2004). Towards a Robust Metric of Opinion. In *AAAI Spring Symposium on Exploring Attitude and Affect in Text.* (pp. 598 – 603).

Pang, B., & Lee, L. (2004). A Sentimental Education: Sentiment Analysis Using Subjectivity Summarization Based on Minimum Cuts. In *Proceedings of the ACL*.

Pang, B., & Lee, L. (2005). Seeing Stars: Exploiting Class Relationships for Sentiment Categorization with Respect to Rating Scales. In *Proceedings of the 43rd Meeting of the ACL* (pp. 115-124).

Pang, B., & Lee, L. (2008). Opinion Mining and Sentiment Analysis. *Foundations and Trends in Information Retrieval, 2*(1-2), 1–135. doi:10.1561/1500000011

Pang, B., Lee, L., & Vaithyanathan, S. (2002). Thumbs up? Sentiment Classification using Machine Learning Techniques. In *Proceedings of EMNLP*.

Rao, D., & Ravichandran, D. (2009). Semi-Supervised Polarity Lexicon Induction. In *Proceedings of the 12th Conference of the European Chapter of the ACL* (pp. 675-682). Athens, Greece.

Salton, G., Wong, A., & Yang, C. S. (1975). A Vector Space Model for Automatic Indexing Communications. *ACM, 11*(18), 613–620. doi:10.1145/361219.361220

Salvetti, F., Lewis, S., & Reichenbach, C. (2004). Automatic Opinion Polarity Classification of Movie Reviews. *Colorado Research in Linguistics, June 2004, 17 (1). Boulder, CO: University of Colorado.*

Sebastiani, F. (2002). Machine Learning in Automated Text Categorization. *ACM Computing Surveys, 34*, 1–47. doi:10.1145/505282.505283

Somasundaran, S., Ruppenhofer, J., & Wiebe, J. (2008). Discourse level Opinion Relations: An Annotation Study. In *SIGdial Workshop on Discourse and Dialogue*.

Stone, P. J., Dunphy, D. C., Smith, M. S., & Oglivie, D. M. (1966). *The General Enquirer: A Computer Approach to Content Analysis*. Cambridge, MA: MIT Press.

Strapparava, C., & Valitutti, A. (2004). WordNet-Affect: An Affective Extension of WordNet. In *Proceedings of the 4th International Conference on Language Resources and Evaluation*.

Strapparava, C., Valitutti, A., & Stock, O. (2006). The Affective Weight of Lexicon. In *Proceedings of the Fifth International Conference on Language Resources and Evaluation*.

Toutanova, K., & Manning, C. (2000). Enriching the Knowledge Sources Used in a Maximum Entropy Part-of-Speech Tagger. In *Proceedings of the Joint SIGDAT Conference on Empirical Methods in Natural Language Processing and Very Large Corpora (EMNLP/VLC-2000)* (pp. 63-70).

Turney, P. (2002). Thumbs up or Thumbs down? Sentiment Orientation Applied to Unsupervised Classification of Reviews. In *Proceedings of the 40th Annual Meeting of the Association of Computational Linguistics – ACL*.

Turney, P., & Littman, M. (2003). Measuring Praise and Criticism: Inference of Semantic Orientation from Association. *ACM Transactions on Information Systems, 4*(21), 315–346. doi:10.1145/944012.944013

Wiebe, J. (1990). Identifying Subjective Characters in Narrative. In *Proceedings of the 13th Conference on Computational linguistics*. Helsinki, Finland, Wiebe, J., & Mihalcea, R. (2006). Word Sense and Subjectivity. In *Proceedings of the 21st International ACL Conference on Computational Linguistics* (pp. 1065-1072).

Wiebe, J., Bruce, R., Martin, M., Wilson, T., & Bell, M. (2004). Learning Subjective Language. *Computational Linguistics, 30*(3), 277–308. doi:10.1162/0891201041850885

Wiebe, J., Bruce, R., Martin, M., Wilson, T., & Bell, M. (2004). Learning Subjective Language. *Computational Linguistics, 30*(3), 277–308. doi:10.1162/0891201041850885

Wiebe, J., Bruce, R., & O'Hara, T. (1999). Development and Use of Gold-Standard Data Set for Subjectivity Classifications. In *Proceedings of the 37th Annual Meeting of the Association of Computational Linguistics – ACL-99* (pp. 246-253).

Wilson, T., Wiebe, J., & Hoffmann, P. (2005). Recognizing Contextual Polarity in Phrase-Level Sentiment Analysis. In *Proceedings of HLT/EMNLP*. Vancouver, Canada.

Yang, K., Yu, N., & Zhang, H. (2007). WIDIT in TREC-2007 Blog Track: Combining Lexicon-based Methods to Detect Opinionated Blogs. In *Proceedings of the 16th Text Retrieval Conference (TREC 2007)*.

Yi, J., Nasukawa, T., Bunescu, R., & Niblack, W. (2003). Sentiment Analyzer: Extracting Sentiments about a given topic using Natural Language Processing Techniques. In *Third IEEE International Conference on Data Mining, ICDM 2003* (pp.427-434).

Yu, H., & Hatzivassiloglou, V. (2003). Towards Answering Opinion Questions: Separating Facts from Opinions and Identifying Polarity in Sentences. In *Proceedings of the 2003 Conference on Empirical Methods in Natural Language Processing* (pp. 129-136).

KEY TERMS AND DEFINITIONS

Knowledge Discovery: Research field in computer science concerned with devising processes and computational methods aiming at automatically detecting novel, useful patterns in very large volumes of data where the use of traditional data analysis techniques relying on human inspection alone are not feasible or too costly.

Opinion Lexicon: A lexical resource in a given language, typically in the form of a machine readable database that categorizes terms according to their subjective content and opinion polarity.

Opinion Mining: Research area concerned with the application of computational methods to the treatment of subjectivity in text. Opinion mining is a cross disciplinary area that leverages and contributes to advances in text mining, natural language processing and machine learning.

Sentiment Classification: In opinion mining, refers to the task of predicting if a given piece of text, known *a priori* to be subjective, conveys positive, negative or neutral sentiment by applying automatic computational methods derived from text mining approaches, or by leveraging natural language processing techniques.

SentiWordNet: An opinion lexicon for the English language built upon the WordNet database of terms and relationships. SentiWordNet is built by expanding from a core of terms known to carry a priori sentiment information (e.g. "good", "bad", etc.) by using WordNet's term relationships and each term's explanatory text, or *glosses*.

Subjectivity Detection: In opinion mining, refers to application of predictive methods to determine the degree of which a given piece of text is subjective.

Subjectivity: In text, refers to the use of language for the expression of private states of mind such as opinions, judgement, evaluations and speculations.

WordNet: WordNet is a database of terms and relationships for the English language, where words are grouped into sets of similar meaning (synsets), and may contain semantic associations such as synonym, antonym, "is-a", etc.

Chapter 14
Analysis and Integration of Biological Data:
A Data Mining Approach using Neural Networks

Diego Milone
Universidad Nacional del Litoral & National Scientific and Technical Research Council, Argentina

Georgina Stegmayer
Universidad Tecnologica Nacional & National Scientific and Technical Research Council, Argentina

Matías Gerard
Universidad Nacional del Litoral & Universidad Tecnologica Nacional & National Scientific and Technical Research Council, Argentina

Laura Kamenetzky
Institute of Biotechnology, INTA & National Scientific and Technical Research Council, Argentina

Mariana López
Institute of Biotechnology, INTA & National Scientific and Technical Research Council, Argentina

Fernando Carrari
Institute of Biotechnology, INTA & National Scientific and Technical Research Council, Argentina

ABSTRACT

The volume of information derived from post genomic technologies is rapidly increasing. Due to the amount of involved data, novel computational methods are needed for the analysis and knowledge discovery into the massive data sets produced by these new technologies. Furthermore, data integration is also gaining attention for merging signals from different sources in order to discover unknown relations. This chapter presents a pipeline for biological data integration and discovery of a priori unknown relationships between gene expressions and metabolite accumulations. In this pipeline, two standard clustering methods are compared against a novel neural network approach. The neural model provides

DOI: 10.4018/978-1-60960-067-9.ch014

a simple visualization interface for identification of coordinated patterns variations, independently of the number of produced clusters. Several quality measurements have been defined for the evaluation of the clustering results obtained on a case study involving transcriptomic and metabolomic profiles from tomato fruits. Moreover, a method is proposed for the evaluation of the biological significance of the clusters found. The neural model has shown a high performance in most of the quality measures, with internal coherence in all the identified clusters and better visualization capabilities.

INTRODUCTION

Nowadays, the biology field is in the middle of a data explosion. A series of technical advances in recent years has increased the amount of data that biologists can record about different aspects of an organism at the genomic, transcriptomic and proteomic levels (Keedwell & Narayanan, 2005).

Nowadays, the discipline of computational biology has allowed biologists to make full use of the advances in computer science and statistics in understanding this information. Due to the amount and nature of the biological data involved (such as noisy and missing data), novel computational methodologies are needed for properly analysing it. Moreover, as the volume of data continues to grow at a high speed, new challenges appear, such as the need to extract information that was not previously known from these databases to supplement current knowledge. For example, the discovery of hidden patterns of gene expression in microarray and metabolite profiles from plants of economic importance to agro-biotechnology, is a current challenge because the use of any algorithm for pattern recognition suffers from the so-called curse of dimensionality. In addition, data integration is also gaining attention given the need for merging and extracting knowledge from signals of different sources and nature. Visualization of results is also an important issue for the understanding and interpretation of hidden relationships (Tasoulis, Plagianakos, & Vrahatis, 2008).

Bioinformatics has evolved over time, mainly from the development of data mining techniques and their application to automatic prediction and discovery of classes, two key tasks for the analysis and interpretation of gene expression data on microarrays (Polanski & Kimmel, 2007). The prediction of classes uses the available information on the expression profiles and the known characteristics of the sets of data or experiments to build classifiers for future data. On the contrary, in the case of classes discovery, data are explored from the viewpoint of the existence or not of unknown relations and a hypothesis to explain them is formulated (Golub et al., 1999). Among class discovery techniques, the Hierarchical Clustering (HC) algorithm is the most commonly used technique in biological data. It is a deterministic method based on a pairwise distance matrix. This algorithm establishes small groups of genes/conditions that have a common expression pattern and then constructs a dendrogram, sequentially, on the basis of the distances between feature vectors. Clusters are obtained by pruning the tree at some level, and the number of clusters is controlled by deciding at which level of the hierarchy of the tree the splitting is performed (Tasoulis et al., 2008). Regarding non-hierarchical algorithms, the distances are calculated from a predetermined number of clusters and the genes are iteratively placed in different groups until minimizing each cluster internal spread. The more representative algorithm of this type is the k-means (KM) algorithm (Duda & Hart, 2003).

NEW TRENDS

One of the current trends in the field is the integration of two types of biological data: metabolic profiles and transcriptional data from microarrays, with the objective of finding hidden relations among them and to infer new knowledge about the biological processes that involve them (Bino et al., 2004). For example, a problem of interest is how to evaluate the presence of genes associated with regulatory mechanisms in metabolic pathways. This is especially important in plants due to the availability of primary and secondary metabolites and the wide variety of genes associated with these pathways. In particular the integration of data of transcriptome and metabolome in plants, correlating gene transcription profiles with variations profiles of a large number of non-protein molecules, can be used for the identification of changes not reflected in the plant morphology (Carrari et al., 2006). This allows having a snapshot of the metabolic pathways from the changes in transcription profiles and the simultaneous analysis of metabolites and their variation in response to a given condition. A metabolic network can be formally defined as a collection of objects and the relationships between them. The objects can be chemical compounds (metabolites), biochemical reactions, enzymes (proteins) and genes. The identification of links between genes, proteins and reactions is not a trivial task, and is of particular interest for the reconstruction of a metabolic network, which could be involved in obtaining a final product (for example tomato plant) with certain desired characteristics (Lacroix, Cottret, Thebault, & Sagot, 2008).

The analysis of large biological datasets resulting from the different "omics" fields (Genomics, proteomics, transcriptomics and metabolomics) is usually focussed on three main goals (Lindon et al., 2007):

1. Determine a significant difference between groups related to an effect of interest.
2. Visualize differences, trends and relationships between samples and variables.
3. Detect which components (for example, genes) are responsible for the changes.

The new challenges that have arisen in computational biology indicates the need for the development of new data mining techniques to overcome the limitations of existing ones in satisfying these three points (Polanski & Kimmel, 2007). Among the current proposals in the area, soft computing tools have been mentioned recently (Keedwell & Narayanan, 2005), in particular artificial neural networks (Kelemen, Abraham, & Chen, 2008; Tasoulis, Plagianakos, & Vrahatis, 2008). Specifically within artificial neural network models, Self-Organizing Maps (SOM) (Kohonen, 1982; Kohonen et al., 2005) have proven to be adequate for handling large data volume and projecting them in low dimensional maps while showing, at the same time, hidden relationships. In fact, SOMs have been applied to analyse expression profiles in several systems biology studies lately, and it was one of the first machine learning techniques used for these kind of analysis (Quackenbush, 2001).

In Hirai et al. (2004) a SOM model is proposed for the integrated analysis of *Arabidopsis thaliana* metabolome and transcriptome datasets. A related work in Yano et al. (2006) shows that the clustering performance of SOM helped in the elucidation of a metabolic mechanism responding to sulfur deficiency. The results showed that functionally related genes were clustered in the same or neighbour neurons. The examination of each cluster "by hand" helped in the deduction of putative functions of genes involved in glucosinolate biosynthesis. However, the experiments and the model were specifically set for following the evolution of a previously-established condition (sulfur and nitrogen deficiency) over time, and therefore it was used for hypotheses corroboration rather than knowledge discovery. However, in most cluster analyses, groups are not known *a priori* and the interest is focused on finding them without the help of a response variable, like in Saito et al. (2008).

In many cases, the biological experiment does not involve time evolution of a particular condition, but the interest focuses on the study of the differences among several plant genomes. It may involve an original genome that has been modified by introgression lines of wild species alleles (cisgenic plants) or transgenic plants over expressing a gene of interest. An *Introgression Line* (IL) is defined as a genotype that carries genetic material derived from a similar species, for example a "wild" relative. Or the focus may be the identification of meaningful biological points (markers) that are hidden within large-scale analytical intensity measurements from metabolomic experiments. For these tasks, many software computing tools implementing the use of SOMs have appeared lately, such as Kaever et al. (2009), which performs data mining on intensity-based profiles using one-dimensional self-organizing maps; or (Tokimatsu et al., 2005) which is a web-based tool for representing quantitative data for individual transcripts and/or metabolites on plant metabolic pathway maps.

Differently from the previous mentioned approaches, in this chapter a methodology for finding relationships among introgression lines compared to a wild type control, instead of data evolving over time is presented. An important contribution of this chapter consists in the presentation of a pipeline for biological data pre-processing, integration and mining towards the discovery of metabolic pathways. Furthermore, the proposed methodology is oriented towards discovering new and unknown relationships among transcriptional and metabolic data, instead of verifying an *a priori* condition or performing a guided analysis. The authors propose the use of different kind of measurements for evaluating the quality of the clusters found by different clustering techniques. In the case of the neural clustering (Stegmayer, Milone, Kamenetzky, Lopez, & Carrari, 2009), the model also provides a simple visualization interface for the identification of co-expressed and co-accumulated genes and metabolites. The focus is on the easy identification of groups of different kinds of patterns, independently from the number of formed clusters. This kind of analysis

may be useful for inference of unknown metabolic pathways involving the grouped data.

This chapter is organized as follows. First, a brief review of standard clustering algorithms is given. Second, the most relevant quality measures are presented. In the next section, the pipeline for integration and analysis of introgression lines will be detailed. In this sequence of steps, visualization capabilities, quality measures and biological assessments will be shown for a case of study involving transcriptional and metabolic data of tomato fruits. Finally, the chapter ends with the conclusion.

BACKGROUND

Data mining methods may be categorized as either supervised or unsupervised. In unsupervised methods, no target variable is identified. Instead, the data mining algorithm searches for patterns and structure among all the variables. The most common unsupervised data mining method is clustering (Olson & Delen, 2008). Clustering refers to the grouping of records, observations or cases into classes of similar objects. A cluster is a collection of records that are similar to one another and dissimilar to records in other clusters. The clustering task does not try to classify, estimate or predict the value of a target variable. Instead, clustering algorithms seek to segment the entire data set into relatively homogeneous subgroups or clusters, where the similarity of the records within the cluster is maximized, and the similarity to records outside this cluster is minimized (Larose, 2005).

The result of clustering can be expressed in different ways. The groups that are identified may be exclusive so that any instance belongs to only one group. Or they may be overlapping so that an instance may fall into several groups. Furthermore, they may be probabilistic (or fuzzy), where an instance belongs to each group with a certain

Figure 1. Agglomerative Hierarchical Clustering (HC)

Data:
    X: dataset
    k: number of clusters
Results:
    Ω: clusters
    W: centroids
begin
    $N \leftarrow \text{size}(X)$
    Start with N singleton clusters: $\mathbf{w}_i = \mathbf{x}_i, \quad i = 1, \ldots, N$
    Calculate the proximity matrix: $\delta_{ij} = \|\mathbf{w}_i - \mathbf{w}_j\|, \quad 0 < i \neq j \leq N$
    while $N > k$ **do**
        Search the minimal distance $i^*j^* = \arg\min_{\forall i, \forall j}\{\delta_{ij}\}$
        Combine clusters Ω_{i^*} and Ω_{j^*} into a new cluster Ω_{ij^*}
        Remove clusters Ω_{i^*} and Ω_{j^*} from δ
        Update δ by computing the distances to and from Ω_{ij^*}
        Update clusters in the HC tree
        $N \leftarrow N - 1$
    $\Omega \leftarrow$ patterns in the HC tree branches at top level reached
    $W \leftarrow$ centroids of clusters in Ω
end

---

probability (or fuzzy membership) (Chakrabarti et al., 2009).

In the following subsections, the fundamentals of the basic clustering algorithms used in this chapter and some basic concepts regarding the validation of the found clusters are presented. In the next sections the following notation will be used: X is the dataset formed by x_i data samples; Ω is the set of samples that have been grouped in a cluster and W is the set of w_i centroids of the clusters in Ω.

Hierarchical Clustering

One of the simplest and most popular unsupervised method in post-genomic data analysis is Hierarchical Cluster (HC) analysis. This method clusters the data forming a tree diagram, or dendrogram, which shows the relationships between samples according to a proximity matrix. The root node of the dendrogram represents the whole data set, and each leaf node is regarded as a data point. The intermediate nodes describe how the samples are proximal to each other; and the height of the dendrogram usually expresses the distance between each pair of data points or clusters, or a data point

and a cluster. The clusters are obtained by cutting the dendrogram at different levels (Larose, 2005).

HC groups data with a sequence of nested partitions, either from singleton clusters to a cluster including all individuals or vice-versa. The former is known as agglomerative HC, and the latter is called divisive HC. Agglomerative HC clustering starts with N clusters, each of which includes exactly one data point. The algorithm then computes the distances between all pairs of data points in the multidimensional parameter space. This is usually computed on a Euclidean basis, though other distance metrics can be used. A series of merge operations is then followed that eventually forces all objects into the same group. In the proximity matrix, the minimal distance between two clusters is searched and those two clusters are then combined into a new one. After that, the proximity matrix is updated by computing the distances between the new cluster and the other clusters. These steps are repeated until only one cluster remains. The HC method is shown in Figure 1.

Figure 2. K-means (KM) Clustering

Data:
  X: dataset
  k: number of clusters
Results:
  Ω: clusters
  W: centroids
begin
  $N \leftarrow \text{size}(X)$
  Randomly initialize centroids: $\mathbf{w}_i = \mathbf{x}_{\text{rnd}(1,\ldots,N)}, \quad i = 1,\ldots,k$
  repeat
    foreach $\mathbf{x}_j \in X$ **do**
      Search the minimal distance $i_j^* = \arg\min_{\forall i}\{\|\mathbf{w}_i - \mathbf{x}_j\|\}$
      Assign pattern $\mathbf{x}_j$ to cluster $\Omega_{i_j^*}$
    Recalculate centroids $\mathbf{w}_i = \frac{1}{|\Omega_i|}\sum_{\mathbf{x}_j \in \Omega_i}\mathbf{x}_j$
  until W *do not change*
end

K-Means

The *k*-means (KM) algorithm is one of the best-known and most popular clustering algorithms (Forgy, 1965; Duda & Hart, 2003). Figure 2 shows its functioning. It begins by selecting the desired number of *k* clusters and assigning their centroids to data points randomly chosen from the training set. At each iteration, data points are classified by assigning them to the cluster whose centroid is closest and then new cluster centroids are computed as the average of all the points belonging to each cluster. This process continues until both the cluster centroids and the class assignments no longer change.

This technique inherently looks for compact, spherical clusters. The KM algorithm has become one of the most widely used clustering approaches finding many applications in post-genomics, especially in the analysis of transcriptomic data (Lindon et al., 2007). KM assumes that the number of clusters *k* is already known by the user, which, unfortunately, usually is not true in practice. Like for cluster initialization, there are no efficient and universal methods for the selection of *k* (Xu & Donald, 2009).

Neural Networks

Neural networks have solved a wide range of problems and have good learning capabilities. Neural network based clustering is closely related to the concept of competitive learning, which is based on the idea of units (neurons) that compete in some way to respond to a given subset of inputs. The nodes in the input layer admit input patterns and they are fully connected to the output nodes in the competitive layer. Each output node corresponds to a cluster and is associated with a prototype or synaptic weight vector (Xu et al., 2009).

Given an input pattern, its similarity (or distance) to the weights vectors is computed. The neurons in the competitive layer then compete with each other, and only the one closest to the input becomes activated or fired. The weight vector of this winning neuron is further moved towards the input pattern. This competitive learning paradigm only allows learning for a particular winning neuron that best matches the given input pattern and it is also known as winner-takes-all learning (Haykin, 2007).

Self-organizing maps were introduced in 1982 by Kohonen (1982). They represent a special class of neural networks that use competitive learning.

Figure 3. Self-Organizing Map (SOM) Training

```
Data:
    X: input vector
    k: number of neurons for a k = n × n map
Results:
    Ω: clusters
    W: centroids
begin
    N ← size(X)
    Define neurons neighborhood function Λ(n)
    Initiliaze the map by choosing random weights values
    wᵢⱼ ∈ [−0.5, +0.5]
    repeat
        Select a pattern at random xᵣ = x_rnd(1,...,N)
        Search for the winning neuron: j* = arg min {‖wⱼ − xᵣ‖}
                                              ∀j
        Adapt weights: wⱼ ← { wⱼ + η(xᵣ − wⱼ)  if j ∈ Λⱼ* }
                            { wⱼ                if j ∉ Λⱼ* }
    until no significative changes in wⱼ
    Ωⱼ ← {xₗ/‖wⱼ − xₗ‖ < ‖wᵢ − xₗ‖ ∀i ≠ j, 0 < i ≤ k}
end
```

The goal of self-organizing maps is to represent complex high-dimensional input patterns into a simpler low-dimensional discrete map, with prototype vectors that can be visualized in a two-dimensional lattice structure, while preserving the proximity relationships of the original data as much as possible (Kohonen et al., 2005). Thus, SOMs can be appropriate for cluster analysis when looking for underlying hidden patterns in data. A SOM structures the output nodes (neurons) into clusters of nodes, where nodes in closer proximity are more similar to each other than to other nodes that are farther apart. A neighbourhood function is defined for each neuron. When competition among the neurons is complete, SOM updates a set of weight vectors within the neighbourhood of the winning neuron (see Figure 3).

Having finished the training, neighbouring input patterns are projected into the lattice, corresponding to adjacent neurons connected to each other through the neighbourhood function, giving a clear topology of how the network fits into the input space. Therefore, the regions with a high probability of occurrence of sampled patterns will be represented by larger areas in the feature map (Haykin, 2007). In this sense, some authors prefer to think of SOM as a method of displaying latent data structures in a visual way rather than through a clustering approach (Xu et al., 2009).

CLUSTERING VALIDATION FOR THE COMPARISON OF ALGORITHMS

Given a data set, each clustering algorithm can always produce a partition whether or not there really is a particular structure in the data. Moreover, different clustering approaches usually lead to different clusters of data, and even for the same algorithm, the selection of a parameter or the presentation order of input patterns may affect the final results. Therefore, effective evaluation standards and criteria are critically important to provide users with a degree of confidence for the clustering results.

The discovery of novel biological knowledge from the analysis of post-genomic data relies upon the use of unsupervised processing methods, in particular clustering techniques. Much recent research in bioinformatics has therefore been focused on the transfer of clustering methods introduced in other scientific fields and on the development of novel algorithms specifically designed to tackle the challenges posed by post-genomic data. To avoid inconsistencies in the results and to assure that the resulting clusters are reflective of the general population, the clustering solution should be validated (Larose, 2005). The partitions returned by a clustering algorithm are commonly validated using visual inspection and concordance with prior biological knowledge. Suitable computational cluster validation techniques are available in the general data-mining literature, but have been given only a fraction of the same attention in bioinformatics (Handl et al., 2005).

The data-mining literature provides a range of different validation techniques, distinguishing between external and internal validation measures. External validation measures comprise all those methods that evaluate a clustering result based on the knowledge of the correct class labels. Internal measures take a clustering and the underlying dataset as the input, and use information intrinsic to the data to assess the quality of the clustering (Halkidi, 2001).

When clustering a novel biological dataset, cluster validation plays a very different role. A completely objective validation of cluster quality is usually impossible in such a case, but the use of cluster validation during the clustering process can help to improve the quality of results, and increase the confidence in the final result. No reliable method exists to identify the number of clusters in an unknown dataset, and the choice of the best number of clusters may well depend on the clustering method used. A cluster analysis should therefore always be performed for a (sensible) range of different numbers of clusters. Internal validation measures should be used to provide feedback on the quality of the data and to check whether a given partitioning is justified in terms of the underlying data distribution. A good clustering solution will tend to perform reasonably well under multiple measures.

Internal measures can be grouped according to the particular notion of clustering quality that they employ. In Handl et al. (2005) the following classification of internal measures is proposed:

Type I measures (*Compactness*): It comprises validation measures assessing cluster compactness or homogeneity. Intracluster variance is their most popular representative:

$$\overline{C}_j = \frac{1}{|\Omega_j|} \sum_{\forall \mathbf{x}_i \in \Omega_j} \left\| \mathbf{x}_i - \mathbf{w}_j \right\|_2, \tag{1}$$

where is the number of patterns in node j. As a global measure of compactness, the average over all nodes is calculated as $\overline{C} = \frac{1}{k} \sum_j \overline{C}_j$. Values of $\overline{C}$ close to 0 indicate more compact nodes.

Type II measures (*Separation*): This group includes all those measures that quantify the degree of separation between individual clusters. It can be evaluated measuring mean, minimum and maximum Euclidean distance among cluster centroids, according to:

$$\overline{S} = \frac{2}{k^2 - k} \sum_{i=1}^{k} \sum_{j=i+1}^{k} \left\| \mathbf{w}_i - \mathbf{w}_j \right\|_2, \tag{2}$$

$$S_m = \min_{0 < i \neq j \leq k} \left\{ \left\| \mathbf{w}_i - \mathbf{w}_j \right\|_2 \right\}, \tag{3}$$

$$S_M = \max_{0 < i \neq j \leq k} \left\{ \left\| \mathbf{w}_i - \mathbf{w}_j \right\|_2 \right\}, \tag{4}$$

where $\overline{S}$ close to zero indicates closer nodes.

Type III measures: These are *combinations* of the mentioned two types of measures and they are the most popular because they exhibit opposing trends. For example, while compactness improves with an increasing number of clusters, the distance between clusters tends to deteriorate.

The first combined measurement used in this work is the Davies-Bouldin index (Davies & Bouldin, 1979), defined as

$$DB = \frac{1}{k} \sum_{i=1}^{k} \max_{j \neq i} \left(\frac{\overline{C}_i + \overline{C}_j}{\left\| \mathbf{w}_i - \mathbf{w}_j \right\|_2} \right). \tag{5}$$

This index is a function of the ratio of the sum of within-cluster scatter to between-cluster separation. It measures the distance between the cluster centroid and the other points over the between-cluster distance. This is an indication of clusters overlap, therefore a *DB* close to zero indicates that the clusters are compact and far from each other.

The other combined measurement used is the internal cluster dispersion rate of the final partition defined as Mingoti and Lima (2006)

$$Y = 1 - \frac{\sum_{j=1}^{k} \left\| \mathbf{w}_j - \left(\frac{1}{N} \sum_{\ell=1}^{N} \mathbf{x}_\ell \right) \right\|_2}{\sum_{i=1}^{N} \left\| \mathbf{x}_i - \left(\frac{1}{N} \sum_{\ell=1}^{N} \mathbf{x}_\ell \right) \right\|_2} \qquad (6)$$

The numerator in (6) corresponds to the sum of the distances among the centroids and the overall sample mean vector; the denominator is the sum of the distances between each pattern and the overall sample mean vector. The smaller the value of Y, the smaller the intraclass clusters dispersion.

PIPELINE FOR INTEGRATION AND ANALYSIS OF INTROGRESSION LINES

Since the completion of genome sequences, functional identification of unknown genes has become a principal challenge in systems biology. The analysis of biological data, such as, for example, gene expression data and metabolic profiles in plants of agro-economical interest, is based on the idea that genes (and metabolites) that are involved in a particular metabolic pathway should be co-regulated and therefore should exhibit similar patterns of expression. Thus, a fundamental task for their analysis is to identify groups of data samples showing similar expression patterns. For this task, clustering has become a fundamental approach. It

can support the identification of existing underlying relationships among a set of variables such as biological conditions or perturbations. Clustering may, even, allow the discovery of new biological knowledge.

As shown in Background section, there are several clustering algorithms and most of them, at least indirectly, assume that the cluster structure of the data under consideration exhibits particular characteristics. For instance, HC assumes that the clusters are well separated and KM supposes that the shape of the clusters is spherical (Azuaje & Bolshakova, 2002). Unfortunately, this type of knowledge may not always be available beforehand in biology (as in other applications). In general, the application of two or more clustering techniques may provide a basis for the synthesis of accurate and reliable results, especially if similar results are obtained by using different techniques. However, from the application point of view, it is important to be able to quantify the confidence in each method, in particular when new biological inferences could be made from the analyzed data.

In this section, authors present a pipeline of steps that can be followed to help the discovery of gene-to-gene and metabolite-to-gene networks thanks to the integration of metabolomics with transcriptomics. It is oriented towards the cases where a biological experiment is focused in the study of the differences among several plant genomes, involving an original genome that has been modified by introgression of another species genome.

As part of the process, a specific step that can help in assessing the validity of one clustering algorithm over another one is proposed, not only from the point of view of the quality of the clusters found, but also from the biological meaning of the found relations. Several measures that can be applied to the clusters and biological criteria to verify their biological value is also introduced. This last step presents a strategy that can be of help for the identification of novel metabolic pathways.

Figure 4. Pipeline for integration and analysis of biological (metabolic and transcriptomic) data of introgression lines

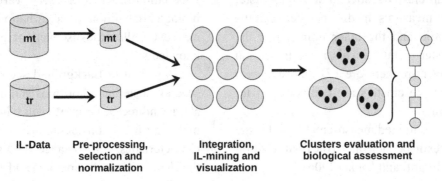

IL-Data Pre-processing, Integration, Clusters evaluation and
selection and IL-mining and biological assessment
normalization visualization

Figure 4 shows the proposed process, which consists of the following steps:

1. **IL-Data understanding**: It involves the definition of the biological data, the ILs involved in the study, the kind and number of data types (for example, metabolites and transcripts), the number of experiments and repetitions for each of them, as well as the structure and type of data files that contain them (such as raw quantified array data from micro array specific software).

2. **Pre-processing, selection and normalization**: It involves the cleaning and error elimination from data, as well as the application of appropriate selection criteria with the objective of including only sufficiently expressed data in the analysis (Baxter, Sabar, Quick, & Sweetlove, 2005). This step needs also a normalization of the log ratio of the expression intensity values over the control sample in the case of data coming from micro array experiments (Causton, Quackenbush, & Brazma, 2003).

3. **Integration, IL-mining and visualization**: With an appropriate normalization, metabolobome and transcriptome data obtained from the same plant material can be integrated into a single multivariate dataset suitable for further analysis with a clustering technique. Several data mining algorithms should be applied, whose relevance is later determined in the next pipeline step. Simple and easy to understand visualization of results are used for the interpretation of hidden relationships among co-expressed and co-accumulated genes and metabolites, in particular, groups of different kind of patterns. This kind of feature can be useful for a preliminary evaluation of the clusters.

4. **Clusters evaluation and biological assessment**: For choosing an adequate clustering technique for the data, comparison of several methods through clustering measurements (that will indicate the quality of the clusters found) and through a biological assessment of the clusters that integrate different kinds of data (that will indicate biological significance of the found groups) are proposed.

The following subsections describe the proposed steps of the pipeline in detail, through the application of the proposal to a case of study involving a commercial tomato database (http://ted.bti.cornell.edu).

IL-Data Understanding

The metabolome is the final product of a series of gene actions. Hence, metabolomics has a po-

Figure 5. Introgression Lines (ILs): the portion of introgressed genome is marked in each IL with a red line

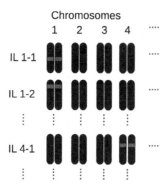

tential to elucidate gene functions and networks, especially when integrated with transcriptomics (Hirai et al., 2005). Like it was mentioned before, there are many cases where a biological experiment is focused in the study of the differences among several plant genomes. It may involve an original genome that has been modified by introgression of wild species alleles or transgenic plants over expressing a gene of interest. The use of introgression lines allows the study and creation of new varieties by introducing exotic traits and constitute a useful tool in crop domestication (and breeding) (Rieseberg & Wendel, 1993; Lippman & D, 2007).

The case of study presented in this chapter involves the analysis of metabolic and transcriptional profiles data from ILs of tomato (Solanum lycopersicum) which posses, at certain chromosomes segments, introgressed portions of a wild tomato species (Solanum pennelli). The interest in comparing the cultivated tomato against the different ILs, lies on the fact that it has been proven that some wild tomato fruits can be sources of several specific agronomical characters of interest which could be used for the improvement of commercial tomato lines. Figure 5 shows a scheme of the chromosomes of this plant population.

The metabolic data have been obtained analyzing polar extracts of tomato fruits, through Gas Chromatography coupled to Mass Spectrometry. The peak intensities have been normalized to the quantity of material used. The metabolite profiling technique used allows the identification of approximately 80 primary metabolic compounds (Carrari et al., 2006).

Transcriptional levels have been obtained from hybridization chips having all the genes of the material of interest (all ≈25000 tomato genes) ordered into spots, previously marked with two fluorescence channels. The tomato gene expression database used contains annotation and sequence information of all probes on the tomato oligo array by micro array hybridization mRNA expression techniques for ≈13000 genes. $P=21$ ILs have been analyzed, with introgressions in chromosomes: 1, 2, 3, 5, 8, 10, 11 and 12 (Baxter et al., 2005).

Pre-Processing, Selection and Normalization

The following steps aim at filtering error or missing measurements, NaN values, poor quality spots in the micro array images (according to the flags from the image processing program) and spots not expressed in both channels (such as empty spots or spots that do not pass a minimum empirical threshold value). The following lines present a detailed description of the pre-processing, selection and normalization steps performed for each type of data type analyzed.

Metabolite Data

Metabolite accumulation measurements are obtained from several replicates of an experiment. Each experiment compares a specific introgression tomato line against a control tomato genome. Metabolites that do not appear in at least two repetitions are marked as missing data for further analysis. For each metabolite in each IL, the log ratio of the mean of the valid replicates is calculated according to

$$\log R_i^m = \log_{10}\left(\frac{\overline{S}_i^m}{\overline{Q}_i^m}\right) \qquad (7)$$

where $\overline{S}_i^m$ is the accumulation mean of the valid replicates for metabolite m at the IL i, and $\overline{Q}_i^m$ is the accumulation mean of the valid replicates for the corresponding control measurement. In the selection step, only metabolites with are kept for data integration and cluster analysis.

Transcriptional Data

Poor quality spots, negative spots, spots not expressed in both channels and empty spots are filtered out. Not expressed spots are detected for IL and control slides according to

$$\overline{F}^t < \overline{B}^t + a\tilde{B}^t \qquad (8)$$

where F^t is the foreground signal mean for the transcript t, $\overline{B}^t$ is the spot mean background, $\tilde{B}^t$ is the spot background standard deviation and α is a quality parameter to be empirically set in the interval [2,3].

The microarray measurements are normalized using the print-tip Lowess normalization strategy (Causton et al., 2003). Spots with at least two valid replicated data points are included for analysis using

$$\log R_{ir}^t = \log_2\left(\frac{\breve{S}_{ir}^t}{\breve{Q}_{ir}^t}\right) \qquad (9)$$

where $\breve{S}_{ir}^t$ is the foreground signal median for the transcript t, in the replicate r at IL i, and $\breve{Q}_{ir}^t$ is the foreground signal median for the transcript t, in the corresponding control replicate r for the same IL i.

The valid replicates are averaged simply as

$$\log R_i^t = \frac{1}{\Gamma_i^t}\sum_{r=1}^{\Gamma_i^t}\log R_{ir}^t, \qquad (10)$$

where Γ_i^t the number of is valid replicates for the transcript t at the IL i.

Normalization

After the pre-processing and selection steps, M=71 metabolites and T=1385 genes have been selected as sufficiently expressed. The resulting log ratios are normalized. For each pattern, the sum of the square of log ratios is set equal to 1 according to

$$x_i^* = \frac{\log R_i^*}{\sum_{j=1}^{P}(\log R_j^*)^2} \qquad (11)$$

where * stands for m or t and P is the total number of available ILs.

Integration, IL-Mining and Visualization

Integration

All normalized data are integrated into a single matrix and arranged in the training set as shown in Figure 6. Various ways of integration are possible. For example, before integration of two data sets, the plus/minus sign of one data set can be reversed to obtain negatively correlated items. To find all possible inverted correlations (direct-direct, direct-inverted), the training set includes the original and the inverted versions of all the patterns. Then, each column/dimension-IL is normalized in the range [0,1] according to histogram equalization.

Figure 6. Data integration into a single training set. Original and inverted versions of all the data samples are include

	IL_1	IL_2	...	IL_i	...	IL_P
Transcripts	$x_1^{t_1}$	$x_2^{t_1}$	...	$x_i^{t_1}$	...	$x_P^{t_1}$
	$x_1^{t_2}$	$x_2^{t_2}$	...	$x_i^{t_2}$	...	$x_P^{t_2}$
	$\vdots$	$\vdots$	$\ddots$	$\vdots$	$\vdots$	$\vdots$
	x_1^{t}	x_2^{t}	...	x_i^{t}	...	x_P^{t}
	$\vdots$	$\vdots$	$\ddots$	$\vdots$	$\vdots$	$\vdots$
	x_1^{T}	x_2^{T}	...	x_i^{T}	...	x_P^{T}
Inverted transcripts	$-x_1^{t_1}$	$-x_2^{t_1}$	...	$-x_i^{t_1}$	...	$-x_P^{t_1}$
	$-x_1^{t_2}$	$-x_2^{t_2}$	...	$-x_i^{t_2}$	...	$-x_P^{t_2}$
	$\vdots$	$\vdots$	$\ddots$	$\vdots$	$\vdots$	$\vdots$
	$-x_1^{t}$	$-x_2^{t}$	...	$-x_i^{t}$	...	$-x_P^{t}$
	$\vdots$	$\vdots$	$\ddots$	$\vdots$	$\vdots$	$\vdots$
	$-x_1^{T}$	$-x_2^{T}$	...	$-x_i^{T}$	...	$-x_P^{T}$
Metabolites	$x_1^{m_1}$	$x_2^{m_1}$	...	$x_i^{m_1}$	...	$x_P^{m_1}$
	$x_1^{m_2}$	$x_2^{m_2}$	...	$x_i^{m_2}$	...	$x_P^{m_2}$
	$\vdots$	$\vdots$	$\ddots$	$\vdots$	$\vdots$	$\vdots$
	x_1^{m}	x_2^{m}	...	x_i^{m}	...	x_P^{m}
	$\vdots$	$\vdots$	$\ddots$	$\vdots$	$\vdots$	$\vdots$
	x_1^{M}	x_2^{M}	...	x_i^{M}	...	x_P^{M}
Inverted metabolites	$-x_1^{m_1}$	$-x_2^{m_1}$	...	$-x_i^{m_1}$	...	$-x_P^{m_1}$
	$-x_1^{m_2}$	$-x_2^{m_2}$	...	$-x_i^{m_2}$	...	$-x_P^{m_2}$
	$\vdots$	$\vdots$	$\ddots$	$\vdots$	$\vdots$	$\vdots$
	$-x_1^{t}$	$-x_2^{t}$	...	$-x_i^{t}$	...	$-x_P^{t}$
	$\vdots$	$\vdots$	$\ddots$	$\vdots$	$\vdots$	$\vdots$
	$-x_1^{M}$	$-x_2^{M}$	...	$-x_i^{M}$	...	$-x_P^{M}$

For the analysis of these biological data, clustering is implemented, under the assumption that behaviourally similar genes could share common pathways. According to this principle, named "guilt-by-association" (Wolfe et al., 2005), a set of genes involved in a biological process are co-expressed under the control of the same regulation network. This way, if an unknown gene is co-expressed with known genes in a biological process, this unknown gene is probably involved in the same metabolic pathway. Similar reasoning can be applied to metabolites.

IL-Mining

In this step, several clustering methods are applied to the IL-data. The proposed pipeline is based on the idea that such a model can make tractable the problem of computational analysis and interpretation of large amounts of data from different nature, such as gene expression and metabolic profiles, for finding relationships among introgressed lines. Therefore, the models for clustering referred in this context are named as IL-HC, IL-KM and IL-SOM. In the case of the IL-SOM model, each node corresponds to a neuron, for IL-HC each branch is a node and in the case of IL-KM the nodes correspond to the *k* parts the data are divided by. Several model topologies, map sizes and initialization strategies are possible in IL-SOM. For the map shape a rectangular lattice has been used. The initial vectors are set by principal component analysis, obtaining a learning process independent of the order of input of vectors, and hence reproducible (http://www.cis.hut.fi/projects/somtoolbox/).

Let us call node to each of the *k* elements of the grouping method. In the three cases, a node is identified with the index *j*, the centroid with and the set of patterns grouped in a node with. The term "integration node" is used to refer a node that contains both different kinds of patterns (metabolites and transcripts). For all the methods, Euclidean distance is used to measure distance between patterns, and clusters are generated for 50 and 200 nodes.

Figure 7 shows the resulting histograms for each method with *k*=50.

As can be seen, IL-HC comprises the vast majority of the patterns in the same branch (Figure 7.a). This constitutes a major drawback to this technique, both from the perspective of its capabilities as a method of grouping this type of data as from the perspective of the information about the biological processes involved that can be inferred from this grouping. It is important to mention that, regardless of the depth at which the branch lines are cut, the method always tends to group the majority of patterns in a few nodes. Another major inconsistency detected in this case is that the original patterns have been grouped together with their inverted (sign) version, in many cases, in the same node.

When comparing the histograms of IL-KM (Figure 7.b) and IL-SOM (Figure 7.c), it can be seen that the distribution in the case of IL-SOM is much more uniform. While IL-KM has several nodes with very few patterns and few nodes with many patterns, the patterns distribution of the

IL-SOM is more balanced across all the nodes. This is mainly due to the influence of the neighbourhood radius during the self-organizing map training process. In IL-KM, each node is trained independently from each other; in the case of SOM, instead, an update of the nodes around the winning neuron is performed, which allows the centroids not to spread so much and the patterns can be more homogeneously distributed in regions of neurons with similar centroids. The more balanced distribution of the patterns and the possibility of analyzing individual neurons also extending the analysis to those located nearby, for several radios, is a distinct advantage of the IL-SOM model in comparison with IL-KM.

The notion of a social network and associated methods of analysis and visualizations is influencing an increasing number of application domains, including bioinformatics and systems biology nowadays. A social network consists of a graph $G=(V,E)$ where there are relations among a set of actors or vertices V and edges E representing relations. From the very beginning, visualization played an important role in social network analysis, not only for presentation, but even more so by facilitating data exploration (Brandes, 2008).

A social graph is proposed for visualization and comparison among clustering methods. For example, once the patterns have been assigned to clusters, it is easy to see, by visual inspection, if the direct and corresponding inverted patterns have been grouped consistently, or not.

For the case study example of tomato metabolites and transcripts, considering only integration nodes for the case k=50, Figure 8 shows, at a glance, that IL-HC has inconsistently grouped direct and inverted sign patterns into one single cluster. IL-KM, instead, has found coherent relationships, but scattered through a different number of integration nodes. Thus, the associations do not always reflected the opposite sign relationships. Differently from the other methods, IL-SOM has always correctly grouped direct and inverted sign data into different (in fact, opposite) clusters in the

Figure 7. Patterns distribution histograms by clustering method (grey for transcripts, black for metabolites). a) IL-Hierarchical clustering; b) IL-k-means; c) IL-Self-organizing maps

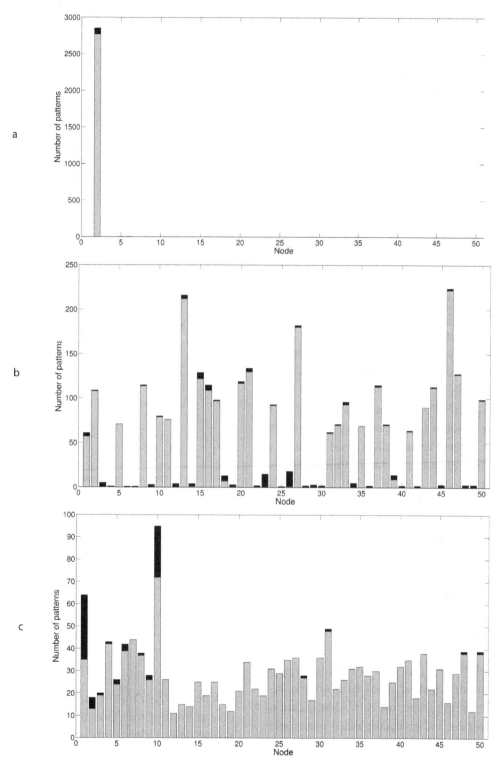

feature map. For the special case of the IL-SOM, many interesting representations of clusters can be obtained form the projection of the patterns in the lattice of neurons. If the dataset includes the original data plus the original data with inverted sign, the resulting map shows a symmetrical "triangular" configuration. This means that the top-right and down-left zones of the map group exactly the same data but having opposite sign. This allows seeing, at once, directs (up-regulated genes and metabolites, down-regulated genes and metabolites) and inverted (down-regulated genes grouped together with up-regulated metabolites) relations among data. There is a specific zone in the map where the exactly opposite behaviour per IL can be found, which is useful for associating specific genes/metabolites to specific IL. For example, one gene similarly expressed in several ILs but up-regulated in a determined IL, which will be down-regulated in it if its sign is inverted. These kind of analysis may be of help for the further inference of a-priori unknown metabolic pathways involving the grouped data.

In a standard SOM map, clusters are recognized as a group of nodes rather than considering each node as a cluster. The identification of clusters is mainly achieved through visualization methods such as the U-matrix (Ultsch, 1999). It computes the average distance between the codebook vectors of adjacent nodes, yielding a landscape surface where light-colours stands for short distance (a valley) and dark-colours for larger distance (a hill). Then, the number of underlying clusters must be determined by visual inspection.

Visualization

The visualizations provided by the proposed IL-SOM model, instead, provide a simple interface for helping the quickly identification of co-expressed and co-accumulated genes and metabolites through a simple colour code for the integration nodes. The focus is on the easily identification of groups of different types of patterns,

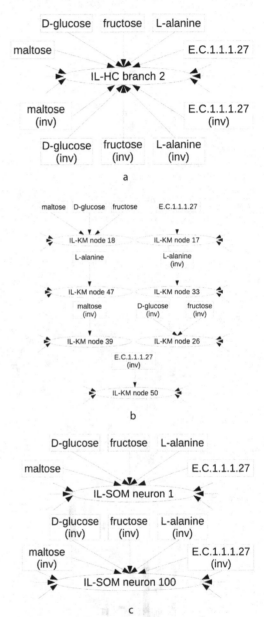

Figure 8. Social net graphs for clusters visualization: a) inconsistent cluster in IL-HC; b) scattered patterns in IL-KM and c) a coherent grouping of patterns in IL-SOM

independently from the number of neurons in a cluster. Furthermore, the setting of several possible visualization neighbourhoods (Vn) of a neuron is also helpful for the easy detection of groups of combined data types, avoiding the need for the

Figure 9. Activation SOM resulting from the integrated analysis of 1385 genes and 71 metabolites from 21 tomato ILs. Map topology of 40x40 neurons with a) Vn=1 and b) Vn=2

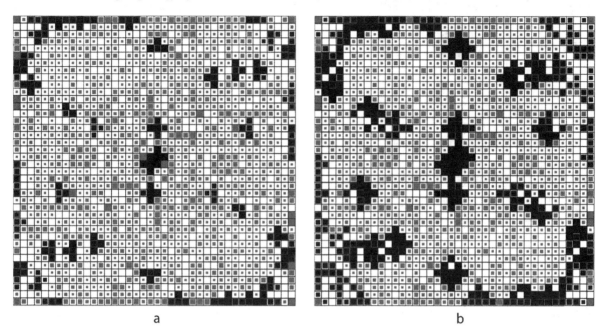

a   b

identification of neuron clusters. When a Vn is defined, all the neighbourhood neurons (according to the neighbourhood radius set) are considered as a group and treated altogether accordingly, also for counting whether there are metabolites and transcripts grouped.

The following visualizations are supported by the ILSOM model:

- **Easy identification of clusters of combined data types:** Figure 9 shows different marker colours which indicate the kind of pattern grouped in the neuron: black for combined data types, blue for only metabolites and red for only transcripts. Also the marker size indicates the number of patterns grouped. The figure shows the activation map resulting from the integrated analysis of 21 tomato ILs with a 40x40 neuron topology, with Vn=1 and Vn=2.

- **Detail view of original data measurements:** Figure 10 shows some visualization provided by the software that has been

designed for the IL-SOM. The figure shows, in the upper left, the resulting IL-SOM integrated model for the 21 ILs dataset (map with 20x20 neurons). The curves presented in the right part of the figure show a detail of the normalized patterns which have all been clustered together in the neuron 604: the metabolite Pyroglutamic Acid., and the metabolites Aspartic acid L and Calystegine B2, together with the inverted sign transcripts LE12J18, LE13G19 and LE22O03. For this metabolite the upper right plot shows its denormalized (original) log ratios. The down left part of the figure shows a decodification of the LE33K02 transcript according to its probe code, which has been automatically translated into its corresponding Arabidopsis (www.arabidopsis.org) (At.3g16720.1) and Unigene (www.sgen.cornell.edu) (SGN-U217330) annotations. In the denormalized plot, missing data (samples in a IL not having enough valid

Figure 10. Integration model visualizations

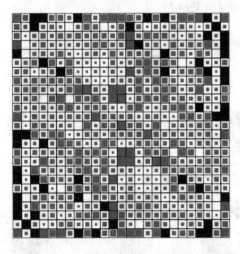

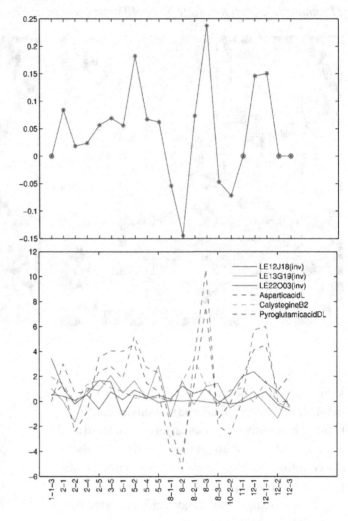

LE12J18: SGN-U215829 - At4g25700.1
68411.m03367 beta-carotene
hydroxylase identical to GI:1575296 -
gi|5870598|emb|CAB55625.1| beta-carotene
hydroxylase [Lycopersicon esculentum]
LE13G19: SGN-U215730 - At1g78240.1
68408.m08365 dehydration-induced
protein-related similar to
early-responsive to dehydration stress
ERD3 protein [Arabidopsis thaliana]
GI:15320410; contains Pfam profile
PF03141: Putative methyltransferase
- gi|42563316|ref|NP_177948.3|
dehydration-responsive protein-related
[Arabidopsis thaliana]
LE22O03: SGN-U218245 -
At4g20850.1 68411.m02765 expressed
protein tripeptidyl-peptidase II -
gi|30685230|ref|NP_193817.2| expressed
protein [Arabidopsis thaliana]

replicates experiments for the average log ratio calculation) are indicated with a red circle.

- **Visualization of clusters inside a specific chromosome:** Another possibility is the visualization of clusters inside a specific chromosome, for all the included ILs in it. This allows the comparison of patterns expressions according to a colour scale that paints only neurons having patterns with an important deviation from the neuron mean, for each dimension/IL. That is, the neuron where at least one pattern has a value greater than the mean plus one stan-

dard deviation in the corresponding IL is depicted in green. If in this IL there is at least one pattern in the neuron with a value lower than the mean plus one standard deviation, the neuron is painted in grey. The variations in the expression levels of the grouped patterns may provide useful information regarding genes/metabolites specifically associated to certain mechanisms in each particular IL. The visualization of these patterns outliers (or special patterns), IL against IL, may highlight interest characteristics of a specific IL that may differentiate it from the other ones.

Figure 11. SOM activation map for the tomato chromosome 12, introgression lines 12-1-1, 12-1, 12-2 and 12-3

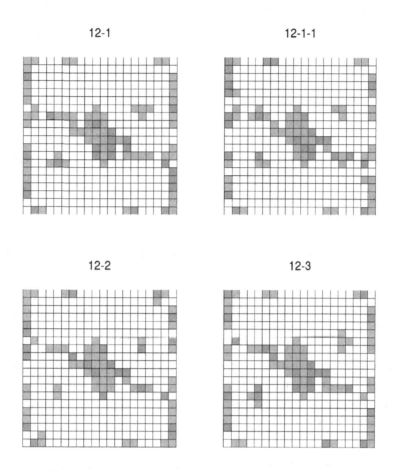

Figure 11 shows the activations per IL of a 20x20 map for the tomato chromosome 12: 12-1, 12-1-1, 12-2 and 12-3 ILs, with Vn=1. For example, in the patterns inside neuron (1,1), the Citric acid (Citrate) metabolite can be found. A detailed analysis of the grouped pattern shows that the Citric acid is the only responsible for the neuron being painted green in the IL 12-1 (while its values on the other ILs remain inside the average). This is an important clue regarding the metabolite location being highly tightened to this specific IL. Other similar relations can be drawn with this type of visualization capability.

It is quite important to be able to evaluate the quality of several clustering algorithm when ap-plied to biological data, in particular if later bio-logical inferences should be made. This is the objective of the next step of the proposed bio-logical data pipeline.

Clusters Evaluation and Biological Assessment

Several clustering algorithms have been employed to analyse the available IL expression data. How-ever, a quality or confidence measure is necessary for each technique to assess the quality of their outcomes. This step provides a cluster validity framework to get insights into the clustering method selection for the biological data under

Figure 12. Quality measurements for the clustering methods compared

Type	Measure	IL-HC		IL-KM		IL-SOM	
		50	200	50	200	50	200
I	$\overline{C}$	4.728	3.511	4.608	3.167	<u>3.433</u>	<u>3.294</u>
II	$\overline{S}$	21.51	13.57	12.29	9.577	<u>1.344</u>	<u>2.118</u>
II	S_m	8.635	4.159	1.892	1.369	<u>0.239</u>	<u>0.196</u>
II	S_M	45.92	45.92	45.92	45.92	<u>3.483</u>	<u>7.363</u>
III	DB	<u>2.280</u>	<u>2.901</u>	5.764	3.630	24.42	20.67
III	Υ	0.936	0.842	0.967	0.895	<u>0.995</u>	<u>0.971</u>

analysis. The results obtained for the case of study indicate that this systematic evaluation approach may support the process for knowledge discovery applications over IL-data.

According to Guillet and Hamilton (2007), comparison between clustering methods can be performed using objective and/or subjective measures. An objective measure is based on only the raw data. No additional knowledge about the data is required. A subjective measure is a one that takes into account both the data and the user who uses the data. To define a subjective measure, the user domain or background knowledge about the data is needed. The key issue for mining patterns based on subjective measures is the representation of user knowledge.

For the comparisons among clustering methods in this pipeline step, the use of two categories of measures is proposed: i) objective or clustering measurements, that measure the quality of the clusters found with each technique, regardless of their biological meaning; and ii) biological criteria have been defined for the assessment of the clusters that integrate metabolites with transcripts, from the point of view of the metabolic pathways that should involve them.

Comparison Based on Objective Clustering Measures

In this step, the applied clustering method is compared according to the clustering measures that have been defined in Clustering Validation for the Comparison of Algorithms section. Figure

12 shows the results obtained in the comparison of the three methods, for different numbers of nodes. The method of IL-HC has concentrated more than 85% of the patterns in a single node, including direct and inverted data. This is a strong indication that it would not be a valid method for detecting coordinated changes in these kinds of patterns. More compact nodes and having low internodes spacing ($\overline{C}$ and $\overline{S}$) have been obtained by IL-SOM. As for separation, it was noted that IL-HC and IL-KM tend to locate a centroid in each of the more distant patterns of the data set analyzed. The self-organizing maps are more robust, keeping the distances between neurons centroids through the neighbourhood update during the early stages of the training algorithm. Clearly, by increasing the number of neurons in the map, the degrees of freedom are increased and the outer centroids of the map may get closer to the data patterns that are farther apart from the whole dataset. It can be noticed that the minimum separation is reduced in the IL-SOM in comparison to the other methods, which allows looking at the map with greater confidence that the changes between nearby nodes are gradual and can form clusters of more biological interest.

With respect to Type III measurements, it has to be considered that intranode dispersion is always greater for IL-SOM, regardless of the number of nodes. This means that the average distance between IL-SOM centroids and the global centre of the patterns is lower (in relation to the total patterns dispersion) than the average distance of the other methods centroids. Since IL-HC finds a

Figure 13. Quality measurements for the clustering methods compared, considering only integration nodes

Type	Measure	IL-HC		IL-KM		IL-SOM	
		50	200	50	200	50	200
	N	1	13	26	35	13	21
I	$\overline{C}$	3.787	3.356	3.638	3.588	4.104	4.660
II	$\overline{S}$	–	7.493	4.214	6.591	1.609	2.913
II	S_m	–	4.372	1.892	2.733	0.302	0.371
II	S_M	–	12.51	11.02	15.14	3.483	6.118
III	DB	–	2.516	2.472	3.274	18.13	11.28
III	Υ	–	0.994	0.993	0.986	0.998	0.995

large node containing most of the patterns and IL-KM forms many spread nodes with a few patterns, all the distances among scattered nodes (and their centroids) are greater. Because of this, the DB index is the lowest for the case of IL-HC. This is not happening in IL-SOM because the distances between centroids are always smaller, since they are better distributed and centroids are not associated to remote and isolated patterns There are more centroids to be distributed for sharing and it is not forced to concentrate many patterns in few centroids. Moreover, since the farther away patterns (probably outliers) have to be associates to any centroid, also nodes compactness decreases and hence the DB index is the highest.

Figure 13 shows the results obtained in the comparison of the three methods, considering in this case only integration nodes. The interest of this particular analysis lies in the fact that the patterns grouped into these nodes may be parts of the same metabolic pathway. As can be seen, a row has been added to the table with the number of integration nodes found by each technique. As expected, adding more degrees of freedom to the techniques, more nodes of this type are found. IL-KM is the method that founds the higher number of integration nodes having also high cohesion. However, the detail of these clusters indicates that patterns have not been grouped coherently in all cases: there are nodes grouping non-inverted versions of patterns but their inverted versions have been dispersed along several nodes, even mixing non-inverted and inverted versions of data

in some cases (which is also inconsistent). On the other hand, IL-HC finds the least amount of nodes, but with the problems highlighted above regarding grouping, in the same node, a direct and an inverted version of the patterns, which is meaningless from the mathematical as well as from the biological viewpoint. IL-SOM, instead, always finds consistently grouped data.

As for Type II measures, IL-SOM has obtained the best rates in terms of minimum, maximum and average integration nodes separation. The IL-HC technique with k=50 has found a single integration node with 98% of the data. Measures of Type II can not be calculated for this case because there is no separation between nodes (there is a single integration node). Similarly, combined measures cannot be calculated for this case because it is meaningless to measure the overlap of a single node. The intercluster dispersion is best for the SOM, although very close to 1.0 in all the other methods. For the same reasons discussed above, the SOM is still having the highest rate of clusters overlap and the lowest spacing between nodes. The DB index favours compact clusters, well separated from each other, which, as already said, is the opposite way in which the self-organizing maps forms the clusters. However, from a biological point of view, it would be useful to have groups with a high DB index, because there are patterns that should be close to many other patterns, if the groupings reflect components of common metabolic pathways and that there are patterns that can participate in several pathways, simultaneously.

Comparison Based on Biological Assessment Criteria

To assess the significance of the clusters from the viewpoint of their biological meaning, a detailed inspection to verify the membership of the patterns grouped in integration nodes (clusters grouping both metabolites and transcripts data types) to any known metabolic pathway should be performed. In the example given here, only integration nodes found by the three methods have been analyzed.

For this analysis, well known metabolic pathways occurring in tomato fruits have been considered (LycoCyc:http://solcyc.sgn.cornell.edu/LYCO/server.html), related to energy production (glycolysis and TCA cycle) and few associated reactions, due to their importance in all living organisms and the large amount of available data. Furthermore, except in few cases, the choice of biological processes common to the vast majority of organisms is an important starting point for comparison, because it is assumed that any clustering method used to analyze these data should be able to find such relations.

Figure 14 shows a simplified diagram of the metabolic pathways found for a preliminary analysis with k=50. For the transcripts, the EC codes have been used, corresponding to the standard nomenclature for enzymes. The metabolites and transcripts that are part of the pathway and that are present in the training set have been highlighted with a rectangle and highlighted in bold, respectively. The remaining compounds (in italics) will not be taken into account in this analysis because they have not been measured. In this figure, it is highlighted the number of integrative node in which each compound has been found, distinguishing between the SOM method (node number to the right) and IL-KM method (number to the left). In the case of enzymes that are encoded by more than one gene, all the nodes in which each gene

has been clustered are indicated. To simplify the notation in the following analysis, the compounds that have been grouped together in the same integration node are indicated between brackets [...].

IL-KM has found coherent relationships, but scattered through a different number of integration nodes. For example, this can be observed in the following nodes: [glucose and F6P], [succinate and fumarate], [glycine, serine and GABA(4-aminobutyrate)], [EC 4.2.1.2 and 1 gene from EC 4.1.1.31], [malate and 1 gene from EC 1.1.1.1], and [ascorbate and EC 1.1.1.29].

However, the associations do not always reflected the opposite relationships, such as the case of [maltose and glucose], [glutamate and EC 1.1.1.29], [fumarate and EC 4.2.1.2], among others, where for a sign configuration there have been grouped together in the same node, but when the sign is inverted, they have been split into different groups. These inconsistencies, if not so significant as in the case of IL-HC, are a limit to the method and throws doubts over the method regarding its applicability to these kinds of biological data, specially when looking for unknown relationships among them.

Even when IL-SOM has generated half the number of integrators nodes than IL-KM (as can be seen in Figure 13), differently from this last one, the patterns associations has been consistent as much for the directed as for the inverted sign cases, and the clusters clearly have associated more compounds in the same pathway in less integration nodes. This has been the case of [maltose, glucose, fructose, F6P, alanine, glycine, glycerol 3P, EC 1.1.1.27, EC 4.2.1.2 and 1 gene from EC 4.1.1.31] and of [citrate, glutamate, succinate, malate and sucrose].

The IL-SOM model allows, also, analyzing relationships with different neighbourhood radius in the IL-SOM map (Stegmayer et al., 2009), which offers an extra level of analysis in relation to the other methods. If the first neighbours of each neuron are considered (that is to say, Vn=1), another relationships of interest (for the pathway

Figure 14. Simplified schematics of glycolisis, TCA cycle and associated reactions

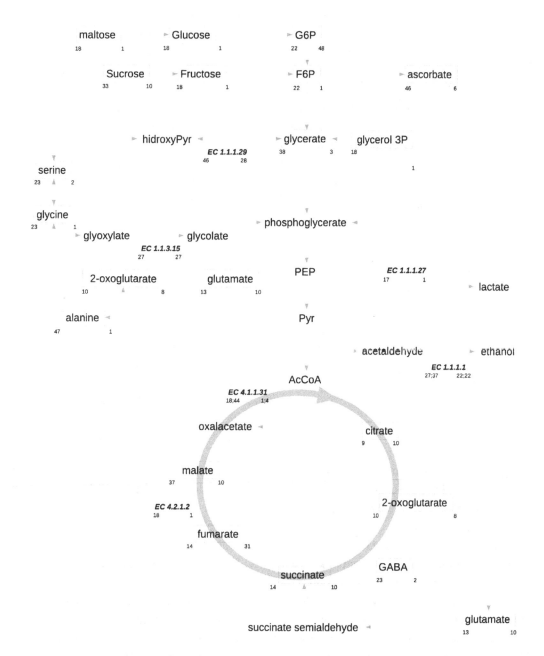

under analysis) can be found, such as [glycine, serine, glicerate, GABA (4-aminobutyrate) and EC 4.1.1.31], [EC 1.1.1.29 and EC 1.1.3.15], and [fumarate and 2 genes from EC 1.1.1.1]. In the first group, compounds that have been grouped by IL-KM but not by IL-SOM with neighbourhood radius = 0, can be found. Additionally, both genes that codify for the EC 1.1.1.1 enzyme have been now grouped in the same cluster.

A deeper analysis has been performed over the available data, considering now k=625, which corresponds to an IL-SOM of 25×25 neurons. Figure 15 shows a schematic diagram of the reconstructed pathways by analyzing, in the new

Figure 15. Primary carbon metabolism in tomato fruits

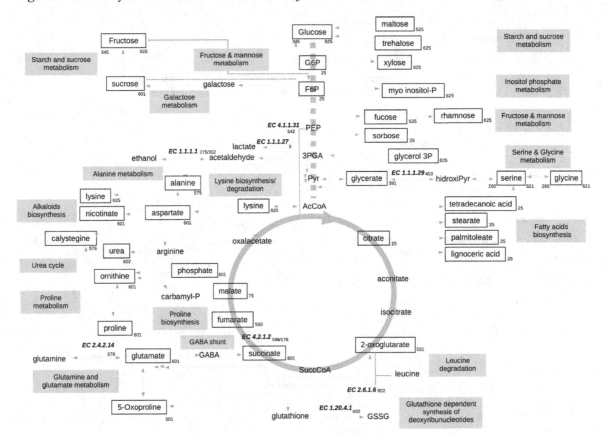

map, neurons 25, 601 and 625 and their neighbours. These neurons were chosen because they grouped most of the glycolytic and TCA cycle intermediates and enzyme encoding genes connecting these pathways with amino acids metabolism. This IL-SOM model, similarly to the presented above also groups known components of biochemical pathways in few neurons. In many cases, what has been grouped in the same neuron in the IL-SOM map of 20×20 neurons, now appears more spread because of the new size of the map and, as previously mentioned, wider visualization radius should be used. As can be seen from the figure, most of the pathway components are grouped in neuron 625 or its neighbours (599, 575, 621). Conversely, other well characterized intermediates of the TCA cycle were not found in neighbouring neurons such as the case of 2-oxoglutare (grouped

in neuron 531). This could either be interpreted as a limitation of the "guilt-by-association" assumption or as a restriction in the SOM model and surely further investigations are needed to elucidate this point.

Furthermore, this model allows the discovery of a new relationship such as the case of the glutaredoxin (EC 1.20.4.1) encoding gene found in neuron 602. The function of this enzyme is widely described in the literature in many organisms (Holmgren, 1989), but its metabolic linkage with primary carbon metabolism is not known in tomato fruits. This example highlights the potential of the method used here to propose experiments in order to test new emerging hypotheses.

In comparison, IL-KM has grouped these TCA fundamental compounds (malate and 2-oxoglutare) in different clusters, and similarly to the previous analysis, the patterns are scattered all over the cluster space. In the figure, only IL-KM coherent groupings are indicated with its corresponding cluster number on the left for the following metabolites [fructose and glucose] and [serine and glycine]. On all other cases, the metabolites and enzymes are spread over several different clusters.

FUTURE RESEARCH DIRECTIONS

As future work, the proposed pipeline will be extended to allow finding new relationships within known metabolic pathways. This will be done by checking integration nodes against online available metabolic pathways (for example, the Kyoto Encyclopedia of Genes and Genomes) for finding candidates genes and metabolites belonging to new metabolic pathways.

Regarding applications, it is feasible to explore the application of this pipeline on other plants or animals, but always depending on data availability.

CONCLUSION

This chapter presents a pipeline for data integration and discovery of *a priori* unknown relationships among introgression lines transcriptional and metabolic data. The pipeline includes four steps: 1) IL-Data understanding, 2) Pre-processing, selection and normalization, 3) Integration, IL-mining and visualization; and 4) Clusters evaluation and biological assessment. Each step of the proposed methodology has been explained in detail, through a case study, which involved genes micro array measurements and metabolite profiles from tomato fruits.

In this pipeline, two standard clustering methods (hierarchical clustering and k-means) are compared against a novel neural network approach named IL-SOM, oriented towards IL-data mining, also providing simple visualizations for identification of co-expressed genes and co-accumulated metabolites. The methods have been compared through objective measures, to analyze the quality of the found clusters. Moreover, a way of measuring their biological significance has been proposed as well, which was addressed from the perspective of the usefulness of the groupings to identify those patterns that change in coordination and therefore belong to common pathways of metabolic regulation. The IL-SOM model has shown high performance in most objective quality measures, plus the maximum coherence from the viewpoint of the biological significance of the relationship between metabolites and transcripts obtained.

REFERENCES

Azuaje, F., & Bolshakova, N. (2002). *Clustering Genome Expression Data: Design and Evaluation Principles*. Springer.

Baxter, C. J., Sabar, M., Quick, W. P., & Sweetlove, L. J. (2005). Comparison of changes in Fruit Gene Expression in Tomato Introgression Lines provides evidence of Genome-wide Transcriptional changes and reveals links to Mapped Qtls and Described Traits. *Journal of Experimental Botany*, 56, 1591–1604. doi:10.1093/jxb/eri154

Bino, R., Hall, R., Fiehn, O., Kopka, J., Saito, K., & Draper, J. (2004). Potential of Metabolomics as a functional Genomics Tool. *Trends in Plant Science*, 9(9), 418–425. doi:10.1016/j.tplants.2004.07.004

Brandes, U. (2008). Social Network Analysis and Visualization. *IEEE Signal Processing Magazine*, 25(6), 147–151. doi:10.1109/MSP.2008.929814

Carrari, F., Baxter, C., Usadel, B., Urbanczyk-Wochniak, E., Zanor, M.-I., & Nunes-Nesi, A. (2006). Integrated Analysis of Metabolite and Transcript Levels reveals the Metabolic Shifts that underlie Tomato Fruit Development and highlight regulatory aspects of Metabolic Network Behavior. *Plant Physiology, 142*, 1380–1396. doi:10.1104/pp.106.088534

Causton, C., Quackenbush, J., & Brazma, A. (2003). *Microarray Gene Expression Data Analysis: A Beginner's Guide*. Blackwell Publishers.

Chakrabarti, S., Cox, E., Frank, E., Goting, R., Han, J., & Jiang, X. (2009). *Data Mining. Know it All*. Elsevier.

Davies, D., & Bouldin, D. (1979). A Cluster Separation Measure. *IEEE Transactions on Pattern Analysis and Machine Intelligence, 1*(4), 224–227. doi:10.1109/TPAMI.1979.4766909

Duda, R., & Hart, P. (2003). *Pattern Classification and Scene Analysis*. New York: Wiley.

Forgy, E. (1965). Cluster Analysis of Multivariate Data: Efficiency vs. Interpretability of Classifications. *Biometrics, 21*(1), 768–780.

Golub, T., Slonim, D., Tamayo, P., Huard, C., Gaasenbeek, M., & Mesirov, J. (1999). Molecular Classification of Cancer: Class Discovery and Class Prediction by Gene Expression Monitoring. *Science (New York, N.Y.), 286*, 531–537.

Guillet, F., & Hamilton, H. J. (2007). *Quality Measures in Data Mining. Studies in Computational Intelligence*. Springer.

Halkidi, M. a. (2001). On Clustering Validation Techniques. *Journal of Intelligent Information Systems, 17*(1), 107–145. doi:10.1023/A:1012801612483

Handl, J., Knowles, J., & Kell, D. B. (2005). Computational Cluster Validation in Post-genomic Data Analysis. *Bioinformatics (Oxford, England), 21*(15), 3201–3212. doi:10.1093/bioinformatics/bti517

Haykin, S. (2007). *Neural Networks: A Comprehensive Foundation* (3rd ed.). Upper Saddle River, NJ: Prentice-Hall, Inc.

Hirai, M., Klein, M., Fujikawa, Y., Yano, M., Goodenowe, D., & Yamazaki, Y. (2005). Elucidation of Gene-to-Gene and Metabolite-to-Gene Networks in Arabidopsis by Integration of Metabolomics and Transcriptomics. *The Journal of Biological Chemistry, 280*(27), 25590–25595. doi:10.1074/jbc.M502332200

Hirai, M. Y., Yano, M., Goodenowe, D. B., Kanaya, S., Kimura, T., Awazuhara, M., et al. (2004). Integration of Transcriptomics and Metabolomics for understanding of global responses to Nutritional Stresses in Arabidopsis Thaliana. In *Proceedings of the National Academy of Sciences of the United States of America* (pp.10205–10210).

Holmgren, A. (1989). Thioredoxin and Glutaredoxin Systems. *The Journal of Biological Chemistry, 264*, 13963–13966.

Kaever, A., Lingner, T., Feussner, K., Gobel, C., Feussner, I., & Meinicke, P. (2009). *Marvis: A Tool for Clustering and Visualization of Metabolic Biomarkers*. BMC Bioinformatics.

Keedwell, E., & Narayanan, A. (2005). *Intelligent Bioinformatics: The Application of Artificial Intelligence Techniques to Bioinformatics Problems*. New York: Wiley. doi:10.1002/0470015721

Kelemen, A., Abraham, A., & Chen, Y. (2008). *Computational Intelligence in Bioinformatics*. New York: Springer.

Kohonen, T. (1982). Self-organized Formation of Topologically Correct Feature Maps. *Biological Cybernetics, 43*, 59–69. doi:10.1007/BF00337288

Kohonen, T., Schroeder, M. R., & Huang, T. S. (2005). *Self-Organizing Maps*. New York: Springer-Verlag.

Lacroix, V., Cottret, L., Thebault, P., & Sagot, M.-F. (2008). An Introduction to Metabolic Networks and their Structural Analysis. *IEEE Transactions on Computational Biology and Bioinformatics*, *5*(4), 594–617. doi:10.1109/TCBB.2008.79

Larose, D. (2005). *Discovering Knowledge in Data: An Introduction to Data Mining*. Wiley-Interscience.

Lindon, J. C., Nicholson, J. K., & Holmes, E. (2007). *The Handbook of Metabonomics and Metabolomics*. Elsevier.

Lippman, Z.B., S. Y., & D., Z. (2007). An Integrated view of Quantitative Trait Variation using Tomato Interspecific Introgression Lines. *Current Opinion in Genetics & Development*, *17*, 1–8. doi:10.1016/j.gde.2007.07.007

Mingoti, S. A., & Lima, J. O. (2006). Comparing SOM Neural Network with Fuzzy c-means, k-means and Traditional Hierarchical Clustering Algorithms. *European Journal of Operational Research*, *174*(3), 1742–1759. doi:10.1016/j.ejor.2005.03.039

Olson, D., & Delen, D. (2008). *Advanced Data Mining*. New York: Springer.

Polanski, A., & Kimmel, M. (2007). *Bioinformatics*. New York: Springer-Verlag.

Quackenbush, J. (2001). Computational Analysis of Microarray Data. *Nature Reviews. Genetics*, *2*(6), 18–427. doi:10.1038/35076576

Rieseberg, L., & Wendel, J. (1993). *Introgression and its consequences in Plants*. Oxford, UK: Oxford University Press.

Saito, K., Hirai, M. Y., & Yonekura-Sakakibara, K. (2008). Decoding Genes with Coexpression Networks and Metabolomics - Majority report by Precogs. *Trends in Plant Science*, *13*, 36–43. doi:10.1016/j.tplants.2007.10.006

Stegmayer, G., Milone, D., Kamenetzky, L., Lopez, M., & Carrari, F. (2009). Neural Network Model for Integration and Visualization of Introgressed Genome and Metabolite Data. In *International Joint Conference on Neural Networks* (pp. 2983-2989).

Tasoulis, D., Plagianakos, V., & Vrahatis, M. (2008). *Computational Intelligence in Bioinformatics. Studies in Computational Intelligence*. New York: Springer.

Tokimatsu, T., Sakurai, N., Suzuki, H., Ohta, H., Nishitani, K., & Koyama, T. (2005). Kappa-view: A Web-based Analysis Tool for Integration of Transcript and Metabolite Data on Plant Metabolic Pathway Maps. *Plant Physiology*, *138*(3), 1289–1300. doi:10.1104/pp.105.060525

Ultsch, A. (1999). *Data Mining and Knowledge Discovery with Emergent Self-organizing Feature Maps for Multivariate Time Series in Kohonen Maps*. Elsevier.

Wolfe, C. J., Kohane, I. S., & Butte, A. J. (2005). Systematic survey reveals general applicability of "guilt-by-association" within Gene Coexpression Networks. *BMC Bioinformatics*, *6*, 227. doi:10.1186/1471-2105-6-227

Xu, R., & Donald, C. Wunsch, I. (2009). *Clustering*. New York: Wiley and IEEE Press.

Yano, M., Kanaya, S., Altaf-Ul-Amin, M., Kurokawa, K., Hirai, M. Y., & Saito, K. (2006). Integrated Data Mining of Transcriptome and Metabolome based on BLSOM. *Journal of Computer Aided Chemistry*, *7*, 125–136. doi:10.2751/jcac.7.125

KEY TERMS AND DEFINITIONS

Hierarchical Clustering: Unsupervised data mining algorithm. It clusters the data forming a tree diagram, or dendrogram, which shows the relationships between samples according to a proximity matrix. The root node of the dendrogram represents the whole data set, and each leaf node is regarded as a data point. The clusters are obtained by cutting the dendrogram at different levels

IL-Mining: Data mining algorithms applied over a biological database containing different types of data (for example: metabolic profiles and transcriptional data from microarrays) from an original genome that that has been modified by introgression lines of wild species alleles (cisgenic plants) or transgenic plants overexpressing a gene of interest. An introgression line (IL) is defined as a genotype that carries genetic material derived from a similar species, for example a "wild" relative. The IL-mining objective is finding hidden relations among the IL-data to infer new knowledge about the biological processes that involve them

K-means: It is one of the best-known and most popular clustering algorithms. It begins by selecting a desired number of *k* clusters and assigning their centroids to data points randomly chosen from the data set. At each iteration, data points are classified by assigning them to the cluster whose centroid is closest and then new cluster centroids are computed as the average of all the points belonging to each cluster.

Metabolite: The metabolome forms a large network of metabolic reactions, where outputs from one enzymatic chemical reaction are inputs to other chemical reactions. Metabolites are the intermediates and products of metabolism. A primary metabolite is directly involved in normal growth, development, and reproduction. A secondary metabolite is not directly involved in those processes, but usually has an important ecological function.

Objective Clustering Measurement: An objective measure is based on only the raw data. No additional knowledge about the data is required. An objective measure usually represents the correlation or distribution of the data. In the case of clustering, objective measurements evaluate the quality the clusters found by a data mining algorithm.

Pathway: Series of chemical reactions catalyzed by enzymes and connected by their intermediates, i.e. the reactants of one reaction are the products of the previous one, and so on. Reconstructing a metabolic pathway consists in inferring the relations between genes, proteins (enzymes), and reactions in a given metabolic system.

Self-organizing Maps: Neural networks that use competitive learning. They can represent complex high-dimensional input patterns into a simpler low dimensional discrete map, with prototype vectors that can be visualized in a two-dimensional lattice structure, while preserving the proximity relationships of the original data as much as possible.

Subjective Clustering Measure: A subjective measure takes into account both the data and the user domain or background knowledge about the data. In the case of clustering, subjective measurements evaluate the validity of the clusters found by a technique from the application point of view (for example, for a biological database, the biological validity of the groupings found).

Transcript: An RNA molecule, a type of compound produced directly from genes. Transcription levels are obtained from hybridation chips containing all genes of the material of interest ordered into spots that are incubated with the transcriptes obtained from the material. They are marked with fluorescence and the results are observed as quantifiable intensity peaks.

Chapter 15
Internet Forums:
What Knowledge can be Mined from Online Discussions

Mikołaj Morzy
Poznan University of Technology, Poland

ABSTRACT

An Internet forum is a web application for publishing user-generated content under the form of a discussion. Messages posted to the Internet forum form threads of discussion and contain textual and multimedia contents. An important feature of Internet forums is their social aspect. Internet forums attract dedicated users who build tight social communities. There is an abundance of Internet forums covering all aspects of human activities: politics, sports, entertainment, science, religion, leisure, hobbies, etc. With large user communities forming around popular Internet forums it is important to distinguish between knowledgeable users, who contribute high quality contents, and other types of users, such as casual users or Internet trolls. Therefore, social role discovery becomes an important issue in discovery of valuable knowledge from Internet forums. This chapter provides an overview of Internet forum technology. It discusses the architecture of Internet forums, presents an overview of data volumes involved and outlines technical challenges of scraping Internet forum data. A broad summary of all research conducted on mining and exploring Internet forums for social role discovery is presented. Next, a multi-tier model for Internet forum analysis (statistical analysis, index analysis, and network analysis) is introduced. Social roles are automatically attributed to Internet forum users based on egocentric graphs of user activity. The issues discussed in the chapter are illustrated with real-world examples. The chapter concludes with a brief summary and a future work agenda.

INTRODUCTION

In this section a brief introduction to the problem of mining Internet forums is presented. Introduc-

tion begins with defining what data mining is and what types of methods are commonly employed to discover knowledge in large repositories of data. Next, the description of Internet forums, a new technology enabling social conversations in the Web 2.0 era is presented.

DOI: 10.4018/978-1-60960-067-9.ch015

Mining Knowledge from Data

Contemporary information systems contain limitless volumes of data. Valuable knowledge is hidden in these data under the form of trends, regularities, correlations, and outliers. Traditional querying models utilized by database systems or data warehouses are not sufficient to extract this knowledge. The value of the data can be greatly increased by adding means to automatically discover useful knowledge from large volumes of gathered data. Recent advances in data capture and data harvesting further increase the amount of data which are continuously loaded into contemporary database systems. Unfortunately, the advances in data gathering techniques are not followed by the increased ability to process and utilize the data. The amount of data to be processed grows quicker than the ability to process it. Therefore, advanced systems are required to automatically process very large amounts of data and acquire useful knowledge from the data self-reliantly. Data mining is the discipline which aims at "… the discovery and extraction of useful, previously unknown, non-trivial, and ultimately understandable patterns from large databases and data warehouses" (Fayyad, Piatetsky-Shapiro, Smyth, & Uthurusamy, 1996). Also brings together databases, decision support systems, machine learning, artificial intelligence, statistics, data visualization, and several other disciplines. Data mining uses different models of knowledge to present patterns discovered in raw data. These models include, but are not limited to, association rules, cyclic rules, characteristic and discriminant rules, classifiers, decision trees, sequential patterns, clusters, time series, and outliers. In parallel, numerous algorithms have been developed to discover and maintain patterns.

Data mining methods can be generally divided into two classes: Predictive tasks and Descriptive tasks. Predictive tasks apply algorithms and techniques to discover hidden patterns in the data and, based on discovered regularities, to provide predictive information which can be used to infer unknown values of attributes or to forecast future behavior. An example of a predictive task is the identification of target customer groups, customer retention analysis, prediction of the future behavior of customers, etc. Descriptive tasks aim at the discovery of patterns which can be used to describe the existing data concisely and to capture general data properties. A typical example of a descriptive task is the discovery of similar customer groups, the discovery of groups of products often purchased together, or the identification of outliers in a dataset. A data mining technique used to discover the hidden knowledge in social structures formed in online Internet forum communities is presented in this chapter.

Internet Forums as New Means of Communication

An Internet forum is a web application for publishing user-generated content under the form of a discussion. Usually, the term *forum* refers to the entire community of users. Discussions considering particular subjects are called *topics* or *threads*. Internet forums (The Latin plural *fora* may also occasionally be used) are sometimes called web forums, discussion boards, message boards, discussion groups, or bulletin boards. Internet forums are not new to the network community. They are successors of tools such as Usenet Newsgroups and Bulletin Board Systems (BBS) that were popular before the advent of the World Wide Web. Messages posted to a forum can be displayed either chronologically, or using threads of discussion. Most forums are limited to textual messages with some multimedia content embedded (such as images or flash objects). Internet forum systems also provide sophisticated search tools that allow users to search for messages containing search criteria, to limit the search to particular threads or sub-forums, to search for messages posted by a particular user, to search within the subject or body of the post, etc.

The most important feature of Internet forums is their social aspect. Many forums are active for a long period of time and attract a group of dedicated users, who build a tight social community around a forum. With great abundance of forums devoted to every possible aspect of human activity, such as politics, religion, sports, technology, entertainment, economy, fashion, and many more, users are able to find a forum that perfectly suits their needs and interests (Hanna & De Nooy, 2009). Usually, upon joining the forum a user pledges to adhere to the netiquette of a forum, i.e., the set of rules governing the accepted format and content of posts. Some forums are very strict about enforcing netiquette rules (e.g., a family forum may not tolerate any form of cursing or sexually explicit content), and some forums do not enforce netiquette rules at all. Two types of special users are present to protect the forum and enforce the netiquette. Administrators have a complete set of rights and permissions to edit and delete abusing posts, to manage threads of discussion, to change global forum settings, to conduct software upgrades, to manage users and their accounts, to ban users who do not comply with the netiquette, and to stick popular threads and create word filters for posts.

Moderators enjoy a subset of rights and permissions granted to administrators. Moderators are commonly assigned the task to run a single forum or a single thread and moderate the discussion by issuing warnings to users who do not comply with the netiquette. Moderators can suspend users, edit and delete questionable posts, and temporarily ban users who breach the rules of the forum. Forums may require a registration and a login prior to posting a message, but there are also popular forums where anonymous users are allowed to post. Anonymity and pseudo-anonymity drastically lower the quality of data and information available on a forum. Besides, the registration requirement creates a strong liaison between a user and a forum, building durable social bindings. Unfortunately, even registration does not shield forum community from trolls, malevolent users whose sole intention is to spark heated discussion, ignite controversy, or post offensive and abusive contents. Trolls usually have no other merit or purpose than to irritate and offend other users, misusing pseudo-anonymity offered by the Internet. Trolling is just one example of the obtrusive social cost of cheap pseudonyms which can be created and used at no cost. Indeed, trolls fear no real retaliation for their vandalizing behavior other than a ban on a given identity. As the registration is almost always free of charge, there is no incentive for a troll to preserve his/her identity.

As noted earlier, Internet forums are not a new concept, but merely an improvement over Usenet Newsgroups and Dial-up Bulletin Boards. They differ from Usenet groups in that they do not use email interface or specialized news reader, but utilize a standard web interface accessible from a standard browser. They differ from blogs, because they use the pull architecture (as opposed to the push architecture commonly used by blog readers) and they support the model of "many writers, many readers" (as opposed to the model of "one writer, many readers" employed by blogs). Also, the ability to create strong social bonds among members of a forum is quite unique with respect to other Web 2.0 technologies. This distinctive feature of Internet forums is used to mine forum data in search of social roles of participants.

LITERATURE OVERVIEW

Data mining is a well-established discipline within the computer science domain, with many excellent textbooks covering the entire field. A thorough introduction to data mining and knowledge discovery can be found in Tan et al. (2005). A database perspective on data mining methods and algorithms is presented in Han et al. (2005). Many practical aspects of data mining algorithm design and deployment are discussed in Witten and Frank (2005).

The data acquired from the web has its own distinct properties and characteristics that make these data particularly difficult to mine. Web mining has recently emerged as a new field of research, which copes with the task of designing efficient and robust algorithms for mining internet data. A very good introduction to web mining methods and models can be found in Chakrabarti (2002). Much research has been conducted on text mining and knowledge discovery from unstructured data. An interested reader may find a detailed summary of recent findings in this domain in Feldman and Sanger (2006) and Weiss et al. (2004). In addition, much work has been done on statistical natural language processing. Statistical methods for text mining are described and discussed in detail in Manning and Schuetze (1999).

Analysis of threaded conversations, which are the predominant pattern of communications in the contemporary web, is an actively researched domain. In particular, many proposals have been submitted to derive social roles solely based on the structural patterns of conversations. Examples of earlier proposals include (White, Boorman, & Breiger, 1976 ; Viegas & Smith, 2004 ; Fisher, Smith, & Welser, 2006). A thorough overview of structural patterns associated with particular social roles, that can be used as structural signatures, can be found in Skvoretz and Faust (2002). Most of the recent work has been performed on the basis of social network analysis methods (Hanneman & Riddle, 2005 ; Brandes & Erlebach, 2005 ; Carrington, Scott, & Wasserman, 2005), but the investigation of role typology has been an important challenge in sociology (Parsons, 1951; Merton, 1968). Recently, more attention has been given to the identification of social roles that are not general, but specific to online communities. The existence of local experts, trolls, answer people, fans, conversationalists, etc. has been verified (Burkharter & Smith, 2004 ; Golder, 2003 ; Turner, Smith, Fisher, & Welser, 2005; Marcoc-

cia, 2004). Moreover, the benefits of being able to deduce the social role of an individual without having to analyze the contents generated by that individual are becoming apparent (Wenger, 1999 ; Wenger & Snyder, 2000; Wenger, McDermott, & Snyder, 2002).

MINING INTERNET FORUMS

In this section, the characteristics of the data harvested from Internet forums is discussed and the challenges and problems involved in knowledge acquisition from Internet forums were outlined. The author then proceeds to the presentation of his model for Internet forum mining, where multi-tier analysis of Internet forum data reveals interesting patterns and characteristics of forums, threads, and individual users.

Data from Internet Forums

Internet forums have recently become the leading form of peer communication in the Internet. Many software products are available for creating and administering Internet forums. Usually, Internet forums are complex scripts prepared in the technology of choice: PHP, CGI, Perl, ASP.NET, or Java. Threads and posts are stored either in a relational database or in a flat file. Internet forums vary in terms of functions offered to its users. The simplest forums allow only to prepare textual messages that are displayed chronologically using threads of discussion. Sophisticated forum management systems allow users to prepare posts using visual editors and markup languages, such as BBCode (Bulleting Board Code) or HTML, and to address replies to individual posts. In particular, using BBCode tags makes the analysis and parsing of forum posts difficult. BBCode is a lightweight markup language used to beautify discussion list posts. The use of BBCode allows forum administrators to turn off the ability to embed HTML content in forum posts for security reasons, at the same time allowing users to prepare visually attractive posts. Unfortunately, different implementations of the BBCode markup are not compatible across Internet forum management systems, with varying keyword lists or inconsistencies in enforcing capital letters in BBCode tags.

Among many competing platforms for Internet forum management three platforms are of particular interest to the research presented in this chapter. The first one, PHP Bulletin Board (PhpBB) is a very popular Internet forum software written entirely using PHP programming language and distributed using the GNU (General Public License) as open source software. Since its publication in the year 2000, PhpBB has become undoubtedly the most popular open source software for managing Internet forums. PhpBB is characterized by a simple and intuitive installation process, overall friendliness of the interface, high efficiency, flexibility and customizability. An additional advantage of PhpBB is a very large and supportive user community providing inexperienced users with many tutorials and guidelines. PhpBB is one of the very few solutions that provide interfaces to almost all contemporary database management systems, among others, to MySQL, PostgreSQL, SQL Server, FireBird, Oracle, and SQLite. The second Internet forum management system is the Invision Power Board (IPB) produced by Invision Power Services Inc. IPB is a commercial product popular among companies and organizations due to its low cost of maintenance and effective support. IPB provides interfaces only to the most popular databases: MySQL, Oracle, and SQL Server.

Differently from PhpBB, IPB is a fully-fledged content management system, which releases administrators from the bulk of manually creating and managing HTML pages. In addition, IPB fully utilizes newest capabilities of asynchronous data transfer using AJAX and JavaScript calls, and supports a modular forum design using the technology of plugins. The third platform for Internet forum management discussed in this chapter is the dedicated software script developed by gazeta. pl, a popular web portal of the leading Polish newspaper "*Gazeta Wyborcza*". The spectrum of forums offered by the portal gazeta.pl is very broad, one may find highly specialized forums devoted to sports, technology, economy, politics, health, entertainment, and many more. As of the time of writing gazeta.pl hosts 4895 forums containing 79 346 874 posts. The gazeta.pl forum management system is an example of a custom software script that required developing a dedicated crawler for Internet forum data acquisition.

In order to better understand scalability-related challenges of mining Internet forum data, statistics on selected forums were presented. All statistics were gathered by Big Boards (http://www.bigboards.com), the catalog of the biggest Internet forums exceeding 500,000 posts. Estimating the size of a forum is a difficult and error-prone task. By far the most popular metric is the total number of posts. This metric can be biased by the presence of automatically generated spam messages, but other metrics are also susceptible to manipulation. For instance, measuring the number of registered users may be tricky, because many Internet forums allow posts not only from directly registered users, but from users who registered to other parts of a portal as well. Similarly, the frequency of posting per registered user may be biased by the vague definition of the term "registered user". Table 1 summarizes the Top 10 Biggest Internet Forums list. This list is very interesting as it clearly demonstrates the diversity of Internet forums. The biggest forum, Gaia Online, is an anime role-playing community, with a huge base of members. FaceTheJury is a set of real-life picture rating forums and 4chan is a message board for discussing topics related to Japanese culture. The numbers behind these forums demonstrate the unprecedented sizes of virtual communities emerging around Internet forums. It is clear that such vast repositories of data and information cannot be analyzed and browsed manually, and

Table 1. Top 10 biggest Internet forums

S.No	Name	Technology	Number of posts	Number of users
1	Gaia Online	phpBB	1632265797	19086312
2	4chan	custom	306973518	29417
3	D2jsp	custom	221897454	493344
4	IGN boards	IGN boards	199510907	1255254
5	Nexopia	custom	182602864	1424092
6	FaceTheJury	custom	156252488	552000
7	Jogos	phpBB	142582510	186353
8	Vault Network boards	IGN boards	121786165	626203
9	Offtopic.com	vBulletin	119930222	209456
10	Doctissimo.fr	custom	98185241	1456507

Table 2. Top 10 Internet forum technologies

S.No	Technology	Number of forums	Percent of forums
1	vBulletin	1411	63%
2	IGN Boards	289	13%
3	phpBB	253	11%
4	custom	108	4%
5	SMF	47	2%
6	UBB	41	2%
7	ezBoard	37	2%
8	MesDiscussions. net	18	1%
9	ASP Playground	16	1%
10	Burning Board	15	1%

Table 3. Top Internet forum implementation languages

S.No	Language	Number of forums	Percent of forums
1	PHP	2186	94%
2	ASP.NET	49	2%
3	Perl/CGI	44	2%
4	SmallTalk	22	1%
5	ColdFu- sion	11	1%

that automated methods for knowledge discovery and extraction are necessary.

Table 2 presents the list of top 10 Internet forum software technologies. This list presents the distribution of Internet forum software technologies only for Internet forums indexed by Big Boards. From the results it may be concluded that the majority of popular Internet forum software technologies are commercial products (vBulletin, IGN Boards, UBB, ezBoard, MesDiscussions. net, or Burning Board), but open source solutions are paving their way (PhpBB, SMF).

As for the programming language of choice, Table 3 shows that the overwhelming majority of Internet forums are implemented in PHP, with negligible presence of ASP.NET and Perl/CGI.

Initially, main subjects of discussions on Usenet groups and bulletin boards were related to computers and technology. With the widespread adoption of the Internet within the society, discussion boards and Internet forums were quickly attracting more casual users. Today, entertainment, recreation, and computer games are the most popular categories of discussions. Table 4 summarizes the most popular categories of Internet forums. The data clearly shows that Internet forums span a very broad spectrum of subjects and, importantly, there is no dominant category or subject.

Table 4. Top 10 Internet forum categories

S.No	Category	Number of forums	Percent of forums
1	Entertainment	438	17%
2	Recreation	408	16%
3	Games	391	15%
4	Computers	324	13%
5	Society	257	10%
6	Sports	221	9%
7	General	218	9%
8	Art	138	5%
9	Home	79	3%
10	Science	70	3%

Table 5. Top 10 Internet forum languages

S.No	Language	Number of forums	Percent of forums
1	English	1758	79%
2	German	143	6%
3	French	76	3%
4	Dutch	54	2%
5	Russian	49	2%
6	Spanish	47	2%
7	Turkish	36	2%
8	Italian	35	2%
9	Swedish	20	1%
10	Chinese	19	1%

Finally, let us consider the degree of internationalization of Internet forum communities. Table 5 presents the distribution of languages spoken on Internet forums. As expected, Internet forums are dominated by English, followed by European languages (German, French, Dutch, etc.). What comes as a surprise is that Chinese is not very popular among Internet forum users.

Crawling Internet Forums

Analysis and mining of Internet forum data requires data to be cleansed, pruned, pre-processed, and stored conveniently, most favorably in a relational database due to the maturity of the relational database technology and the broad availability of tools for mining relational databases. Unfortunately, crawling Internet forums is a daunting and difficult task (Wang, Yang, Lai, Cai, Zhang, & Ma, 2008). Forum discussions can lead to tree-like structures of arbitrary depths, posts pertaining to a single discussion can be paginated, and Internet forum engines, such as PhpBB, can be personalized, leading to HTML code that is different from the original engine HTML output. Therefore, a robust and reliable method for crawling and harvesting Internet forum pages into a structured form must have been developed.

The first step in Internet forum analysis is the development of a web crawler capable of crawling and downloading an entire forum identified by its URL address (Cai, Yang, Lai, Wang, & Zhang, 2008). At this stage an open-source library WebSphinx (http://www.cs.cmu.edu/~rcm/websphinx) has been used to automate the majority of repetitive and difficult tasks. Among others, the WebSphinx library takes care of the following tasks: maintaining the cache of URL addresses to visit, scheduling requests, conforming to the netiquette, and managing the set of threads that access the address cache in parallel. For each document processed by the crawler, the method void visit(Page) is called to parse and analyze the contents of the document.

In addition, for each link encountered on the processed page the result of the method boolean shouldVisit(Link) indicates whether the link should be followed, i.e., whether the link should be added to the address cache. The address cache is accessed in parallel by multiple threads of the crawler, where each thread picks a single address from the cache and processes it. Additional parameters can be set that govern the behavior of the crawler, e.g., the depth of the crawl or the maximum size of documents to be fetched. To make the crawler general enough to handle different Internet forums, the crawler is implemented using abstract classes for document processing and URL analysis. In this way, adding a new Internet forum engine template to the crawler is simplified and the architecture of the crawler becomes flexible and extensible.

Downloaded documents are parsed in search of topics and posts. Then, the discovered structures are loaded into the database. The database schema for the Internet forum analysis is fairly simple and consists of seven tables joined by several foreign keys. Main tables include PARENT_FORUM and FORUM for storing hierarchical structure of Internet forums, AUTHOR and AUTHOR COMM tables for storing information on users and their communication, TOPIC, POST, and ENTITY tables for storing information on topics and posts, as well as named entities referenced in posts. The latter is required for discovering experts and trend setters among users. In addition to tables, several B-tree indexes are created to speed up query processing. During crawling and initial processing of Internet forum data, several obstacles may appear. First of all, automatic threaded crawler may overload the forum server, even when it conforms to the netiquette and follows robots. txt and <META> protocols. In such case, no new session can be created on the server.

The crawler must be robust and must handle such situations. Secondly, many links are duplicated across the forum. Duplication helps humans to better navigate the forum, but is very troublesome for web crawlers. In particular, the links leading to the same document can differ, e.g., in parameter lists. In such case, the crawler cannot recognize an already visited document, which, in turn, leads to parsing the same document several times. Lastly, many methods for forum analysis rely on the chronological order of topics and posts. Unfortunately, parsing the date is an extremely difficult task. There are no fixed formats for displaying dates and each date can be displayed differently depending on the language being used.

In addition, some Internet forum engines display dates using relative descriptions, e.g. "yesterday" or "today". These differences must be accounted for when customizing the crawler for a particular forum.

Challenges in Mining Internet Forums

As a summary, the main technological and research problems and challenges in mining Internet forums were identified so far. Traditional data mining algorithms are tailored to highly structured relational data first. Unfortunately, data harvested from the web differ significantly from the relational data. Main differences arise from the way social data are generated, acquired, and used. For example, data acquired from Internet forums are incomplete (e.g. because of the imminent limitations of Internet crawlers) and dirty (due the amount of spam and bot-generated contents). As seen already, there are no agreed upon standards with respect to the format of the data. The ability to derive structure is crucial in mining any type of data. Unfortunately, with web data it is very difficult to assume anything about the structure and the format of data acquired from crawlers. The primary cause of this difficulty is the lack of standards regarding such data, because every website uses custom data structures. As the consequence, a tailor-made mapping must be constructed for each single website to cast the data harvested by a crawler into a database. Needless to say, this requirement makes Internet forum data acquisition expensive and cumbersome.

A very important aspect of Internet forum data is its mutability and scale-free networking properties. Internet forum data are usually presented in the form of a graph or a network. Nodes in the network appear and disappear freely, relationships forming edges in the network may fade over time, and the topology of the network changes constantly. As a result, constructing a static view of the network may be difficult, if not impossible. The lack of a single unifying view of the network makes the transition between network states indeterministic and must be accounted for in every algorithm for mining the data. On the other hand, Internet forum data, like the majority of social-driven data, usually form a scale-free network (Barabasi & Bonabeau, 2003), with the distribution of node degrees given by $P(k) \sim k^{\gamma}$ where $P(k)$ is the probability that a node has the degree of k, and the coefficient γ usually varies between 2 and 3. In other words, a scale-free network consists of a small number of high degree nodes, called hubs, and a large number of nodes with low degree. Because social networks grow accordingly to the Barabási-Albert model (Barabási & Albert, 1999) (also known as the preferential attachment), the resulting network is a scale-free network.

One of the most important properties of scale-free networks is their robustness and resistance to failures. If nodes in the network fail with equal probability, then a failure of an ordinary node does not affect the rest of the network, these are only failures of hubs that may influence the network as a whole. Because the number of hubs is negligible when compared to the size of the network, the peril of bringing the network down is minimal. In addition, every change of an ordinary node passes almost unnoticed. From the algorithmic point of view, only a small percentage of data alterations is interesting, and all alterations of ordinary nodes may be ignored without significant loss of precision, because the alterations of ordinary nodes do not affect the global properties of the network. As the result, mining algorithms may concentrate only on nodes belonging to the core of the network, thus effectively reducing computational costs, but the problem of determining the set of core nodes remains to be solved.

Finally, most of the content of Internet forums is textual. The informality of the language being used, presence of acronyms, fast-changing jargon, abbreviations, spelling errors, and multi-linguicity all contribute to the fact that employing Natural Language Processing (NLP) techniques to Internet forum data is extremely difficult. A true research challenge is therefore the design and implementation of data mining methods capable of discovering valuable knowledge (e.g. expertise levels of users) solely from the structure of the network, without resorting to text mining methods.

Multi-Tiered Analysis of Internet Forums

Statistical Analysis

A statistical analysis of an Internet forum consists in identifying basic building blocks for indexes. Basic statistics on topics, posts, and users are used to define activity, controversy, popularity, and other measures introduced in the next section. The analysis of these basic statistics provides great insight into the characteristics of Internet forums. Basic statistics can be computed during the loading of an Internet forum into the database, or on demand upon the analysis of a forum. The latter technique is used for statistics that are time-bound, for instance, when calculating the activity of an Internet forum relative to the date of the analysis. In this section the results of the analysis of an exemplary Internet forum that gathers bicycle lovers is presented. As of the day of the analysis the forum contained 1099 topics with 11595 posts and 2463 distinct contributors. Due to the lack of space only selected figures illustrating presented distributions is included.

The most important factor in the analysis of Internet forums is the knowledge embedded in Internet forum topics. A variety of topics provides users with a wealth of information, but, at the same time, makes searching for particular knowledge difficult. The main aim of mining Internet forums is to provide users with automatic means of discovering useful knowledge from these vast amounts of textual data. The basic statistics on topics gathered during the crawling and parsing phases is given below.

Most topics contain a single post. This is either a question that has never been answered, or a post that did not spark any discussion. Posts leading to long heated discussions with many posts are very rare, and if a post generates a response, then continuing the discussion is not very likely. Almost every Internet forum has a small set of discussions that are very active (these are usually "sticky" topics). The biggest number of posts per topic can be generated by the most controversial posts that provoke heated disputes. Topic depth may be computed only for Internet forums that allow for threaded discussions. Flat architectures, such as PhpBB, where each post is a direct answer to the previous post, do not allow to create deeply threaded discussions. The depth of a topic is a very good indicator of topic's controversy. Controversial topics usually result in long, deeply threaded discussions between small subsets of participants. Deeply threaded discussions (8-16 responses) are not frequent (although not negligible) and the majority of topics is either almost flat (1-2 responses), or slightly threaded (3-7 responses). Another important statistic concerns the number of distinct users who participate in and contribute to the topic. Most topics attract a small number of users (2-3 users). Sometimes, there is only one user posting to a topic (an example is a question that was answered by no one) or just two users (an example could be a question with a single answer). Some questions may encourage a dispute among experts, in such case a single question may generate a few conflicting answers from several users. Finally, certain topics stimulate many users to post (10-20 users), especially if the subject of the opening post, or some subsequent answers, are controversial.

This statistic is useful when assessing the popularity and interestingness of a topic, under the assumption that interesting topics attract many users. This statistic can also be used to measure the controversy surrounding a topic. If a topic is controversial, more users are likely to express their views and opinions on such topic. Combined with the analysis of the depth of the discussion, this statistic allows to quickly discover the most controversial topics. Finally, for each topic a statistic on the average number of posts per day is collected. Most topics are not updated frequently, with the average number of posts ranging from 1 to 5, but there is also a significant number of hot topics that gather numerous submissions. If a topic concerns a recent development, e.g. a political event, many users are likely to share their thoughts and opinions. Also, some posts are labeled as urgent and the utility of an answer is directly related to the promptness of the answer.

Interesting statistics can be gathered at the granularity level more detailed than a topic, namely, by analyzing individual posts. Posts may differ significantly by content, length, information value, etc. The main goal is to derive as much knowledge as possible by analyzing only the structure of the social network, and not its contents. Therefore, the author deliberately refrain from using well-established methods of natural language processing and uses only the most elementary statistics. The distributions of post lengths measured in the number of words and characters is collected. Figure 1 presents the distribution of post lengths measured in terms of number of words.

The shapes of these distributions are naturally very similar, but there are subtle differences. Both statistics have been chosen to account for the variability in vocabulary used in different forums. The language used by many Internet forum participants is a form of an Internet slang, full of abbreviations and acronyms. When a post is written using this type of language, then measuring the number of words is more appropriate to assess the information value of the post. On the other hand, forums that attract eloquent and educated people usually uphold high standards of linguistic correctness and measuring the information value of a post using the number of characters may be less biased.

Figure 1. The distribution of post lengths measures in terms of number of words

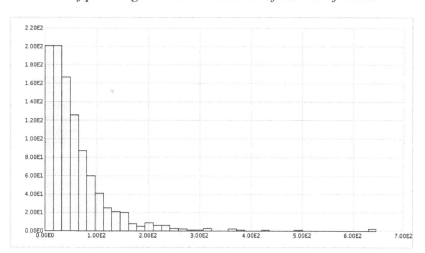

Apart from statistically measuring topics and posts, a fair amount of statistics describing the behavior of users have been collected. Users are the most important asset of every Internet forum, they provide knowledge and expertise, moderate discussions, and form the living backbone of the Internet forum community. The most interesting aspect of the Internet forum analysis is the clustering of users based on their social roles. Some users play the role of experts, answering questions and providing invaluable help. Other users play roles of visitors, newbies, or even trolls. Basic statistics gathered during downloading and parsing of an Internet forum provide building blocks that will further allow us to attribute certain roles to users.

The simplest measure of user activity and importance is the number of posts submitted by a user. The overwhelming majority of users appears only once to post a single message, presumably a question. These users do not contribute to the forum, but benefit from the presence of experts who volunteer to answer their questions. Such distribution is very characteristic of anonymous or semi-anonymous Internet forums (i.e., forums that allow to post messages either anonymously, or using a pseudonym, but without the requirement to register).

The number of posts created by a user may be somehow misleading. Consider two posts, the first one with a detailed description of how to solve a complex problem, and another post with a simple "thank you" message. Both posts equally contribute to the previous statistic. Therefore, to include another statistic that measures the average length of a post per user expressed as the number of characters is chosen. Most posts are relatively short, rarely exceeding four sentences. The average English world length is 5.10 letters, and the average English sentence length is 14.3 words, which results in the average of 72.93 letters per sentence. Most users submit short posts, up to 50 words (which translates roughly into 5 sentences). Both above statistics require a word of caution. It is very common for Internet forum posts to include quotations from other sources. Often, a user posting an answer to a query uses the text originating from another site to validate and endorse the answer. In such case, both statistics favor users who quote other material and make their submissions longer. On the other hand, identifying and removing quoted contents is very difficult, or even impossible. Other popular form of quotation consists in including a hyperlink to the quoted contents. Such post is much shorter,

Figure 2. Weekly activity chart of a forum

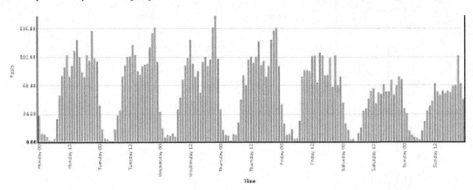

but interested users can follow the hyperlink to find relevant and useful information.

The final statistic considers the average number of topics in which a given user has participated. The rationale behind this statistic is twofold. First, it measures the versatility of a user. Users participating in many topics are usually capable of answering a broad spectrum of questions, and therefore can be perceived as experts. On the other hand, users who post questions to many topics are actively seeking for information and knowledge. Secondly, this statistic measures the commitment of a user. Users who participate in many topics contribute to the existence and vitality of the Internet forum community. The data shows that most users participate in a single topic and the community of Internet forum users is dominated by one-time visitors who post a question, receive an answer, and never come back to the Internet forum. Of course, all these statistics consider only active participants and do not consider consumers of information, who read but do not post.

Selected measures for assessing the importance and quality of Internet forums is presented next. The author refrain from creating a universal ranking among Internet forums and dido not try to derive a single unifying measure for all Internet forums. Instead, several indexes which utilize the basic statistical measures presented in the previous section were constructed. These indexes can be manipulated and validated by users, who subjectively rank forums, topics, and posts using the multi-criterion rankings.

Prior to define indexes used to rank individual topics, posts, and users, two additional measures have been introduced that can be used to characterize the entire forum. These measures are related to the activeness of the forum. The first measure is the activity of a forum (measured as the number of posts per day) since the creation of the forum. This measure allows to assess the liveliness of the forum and to follow the development of the forum, from its infancy, throughout adolescence and maturity, until its sunset years. In addition, the development trend of the forum can be deduced, as well as the stability of the forum and its dynamics. Another interesting time-related measure is the chart of the weekly activity of the Internet forum, again, measured as the number of posts submitted daily. An example of such a chart is presented in Figure 2. The shape of this chart discloses much about the Internet forum community. Some Internet forums gather professionals and are used mainly to solve problems that occur during work. Such Internet forums have the main peak of their activity on working days from 9am to 4pm. Other Internet forums may serve as the meeting point for hobbyists, who discuss issues in their spare time, usually in the evenings and over weekends. After identifying the main type of the Internet forum (morning activity, weekend activity, evening and night activity, etc.) its participants and contributors may be additionally tagged based on this type.

Index Analysis

At the heart of every Internet forum lie discussion topics. The main emphasis of every analysis of Internet forums must focus on topics. It is the topic that attracts the activity and productivity of users. Since most Internet forums are very versatile, they contain topics that are active and passive, interesting and useless, popular and interesting only to a small fraction of users. In other words, topics within a single Internet forum may be very different and a robust method of topic analysis is required to unearth interesting, intriguing and stimulating discussions. This section begins by presenting indexes for topic analysis, indexes for user analysis is proceeded, and finally concludes with the presentation of indexes for post analysis. Topics can be ranked according to a plethora of criteria. Three exemplary indexes that can be constructed using the basic statistics introduced previously is presented below:

Activity

Topic activity, similarly to Internet forum activity, is always defined in the context of a given time period. To help identify the most active topics that attract vivid discussions, Topic Activity Index (TAI) is defined that measures the number of posts submitted during days preceding the given date. Posts are aged relatively to the given date, so the posts submitted earlier have lower weight. Formally, TAI is defined as

$$TAI = w_1 * P_{0,1} + w_2 * P_{1,2} + w_3 * P_{2,4} + w_4 * P_{4,10}$$

where $P_{i,j}$ denotes the number of posts submitted to the topic between i and j days before the date of the analysis, and w_i are arbitrary weights such that $\sum_i w_i = 1$. The coefficients were chosen empirically as the result of the analysis of

several different Internet forums and set in the following way: $w_1 = 0.4$, $w_2 = 0.3$, $w_3 = 0.2$, $w_4 = 0.1$. The author decided to remove from consideration posts older than 10 days. In addition, the TAI measure strongly favors topics that attract many submissions as of the time of the analysis, and prunes topics that were suspended, became quiet, or simply lost popularity. The last case is often seen on Internet forums discussing newest developments in politics, entertainment, and sports, where very popular topics appear instantly with the discussed event, and then quickly loose freshness and relevance.

Popularity

The Popularity Index (PI) measures the overall popularity of a topic, outside of the context of the current analysis. Therefore, the popularity index of a topic is a monotonically increasing measure. PI is defined as

$$PI = w_1 * U + w_2 * P$$

where U denotes the number of users contributing to the topic, P denotes the number of posts submitted to the topic, and w_1, w_2 are arbitrary weights such that $\sum_i w_i = 1$. It has been found that the most reliable results can be achieved for w_1 significantly greater than w_2, e.g. $w_1 = 0.75$, $w_2 = 0.25$.

Controversy

The Controversy Index (CI) aims at identifying the most interesting and heated discussions. Controversy may result from two different reasons. Firstly, a topic may have been started by a controversial question or may touch an issue on which there are conflicting views within the community. Secondly, a topic may be fueled by trolling or flaming (i.e. posting intentionally abusive and conflicting posts with the sole purpose of irritating and annoying other members of the community). Of course, the aim of the analysis is to identify the first type of the controversy present in topic posts. The main difficulty in designing of the Controversy Index is a very high subjectivity of what should be considered controversial. Users vary significantly in their tolerance to emotional language, cursing, or critically attacking sensitive issues. Other users take such posts very personally and do not tolerate any controversy. One good marker of the type of the controversy is the depth of the discussion tree. Users, who feel offended by a controversial post, tend to express their contempt but, usually, they do not continue the discussion.

On the other hand, if the controversy stems from the natural disagreement on a given issue, then participants are far more likely to continue the discussion with the aim of convincing their adversary. In addition to measuring the depth of the discussion, the number of distinct users who submitted posts below a given discussion depth threshold is also measured. This additional measure allows to decide whether the discussion was a heated exchange of opinions between two quarreling users, or the subject was interesting for a broader audience. Combining these two numbers allows to prune discussions where only two users participate and the community is indifferent to the issue. The last building block of the CI is the emotionality of posts submitted to the topic. The emotionality measure is defined a little further when discussing measures for individual post ranking. Suffice to say, high emotionality characterizes posts that either contain emotional words, or their punctuation indicates strong emotions. Formally, the CI is defined as

$$CI = w_1*avg(E)+w_2*U+w_3*W$$

where avg(E) denotes the average emotionality of a post submitted to the topic, U denotes the number of distinct contributors who have passed the topic depth threshold, W denotes the number of posts, and w_1,w_2,w_3 are arbitrary weights such that $\sum_i w_i = 1$. In the experiments it has been found that the following values of weights produce high quality results: $w_1 = 0.5$, $w_2 = 0.375$, and $w_3 = 0.125$.

Another dimension of the Internet forum mining is the analysis of users. As in case of topics, users may be ranked according to several different, and sometimes conflicting, criteria. Two simple indexes that can be used to rank Internet forum users by employing basic statistics introduced previously is described below:

Activity

User activity may be measured primarily by the number of posts submitted to the forum, but there is a subtle difference between submitting ten posts to a single topic, and submitting one post to ten topics. Users who participate in many discussions and who post to different topics or maintain a high average of posts per day are likely to be the most valuable users of the Internet forum. Participation in several topics signals not only the versatility of the user, but her commitment to the Internet forum community. The Activity Index for Users (AIU) considers both the number of posts submitted by the user, and the number of distinct topics in which the user has participated. Formally, the AIU is defined as

$$AIU = w_1*T+w_2*W$$

where T denotes the number of topics in which the user took part, W is the number of posts submitted by the user, and w_1,w_2 are arbitrary weights such that $\sum_i w_i = 1$. The author strongly suggest that $w_1 > w_2$, which allows to prune users who post selectively, but their activity is limited to a small number of topics.

Productivity

The Productivity Index (PI) of a user captures the efficiency of the user in passing knowledge. This index computes the total length of all posts submitted by the user. However, the PI can be misleading, because it favors users who write long posts, but severely punishes users who reply by pointing to external resources (FAQs, wikis, etc.) providing the URL of the external resource. In such case, the user may provide valid and valuable knowledge by passing a relatively short text. On the other hand, the majority of posts consists only of one or two words, which are either pointers to external resources, links leading to unrelated sites as the result of spamming, or useless text such as "thank you", "wow!", and the like. The Productivity Index helps to sieve through these short texts at the cost of ignoring some valuable submissions.

The final dimension of Internet forum mining is the analysis of individual posts. As mentioned earlier, for each post all possible statistics are collected, such as the length of the post in characters, the number of words in the post, the number of entities in the post, and the post's depth in the topic tree (where applicable). An exemplary index that can be constructed from these basic statistics is presented below.

Emotionality

The Emotionality Index (EI) serves at least three different purposes. Firstly, it allows to assess the temperature of the discussion. Secondly, it shows the mutual relationships between users. Finally, it may be used to compute the degree of controversy around a given topic. Unfortunately, similarly to the controversy, individual perception of emotionality in a post is a highly subjective matter. A method similar to the method presented in Alm et al. (2005) is used. The emotionality of a post is estimated using two factors. The first factor is the number of words in the post that bear strong emotional weight. The words using a predefined vocabulary of emotional words and the semantic lexicon WordNet were found. The second factor utilizes emoticons (dots, commas, and combinations of special characters) and punctuation used in the text. The presence of certain emoticons in the

text may very well account for certain emotional state of writing.

Network Analysis

A social network is a structure made of entities that are connected by one or more types of interdependency. Entities constituting a social network represent individuals, groups or services, and relationships between entities reflect real-world dependencies. Social networks are best represented by sociograms, which are graphic representations of social links connecting individuals within the network. Nodes in a sociogram represent individuals, and edges connecting nodes represent relationships. Edges can be directed (e.g., a relationship of professional subordination), undirected (e.g., a relationship of acquaintance), one-directional (e.g., a relationship of trust), and bi-directional (e.g., a relationship of discussion). Sociograms are the main tool used in sociometry, a quantitative method of measuring features of social links, such as expertise levels of individuals (Zhang, Ackerman, & Adamic, 2007).

In order to compute the measures of social importance and coherence of Internet forums, a model of a social network for Internet forums should be created first. When developing a model of a social network for a given domain, one must carefully design the sociogram for the domain: what constitutes nodes and edges of the sociogram, are there any weights associated with edges, and whether edges are directed or undirected. Let us first consider the choice of nodes, and then to proceed to the design of edges.

The participation in an Internet forum is tantamount to the participation in an established social community defined by the Internet forum subject. The degree of coherence of the community may vary from very strict (a closed group of experts who know each other), through moderate (a semi-opened group consisting of a core of experts and a cloud of visitors), to loose (fully opened group of casual contributors who participate sporadically in selected topics). The degree of coherence informs about information value of the forum. Opened forums are least likely to contain interesting and valuable knowledge content. These forums are dominated by random visitors, and sometimes attract a small group of habitual guests who tend to come back to the forum on a regular basis. Discussions on opened forums are often shallow, emotional, inconsistent, lacking discipline and manners. Opened forums rarely contain useful practical knowledge or specialized information.

On the other hand, opened forums are the best place to analyze controversy, emotionality, and social interactions between participants of the discussion. Their spontaneous and impulsive character encourages users to form their opinions openly, so opened forums may be perceived as the main source of information about attitudes and beliefs of John Q Public. On the opposite side lie closed specialized forums. These forums provide high quality knowledge on selected subject, they are characterized by discipline, consistency, and credibility. Users are almost always well known to the community, random guests are very rare, and users pay attention to maintain their status within the community by providing reliable answers to submitted questions. Closed forums account for a small fraction of the available Internet forums. The majority of forums are semi-opened forums that allow both registered and anonymous submissions. Such forums may be devoted to a narrow subject, but may also consider a broad range of topics. Usually, such forum attracts a group of dedicated users, who form the core of the community, but casual users are also welcomed. These forums are a compromise between the strictly closed specialized forums and the totally opened forums. One may dig such forum in search of practical information, or browse through the forum with no particular search criterion.

The first assumption behind the sociogram of the social network formed around the Internet forum concerns users. The author decided to consider only regular users as the members of the social network. Casual visitors, who submit a single question and never return to the forum, are marked as outliers and do not form nodes in the sociogram. This assumption is perfectly valid and reasonable, as casual users do not contribute to the information contents of the forum and provide no additional value to the forum. The threshold for considering a given user to be a regular user depends on the chosen forum and may be defined using the number of submitted posts and the frequency of posting. The second assumption used during the construction of the sociogram is that edges in the sociogram are created on the basis of participation in the same discussion within a single topic. Again, this assumption is natural in the domain of Internet forums. The core functionality of the Internet forum is to allow users to discuss and exchange views, opinions, and remarks. Therefore, the relationships mirrored in the sociogram must reflect real-world relationships between users. These relationships, in turn, result from discussing similar topics.

The more frequent the exchange of opinions between two users, the stronger the relationship binding these users. Of course, the nature of this relationship may be diverse. If two users frequently exchange opinions, it may signify an antagonism, contrariness, and dislike, but it may also be used to reflect strong interaction between users. In the model used the nature of the relationship between two users is reflected in the type of the edge connecting these two users in the sociogram: if the edge is bi-directional, then it represents a conflict, if the edge is one-directional, then it represents a follow-up (usually an answer to a question), and if the edge is undirected, then the nature of the relationship cannot be determined. The final element of the sociogram is the computation of edge weights. In a more sophisticated model the weight of an edge could represent the emotionality of the relationship (e.g., friendliness, enmity, or indifference). Such emotionality could be determined by analyzing posts and computing their emotionality. Unfortunately, this would require the employment of natural language processing techniques to analyze not only the structure, but the semantics of posts as well.

The definition of the participation in the same discussion requires a few words of explanation. Many Internet forum engines allow for threaded discussions, where each post can be directed as the reply to a particular previous post. In the case of such engines the entire topic can be drawn as a tree structure with a single initial post in the root of the tree, and all subsequent posts forming branches and leaves of the tree. With threaded Internet forum engines the author distinguishes between participating in the same topic, participating in the same thread of the discussion (i.e., posting in the same branch of the discussion), and direct communication (i.e., replying directly to a post). A well-balanced tree of discussion represents an even and steady flow of the discussion, whereas a strongly unbalanced tree represents a heated discussion characterized by frequent exchange of posts.

Unfortunately, most Internet forum engines do not allow for threading. Usually, every post is appended to the sequential list of posts ordered chronologically. Users, who want to reply to a post other than the last one, often quote the original post, or the parts thereof. Due to message formatting and different quoting styles, determining the true structure of such flat Internet forum is very difficult, if impossible. In the model it has assumed that in the case of flat forums, where no threading is available, each post is the reply to the precedent post. This somehow simplistic assumption may introduce a slight bias during the analysis, but the empirical observations justify such assumption. In addition, imposing virtual threads onto flat forum structure allows to compute the depth of a submission as one of the basic statistics. The depth of a post is computed using a sliding window technique with the width of 5 subsequent posts (the threshold has been set up experimentally). For each post, the author is looking for another post submitted by the same author within the last five posts. If

such post is encountered, the depth of the current post is increased, otherwise the post is treated as the new branch of the discussion.

The social network built on top of the Internet forum community accounts for the following types of users:

- **key users** who are placed in the center of the discussion.
- **casual users** who appear on the outskirts of the network.
- **commenting users** who answer many questions but receive few replies.
- **hot users** who receive many answers from many other users (e.g., authors of provoking and controversial posts).

The above-mentioned types of users are clearly visible from the shape of the social network. Figure 3 presents an example of a social network derived from the Internet forum on bicycles. Weights of edges represent the number of posts exchanged between users represented by respective nodes. For clarity, only the strongest edges are drawn on the sociogram. Small isolated groups consisting of a few users in the left-hand side of the sociogram can be seen clearly. The number of posts exchanged between users and isolation from other users suggest, that these nodes represent a long dispute between the users, most often, being the result of a controversial post. A central cluster of strongly interconnected users visible in the right-hand side of the sociogram is also seen. Within the cluster a few nodes tend to collect more edges, but there is no clear central node in this network. Interestingly, most edges in the cluster are bi-directional, which implies a balanced and popular discussion, where multiple users are involved.

Another type of a sociogram is presented in Figure 4. The Internet forum, for which the sociogram is computed, is devoted to banks, stock exchange, and investment funds. The central and the most important node in the sociogram is **krzysztofsf**. This user always answers and never

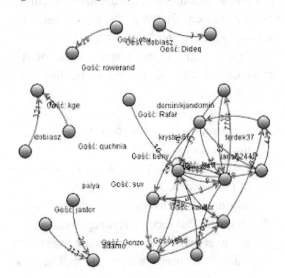

Figure 3. Sociogram for the forum on bicycles

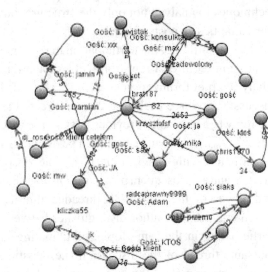

Figure 4. Sociogram for the forum on banks

asks questions or initializes a topic. Clearly, this user is an expert providing answers and expertise to other members of the community. In particular, observe the weight of the edge connecting **krzysztofsf** to **Gość:gość** (which denotes an anonymous login). This single expert has posted 2652 replies to questions asked by casual visitors! Another very interesting formation is visible to the bottom of the figure. There is a linked list of users connected mostly by one-directional edges and isolated from the main cluster. It has been suspected that this formation denotes a small community within the Internet forum community. It may be an openly acknowledged group of users, but it may also be an informal group that continues their discussions on very narrowly defined subjects.

Apart from analyzing the social network of users participating in a given forum or topic, it should also analyze individual users in terms of their global relationships. The sociogram centered on a particular node is called an egocentric graph and it can be used to discover the activity of the node, the nature of the communication with other nodes, and thus, to attribute a given social role to the node. The egocentric graph for a given user consists of the node representing the user, the nodes directly connected to the central node,

and all edges between nodes included in the egocentric graph. Figure 5 presents the egocentric graph for the user **wieslaw.tomczyk**. A star pattern is seen clearly, where the node in the center connects radially by one-directional edges with multiple nodes, and those nodes are not connected by edges. This pattern is characteristic of experts who answer many questions, and users who ask questions do not form any relationships (usually, these are casual users who seek an advice on a particular subject).

A very different egocentric graph is presented in Figure 6. Here, the user **kris 46** belongs to a small and strongly tied community consisting of five more users forming almost a clique. Apart from the core group including users **kazimierzp**, **polu**, **bondel**, and **zenon5**, user **kris 46** occasionally communicates with a few other users, who lie outside of the core group. This cloud structure consisting of a densely connected core and loosely connected outlier nodes is characteristic for users who participate in the forum community for a longer period of time. This long participation allows them to form substructures within the community that harden their commitment to the community.

Figure 5. Egocentric graph for the user **wieslaw. tomczyk**

Figure 6. Egocentric graph for the user **kris 46**

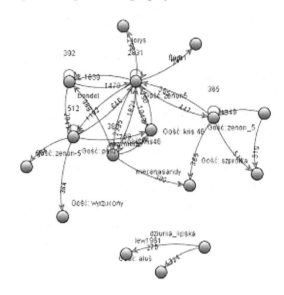

One of the most interesting and challenging problems in mining Internet forum communities is the discovery and attribution of social roles in the social network of users (Fisher, Smith, & Welser, 2006)

(Welser, Gleave, Fisher, & Smith, 2007). Social roles may be statically attributed to users, or may be dynamically assigned to users for each discussion. The latter solution is more flexible, because it accounts for the situation where a user may act as an expert on one topic, and a commenter on another topic. For the sake of simplicity the static attribution of social roles to users is assumed.

Many different social roles may be derived from the social network of Internet forum users. Every role should be distinct from other roles and identifiable from the structure of the social network only, i.e., the identification of the social role for a given user must not require the semantic analysis of posts submitted by the user. An exemplary classification of social roles is given below:

- **newbie:** a user who a few questions and then disappears from the community, very easy to discover because her egocentric graph is empty,

- **observer:** similar to a newbie, but participates in the community on a regular basis, rarely posts, her egocentric graph is sparse,

- **expert:** a comprehensive user with high authority, does not ask questions, participates in discussions on multiple topics, her egocentric graph follows the star pattern,

- **commentator:** a comprehensive user, answers many questions, often follows an expert and adds comments and remarks, similar to an expert, but the average length of posts is much shorter,

- **troll:** a provoking and irritating user, initiates many discussions characterized by the high controversy and temperature, her egocentric graph often follows the inverted star pattern (many users answer the troll).

Of course, social role identification serves a more important goal than just tagging users. For a closed specialized forum identifying experts is crucial for interacting with knowledge contents hidden within the Internet forum. One may quickly rank users by their authority and focus on reading posts written by experts. Another possibility is an automatic knowledge acquisition, where posts submitted by experts may be retrieved and parsed in search for named entity references. For common opened forums one may want to identify trolls in order to create spam filters for the forum. Usually, discussions stoked by trolls bear little knowledge contents and following these discussions is a waste of time. The identification of social roles based solely on the shape of the egocentric graph for a given user is difficult and error-prone. Additional statistics are useful to improve the precision and recall of social role attribution. For instance, in order to identify an expert the following basic statistics: the number of distinct topics with user submissions (must be large), the depth of the discussion following an expert's post (expert opinions tend to close the discussion and do not spark long disputes), the average length of a post (moderate, neither too long nor too short) shall be considered. Similar additional basic statistics can be derived for other social roles.

FUTURE RESEARCH DIRECTIONS

The results of the research presented in this chapter reaches beyond the interests of the academic community. The ability to mine knowledge hidden in Internet forums, to discover emerging trends and fashions, to compute social reception of brands and products, all these are of extreme interest to the marketing industry. Pollsters, advertisers, and media monitors are among those who may profit from the development of the presented technology. This initial research into the topic of mining Internet forums can be extended in several directions. A possible future work agenda includes, among others, the investigation into the Internet forum evolution, the analysis of macro- and micro-measures pertaining to the social network of Internet forum users, and further examination of social roles.

CONCLUSION

In this chapter a methodology of mining the most popular Internet discussion engine – Internet forums is presented. First, the nontrivial process of data acquisition by crawling Internet forums is described. Then, the three levels of Internet forum analysis: the statistical analysis, the index analysis, and the network analysis. On each level, interesting knowledge can be discovered and presented to the user. The author have designed a few indexes that allow users to rank forum topics, posts, and users, according to a plethora of criteria: the most controversial, the most active, the most popular, etc. Finally, the process of modeling a forum as a social network linking users through discussions is discussed. Finally, how analysis of such a social network allows to discover social roles of users, and, in result, to filter interesting knowledge from huge volumes of posts is shown.

The abundance of Internet forums, ranging from specialized to popular, makes the subject of mining Internet forums both interesting and very desirable. Internet forums hide enormous amounts of high quality knowledge generated by immense communities of users. Unfortunately, the lack of structure and standards makes the acquisition of this knowledge very difficult. Research presented in this chapter is a step towards automatic knowledge extraction from these opened repositories of knowledge. The statistics, heuristics and indexes are fairly simple, but work surprisingly well in the real world. It has found that the prototype generated high quality rankings of topics and users for a wide variety of Internet forums.

REFERENCES

Alm, C. O., Roth, D., & Sproat, R. (2005). Emotions from Text: Machine Learning for Text-based Emotion Prediction. In *Human Language Technology Conference and Conference on Empirical Methods in Natural Language Processing* (pp. 579-586). Vancouver, Canada: Association for Computational Linguistics.

Barabási, A. L., & Albert, R. (1999, October). Emergence of Scaling in Random Networks. *Science, 286*(5439), 509–512. doi:10.1126/science.286.5439.509

Barabási, A. L., & Bonabeau, E. (2003). Scale-free Networks. *Scientific American*, (May): 2003.

Brandes, U., & Erlebach, T. (2005). *Network Analysis, Methodological Foundations*. New York: Springer.

Burkharter, B., & Smith, M. (2004). Inhabitant's Uses and Reactions to Usenet Social Accounting Data. In Snowdon, D., Churchill, E. F., & Frecon, E. (Eds.), *Inhabited Information Spaces* (pp. 291–305). Springer. doi:10.1007/1-85233-862-8_15

Cai, R., Yang, J.-M., Lai, W., Wang, Y., & Zhang, L. (2008). iRobot: An Intelligent Crawler for Web Forums. In *17th International Conference on World Wide Web*, Beijing (pp.447-456). New York: ACM Press.

Carrington, P. J., Scott, J., & Wasserman, S. (2005). *Models and Methods in Social Network Analysis*. Cambridge, UK: Cambridge University Press.

Chakrabarti, S. (2002). *Mining the Web: Discovering Knowledge from Hypertext Data*. San Francisco: Morgan Kaufmann.

Fayyad, U. M., Piatetsky-Shapiro, G., Smyth, P., & Uthurusamy, R. (1996). *Advances in Knowledge Discovery and Data Mining*. AAAI/MIT Press.

Feldman, R., & Sanger, J. (2006). *The Text Mining Handbook: Advanced Approaches in Analyzing Unstructured Data*. Cambridge, UK: Cambridge University Press. doi:10.1017/CBO9780511546914

Fisher, D., Smith, M., & Welser, H. T. (2006). You Are Who You Talk To: Detecting Roles in Usenet Newsgroups. In *39th Annual Hawaii International Conference on System Sciences*. Kauai: IEEE Computer Society.

Golder, S. A. (2003). A Typology of Social Roles in Usenet. *A thesis submitted to the Department of Linguistics*. Boston: Harvard University.

Han, J., Kamber, M., & Pei, J. (2005). *Data Mining: Concepts and Techniques* (2nd ed.). San Francisco: Morgan Kaufmann.

Hanna, B., & De Nooy, J. (2009). *Learning Language and Culture via Public Internet Discussion Forums*. Palgrave Macmillan. doi:10.1057/9780230235823

Hanneman, R., & Riddle, M. (2005). *Introduction to Social Network Methods*. University of California, Riverside.

Manning. Ch, D., & Schuetze, H. (1999). *Foundations of Statistical Natural Language Processing*. Cambridge, MA: MIT Press.

Marcoccia, M. (2004). On-line Polylogues: Conversation Structure and Participation Framework in Internet Newsgroups. *Journal of Pragmatics, 36*(1), 115–145. doi:10.1016/S0378-2166(03)00038-9

Merton, R. K. (1968). *Social Theory and Social Structure*. New York: Free Press.

Parsons, T. (1951). *The Social System*. Routledge & Kegan Paul Ltd.

Skvoretz, J., & Faust, K. (2002). Relations, Species, and Network Structure. *Journal of Social Structure, 3*(3).

Tan, P.-N., Steinbach, M., & Kumar, V. (2005). *Introduction to Data Mining*. Reading, MA: Addison Wesley.

Turner, T. C., Smith, M., Fisher, D., & Welser, H. T. (2005). Picturing Usenet: Mapping Computer-Mediated Collective Action. *Journal of Computer-Mediated Communication, 10*(4).

Viegas, F. B., & Smith, M. (2004). Newsgroup Crowds and AuthorLines: Visualizing the Activity of Individuals in Conversational Cyberspaces. In *37th Annual Hawaii International Conference on System Sciences (HICSS'04) - Track 4*. Kauai: IEEE Computer Society.

Wang, Y., Yang, J.-M., Lai, W., Cai, R., Zhang, L., & Ma, W.-Y. (2008). Exploring Traversal Strategy for Web Forum Crawling. In *31st International ACM SIGIR Conference on Research and Development in Information Retrieval* (pp.459-466). New York: ACM Press.

Weiss, S., Indurkhya, N., Zhang, T., & Damerau, F. (2004). *Text Mining: Predictive Methods for Analyzing Unstructured Information*. Springer.

Welser, H. T., Gleave, E., Fisher, D., & Smith, M. (2007). Visualizing the Signatures of Social Roles in Online Discussion Groups. *Journal of Social Structure, 8*(2).

Wenger, E. (1999). *Communities of Practice: Learning, Meaning, and Identity*. Cambridge, UK: Cambridge University Press.

Wenger, E., McDermott, R., & Snyder, W. S. (2002). *Cultivating Communities of Practice: A Guide to Managing Knowledge*. Boston: Harvard Business School Press.

Wenger, E., & Snyder, M. (2000). Communities of Practice: The Organizational Frontier. *Harvard Business Review*, 139–145.

White, H. C., Boorman, S. A., & Breiger, R. L. (1976). Social-Structure from Multiple Networks: 1. Blockmodels of Roles and Positions. *American Journal of Sociology, 81*(4), 730–780. doi:10.1086/226141

Witten, I., & Frank, E. (2005). *Data Mining: Practical Machine Learning Tools and Techniques* (2nd ed.). San Francisco: Morgan Kaufmann.

Zhang, J., Ackerman, M. S., & Adamic, L. (2007). Expertise Networks in Online Communities: Structure and Algorithms. In *16th International Conference on World Wide Web*, Banff, Alberta, Canada. ACM Press.

KEY TERMS AND DEFINITIONS

Crawler: A specialized software for reading data directly from websites.

Data Mining: A discipline aiming at the discovery of useful knowledge from vast repositories of data.

Internet Forum: Web application for publishing user-generated content under the form of a chronologically ordered discussion.

Social Network Analysis: (SNA): A set of theorems, methods and models originating in network theory, applied to complete social networks and egocentric graphs of individual nodes.

Social Network: A structure consisting of nodes, which represent people or organizations, and edges depicting various types of relations between nodes, e.g., friendship, kinship, trust, dislike, distrust, authority, influence, etc.

Social Role: A set of behaviors and duties applicable to a given situation; an expected behavior of an individual with a given social status and prestige in a given situation.

Sociogram: A graphical representation of a social network; a chart plotting the structure of relations between the participants of a social network.

Compilation of References

Abbasi, A., Chen, H., & Salem, A. (2008). Sentiment Analysis in Multiple Languages: Feature Selection for Opinion Classification in Web Forums. *ACM Transactions on Information Systems*, *26*(3), 1–34. doi:10.1145/1361684.1361685

Adomavicius, G., & Tuzhilin, A. (2001). Expert-driven Validation of Rule-based User Models in Personalization Applications. *Data Mining and Knowledge Discovery*, *5*(1-2), 33–58. doi:10.1023/A:1009839827683

Adverse Event Reporting System (AERS). Retrieved June 1, 2009, from U.S. Food and Drug Administration: http://www.fda.gov/cder/aers/default.htm

Agrawal, R., & Srikant, R. (1994). *Fast Algorithms for Mining Association Rules* (pp. 487–499). VLDB.

Agrawal, A., & Mitta, A. (2005). Identifying Temporal Gene Networks Using Signal processing Metrics on Time-Series Gene Expression Data. In *Proceedings of 3rd IEEE ICISIP Conference* (pp. 86-92).

Agrawal, R., & Srikant, R. (1994). Fast Algorithm for Mining Association Rules. In *Proceedings of the 20th International Conference on Very Large Data Bases (VLDB-94)* (pp. 487-499). Santiago de Chile, Chile: Morgan Kaufmann Publishers.

Agrawal, R., & Srikant, R. (1994). Fast Algorithms for Mining Association Rules. In *Proceedings VLDB Conference.*

Agrawal, R., Imielinski, T., & Swami, A. (1993). Mining Association Rule between Sets of Items in Large Databases. In *Proceedings of the 1993 ACM SIGMOD International Conference on Management of Data* (pp. 207-216). Washington D.C.: ACM Press.

Agrawal, R., Lin, K. I., Sawhney, H. S., & Shim, K. (1995). Fast similarity search in the presence of Noise, Scaling and Translation in Time Series Databases. In *Proceedings of 21" International Conference on Very Large Data Bases (VLDB 95)* (pp. 490-501).

Agrawal, S., Godbole, S., Punjani, D., & Roy, S. (2007). How much noise is too much: A study in Automatic Text Classification. In *Proceedings of the 7th IEEE International Conference on Data Mining (ICDM-07)* (pp. 3-12). Omaha, NE, USA: IEEE Computer Society.

Ahmad, K., Cheng, D., & Almas, Y. (2006). Multi-lingual Sentiment Analysis of Financial News Streams. In *Proceedings of the 1st International Conference on Grid in Finance*. Palermo.

Akehurst, G. (2009). User generated content: The use of Blogs for Tourism Organizations and Tourism Consumers. *Service Business*, *3*(1), 51–61. doi:10.1007/s11628-008-0054-2

Akerkar, R. A., & Sajja, P. S. (2009). *Knowledge-based Systems*. Sudbury, MA: Jones & Bartlett Publishers.

Ale, J., & Rossi, G. (2000). An Approach to Discovering Temporal Association Rules. *Symposium on Applied Computing.*

Ali, K., Manganaris, S., & Srikant, R. (1997). Partial Classification using Association Rules. In *Proceedings of the 3rd International Conference on Knowledge Discovery and Data Mining* (pp. 115-118). Newport Beach, CA, USA: AAAI Press.

Allcock, W., Chervenak, A., Foster, I., Kesselman, C., Salisbury, C., & Tuecke, S. (2001). The Data Grid: Towards an Architecture for the Distributed Management and Analysis of Large Scientific Datasets. *Journal of Network and Computer Applications, 23*, 187–200.

Alm, C. O., Roth, D., & Sproat, R. (2005). Emotions from Text: Machine Learning for Text-based Emotion Prediction. In *Human Language Technology Conference and Conference on Empirical Methods in Natural Language Processing* (pp. 579-586). Vancouver, Canada: Association for Computational Linguistics.

Alon, J., Sclaroff, S., Kollios, G., & Pavlovic, V. (2003). Discovering Clusters in Motion Time Series Data. In *Proceedings of 2003 IEEE Comput. Soc. Conf. on Computer Vision and Pattern Recognition* (pp. I.375– I.381).

Alon, U., Barkai, N., Notterman, D., Gish, K., Ybarra, S., Mack, D., & Levine, A. (1999). Broad Patterns of Gene Expression Revealed by Clustering Analysis of Tumor and Normal Colon Tissues Probed by Oligonucleotide Array. In *Proceedings of National Academy Science* (pp. 6745-6750). USA.

Alonso, F., Caraça-Valente, J. P., Martínez, L., & Montes, C. (2003). Discovering Similar Patterns for Characterising Time Series in a Medical Domain. *Knowledge and Information Systems: An International Journal, 5*(2), 183–200. doi:10.1007/s10115-003-0098-5

Alonso, F., Martínez, L., Pérez, A., Santamaría, A., & Valente, J. P. (2006). Symbol Extraction Method and Symbolic Distance for Analyzing Medical Time Series. In *Proceedings of International Symposium on Biological and Medical Data Analysis.* [Berlin: Springer.]. *Lecture Notes in Computer Science, 4345*, 311–322. doi:10.1007/11946465_28

Alonso, F., Caraça-Valente, J. P., Martínez, L., & Montes, C. (2005). Discovering Patterns and Reference Models in the Medical Domain of Isokinetics. In Kantardzic, M., & Zurada, J. (Eds.), *Next Generation of Data-Mining Applications* (pp. 393–414). New York: Wiley-IEEE Press.

American National Election Studies (ANES). (2005). *Center for Political Studies*. Ann Arbor, MI: University of Michigan.

Ammons, G., Bodik, R., & Larus, J. R. (2002). Mining Specifications. *ACM SIGPLAN Notices, 37*(1), 4–16. doi:10.1145/565816.503275

Andreevskaya, A., & Bergler, S. (2006). Mining WordNet for Fuzzy Sentiment: Sentiment Tag Extraction from WordNet Glosses. In *Proceedings of EACL.*

Ansari, Asim., & Mela, Carl F. (2003). E-customization. *JMR, Journal of Marketing Research, 40*, 131–145. doi:10.1509/jmkr.40.2.131.19224

Antonie, M. L., & Zaiane, O. R. (2002). Text Document Categorization by Term Association. In *Proceedings of the 2002 IEEE International Conference on Data Mining* (pp. 19-26). Maebashi City, Japan: IEEE Computer Society.

Apte, C., Grossman, E., Pednault, E. P. D., Rosen, B. K., Tipu, F. A., & White, B. (1999). Probabilistic Estimation-Based Data Mining for Discovering Insurance Risks. *IEEE Intelligent Systems, 14*(6), 49–58. doi:10.1109/5254.809568

Arnott, D., & Pervan, G. (2008). Eigth Key Issues for the Decision Support Systems Discipline. *Decision Support Systems, 44*(3), 657–672. doi:10.1016/j.dss.2007.09.003

Aslandogan, Y. A., Mahajani, G. A., & Taylor, S. (2004). Evidence combination in Medical Data Mining. In *Proceedings of International Conference on Information Technology: Coding and Computing (ITCC'04), Vol. 2*, (pp.465-469). Las Vegas, NV.

Attaluri, Gopi, K., & Salem, K. (2002). The Presumed-Either Two-Phase Commit Protocol. *IEEE Transactions on Knowledge and Data Engineering, 14(*5), 1190-1196.

Atzeni, P., & Antonellis, V. D. (1993). *Relational Database Theory*. Redwood, CA, USA: Benjamin-Cummings Publishing Co.

Au, W., Chan, K., Wong, A., & Yang, W. (2005). Attribute Clustering for Grouping, Selection, and Classification of Gene Expression Data. *IEEE/ACM Transactions on Computational Biology and Bioinformatics, 2*(2), 83–101. doi:10.1109/TCBB.2005.17

Ayad, A. M., El-Makky, N. M., & Taha, Y. (2001). Incremental Mining of Constrained Association Rules. In *Proceedings of the First Conference on Data Mining.*

Azevedo, A., & Santos, M. F. (2008). KDD, SEMMA and CRISP-DM: A Parallel Overview. In. *Proceedings of the IADIS European Conference on Data Mining, DM2008*, 182–185.

Azevedo, A., & Santos, M. F. (2009). Business Intelligence: State of the Art, Trends, and Open Issues. In *Proceedings of the First International Conference on Knowledge Management and Information Sharing - KMIS 2009* (pp.296-300).

Azuaje, F., & Bolshakova, N. (2002). *Clustering Genome Expression Data: Design and Evaluation Principles*. Springer.

Babu, T. R., Murty, M. N., & Agrawal, V. K. (2004). Hybrid Learning Scheme for Data Mining Applications. In *Fourth International Conference on Hybrid Intelligent Systems (HIS'04)* (pp. 266-271). Kitakyushu, Japan.

Baccianella, S., Esuli, A., & Sebastiani, F. (2009). Multifacet Rating of Product Reviews. In *Proceedings of the 31th European Conference on IR Research on Advances in Information Retrieval.* Toulouse, France.

Bachman, K. (2000). *Corporate e-Learning: Exploring a new frontier*. W.R. Hambrecht and Co.

Bagui, S. (2006). An approach to Mining Crime Patterns. *International Journal of Data Warehousing and Mining, 2*(1), 50–80.

Bagui, S., Just, J., & Bagui, S. C. (2008). Deriving Strong Association Mining Rules using a Dependency Criterion, the Lift Measure. *International Journal of Data Analysis Techniques and Strategies, 1*(3), 297–312. doi:10.1504/IJDATS.2009.024297

Baldi, P., Chauvin, Y., Hunkapiller, T., & McClure, M. (1994). Hidden Markov models of Biological Primary Sequence Information. In *Proceedings of National Academy Science* (pp. 1059-1063). USA 91.

Barabási, A. L., & Albert, R. (1999, October). Emergence of Scaling in Random Networks. *Science, 286*(5439), 509–512. doi:10.1126/science.286.5439.509

Barabási, A. L., & Bonabeau, E. (2003). Scale-free Networks. *Scientific American*, (May): 2003.

Baralis, E., Bruno, G., & Ficarra, E. (2008). Temporal Association Rules for Gene Regulatory Networks. In *IEEE International Conference on Intelligent Systems.*

Barnes, S. J., & Scornavacca, E. (2008). The Strategic value of Enterprise Mobility: Case study insights. *Information-Knowledge-Systems Management, 7*(1-2), 227–241.

Baru, C., Moore, R., Rajasekar, A., & Wan, M. (1998). The SDSC storage resource broker. In *Proceedings of CASCON'98 Conference*, Toronto, Canada.

Barwise, P., & Strong, C. (2002). Permission-based Mobile Advertising. *Journal of Interactive Marketing, 16*(1), 14–24. doi:10.1002/dir.10000

Battiato, S., Farinella, G. M., Giuffrida, G., Sismeiro, C., & Tribulato, G. (2009b). Using Visual and Text Features for Direct Marketing on Multimedia Messaging Services Domain. *Multimedia Tools and Applications, 42*(1), 5–30. doi:10.1007/s11042-008-0250-z

Battiato, S., Farinella, G.M., Giuffrida, G., Sismeiro, C., & Tribulato, G. (2009a). Exploiting Visual and Text Features for Direct Marketing Learning in Time and Space Constrained Domains. *Pattern Analysis and Applications Multimedia Tools and Applications Journal - Special Issue on Metadata Mining for Image Understanding, 42*(1), 5-30.

Battula, V. L., Bareiss, P. M., Treml, S., Conrad, S., Albert, I., & Hojak, S. (2007). Human Placenta and Bone Marrow derived MSC cultured in Serum-free, b-FGF-containing medium express cell surface frizzled-9 and SSEA-4 and give rise to multilineage differentiation. *Differentiation, 75*(4), 279–291. doi:10.1111/j.1432-0436.2006.00139.x

Bauer, H. H., Neumann, M., & Reichardt, T. (2005). Driving Consumer Acceptance of Mobile Marketing - A Theoretical Framework and Empirical Study. In *Proceedings of the 4th International Marketing Trends Congress, ESCP-EAP Annual Conference* (pp. 181-192). Paris.

Baxter, C. J., Sabar, M., Quick, W. P., & Sweetlove, L. J. (2005). Comparison of changes in Fruit Gene Expression in Tomato Introgression Lines provides evidence of Genome-wide Transcriptional changes and reveals links to Mapped Qtls and Described Traits. *Journal of Experimental Botany, 56*, 1591–1604. doi:10.1093/jxb/eri154

Beeres, S. L., Atsma, D. E., van der Laarse, A., Pijnappels, D. A., van Tuyn, J., & Fibbe, W. E. (2005). Human Adult Bone Marrow Mesenchymal Stem Cells repair experimental conduction block in rat Cardiomyocyte Cultures. *Journal of the American College of Cardiology, 46*(10), 1943–1952. doi:10.1016/j.jacc.2005.07.055

Belen, R. (2009). *Detecting disguised missing data.* Unpublished MSc thesis, Ankara Turkey: ODTU

Berault, J. (2001). Data mining diabetic databases: Are rough sets a useful addition? In *Proceedings of. 33rd Symposium on the Interface, Computing Science and Statistics, Fairfax.* Fairfax, VA. Costa Mesa (CA): The Interface Foundation of North America.

Bergmann, S., Ihmels, J., & Barkai, N. (2003). Iterative Signature Algorithm for the Analysis of Large-Scale Gene Expression Data. *Physical Review, 67*(3).

Berners-Lee, T., Hendler, J., & Lassila, O. (2001). The Semantic Web. *Scientific American, 279*(5), 34–43. doi:10.1038/scientificamerican0501-34

Bestavros, A. (1992). Speculative Concurrency Control. *Technical Report TR-16-92.* Boston University, Boston, MA.

Bestavros, A., & Braoudakis, S. (1995). Value Cognizant Speculative Concurrency Control. In *21st VLDB Conference.* Zurich, Switzerland.

Bestavros, A., Braoudakis, S., & Panagos, E. (1993). Performance Evaluation of Two-Shadow Speculative Concurrency Control. *Technical Report 1993-001.* Boston University, Boston, MA.

Bethel, C. L., Hall, L. O., & Goldgof, D. (2006). Mining for Implications in Medical Data. In Y.Y. Tang, S.P. Wang, G. Lorette, D.S. Yeung & H. Yan (Eds.), *Proceedings of the 18th International Conference on Pattern Recognition* (pp. 1212-1215). Los Alamitos, CA: IEEE Computer Society.

Bhandari, I., Colet, E., Parker, J., Pines, Z., Pratap, R., & Ramanujam, K. (1997). Advanced Scout: Data Mining and Knowledge Discovery in NBA Data. *Data Mining and Knowledge Discovery, 1*(1), 121–125. doi:10.1023/A:1009782106822

Bianco, P., Riminucci, M., Gronthos, S., & Robey, P. G. (2001). Bone Marrow Stromal Stem Cells: Nature, Biology, and Potential applications. *Stem Cells (Dayton, Ohio), 19*(3), 180–192. doi:10.1634/stemcells.19-3-180

Bino, R., Hall, R., Fiehn, O., Kopka, J., Saito, K., & Draper, J. (2004). Potential of Metabolomics as a functional Genomics Tool. *Trends in Plant Science, 9*(9), 418–425. doi:10.1016/j.tplants.2004.07.004

Bobek, S., & Perko, I. (2006). Intelligent Agent-Based Business Intelligence. *Current Developments in Technology-Assisted Education,* FORMATEX, 1047-1051.

Boehm, B. W., Brown, J. R., & Lipow, M. (1976). Quantitative Evaluation of Software Quality. In *The 2nd International Conference on Software Engineering* (pp. 592-605). San Francisco, CA: IEEE Computer Society Press.

Bonchi, F., Giannotti, F., Lucchesse, C., Orlando, S., Perego, R., & Trasarti, R. (2007). On Interactive Pattern Mining from Relational Databases. In S.Dzeroski & J. Struyf (Eds.), *Lecture Notes in Computer Science: Vol. 4747, Knowledge Discovery in Inductive Databases - 5th International Workshop - KDID 2006* (pp. 42-62). Berlin, Heidelberg: Springer-Verlag.

Boser, B. E., Guyon, I. M., & Vapnik, V. N. (1992). A Training Algorithm for Optimal Margin Classifiers. In *Proceedings of the 5th ACM Annual Workshop on Computational Learning Theory* (pp. 144-152). Pittsburgh, PA, USA: ACM Press.

Botta, M., Boulicaut, J., Masson, C., & Meo, R. (2004). Query Languages Supporting Descriptive Rule Mining: A Ccomparative Study. In R. Meo, P.L. Lanzi & Mika Klemettinen (Eds.), *Lecture Notes on Artificial Intelligence: Vol. 2682, Database Support for Data Mining Applications - Discovering Knowledge with Inductive Queries* (pp. 24-51). Berlin, Heidelberg: Springer-Verlag.

Boulicaut, J., Klemettinen, M., & Mannila, H. (1999). Modeling KDD Processes within the Inductive Database Framework. In M. Mohania & A. M. Tjoa (Eds.), *Lecture Notes on Computer Science: Vol. 1676, Data Warehousing and knowledge Discovery - 1st International Conferense DaWak99* (pp. 193-202). Berlin, Heidelberg: Springer-Verlag.

Box, G. E. P., Jenkins, G. M., & Reinsel, G. C. (1994). *Time Series Analysis: Forecasting and Control*. Singapore: Pearson Education Inc.

Braga-Neto, U., & Dougherty, E. (2004). Is Cross-validation valid for Small-Sample Microarray Classification? *Bioinformatics (Oxford, England)*, *20*(3), 374. doi:10.1093/bioinformatics/btg419

Brandes, U. (2008). Social Network Analysis and Visualization. *IEEE Signal Processing Magazine*, *25*(6), 147–151. doi:10.1109/MSP.2008.929814

Brandes, U., & Erlebach, T. (2005). *Network Analysis, Methodological Foundations*. New York: Springer.

Breiman, L. (2001). Random Forests. *Machine Learning*, *45*(1), 5–32. doi:10.1023/A:1010933404324

Breiman, L., Friedman, J., Olshen, R., & Stone, C. (1984). *Classification and Regression Trees*. Boca Raton, FL: Chapman & Hall/CRC Press LLC.

Brin, S. J., & Rajeev Motwani, D. (1997). Dynamic Itemset Counting. In *Proceedings of ACM SIGMOD Conference* (pp. 255-264).

Brin, S., Motwani, R., Ullman, J. D., & Tsur, S. (1997). Dynamic Itemset counting and Implication Rules for Market Basket Data. In *Proceedings of the 1997 ACM SIGMOD International Conference on Management of Data* (pp. 255-264). Tucson, Arizona, USA: ACM Press.

Brisson, L., & Collard, M. (2008). How to Semantically Enhance a Data Mining Process? In J. Filipe & J. Cordeiro (Eds.), *10th International Conference, ICEIS 2008, Revised Papers. Lecture Notes in Business Information Processing*, 19 (pp. 103-116). Berlin/Heidelberg: Springer.

Bulashevska, S., & Eils, R. (2005). Inferring Genetic Regulatory Logic from Expression Data. *Bioinformatics (Oxford, England)*, *21*(11), 2706–2713. doi:10.1093/bioinformatics/bti388

Burkharter, B., & Smith, M. (2004). Inhabitant's Uses and Reactions to Usenet Social Accounting Data. In Snowdon, D., Churchill, E. F., & Frecon, E. (Eds.), *Inhabited Information Spaces* (pp. 291–305). Springer. doi:10.1007/1-85233-862-8_15

Bushel, P., Wolfinger, R., & Gibson, G. (2007). Simultaneous Clustering of Gene Expression Data with Clinical Chemistry and Pathological Evaluations Reveals Phenotypic Prototypes. *BMC Systems Biology*, *1*(1), 15. doi:10.1186/1752-0509-1-15

Cadez, I., Heckerman, D., Meek, C., Smyth, P., & White, S. (2000). *Model-based Clustering and Visualization of Navigation Patterns on a Website. Technical Report CA 92717-3425*. Irvine, CA: Dept. of Information and Computer Science, University of California.

Cai, R., Yang, J.-M., Lai, W., Wang, Y., & Zhang, L. (2008). iRobot: An Intelligent Crawler for Web Forums. In *17th International Conference on World Wide Web*, Beijing (pp.447-456). New York: ACM Press.

Calders, T., Lakshmanan, L. V. S., Ng, R. T., & Paredaens, J. (2006). Expressive Power of an Algebra for Data Mining. *ACM Transactions on Database Systems*, *31*(4), 1169–1214. doi:10.1145/1189769.1189770

Calders, T., Goethals, B., & Prado, A. (2006). Integrating Pattern Mining in Relational Databases. In J. Fürnkranz, T. Scheffer & M. Spiliopoulou (Eds.), *Lecture Notes on Artificial Intelligence: Vol. 4213, Knowledge Discovery in Databases - 10th European Conference on Principles and Practice of Knowledge Discovery in Databases - PKDD2006* (pp. 454-461). Berlin, Heidelberg: Springer-Verlag.

Cannataro, M., & Talia, D. (2003). Knowledge grid: An architecture for distributed knowledge discovery. *Communications of the ACM, 46*(1), 89–93. doi:10.1145/602421.602425

Cannataro, M., & Talia, D. (2004). Semantics and Knowledge Grids: Building the Next-Generation Grid. *IEEE Intelligent Systems, 19*(1), 56–63. doi:10.1109/MIS.2004.1265886

Capuano, N., Marsella, M., & Salerno, S. (2000). ABITS: An Agent-based Intelligent Tutoring System for Distance Learning. In *Proceedings of ITS 2000*, Montreal, Canada. Retrieved from http://www.capuano.biz/Papers/ITS_2000.pdf

Carmona-Saez, P., Chagoyen, M., Rodriguez, A., Trelles, O., Carazo, J., & Pascual-Montano, A. (2006). Integrated Analysis of Gene Expression by Association Rules Discovery. *BMC Bioinformatics, 7*(1), 54. doi:10.1186/1471-2105-7-54

Carrari, F., Baxter, C., Usadel, B., Urbanczyk-Wochniak, E., Zanor, M.-I., & Nunes-Nesi, A. (2006). Integrated Analysis of Metabolite and Transcript Levels reveals the Metabolic Shifts that underlie Tomato Fruit Development and highlight regulatory aspects of Metabolic Network Behavior. *Plant Physiology, 142*, 1380–1396. doi:10.1104/pp.106.088534

Carrington, P. J., Scott, J., & Wasserman, S. (2005). *Models and Methods in Social Network Analysis*. Cambridge, UK: Cambridge University Press.

Casanova, M. A. (2005). *Grid Computing – Introduction*. Retrieved from http://www.inf.puc-rio.br/~casanova/INF2328-Topicos-WebBD/modulo6-Topicos/modulo6a-grid.PDF

Catania, B., Maddalena, A., Mazza, M., Bertino, E., & Rizzi, S. (2004). A Framework for Data Mining Pattern Management. In J. Boulicaut, F. Esposito & F. Giannotti (Eds.), *Lecture Notes on Artificial Intelligence: Vol. 3202, Knowledge Discovery in Databases - 8th European Conference on Principles and Practice of Knowledge Discovery in Databases - PKDD2004* (pp. 87-98). Berlin, Heidelberg: Springer-Verlag.

Causton, C., Quackenbush, J., & Brazma, A. (2003). *Microarray Gene Expression Data Analysis: A Beginner's Guide*. Blackwell Publishers.

Celotti, F., Colciago, A., Negri-Cesi, P., Pravettoni, A., Zaninetti, R., & Sacchi, M. C. (2006). Effect of Platelet-rich plasma on Migration and Proliferation of SaOS-2 Osteoblasts: Role of Platelet-derived Growth Factor and Transforming Growth Factor-beta. *Wound Repair and Regeneration, 14*(2), 195–202. doi:10.1111/j.1743-6109.2006.00110.x

Chakrabarti, S., Cox, E., Frank, E., Goting, R., Han, J., & Jiang, X. (2009). *Data Mining. Know it All*. Elsevier.

Chakrabarti, S. (2002). *Mining the Web: Discovering Knowledge from Hypertext Data*. San Francisco: Morgan Kaufmann.

Chan, P. K., Fan, W., Prodromidis, A. L., & Stolfo, S. J. (1999). Distributed Data Mining in Credit Card Fraud Detection. *IEEE Intelligent Systems, 14*(6), 67–74. doi:10.1109/5254.809570

Chandra, C., & Grabis, J. (2008). A Goal Model-driven Supply Chain Design. *International Journal of Data Analysis Techniques and Strategies, 1*(3), 224–241. doi:10.1504/IJDATS.2009.024294

Chang, S. F., Chen, W., Men, J., Sundaram, H., & Zhong, D. (1998). A Fully Automated Content based Video Search Engine supporting Spatio-temporal Queries. *IEEE Transactions on Circuits and Systems for Video Technology, 8*(5), 602–615. doi:10.1109/76.718507

Chang, C., & Lin, C. (2001). *LIBSVM: A Library for Support Vector Machines*. Retrieved from http://www.csie.ntu.edu.tw/~cjlin/libsvm

Chang, F., & Ren, J. (2007). Validating System Properties Exhibited in Execution Traces. In *IEEE/ACM International Conference on Automated Software Engineering* (pp. 517-520). Atlanta, GA: ACM.

Chapman, W., Bridewell, W., Hanbury, P., Cooper, G., & Buchanan, B. (2001). Evaluation of Negation Phrases in Narrative Clinical Report, In *Proceedings of 2001 AMIA Symposium*. (pp 105-109).

Chatfield, C. (1996). *The Analysis of Time Series*. New York, NY: Chapman and Hall.

Chatterjee, Patrali, & Hoffman, Donna, L., Novak, & Thomas, P. (2003). Modeling the Clickstream: Implications for Web-Based Advertising Efforts. *Marketing Science*, *22*(4), 520–541. doi:10.1287/mksc.22.4.520.24906

Chazard, E., Preda, C., Merlin, B., Ficheur, G., & Beuscart, R. (2009). Data-Mining-based Detection of Adverse Drug Events. In H. -P Adlassnig, B. Blobel, J. Mantas & I. Masic (Eds.), *Medical Informatics in a United and Healthy Europe, Proceedings of MIE 2009. Studies in Health Technology and Informatics*, 150 (pp. 552-556). Amsterdam: IOS Press.

Chen, M., Han, J., & Yu, P. S. (1996). Data Mining: An Overview from a Database Perspective. *IEEE Transactions on Knowledge and Data Engineering*, *8*(6), 866–883. doi:10.1109/69.553155

Chen, Q., Dayal, U., & Hsu, M. (2000). OLAP-Based Data Mining for Business Intelligence Applications in Telecommunications and E-commerce. In Bhalla, S. (Ed.), *Proceedings of Databases in Networked Information Systems, International Workshop DNIS 2000* (pp. 1–19). Aizu, Japan. doi:10.1007/3-540-44431-9_1

Chen, X., & Petr, I. (2000). Discovering Temporal Association Rules: Algorithms, Language and System. In *International Conference of Data Engineering*.

Cheng, Y., & Church, G. (2000). Biclustering of Expression Data. In *Proceedings of Eighth International Conference Intelligent Systems for Molecular Biology* (pp.93-103).

Chiang, I., Shieh, M., & Hsu, J., Y. & Wong, J. (2005). Building a Medical Decision Support System for Colon Polyp Screening by Using Fuzzy Classification Trees. *Applied Intelligence*, *22*(1), 61–75. doi:10.1023/B:APIN.0000047384.85823.f6

Clark, T. D., Jones, M. C., & Armstrong, C. P. (2007). The Dynamic Structure of Management Support Systems: Theory Development, Research, Focus, and Direction. *Management Information Systems Quarterly*, *31*(3), 579–615.

Close, K. J., Pedrycz, W., Swiniarski, R. W., & Kurgan, L. A. (2007). *Data Mining: A Knowledge Discovery Approach*. Springer.

Codd, E. F. (1970). A Relational Model of Data for Large Shared Data Banks. *Communications of the ACM*, *13*(6), 377–387. doi:10.1145/362384.362685

Codd, E. F. (1982). Relational Database: A Practical Foundation for Productivity. *Communications of the ACM*, *25*(2), 109–117. doi:10.1145/358396.358400

Cody, G. D., Boctor, N. Z., Filley, T. R., Hazen, R. M., Scott, J. H., & Sharma, A. (2000). Primordial Carbonylated Iron-Sulfur compounds and the synthesis of Pyruvate. *Science*, *289*(5483), 1337–1340. doi:10.1126/science.289.5483.1337

Coenen, F., & Leng, P. (2007). The Effect of Threshold Values on Association Rule based Classification Accuracy. *Journal of Data and Knowledge Engineering*, *60*(2), 345–360. doi:10.1016/j.datak.2006.02.005

Coenen, F., Leng, P., & Ahmed, S. (2004). Data Structures for Association Rule Mining: T-trees and P-trees. *IEEE Transactions on Data and Knowledge Engineering*, *16*(6), 774–778. doi:10.1109/TKDE.2004.8

Coenen, F. P., Leng, P., & Goulbourne, G. (2004). Tree Structures for Mining Association Rules. *Journal of Data Mining and Knowledge Discovery*, *8*(1), 25–51. doi:10.1023/B:DAMI.0000005257.93780.3b

Coenen, F. (2004). The LUCS-KDD Apriori-T Association Rule Mining Algorithm. *Department of Computer Science, The University of Liverpool, UK*. Retrieved from http://www.cxc.liv.ac.uk /~frans/ KDD/ Software/ Apriori_T/aprioriT.html.

Coenen, F., & Leng, P. (2002). Finding Association rules with some very Frequent Attributes. In *Proceedings of the 6th European Conference on Principles and Practice of Knowledge Discovery in Databases* (pp. 99-111). Helsinki, Finland: Springer-Verlag.

Coenen, F., & Leng, P. (2004). An Evaluation of Approaches to Classification Rule Selection. In *Proceedings of the 4th IEEE International Conference on Data Mining* (pp. 359-362). Brighton, UK: IEEE Computer Society.

Coenen, F., Goulbourne, G., & Leng, P. (2001). Computing Association Rules using partial totals. In *Proceedings of the 5th European Conference on Principles and Practice of Knowledge Discovery in Databases* (pp. 54-66). Freiburg, Germany: Springer-Verlag.

Coenen, F., Leng, P., & Zhang, L. (2005). Threshold Tuning for improved Classification Association Rule Mining. In *Proceedings of the 9th Pacific-Asia Conference on Knowledge Discovery and Data Mining* (pp. 216-225). Hanoi, Vietnam: Springer-Verlag.

Cohen, J. (2004). Bioinformatics – An Introduction for Computer Scientists. *ACM Computing Surveys, 36*(2), 122–158. doi:10.1145/1031120.1031122

Cohen, W. W. (1995). Fast Effective Rule Induction. In *Proceedings of the 12th International Conference on Machine Learning* (pp. 115-123). Tahoe City, CA, USA: Morgan Kaufmann Publishers.

Cooke, C. D., Santana, C. A., Morris, T. I., DeBraal, L., Ordonez, C., & Omiecinski, E. (2000). Validating Expert System Rule Confidences Using data Mining of Myocardial Perfusion SPECT Databases. *IEEE Computers in Cardiology, 27*, 785–788.

Corchado, J. M., Mata, A., Paz, F. D., & Pozo, D. D. (2008). A Case-Based Reaosoning System to Forecast the Presence of Oil Slicks. In. *Proceedings of the IADIS European Conference on Data Mining, 2008*, 3–10.

Cornelis, C., Yan, P., Zhang, X., & Chen, G. (2006). Mining Positive and Negative Association Rules from Large Databases. *Proceedings of the 2006 IEEE International Conference on Cybernetics and Intelligent Systems* (pp. 613-618). Bangkok, Thailand: IEEE Computer Society.

Corpet, F. (1988). Multiple Sequence Alignment with Hierarchical Clustering. *Nucleic Acids Research, 16*, 10881–10890. doi:10.1093/nar/16.22.10881

Cover, T., & Hart, P. (1967). Nearest Neighbor Pattern Classification. *IEEE Transactions on Information Theory, 13*(1), 21–27. doi:10.1109/TIT.1967.1053964

Cox, K. C., Eick, S. G., Wills, G. J., & Brachman, R. J. (1997). Visual Data Mining: Recognizing Telephone Calling Fraud. *Data Mining and Knowledge Discovery, 1*(2), 225–231. doi:10.1023/A:1009740009307

Creighton, C., & Hanash, S. (2003). Mining Gene Expression Databases for Association Rules. *Bioinformatics (Oxford, England), 19*(1), 79–86. doi:10.1093/bioinformatics/19.1.79

Cui, H., Mittal, V., & Datar, M. (2006). Comparative Experiments on Sentiment Classification for Online Product Reviews. In *Proceedings of the National Conference on Artificial Intelligence* (pp. 1265-1270). AAAI Press.

Dan, G., Florin, L., & Mihai, H. (2003). e-Learning distributed framework using intelligent agents. *New Trends in Computer Science and Engineering*, Anniversary Volume, Technical University Gh. Asachi, Polirom Press, Iaşi, 159-163.

Darrell, T., & Pentland, A. (1993). Space-time Gestures. In *Proceedings of 1993 IEEE Comput. Soc. Conf. on Computer Vision and Pattern Recognition* (pp. 335–340).

Das, G., Mannila, H., & Smyth, P. (1998). *Rule Discovery from Time Series* (pp. 16–22). KDD.

Dasu, T. J. T. (2003). *Exploratory Data Mining and Data Cleaning*. New York: Wiley-Interscience.

Data Mining Group. (2009). Predictive Model Markup Language (PMML). Retrieved August 1, 2009, from http://www.dmg.org/.

Date, C. J. (2004). *An Introduction to Database Systems.* Upper Sadle River, New Jersey: Pearson Education.

Datta, S., & Datta, S. (2006). Evaluation of Clustering Algorithms for Gene Expression Data. *BMC Bioinformatics, 7*(Suppl 4), S17. doi:10.1186/1471-2105-7-S4-S17

Dave, K., Lawrence, S., & Pennock, D. (2003). Mining the Peanut Gallery: Opinion Extraction and Semantic Classification in Product Reviews. In *Proceedings of the 12ᵗʰ International Conference on the World Wide Web - ACM WWW2003.* Budapest, Hungary.

Davies, L., & Gather, U. (1993). The identification of Multiple Outliers. *Journal of the American Statistical Association, 88,* 782–801. doi:10.2307/2290763

Davies, D., & Bouldin, D. (1979). A Cluster Separation Measure. *IEEE Transactions on Pattern Analysis and Machine Intelligence, 1*(4), 224–227. doi:10.1109/TPAMI.1979.4766909

Davis, R., Buchanan, B., & Shortliffe, E. H. (1977). Production Rules as a representation for a Knowledge-based Consultation Program. *Artificial Intelligence, 8*(1), 15–45. doi:10.1016/0004-3702(77)90003-0

De Hoon, M. (2002). Cluster 3.0 for Windows, Mac OS X, Linux, Unix. Retrieved August 18, 2009, from http://bonsai.ims.u-tokyo.ac.jp/~mdehoon/software/cluster/

De Raedt, L. (2003). A Perspective on Inductive Databases. *SIGKDD Explorations, 4*(2), 69–77. doi:10.1145/772862.772871

De Raedt, L. (2002). Data Mining as Constraint Logic Programming. In A.C.Kakas & F. Sadri (Eds.), *Lecture Notes on Artificial Intelligence: Vol. 2408, Computational Logic: Logic Programming and Beyond - Essays in Honour of Robert A. kowalski - Part II* (pp. 526-547). Berlin, Heidelberg: Springer-Verlag.

De Soto, A. R., Capdevila, C. A., & Fernández, E. C. (2003). Fuzzy Systems and Neural Networks XML Schemas for Soft Computing. *Mathware & Soft Computing, 10*(2-3), 43–56.

Dellarocas, C. (2003). The Digitization of Word of Mouth: Promise and Challenges of Online Feedback Mechanisms. *Management Science.* Institute for Operations Research and Management Sciences, 1407-1424.

Dembélé, D., & Kastner, P. (2003). Fuzzy C-means method for Clustering Microarray Data. *Bioinformatics (Oxford, England), 19*(8), 973–980. doi:10.1093/bioinformatics/btg119

Denmat, T., Ducasse, M., & Ridoux, O. (2005). Data Mining and Cross-checking of Execution Traces: A Reinterpretation of Jones, Harrold and Stasko Test Information Visualization. In *20th IEEE/ACM International Conference on Automated Software Engineering* (pp. 396 – 399). Long Beach, CA: ACM/IEEE. Denton, T., Jones, E., Srinivasan, S., Owens, K., & Buskens, R.W. (2008). NAOMI – An Experimental Platform for Multi-modeling. In *ACM/IEEE 11th International Conference on Model Driven Engineering Languages & Systems.* Toulouse, France.

Derubeis, A. R., & Cancedda, R. (2004). Bone Marrow Stromal Cells (BMSCs) in Bone Engineering: Limitations and Recent Advances. *Annals of Biomedical Engineering, 32*(1), 160–165. doi:10.1023/B:ABME.0000007800.89194.95

Deshpande, M., & Karypis, G. (2002). Using Conjunction of Attribute Values for Classification. In *Proceedings of the Eleventh International Conference on Information and Knowledge Management* (pp.356-364). McLean, VA.

Devitt, A., & Ahmad, K. (2007). Sentiment Polarity Identification in Financial News: A Cohesion Based Approach. In *Proceedings of the 45th Annual Meeting of the Association of Computational Linguistics* (pp. 984–991). Prague, Czech Republic.

Dhillon, I. S., & Modha, D. S. (2001a). Concept Decompositions for Large Sparse Text Data using Clustering. *Machine Learning, 42*(1),143–175. Also appears as *IBM Research Report RJ 10147,* 1999.

Dhillon, I. S., Fan, J., & Guan, Y. (2001b). Efficient Clustering of Very Large Document Collections. *Data Mining for Scientific and Engineering Applications,* 357–381.

Dìaz-Uriarte, R., & Alvarez de Andres, S. (2006). Gene selection and classification of microarray data using random forest. *BMC Bioinformatics*, *7*(3), 1471–2105.

Dietterich, T. G. (2000). Ensemble methods in Machine Learning. In *Proceedings of the First International Workshop on Multiple Classifier Systems* (pp.1-15). Cagliari, Italy.

Ding, C. (2003). Unsupervised feature selection via Two-Way Ordering in Gene Expression Analysis. *Bioinformatics (Oxford, England)*, *19*(10), 1259–1266. doi:10.1093/bioinformatics/btg149

Ding, C., & Peng, H. (2005). Minimum Redundancy Feature selection from Microarray Gene Expression Data. *Journal of Bioinformatics and Computational Biology*, *3*(2), 185–206. doi:10.1142/S0219720005001004

Domingos, P., & Pazzani, M. (1997). On the Optimality of the Simple Bayesian Classifier under Zero-One Loss. *Machine Learning*, *29*, 103–130. doi:10.1023/A:1007413511361

Downs, E., Clare, P., & Coe, I. (1988). *Structured Systems Analysis and Design Method: Application and Context.* Hertfordshire, UK: Prentice Hall International (UK) Ltd.

Draminski, M., Rada-Iglesias, A., Enroth, S., Wadelius, C., Koronacki, J., & Komorowski, J. (2008). Monte Carlo feature selection for Supervised Classification. *Bioinformatics (Oxford, England)*, *24*(1), 110. doi:10.1093/bioinformatics/btm486

Drucker, P. (2000). Need to know: Integrating e-Learning with high-velocity value chains. *A Delphi Group White Paper*. Retrieved from http://www.delphigroup.com/research/ whitepaper_request_download.htm

Duda, R., & Hart, P. (2003). *Pattern Classification and Scene Analysis*. New York: Wiley.

Duda, R., Hart, P., & Stork, D. (2001). Pattern Classification.

Dudoit, S., Fridlyand, J., & Speed, T. (2002). Comparison of Discrimination methods for the classification of Tumors using Gene Expression Data. *Journal of the American Statistical Association*, *97*(457), 77–88. doi:10.1198/016214502753479248

Dy, J. G., & Brodley, C. E. (2004). Feature Selection for Unsupervised Learning. *Journal of Machine Learning Research*, *5*, 845–889.

Dzeroski, S. (2007). Towards a General Framework for Data Mining. In S. Dzeroski & J. Struyf (Eds.), *Lecture Notes in Computer Science: Vol. 4747, Knowledge Discovery in Inductive Databases - 5th International Workshop, KDID 2006* (pp. 259-300). Berlin, Heidelberg: Springer-Verlag.

Dzieciolowski, K., & Kina, D. (2008). Data Mining in Marketing Acquisition Campaigns. In. *Proceedings of the IADIS European Conference on Data Mining, 2008*, 173–175.

Eckerson, W. W. (2009). Research Q&A: Performance Management Strategies. *Business Intelligence Journal*, *14*(1), 24–27.

Edsall, T. B. (2006). Democrats' Data Mining Stirs an Intraparty Battle. *The Washington Post*, March 8, A1.

Eisen, M., Spellman, P., Brown, P., & Botstein, D. (1998). Cluster Analysis and Display of Genome-wide Expression Patterns. In *Proceedings of National Academy of Science* (pp. 14863-14868). *USA*.

El-Gendy, M. A., Bose, A., & Shin, K. (2003). Evolution of the Internet QoS and Support for Soft Real-time Applications. In *Proceedings of the IEEE* (pp. 1086-1104), 91 (7).

El-Hajj, M., & Zaiane, O. R. (2003). Inverted Matrix: Efficient Discovery of Frequent Items in Large Datasets in the context of Interactive Mining. In *Proceedings of the 9th ACM SIGKDD International Conference on Knowledge Discovery and Data Mining* (pp. 109-118). Washington, DC: ACM Press.

Elmasri, R., & Navathe, S. B. (2007). *Fundamentals of Database Systems*. Upper Sadle River, New Jersey: Pearson Education.

Eshghi, A., Haughton, D., & Topi, H. (2007). Determinants of Customer Loyalty in the Wireless Telecommunications Industry. *Telecommunications Policy*, *31*, 93–106. doi:10.1016/j.telpol.2006.12.005

Esuli, A., & Sebastiani, F. (2005). Determining the Semantic Orientation of terms through Gloss Classification. In *Proceedings of the 14th ACM International Conference on Information and Knowledge Management* (pp. 617-624). Bremen, Germany.

Esuli, A., & Sebastiani, F. (2006). SentiWordNet: A Publicly Available Lexical Resource for Opinion Mining. In *Proceedings of the International Conference on Language Resources and Evaluation (LREC)*. Genoa.

Ewens, W. J., & Grant, G. R. (2001). *Statistical methods in Bioinformatics: An Introduction*. New York: Springer-Verlag.

Ezawa, K. J., & Norton, S. W. (1996). Constructing Bayesian Networks to Predict Uncollectible Telecommunications Accounts. *IEEE Expert, 11*(5), 45–51. doi:10.1109/64.539016

Ezawa, K., & Norton, S. (1995). Knowledge Discovery in Telecommunication Services Data Using Bayesian Network Models. In U. Fayyad & R. Uthurusamy (Eds.), Proceedings of the First International Conference on Knowledge Discovery & Data Mining, Montreal (pp. 100-105). Canaak, AAAI Press, Menlo Park, CA.

Fadili, M. J., Ruan, S., Bloyet, D., & Mazoyer, B. (2000). A Multistep Unsupervised Fuzzy Clustering Analysis of fMRI Time Series. *Human Brain Mapping, 10*, 160–178. doi:10.1002/1097-0193(200008)10:4<160::AID-HBM20>3.0.CO;2-U

Faloutsos, C., Ranganatha, M., & Manolopoulos, Y. (1994). Fast subsequence matching in Time Series Databases. In *Proceedings of the 3rd International Conference on Knowledge Discovery and Data Mining* (pp. 24-30). Menlo Park, CA: AAAI Press.

Fard, A. M., Kamyar, H., & Naghibzadeh, M. (2008). Multi-expert Disease Diagnosis System over Symptom Data Grids on the Internet. *World Applied Science Journal, 3*(2), 244–253.

Farhoomand, A., & Drudy, D. H. (2002). Managerial Information Overload. *Communications of the ACM, 45*(10), 127–131. doi:10.1145/570907.570909

Fawcett, T., & Provost, F. (1997). Adaptive Fraud Detection. *Data Mining and Knowledge Discovery, 1*(3), 291–316. doi:10.1023/A:1009700419189

Fayyad, U. M. (1996). Data Mining and Knowledge Discovery: Making Sense Out of Data. *IEEE Expert, 11*(5), 20–25. doi:10.1109/64.539013

Fayyad, U., Piatetsky-Shapiro, G., & Smyth, P. (1996, November). The KDD Process for Extracting useful Knowledge from Volumes of Data. *Communications of the ACM, 11*(39), 27–34. doi:10.1145/240455.240464

Fayyad, U. M., Piatetsky-Shapiro, G., Smyth, P., & Uthurusamy, R. (1996). *Advances in Knowledge Discovery and Data Mining*. AAAI/MIT Press.

Fayyad, U. M., Piatetski-Shapiro, G., & Smyth, P. (1996). From Data Mining to Knowledge Discovery: An Overview. In Fayyad, U. M., Piatetski-Shapiro, G., Smyth, P., & Uthurusamy, R. (Eds.), *Advances in Knowledge Discovery and Data Mining* (pp. 1–34). Menlo Park, California: AAAI Press/The MIT Press.

Feldman, R., & Sanger, J. (2006). *The Text Mining Handbook: Advanced Approaches in Analyzing Unstructured Data*. Cambridge, UK: Cambridge University Press. doi:10.1017/CBO9780511546914

Fennell, G., Allenby, G. M., Yang, S., & Edwards, Y. (2003). The Effectiveness of Demographic and Psychographic Variables for Explaining Brand and Product Category Use. *Quantitative Marketing and Economics, 1*(2), 223–244. doi:10.1023/A:1024686630821

Fink, E., Kokku, P. K., Nikiforou, S., Hall, L. O., Goldgof, D. B., & Krischer, J. P. (2004). Selection of Patients for Clinical Trials: An Interactive Web-Based System. *Artificial Intelligence in Medicine, 31*(3), 241–254.

Fisher, D., Smith, M., & Welser, H. T. (2006). You Are Who You Talk To: Detecting Roles in Usenet Newsgroups. In *39th Annual Hawaii International Conference on System Sciences*. Kauai: IEEE Computer Society.

Fitzgerald, S., Foster, I., Kesselman, C., vonLaszewski, G., Smith, W., & Tuecke, S. (1997). A Directory Service for Configuring High-performance Distributed Computations. In *Proceedings of 7th IEEE Symposium on High Performance Distributed Computing* (pp.365-375).

Forgy, E. (1965). Cluster Analysis of Multivariate Data: Efficiency vs. Interpretability of Classifications. *Biometrics, 21*(1), 768–780.

Foster, I., & Kesselman, C. (1999). *The Grid: Blueprint for a new computing infrastructure*. San Francisco: Morgan Kaufmann.

Foster, I., Kesselman, C., & Tuecke, S. (2001). The Anatomy of the Grid: Enabling Scalable Virtual Organizations. *The International Journal of Supercomputer Applications, 15*(3), 6–13.

Freitas, A. A. (2002). *Data Mining and Knowledge Discovery with Evolutionary Algorithm*. Germany: Springer-Verlag Berlin Heidelberg.

Freund, Y., & Schapire, R. E. (1997). A Decision-Theoretic Generalization of On-line Learning and an application to Boosting. *Journal of Computer and System Sciences, 55*, 1–34. doi:10.1006/jcss.1997.1504

Frietman, E., Hill, M., & Khoe, G. (2001). A Kohonen Neural Network Controlled All-Optical Router System. *International Journal of Computer Research, 10*(2), 251–267.

Fromont, É., Blockeel, H., & Struyf, J. (2007). Integrating Decision Tree Learning into Inductive Databases. In S. Dzeroski & J. Struyf (Eds.), *Lecture Notes in Computer Science: Vol. 4747. Knowledge Discovery in Inductive Databases - 5th International Workshop, KDID 2006* (pp. 81-96). Berlin, Heidelberg: Springer-Verlag.

Fu, L., & Medico, E. (2007). FLAME, A Novel Fuzzy Clustering method for the analysis of DNA Microarray Data. *BMC Bioinformatics, 8*(1), 3. doi:10.1186/1471-2105-8-3

Fu, X., & Wang, L. (2005). Data Dimensionality Reduction with application to improving Classification Performance and explaining Concepts of Data Sets. *International Journal of Business Intelligence and Data Mining, 1*(1), 65–87. doi:10.1504/IJBIDM.2005.007319

Fung, G., & Stoeckel, J. (2007). SVM feature selection for classification of SPECT images of Alzheimer's disease using spatial information. *Knowledge and Information Systems, 11*(2), 243–258. doi:10.1007/s10115-006-0043-5

Gago, P., Fernandes, C., Pinto, F., & Santos, M. F. (2009). INTCare: On-line Knowledge Discovery in the Intensive Care Unit. In. *Proceedings of INES, 2009*, 159–164.

Gago, P., & Santos, M. F. (2008). Towards an Intelligent Decision Support System for Intensive Care Units. In O. Okun & G. Valentini (Eds.), *Proceedings of the 18th European Conference on Artificial Intelligence: Vol. 1. Workshop on Supervised and Unsupervised Ensemble Methods and their Applications* (pp. 21-25). Patras, Greece.

Gamon, M. (2004). Sentiment Classification on Customer Feedback Data: Noisy Data, Large Feature Vectors, and the Role of Linguistic Analysis. In *Proceedings of the 20th International Conference on Computational Linguistics* (pp. 841). Geneva, Switzerland.

Garofalakis, M., & Rastogi, R. (2001). The NEMESIS. In *Proceedings of Data Mining and Knowledge Discovery DMKD 2001*. Santa Barbara, CA: Data Mining Meets Network Management.

Gehrke, J., Ramakrishnan, R., & Ganti, V. (1998). RainForest: A Framework for Fast Decision Tree Construction of Large Datasets. In *Proceedings of International Conference on Very Large Data Bases* (pp. 416-427). New York, USA.

Geiger, J. (2004). Data Quality Management The Most Critical Initiative You Can Implement. In *Proceedings of the Twenty-Ninth Annual SAS® Users Group International Conference*. Montreal, Canada: SAS Institute Inc.

Geng, L., & Hamilton, H. J. (2006). Interestingness measures for Data Mining: A Survey. *ACM Computing Surveys, 38*(3), 9–14. doi:10.1145/1132960.1132963

Gerber, L., & Fernandes, A. A. A. (2004). An Abstract Algebra for Knowledge Discovery in Databases. In Benczúr, A., Demetrovics, J., & Gottlob, G. (Eds.), *Advances in Database and Information Systems* (pp. 83–98). Berlin, Heidelberg: Springer-Verlag.

Geurts, P. (2001). Pattern Extraction for Time Series Classification. In *Principles of Data Mining and Knowledge Discovery, 5th European Conference, PKDD 2001. Lecture Notes in Computer Science*, 2168 (pp. 115-127). Berlin/Heidelberg: Springer. doi:10.1007/3-540-44794-6.

Ghanem, M., Guo, Y., Rowe, A., & Wendel, P. (2002). Grid-based Knowledge Discovery Services for High Throughput Informatics. In *Proceedings of 11ᵗʰ IEEE International Symposium on High Performance Distributed Computing* (pp. 416). Washington, DC: IEEE CS Press.

Ghias, A., Logan, J., Chamberlin, D., & Smith, B. C. (1995). Query by Humming – Musical Information Retrieval in an Audio Database. In *Proceedings of ACM Multimedia 95.* San Francisco, CA.

Ghose, A., & Yang, S. (2009). (forthcoming). An Empirical Analysis of Search Engine Advertising: Sponsored Search in Electronic Markets. *Management Science*. doi:10.1287/mnsc.1090.1054

Ghosh, J., & Strehl, A. (2005). Clustering and Visualization of Retail Market Baskets. In Pal, N. R., & Jain, L. (Eds.), *Advanced Techniques in Data Mining and Knowledge Discovery* (pp. 75–102). London, UK: Springer-Verlag. doi:10.1007/1-84628-183-0_3

Giotopoulos, K., Alexakos, C., Beligiannis, G., & Likothanassis, S. (2007). Integrating Computational Intelligence Techniques and Assessment Agents in e-Learning Environments. *International Journal of Computational Intelligence*, 3(4), 328–337.

Giuffrida, G., Sismeiro, C., & Tribulato, G. (2008). Automatic Content Targeting on Mobile Phones. In *Proceedings of the 11ᵗʰ International Conference on Extending Database Technology: Advances in Database Technology* (pp. 630-639). Nantes, France. *EDBT '08*, Vol. 261.New York: ACM.

Glance, N., Hurst, M., Nigam, K., Siegler, M., Stockton, R., & Tomokiyo, T. (2005). Deriving Marketing Intelligence from Online Discussion. In *Proceedings of the 11ᵗʰ ACM SIGKDD International Conference on Knowledge Discovery in Data Mining* (pp. 419 – 428).

Gleeson, N. P., & Mercer, T. H. (1996). The utility of Isokinetics Dynamometry in the Assessment of Human Muscle Function. *Sports Medicine (Auckland, N.Z.)*, 21(1), 18–34. doi:10.2165/00007256-199621010-00003

Gold, B., & Morgan, N. (2000). *Speech and Audio Signal Processing: Processing and Perception of Speech and Music*. New York: John Wiley & Sons.

Golder, S. A. (2003). A Typology of Social Roles in Usenet. *A thesis submitted to the Department of Linguistics*. Boston: Harvard University.

Golfarelli, M., Rizzi, S., & Cella, I. (2004). What`s Next in Business Intelligence. In *DOLAP '04* (pp. 1–6). Beyond Data Warehousing.

Golub, T. (1999). Molecular Classification of Cancer: Class Discovery and Class Prediction by Gene Expression Monitoring. *Science*, 286(5439), 531–537. doi:10.1126/science.286.5439.531

Golub, T., Slonim, D., Tamayo, P., Huard, C., Gaasenbeek, M., & Mesirov, J. (1999). Molecular Classification of Cancer: Class Discovery and Class Prediction by Gene Expression Monitoring. *Science (New York, N.Y.)*, 286, 531–537.

Gotschall, M. (2000). e-Learning strategies for Executive Education and Corporate Training. *Fortune*, 141(10), S5–S59.

Gray, J. (1978). Notes on Database Operating Systems. Operating Systems: An Advanced Course. *Lecture Notes in Computer Science, Springer Verlag*, 60, 393–481.

Gray, J., & Reuter, A. (1993). *Transaction Processing: Concepts and Technique*. San Mateo, CA: Morgan Kaufman.

Gray, J., Tolvanen, J. P., Kelly, S., Gokhale, A., Neema, S., & Sprinkle, J. (2007). Domain-Specific Modeling. In P. Fishwick, *CRC Handbook on Dynamic System Modeling* (pp. 7.1-7.20). CRC Press.

Grefenstette, G., Qu, Y., Shanahan, J., & Evans, D. (2004). Coupling Niche Browsers and Affect Analysis for an Opinion Mining Application. In. *Proceedings of the RIAO, 2004*, 186–194.

Griffith, L. G., & Swartz, M. A. (2006). Capturing complex 3D Tissue physiology in vitro. *Nature Reviews. Molecular Cell Biology*, 7(3), 211–224. doi:10.1038/nrm1858

Grzymala-Busse, J. W., & Hu, M. (2001). A Comparison of several approaches to missing attribute values in Data Mining. *Lecture Notes in Computer Science*, 378–385. doi:10.1007/3-540-45554-X_46

Gu, J., & Liu, J. (2008). Bayesian Biclustering of Gene Expression Data. *BMC Genomics*, 9(Suppl. 1), S4. doi:10.1186/1471-2164-9-S1-S4

Guillet, F., & Hamilton, H. J. (2007). *Quality Measures in Data Mining. Studies in Computational Intelligence.* Springer.

Guimarães, G. (2000). *The Induction of Temporal Grammatical Rules from Multivariate Time Series* (pp. 127–140). ICGI.

Gupta, R. Haritsa, J. R., & Ramamritham, K. (1997). More Optimism About Real-Time Distributed Commit Processing. *Technical Report TR-97-04.* Database System Lab, Supercomputer Education and Research Centre, I.I.Sc. Bangalore, India

Gupta, R., Haritsa, J. R., Ramamritham, K., & Seshadri, S. (1996). Commit Processing in Distributed Real Time Database Systems. *Real-time Systems Symposium.* Washington DC, San Francisco.

Guyon, I., Weston, J., Barnhill, S., & Vapnik, V. (2002). Gene selection for Cancer Classification using Support Vector Machines. *Machine Learning*, 46(1), 389–422. doi:10.1023/A:1012487302797

Haider, K., Tweedale, J., & Jain, L. (2009). An Intelligent Decision Support System Using Expert Systems in a MAS. In Nakamatsu, K., Phillips-Wren, G., Jain, L. C., & Howlett, R. J. (Eds.), *New Advances in Intelligent Decision Technologies. Studies in Computational Intelligence, 199* (pp. 213–222). Berlin, Heidelberg: Springer. doi:10.1007/978-3-642-00909-9_21

Hajek, P., Havel, I., & Chytil, M. (1966). The GUHA Method of Automatic Hypotheses Determination. *Computing, 1*, 293–308. doi:10.1007/BF02345483

Halkidi, M. a. (2001). On Clustering Validation Techniques. *Journal of Intelligent Information Systems, 17*(1), 107–145. doi:10.1023/A:1012801612483

Han, J., & Kamber, M. (2001). *Data Mining: Concepts and Techniques.* San Francisco: Morgan Kaufmann Publishers.

Han, J., Dong, G., & Yin, Y. (1998). Efficient Mining of Partial Periodic Patterns in Time Series Database. In *Proceedings of the 4th International Conference on Knowledge Discovery and Data Mining* (pp. 214-218). Menlo Park, CA: AAAI Press.

Han, J., Fu, Y., Wang, W., Koperski, K., & Zaiane, O. (1996). DMQL: A Data Mining Query Language for Relational Databases. In *Proceedings of the SIGMOD '96 Workshop on Research Issues on Data Mining and Knowledge Discovery (DMKD '96)* (pp. 27-34).

Han, J., Pei, J., & Yin, Y. (2000). Mining Frequent Patterns without Candidate Generation. In *Proceedings of the 2000 ACM SIGMOD International Conference on Management of Data* (pp. 1-12). ACM Press, Dallas, TX, USA.

Hanada, K., Dennis, J. E., & Caplan, A. I. (1997). Stimulatory effects of basic Fibroblast Growth Factor and Bone Morphogenetic Protein-2 on Osteogenic differentiation of Rat Bone Marrow-derived Mesenchymal Stem Cells. *Journal of Bone and Mineral Research, 12*(10), 1606–1614. doi:10.1359/jbmr.1997.12.10.1606

Hanczar, B., Courtine, M., Benis, A., Hennegar, C., Clement, K., & Zucker, J. (2003). Improving Classification of Microarray Daya using Proptotype-based Feature Selection. *SIGKDD Explorations, 5*(2), 23–30. doi:10.1145/980972.980977

Hand, D., Mannila, H., & Smyth, P. (2001). *Principles of Data Mining*. Cambridge, MA: The MIT Press.

Handl, J., Knowles, J., & Kell, D. B. (2005). Computational Cluster Validation in Post-genomic Data Analysis. *Bioinformatics (Oxford, England)*, *21*(15), 3201–3212. doi:10.1093/bioinformatics/bti517

Hanna, B., & De Nooy, J. (2009). *Learning Language and Culture via Public Internet Discussion Forums*. Palgrave Macmillan. doi:10.1057/9780230235823

Hanneman, R., & Riddle, M. (2005). *Introduction to Social Network Methods*. University of California, Riverside.

Hannula, M., & Pirttimäki, V. (2003). Business Intelligence Empirical Study on the Top 50 Finnish Companies. *Journal of American Academy of Business*, *2*(2), 593–599.

Harel, D. (1987). Statecharts: A Visual Formalism for Complex Systems. *Science of Computer Programming*, *8*(3), 231–274. doi:10.1016/0167-6423(87)90035-9

Haritsa, J. R., Ramamritham, K., & Gupta, R. (2000). The PROMPT Real Time Commit Protocol. *IEEE Transactions on Parallel and Distributed Systems*, *11*(2), 160–181. doi:10.1109/71.841752

Hartigan, J. (1972). Direct Clustering of a Data Matrix. *Journal of the American Statistical Association*, *67*(337), 123–129. doi:10.2307/2284710

Haselsteiner, E., & Pfurtscheller, G. (2000). Using Time-dependent Neural Networks for EEG Classification. *IEEE Trans. Rahab. Eng*, *8*, 457–463. doi:10.1109/86.895948

Hastie, T., Tibshirani, R., & Friedman, J. (2001). *The Elements of Statistical Learning: Data mining, Inference and Prediction*. New York: Springer-Verlag.

Hatzivassiloglou, V., & McKeown, K. (1997). Predicting the Semantic Orientation of Adjectives. In *Proceedings of the 35ᵗʰ Annual Meeting of the Association of Computational Linguistics (ACL'97)* (pp. 174-181). Madrid, Spain.

Haykin, S. (2007). *Neural Networks: A Comprehensive Foundation* (3rd ed.). Upper Saddle River, NJ: Prentice-Hall, Inc.

Haynesworth, S. E., Baber, M. A., & Caplan, A. I. (1996). Cytokine expression by Human Marrow-derived Mesenchymal Progenitor Cells in vitro: Effects of Dexamethasone and IL-1 Alpha. *Journal of Cellular Physiology*, *166*(3), 585–592. doi:10.1002/(SICI)1097-4652(199603)166:3<585::AID-JCP13>3.0.CO;2-6

He, X., Cai, D., & Niyogi, P. (2006). Laplacian Score for Feature Selection. *Advances in Neural Information Processing Systems*, *18*, 507.

Heckert, A. (2006). Chi Square Two Sample. *Tarihinde*, Retrieved June 11, 2009, from http://www.itl.nist.gov: http://www.itl.nist.gov/div898/software/dataplot/refman1/auxillar/ chi2samp.htm

Heineman, G. T., & Councill, W. T. (2001). *Component-based Software Engineering: Putting the Pieces Together*. Boston, MA: Addison-Wesley Longman Publishing Co., Inc.

Hersh, W. (2008). *Information Retrieval: A Health and Biomedical Perspective*. Springer Verlag.

Hidber, C. (1999). Online Association Rule Mining. In *Proceedings of the 1999 ACM SIGMOD International Conference on Management of Data* (pp. 145-156). Philadelphia, Pennsylvania, USA: ACM Press.

Hill, J. H., & Gokhale, A. (2007). Model-driven Engineering for Early QoS Validation of Component-based Software Systems. *Journal of Software*, *2*(3), 9–18. doi:10.4304/jsw.2.3.9-18

Hill, J. H., Schmidt, D. C., Slaby, J., & Porter, A. (2008). CiCUTS: Combining System Execution Modeling Tools with Continuous Integration Environments. In *15th Annual IEEE International Conference and Workshops on the Engineering of Computer Based Systems* (pp. 66-75). Belfast, Northern Ireland: IEEE Computer Society.

Hill, J. H., Slaby, J. M., Baker, S., & Schmidt, D. (2006). Applying System Execution Modeling Tools to Evaluate Enterprise Distributed Real-time and Embedded System QoS. In *12th International Conference on Embedded and Real-Time Computing Systems and Applications* (pp. 350-362). Sydney, Australia: IEEE Computer Society.

Hill, L. (2003). *Implementing a Practical e-Learning System*. Retrieved from http://agora. lakeheadu.ca /pre2004/ december2002/elearning.html

Hinke, T., & Novotny, J. (2000). Data Mining on NASA's Information Power Grid. In *Proceedings of 9th IEEE International Symposium on High Performance Distributed Computing* (pp.292-293). IEEE CS Press.

Hipp, J., Guntzer, U., & Nakhaeizadeh, G. (2000). Algorithms for Association Rule Mining – A General Survey and Comparison. *SIGKDD Explorations, 2*(1), 58–64. doi:10.1145/360402.360421

Hipp, J., Güntzer, U., & Grimmer, U. (2001). *Data Quality Mining: Making a Virtue Neccessity.*

Hirai, M., Klein, M., Fujikawa, Y., Yano, M., Goodenowe, D., & Yamazaki, Y. (2005). Elucidation of Gene-to-Gene and Metabolite-to-Gene Networks in Arabidopsis by Integration of Metabolomics and Transcriptomics. *The Journal of Biological Chemistry, 280*(27), 25590–25595. doi:10.1074/jbc.M502332200

Hirai, M. Y., Yano, M., Goodenowe, D. B., Kanaya, S., Kimura, T., Awazuhara, M., et al. (2004). Integration of Transcriptomics and Metabolomics for understanding of global responses to Nutritional Stresses in Arabidopsis Thaliana. In *Proceedings of the National Academy of Sciences of the United States of America* (pp.10205–10210).

Hoffman, T. (2009). 9 Hottest Skills for '09. *Computer World, January 1* (1), 26-27.

Hoffmann, R., & Valencia, A. (2005). Implementing the iHOP concept for navigation of Biomedical Literature. *Bioinformatics (Oxford, England), 21*(2). doi:10.1093/ bioinformatics/bti1142

Holmgren, A. (1989). Thioredoxin and Glutaredoxin Systems. *The Journal of Biological Chemistry, 264*, 13963–13966.

Horrigan, J. (2008). Online Shopping. *Pew Internet and American Life Project – Research Report.*

Houtsma, M., & Swami, A. (1995). Set-oriented Mining of Association Rules in Relational Databases. In *Proceedings of the 11th International Conference on Data Engineering* (pp. 25-33). Taipei, Taiwan: IEEE Computer Society.

Hsu, C., Chung, H., & Huang, H. (2004). Mining Skewed and Sparse Transactions Data for Personalized Shopping Recommendation. *Machine Learning, 57*(1-2), 35–59. doi:10.1023/B:MACH.0000035471.28235.6d

Hsu, J. (2002). Data Mining Trends and Developments: The Key Data Mining Technologies and Applications for the 21st Century. In *Proceedings of 19th Annual Conference for Information Systems Education (ISECON 2002),* (Art 224b). San Antonio, TX.

Hu, X. (2005). A Data Mining Approach for Retailing Bank Customer Attrition Analysis. *Applied Intelligence, 22*(1), 47–60. doi:10.1023/B:APIN.0000047383.53680.b6

Hua, M., & Pei, J. (2007). Cleaning Disguised Missing Data: A Heuristic Approach. In *Proceedings of the 13th ACM SIGKDD International Conference on Knowledge Discovery and Data Mining* (pp. 950-958). California: IEEE.

Huang, D., & Pan, W. (2006). Incorporating biological knowledge into distance-based clustering analysis of microarray gene expression data. *Bioinformatics (Oxford, England), 22*(10), 1259–1268. doi:10.1093/bioinformatics/btl065

Huang, J. (1991). *Real Time Transaction Processing: Design, Implementation and Performance Evaluation.* Unpublished doctoral dissertation, University of Massachusetts, USA.

Huang, Y., & Lowe, H. (2007). A Novel Hybrid Approach to Automated Negation Detection in Clinical Radiology Reports. *Journal of the American Medical Informatics Association, 14*(3), May/June 2007.

Hyunsoo, K., Golub, G., & Park, H. (2005). Missing Value Estimation for DNA Microarray Gene Expression Data: Local Least Squares Imputation. *Bioinformatics (Oxford, England), 21*(2), 187–198.

Imielinski, T., & Mannila, H. (1996). A Database Perspective on Knowledge Discovery. *Communications of the ACM, 39*(11), 58–64. doi:10.1145/240455.240472

Imielinski, T., & Virmani, A. (1999). MSQL: A Query Language for Database Mining. *Data Mining and Knowledge Discovery, 3*(4), 373–408. doi:10.1023/A:1009816913055

Inseon, L., & Yeom, H. Y. (2002). A Single Phase Distributed Commit Protocol for Main Memory Database Systems. In *16th International Parallel & Distributed Processing Symposium (IPDPS 2002).* Ft. Lauderdale, Florida, USA.

ITU-T E.800 (1994). Terms And Definitions Related to Quality of Service And Network Performance Including Dependability. ITU-T Recommendation E.800.

James, M. (1985). *Classification Algorithm.* New York: Wiley-Interscience.

Jamil, H. M. (2004). Declarative Data Mining Using SQL3. In R. Meo, P. Lanzi & M. Klemettinen (Eds.), *Lecture Notes on Artificial Intelligence: Vol. 2682, Database Support for Data Mining Applications - Discovering Knowledge with Inductive Queries* (pp. 52-75). Berlin, Heidelberg: Springer-Verlag.

Jaroszewicz, S., & Simovici, D. A. (2004). Interestingness of Frequent Itemsets using Bayesian Networks as Background Knowledge. In *Proceedings of 10th ACM SIGKDD International Conference on Knowledge Discovery and Data Mining* (pp.178-186). Seattle, WA.

Jeffery, I., Higgins, D., & Culhane, A. (2006). Comparison and Evaluation of methods for generating Differentially Expressed Gene Lists from Microarray. *BMC Bioinformatics, 7*(1), 359. doi:10.1186/1471-2105-7-359

Jiang, D., Tang, C., & Zhang, A. (2004). Cluster Analysis for Gene Expression Data: A Survey. *IEEE Transactions on Knowledge and Data Engineering, 16*(11), 1370–1386. doi:10.1109/TKDE.2004.68

Jiang, H., Deng, Y., Chen, H., Tao, L., Sha, Q., & Chen, J. (2004). Joint Analysis of Two Microarray Gene-Expression Data Sets to Select Lung Adenocarcinoma Marker Genes. *BMC Bioinformatics, 5*(1), 81. doi:10.1186/1471-2105-5-81

Jiang, X., & Gruenwald, L. (2005). Microarray Gene Expression Data Association Rules Mining based on BSC-tree and FIS-tree. *Data & Knowledge Engineering, 53.*

Jiang, D., Pei, J., & Zhang, A. (2003). DHC: A Density-based Hierarchical Clustering method for Time Series Gene Expression Data. In *Proceedings of the IEEE Symposium on Bioinformatics and Bioengineering* (pp.393-400).

Jilani, A. A., Nadeem, A., Kim, T.-h., & Cho, E.-s. (2008). Formal Representations of the Data Flow Diagram: A Survey. *Advanced Software Engineering and Its Applications,* 153-158.

Jin, X., Li, Y., Mah, T., & Tong, J. (2007). Sensitive Webpage Classification for Content Advertising. In *Proceedings of the 1st International Workshop on Data Mining and Audience Intelligence for Advertising* (pp. 28-33).

John, G. H., Miller, P., & Kerber, R. (1996). Stock Selection Using Rule Induction. *IEEE Expert, 11*(5), 52–58. doi:10.1109/64.539017

Johnstone, B., Hering, T. M., Caplan, A. I., Goldberg, V. M., & Yoo, J. U. (1998). In vitro Chondrogenesis of Bone Marrow-derived Mesenchymal Progenitor Cells. *Experimental Cell Research, 238*(1), 265–272. doi:10.1006/excr.1997.3858

Jones, J. A., Harrold, M. J., & Stasko, J. (2002). Visualization of Test Information to Assist Fault Localization. In *24th International Conference on Software Engineering* (pp. 467 – 477). Orlando, FL: ACM.

Joshy, J., & Craig, F. (2004). *Introduction to Grid Computing.* Upper Saddle River, NJ: Prentice Hall.

Joukov, N., Wong, T., & Zadok, E. (2005). Accurate and Efficient Replaying of File System Traces. In *4th Conference on USENIX Conference on File and Storage Technologies* (p. 25). San Francisco, CA: USENIX Association.

Juan, M. Ale., Gustavo, H., & Rossi, R. (2000). An Approach to Discovering Temporal Association Rules. In *ACM SIGDD.*

Juang, B. H., & Rabiner, L. (1993). *Fundamentals of Speech Recognition.* Englewood Cliffs, NJ: Prentice Hall.

Julesz, B. (1981). Textons, the elements of Texture Perception, and their Interactions. *Nature, 290,* 91–97. doi:10.1038/290091a0

Juliusdottir, T., Keedwell, E., Corne, D., & Narayanan, A. (2005). Two-Phase EA/k-NN for Feature selection and Classification in Cancer Microarray Datasets. In *Proceedings of IEEE Symposium on Computer Intelligence in Bioinformatics and Computing Biology* (pp.1-8).

Kaever, A., Lingner, T., Feussner, K., Gobel, C., Feussner, I., & Meinicke, P. (2009). *Marvis: A Tool for Clustering and Visualization of Metabolic Biomarkers.* BMC Bioinformatics.

Kahveci, T., & Singh, A. (2001). Variable Length Queries for Time Series Data. In *Proceedings of the 17th International Conference of Data Engineering* (pp 273-282). Heidelberg, Germany. doi: 10.1109/ICDE.2001.914838

Kalpakis, K., & Puttagunta, D. G. V. (2001). Distance measures for Effective Clustering of ARIMA Time Series. *IEEE International Conference on Data Mining.* San Jose, CA.

Kamps, J., Marx, M., Mokken, R. J., & De Rijke, M. (2004). Using WordNet to measure Semantic Orientation of Adjectives. In *Proceedings of the 4th International Conference on Language Resources and Evaluation (LREC 2004)* (pp. 1115-1118).

Kanendran, T. A., Johnny, S., & Durga, B. V. (2004). Technical report: Issues and strategies of e-Learning. *Sunway College Journal, 1,* 99–107.

Kargupta, H., & Chan, P. (1999). *Advances in Distributed and Parallel Knowledge Discovery.* AAAI Press.

Kaufer, D. (2000) Flaming: A White Paper. *Carnegie Mellon Dept. of English.*

Kaynar, D. K., Lynch, N., Segala, R., & Vaandrager, F. (2006). *The Theory of Timed I/O Automata.* San Rafael, CA, USA: Morgan and Claypool Publishers.

KDNuggets. (2009). Data Mining Software Suites. Retrieved August 5, 2009, from http://www.kdnuggets.com/software/suites.html.

Keedwell, E., & Narayanan, A. (2005). *Intelligent Bioinformatics: The Application of Artificial Intelligence Techniques to Bioinformatics Problems.* New York: Wiley. doi:10.1002/0470015721

Kelemen, A., Abraham, A., & Chen, Y. (2008). *Computational Intelligence in Bioinformatics.* New York: Springer.

Kennedy, A., & Inkpen, D. (2006). Sentiment Classification of Movie Reviews Using Contextual Valence Shifters. *Computational Intelligence, 22,* 110–125. doi:10.1111/j.1467-8640.2006.00277.x

Kerris, N., & Bowcock, J. (2009). *Apple's App Store Downloads Top 1.5 Billion in First Year.* Retrieved August 18, 2009, from http://www.apple.com/pr/library/2009/07/14apps.html

Kim, S., & Hovy, E. (2004). Determining the Sentiment of Opinions. In *Proceedings of Conference on Computational Linguistics (COLING-04)* (pp.1367-1373). Geneva, Switzerland.

Klementtinen, M. (1999). A Knowledge Discovery Methodology for Telecommunication Network Alarm Databases. Thesis (PhD), University of Helsinki.

Klemettinen, M., Mannila, H., Ronkainen, P., Toivonen, H., & Verkamo, A. I. (1994). Finding Interesting Rules from Large Sets of Discovered Association Rules. In *Proceedings of Third International Conference on Information and Knowledge Management (CIKM'94)* (pp. 401-408). Gaithersburg, Maryland, USA.

Klosgen, W., & Zytkow, J. (1996). Knowledge Discovery in Databases Terminology. In Fayyad, U., Piatetsky-Shapiro, G., Smyth, P., & Uthurusamy, R. (Eds.), *Advances in Knowledge Discovery and Data Mining* (pp. 573–592). Cambridge, MA: The MIT Press.

Kohonen, T. (1982). Self-organized Formation of Topologically Correct Feature Maps. *Biological Cybernetics, 43,* 59–69. doi:10.1007/BF00337288

Kohonen, T., Schroeder, M. R., & Huang, T. S. (2005). *Self-Organizing Maps.* New York: Springer-Verlag.

König, A., & Gratz, A. (2005). Advanced Methods for the Analysis of Semiconductor Manufacturing Process Data. In Pal, N., & Jain, L. (Eds.), *Advanced Techniques in Data Mining and Knowledge Discovery* (pp. 27–74). London, UK: Springer-Verlag. doi:10.1007/1-84628-183-0_2

König, A. C., & Brill, E. (2006). Reducing the Human Overhead in Text Categorization. In *Proceedings of the 12th ACM SIGKDD International Conference on Knowledge Discovery and Data Mining - KDD '06* (pp. 598-603). Philadelphia, PA, USA.

Koppel, M., & Shtrimberg, I. (2004). Good news or bad news? Let the market decide. *AAAI Spring Symposium on Exploring Attitude and Affect in Text*, 86-88. Springer.

Krallinger, M., Valencia, A., & Hirschman, L. (2008). Linking Genes to Literature: Text Mining, Information Extraction, and Retrieval Applications for Biology. *Genome Biology*, 9(2), S8. doi:10.1186/gb-2008-9-s2-s8

Kramer, S., Aufschild, V., Hapfelmeier, A., Jarasch, A., Kessler, K., Reckow, S., et al. (2006). Inductive Databases in the Relational Model: The Data as the Bridge. In F.Bonchi & J. Boulicault (Eds.), *Lecture Notes on Computer Science: Vol. 3933. Knowledge Discovery in Inductive Databases - 4th International Workshop - KDID2005* (pp. 124-138). Berlin, Heidelberg: Berlin-Verlag.

Krampera, M., Glennie, S., Dyson, J., Scott, D., Laylor, R., & Simpson, E. (2003). Bone Marrow Mesenchymal Stem Cells inhibit the response of naive and memory antigen-specific T cells to their Cognate Peptide. *Blood*, 101(9), 3722–3729. doi:10.1182/blood-2002-07-2104

Kruskal, J. B. (1983). An Overview of Sequence Comparison: Time warps, String edits and Macromolecules. *SIAM Review*, 21, 201–237. doi:10.1137/1025045

Kuan-Ching, L., Chuan-Ko, T., Yin-Te, T., & Hsiao-His, W. (2006). Towards design of e-Learning platform in Grid Environments. In *Proceedings of the 2006 International Conference on Grid Computing & Applications*. Las Vegas, Nevada.

Kudyba, S., & Hoptroff, R. (2001). *Data Mining and Business Intelligence: A Guide to Productivity*. Hershey, PA: Idea Group Publishing.

Kumar, D. A., & Ravi, V. (2008). Predicting Credit Card Customer Churn in Banks using Data Mining. *International Journal of Data Analysis Techniques and Strategies*, 1(1), 4–28. doi:10.1504/IJDATS.2008.020020

Kumpulainen, P., Hätönen, K., & Vehviläinen, P. (2003). Automatic Discretization in Preprocessing for Data Analysis in Mobile Network. In XVII IMEKO World Congress Metrology in the 3rd Millennium. Cavtat- Dubrovnik, Croatia.

Kundu, A., He, Y., & Bahl, P. (1988). Word Recognition and Word Hypothesis generation for Handwritten Script: A Hidden Markov Model based approach. In *Proceedings 1988 IEEE Comput. Soc. Conf. on Computer Vision and Pattern Recognition* (pp. 457–462).

Kuznetsov, S. A., Friedenstein, A. J., & Robey, P. G. (1997). Factors required for Bone Marrow Stromal Fibroblast Colony Formation in vitro. *British Journal of Haematology*, 97(3), 561–570. doi:10.1046/j.1365-2141.1997.902904.x

Lacroix, V., Cottret, L., Thebault, P., & Sagot, M.-F. (2008). An Introduction to Metabolic Networks and their Structural Analysis. *IEEE Transactions on Computational Biology and Bioinformatics*, 5(4), 594–617. doi:10.1109/TCBB.2008.79

Lai, C., Reinders, M., Van't Veer, L., & Wessels, L. (2006). A Comparison of Univariate and Multivariate Gene Selection Techniques for Classification of Cancer Datasets. *BMC Bioinformatics*, 7(1), 235. doi:10.1186/1471-2105-7-235

Lai, C., Reinders, M., & Wessels, L. (2005). Multivariate Gene Selection: Does it help? In *Proceedings of the IEEE CSB Conference Workshops*.

Laiho, J. (2002). Radio Network Planning and Optimizations for WCDMA. Thesis (Doc. Tech.), Helsinki University of Technology.

Lam, K. Y. (1994). *Concurrency Control in Distributed Real-Time Database Systems*. Unpublished doctoral dissertation, City University of Hong Kong, Hong Kong.

Lam, K. Y., Hung, S. L., & Son, S. H. (1997). On Using Real-Time Static Locking Protocols for Distributed Real-Time Databases. *Real-Time Systems*, *13*, 141–166. doi:10.1023/A:1007981523223

Lam, K. Y., Pang, C., Son, S. H., & Cao, J. (1999). Resolving Executing-Committing Conflicts in Distributed Real - time Database Systems. *Journals of Computer*, *42*(8), 674–692. doi:10.1093/comjnl/42.8.674

Lama, E., Mello, P., Nanetti, A., Riguzzi, F., Storari, S., & Valastro, G. (2006). Artificial Intelligence Techniques for Monitoring Dangerous Infections. *IEEE Transactions on Information Technology in Biomedicine*, *10*(1), 143–155. doi:10.1109/TITB.2005.855537

Lane, T., & Brodley, C. E. (2003). An Empirical Study of Two Approaches to Sequence Learning for Anomaly Detection. *Machine Learning*, *51*(1), 73–107. doi:10.1023/A:1021830128811

Lappas, G. (2009). Machine Learning and Web Learning: Methods and Applications in Societal Benefit areas. In Rahman, H. (Ed.), *Data Mining Applications for Empowering Knowledge Societies* (pp. 76–95). Hershey, PA: IGI Publishing. doi:10.4018/978-1-59904-657-0.ch005

Larose, D. (2005). *Discovering Knowledge in Data: An Introduction to Data Mining*. Wiley-Interscience.

Law, M. H., & Kwok, J. T. (2000). Rival penalized competitive learning for Model-based Sequence Clustering. In *Proc. IEEE Int. Conf. on Pattern Recognition*. Barcelona, Spain.

Ledeczi, A., Bakay, A., Maroti, M., Volgyesi, P., Nordstrom, G., & Sprinkle, J. (2001). Composing Domain-Specific Design Environments. *IEEE Computer*, *34*(11), 44–51.

Ledeczi, A., Maroti, M., Karsai, G., & Nordstrom, G. (1999). Metaprogrammable Toolkit for Model-Integrated Computing. In *IEEE International Conference on the Engineering of Computer-Based Systems Conference*. Nashville, TN: IEEE Computer Society.

Lee, E. A., & Parks, T. M. (2002). *Dataflow Process Networks*. Norwell, MA, USA: Kluwer Academic Publishers.

Lee, T. B., & Fischetti, M. (1999). *Weaving the Web*. Harper, San Francisco.

Lee, Victor C. S., Lam, K. Y., & Kao, B. (1999). Priority Scheduling of Transactions in Distributed Real - Time Databases. *International Journal of Time-Critical Computing Systems*, *16*, 31–62.

Lempilainen, J., & Manninen, M. (2001). *Radio Interface System Planning for GSM/GPRS/UMTS*. Dordrecht, The Netherlands: Kluwer Academic Publishers.

Lennon, D. P., Haynesworth, S. E., Young, R. G., Dennis, J. E., & Caplan, A. I. (1995). A Chemically defined medium supports in vitro proliferation and maintains the osteochondral potential of Rat Marrow-derived Mesenchymal Stem Cells. *Experimental Cell Research*, *219*(1), 211–222. doi:10.1006/excr.1995.1221

Leppaniemi, M., & Karjaluoto, H. (2007). Mobile Marketing: From Marketing Strategy to Mobile Marketing Campaign Implementation. In *Proceedings of the 6th Annual Global Mobility Roundtable Conference*. Los Angeles.

Létourneau, S., Famimi, F., & Matwin, S. (1999). Data Mining to Predict Aircraft Component Replacement. *IEEE Intelligent Systems*, *14*(6), 59–65. doi:10.1109/5254.809569

Li, J., Zhang, X., Dong, G., Ramamohanarao, K., & Sun, Q. (1999). *Efficient Mining of High Confidence Association Rules without Support Thresholds* (pp. 406–411). PKDD.

Li, T., Zhang, C., & Ogihara, M. (2004). A Comparative Study of Feature Selection and Multiclass Classification methods for Tissue Classification based on Gene Expression. *Bioinformatics (Oxford, England)*, *20*(15), 2429–2437. doi:10.1093/bioinformatics/bth267

Li, X., Rao, S., Jiang, W., Li, C., Xiao, Y., & Guo, Z. (2006). Discovery of Time-delayed Gene Regulatory Networks based on Temporal Gene Expression Profiling. *BMC Bioinformatics, 7*(26).

Li, J., Tang, J., Li, Y., & Luo, Q. (2009). RiMOM: A Dynamic Multistrategy Ontology Alignment Framework. *IEEE Transactions on Knowledge and Data Engineering, 21*(8), 1218–1232. doi:10.1109/TKDE.2008.202

Li, W., Han, J., & Pei, J. (2001). CMAR: Accurate and Efficient Classification based on Multiple Class-Association Rules. In *Proceedings of the 2001 IEEE International Conference on Data Mining* (pp. 369-376). San Jose, CA: IEEE Computer Society.

Li, Y., Xu, X., & Songram, P. (2009). A Novel Model for Customer Retention. In H. Wang, Y. Shen, T. Huang & Z. Zeng (Eds.), *Sixth International Symposium on Neural Networks (ISNN 2009). Advances in Intelligent and Soft Computing, 56* (pp. 739-747). Berlin/Heidelberg: Springer. doi: 10.1007/978-3-642-01216-7.

Liabotis, I., Theodoulidis, B., & Saraaee, M. (2006). Improving Similarity Search in Time Series Using Wavelets. *International Journal of Data Warehousing and Mining, 2*(2), 55–81.

Linder, R., Richards, T., & Wagner, M. (2007). Microarray Data classified by Artificial Neural Networks. *Methods in Molecular Biology-Clifton Then Totowa, 382*, 345.

Lindon, J. C., Nicholson, J. K., & Holmes, E. (2007). *The Handbook of Metabonomics and Metabolomics*. Elsevier.

Ling, N., & Hasan, Y. (2006). Classification on Microarray Data. In *Proceedings of the 2nd IMT-GT Regional Conference on Mathematics, Statistics and Applications*.

Linoff, G. S. (2008). Survival Data Mining Using Relational Databases. *Business Intelligence Journal, 13*(3), 20–30.

Lippman, Z. B., S. Y., & D., Z. (2007). An Integrated view of Quantitative Trait Variation using Tomato Interspecific Introgression Lines. *Current Opinion in Genetics & Development, 17*, 1–8. doi:10.1016/j.gde.2007.07.007

Liu, C. H., Wu, M. L., & Hwang, S. M. (2007). Optimization of Serum free medium for Cord Blood Mesenchymal Stem Cells. *Biochemical Engineering Journal, 33*(1), 1–9. doi:10.1016/j.bej.2006.08.005

Liu, B., Hsu, W., & Ma, Y. (1998). Integrating Classification and Association Rule Mining. In *Proceedings of the 4th International Conference on Knowledge Discovery and Data Mining* (pp. 80-86). New York City: AAAI Press.

Liu, J. (2003). Web Intelligence (WI): What makes Wisdom Web? In *Proceedings of the 18th International Joint Conference on Artificial Intelligence (IJCAI-03)* (pp.1596-1601). Acapulco, Mexico.

Liu, J., Pan, Y., Wang, K., & Han, J. (2002). Mining Frequent Item Sets by Opportunistic Projection. In *Proceedings of the 8th ACM SIGKDD International Conference on Knowledge Discovery and Data Mining* (pp. 229-238). Edmonton, Alberta, Canada: ACM Press.

Lo, D., & Khoo, S. (2006). SMArTIC: Towards Building an Accurate, Robust and Scalable Specification Miner. In *14th ACM SIGSOFT International Symposium on Foundations of Software Engineering* (pp. 265 – 275). Portland, OR: ACM.

Lo, D., Khoo, S., & Liu, C. (2008). Mining Past-time Temporal Rules from Execution Traces. In *International Workshop on Dynamic Analysis* (pp. 50 – 56). Seattle, WA: ACM.

Lo, D., Maoz, S., & Khoo, S. (2007). Mining Modal Scenario-based Specifications from Execution Traces of Reactive Systems. In *22nd IEEE/ACM International Conference on Automated Software Engineering* (pp. 465 – 468). Atlanta, GA: IEEE/ACM.

Loo, L., Roberts, S., & Hrebien, L. (2007). New Criteria for Selecting Differentially Expressed Genes. *IEEE Engineering in Medicine and Biology Magazine, 26*(2), 17–26. doi:10.1109/MEMB.2007.335589

Lowd, D., & Domingos, P. (2005). Naive Bayes Models for Probability Estimation. In *Proceedings of the 22nd International Conference on Machine Learning* (pp. 529-536). Bonn, Germany: ACM Press.

Loyall, J., Carvalho, M., Schmidt, D., Gillen, M., Martignoni, A. III, & Bunch, L. (2009). *QoS Enabled Dissemination of Managed Information Objects in a Publish-Subscribe-Query Information Broker*. Orlando, FL: Defense Transformation and Net-Centric Systems.

Lu, H., Han, J., & Feng, L. (1998). Stock Price Movement Prediction and N-Dimensional Inter-Transaction Association Rules. In *ACM SIGMOD Workshop on Research Issues in Data Mining and Knowledge Discovery* (pp.12.1-12.7).

Luck, D. (2009). The Importance of Data Within Contemporary CRM. In Rahman, H. (Ed.), *Data Mining Applications for Empowering Knowledge Societies* (pp. 96–109). Hershey, PA: IGI Publishing. doi:10.4018/978-1-59904-657-0.ch006

Lui, B., Li, X., Lee, W. S., & Yu, P. S. (2004). Text Classification by Labeling Words. In *Proceedings of the 19th National Conference on Artificial Intelligence*. San Josè, California.

Lunh, H. P. (1958). A Business Intelligence System. *IBM Journal of Research and Development*, *2*(4), 314–319. doi:10.1147/rd.24.0314

Mackay, A. M., Beck, S. C., Murphy, J. M., Barry, F. P., Chichester, C. O., & Pittenger, M. F. (1998). Chondrogenic differentiation of Cultured Human Mesenchymal Stem Cells from Marrow. *Tissue Engineering*, *4*(4), 415–428. doi:10.1089/ten.1998.4.415

MacQueen, J. B. (1967). Some Methods for Classification and Analysis of Multivariate Observations. In *Proceedings of 5-th Berkeley Symposium on Mathematical Statistics and Probability* (pp.281-297).

Magaki, T., Kurisu, K., & Okazaki, T. (2005). Generation of Bone Marrow-derived Neural Cells in Serum-free Monolayer Culture. *Neuroscience Letters*, *384*(3), 282–287. doi:10.1016/j.neulet.2005.05.025

Mania, D., Murphy, J., & McManis, J. (2002). *Developing Performance Models from Nonintrusive Monitoring Traces*. IT & T.

Mann, J. (1996). *The Role of Project Escalation in Explaining Runaway Information Systems Development Projects: A Field Study*. Atlanta, GA: Georgia State University.

Mannila, H. (2000). Theoretical Frameworks for Data Mining. *SIGKDD Explorations*, *1*(2), 30–32. doi:10.1145/846183.846191

Mannila, H., Toivonen, H., & Verkamo, A. 1. (1994). Efficient Algorithms for Discovering Association Rules. In *Proceedings of the 1994 AAAI Workshop on Knowledge Discovery in Databases* (pp. 181-192). Seattle, Washington, USA: AAAI Press.

Manning. Ch, D., & Schuetze, H. (1999). *Foundations of Statistical Natural Language Processing*. Cambridge, MA: MIT Press.

Marcoccia, M. (2004). On-line Polylogues: Conversation Structure and Participation Framework in Internet Newsgroups. *Journal of Pragmatics*, *36*(1), 115–145. doi:10.1016/S0378-2166(03)00038-9

Markov, Z., & Larose, D. T. (2007). *Data mining the Web: Uncovering Patterns in Web content, Structure, and Usage*. Hoboken, New Jersey: Wiley-Interscience.

Maron, M. E. (1961). Automatic Indexing: An Experimental Inquiry. [JACM]. *Journal of the ACM*, *8*(3), 404–417. doi:10.1145/321075.321084

Martinez, R., Pasquier, N., & Pasquier, C. (2008). *GenMiner: Mining Informative Association Rules from Integrated Gene Expression Data and Annotations*. Bioinformatics.

Matsumura, Y., Matsunaga, T., Maeda, Y., Tsumoto, S., Matsumura, H., & Kimura, M. (1988). Consultation System for Diagnoses of Headache and Facial Pain: RHINOS. *Medical Informatics*, *11*, 145–157. doi:10.3109/14639238609001367

Mattison, M. (1997). *Data Warehousing and Data Mining for Telecommunications*. Norwood, MA, USA: Artech House, Inc.

Maydanchik, A. (2007). *Data Quality Assessment (Data Quality for Practitioners Series). Technics Publications*. LLC.

McCallum, A., & Nigam, K. (1999). Text Classification by Bootstrapping with Keywords, EM and Shrinkage. In *ACL99* (pp. 52–58). Workshop for Unsupervised Learning in Natural Language Processing.

McKnight, W. (2002). Briging Data Mining to the Front Line, Part 1. *Information Management magazine, November* (2002), Retrieved July 16, 2009, from http://www.information-management.com/issues/200211001/5980-1.html.

Meo, R., Psaila, G., & Ceri, S. (1998). An Extension to SQL for Mining Association Rules. *Data Mining and Knowledge Discovery, 2*(2), 195–224. doi:10.1023/A:1009774406717

Meo, R., & Psaila, G. (2006). An XML-Based Database for Knowledge Discovery. In T. Grust, H. Höpfner, A. Illarramendi, S. Jablonski, M. Mesiti, S. Müller, P. Patranjan, S. Kai-Uwe, M. Spiliopoulou & J. Wijsen (Eds.), *Lecture Notes in Computer Science: Vol. 4254. Current Trends in Database Technology EDTB 2006 Workshops* (pp. 814-828). Berlin, Heidelberg: Springer-Verlag.

Merton, R. K. (1968). *Social Theory and Social Structure*. New York: Free Press.

Meuleman, N., Tondreau, T., Delforge, A., Dejeneffe, M., Massy, M., & Libertalis, M. (2006). Human Marrow Mesenchymal Stem Cell Culture: Serum-free Medium allows better expansion than Classical Apha-MEM medium. *European Journal of Haematology, 76*(4), 309–316. doi:10.1111/j.1600-0609.2005.00611.x

Michalewicz, Z., Schmidt, M., Michalewicz, M., & Chiriac, C. (2007). *Adaptive Business Intelligence*. Berlin, Heidelberg: Springer-Verlag.

Michalski, R., & Kaufman, K. (2001). Learning Patterns in Noisy Data: The AQ Approach. *Machine Learning and its Applications*, 22-38.

Mielikäinen, T. (2004). Inductive Databases as Ranking. In Y. Kambayashi, M. Mohania & W. Wöb (Eds.), *Lecture Notes on Computer Science: Vol. 3181, Data Warehousing and Knowledge Discovery - 6th International Conference DaWak2004* (pp. 149-158). Berlin, Heidelberg: Springer-Verlag.

Mierswa, I., Wurst, M., Klinkenberg, R., Scholz, M., & Euler, T. (2006). YALE: Rapid Prototyping for Complex Data Mining Tasks. In *Proceedings of the 12th ACM SIGKDD International Conference on Knowledge Discovery and Data Mining (KDD-06)*.

Mihalcea, R., & Strapparava, C. (2005). Making Computers Laugh: Investigations in Automatic Humour Recognition. In *Joint Conference on Human Language Technology/Empirical Methods in Natural Language Processing (HLT/EMNLP)*.

Miller, G. A., Beckwith, R., Fellbaum, C., Gross, D., & Miller, K. J. (1990). Introduction to Wordnet: An On-line Lexical Database. *International Journal of Lexicography, 3*(4), 235–244. doi:10.1093/ijl/3.4.235

Mingoti, S. A., & Lima, J. O. (2006). Comparing SOM Neural Network with Fuzzy c-means, k-means and Traditional Hierarchical Clustering Algorithms. *European Journal of Operational Research, 174*(3), 1742–1759. doi:10.1016/j.ejor.2005.03.039

Misikangas, P. (1997). *2PL and its Variants.* Seminar on Real - Time Systems. Department of Computer Science, University of Helsinki.

Mitra, P., Murthy, C., & Pal, S. (2002). Unsupervised Feature Selection Using Feature Similarity. *IEEE Transactions on Pattern Analysis and Machine Intelligence*, 301–312. doi:10.1109/34.990133

Moe, J., & Carr, D. A. (2001). Understanding Distributed Systems via Execution Trace Data. In *9th International Workshop on Program Comprehension* (pp. 60). Toronto, Canada: IEEE Computer Society.

Mohan, C., Lindsay, B., & Obermarck, R. (1986). Transaction Management in the R* Distributed Database Management System. *ACM Transactions on Database Systems, 11*(4). doi:10.1145/7239.7266

Montgomery, A. L. (1999). *Using Clickstream to predict WWW usage*. Retrieved August 19, 2009, from http://www.andrew.cmu.edu/user/alm3/papers/predicting%20www%20usage.pdf

Moore, R. (2001). Knowledge-based Grids. In *Proceedings of the Eighteenth IEEE Symposium on Mass Storage Systems and Technologies* (pp. 29). San Diego, California

Mos, A. M., & Murphy, J. (2001). Performance Monitoring of Java Component-Oriented Distributed Applications. In *9th International Conference on Software, Telecommunications and Computer Networks* (pp. 9-12). Dubrovnik, Croatia.

Moss, L. T., & Shaku, A. (2003). *Business Intelligence Roadmap: The Complete Project Lifecycle for Decision-Support Applications*. Upper Saddle River, NJ: Pearson Education.

Mullen, T., & Collier, N. (2004). Sentiment Analysis using Support Vector Machines with diverse Information Sources. In *Proceedings of EMNLP*.

Mullen, T., & Malouf, R. (2006). A Preliminary Investigation into Sentiment Analysis of Informal Political Discourse. In *Proceedings of the AAAI Symposium on Computational Approaches to Analyzing Weblogs* (pp.159-162).

Muller, I., Kordowich, S., Holzwarth, C., Spano, C., Isensee, G., & Staiber, A. (2006). Animal Serum-free culture conditions for Isolation and Expansion of Multipotent Mesenchymal Stromal Cells from Human BM. *Cytotherapy*, 8(5), 437–444. doi:10.1080/14653240600920782

Murray, G. R., Riley, C., & Scime, A. (2009). Pre-election Polling: Identifying likely voters using Iterative Expert Data Mining. *Public Opinion Quarterly*, 73(1), 159–171. doi:10.1093/poq/nfp004

Murray, G. R., & Scime, A. (2010). Microtargeting and Electorate Segmentation: Data Mining the American National Election Studies. *Journal of Political Marketing*, 9(3), 143–166. doi:10.1080/15377857.2010.497732

Murray, G. R., Riley, C., & Scime, A. (2007). *A New Age Solution for an Age-old problem: Mining Data for Likely Voters*. Paper presented at the 62nd Annual Conference of the American Association of Public Opinion Research, Anaheim, CA.

Mutalik, P., Deshpande, A., & Nadkardi, P. (2001). Use of General-Purpose Negation Detection to Augment Concept Indexing of Medical Documents. *Journal of the American Medical Informatics Association*, 8(6).

Nag, R., Wong, K. H., & Fallside, F. (1986). Script recognition using Hidden Markov Models. In *Proceedings of 1986 IEEE Int. Conf. on Acoustics, Speech and Signal Processing* (pp. 2071–2074).

Nalwa, V. S. (1997). Automatic On-line Signature Verification. *Proceedings of the IEEE*, 85, 215–239. doi:10.1109/5.554220

Nam, H., Lee, K., & Lee, D. (2009). Identification of Temporal Association Rules from Time-Series Microarray Data Sets. *BMC Bioinformatics*, 10.

Nash, E. (2000). *Direct Marketing: Strategy, Planning, Execution*. New York: McGraw-Hill Education.

National Academy of Sciences. (2008). *Science, Evolution, and Creationism*. Washington, D.C.: National Academies Press.

National Security Agency. (2009, June 28). *Global Information Grid*. Retrieved August 5, 2009, from http://www.nsa.gov/ia/programs/ global_industry_grid/ index. shtml

NCCLS. (2005). *National Committee for Clinical Laboratory Standards (NCCLS)*. Retrieved 2005, from http://www.nccls.org.

Needleman, S. B., & Wunsch, C. D. (1970). A General method applicable to the search for Similarities in the Amino Acid Sequences of Two Proteins. *Journal of Molecular Biology*, 48, 443–453. doi:10.1016/0022-2836(70)90057-4

Negash, S. (2004). Business Intelligence. *Communications of the Association for Information Systems*, 13(1), 177–195.

Nemati, H. R., Steiger, D. M., Iyer, L. S., & Herschel, R. T. (2002). Knowledge Warehouse: An Architectural Integration of Knowledge Management, Decision Support, Artificial Intelligence and Data Warehousing. *Decision Support Systems*, 33(1), 143–161. doi:10.1016/S0167-9236(01)00141-5

Ngai, E. W. T., & Gunasekaran, A. (2007). A Review for Mobile Commerce Research and Applications. *Decision Support Systems, 43,* 3–15. doi:10.1016/j.dss.2005.05.003

Ni, B., & Liu, J. (2004). A Hybrid Filterwrapper Gene Selection Method for Microarray Classification. In *Proceedings of the Third International Conference on Machine Learning and Cyherneucs.*

Ni, S. (2001). Network Capacity and Quality of Service Management in F/TDMA Cellular Systems. Thesis (Doc. Tech.), Helsinki University of Technology.

Nigam, K., & Hurst, M. (2004). Towards a Robust Metric of Opinion. In *AAAI Spring Symposium on Exploring Attitude and Affect in Text.* (pp. 598 – 603).

Niijima, S., & Okuno, Y. (2007). Laplacian Linear Discriminant Analysis Approach to Unsupervised Feature selection. *IEEE/ACM Transactions on Computational Biology and Bioinformatics, 10,* 20.

Nijssen, S., & De Raedt, L. (2007). IQL: A Proposal for an Inductive Query Language. In S. Dzeroski & J. Struyf (Eds.), *Lecture Notes in Computer Science: Vol. 4747, Knowledge Discovery in Inductive Databases - 5th International Workshop, KDID 2006* (pp. 189-209). Berlin, Heidelberg: Springer-Verlag.

Nlenanya, I. (2009). Building an Environmental GIS Knowledge Infrastucture. In Rahman, H. (Ed.), *Data Mining Applications for Empowering Knowledge Societies* (pp. 262–279). Hershey, PA: IGI Publishing.

Nokia Inc. (2003). *A History of Third Generation Mobile 3G.* Nokia Inc.

O'Shaughnessy, D. (2003). *Speech Communications: Human and Machine.* Piscataway, NJ: IEEE Press.

Object Management Group. (2008). Knowledge Discovery Model (KDM). Retrieved August 1, 2009, from http://kdmanalytics.com/kdm/index.php.

O'Connell, S. M., Impeduglia, T., Hessler, K., Wang, X. J., Carroll, R. J., & Dardik, H. (2008). Autologous Platelet-rich Fibrin Matrix as Cell Therapy in the Healing of Chronic Lower-extremity Ulcers. *Wound Repair and Regeneration, 16*(6), 749–756. doi:10.1111/j.1524-475X.2008.00426.x

Olson, J. E. (2003). *Data Quality: The Accuracy Dimension.* San Francisco: Morgan Kaufmann.

Olson, D., & Delen, D. (2008). *Advanced Data Mining.* New York: Springer.

Osborne, J., Zhu, L., Lin, S., & Kibbe, W. (2007). Interpreting Microarray results with Gene Ontology and MeSH. *Methods in Molecular Biology-Clifton then Totowa, 377,* 223.

Ozden, B., Ramaswamy, S., & Silberschatz, A. (1998). Cyclic Association Rules. In *Proceedings of 14th International Conference on Data Engineering (ICDE'98)* (pp.412-421). Orlando, Florida.

Padmanabhan, B., & Tuzhilin, A. (2000). Small is Beautiful: Discovering the minimal set of Unexpected Patterns. In *Proceedings of the Sixth ACM SIGKDD International Conference on Knowledge Discovery and Data Mining* (pp.54-63). Boston, MA.

Pan, J., Yang, Q., Yang, Y., Li, L., Li, F. T., & Li, G. W. (2007). Cost-Sensitive-Data Preprocessing for Mining Customer Relationship Management Databases. *IEEE Intelligent Systems, 22*(1), 46–51. doi:10.1109/MIS.2007.7

Pang, B., & Lee, L. (2008). Opinion Mining and Sentiment Analysis. *Foundations and Trends in Information Retrieval, 2*(1-2), 1–135. doi:10.1561/1500000011

Pang, B., & Lee, L. (2004). A Sentimental Education: Sentiment Analysis Using Subjectivity Summarization Based on Minimum Cuts. In *Proceedings of the ACL.*

Pang, B., & Lee, L. (2005). Seeing Stars: Exploiting Class Relationships for Sentiment Categorization with Respect to Rating Scales. In *Proceedings of the 43rd Meeting of the ACL* (pp. 115-124).

Pang, B., Lee, L., & Vaithyanathan, S. (2002). Thumbs up? Sentiment Classification using Machine Learning Techniques. In *Proceedings of EMNLP.*

Pang, C. L., & Lam, K. Y. (1998). On Using Similarity for Resolving Conflicts at Commit in Mixed Distributed Real-time Databases. In *5th International Conference on Real - Time Computing Systems and Applications.*

Pankratius, V., & Vossen, G. (2003). Towards e-Learning Grids: Using Grid Computing in Electronic. Learning. In *Proceedings of IEEE Workshop on Knowledge Grid and Learning Grid Intelligence* (pp.4-15). Halifax, Canada.

Papachristoudis, G,, Diplaris, S., & Mitkas, P. (2009). SoFoCles: Feature filtering for Microarray Classification based on Gene Ontology. *Journal of Biomedical Informatics*.

Parsons, T., Mos, A., & Murphy, J. (2006). J2EE Systems. In *IEE Proceedings-Software*. Non-Intrusive End-to-End Runtime Path Tracing.

Parsons, T. (1951). *The Social System*. Routledge & Kegan Paul Ltd.

Pasquier, N., Bastide, Y., Taouil, R., & Lakhal, L. (1999). Efficient Mining of Association Rules using Closed Itemset Lattices. *Information Systems, 24*(1), 25–46. doi:10.1016/S0306-4379(99)00003-4

Pawlak, Z. (1982). Rough Sets. *International Journal of Computer and Information Sciences, 11*(5), 341–356. doi:10.1007/BF01001956

Pearson, R. K. (2006). The Problem of Disguised Missing Data. *ACM SIGKDD Explorations Newsletter, 8*(1), 83–92. doi:10.1145/1147234.1147247

Pearson, R., Gonye, G., & Schwaber, J. (2003). *Outliers in Microarray Data Analysis*. Springer.

Pekko, V. (2004). Data Mining for Managing Intrinsic Quality of Service in Digital Mobile Telecommunications Networks. (Thesis) Ph.D, Tampere University of Technology Publications.

Peng, H., Long, F., & Ding, C. (2005). Feature selection based on mutual information: Criteria of max-dependency, max-relevance, and min-redundancy. *IEEE Transactions on Pattern Analysis and Machine Intelligence, 27* (8), 1226-1238.*Pima Indians Diabetes Data Set*. (2009). Retrieved June 21, 2009, from http://archive.ics.uci.edu/ml/ datasets/Pima+Indians+Diabetes

Penttinen, I., & Ritala, R. (2002). *2002* (pp. 154–158). Stockholm, Sweden: XML-Based Process Control. In Proceedings of Control Systems.

Penttinen, J. (2001). *GSM-tekniikka. Järjestelmän toiminta ja kehitys kohti UMTS-aikakautta*. Helsinki: WSOY. (In Finnish)

Pereira, R. H., Azevedo, A., & Castilho, O. (2007). Secretaria On-Line From Iscap: A Case of Innovation. In *Proceedings of the IADIS International Conference WWW/Internet 2007* (pp.301-305).

Perng, C., Wang, H., Zhang, S. R., & Parker, D. S. (2000). Landmarks: A New Model for Similarity-Based Pattern Querying in Time Series Databases *ACDE*, 33-44.

Pezzini, M., & Natis, Y. V. (2007). *Trends in Platform Middleware: Disruption Is in Sight*. Retrieved June 10, 2008, from www.gartner.com/DisplayDocument?doc_cd=152076

Phuong, N. H., Hung, D. H., Co, N. V., Duong, B. D., Thinh, P. T., Hoa, N. P., & Linh, N. N. (1999). TUBERDIAG: An Expert system for Pulmonary Tuberculosis Diagnosis. *International Journal of Uncertainty. Fuzziness and Knowledge Based Systems, 7*(4), 371–382. doi:10.1142/S0218488599000325

Piatetsky-Shapiro, G., & Tamayo, P. (2003). Microarray Data Mining: Facing the Challenges. *SIGKDD Exploration Newsletter, 5*(2), 1–5. doi:10.1145/980972.980974

Pinto, F., Gago, P., & Santos, M. F. (2006). Data Mining as a New Paradigm for Business Intelligence in Database Marketing Projects. In *Proceedings of the 8th International Conference on Enterprise Information Systems - ICEIS 2006* (pp.144-149).

Pirooznia, M., Yang, J., Yang, M., & Deng, Y. (2008). A Comparative Study of Different Machine Learning Methods on Microarray Gene Expression Data. *BMC Genomics, 9*(Suppl. 1), S13. doi:10.1186/1471-2164-9-S1-S13

Pittenger, M. F., Mackay, A. M., Beck, S. C., Jaiswal, R. K., Douglas, R., & Mosca, J. D. (1999). Multilineage potential of Adult Human Mesenchymal Stem Cells. *Science, 284*(5411), 143–147. doi:10.1126/science.284.5411.143

Polanski, A., & Kimmel, M. (2007). *Bioinformatics*. New York: Springer-Verlag.

Pomeroy, S., Tamayo, P., Gaasenbeek, M., Sturla, L., Angelo, M., & McLaughlin, M. (2002). Prediction of Central Nervous System Embryonal Tumour Outcome based on Gene Expression. *Nature*, *415*(6870), 436–442. doi:10.1038/415436a

Ponzoni, I., Azuaje, F., Augusto, J., & Glass, D. (2007). Inferring Adaptive Regulation Thresholds and Association Rules from Gene Expression Data through Combinatorial Optimization Learning. *IEEE/ACM Transactions on Computational Biology and Bioinformatics*, *4*(4), 624–634. doi:10.1109/tcbb.2007.1049

Pyle, D. (1999). *Data Preparation for Data Mining. The Morgan Kaufmann Series in Data Management Systems*. San Francisco: Morgan Kaufmann.

Qi, J., & Tang, J. (2007). Integrating Gene Ontology into Discriminative Powers of Genes for Feature Selection in Microarray Data. In *Proceedings of 2007 ACM Symposium on Applied Computing* (pp.434).

Qin, B., & Liu, Y. (2003). High Performance Distributed Real-time Commit Protocol. *Journal of Systems and Software, Elsevier Science Inc.*, *68*(2), 145–152.

Qin, B., Liu, Y., & Yang, J. C. (2003). A Commit Strategy for Distributed Real-Time Transaction. *Journal of Computer Science and Technology*, *18*(5), 626–631. doi:10.1007/BF02947122

Quackenbush, J. (2001). Computational Analysis of Microarray Data. *Nature Reviews. Genetics*, *2*(6), 18–427. doi:10.1038/35076576

Quinlan, J. (1986). Induction of Decision Trees. *Machine Learning*, *1*, 81–106. doi:10.1007/BF00116251

Quinlan, J. R. (1993). *C4.5: Programs for Machine Learning*. San Mateo, CA, USA: Morgan Kaufmann Publishers.

Quinlan, J. R., & Cameron-Jones, R. M. (1993). FOIL: A Midterm Report. In *Proceedings of the 1993 European Conference on Machine Learning (ECML-93)* (pp. 3-20). Vienna, Austria: Springer-Verlag.

Quintela, H., Santos, M. F., & Cortez, P. (2007). Real-Time Intelligent Decision Support System for Bridges Structures Behavior Prediction. In J. Neves, M.F. Santos & J.Machado (Eds.), *LNAI: Vol. 4874, Proceedings of the 13th Portuguese Conference on Aritficial Intelligence, EPIA 2007* (pp. 124-132). Berlin Heidelberg, Germany: Springer-Verlag.

Raisinghani, M. (2004). *Business Intelligence in the Digital Economy: Opportunities, Limitations and Risks*. Hershey, PA: Idea Group Publishing.

Rajasethupathy, K., Scime, A., Rajasethupathy, K. S., & Murray, G. R. (2009). Finding "Persistent Rules": Combining Association and Classification Results. *Expert Systems with Applications*, *36*(3P2), 6019-6024.

Ramamritham, K., & Chrysanthis, P. K. (1996). A Taxonomy of Correctness Criteria in Database Applications. *Journal of the VLDB*, *5*, 85–97. doi:10.1007/s007780050017

Ramaswamy, S., Mahajan, S., & Silberschatz, A. (1998). *On the Discovery of Interesting Patterns in Association Rules* (pp. 368–379). VLDB.

Ramu, K., & Ravi, V. (2008). Privacy preservation in Data Mining using Hybrid Perturbation methods: An application to Bankruptcy Prediction in Banks. *International Journal of Data Analysis Techniques and Strategies*, *1*(4), 313–331. doi:10.1504/IJDATS.2009.027509

Rantzau, R. (2004). Frequent Itemset Discovery with SQL Using Universal Quantification. In R. Meo, P. Lanzi & M. Klemettinen (Eds.), *Lecture Notes on Artificial Intelligence: Vol. 2682. Database Support for Data Mining Applications - Discovering Knowledge with Inductive Queries* (pp. 194-213). Berlin, Heidelberg: Springer-Verlag.

Rao, D., & Ravichandran, D. (2009). Semi-Supervised Polarity Lexicon Induction. In *Proceedings of the 12th Conference of the European Chapter of the ACL* (pp. 675-682). Athens, Greece.

Redman, T. C. (1997). *Data Quality for the Information Age*. Norwood, MA, USA: Artech House Publishers.

Renninger, L. W., & Malik, J. (2004). When is Scene Recognition just Texture Recognition? *Vision Research, 44*, 2301–2311.

Ricci, R., Alfred, C., & Lepreau, J. (2003). A Solver for the Network Testbed Mapping Problem. *SIGCOMM Computer Communications Review, 33*(2), 30–44.

Richards, A., Holmans, P., O'Donovan, M., Owen, M., & Jones, L. (2008). A Comparison of Four Clustering methods for Brain Expression Microarray Data. *BMC Bioinformatics, 9*(1), 490. doi:10.1186/1471-2105-9-490

Richardson, J., Schlegel, K., & Hostmann, B. (2009). *Magic Quadrant for Business Intelligence Platforms.* Core Research Note: G00163529, Gartner.

Richardson, J., Schlegel, K., Hostmann, B., & McMurchy, N. (2008). *Magic Quadrant for Business Intelligence Platforms, 2008.* Core Research Note: G00154227, Gartner.

Rieseberg, L., & Wendel, J. (1993). *Introgression and its consequences in Plants.* Oxford, UK: Oxford University Press.

Rittel, H., & Webber, M. (1973). Dilemmas in a General Theory of Planning. *Policy Sciences, 4*(2), 155–169. doi:10.1007/BF01405730

Roddick, J., & Spiliopoulou, M. (2001). A Survey of Temporal Knowledge Discovery Paradigms and Methods. *IEEE Transactions on Knowledge and Data Engineering, 13*.

Roelen, B. A., & Dijke, P. (2003). Controlling Mesenchymal Stem Cell differentiation by TGFBeta Family Members. *Journal of Orthopaedic Science, 8*(5), 740–748. doi:10.1007/s00776-003-0702-2

Romei, A., Ruggieri, S., & Turini, F. (2006). KDDML: A Middleware Language and System for Knowledge Discovery in Databases. *Data & Knowledge Engineering, 57*(2), 179–220. doi:10.1016/j.datak.2005.04.007

Ruiz, R., Riquelme, J., & Aguilar-Ruiz, J. (2006). Incremental Wrapper-based Gene Selection from Microarray Data for Cancer Classification. *Pattern Recognition, 39*(12), 2383–2392. doi:10.1016/j.patcog.2005.11.001

Russell, N., van der Aalst, W. M., ter Hofstede, A. H., & Wohed, P. (2006). On the Suitability of UML 2.0 Activity Diagrams for Business Process Modelling. In *3rd Asia-Pacific Conference on Conceptual Modelling* (pp. 95 – 104). Hobart, Australia: Australian Computer Society, Inc.

Rymon, R. (1992). Search through Systematic Set Enumeration. In *Proceedings of the 3rd International Conference on Principles of Knowledge Representation and Reasoning* (pp. 539-550). Cambridge, MA, USA: Morgan Kaufmann Publishers.

Sairafi, S. A., Emmanouil, F. S., Giannadakis, M., Guo, Y., Kalaitzopolous, D., & Osmond, M. (2003). The design of Discovery Net: Towards Open Grid services for Knowledge Discovery. *International Journal of High Performance Computing Applications, 17*(3).

Saito, K., Hirai, M. Y., & Yonekura-Sakakibara, K. (2008). Decoding Genes with Coexpression Networks and Metabolomics - Majority report by Precogs. *Trends in Plant Science, 13*, 36–43. doi:10.1016/j.tplants.2007.10.006

Sajja, P. S. (2006). Parichay: An Agent for Adult Literacy. *Prajna, 14*, 17–24.

Sajja, P. S. (2007). Knowledge representation using Fuzzy XML Rules for Knowledge-based Adviser. *International Journal of Computer. Mathematical Sciences and Applications, 1*(2-4), 323–330.

Sajja, P. S. (2008). Enhancing Quality in e-Learning by Knowledge-based IT support. *International Journal of Education and Development Using Information and Communication Technology, 4*(1).

Sajja, P. S. (2009). Multi-tier Knowledge-based System accessing Learning Object Repository using fuzzy XML. In Yang, H., & Yuen, S. (Eds.), *Handbook of Research on Practices and Outcomes in e-Learning: Issues and Trends*. Hershey, PA: IGI Global Book Publishing.

Sajja, P. S., & Chourasia, N. N. (2005). Knowledge Representation Using XML in a Multi-Layer Knowledge-Based Adviser for Small-Scale and Cottage Industries. In *Proceedings of 2nd National Seminar on Data and Knowledge Engineering*, India.

Salo, J., & Tahtinen, J. (2005). Retailer use of Permission-based Mobile Advertising. In I.Clarke & Flaherty Theresa (Eds.), *Advances in Electronic Marketing, Idea Group Inc* (pp.140-156).

Salton, G., Wong, A., & Yang, C. S. (1975). A Vector Space Model for Automatic Indexing Communications. *ACM, 11*(18), 613–620. doi:10.1145/361219.361220

Salvetti, F., Lewis, S., & Reichenbach, C. (2004). Automatic Opinion Polarity Classification of Movie Reviews. *Colorado Research in Linguistics, June 2004, 17 (1). Boulder, CO: University of Colorado.*

Salzberg, S. L. (1999). Gene Discovery in DNA Sequences. *IEEE Intelligent Systems, 14*(6), 44–48. doi:10.1109/5254.809567

Santos, M. F., Cortez, P., Pereira, J., & Quintela, H. (2006). Corporate Bankruptcy Prediction Using Data Mining Techniques. In A. Zanasi, C.A. Brebbia & N.F.F. Ebecken (Eds.), *WIT Transactions on Information and Communication Tecchnologies: Vol. 37, Data Mining VII: Data, Text and Web Mining and their Business Applications* (pp. 349-357). Southampton, UK: WIT Press.

Santos, M. F., Cortez, P., Quintela, H., & Pinto, F. (2005). A Clustering Approach for Knowledge Discovery in Database Marketing. In A.Zanasi, C.A. Brebbia & N.F.F. Ebecken (Eds.), *WIT Transactions on Information and Communication Tecchnologies: Vol. 35. Data Mining VI: Data, Text and Web Mining and their Business Applications* (pp. 367-376). Southampton, UK: WIT Press.

Santos, M. F., Cortez, P., Quintela, H., Neves, J., Vicente, H., & Arteiro, J. (2005). Ecological Mining - A Case Study on Dam Water Quality. In A. Zanasi, C.A. Brebbia & N.F.F. Ebecken (Eds.), *WIT Transactions on Information and Communication Tecchnologies: Vol. 35. Data Mining VI: Data mining, Text Mining and their Business Applications* (pp. 481-489). Southampton, UK: WIT Press.

Santos, M., Pereira, J., & Silva, Á. (2005). A Cluster Framework for Data Mining Models: An application to intensive medicine. In *Proceedings of the 7th International Conference on Enterprise Information Systems - ICEIS 2005* (pp.163-168).

Sarawagi, S., Thomas, S., & Agrawal, R. (2000). Integrating Association Rule Mining with Relational Database Systems: Alternatives and Implications. *Data Mining and Knowledge Discovery, 4*(2-3), 89–125. doi:10.1023/A:1009887712954

Sarwar, B., Karypis, G., Konstan, J., & Reidl, J. (2001). Item-based collaborative filtering recommendation algorithms. In *Proceedings of the 10ᵗʰ International Conference on World Wide Web* (pp. 285-295). Hong Kong.

Sasisekharan, R., Seshadri, V., & Weiss, S. (1996). Data Mining and Forecasting in Large-Scale Telecommunication Networks. *IEEE Expert, 11*(1), 37–43. doi:10.1109/64.482956

Sasisekharan, R., Hsu, Y., & Simen, D. (1993). SCOUT: An approach to Automating Diagnoses of Faults in Large Scale Networks. In Technical Program Conference Record, GLOBECOM '93, Global Telecommunications Conference (pp. 212-216).

Savasere, A., Omiecinski, E., & Navathe, S. (1995). An Efficient Algorithm for Mining Association Rules in Large Databases. In *Proceedings of the 21st International Conference on Very Large Data Bases* (pp. 432-444). Zurich, Switzerland: Morgan Kaufmann Publishers.

Schaffer, C. (1993). Selecting a Classification Method by Cross-Validation. *Machine Learning, 13*(1), 135–143. doi:10.1007/BF00993106

Schmidt, D. C. (2006). Model-Driven Engineering. *IEEE Computer, 39* (2).

Schreiber, T., & Schmitz, A. (1997). Classification of Time Series data with Nonlinear Similarity Measures. *Physical Review Letters, 79*, 1475–1478. doi:10.1103/PhysRevLett.79.1475

Scime, A., & Murray, G. R. (2007). Vote prediction by Iterative Domain Knowledge and Attribute Elimination. *International Journal of Business Intelligence and Data Mining, 2*(2), 160–176. doi:10.1504/IJBIDM.2007.013935

Scime, A., Murray, G. R., & Hunter, L. Y. (2010). Testing Terrorism Theory with Data Mining. *International Journal of Data Analysis Techniques and Strategies, 2*(2), 122–139. doi:10.1504/IJDATS.2010.032453

Sclaroff, S., Kollios, G., Betke, M., & Rosales, R. (2001). Motion Mining. In *Lecture notes in Computer Science; Proc. 2ⁿᵈ Intl. Workshop on Multimedia Databases and Image Communication.* Heidelberg: Springer-Verlag.

Sebastiani, F. (2002). Machine Learning in Automated Text Categorization. *ACM Computing Surveys, 34*, 1–47. doi:10.1145/505282.505283

Segal, E., Battle, A., & Koller, D. (2003). Decomposing Gene Expression into Cellular Processes. In *Proceedings of Pacific Symposium on Biocomputing* (pp.89-100).

Seifert, J. W. (2006). Data Mining: An Overview. In Pegarkov, D. D. (Ed.), *National Security Issues* (pp. 201–217). Haupauge, NY: Nova Science Publishers.

Seroussi, B., Bouaud, J., & Antoine, E. C. (2001). ONCODOC: A Successful Experiment of Computer-supported Guideline Development and Implementation in the treatment of Breast Cancer. *Artificial Intelligence in Medicine, 22*(1), 43–64. doi:10.1016/S0933-3657(00)00099-3

Shamir, R., & Sharan, R. (2001). *Algorithmic Approaches to Clustering Gene Expression Data*. Current Topics in Computational Biology.

Shanker, U. (2006). *Some Performance Issues in Distributed Real Time Database Systems*. Unpublished doctoral dissertation, Department of Electronics & Computer Engineering, Indian Institute of Technology Roorkee, India.

Shanker, U., & Misra, M. Sarje, Anil K., & Shisondia, R. (2006). Dependency Sensitive Shadow SWIFT. In *10ᵗʰ International Database Applications and Engineering Symposium* (pp. 373-376). Delhi, India.

Shanker, U., Misra, M., & Sarje, Anil K. (2001). Hard Real-Time Distributed Database Systems: Future Directions. In *All India Seminar on Recent Trends in Computer Communication Networks* (pp. 172-177). Department of Electronics & Computer Engineering, Indian Institute of Technology Roorkee, India.

Shanker, U., Misra, M., & Sarje, Anil K. (2006). SWIFT-A New Real Time Commit Protocol. [Springer Verlag]. *International Journal of Distributed and Parallel Databases, 20*(1), 29–56. doi:10.1007/s10619-006-8594-8

Shanker, U., Misra, M., & Sarje, Anil K. (2008). Distributed Real Time Database Systems: Background and Literature Review. [Springer Verlag.]. *International Journal of Distributed and Parallel Databases, 23*(2), 127–149. doi:10.1007/s10619-008-7024-5

Shidara, Y., Nakamura, A., & Kudo, M. (2007). CCIC: Consistent Common Itemsets Classifier. In *Proceedings of the 5th International Conference on Machine Learning and Data Mining (MLDM-07)* (pp. 490-498). Leipzig, Germany: Springer-Verlag.

Shim, J. P., Warkentin, M., Courtney, J. F., Power, D. J., Sharda, R., & Carlsson, C. (2002). Past, Present, and Future of Decision Support Technology. *Decision Support Systems, 32*(1), 111–126. doi:10.1016/S0167-9236(01)00139-7

Shortliffe, E. H., Scott, A. C., Bischoff, M. B., Campbell, A. B., van Melle, W., & Jacobs, C. D. (1981). ONCOCIN: An Expert System for Oncology Protocol Management. In *Proceedings of the Seventh International Joint Conference on Artificial Intelligence* (pp. 876-881). Vancouver, Canada: IJAI.

Shreiber, D. A., & Berge, Z. L. (1998). *Distance training: How innovative organizations are using technology to maximize learning and business objectives*. San Francisco: Jossey-Bass.

Silberschatz, A., & Tuzhilin, A. (1996). What makes Patterns interesting in Knowledge Discovery. *IEEE Transactions on Knowledge and Data Engineering, 8*(6), 970–974. doi:10.1109/69.553165

Silva, M. S., Câmara, G., & Escada, M. I. (2009). Image Mining: Detecting Deforestation Patterns Through Satellites. In Rahman, H. (Ed.), *Data Mining Applications for Empowering Knowledge Societies* (pp. 55–75). Hershey, PA: IGI Publishing.

Simoudis, E. (1996). Reality Check for Data Mining. *IEEE Expert, 11*(5), 26–33. doi:10.1109/64.539014

Singhal, M., & Shivaratri, N. G. (1994). *Advanced Concepts in Operating Systems*. New York, NY, USA: McGraw-Hill, Inc.

Skvoretz, J., & Faust, K. (2002). Relations, Species, and Network Structure. *Journal of Social Structure, 3*(3).

Smith, C., & Williams, L. (2001). *Performance Solutions: A Practical Guide to Creating Responsive, Scalable Software*. Boston: Addison-Wesley Professional.

Smyth, P. (1997). Clustering Sequences with Hidden Markov Models. *Adv. Neural Inf. Process, 9*, 648–655.

Snow, A., & Keil, M. (2001). The Challenges of Accurate Project Status Reporting. In *34th Annual Hawaii International Conference on System Sciences*. Maui, Hawaii: ACM.

Software Engineering Institute. (2006). *Ultra-Large-Scale Systems: Software Challenge of the Future. Carnegie Mellon University*. Pittsburgh, PA: Carnegie Mellon.

Somasundaran, S., Ruppenhofer, J., & Wiebe, J. (2008). Discourse level Opinion Relations: An Annotation Study. In *SIGdial Workshop on Discourse and Dialogue*.

Soparkar, N., Levy, E., Korth, H. F., & Silberschatz, A. (1994). Adaptive Commitment for Real - Time Distributed Transaction. In *3rd International Conference on Information and Knowledge Management* (pp.187-104). Gaithersburg, Maryland, United States.

Spiliopoulou, M., Kalousis, A., Faulstich, C., & Theoharis, T. (1998). NOEMON: An Intelligent assistant for Classifier Selection. In Wysotzki, F., Geibel, P., & Schädler, K. (Eds.), *Beiträge zum Treffen der GI-Fachgruppe 1.1.3 Maschinelles Lernen (FGML98)* (pp. 90–97). TU Berlin.

Srikant, R., & Agrawal, R. (1995). Mining generalized Association Rules. In *Proceedings of the 21st VLDB Conference* (pp. 407-419). Zurich, Switzerland.

Srikant, R., & Agrawal, R. (1996). Mining Quantitative Association Rules in Large Relational Tables. In *Proceedings of the 1996 ACM SIGMOD International Conference on Management of Data* (pp. 1-12). Montreal, Quebec, Canada: ACM Press.

Srivatsan Laxman, & Sastry, P.S. (2006). A Survey of Temporal Data Mining. *Sadhana, 31*, 173–198. doi:10.1007/BF02719780

Starner, T. E., & Pentland, A. (1995). Visual Recognition of American Sign Language. In *Proceedings of 1995 Int. Workshop on Face and Gesture Recognition*. Zurich.

Statistics, N. I. (2000). *2000 National Census Data Set: The Social and Economic attributes of the population*. Ankara: National Institute of Statistics.

Statnikov, A., Aliferis, C., Tsamardinos, I., Hardin, D., & Levy, S. (2005). A Comprehensive Evaluation of Multicategory Classification methods for Microarray Gene Expression Cancer Diagnosis. *BMC Bioinformatics, 21*(5), 631–643.

Stegmayer, G., Milone, D., Kamenetzky, L., Lopez, M., & Carrari, F. (2009). Neural Network Model for Integration and Visualization of Introgressed Genome and Metabolite Data. In *International Joint Conference on Neural Networks* (pp. 2983-2989).

Stekel, D. (2003). *Microarray Bioinformatics*. Cambridge, UK: Cambridge University Press. doi:10.1017/CBO9780511615535

Sterrit, R., Adamson, K., Shapcott, M., & Curran, E. (2000b). Parallel Data Mining of Bayesian Networks from Telecommunications Network Data. In Proceedings of IPDPS 2000 Workshops. Cancun, Mexico.

Sterritt, R., Adamson, K., Shapcott, C., & Curran, E. (2000a). Data Mining Telecommunications Network Data for Fault Management and Development Testing. In Becken, N., & Brebbai, C. (Eds.), *Data Mining II* (pp. 299–308). Southampton: Wit Press.

Stone, P. J., Dunphy, D. C., Smith, M. S., & Oglivie, D. M. (1966). *The General Enquirer: A Computer Approach to Content Analysis*. Cambridge, MA: MIT Press.

Stork, H. (2002). Webs, Grids and Knowledge Spaces - Programmes, Projects and Prospects. *Journal of Universal Computer Science, 8*(9), 848–868.

Strapparava, C., & Valitutti, A. (2004). WordNet-Affect: An Affective Extension of WordNet. In *Proceedings of the 4th International Conference on Language Resources and Evaluation*.

Strapparava, C., Valitutti, A., & Stock, O. (2006). The Affective Weight of Lexicon. In *Proceedings of the Fifth International Conference on Language Resources and Evaluation.*

Styczynski, M., & Stephanopoulos, G. (2005). Overview of Computational Methods for the Inference of Gene Regulatory Networks. *Computers & Chemical Engineering, 29,* 519–534. doi:10.1016/j.compchemeng.2004.08.029

Su, Y., Murali, T., Pavlovic, V., Schaffer, M., & Kasif, S. (2003). RankGene: Identification of Diagnostic Genes based on Expression Data. *Bioinformatics (Oxford, England), 19*(12), 1578. doi:10.1093/bioinformatics/btg179

Su, X., Khoshgoftaar, T. M., & Greiner, R. (2009). Making an Accurate Classifier Ensemble by Voting on Classifications from Imputed Learning Sets. *International Journal of Information and Decision Sciences, 1*(3), 301–322. doi:10.1504/IJIDS.2009.027657

Sugar, C. A., & James, G. M. (2003). Finding the Number of Clusters in a Dataset. *Journal of the American Statistical Association, 98*(463), 750–763. doi:10.1198/016214503000000666

Sun, B., Li, Y., & Zhang, L. (2009). The Intelligent System of Cardiovascular Disease Diagnosis Based on Extension Data Mining. In Y. Shi, S. Wang, Y. Peng, J. Li & Y. Zeng (Eds.), *Cutting-Edge Research Topics on Multiple Criteria Decision Making, Proceedings of 20th International Conference on Multiple Criteria Decision Making. Communications in Computer and Information Science,* 35 (pp. 133-140). Berlin/Heidelberg: Springer. doi: 10.1007/978-3-642-02298-2.

Sutton, R. S. (1988). Learning to predict by method of Temporal Differences. *Machine Learning, 3*(1), 9–44. doi:10.1007/BF00115009

Suutarinen, J. (1994). Performance Measurements of GSM Base Station System. Thesis (Lic.Tech.), Tampere University of Technology.

Sztipanovits, J., & Karsai, G. (1997). Model-Integrated Computing. *IEEE Computer, 30*(4), 110–112.

Tadesse, T., Wardlow, B., & Hayes, M. J. (2009). The Application of Data Mining for Drought Monitoring and Prediction. In Rahman, H. (Ed.), *Data Mining Applications for Empowering Knowledge Societies* (pp. 280–291). Hershey, PA: IGI Publishing.

Taina, J., & Son, S. H. (1999). Towards a General Real-Time Database Simulator Software Library. In *Proceedings of the Active and Real-Time Database Systems.*

Talia, D. (2002). The Open Grid Services Architecture: Where the Grid Meets the Web. *IEEE Internet Computing, 6*(6), 67–71. doi:10.1109/MIC.2002.1067739

Tan, P.-N., Steinbach, M., & Kumar, V. (2006). *Introduction to Data Mining.* Boston: Addison Wesley.

Tang, Z., & MacLennan, J. (2005). *Data Mining with SQL Server 2005.* Indianapolis, IN: Wiley Publishing.

Tari, L., Baral, C., & Kim, S. (2009). Fuzzy c-means Clustering with Prior Biological Knowledge. *Journal of Biomedical Informatics, 42*(1), 74–81. doi:10.1016/j.jbi.2008.05.009

Tasoulis, D., Plagianakos, V., & Vrahatis, M. (2008). *Computational Intelligence in Bioinformatics. Studies in Computational Intelligence.* New York: Springer.

Terplan, K. (2001). *OSS Essentials: Support System Solutions for Service Providers.* Chichester, England: John Wiley & Sons, Ltd.

Thabtah, F., Cowling, P., & Peng, Y. (2005). The Impact of Rule Ranking on the Quality of Associative Classifiers. In *Proceedings of AI-2005, the Twenty-fifth SGAI International Conference on Innovative Techniques and Applications of Artificial Intelligence (AI-05) - Research and Development in Intelligent Systems XXII* (pp. 277-287). Cambridge, UK: Springer-Verlag.

Thalamuthu, A., Mukhopadhyay, I., Zheng, X., & Tseng, G. (2006). Evaluation and Comparison of Gene Clustering methods in Microarray Analysis. *Bioinformatics (Oxford, England), 22*(19), 2405–2412. doi:10.1093/bioinformatics/btl406

The Netsize Guide. (2009). *Mobile Society & Me: When Worlds Combine*. Retrieved from. [available at http://www.netsize.com/]

Thierauf, R. J. (2001). *Effective Business Intelligence Systems*. West Port, CP: Quorum Books.

Tisal, J. (2001). *The GSM Network*. Chichester, England: John Wiley & Sons, Ltd.

TMF. (1999). *Network Management Detailed Operations Map. Evaluation Version 1.0*. TeleManagement Forum.

Toivonen, H. (1996). Sampling Large Databases for Association Rules. In *Proceedings of the 22nd International Conference on Very Large Data Bases* (pp. 134-145). Mumbai (Bombay), India: Morgan Kaufmann Publishers.

Toivonen, H., Klemettinen, M., Ronkainen, P., Hätönen, K., & Mannila, H. (1995). Pruning and Grouping of Discovered Association Rules. In *Proceedings of ECML-95 Workshop on Statistics, Machine Learning, and Discovery in Databases* (pp. 47-52). Heraklion, Crete, Greece.

Tokimatsu, T., Sakurai, N., Suzuki, H., Ohta, H., Nishitani, K., & Koyama, T. (2005). Kappa-view: A Web-based Analysis Tool for Integration of Transcript and Metabolite Data on Plant Metabolic Pathway Maps. *Plant Physiology*, *138*(3), 1289–1300. doi:10.1104/pp.105.060525

Tortonesi, M., Stefanelli, C., Suri, N., Arguedas, M., & Breedy, M. (2006). Mockets: A Novel Message-Oriented Communications Middleware for the Wireless Internet. In *International Conference on Wireless Information Networks and Systems*. Setubal, Portugal.

Toutanova, K., & Manning, C. (2000). Enriching the Knowledge Sources Used in a Maximum Entropy Part-of-Speech Tagger. In *Proceedings of the Joint SIGDAT Conference on Empirical Methods in Natural Language Processing and Very Large Corpora (EMNLP/VLC-2000)* (pp. 63-70).

Tozicka, J., Rovatsos, M., & Pechoucek, M. (2007). A Framework for Agent-based Distributed Machine Learning and Data Mining. In *Proceedings of the 6th International Joint Conference on Autonomous Agents and Multiagent Systems,* (Art 96). Honolulu, HI.

Troyanskaya, O., Cantor, M., Sherlock, G., Brown, P., Hastie, T., & Tibshirani, R. (2001). Missing Value Estimation methods for DNA Microarrays. *Bioinformatics (Oxford, England)*, *17*(6), 520–525. doi:10.1093/bioinformatics/17.6.520

Tsumoto, S. (1999). Discovery of Rules for Medical Expert Systems-Rough Set Approach. In *Proceedings of the Third International Conference on Computational Intelligence and Multimedia Applications* (pp. 212-216). Los Alamitos, CA: IEEE Computer Society.

Tuan, R. S., Boland, G., & Tuli, R. (2003). Adult Mesenchymal Stem Cells and Cell-based Tissue Engineering. *Arthritis Research & Therapy*, *5*(1), 32–45. doi:10.1186/ar614

Turban, E., Sharda, R., Aroson, J. E., & King, D. (2008). *Business Intelligence: A Managerial Approach*. Upper Sadle River, New Jersey: Pearson Prentice Hall.

Turner, T. C., Smith, M., Fisher, D., & Welser, H. T. (2005). Picturing Usenet: Mapping Computer-Mediated Collective Action. *Journal of Computer-Mediated Communication*, *10*(4).

Turney, P., & Littman, M. (2003). Measuring Praise and Criticism: Inference of Semantic Orientation from Association. *ACM Transactions on Information Systems*, *4*(21), 315–346. doi:10.1145/944012.944013

Turney, P. (2002). Thumbs up or Thumbs down? Sentiment Orientation Applied to Unsupervised Classification of Reviews. In *Proceedings of the 40th Annual Meeting of the Association of Computational Linguistics – ACL*.

Tuzhilin, A., & Adomavicius, G. (2002). Handling very large numbers of Association Rules in the Analysis of Microarray Data. In *Proceedings of Eighth ACM SIGKDD International Conference on Data Mining and Knowledge Discovery* (pp.396-404).

Ultsch, A. (1999). *Data Mining and Knowledge Discovery with Emergent Self-organizing Feature Maps for Multivariate Time Series in Kohonen Maps*. Elsevier.

Ulusoy, O. (1992). *Concurrency Control in Real-time Database Systems*. Unpublished doctoral dissertation, Department of Computer Science, University of Illinois, Urbana-Champaign, USA.

Unwin, D. (2003). Information support for e-Learning: principles and practice. *UK eUniversities Worldwide Summer.*

Vapnik, V. (1998). *Statistical Learning Theory*. Wiley.

Varshavsky, R., Gottlieb, A., Linial, M., & Horn, D. (2006). Novel Unsupervised Feature Filtering of Biological Data. *Bioinformatics (Oxford, England), 22*(14). doi:10.1093/bioinformatics/btl214

Vatsavai, R. R., & Bhaduri, B. (2007). A Hybrid Classification Scheme for Mining Multisource Geospatial Data. In *Proceedings of the Seventh IEEE International Conference on Data Mining Workshops (ICDMW 2007)* (pp. 673-678). Omaha, NE.

Vazhkudai, S., Tuecke, S., & Foster, I. (2001). Replica Selection in the Global Data Grid. In *Proceedings of the 1st International Symposium on Cluster Computing and the Grid. Brisbane*, Australia.

Vazquez, F. (1994). Identification of Complete Dataflow Diagrams. *SIGSOFT Software Engineering Notes, 19*(3), 36–40. doi:10.1145/182824.182832

Vercellis, C. (2009). *Business Intelligence: Data Mining and Optimization for Decision Making*. West Sussex, United Kindgom: John Wiley & Sons.

Vesanto, J., Himberg, J., Alhoniemi, E., & Parhankangas, J. (2000). *SOM Toolbox for Matlab 5*. Helsinki, Finland: Helsinki University of Technology.

Vesanto, J. (2002). Data Exploration Based on the Self-Organizing Map. Thesis (Doc. Tech.), Helsinki University of Technology.

Viegas, F. B., & Smith, M. (2004). Newsgroup Crowds and AuthorLines: Visualizing the Activity of Individuals in Conversational Cyberspaces. In *37th Annual Hawaii International Conference on System Sciences (HICSS'04) - Track 4*. Kauai: IEEE Computer Society.

Wagstaff, K., Cardie, C., Rogers, S., & Schrödl, S. (2001). Constrained k-means Clustering with Background Knowledge. In *Proceedings of the Eighteenth International Conference on Machine Learning* (pp. 577-584). Williamstown, MA.

Wang, Y., Makedon, F., Ford, J., & Pearlman, J. (2005). HykGene: A Hybrid Approach for Selecting Marker Genes for Phenotype Classification using Microarray Gene Expression Data. *Bioinformatics (Oxford, England), 21*(8), 1530–1537. doi:10.1093/bioinformatics/bti192

Wang, Z., Yan, P., Potter, D., Eng, C., Huang, T., & Lin, S. (2007). Heritable Clustering and Pathway Discovery in Breast Cancer Integrating Epigenetic and Phenotypic Data. *BMC Bioinformatics, 8*(1), 38. doi:10.1186/1471-2105-8-38

Wang, Y., Zhang, Y., Xia, J., & Wang, Z. (2008). Segmenting the Mature Travel Market by Motivation. *International Journal of Data Analysis Techniques and Strategies, 1*(2), 193–209. doi:10.1504/IJDATS.2008.021118

Wang, H., & Wang, S. (2008). A Knowledge Management Approach to Data Mining Process for Business Intelligence. *Industrial Management & Data Systems, 108*(5), 622–634. doi:10.1108/02635570810876750

Wang, W., Wang, Y. J., Bañares-Alcántara, R., Coenen, F., & Cui, Z. (in press). Analysis of Mesenchymal Stem Cell differentiation in vitro using Classification Association Rule Mining. *Journal of Bioinformatics and Computational Biology.*

Wang, Y. J., Xin, Q., & Coenen, F. (2008). Hybrid rule ordering in Classification Association Rule Mining. *Transactions on Machine Learning and Data Mining, 1*(1), 1–15.

Wang, G., Zhang, C., & Huang, L. (2008). A Study of Classification Algorithm for Data Mining based on Hybrid Intelligent Systems. In *Ninth ACIS International Conference on Software Engineering, Artificial Intelligence, Networking, and Parallel/Distributed Computing* (pp. 371-375). Phuket Thailand.

Wang, H., Wang, W., Yang, J., & Yu, P. (2002). Clustering by Pattern Similarity in Large Data Sets. In *Proceedings ACM SIGMOD International Conference on Management of Data* (pp.394-405).

Wang, J. T.-L., Chirn, G.-W., Marr, T. G., Shapiro, B., Shasha, D., & Zhang, K. (1994). Combinatorial Pattern Discovery for Scientific Data: Some Preliminary Results. In *Proceedings of 1994 ACM SIGMOD International Conference on Management of Data* (pp. 115-125). Minneapolis, Minnesota.

Wang, W., Wang, Y. J., Bañares-Alcántara, R., Cui, Z., & Coenen, F. (2009). Application of Classification Association Rule Mining for Mammalian Mesenchymal Stem Cell differentiation. In *Proceedings of the 9th Industrial Conference on Data Mining (ICDM-09) — Advances in Data Mining Applications and Theoretical Aspects* (pp. 51-61). Leipzig, Germany: Springer-Verlag Berlin Heidelberg.

Wang, Y. J., Xin, Q., & Coenen, F. (2007). A Novel Rule Ordering Approach in Classification Association Rule Mining. In *Proceedings of the 5th International Conference on Machine Learning and Data Mining* (pp.339-348). Leipzig, Germany: Springer-Verlag.

Wang, Y., Yang, J.-M., Lai, W., Cai, R., Zhang, L., & Ma, W.-Y. (2008). Exploring Traversal Strategy for Web Forum Crawling. In *31st International ACM SIGIR Conference on Research and Development in Information Retrieval* (pp.459-466). New York: ACM Press.

Webb, G. I., & Zheng, Z. (2004). Multistrategy Ensemble Learning: Reducing Error by Combining Ensemble Learning Techniques. *IEEE Transactions on Knowledge and Data Engineering, 16*(8), 980–991. doi:10.1109/TKDE.2004.29

Wehmeyer, K. (2007). Mobile Ad Intrusiveness – The effects of Message type and Situation. In *Proceedings of the 20th Bled eConference eMergence.* Bled, Slovenia.

Weiss, S., Indurkhya, N., Zhang, T., & Damerau, F. (2004). *Text Mining: Predictive Methods for Analyzing Unstructured Information.* Springer.

Weiss, G. M., Eddy, J., & Weiss, S. (1998). Intelligent Telecommunication Technologies. In Jain, L. C., Johnson, R. D., Takefuji, Y., & Zadeh, L. A. (Eds.), *Knowledge-based Intelligent Techniques* (pp. 249–275). Boca Raton, Florida: CRC Press.

Welser, H. T., Gleave, E., Fisher, D., & Smith, M. (2007). Visualizing the Signatures of Social Roles in Online Discussion Groups. *Journal of Social Structure, 8*(2).

Wenger, E. (1999). *Communities of Practice: Learning, Meaning, and Identity.* Cambridge, UK: Cambridge University Press.

Wenger, E., McDermott, R., & Snyder, W. S. (2002). *Cultivating Communities of Practice: A Guide to Managing Knowledge.* Boston: Harvard Business School Press.

Wenger, E., & Snyder, M. (2000). Communities of Practice: The Organizational Frontier. *Harvard Business Review,* 139–145.

White, H. C., Boorman, S. A., & Breiger, R. L. (1976). Social-Structure from Multiple Networks: 1. Blockmodels of Roles and Positions. *American Journal of Sociology, 81*(4), 730–780. doi:10.1086/226141

Wiebe, J., Bruce, R., Martin, M., Wilson, T., & Bell, M. (2004). Learning Subjective Language. *Computational Linguistics, 30*(3), 277–308. doi:10.1162/0891201041850885

Wiebe, J., Bruce, R., Martin, M., Wilson, T., & Bell, M. (2004). Learning Subjective Language. *Computational Linguistics, 30*(3), 277–308. doi:10.1162/0891201041850885

Wiebe, J. (1990). Identifying Subjective Characters in Narrative. In *Proceedings of the 13th Conference on Computational linguistics.* Helsinki, Finland, Wiebe, J., & Mihalcea, R. (2006). Word Sense and Subjectivity. In *Proceedings of the 21st International ACL Conference on Computational Linguistics* (pp. 1065-1072).

Wiebe, J., Bruce, R., & O'Hara, T. (1999). Development and Use of Gold-Standard Data Set for Subjectivity Classifications. In *Proceedings of the 37th Annual Meeting of the Association of Computational Linguistics – ACL-99* (pp. 246-253).

Wilson, T., Wiebe, J., & Hoffmann, P. (2005). Recognizing Contextual Polarity in Phrase-Level Sentiment Analysis. In *Proceedings of HLT/EMNLP*. Vancouver, Canada.

Winn, J., Criminisi, A., & Minka, T. (2005). Object categorization by Learned Universal Visual Dictionary. In *Proceedings of the Tenth IEEE International Conference on Computer Vision* (pp. 1800-1807). Washington, DC, USA.

Witten, I. H., & Frank, E. (2005). *Data Mining: Practical Machine Learning Tools and Techniques* (2nd ed.). San Francisco: Morgan Kaufman.

Wolfe, C. J., Kohane, I. S., & Butte, A. J. (2005). Systematic survey reveals general applicability of "guilt-by-association" within Gene Coexpression Networks. *BMC Bioinformatics*, *6*, 227. doi:10.1186/1471-2105-6-227

Woodside, M., Franks, G., & Petriu, D. C. (2007). *The Future of Software Performance Engineering* (pp. 171–187). Minneapolis, MN: The Future of Software Engineering.

World, G. S. M. (2003). Website of the GSM Association [online]. Retrieved August 6, 2003, from: - http://www.gsmworld.com/index.shtml.

Wormus, T. (2008). Complex Event Processing: Analytics and Complex Event Processing: Adding Intelligence to the Event Chain. *Business Intelligence Journal*, *13*(4), 53–58.

Wray, R. (2009). *Orange to offer free gifts to students who agree to receive Ads on Mobiles*. Retrieved August 19, 2009, from http://www.guardian.co.uk/business/2009/jul/22 /orange-free-gifts-advertising-blyk

Wright, P. (1998). Knowledge Discovery PreProcessing: Determining Record Usability. In Proceedings of the 36th Annual ACM Southeast Regional Conference (pp. 283-288). Marietta, GA, USA.

Wroe, C., Stevens, R., Goble, C., Roberts, A., & Greenwood, M. (2003). A Suite of DAML+OIL Ontologies to describe Bioinformatics Web Services and Data. *International Journal of Cooperative Information Systems*, *12*(2), 197–224. doi:10.1142/S0218843003000711

Wu, F. (2008). Genetic Weighted k-means Algorithm for Clustering Large-scale Gene Expression Data. *BMC Bioinformatics*, *9*.

Wu, S., & Manber, U. (1992). Fast Text searching allowing Errors. *Communications of the ACM*, *35*(10), 83–91. doi:10.1145/135239.135244

Wu, C., Yu, L., & Jang, F. (2005). Using Semantic Dependencies to Mine Depressive Symptoms from Consultation Records. *IEEE Intelligent Systems*, *20*(6), 50–59. doi:10.1109/MIS.2005.115

Wu, Z., Chen, H., & Xu, J. (2003). Knowledge Base Grid: A Generic Grid Architecture for Semantic Web. *Journal of Computer and Technology*, *18*(4), 462–473. doi:10.1007/BF02948920

Wu, C., Berry, M., Shivakumar, S., & McLarty, J. (1995). Neural Networks for Full-scale Protein Sequence Classification: Sequence Encoding with Singular Value Decomposition. *Machine Learning, Special issue on applications in Molecular Biology*, *21*(1-2), 177-193.

Xin, T. (2006). *A Framework for Processing Generalized Advanced Transactions*. Unpublished doctoral dissertation, Department of Computer Science, Colorado State University, USA.

Xiong, Y., & Yeung, D. Y. (2002). Mixtures of ARMA models for Model-based Time Series Clustering. In *2002 IEEE International Conference on Data Mining* (pp. 717-720). Maebashi City, Japan.

Xu, B., & Liu, L. Q. (2008). Research of Litchi Diseases Diagnosis Expert System Based on RBR and CBR. In D. Li & C. Zhao (Eds.), *The Second IFIP International Conference on Computer and Computing Technologies in Agriculture (CCTA2008). IFIP Advances in Information and Communication Technology*, 293 (pp. 681-688). Boston: Springer.

Xu, R., & Donald, C. Wunsch, I. (2009). *Clustering*. New York: Wiley and IEEE Press.

Yamato, J., Ohya, J., & Ishii, K. (1992). Recognizing Human action in Time-sequential Images using Hidden Markov Model. In *Proceedings of 1992 IEEE Comput. Soc. Conf. on Computer Vision and Pattern Recognition* (pp. 379-385). Champaign, IL.

Yang, K., Yu, N., & Zhang, H. (2007). WIDIT in TREC-2007 Blog Track: Combining Lexicon-based Methods to Detect Opinionated Blogs. In *Proceedings of the 16th Text Retrieval Conference (TREC 2007)*.

Yang, L., Widyantoro, D. H., Ioerger, T., & Yen, J. (2001). An entropy-based adaptive Genetic Algorithm for learning Classification Rules. In *Proceedings of the 2001 Congress on Evolutionary Computation (CEC-01)* (pp. 790-796). Seoul, South Korea: IEEE Computer Society.

Yano, M., Kanaya, S., Altaf-Ul-Amin, M., Kurokawa, K., Hirai, M. Y., & Saito, K. (2006). Integrated Data Mining of Transcriptome and Metabolome based on BLSOM. *Journal of Computer Aided Chemistry, 7*, 125–136. doi:10.2751/jcac.7.125

Yeung, K., & Bumgarner, R. (2003). Multiclass Classification of Microarray Data with Repeated Measurements: Application to Cancer. *Genome Biology, 4*.

Yi, J., Nasukawa, T., Bunescu, R., & Niblack, W. (2003). Sentiment Analyzer: Extracting Sentiments about a given topic using Natural Language Processing Techniques. In *Third IEEE International Conference on Data Mining, ICDM 2003* (pp.427-434).

Yin, X., & Han, J. (2003). CPAR: Classification based on predictive Association Rules. In *Proceedings of the 3rd SIAM International Conference on Data Mining (SDM-03)* (pp. 331-335). San Francisco, CA, USA: SIAM.

Yingjiu Li. Peng Ning, X., Sean Wang., & Sushil Jajodia, R. (2003). Discovering Calendar-based Temporal Association Rules. *Data & Knowledge Engineering,* Vol. 4, Elesvier Publisher,193-214.

Yoon, Y., & Lee, G. G. (2005). Practical Application of Associative Classifier for Document Classification. In *Proceedings of the Second Asia Information Retrieval Symposium* (pp. 467-478). Jeju Island, Korea: Springer-Verlag.

Yu, J., Cheng, F., Xiong, H., Qu, W., & Chen, X. (2008). A Bayesian Approach to Support Vector Machines for the Binary Classification. *Neurocomputing, 72*(1-3), 177–185. doi:10.1016/j.neucom.2008.06.010

Yu, H., & Hatzivassiloglou, V. (2003). Towards Answering Opinion Questions: Separating Facts from Opinions and Identifying Polarity in Sentences. In *Proceedings of the 2003 Conference on Empirical Methods in Natural Language Processing* (pp. 129-136).

Zadeh, L. A. (1965). Fuzzy Sets. *Journal of Information and Control, 8*, 338–353. doi:10.1016/S0019-9958(65)90241-X

Zahurak, M., Parmigiani, G., Yu, W., Scharpf, R., Berman, D., & Schaeffer, E. (2007). Pre-processing Agilent Microarray Data. *BMC Bioinformatics, 8*(142), 1471–2105.

Zaki, M. J. (2004). Mining Non-redundant Association Rules. *Data Mining and Knowledge Discovery, 9*, 223–248. doi:10.1023/B:DAMI.0000040429.96086.c7

Zelezný, F., Mikšovský, P., Štepánková, O., & Zídek, J. (2000). KDD in Telecommunications. In DDMI 2000 Workshop (pp. 103-112). Porto: University of Porto.

Zeller, J. (2007). Business Intelligence: The Chicken or the Egg. Retrieved from http://www.information-management.com/bissues/20070601/2600340-1.html.

Zeller, J. (2008). Business Intelligence: The Road Trip. *Information Management Special Reports, December 2, 2008,* Retrieved from http://www.information-management.com/specialreports/2008112/100002266-1.html.

Zhang, X., Hu, X., Xia, J., Zhou, X., & Achananuparp, P. (2008). A Graph-Based Biomedical Literature Clustering Approach Utilizing Term's Global and Local Importance Information. *International Journal of Data Warehousing and Mining, 4*(4), 84–101.

Zhang, Y., Li, C., Jiang, X., Zhang, S., Wu, Y., & Liu, B. (2004). Human placenta-derived Mesenchymal Progenitor Cells support culture expansion of long-term culture-initiating cells from Cord blood CD34+ cells. *Experimental Hematology, 32*(7), 657–664. doi:10.1016/j.exphem.2004.04.001

Zhang, J., Ackerman, M. S., & Adamic, L. (2007). Expertise Networks in Online Communities: Structure and Algorithms. In *16th International Conference on World Wide Web,* Banff, Alberta, Canada. ACM Press.

Zhao, Y., Zhang, C., & Zhang, S. (2005). Discovering Interesting Association Rules by Clustering. *AI 2004: Advances in Artificial Intelligence*, 3335, 1055-1061. Heidelberg: Springer.

Zheng, G., George, E., & Narasimhan, G. (2005). *Neural Network Classifiers and Gene Selection methods for Microarray Data on Human Lung Adenocarcinoma.* Methods of Microarray Data Analysis IV.

Zheng, Q., & Wang, X. (2008). GOEAST: A Web-based Software Toolkit for Gene Ontology Enrichment Analysis. *Nucleic Acids Research, 36,* W358. doi:10.1093/nar/gkn276

Zhong, N., Yao, Y. Y., Ohshima, M., & Ohsuga, S. (2001). Interestingness, Peculiarity, and Multi-database Mining. In *First IEEE International Conference on Data Mining (ICDM'01)* (pp.566-574). San Jose, California.

Zhong, S. (2005). Efficient Online Spherical k-means Clustering. *Neural Networks, IJCNN'05,* 5, 3180-3185.

Zhuge, H. (2004a). Semantics, Resource and Grid. *Future Generation Computer Systems, 20*(1), 1–5. doi:10.1016/S0167-739X(03)00159-6

Zhuge, H. (2004b). *The Knowledge Grid.* China: Chinese Academy of Sciences.

Zhuge, H. (2004c). China's e-Science Knowledge Grid Environment. *IEEE Intelligent Systems, 19*(1), 13–17. doi:10.1109/MIS.2004.1265879

About the Contributors

A.V. Senthil Kumar is presently working as a Director in the Department of MCA, Hindusthan College of Arts and Science, Coimbatore, Tamilnadu, India. He has written many articles/papers in Computer Science. He is an Editorial Board Member and Reviewer for various International Journals; Committee member for various International Journals and member of various Computer Science as¬sociations. He has more than 13 years of teaching and 5 years of industrial experience. He has obtained his B.Sc Degree (Physics) in 1987, Post Graduate Diploma in Computer Applications in 1988, Master of Computer Applications in 1991 from Bharathiar University. He has done his Master of Philosophy in Computer Science from Bharathidasan University and completed his PhD in Computer Science from the Vinayaka Missions University, Salem, Tamilnadu, India in 2009.

* * *

Abhinav Anand was born in Gorakhpur in 1985. He moved to M. M. M. Engineering College, Gorakhpur-273010, India for his undergraduate study in 2005 after completion of basic education. Presently, he is working as a project engineer in WIPRO Technologies. His one of the specialized area of interests is Database Systems.

Abhay N. Singh was born in 1986. He has completed his undergraduate study from Madan Mohan Malviya Engineering College, Gorakhpur-273010, India. Presently, he is pursuing his graduate degree from Department of Electronics and Computer Engineering, Indian Institute of Technology Roorkee, Roorkee-247 667, India. His main research interests include Distributed Database System.

Alessandro Fiori is PhD Student in Information and System Engineering at Politecnico di Torino. His research activity is focused on the analysis of gene expression data and on the knowledge extraction from biological documents. He has been working on feature selection algorithms to select the most relevant genes under determinate conditions. Moreover, he is investigating clustering techniques which weight differently specific features of data in similarity measure computation. His current research interests include an approach to validate biological analysis results using the knowledge retrieved from published literature.

Ana Azevedo teaches Information Systems and Technologies at the School of Accounting and Administration, Polytechnic Institute of Porto, Portugal. She is a PhD Student in Information Systems and Technologies at the department of information systems, University of Minho, Guimarães, Portugal. She is a researcher of the Algoritmi Research Center and of CEISE/STI research center. She is involved in the implementation of a BI system in a Higher Education Institution. Her research interests include Decision Support Systems, Data mining, e-Learning. She is involved in several research projects.

Anthony Scime currently is an Associate Professor of Computer Science at The College at Brockport, State University of New York. His work in data mining has been published in Expert Systems with Applications, the International Journal of Business Intelligence and Data Mining, Data Mining and Knowledge Discovery Technologies, and Public Opinion Quarterly. Idea Group Publishing published his book Web Mining: Applications and Techniques. His current research interests include Web mining, data mining in the social and behavioral sciences, and computing education.

Aurora Pérez received her BS and PhD degrees in Computer Science from Universidad Politécnica de Madrid (UPM) in 1987 and 1991, respectively. Dr. Perez's PhD dissertation merited the distinction of university prize.She is currently an Associate Professor of Computer Science and Assistant Director of the Department of Languages and Systems at the Universidad Politécnica de Madrid. She is also the Department's Postgraduate Studies Coordinator. She was a guest researcher at Carnegie Mellon University in 1993 and 1994. She has published several papers in refereed journals and international conferences. Her research interests include data mining and scientific discovery.

Brendan Tierney is a lecturer with the School of Computing at the Dublin Institute of Technology, Ireland. Brendan obtained a Diploma in Applied Science and a BSc (Hons) in Applied Science at DIT in 1993. He completed his MSc. in DCU in 1998 and a Diploma in Applied Project Management from the Institute of Project Management of Ireland and University College Cork in 2001.

Bruno Ohana is a PhD researcher with the School of Computing at the Dublin Institute of Technology (DIT), Ireland with research interests in data mining, natural languages and opinion mining. Bruno obtained a bachelor degree in Computer Science at São Paulo University – Brazil, and has completed his MSc. at DIT in the area of Knowledge Management and Data Mining in 2009.

Catarina Sismeiro is Associate Professor at Imperial College Business School, Imperial College London. She received her Ph.D. in Marketing from the University of California, Los Angeles, and her Licenciatura in Management from the University of Porto, Portugal. Before joining Imperial College Catarina had been an Assistant Professor at Marshall School of Business, University of Southern California. She received the 2003 Paul Green Award, was the finalist of the 2007 and 2008 O'Dell Awards, and was a 2007 MSI Young Scholar, Catarina is currently on the editorial board of the International Journal of Research in Marketing.

Chandra Sekhar Pedamallu has his B.Tech. (1999) in Mechanical Engineering from Nagarjuna University, India, M.Tech. (2001) in Industrial Management from Indian Institute of Technology Madras, India and Ph.D (2007) from the Division of Systems Engg. And Mgmt., Nanyang Technological University, Singapore. He has worked as Visiting Scientist and Project Leader in New England Biolabs Inc., USA and Indonet Global Limited (Division of Subuthi Overseas Inc., USA), India respectively. He is currently working as Postdoctoral Research Fellow in Bioinformatics at New England Biolabs,

Inc., USA. His research interests are in the areas of bioinformatics, computational biology, data mining, global optimization, parallel algorithms, interval-symbolic applications in nonlinear programming and applications of meta-heuristics on OR problems. Dr. Pedamallu is an editorial board member of three research journals and founding /active member of several European working groups on OR.

Diego Milone received the Bioengineer degree (Hons.) from National University of Entre Rios (Argentina) in 1998, and the Ph.D. in Microelectronics and Computer Architectures from Granada University, Spain, in 2003. He is Full Professor in the Department of Informatics at National University of Litoral and Associate Researcher at the National Council of Scientific and Technological Research. Prof. Milone served as Associate Dean for Science and Technology, as Director of the Laboratory for Signals and Computational Intelligence and he is currently Director of the Department of Informatics. His research interests include statistical learning, pattern recognition, signal processing, neural and evolutionary computing.

Diego Reforgiato Recupero has been a Post Doctoral Researcher at the Department of Computer Science and Telecommunications Engineering (DIIT) working on peer-to-peer video since 3/11/2008. The support for this fellowship has been given by PROVIDEO, a Marie Curie International Grant (IRG) that Dr. Reforgiato won in summer 2008 together with the University of Catania. From 4/1/2005 to 5/1/2008 Dr. Reforgiato was a Post Doctoral Researcher at the Institute for Advanced Computer Studies, University of Maryland College Park, working with Prof. V.S. Subrahmanian. Dr. Reforgiato received the PhD in December 2004, from the University of Naples Federico II in Computer Sciences.

Fernando Alonso received his PhD in Computer Science in 1985 from the Universidad Politécnica de Madrid (UPM). His PhD dissertation merited the distinction of university prize. He has been a Professor of Computer Science at the UPM's School of Computing since 1989. He is also the R&D Director of the Centre of Computing and Communications Technology Transfer (CETTICO) based at the UPM. His major field of study is software and knowledge engineering and e-learning. He has authored or co-authored 18 books and over 70 papers published in international and national journals.

Fernando Carrari received his PhD in Plant Molecular Genetics from Universidad de Buenos Aires (Argentina) in 2001. Up to 2004 he hold a Post-doctoral Research Associate position at the Max Planck Institute for Molecular Plant Physiology. He is Associate Professor at the Facultad de Agronomia of the Universidad de Buenos Aires and Associate Researcher of the National Council for Science and Technology. His current research interest is focussed on Crop Plants Metabolism.

Frans Coenen has a general background in AI, and has been working in the field of data mining and Knowledge Discovery in Data (KDD) for the last twelve years. He is particularly interested in: Social Network Mining; Trend Mining; the mining of non-standard data sets such a Graph, Image and document bases; and the practical application of data mining in its many forms. He currently leads a small research group (11 PhDs and 2 RAs) working on many aspect of data mining and KDD. He has some 170 refereed publications on KDD and AI related research, and has been on the programme committees for many KDD events. He is currently a senior lecturer within the Department of Computer Science at the University of Liverpool where he is the director of studies for the department's on-line provision.

Georgina Stegmayer received the Eng. degree in Information Systems Engineering from Universidad Tecnologica Nacional - Facultad Regional Santa Fe (Argentina) in 2000, and the Ph.D. in electronic devices in 2006 at Politecnico di Torino (Italy). Since 2007, she has been an Assistant Research Scientist at the National Council of Scientific and Technological Research. She is currently professor at Universidad Tecnologica Nacional and Department of Informatics, National University of Litoral. Her current research interests are Artificial Intelligence, Neural Networks, Data mining and Bioinformatics.

Giovanni Giuffrida is an assistant professor at University of Catania, Italy. He received a degree in Computer Science from the University of Pisa, Italy in 1988 (summa cum laude), a Master of Science in Computer Science from the University of Houston, Texas, in 1992, and a Ph.D. in Computer Science, from the University of California in Los Angeles (UCLA) in 2001. He served as CTO and CEO in the industry and for various organizations. His research interest is on optimizing content delivery on new media such as Internet, mobile phones, and digital tv. He is a member of ACM and IEEE.

Giulia Bruno is a post-doc researcher at the Database and Data Mining group of Politecnico di Torino. She is currently working in the field of data mining and bioinformatics. Her activity is focused on the analysis of microarray gene expression data to propose algorithms for selecting genes relevant for tumor classification and to detect gene regulatory networks through the application of temporal association rules. Furthermore, she is investigating issues related to data cleaning and semantic information discovery in XML and biological databases. Her research activities are also devoted to data mining techniques for monitoring patient conditions and detect unsafe events.

Giuseppe Tribulato was born in Messina, Italy, in 1979. He received the degree in Computer Science (summa cum laude) in 2004 and his Ph.D in Computer Science in 2008. From 2005 he has lead the research team at Neodata Group. His research interests include data mining techniques, recommendation systems and customer targeting.

Gregg R. Murray is an Assistant Professor of Political Science at Texas Tech University. His research focuses on political behavior, including voting, leadership preferences, and public opinion. As part of his research on political behavior, he works on the development of techniques to analyze the numerous, and often under-analyzed, large-scale data sets created by government and other public institutions.

Ibrahim M. El Emary received the Dr. Eng. Degree in 1998 from the Electronic and Communication Department, Faculty of Engineering, Ain shams University, Egypt. From 1998 to 2002, he was an Assistant Professor of Computer science in different faculties and institutes in Egypt. Currently, he is a Visiting Associate Professor at King Abdul Aziz University, Jeddah, Kingdom of Saudi Arabia. His research interests include: analytic simulation techniques, performance evaluation of communication networks, application of intelligent techniques in managing computer communication network, bioinformatics and business intelligence as well as performing a comparative studies between various policies and strategies of routing, congestion, sub netting of computer communication networks. He published more than 100 articles in international refereed journals and conferences.

Ibarahim.S.Alrabea received the Dr. Eng. Degree in 2004 from the Electronic and Communication Department, Faculty of Engineering, Donetsk University, Ukraine. He is a visiting Assistant Professor and Assistant dean of Prince Abdullah Bin Ghazi Faculty of Science and Information technology at Al-Balqa Applied University, Assalt, Jordan. His research interests cover: analyzing the various types of analytic and discrete event simulation techniques, performance evaluation of communication networks, application of intelligent techniques in managing computer communication network, and performing comparative studies between various policies and strategies of routing, congestion control, sub netting of computer communication networks. He published 6 articles in various refereed international journals and conferences covering: Computer Networks, Expert Systems, Software Agents, E-learning, Image processing, wireless sensor networks and Pattern Recognition. Also, in the current time, he is too interested in making a lot of scientific research in wireless sensor networks in view point of enhancing its algorithms of congestion control as well as routing protocols.

James H. Hill is an Assistant Professor in the Department of Computer and Information Science at Indiana University-Purdue University Indianapolis (IUPUI) in Indianapolis, IN. He received his Ph.D. and M.S. in Computer Science from Vanderbilt University, and B.S. in Computer Science from Morehouse College. Dr. Hill's research focuses on techniques for validating enterprise distributed system quality-of-service properties continuously throughout the software lifecycle on the target architecture, as opposed to waiting until complete system integration time. His research in this area has led to the development of an open-source research-based system execution tool called the Component Workload Emulator (CoWorkEr) Utilization Test Suite (CUTS), which has been used in academic- and industry-related projects/settings throughout the world, including mission-critical systems at the Australian Defense Science and Technology Organization, DARPA, General Electric Research, Northrop Grumman, Raytheon, and Lockheed Martin.

Juan Pedro Caraça-Valente Hernández received his BS and PhD in Computer Science from Universidad Politécnica de Madrid, where he has lectured and researched since 1990. His research interests lie in artificial intelligence and databases. His recent research work has focused on the field of data mining applied to time series, especially in medical and sports domains like posturography and stabilometry. He has published the results of his research in several journals articles, book chapters and many papers at international scientific congresses.

Karthik Rajasethupathy is currently at Cornell University, Ithaca, NY working in Mathematics and Economics. His work in data mining has been published in Expert Systems with Applications. His research interests include data security & privacy and data mining.

Kulathur Rajasethupathy is a Professor of Computer Science at The College at Brockport, State University of New York, Brockport, NY. He has published in the area of formal languages, compiling, algorithms and data mining. He can be reached at kraja at brockport dot edu.

Laura Kamenetzky received the PhD in Biology Sciences from Universidad Nacional de Buenos Aires (Argentina) in 2007. She has a Post-doctoral position of the National Council for Science and Technology. She is Lecturer at the Facultad de Ciencias Exactas y Naturales on the Universidad de Buenos Aires and research assistant of CONICET. She is member of the partner group of Max Planck Institute for Molecular Plant Physiology (Germany). Her current research interest is focused on Crop Plant Molecular Biology and Metabolism.

Loïc Martínez received his BS and the PhD in Computer Science from the Universidad Politécnica de Madrid (UPM) in 1993 and 2003, respectively. He is currently Associate Professor of Computing at the UPM's School of Computing. He has co-authored four books, eight book chapters and over 60 papers published in international journals and congresses. His major fields of study and research are accessibility for people with disabilities to information technologies, software development methodologies and data mining techniques, in which he has participated as a researcher in over 40 European or Spanish research projects.

Manuel Filipe Santos is an auxiliary professor in the department of information systems, University of Minho, Guimarães, Portugal. Holds a PhD in computer science (artificial intelligence) and is a researcher of the Algoritmi center leading the Business Intelligence group. Research interests include Knowledge Discovery from Data bases and Intelligent Decision Support Systems. He is involved in various projects with application in areas like the intensive medicine, database marketing and grid data mining.

Mariana López received the PhD in Biology Sciences from Universidad Nacional de Buenos Aires (Argentina) in 2008. She has a Post-doctoral position of the National Council for Science and Technology. She is member of the partner group of Max Planck Institute for Molecular Plant Physiology (Germany). Her current research interests are Crop Plant Metabolism and GC-MS Technologies.

Matias Gerard received his Lic. degree in Biotechnology from Universidad Nacional del Litoral (Argentina) in 2007. He is a PhD student at Universidad Nacional del Litoral, with a Doctoral Scholarship from National Council of Scientific and Technical Research. His current research interests are Bioinformatics, Data Mining, Artificial Intelligence and Omic Sciences.

Mikolaj Morzy, Ph.D., is an assistant professor in the Institute of Computing Science at Poznan University of Technology, Poland. He received his M.Sc. and Ph.D. degrees in computer science from Poznan University of Technology in 1998 and 2004, respectively. He worked at the university in Muenster, Germany, and at the Loyola University in New Orleans, USA. His research interests include data mining, database systems, and data warehouses. Currently, his main domain of research activities is social network analysis, with a special emphasis on reputation and recommender systems. He has authored and coauthored over 50 scientific papers published in international journals, conference proceedings and books.

Priti Srinivas Sajja (b.1970) joined the faculty of the Department of Computer Science, Sardar Patel University, India in 1994 and presently working as a Reader. She received her M.S. (1993) and Ph.D (2000) in Computer Science from the Sardar Patel University. Her research interests include knowledge-based systems, soft computing, multiagent systems, semantic web and software engineering. She has more than 60 publications in books, journals and in the proceedings of national and international conferences. Two of her publications have won best research paper awards. She is co-author of book 'Knowledge-Based Systems' published by Jones & Bartlett Publishers, USA. She is member in editorial board of four international science journals and served as program committee member for many international conferences.

Rahime Belen received her B.Sc. degree in 2006 from Computer Engineering Department of Başkent University and her M.Sc degree in 2009 from Information Systems Department of Graduate School of Informatics at Middle East Technical University. She is currently studying in the same department for her Ph.D.

René Bañares-Alcántara has a BSc in Chemical Engineering from the Universidad Nacional Autónoma de México. He then obtained an MSc and PhD degrees in Chemical Engineering from Carnegie Mellon University. Upon completion of his studies, he worked for various academic institutions including the Instituto de Investigaciones Eléctricas, Facultad de Química (UNAM) and the University of Edinburgh; he has been a Reader in Engineering Science at Oxford since 2003. Since 1980, his general research interest has been the application of Computer Science techniques in Engineering, focusing on the use of Artificial Intelligence techniques for engineering design, synthesis and diagnosis.

Saurabh Agrawal has completed intermediate from Mahatma Gandhi Inter College, Gorakhpur, India in the year 2003. He has acquired B. Tech. degree from Madan Mohan Malviya Engineering College, Gorakhpur-273010, India. His Areas of Interest are Database Management System, Distributed Real Time Systems and Pear-to-Pear Computing.

Tugba Taskaya Temizel received her BSc degree in Computer Engineering from Dokuz Eylul University, Izmir, Turkey (1999) and her PhD degree from Computing Department, University of Surrey, UK (2006). In 1999, she worked as a research assistant in Dokuz Eylul University. Between 2000 and 2003, she worked as a research officer in two EU 5th Framework projects, called IRAIA and GIDA in Queen's University of Belfast and University of Surrey respectively. Between 2003 and 2004 she was a research fellow in ESRC project called Fingrid. Between 2004 and July 2006, she worked as a tutor in Grid computing. Since July 2006, she is assistant professor in Graduate School of Informatics, METU.

Udai Shanker received his B.E. degree in Electrical Engineering from M. M. M. Engineering College Gorakhpur, India in 1986 and .M.E. degree in Computer Engineering from Jadavpur University, Calcutta, India in 1998. He did his PhD degree from Indian Institute of Technology Roorkee, Roorkee-247 667 in 2006. Presently, he is working as professor & head in Department of Computer Science & Engineering, M. M. M. Engineering College, Gorakhpur-273010, India. He has published many research papers in international and national journals/conferences. He has also served as referee for many international journals/conferences His current research interest includes Distributed Real Time Database Systems, Mobile Database Systems and Grid Databases.

Qin Xin graduated with his Ph.D from the University of Liverpool in December, 2004. Currently, he is working as a postdoc at Simula Research Laboratory, Norway. Prior to joining Simula, he spent two years for the postdoc position at University of Bergen, Norway. His main research focus is on algorithms for various problems related to wireless communication networks. He has published roughly 30 papers in the international prestigious conferences or journals on communication theory, algorithms, foundation of computing, and distributed computing including ICALP, PODC, IEEE MASS, ISAAC, ICC, Algorithmica, Theoretical Computer Science and Distributed Computing.

Weiqi Wang got his BSc in University of Science & Technology Beijing (USTB), China. He is currently a PhD student in Chemical Engineering Department, Oxford University, UK. His PhD project is on application of data mining techniques in mesenchymal stem cell related research.

Yanbo J. Wang was awarded a Bachelor of Administrative Studies in IT by York University (Canada, 2003), and a PhD in Computer Science by University of Liverpool (UK, 2008). After his PhD viva, Dr. Wang joined the School of Computer Science at University of Manchester (UK) for a "short-term" position of Postdoctoral Researcher. His main research focuses on Data Mining and Text Mining. Currently, Dr. Wang works as an IT manager in the Information Management Center, China Minsheng Banking Corporation Ltd. (China), who is in charge of constructing a Data Mining platform for the bank.

Zhanfeng Cui is the Donald Pollock Professor of Chemical Engineering, University of Oxford since the Chair was established in 2000. He is the founding Director of the Oxford Centre for Tissue Engineering and Bioprocessing (OCTEB). He was educated in China and got his BSc from Inner Mongolia University of Technology (1982) and MSc (1984) and PhD (1987) from Dalian University of Technology. After a postdoctoral experience in STrathclyde University in Scotland, he joined Edinburgh University as a Lecturer in Chemical Engineering (1991). He then held academic appointments at Oxford Engineering Science Department as University Lecturer (1994-1998) and Reader (1999-2000). He was a Visiting Professor of Georgia Institute of Technology, USA (1999), the Brown Intertec Visiting Professor to University of Minnesota, USA (2004), and a Chang-Jiang Visiting Professor to Dalian University of Technology, China (2005). He is a Chartered Engineer, a Chartered Scientist, and a Fellow of the Institution of Chemical Engineers. In 2009 he was award a Doctor of Science (DSc) by Oxford University to recognize his research achievement. His research interests are tissue engineering and stem cell technologies, bioseparation and bioprocessing, and membrane science and technology. He and his co-workers have published over 100 articles in refereed journal papers and filed 7 patent applications in the last 5 years.

Index

Symbols

4ESS switch 72, 73

A

ABORT 132
Abort Dependency (AD) 138, 139
ACK 132
Activity Index for Users (AIU) 328
Adverse Drug Events (ADEs) 205
Adverse Event Reporting System (AERS) 6, 21
affective computing 269, 275
Agglomerative algorithms 34
aggregation 181, 186, 187
American National Election Studies (ANES) Cumulative Data File 85, 87, 92, 93, 94, 99, 101, 105
anomalous data points 25
ANOVA 29
ANSWER expert system 72, 74
Apple 152, 172
App Store 152, 172
a priori knowledge 176, 177, 179
Architecture 112, 121, 129
ARC: total number of Instances Correctly Classified with respect to the Association Rule 91
ARIMA 51, 62
ARMA models 53, 63
Artificial Neural Networks (ANN) 26, 27, 43
association mining 85, 86, 87, 88, 89, 90, 93, 95, 99, 104
association mining algorithms 1
Association Rule (AR) 228, 229, 243

Association Rule Mining (ARM) 23, 35, 36, 37, 38, 46, 226, 228, 229, 230, 232, 243
association rules 49, 50, 54, 55, 56, 60, 61, 62, 63, 64, 65, 85, 86, 88, 89, 91, 92, 94, 95, 96, 99, 100, 103, 104
Associative Classification (AC) 223, 225, 226, 229, 231, 233, 234, 235, 236, 237, 243
Attribute Cluster Algorithm (ACA) 33
Automatic Decision Systems (ADS) 112

B

Backward Elimination (BE) 29
Bayesian Classifiers 26
Bayes theorem 26
Begin-on-Abort Dependency (BAD) 138, 139, 141
Biclustering 35, 40, 41, 46
biochemical reactions 289
bioinformatics 25, 35, 40, 41, 42, 44, 45, 46
biological data 287, 288, 290, 295, 296, 299, 305, 308
biologists 288
biology 288, 289, 295, 300
biomedical informatics research networks (BIRN) 246
biomedicine 23
biotechnologies 23
blogs 267, 317
bootstrap 27, 28, 39
broadband wireless channels 246
BSC databases 79
BSS 78
bulletin board systems (BBS) 316
Bulleting Board Code (BBCode) 318, 319
Business Activity Monitoring (BAM) 112